The Mill-Race Quartet

Pamela Street was born in Wilton, Wiltshire,
the only daughter of the late A. G. Street.
She was educated at the Godolphin School, Salisbury.
Her first book, a biography
entitled *My Father, A. G. Street*, was published
in 1969 and has been reprinted several times.
This was followed in 1971 by *Portrait of Wiltshire*,
which is now available in a completely revised
and illustrated edition. In 1979 her biography
Arthur Bryant: Portrait of a Historian was
published. Since then she has concentrated on
writing fiction and has just completed her
tenth novel.

Pamela Street

The Mill-Race Quartet

Pan Books
London, Sydney and Auckland

The Mill-Race first published 1983
by Robert Hale Ltd
First Pan Books edition published 1984
© Pamela Street 1983

The Way of the River first published 1984
by Robert Hale Ltd
First Pan Books edition published 1985
© Pamela Street 1984

Many Waters first published 1985
by Robert Hale Ltd
First Pan Books edition published 1986
© Pamela Street 1985

Unto the Fourth Generation first published 1985
by Robert Hale Ltd
First Pan Books edition published 1986
© Pamela Street 1985

This collected Pan edition published 1988
by Pan Books Ltd, Cavaye Place, London SW10 9PG
9 8 7 6 5 4 3 2 1
ISBN 0 330 30491 7

Phototypeset by Input Typesetting Ltd, London
Printed and bound in Great Britain by
Richard Clay, Bungay, Suffolk

In affectionate memory of my parents
Vera Florence (née Foyle)
and
Arthur George Street

Contents

The Mill-Race

1

She could hear the water, slapping, gurgling and rising beneath the downstair floorboards, as she lay but a few feet overhead in the small back bedroom. It was a far more urgent and ominous sound than the one to which she had become so accustomed during her married life. For thirty-two years the mill-race had simply been an echo in the background, albeit a relentless, insistent one, yet as much a part of her existence as the mill hooter which marked the passing of the hours on weekdays, and the bells of St Mark's, which helped her to chivvy the various members of her family to church on Sundays.

Tonight, a little earlier on, those bells had been ringing out for well over an hour, for the rector was a firm believer in practice making perfect and Christmas 1918 was only two days away. Sadly, she realized that there would be no question of her going to any of the services, unless the man beside her in the bed took a turn for the better and she felt able to slip away to midnight mass. But she doubted that would be the case. Propped up by bolster and pillows, her husband, Sidney Lodge, lay awake restlessly, the cough which she had come to dread as the winter months closed in each year now seeming a greater threat than the floods which so often accompanied it.

Above them, in the attic which stretched out, mercifully, not only over the tiny cramped house, but also for at least twenty feet along the top of one of the adjacent mill buildings, the girls – as she always thought of them – lay sleeping: Florence, thirty next birthday; May, twenty-seven; and little Katy, not yet seventeen. In the front bedroom, leading – as did the attic steps – straight from her own, she was aware, as she had been aware for nearly twenty-one years, of Neil, her youngest son, who, because he was a simpleton, would never really come of age. When

11

Henry, her middle boy, came home from France, they would have to share the same bed. Of Frank, her first-born, who had been killed on the Somme, she tried not to think.

'Sid,' she said, after the latest bout of coughing had left her husband exhausted. 'Sid, please go and stay with Edith tomorrow. She's asked again.' Edith was their only married daughter.

'No, Sarah.' In spite of his lack of breath, a fierce, almost frenzied tone had crept into his voice. 'You know I shall never set foot in Edith's home, however much she goes on about it.'

'But it's so much higher and drier, Sid, on downside. You'd get better quicker. It's no good staying here. The Willon's getting up every minute. I reckon we shall have a foot of water in the house by Christmas Day, maybe two. You know how it was the first winter of the war. And it took five weeks to go down. Five weeks, Sid.'

The man beside her became even more agitated. His hands plucked at the coarse sheet. He was not, normally, an irascible character, but any mention of visiting Edith, his once favourite daughter, always seemed to make him so. For the girl, as far as he was concerned, had defied him. She had wilfully become the wife of Herbert Lench, a mill-hand. He, Sidney Lodge, was the mill manager, despite the near-slum in which the mill owners – a brother and sister called Fielding – appeared to think it fitting that he and his family should dwell.

Yet, as he had pointed out to Sarah when he had first been offered the job and immediately proposed to her on the strength of it, there were definite compensations. They might not have a tap indoors but, because it was a felt mill, there were huge vats of hot soapy water where she would be allowed to do her washing. There was a large garden where he could grow all the vegetables she might require. And even the earth closet at the bottom of it, with its adjoining wood and concrete shed, was prettily covered with honeysuckle. Besides, they would be the occupants of what had always been known as the Mill House. She would be able to put that at the top of her letters when she wrote home. It was this last advantage which had finally won Sarah's hand. Her parents – well-to-do West of England clothiers – had been just as much against her marrying Sidney – the seventh son of an impoverished farmer's widow – as he himself had been against Edith marrying Herbert; although she had had the good sense never to remind him about this.

Sarah could recall many a conversation they had had about Edith and Herbert during the summer of 1914, just before war broke out, particularly one evening in June when they had taken a walk together along the river path through the water-meadows. 'Sid,' she had said, 'Herbie's not a bad lad. He's a good time-keeper. Never been in any trouble.' And she could remember clearly her husband's reply: 'Oh, I know, Sarah. But he's a station below. I have to pay him each week, don't I? He stands in line wi' all the others in Main Building. He'll never get anywhere. Too meek and mild. It's not as if he could ever take over from me one of these days. There's no initiative there, unless . . .', and here, Sidney had hesitated a little before going on, 'unless you count courting Edith. But I daresay she made most of the running.'

Sarah had sighed, knowing only too well how she had been constantly having to chide her headstrong, nineteen-year-old daughter for standing about outside the house when the mill hooter went for the men to clock on or off. She was a beauty all right, their Edith, with her mass of auburn hair and bright blue eyes, always laughing and singing and keeping the two younger children, poor Neil and little Katy, amused. She made no bones about the fact that she wanted to get married and have children of her own as soon as she could. Sarah and Sidney had already managed, albeit not without difficulty, to put a stop to more than one unsuitable youthful romance. But although she, too, would have preferred a better match for the girl, 'We can't keep thwarting her, Sid,' Sarah had said after his last remark. 'She needs a husband. If we tell her she can't marry Herbie, goodness knows what might happen.' And then, for ever afterwards, in her mind's eye, she had retained a picture of her husband standing stockstill under the Black Arch, where the South-Western Railway line crossed the valley, and thundering, 'What do you mean, Sarah? If Edith, or any child of mine for that matter, brings disgrace on our home, they shall never set foot in it again.'

Yet she knew that her words must have had some effect. After that, Sidney no longer showed quite such open opposition. He simply got up and left the room at any mention of Herbert's name. Plans for the wedding were undertaken, conspiratorially, by the distaff side of the family. Edith's wedding dress, made by her two elder sisters, was kept hidden in one of the attic cupboards. There then came a Friday when Sidney Lodge paid his future son-in-law in the evening and, barely audibly, gave his daughter away to him in St Mark's church on East Street the following afternoon.

Soon after that war was declared and the army medical authorities discovered that Herbert Lench was unfit for service owing to a weak heart; although not weak enough, Sidney was sometimes apt to remark uncharitably, to beget a son nine months after the wedding and twin girls after a further eleven. Funny-looking children, he'd always thought them. Ugly. Not a bit like their mother. Only yesterday, when Edith had brought them down to the mill and asked if he would like to take a quick look at them, he'd said no – he only wanted to see Edith by herself for a while. He was always glad to have her visit him in his own home, just as long as Herbert was never brought into it. But he supposed that after sitting by his bed and hearing him cough, she must have gone straight downstairs and said something to her mother again about wanting to nurse him up on downside. Silly girl. She ought to have known better. So ought Sarah. If they thought that he was going to accept Herbert Lench's charity because he happened to be ill, then they must want their heads seeing to. He, Sidney Lodge, had lived at the Felt Mills for thirty-two years and a foot or two of water in his living-room wasn't going to drive him out now, bronchitis or no bronchitis. Besides, Sarah could be wrong about the floods. He'd known them go down quite quickly sometimes. True, both they and his cough had started early this year. Usually February was the worst month. February filldike.

'Sarah,' he now said, suddenly, 'tomorrow morning, first thing, I want you to get our Katy to take a note up to Ted Shergold. I reckon he hasn't got them hatches working properly near Bulbarrow sluice. There's probably not enough water getting away through Lower Croft. Silly young fool. He'll never make the drowner his father was. Maybe he didn't do that repair job on 'em that I warned him about back in the summer when the Willon was low.'

'All right, Sid.' Wearily, Sarah leant over and blew out the candle on her side of the bed, making a mental note that she must warn Katy to go up to the Shergolds' cottage through East Street and not take the river path. Anyone who slipped on the planks that had recently been put there could be carried away in no time. It was curious, she reflected, considering all the water which had surrounded them these many years, that none of her children had learnt to swim, not that that would be much help with the currents as swift as they were now.

She wished that she could send silly, simple Neil on this sort of errand instead of Katy. She was such a fragile little thing. Sometimes Sarah wondered how she had ever managed to rear her. All those broken nights, nursing her through one childish illness after another, that terrible year when she had caught diphtheria and then developed meningitis almost straight away afterwards; although by that time Flo and May had been old enough to help her, just as they were doing their best to help her now over their father's illness. They were good girls. All of them were good girls. Still, it wasn't quite the same as having a stalwart man about the place. It would be nice when Henry was demobilized and came home. She was more worried about her husband than she cared to admit, even to Flo. His chest was far worse this winter than she'd ever known it. He'd had much more time off sick; and only yesterday, when Miss Fielding had called with some lemons and honey, Sarah had sensed that she and her brother were none too happy about the frequency with which things had had to be handled by Tom Henstridge – the conscientious but far less experienced under-manager – in his absence. It crossed her mind that Sidney might have fallen victim to the terrible epidemic that was sweeping the country – Spanish 'flu they called it, although she couldn't, for the life of her, see what Spain had to do with it – but, so far as she knew, no cases had as yet been reported in Wilhampton, for which, along with all her other prayers, she thanked God on her knees each night, before climbing into bed.

The man beside her was seized by another paroxysm of coughing. If only it would slacken. She'd put the chamber-pot on top of the commode by his side, so that it would be within easy reach if he wanted to spit: but she doubted that he would need it for this purpose tonight. His breathing was too quick, too harsh, his body far too hot beside her own.

2

Katy Lodge was pleased at being sent up to the Shergold cottage soon after it became light on the morning of Christmas Eve. It gave her a sense of importance. As the youngest and frailest of the family, who had always been treated as somewhat of an invalid, it irked her never to have been considered capable of undertaking anything but the most modest of tasks, such as whitening the front step with hearthstone after it had been scrubbed each morning, and then helping Flo and May in their workroom at the bottom of the garden, where all three plied their trade as seamstresses; although, so far, Katy had usually only been entrusted with tacking, hemming or oversewing and was not yet allowed to make buttonholes for the clothes which Lady Fairfax, up at the Hall – and others of her ilk – were constantly ordering.

Happily for Sarah and Sidney Lodge, their two eldest daughters had, over the years, established quite a name for themselves in the dressmaking line, not only in the small town where the family lived, but also in its surrounding neighbourhood. The Misses F & M Lodge of

The Mill House, Wilhampton — as they wrote in firm, immaculate script at the top of their bills — were much in demand, young ladies to be treated with respect and at times, it had to be admitted, a certain amount of judicious flattery — even coaxing — according to the urgency of their customers' desires.

They were never at a loss for work, invariably taking on more than they could accomplish — that is, reasonably accomplish — without having to burn the one oil lamp in the living room of their home well into the night. Kind-hearted, proud, but eager to do their best for all and sundry, they found it as hard to refuse a commission from her ladyship at the Hall as they did from Mrs Perrick, who kept the sweet shop at the top of the lane, charging the former only a fractional amount more for their services than the latter. When both ladies required their respective outfits by a certain date, Katy was sometimes apt to feel used, indignant at being bribed to take out the tacking on Lady Fairfax's two-piece of an evening, with the promise of a little bit of lace left over from their distinguished client's latest ball gown. On such occasions she bitterly resented the short apprenticeship with a certain Miss Maidment in Wilhampton which, at varying times, her mother had forced all her daughters to undergo, wisely deeming it a most prudent measure should they never marry. With Flo and May her foresight had been more than justified. For, despite the fact that both had above average good looks, impeccable dress sense and had never lacked for beaux — particularly of the officer class during the war — they had as yet remained spinsters.

But as far as Katy was concerned, she saw everything rather differently. Like Edith, she reckoned on finding a husband as soon as she could, although there the similarity in their reasons for desiring matrimony ended. The youngest Lodge daughter harboured ideas, ideas altogether too far-fetched and romantic her mother might have said, had she been fully aware of what went on in the child's mind. Katy wanted someone very much better than a mill-hand and privately considered that both Flo and May had been silly in letting several most debonair suitors slip through their fingers during the war. But whereas, in this respect, the same view was held by Sarah, the latter completely failed to understand the vividness of a youthful imagination which so much illness, coupled with a great deal of reading, had only served to foster.

Moreover, having always been the delicate 'baby' of the family, Katy did not particularly yearn after children herself, and could not see what Edith found attractive about looking after them. She thought it would be far better to find a man who would look after *her*, but preferably someone handsome, rich and dashing. (It was a little beyond her at this stage to appreciate that such an individual would be unlikely to possess the attribute of father figure as well.) She felt a tall dark foreigner might do, or possibly an actor, or even, with luck, a potential lord, someone like Lady Fairfax's son and heir who had just married the most ugly duckling, the eldest daughter of Sir Roger Broadbent from Westonbury House. Katy had stood in the crowd outside the church watching the bride both before and after the ceremony, and a plainer young woman all decked out in white velvet it would have been hard to find. But rumour had it, according to Flo and May, that the Broadbents had recently come into money, and everyone knew that the Fairfaxes were short. That was why Lady Fairfax was always getting the Misses Lodge to copy – in different colours and materials – some specimen dress which she had bought in London. Katy thought it was a mean trick. Her sisters' outfits were infinitely better finished. But when she told them how she felt about it she got severely reprimanded and was reminded of how good her ladyship had been in sending down delicacies from the Hall when she had been ill as a little girl. It was flying in the face of Providence, they said, to say things like that about the hand that had fed her.

Katy kept thinking about all this as she dutifully picked her way through the puddles and potholes of East Street that Christmas Eve morning. She wished she could have seen things the way her elder sisters seemed to see them, but somehow she couldn't, not that she hadn't always been most respectful to her ladyship's face whenever the latter had called at the Mill House; although that had been a rare occurrence. Usually, Flo and May were summoned to the Hall at a given time, returning with vivid descriptions of carpets so deep and soft that their feet had sunk into them; of red and gold walls covered with priceless pictures and portraits and tapestries; of ceilings high, white and carved 'like heavenly ivory', May had said – although even Katy's imagination could not quite envisage that. Then there were doors which were opened and shut by noiseless butlers and parlourmaids, and huge windows from which, in summer, they could see lawns, according to May, 'like emerald velvet', ancient spreading cypresses, a fountain – 'and a pergoda', Flo had added.

Katy had had to go and look up the word in the minus-cule dictionary which old Dr Fitzherbert had given her when she was recovering from meningitis. She was upset at not being able to find it. It was not until many years later that she came to learn that Flo had made a mistake and it was a 'pergola' she had been on about.

But it was her elder sisters' most recent visit which had intrigued Katy most. Only a month or so ago, just after the armistice, she had had the vicarious pleasure of hearing how they had gone to the Hall to fit Lady Fairfax's beautiful daughter, the Honourable Alicia, for her wedding dress, and the girl was still in her bath when they had been shown up to her bedroom. Then, quite unexpectedly, Alicia's fiancé, an ADC and a baronet's son, had arrived from London on leave and she had quickly struggled into a rest gown and rushed downstairs to greet him, much to her mother's anger and agitation. 'She was so excited, dear thing,' said May. 'She hardly stopped to dry herself. Of course, we couldn't have expected her to stand still for a fitting after that. It's obviously a love match.'

A love match. That was what Katy was after, even if she only knew these things dimly, as through coloured glass. But it would have to be a love match with someone a little more exciting than Herbie, someone who would sweep her up and away from her present environment, take her to London perhaps, in the same way as the heroine had been transported by the hero in the Elinor Glyn novel she was reading clandestinely each evening when Flo and May spared her the time. She had just got to the place where the girl had 'all but succumbed' to his advances. She wasn't quite sure what the author meant, but she sensed that it must be wildly exciting and she wished someone would enlighten her a little more. But she knew it was no use asking her mother or Flo or May.

Sometimes it seemed to Katy as if there was almost a conspiracy on the part of the distaff side of the family to keep her in the dark about certain things. She knew that her elder sisters strongly disapproved of her reading so much. Quite often she had to smuggle her current book upstairs when she went to bed, and then quickly blow out her candle when she heard Flo or May climbing the narrow wooden steps to the attic. Of course, the trouble was that a rapidly diminished candle always gave one away. Flo, in particular, was adept at gauging by this means just how long she had been reading. 'You'll ruin your eyes, Katy,' she was wont to say. 'Besides, it's wasting candle grease.' Yet she never said anything about eyesight or burning oil when she wanted Katy to go on working downstairs by lamplight, when the Misses F & M Lodge were up against a deadline for delivery.

Katy couldn't understand why her elder sisters objected to what seemed such an innocent pleasure. Considering all the time she had missed at the National School through illness, she felt that they ought to have been glad that she had acquired such a liking for books. It sometimes seemed as if they were fearful of her growing up, as if they wanted her to remain a child. She still hadn't started her periods, and although she knew roughly what to expect and was eagerly awaiting the first 'show' – even if it was accompanied by pain – she sensed that all the women in the family were glad that she was 'on the late side'. ''T'will be time enough,' Flo had said one day. 'You ought to be thankful. Think of all that extra washing every four weeks. You surely don't want that, do you?' And Katy, suddenly reminded of the big slop pails of water kept in the attic at certain times of the month – in which the soiled towels of her elder sisters were put to soak, until they could be taken to wash in the mill of a Saturday afternoon when no men were about – tried to become more resigned.

Yet Flo's and May's obvious relief at her immaturity still puzzled her. In some strange way she believed that it had something to do with Neil. She could recall snippets of conversation, hastily broken off whenever she entered the room: 'Mother should have had him put away.' ''Tisn't fair, with Katy growing up.' 'I don't like the way he keeps looking at her.' 'She's never to be left alone with him.' What, in heaven's name, did they imagine poor simple Neil was going to do to her? She couldn't make it out. Nevertheless, she had begun to watch him covertly, aware now herself of how much he stared at her. She became uneasy in his presence, yet it was an unease she was at a loss to explain.

It was not exactly the same unease which Katy experienced on the morning of Christmas Eve when she at last reached the Shergolds' cottage, but as she tapped the door she definitely felt a certain sense of timidity. She knew that Mrs Shergold, albeit not much older than Flo, had a reputation for being loudmouthed and somewhat of a termagant. It was said that she gave poor Ted a bad time of it, that she was always grumbling about him being down in 'thic medders', despite Sidney Lodge's pronouncement that he wasn't half the man at his job as his father had been. Nancy Shergold now came to her front door, a slatternly figure, wearing on her head an old cloth cap belonging to her husband and clad in a dirty overall, to which two equally dirty-looking children clung at either side.

'Yes?' She scrutinized her young caller with small, black, boot-button eyes.

Silently, Katy handed her the letter. The woman tore it open, although it had been carefully addressed to her husband. She took so long in studying it that Katy began to wonder whether possibly she was unable to read. Presently, when the silence between them became embarrassing, she volunteered, shyly, 'It's from Father. About the hatches near Bulbarrow sluice, I think.'

Nancy Shergold redirected her gaze once more towards

Katy. 'I can see that, little Miss Know-All. What do you think my Ted's doing now? He went down to thic medders wi' a lantern at cockcrow, risking life an' limb. If it wasn't for him all you upstart mill folk would have been washed away in your beds many a time. You can go home and tell Mr Manager Lodge that if he knows a better way to stop his house getting flooded, then he'd better come up here himself, instead of sending a little flibbertigibbet like you with fancy orders.'

'But Father's sick, Mrs Shergold.' She could feel tears of grief and mortification beginning to well up, uncontrollably.

'Sick, is he? My Ted hasn't time to be sick. If it wasn't for him the water'd be all over Wilhampton by now. Good day, young lady.'

Mrs Shergold closed the door. Katy was not even certain whether she would give her husband the note.

She turned and stumbled home, defeated, the troubled grey eyes overlarge in the small white face, the skinny body on its spindly legs slipping from time to time on the planks over the pavements, which had been placed there by the council workers even since she had started out on her errand.

3

Three days after Christmas, Sidney Lodge died.

The end came quite suddenly, soon after midnight. Dr Fitzherbert had come to the mill the previous evening after Flo had gone up to his surgery and said, 'Father's no better, Doctor. He's worse. Can't get his breath.' And the good man had left his other patients and come straight back with her down River Lane. He had wanted to get him into Westonbury Infirmary there and then, but here he came up against a fierce opposition.

Sidney Lodge's refusal to be moved came out between short, sharp gasps. 'I'll not go, Doctor. If I'm . . . to die . . . 't'will be in my . . . own bed. Sarah's the best nurse . . . There's nothing the Infirmary . . . can do for me better.'

And Dr Fitzherbert knew, despite the foot of water downstairs in his patient's living room, that it was probably best to let Sidney Lodge go to his Maker in the way he wanted. His condition was too advanced, now, to remedy. One lung was completely collapsed. The Infirmary could not do much more than prolong life a day or so. Moreover, the move, in itself, might even hasten the end.

Sarah took to widowhood hardly. Many was the day she lay in bed grieving, the small paraffin heater failing to take the all-pervading dankness out of the atmosphere, just as it had failed so lamentably during Sidney Lodge's last illness. The girls did their best, taking it in turns to see that she was never left alone, constantly reminding her that she had done everything she possibly could for her late husband. Edith, leaving her children in the care of a neighbour, visited her mother daily, bringing meals which could be heated up on a small Primus stove, begging her, as she had so recently begged her father, to come and stay for a while in her own home. But she was met with the same stubborn resistance.

'Here is where I shall stay, Edith. Your father wouldn't have wished it otherwise.'

And Edith would pick her way over the raised duck-boards from the bottom of the narrow winding staircase to the front door, taking a short walk up through the mill buildings to where Herbert was manhandling wool into one of the huge, deafening machines, and report that she had failed in her mission once again.

In their workroom at the end of the garden, which, mercifully, had escaped flooding, Flo and May continued, whenever possible, to execute their orders, while Neil sat, cretinous yet cheerful, in a corner by the small coal fire. Their conversation almost always took the same line.

'D'you think the Fieldings will let Mother stay on?'

'They ought to. When you think of what Father's done all these years. The mill would never be the place it is today but for him.'

'Who d'you think they'll put in his place?'

'The Lord only knows. But I can tell you one thing.

They're not going to get another manager to go into the Mill House, not like it is, anyway.'

'That's what makes me think they'll let her stay. They couldn't turn her out. Not now.'

Their fears and conjectures were eventually silenced one afternoon some six weeks later by the sudden arrival of Ernest Fielding on the Mill House doorstep. He wore a stiff wing-collar and a long, heavy, tweed overcoat draped over his tall ungainly figure. Fortunately, his visit happened to coincide with one of Sarah's better days and, as the floods had subsided, she had been able to get busy early after breakfast with all her customary cleaning. Now, having changed out of her working clothes into a black serge mourning dress, with a little tucker of lace at the neck, she ushered him into her living room, gravely and with composure.

Sarah had never liked Ernest Fielding any more than she had liked Edwina, his sister, but she was well aware that the man before her held the fate of herself and her family in his thin, bony hands.

'May I get you some tea, Mr Fielding, sir? The kettle's all but boiled.'

'Thank you, no, Mrs Lodge.' He spoke authoritatively, yet tinged with a certain unctuousness. It was nothing she could define, but she did not altogether trust him. They now sat, one on either side of the range, and there seemed to be something insensate, even bird-like, about his small head perched on the too-long neck.

'You must have been wondering about the future, Mrs Lodge,' he continued, in a curiously high, nasal voice. 'About this house, for instance.'

'Well, yes, sir. I . . . we . . . couldn't help but want to know.'

He inclined his head and paused, almost as if he was savouring keeping her in suspense. 'Edwina and I,' he went on, at length, 'have been giving a lot of thought to the future management of the mill. Rather than promote Henstridge to your late husband's post, we have engaged an outsider, a young man called Fuller.'

She could feel the colour come to her cheeks, a dampness

in the palms of her hands, which were now clenched. If Henstridge had been given the job he would probably have still remained in Number Ten, River Lane. It was a nice house with a good garden, close enough to keep an eye on things all the time. A new man, this outsider, would want the Mill House, wouldn't he?

'Yes,' she heard her visitor continue, in the same unattractive intonation, 'we felt it best to make a clean break. A new broom, as it were, always sweeps clean ... Not, I may hasten to add, that we have ever had any reason to find fault with your husband's management. On the contrary. We realize only too well that Henstridge would not be able to step into his shoes satisfactorily. The man isn't up to it. That is why we have got Mr Fuller coming from Westonbury.'

'*Westonbury?*' Fear now crept into her voice. Her initial composure vanished. Still the man before her procrastinated.

'Yes. But there are slight problems. Mr Fuller would prefer to stay in the house in which he is now living and in the town where his children are already at school. I understand his wife ... is delicate. He is a little concerned about the water ...' Ernest Fielding broke off suddenly, conscious that he had made a gaffe. It was not his intention to denigrate in any way the magnanimity – or what he felt to be the magnanimity – of the offer he was about to make.

'So the long and short of it is, Mrs Lodge,' he continued, 'that Edwina and I felt that in return for your late husband's services over so many years you should be given six shillings weekly, and allowed to remain at the Mill House for your own lifetime on the understanding that you would still perform certain little duties for us. For example, locking the main gates each night, taking Mr Fuller tea every afternoon in the office we shall be making for him and also ...' and here he coughed slightly, 'watering the plants which, as you know, I like to cultivate in the greenhouse at the back of the main building, which I believe one of your daughters has kindly attended to during these last few weeks. You would, Mrs Lodge, still be the mistress here, as it were. I trust that you find my . . . er . . . our offer completely to your liking.' He smiled, sanctimoniously, showing stained, yellow teeth. He did not say that Dr Fitzherbert had warned him, at the cemetery after Sidney Lodge's funeral, that the Mill House was little more than a deathtrap and ought to be pulled down, and that it would be criminal to put another family there, let alone one with young children.

'Thank you, sir. It's very kind of you, I'm sure.' Although relief had flooded over her, Sarah's hand had instinctively gone to her throat, where she nervously fingered the cameo brooch at its centre. She wondered why her visitor did not now rise and depart. She could hardly wait to go down the garden and tell the girls. But the man in front of her still appeared to have something else to say. As he recrossed his legs and coughed again, he went on, 'There is just one small point, Mrs Lodge, which I feel I should mention at this stage. About Mr Fuller's office.'

'Office?' Sarah frowned uncomprehendingly, unable, for the life of her, to see what the manager's office had to do with her.

'You are well acquainted, I am sure, Mrs Lodge,' Ernest Fielding continued, 'with the layout of the mill,' and here he gave another of what Sarah felt to be his small, false smiles. 'You must know it better than I. You will appreciate that as Mr Fuller will not be resident here he will need a bigger office. I fear we shall have no alternative but to install him in the . . . er . . . workroom which your daughters are at present using.'

'The *workroom*, Mr Fielding? But where would the girls do their sewing?' Anger now had begun to displace fear.

This time it was her visitor who showed unease. 'There must be other premises, Mrs Lodge,' he said, vaguely. 'Or maybe . . .' he looked round the small cramped living room, and she was quick to sense what was going on in his mind.

'They could not possibly do their dressmaking here, sir. All the cutting out . . . the treadle sewing machine. Lady Fairfax could not be expected to . . . to be fitted *here*.' Unconsciously, Sarah had made a diabolically clever reply.

26

Looking back, she wondered how it had come into her head, considering how rare it was for her ladyship to be fitted anywhere other than the Hall.

Ernest Fielding shuffled his feet again. At the mention of Lady Fairfax his attitude seemed to change. His voice became conciliatory. He had not reckoned on her ladyship being brought into this particular little tête-à-tête. He and Edwina were hoping to be invited to a kind of joint reception which he had heard she would be giving for her newly married son and daughter, for all those whom it had been impossible to invite to their respective weddings. He had not appreciated that the Misses Lodge were favoured by her custom. It would not do at all for Lady Fairfax to hear that he had been anything other than immensely generous to the family of the late Sidney Lodge. He seemed to remember Edwina having said that her ladyship had shown especial interest and benignity towards one of the daughters – the youngest one, he believed – when she had been ill as a child. He must be careful. Perhaps, after all, there was some corner in the mill buildings which could be made into a larger office for Mr Fuller without too much cost, possibly partitioning off the long storage room where the bales of wool were kept.

He took a quick look at the handsome, serious-eyed widow opposite him and then back to the fire in the range. He had noticed, reluctantly, the water marks above the wainscoting left by the recent floods. She was no fool, the late manager's wife. He remembered Edwina having once told him that. Seven children in this small, hopelessly inconvenient house. What must it have been like? Trying to rear them in a single downstair living room, where a piece of worn tapestry served as the only door, and a table with a green chenille tasselled overlay took up most of the available space. Yet the general impression of care and cleanliness was unmistakable. It seemed to him that the net curtains at the windows were as white as the lace tucker on Sarah's dress. The walnut grandfather clock in the corner was far more highly polished than his own. The brass candlesticks on either side of the mantelshelf positively gleamed. There was not a speck of dust on the rest of the furniture: the mahogany whatnot with its countless knick-knacks, including a mounted emu's egg and a pewter jug filled with a mass of honesty pods; the upright piano, on which rested a number of family photographs in wooden frames; the glass-fronted cabinet displaying some blue, willow-pattern, Staffordshire china.

Ernest Fielding was not a family man, his imagination was sadly limited, but there was something about the woman before him which commanded respect. 'Naturally,' he said slowly, choosing his words with care, 'we do not want to cause unnecessary hardship after your recent loss. I will have another talk with my sister tonight. I can see that it might be difficult for your daughters to work here. I understand they are most industrious, clever with their needle.'

'Yes, sir. They are all good girls,' Sarah answered simply and, to her relief, her reply now seemed to bring his visit to an end.

As Ernest Fielding got up to take his leave, he had an uneasy feeling that the mistress of the Mill House had quietly got the better of him.

4

The eagerly awaited news of Corporal Henry Lodge's homecoming came one blustery day in the middle of March. Sarah was taking down some washing from the clothes-line in the garden when she saw the telegraph boy cycling through the front gates of the mill. Quickly, she dropped a bolster case into the basket at her feet and went towards him.

'For me, Percy?'

'Yes, Mrs Lodge, ma'am.'

It wasn't so bad nowadays, Percy Hooper thought, being a delivery boy for the Post Office. Not so long ago he had always seemed to be the harbinger of bad news. But he happened to know what was in this particular message, even though he reckoned that there was a bit more to it than Mrs Lodge was expecting. All the same, it wasn't like the one from the War Office which he had had to deliver that autumn morning about two and a half years ago, informing the family that their eldest son had been killed in action. He hadn't quite known what to do when Mrs Lodge fainted. He had somehow managed to ease her fall and then he had run up through the mill to find Mr Lodge. The first person he had come across was Edith's husband and he remembered how Herbie Lench had been quite efficient. He had found the manager almost at once and together they had all three come running back to the house. He and Sidney Lodge had arrived first because poor Herbie got breathless on account of his heart. But by then Flo and May were somehow on the scene and, reluctantly, Percy had had to cycle off. He hadn't seen any of the family for some time after that. They'd kept themselves to themselves. And now Mrs Lodge was a widow, poor thing. Still, she had her daughters to keep her company and soon she'd have a *daughter-in-law*. Percy went off whistling, wondering what she would say to that.

Sarah didn't say anything at all when she first read the telegram. She did not faint, like last time, but she certainly suffered a sense of shock. She went into the house and sat for a while, holding the message in her hand, frowning and looking at it again from time to time. Then, slowly, she got up and walked down the garden path to the workroom.

Flo was bending over the big deal table cutting out a chemise when she entered and remained, at first, concentrated on her task. Neil, sitting on his usual stool by the fireplace, gave her a cheerful vacant smile. Katy was nowhere to be seen. Only May, who had just come to the end of sewing some lace on a collar, looked up and said, 'What is it, Mother?'

Silently, Sarah handed her the piece of paper and sat down in the small armchair, too wrapped in thought to admire the finishing touches which her second daughter had been putting on the stiff, navy-blue moiré dress for Mrs Betts, the new mayoress of Wilhampton, in which she had previously – despite her grieving – shown a certain interest. Had Sidney Lodge lived, Sarah herself would have become the next mayoress.

'Oh, chippatoo! Oh chippatoo!' May, always the most excitable member of the family, made the curious exclamation which she invariably used whenever she was particularly aroused. No one knew from whence she had coined it. It was something she had started saying when she was quite a small girl. Petite and dainty, she now began drumming her little heels on the floor, rocking herself backwards and forwards, her pink and white complexion more flushed than usual, half in surprise, half in pleasure. 'See this, Flo. Our Henry's got himself a wife. French by the sound of her.' She held the telegram out to her elder sister.

Flo put down her scissors and scanned the missive incredulously. Her reactions were always slower than those of her other sisters. She was altogether less spontaneous and, since Sidney Lodge's death, she had assumed an even more sober manner, the weight of responsibility for her mother and the rest of the family hanging heavily on her shoulders. Having read the message once, she now read it again out loud: 'Married last Saturday. Arriving with Marianne Wednesday. Henry.'

Flo took off the steel-framed spectacles she had lately taken to wearing for close work and stared at the three other occupants of the room. Then, with swift practicality, May said, 'Where will they sleep, Mother? At Edith's?'

'I suppose so.' Sarah fingered her cameo brooch, as she so often did in times of stress, well aware that because she and Sidney had hitherto always refused Edith's offers of help, it now made it all the harder to ask for it – not that her married daughter would refuse it. The girl was generous to a fault, even if she and her brother, Henry, had had many a fight as siblings. 'We'd best get a message to her,' she said, at length. 'Where's Katy?'

There was an awkward silence and a certain embarrassment in Flo's voice when she finally spoke. 'She's gone to the fair, Mother . . . The Perrick girl came down after dinner and asked if she could go with her. It was difficult to say no. She'd worked hard all the morning and we

30

thought a bit of fresh air might do her good. She's been looking so peaky ever since . . .' Flo broke off uncertainly, not liking to put into words the simple fact that Katy's periods had started profusely soon after the shock of her father's death.

Sarah Lodge stood, or rather drew herself up. Although, lately, her striking-looking face, with its huge grey eyes and high cheek-bones, still framed by brown hair without a touch of grey, had often seemed worn and haggard and her neat well-corseted figure somewhat bowed, yet, when she wanted, she was still able to take command of a situation, a little as she had done at the end of Ernest Fielding's visit.

'You mean you girls saw fit to give Katy leave to go without asking me?'

'Well, yes, Mother. And we thought you were maybe resting . . .' Flo broke off, once again, uneasily.

This time Sarah rounded on her, the fire and passion in her voice making it easy to see how she had managed to weather so many long years of trial and tribulation. The way she now spoke made her eldest daughter feel about ten again.

'You know perfectly well, my girl, that I have not rested during the daytime these many weeks past. You also know that I expressly asked that you should all honour your late father's memory by behaving in a decent, quiet and seemly fashion. He has not yet been dead three months. Apart from going to church and the cemetery, I have not set foot in the town, nor kept company at home. And now I find that behind my back you have allowed Katy to go to the *fair*. It will be all over Wilhampton by tomorrow. How do you think I shall look, not yet out of mourning?'

Save for a slight crackling in the grate, there was silence in the workroom now. Even Neil appeared to have registered his mother's displeasure, his weak blue eyes, beneath a thatch of fair hair, cast downwards towards his large black boots.

Then, with one hand on the latch, Sarah made her final salvo: 'As Katy is unable to take a message up to Edith, one of you two girls had best go – at once.' She let herself out and went back up the garden, collecting the remainder of her washing on the way. She could not have staged her departure with more effect. Quickly, Flo put on her coat, tied a scarf over her head and set out for downside.

Edith took the news of her brother's marriage and home-coming calmly and good-naturedly. He had always been a happy-go-lucky type, like herself. She would be delighted, she said, to accommodate Henry and Marianne on the brass-railed bedstead in the little back bedroom for as long as they wanted to stay. 'French, you say, Flo? Oh la la. Well, I never. Reckon she'll teach us a thing or two, even if some of our own ancestors did once come from over the water. How's Mother taking it?'

'So, so. I don't suppose she likes it much. I expect she naturally thought that Henry would still be fancy-free and live at home. But right now she's more upset because we let Katy go to the fair.'

'*Did* you, now? Poor kid. She doesn't have much fun on the whole, does she? All that illness. Sometimes I don't think our Katy's quite like the rest of us. Takes after Mother's grandmother, shouldn't wonder.'

'What? The one who ran away and went on the stage?'

'Yes, only we're not meant to know, are we? Anyway, tell Mother I'll start airing the spare mattress straight away. Incidentally, what do you think Henry's going to do now?'

'The Lord only knows. I suppose he must have some plan. He wouldn't have married, else.' Flo stood up. 'I must be going, Edie.'

'You'll not stay for a cup of tea?'

'No thanks. There's so much to do. It's as if half Wilhampton wants new clothes this month. Don't bother to come to the door,' she added, as one of Edith's twins let out a piercing yell, 'it looks as if you've got enough on your hands, too.'

The wind cut across downside as Flo hurried off. High in the tossing elm trees by the allotments, a colony of rooks was noisily going to bed. Below her, the lights of Wilhampton were beginning to appear, one by one. She could still just discern two tall familiar landmarks: the tower of St Mark's and the mill hooter pointing upwards to the darkening sky. It would be good to get home. Although it was downhill all the way, the journey somehow seemed longer this evening. She shivered slightly, the cold, clear air reminding her that she must move the buttons on her new black worsted coat. As it was, they were letting in too much draught, especially since she had lost weight lately. But it had never been a perfect fit, even at the beginning, although that was hardly surprising, she reflected, considering the speed at which all the mourning had had to be made. Some day, if ever she had a moment to spare, she would get down to a whole lot of alterations.

Now, as she turned into River Lane, she wondered whether May would have finished Mrs Betts's dress during her absence. She hoped so. She knew that the mayoress was anxious to have it, even though the reception for which it was wanted was not for another couple of days. It would be nice, if possible, to get it to her tonight. She was apt to be pernickety, fussy about the smallest detail, not that there ever seemed anything to fuss about. Quite often she asked for some minute alteration and then came back next day with a silly affected smile on her face to say, 'You were *quite* right, Miss Lodge. I should *never* have asked you to take that extra tuck. You *always* know best. I do want to wear it at once. Do you think you could possibly . . . ?' And stifling annoyance and resentment, either Flo or May would set to work to do her bidding. A proper old 'tab', the latter was apt to call her on such occasions, although where she got the word from, no one quite knew, just as the family had always been mystified by 'chippatoo'. But proper old tab or no, if her latest dress was now ready and Katy was back, Flo resolved to send her straight up to The Chantry with it just as soon as the child had had her tea.

Katy was indeed back when Flo came into the house; but she was sitting on the old horsehair sofa in tears. Around the table, all set with cups and saucers and plates, Sarah, May and Neil were seated in their customary places. Spread out at one corner on the spotless white cloth there appeared to be a necklace of large, cheap-looking pink pearls, shining – almost defiantly – in the glow of the oil lamp. Flo looked questioningly from one to the other, their faces all turned expectantly towards hers, as if they were waiting for her to act as some kind of referee.

'I am not saying,' Sarah began slowly, after Flo had taken off her coat and was seated at the table herself, 'that it was entirely Katy's fault. Others older than she should have known better than to let her go to the fair in the first place. But what I cannot allow to go unpunished is Katy's own, unthinking, disgraceful behaviour once she got there.' Sarah picked up the bauble by her side, held it disdainfully for a while between finger and thumb and then let it fall, heavily, back on the table. Her action suddenly made Flo think of Edith's remarks about their great-grandmother which had been made but a short while ago. Almost, she felt, Sarah could have been an actress, too. Certainly, in that one small moment of time in the spring of 1919, the living room of The Mill House, Wilhampton, with the lamplight flickering over the faces of the five members of the Lodge family within it, seemed vaguely reminiscent of a stage set.

Flo looked from Sarah towards the smallest, most shadowy figure, still huddled on the sofa. The face alone seemed to stand out, the enormous grey eyes still brimming with tears, the usually chalk-white skin blotched and swollen. If her mother thought that Katy had been unthinking, how much more had she been herself in her initial responsibility for the whole sorry situation. Suddenly, she felt strangely tired, the burden of being eldest of the family altogether too much for her thin square shoulders. She ought to have had more imagination, she should have foreseen what might happen. Although, for the life of her, she couldn't quite see what Katy could have done at the fair to engender quite such wrath on her mother's part. She was sure that she could not have acquired the necklace through any illicit means. She must have won it, although, for all its vulgarity, it was a cut above the usual prizes waiting to be netted or ringed or shot for on the garish tawdry stalls.

'What happened, Katy?' Flo asked, quietly.

But the question only brought a fresh bout of weeping. Sarah had put the fear of the Lord into the girl, all right. She had always been able to do that with all her children, that is, apart from poor Neil, to whom she showed an uncustomary and touching compassion. Now, she simply answered Flo's query herself.

'It seems she won it for acting. There was some extra show this year. Ena and Katy decided to go to it. The stage-manager asked for volunteers.'

'Volunteers?' It was May who now spoke.

'Yes. He offered a prize for the best turn.'

The corner of May's mouth twitched a little. She had always been able to see the funny side of things.

'And what turn did you do, Katy?' Flo spoke gravely but kindly, aware that the sobbing had subsided a little.

'I sang,' came a small muffled voice from the sofa.

'And what did you sing?'

But now Katy was not even given a chance to reply.

'She sang,' Sarah intervened, in a sepulchral voice, ' "Our Lodger's Such a Nice Young Man", with her father not dead three months.'

5

Ever afterwards, Katy always thought of the first day of the Wilhampton spring fair, in 1919, as the day she grew up – or, strictly speaking, perhaps the night she grew up.

She had been sent straight to bed after tea, with the admonishment that there would be no more sustenance forthcoming until morning and on no account was she to read. As for any ablutions, they appeared to have been waived. In any case, the important ones were mostly done of a morning, when members of the family – other than Sarah, for whom a dipper of soapy water was brought up to the washstand in her bedroom – would creep downstairs and into the mill to perform whatever was necessary before the six-thirty hooter sounded and the men arrived for work. Baths, either in a tub by the coal range in the living room, or sometimes in one of the vats in the mill itself, were invariably reserved for weekends.

Katy had not really minded this particular form of punishment. In many ways it was a relief. She had been feeling too sick to manage anything other than a cup of tea; and she was glad to escape from the tense unhappy atmosphere downstairs. As for reading, however much she had been looking forward to getting on with her current book, *A Peep Behind the Scenes* – hopefully hidden beneath her mattress – she was far enough into the tragic story of an ill-treated consumptive wife of a fairground manager to realize that just at the moment the subject was a little too close to real life for her to find altogether enjoyable.

So, having undressed, slipped into a flannelette nightgown and undone her thick brown hair which she had lately taken to pinning up in the fashion adopted by Flo and May, she simply lay in bed, savouring, in retrospect, the extraordinary reception which had followed her début on the small raised platform in the largest tent in the fairground.

Not even Sarah's accusations and anger could take away the exquisite pleasure of seeing and hearing once again, with total recall, the manager coming on to the stage after she had already given three encores, how he had laid one hand on her shoulder and held the other up to the audience, while he had said, 'Ladies and Gentlemen, I think you will agree. We have here a second Marie Lloyd.' And there had been so much thumping and clapping and cheering that Katy had been obliged to do yet another encore, this time with everyone else joining in.

Ena Perrick hadn't said much about it on the way home. It was obvious she was pretty jealous. The poem she had recited – *Lord Ullin's Daughter* – hadn't gone down nearly so well. There had only been a few, perfunctory, half-hearted claps. But so great had been Katy's own triumph that the manager had asked her if she would come back and do an evening performance. She had refused, having the sense to know full well that she would never be able to get away with that. Yet, flushed with temporary euphoria, she had murmured something about possibly returning the following afternoon.

Now, of course, after Sarah's violent reaction there would be nothing like that – nor would there ever be. Her mother had pounced on her as soon as she had entered the door, her eyes immediately spotting a little bit of the necklace showing above the collar of her coat, and then breaking into a merciless castigation. By the time May and Neil had appeared on the scene, she had begun to feel not only wicked but unclean. 'Fair people are dirty folk, Katy. Actors and actresses are worse. How you could *expose* yourself in such a way at a time like this, I simply do not understand.'

In spite of her remorse and wretchedness, Katy had taken special note of the word 'expose'. She couldn't see that she had actually done anything like that. It wasn't as if she'd undressed in public or even made a spectacle of herself. She'd been a success. A great success. Besides, she was vaguely aware that Flo and May used that particular word in relation to something naughty which only men did. She seemed to remember overhearing them whispering in bed one night during the war when they thought she was asleep, and May had referred to having been seen home by a rather elderly colonel who – and here her sister's voice had become more muffled and indistinct – had 'exposed himself in River Lane'. Katy couldn't imagine what poor Colonel Whittingham had done, especially as Sarah or Sidney might easily have been waiting, keys in hand, on the inside of the high heavy mill gates. For, unless it was a very special occasion when, reluctantly, they allowed the small trapdoor to remain open a little longer – on the strict understanding that the latecomer would lock it up carefully with the key hidden inside – 9.30 p.m. was the time they insisted each member of the family should be home. Indeed, Sidney Lodge went even further. Rather like a shepherd, he was not really happy unless his flock was safely indoors by sundown, deeming it somehow unseemly and wrong for anyone – especially women – to be seen after that hour 'howling about at night', as he was apt to put it.

Katy had had no idea exactly when Colonel Whittingham had brought May back to the mill, but she had pondered over the incident a long time, particularly as she became aware that May's association with this seemingly most respectable officer had ceased abruptly from then on; and when, a little later, Sarah had enquired, quite kindly, what had happened to that 'nice Colonel Whittingham', May had all at once appeared to close up, her manner becoming uncharacteristically terse and defensive as she had replied, 'I really don't know, Mother. He's probably been posted.' Katy knew very well that nothing of the sort had happened because she had seen the Colonel coming out of the Victoria Arms only the day before, but naturally she hadn't said anything. One always stood by one's sisters, even if one did think they might be telling tiny white lies.

Katy wished very much that her mother hadn't used this mysterious word of obviously double meaning in relation to herself; but presently she forgot about it and started drifting off to sleep. The excitement of the afternoon and the emotional upset after it had worn her out. She was therefore quite oblivious to the sound of someone climbing the attic steps until there was a noise right beside her. She sat bolt upright in sudden terror. This was no Flo or May, coming to bed gently and quietly in slippered feet, shading their candles for fear of disturbing her. In the moonlight filtering through the chinks in the curtains, she became aware of a different figure, a large, ungainly man's figure. Neil.

Panic-stricken by she knew not what, Katy opened her mouth to scream, but no scream came. She pushed at him blindly, only to have him come closer. He was kneeling now by her low little bed – not much more than a camp one – and she watched in a kind of fascinated horror as, grunting and gasping, he began fumbling with the lower part of his person.

It was May who found them thus. In later life, with possibly one exception, Katy could never remember being more overcome with relief. Still unable to shout or speak, she watched the light from her sister's candle gradually getting brighter as she mounted the attic steps, the bobbing shadow of her neat, reassuring little figure looming larger every second against the opposite wall.

For a moment May appeared to be unaware of what was happening. Neil also was too engrossed in his clandestine, unwholesome activity to heed her presence. Only when she stooped to place her candle on the floor did May hear the unaccustomed sounds and notice the two figures in the far corner of the attic, the one on the bed, rigid and silent, the other beside it, panting and swaying.

'Oh my God!' May was across the room, pulling her brother away from Katy with all the force of her two tiny arms. Suddenly, the boy seemed to crumple, lying on the floor in an awkward heap.

May turned to her younger sister. 'Lie down, lovey. Keep quiet. I want to get him back to his room before Mother comes up to bed.'

Then, kicking at her brother with her little foot, she hissed, 'Get up, Neil. Get up this instant.' Sheepishly, the boy did as he was told. Putting a finger to her lips – one of the signs she knew he was quite capable of understanding – she more or less manhandled him across the room and led him down the attic steps.

When she returned five minutes later, Katy was trembling uncontrollably. 'Did he,' May said, and this time, in her agitation, she spoke almost harshly, 'Did he . . . ?' To her relief, before she could quite bring herself to finish the difficult question, Katy shook her head, even though she was only half cognizant of the exact intricacies of the function to which May was alluding. All she did know was that her sister's eyes seemed to be searching and probing, travelling all over her hunched, skinny body, willing it not to have been violated.

'But he exposed himself!' her elder sister said, at length.

'Yes.' Katy now understood only too well the coarser meaning of the word.

'For how long?'

'I don't know. A minute. Maybe two.'

'He didn't come?'

'Come?' This time Katy was really puzzled again. How

could May say Neil hadn't come, when he had very definitely come up to the attic? Was she trying to make her pretend that the incident hadn't happened? 'Come?' she said, again, wonderingly.

'Oh, Katy dear. I'm sorry. How should you know?' May sat on the bed and put her arms round the still-shaking body. 'It won't happen again, I promise you, although I don't think we'll let Mother know about it just yet. You've had enough trouble for the time being. Suppose you come and sleep in my bed tonight?' And when Flo came upstairs, some half an hour later, she remained unaware till morning of the two forms huddled up together, the younger one fast asleep in her elder sister's arms.

But though Katy had soon dropped off in May's comforting embrace, the latter, her body cramped and her mind racing, had stayed awake most of the night. She knew something would have to be done about Katy. If her mother wouldn't have Neil taken away, then she and Flo would have to see whether they could find a job for their youngest sister which would enable her to live away from home. They had probably already made a mistake in trying to shield the girl for so long from the facts of life; but she had seemed such a fey, capricious, innocent little thing, albeit now fast becoming prettier every day. No wonder she had brought the house down with – of all songs – 'Our Lodger's Such a Nice Young Man'. Poor child. She'd had a rude awakening tonight. May still wasn't quite sure how much she understood. Tomorrow, she would try to have a serious talk with her. But then she remembered that Henry would be arriving with Marianne, and there might not be much opportunity.

During that long, uncomfortable night, May thought back to her own initiation into the mysteries of sex. Sarah had never said a word of enlightenment. It was Lilian Perrick, oddly enough, who had lent her a book called *The Cradle Ship*, which had given her a lot to think about, although it had been altogether too vague and allusory for her liking: all about a young wife and mother-to-be thinking beautiful thoughts every day for nine months in order that she should grow a beautiful baby inside her tummy. It never went into any details about how the baby got into it in the first place. There were a great many pictures of the woman wearing lovely, long, loose-fitting garments and, in each one, her husband seemed to be hovering somewhere in the background. Because of this and constant references to his presence in the text, May – who had been thirteen at the time – gathered that a man was somehow necessary for producing a child; but she had sent Lilian Perrick into fits of laughter when, on returning the book, she had asked whether, if Lady Fairfax had not married Lord Fairfax, she could nevertheless still have had all her babies because she always had a butler around.

May had certainly become much more enlightened about such things during her teens, but it was really the war which had opened both her and Flo's eyes a great deal further. Wilhampton lay in one of the valleys south of Salisbury Plain where, it seemed, most of the British Army was stationed at one time or another. There was never any shortage of men anxious to have and – up to a point – willing to give a good time. May, especially, had learnt how to flirt and use her big blue eyes. She was reputed to have the smallest waist in Wilhampton and was well aware that she was attractive to the opposite sex; but neither she nor Flo would ever have dreamt of letting any man go further than a kiss or a cuddle. There were too many veiled – and not so veiled – parental threats of 'never darkening my door again' if they misbehaved, even though the misbehaviour might not have been spelled out in so many words.

All the same, there had been that one terrible occurrence which Sarah and Sidney, thanks be, had never known about and which, to this day, May had done her best to forget. But somehow, the recent events had unhappily brought it all back as if it were yesterday. She recalled how Major Walter Perkins – by far the most handsome and amusing of her beaux – had asked her to lunch with him one Sunday in April at the White Lion in Westonbury. In her new beige outfit and white and beige beribboned hat, she had walked the three miles into the town in high anticipation. She knew him to be fancy-free and that many a local girl was after him, for he was a real charmer and it was quite a feather in her cap to have had this particular invitation.

As she had hurried along that morning after church – her new, narrow, pointed shoes pinching her small feet on the uneven, dusty, white road – she began to wonder whether, if he *asked*, she might say yes. It wouldn't have been her first proposal by any means, but possibly because she had already been a little spoilt by the sheer number of suitors dancing attendance on her, she had been apt to play one off against the other, feeling that there was still plenty of time and she could afford to be choosy. One day 'Mr Right' was sure to come along. But what had taken place in the spring of 1916 had certainly altered her ideas about men. Although, afterwards, she had still gone out with them and enjoyed having compliments paid her, she managed to keep them at a distance. She was not at all sure that she wished to marry. She did not think she could face up to the physical side of such a relationship; and Flo, sharing vicariously her sister's experience and subsequently undergoing a rather different kind of disillusionment with a member of the opposite sex, had begun to think likewise.

For when May had arrived at the White Lion that day, Major Perkins was not waiting to greet her in the lounge, as she had been given to understand. When she enquired for him at the desk, she was told that he was indisposed and had asked if she would go up to his suite. It did not occur to her to think that there was anything dubious about such a request, despite the rather sour, disapproving look on the face of the porter who showed her the way. For all her twenty-four years, there was then still a charming naïveté about her. Because Walter was an officer, she took it for granted that he was a gentleman. As far as she was concerned, the poor man was ill. She could, perhaps, do something for him before going home.

She found him to be not exactly ill, but certainly strangely flushed and over-animated. He opened the door in answer to her light tap, wearing a silk dressing gown over what appeared to be a pair of fawn mufti trousers. Behind him, in the sitting-room, there was a table laid for luncheon, on which resided a bucket with two bottles of champagne, one of which had already been opened.

Walter Perkins had tried to gather her in his arms at once, but she had held back, fear and suspicion quickly dispelling any previous feelings of trust and hope. There was something wrong. She should never have agreed to come upstairs. Whereas his words, 'May-darling-you-look-good-enough-to-eat — I-adore-you', would, in any other circumstances, have sent her spirits soaring, now, in this silent, second-floor, private suite of the White Lion, they had the reverse effect.

'I only came up because I thought you were ill, Walter,' she remembered saying, primly, once she had got her breath. His own smelled of alcohol. She had tried to leave, but he had forestalled her. She could recall, clearly, how his manner had suddenly changed, that it became petulant and he had more or less dragged her across the room, thrusting a glass of champagne into her unwilling hand, telling her that it would help to chase away 'that ridiculous, Victorian conventionality imposed on you by your misguided mother'.

It was the contemptuous reference to Sarah which had made May fighting mad. Had she been more experienced, more a woman of the world and aware that he had been drinking quite heavily, she might have been able, with a certain amount of tact, to have extricated herself forthwith from the whole unfortunate situation. As it was, she now found herself not only in a mental but also a bitter physical struggle with Major Walter Perkins. It was hardly surprising who had won. He had carried her from the sitting room into his bedroom and there, as she afterwards told Flo, he 'had had his way with her'. Too ashamed and too terrified to make a sound, she had then quickly left his suite, praying that the porter at the White Lion would not notice a certain disarray in her previously immaculate attire.

For eighteen days afterwards, she and Flo had agonized as to whether May would have a period. When, on the nineteenth day, no such occurrence had taken place, she remembered having stood by the mill-race for a long while, watching the water cascading into the boiling inferno below, wondering whether to throw herself into it. But something – God, her parents, fear of dying, even basic love of life – had made her desist. When, that night, she felt the warm welcome wetness between her thighs, she had sent up a little prayer of thanksgiving for deliverance from a fate which had, until those sobering moments by the mill-race, seemed worse than death.

For the remainder of the war, May had known how to take care of herself. She had learnt her lesson. Later on, it had even been reinforced by a second not quite so traumatic one – the whispered account of which Katy had partially overheard – on an evening when she was being escorted back to the mill by someone whom she had considered eminently safe. After this, she felt that no man, not even Colonel Whittingham, MC, who came of good family and had hitherto appeared to have such impeccable manners, could be trusted. For when she had held out her hand to say good night to him, he had suddenly proffered something very different from his own in return. Disgusted, she began to despair of finding a man who did not want 'one thing' and who, on possibly obtaining it, would probably leave a girl with a life sentence: either in the undisguisable form of an illegitimate child or the more nebulous, but sometimes almost as damaging, acquisition of a bad reputation. Though she still could not help harbouring romantic notions of matrimony – a vision of a cream satin wedding dress and a train of Brussels lace floated often into her mind – that, sadly, seemed about as far as she could get.

Neither did Flo fare any better in reaching the altar. The following year, just before Henry was sent to the front, she had been very much in love with a Captain Guy Armitage. He had courted her so assiduously that the Lodges had begun to take it for granted that she would become his wife. Then, for no apparent reason that Flo could see, his attentions had suddenly ceased. No more little notes, flowers or chocolates arrived at the Mill House. Puzzled, she had still gone about her daily duties as conscientiously as ever, but with a heavy heart. One Friday morning, she had happened to glance at the back page of the *Westonbury Journal* before going down to the work-room and was hardly able to believe her eyes when she read:

ARMITAGE–SINCA. On July 7th, in London, CAPTAIN GUY LEONARD ARMITAGE, elder son of Mr and Mrs John Armitage of St Vincent Place, Edinburgh, to GRACE MARY, only daughter of Mr Thomas Sinca and the late Mrs Sinca, of The Warren, Wilhampton.

Flo had rushed out of the house and shut herself in the closet until May, having hastily picked up the discarded paper and seen the news, hurried after her. Here, on the broad, well-scrubbed, wooden seat, she had sat down beside her and, putting her arms around her eldest sister, had done her best to comfort her. When she was at last able to coax Flo out, she insisted that they leave their sewing for a while and take a walk.

May had already heard rumours about Guy and Grace, but she had kept them to herself, hoping the affair would blow over. She was aware that there was always gossip about the Sincas, for their presence on the outskirts of Wilhampton was something of a mystery. They had arrived at the beginning of the war: an ageing invalid father and his bold-eyed, blonde-haired daughter. Possibly because of their foreign-sounding name and Grace's offhand manner and looks, they had never been accepted in the little town. They seemed aliens in every sense of the word. Soon, it was being put about that they were enemy agents and that Grace's entertaining of army personnel was done for a specific reason on her part, even if it was enjoyed for an altogether different reason by the countless uniformed officers who could be seen walking the half mile to and from The Warren at all hours of the day and night.

Aided by shocked but eager denigrators, Grace's reputation became more and more lurid. It was rumoured she made flashing signals from the house after dark, although whether this was for the purpose of attracting lurking German spies or the much more ready and waiting British troops stationed nearby was left to the listener's individual interpretation.

'She'll never make Guy happy, that's for sure,' May had said on their return journey, as Flo strode on unseeingly through the meadows on a day when she would normally have welcomed being out and about, with the lush green countryside lazily enjoying that traditional lull between haymaking and harvest: honeymoon time, as the farming fraternity called it. 'If Guy could fall for a woman like that,' May continued, trying to be as helpful as she could, 'you're well out of it. He's got what's coming to him. She's a . . . Well, *you* know what she is. All Wilhampton does. Percy Hooper's brother said he once went to The Warren to mend the front gate and she was standing at an upstairs window just as God made her. Although . . .' and here May had paused for rather longer, remembering her own misfortune and colouring slightly before going on with a rush, 'well, I mean, she can't have been exactly like that in a long while, can she?'

When, three months later, Guy Armitage had come back from Passchendaele with both his legs blown off, May could not help regretting her harsh words. Nevertheless, she consoled herself by thinking that they had been said in good faith. And if they had helped a sister in distress, it was all that really mattered. That was what families were for.

As time went by, and May and Flo were both in their late twenties, the inhabitants of Wilhampton were invariably surprised that such pleasant, good-looking girls remained spinsters. Little did they guess that, for reasons best known to themselves, the Misses F and M Lodge, though never lacking in admirers – especially while the war had still been on – nevertheless preferred to ply their trade, sitting in their little workroom: cutting, tacking, machining and stitching, having decided, by a mutual, almost unspoken agreement, that for them a husband was a doubtful asset.

46

6

The first thing that Flo noticed when Henry and Marianne alighted from the London train at Wilhampton station was that her new sister-in-law appeared to be most unsuitably dressed. She supposed she was pretty in a dark-eyed, flashy kind of way. She was very obviously foreign, although there seemed to be more of an Italian look about her than a French one – not that Flo knew much about either. It was just that Marianne's olive skin and jet-black hair, done up in tight curls, reminded her of some of the paintings of the Fairfaxes' ancestors up at the Hall, who had reputedly come from Venice.

But it was Marianne's clothes which distressed her more than anything. Flo hardly liked to think the word, let alone use it, but they were *common*. The Lodge family might live in what many people would consider privation, their home one of the most humble and inconvenient in the whole of Wilhampton, yet there was something about them, a *je ne sais quoi* – not that Flo understood about that either – which made them out of the ordinary. Way back, on both sides, there had been *breeding*, even if Sarah's grandmother had run off to go on the stage. For want of a better word, they had style, an unconscious knowledge of what was what, which most plainly revealed itself in the way they dressed. Like the county families they served, they never went in for bright colours. They wore browns, greys, navy or beige and, on occasion, white in summer and, of course, black for mourning.

The young woman now confronting Flo on the windswept platform was wearing a scarlet coat trimmed with some cheap, coarse fur, under which she appeared to have on a dress of shiny blue sateen. Perched on the black curls at a rakish angle there was a tam-o'-shanter of an even brighter blue; on her feet she wore black ankle-strap shoes with at least four-inch heels. To make matters worse, there was about her a smell of cheap scent and round her neck

47

she sported a necklace, not unlike the one which Katy, poor child, had been forced by Sarah to return to the stage manager at the fair that very morning. After they set off for the Mill House – Henry having arranged to collect their luggage a little later on by means of a hand truck borrowed from the mill – Flo wondered how her sister-in-law was going to be able to manage a good mile's walk. And during it, unfortunately, it seemed as if they were destined to meet half Wilhampton.

Henry, with his cheerful, hail-fellow-well-met disposition, had been a popular boy and everyone was glad to think, especially after Sarah's recent widowhood, that he had come home. More than once the little trio was obliged to stop and pass the time of day and the introduction of Marianne naturally caused surprise and sometimes friendly banter; although Flo herself, at these moments, simply stood aside in acute embarrassment, something which gradually increased, with the awareness of many a lace curtain twitching behind a window as they proceeded towards their destination. She dreaded the time when mother-in-law and daughter-in-law met.

Sarah, as Flo had rightly envisaged, was at the door to greet them. Wearing her best black dress, her coiffure immaculate, her work-worn hands clasped a little nervously in front of her, at first it seemed as if her whole countenance lit up on seeing them coming through the mill gates, and then, just as quickly, changed to frowning bewilderment as they drew closer and Henry said, 'Mother, this is Marianne.'

The latter – 'to give her her due', as May, who was standing behind Sarah, remarked afterwards – said, 'Bonjour, Madame,' pleasantly enough, and then kissed her mother-in-law on both cheeks. But, on entering the house, any initial goodwill such gestures might have engendered was quickly dispelled by her looking round, also in obvious astonishment, and saying, 'Plis, la toilette?' She was not the first visitor to discover that the Lodges' actual home by no means came up to the standard automatically presumed by its somewhat grand-sounding name.

It was a rather wan-looking Katy who was detailed to

48

take Marianne down the garden. Here, she shyly pushed open the door of the closet and stood back for this strange, unaccountable sister-in-law to enter, only to be confronted a moment later with a vehement shaking of the tight black curls and a torrent of '*non, merci!*'

Still suffering from the events of the previous twenty-four hours, Katy looked at Marianne dumbly. She knew not one word of French, but it was fairly obvious that some alternative to an earth closet was required. Yet she was painfully aware that this could only be the commode in her mother's bedroom or a chamber-pot in the attic. Neither solution seemed exactly expedient. Why couldn't this silly hoity-toity Frenchwoman do what she needed to do and stop making a fuss. After all, judging by the way she was clad, she did not exactly appear to have come from a palace.

'I'm afraid,' said Katy at length, doing her best to mime her reply, after a further unintelligible spate of French had abated a little, 'we only have this.' Even in her frail, rather shocked state, there was a certain dignity about the child, as she finally spread out her hands in a gesture of despair.

She watched Marianne frown. She had no means of knowing whether she had made herself understood; but she felt that this new wife of Henry's must surely have picked up some English from him by now. To her relief, possibly because of the simple, direct way she had spoken, Katy now saw the newcomer give a little shrug of resignation and disappear into the closet on her ridiculous high heels which she noted, not without satisfaction, had become coated with mud.

Yet the situation was only temporarily alleviated. Once Henry's wife reappeared, she began muttering something which sounded like 'lafay'. In frustration, when this produced no response, she, too, began to mime, making it quite clear that she wished to wash her hands. Miserably, Katy escorted her back to the house, wondering whether her mother would fetch a dipper of hot water from the mill and put it on the table already laid for dinner. But, luckily, this requirement appeared to have been carefully anticipated. May took Marianne up the winding staircase to Sarah's bedroom, where a jug of warm water was standing in the blue and white china basin on the wash-stand, together with some soap and a clean towel.

At last, at 2 p.m., the family sat down to their midday meal, which, owing to the various delays, was not at all as Sarah would have wished. She had asked Mr Pritchett, the butcher, for a special joint in honour of Henry's return, and the good man had delivered what she had told Flo and May was a 'pretty piece of meat', a sirloin of beef which, because of its expense, she would normally never have thought of buying. Now, as she took her first mouthful, having anxiously watched Henry carve none too carefully, she regretted that she had not made an ordinary stew. All the food was overcooked and she noticed that Marianne, Katy, Flo and even May – who, considering her small waist, was nevertheless usually possessed of a hearty appetite – seemed only to make a pretence at eating. Sarah herself also felt totally unable to do justice to the meal. Only the boys, Henry and Neil, tucked in, the former announcing cheerfully – but tactlessly, from his wife's point of view – that there was nothing like a bit of his mother's home cooking.

At last, when the dirty plates had been stacked away behind a curtain in the tiny so-called hall of the house. Sarah broached the question which had been uppermost in her mind since her son had arrived home. She had hoped that he might have brought the subject up himself. As he hadn't, she decided to wait no longer.

'And what, Henry, do you intend to do now?'

There was a momentary silence in the living room. All eyes turned expectantly – with the exception of Neil's vacant ones – towards Henry, those of his wife semi-knowing and supercilious. Suddenly, her husband's breezy self-confidence deserted him. He had forgotten just how forthright and direct his mother could be on occasions. He had known that his future plans would displease her but, with his customary insouciant optimism, had gone ahead, hoped for the best and trusted that he would be able to find a suitably propitious time for imparting his news.

Now, with obvious reluctance, he said, slowly, 'I've signed on, Mother. I'm a regular.'

'You never!' At moments like these, Sarah's grammar was apt to slip. She looked at her son, incredulously. Being a regular soldier would mean he might go anywhere. There would be no chance now of a man about the place. She had neither expected nor wanted him to work in the mill for, with the advent of Mr Fuller, she knew it was unlikely that Henry would be able to follow in his father's footsteps. Besides, he was such an outdoor type. She had reckoned on him obtaining some other sort of job in the district of an individual nature, possibly on the Fairfax estate. After all, head-keeping was quite a good position. Everyone in Wilhampton seemed both to fear and revere the present, ageing Fred Ashford, and although Henry's nature was rather different from that of the stern, tight-lipped Fred, nevertheless he was good with a gun, having been instructed how to use one when still a young lad by none other than Fred himself. Moreover, it was possible, if Henry worked hard, he might do even better. He knew a lot about the countryside, thanks to Fred; indeed, much more than Lilian Perrick's brother had ever done when he had started on the estate, and look where he was now: managing the Fairfaxes' Home Farm. All these things went through Sarah's mind as, in order to gain time and hide her emotion, she bent to make up the fire with hands which shook, partly in anger, partly in grief.

'Where,' asked Flo, trying to ease the tension, 'will they be sending you first, Henry?'

'York,' he replied, quickly. 'I have to report next Wednesday.'

Still with her back towards the others Sarah said, 'Perhaps you'd best be getting off to the station now, Henry, for your luggage. Katy here will take Marianne straight up to Edith's.'

With relief, the little party broke up. While Marianne and Katy were putting on their coats, Flo went into the mill with her brother to look for a suitable hand truck he could borrow.

'It's only natural,' she said quietly, as they went along

the narrow passage leading to the main building in search of the foreman, 'for Mother to take on a bit. I mean, after Frank going and then Father and . . . well, Neil being like he is. We hoped you'd be around somehow.'

Henry's usual carefree countenance had now completely changed. He wore the look of a chastened, crestfallen bloodhound, Suddenly, before they reached the heavy sliding door, he caught hold of Flo's arm and pulled her back.

'Mother would be even more upset if I did stick around,' he said. 'That's why I signed on. You can tell this to May but no one else, mind. Marianne's expecting. She's almost three months gone. I want her to be right out of the district when her time comes. Then we might just be able to get away with saying the baby was premature. Mother would never be able to hold up her head in Wilhampton again, if the truth came out.'

7

It was a chance remark made by Lady Fairfax's daughter one evening in early April which gave Katy Lodge her deliverance from the mill, although not, by any means, in the romantic way she was apt to dream about. No knight in shining armour – or, at least, some eminently desirable personage driving one of the new motor cars which were increasingly to be seen on the Wilhampton streets – arrived to claim and carry her off into the wider world. Her escape was destined to be far more mundane.

It came about because Flo and May had been summoned to the Hall by the now pregnant Honourable Alicia Moreton, who happened to be staying with her mother and wanted some maternity clothes. 'They will be so much better, dear Miss Lodge, than anything I could buy or have made in London,' the charming young mother-to-be said to Flo, as the latter knelt at her feet taking measurements. 'I swear there is no one like you two in the whole of the West End. If you could only set up in Bond Street, you would make a fortune.' And Flo and May had made appropriately appreciative sounds, storing up the conversation to be retailed later on when they got back to the Mill House. In her delight, May had even scrawled Bond Street at the bottom corner of the page in her notebook, where she was writing down such items as Length and Shoulders and Bust, well aware, naturally, that ample allowance must be made for an increase in the latter. Dear Miss Alicia had quite a few months to go yet.

How pretty she was, May thought, as she sat in the chintz-covered window-seat, with pencil poised, while a discussion took place concerning how many inches a certain day dress should be off the ground. At these moments, May was always quite happy to leave the decision to Flo and their client. After all, her sister was the senior in the partnership and it was only right that she should advise on such matters. Fortunately, there had never been any sibling rivalry between them. They worked well in double harness, performing their individual, self-appointed tasks with no other thought than the production of a first-rate garment when these had been completed. In their separate ways, both were perfectionists. May supposed that that was what the Honourable Alicia had been getting at when she had made the flattering remark about setting up in Bond Street. Idly, she wondered what it was like. She had never been to London. She had seen pictures of the capital, of course, sometimes with fashionable ladies and gentlemen strolling about the streets and parks or riding in hansom cabs, but it wasn't the same thing as going there and taking stock with one's own eyes. How wonderful it would have been if she and Flo could have become West End couturiers.

And then, 'as luck would have it' – another of May's pet phrases which she had used to describe the scene afterwards – just as they were leaving, Lady Fairfax had come into the room and her daughter had started reiterating some of her previous remarks about Flo's and May's expertise, but this time adding an even more thought-provoking one: 'So sad, Mummy. Nanny's niece who was coming as nursery maid has been quite ill with rheumatic fever, and her parents don't want her to leave home now.

It's going to be difficult to find someone else whom Nanny Barlow approves of.'

It was then that May's brain, always quicker than Flo's, suddenly got to work. The Fairfaxes' old nanny, who was now safely ensconced in the Moreton household busily preparing for the happy event, knew Katy quite well, didn't she? Katy had to be got away from the mill. From Neil. Katy, being the youngest of the Lodge family, mightn't know quite so much about babies, but she had often been sent up to look after Edith's little ones in emergencies. Besides, she was quick and well-mannered. Katy, under the auspices of Nanny Barlow and this kind, gentle, knowledgeable young matron, could come to no harm, could she? Even in the big city. May did not want to speak out of turn but . . . She looked across at Flo, wondering whether she, too, had grasped the implications, the timeliness of the whole situation. But her elder sister was putting away her tape measure and patterns and samples of material. To May, so much the more impulsive, it seemed now or never. She looked at the Honourable Alicia very directly.

'Then the vacancy for a nursery maid is still open, madam?' she enquired.

'Why, yes,' Lady Fairfax's daughter replied, somewhat in surprise. 'Had you anyone in mind?'

'It's just,' said May, simply, 'I feel that my youngest sister . . .' and here she turned towards Lady Fairfax herself, 'you remember, your ladyship, Katy, the one you have always been so kind to, might possibly be suitable for the position. She has passed her seventeenth birthday now and is quite capable and good with her needle. Her health has much improved. She is altogether fitter these days thanks largely, I am sure, to your ladyship's kindness when she was young.'

'Why, what a perfectly splendid idea.' Lady Fairfax and her daughter spoke almost with one voice. 'Katy is such a sweet, unusual and conscientious young girl.'

'It would, of course,' May added hastily, gaining confidence, albeit trusting she had not gone too far, especially as she had been unable, firstly, to test her elder sister's reactions, 'be for our mother to decide.'

'But naturally, Miss Lodge. Naturally. It would be entirely up to Mrs Lodge. But from our point of view, I cannot think of a happier solution.'

After they had been shown out by a parlourmaid through one of the side entrances, Flo and May elected to take the longer route home through the surrounding parkland. Such licence was one of the little perks connected with their somewhat unusual position, just as long as they were careful – which, of course, went without saying – never to abuse it and meticulously to eschew any of the more formal gardens adjacent to the Hall itself. Now, they took the winding path along by the river, while the evening sunlight came slanting through the willows and a yellow carpet of daffodils tossed hither and thither in a gentle westerly breeze.

'D'you think Mother will let her go?' It was Flo who began the conversation, as she rested for a moment by one of the bridges, her face lined and anxious. May was relieved that her elder sister appeared to have accepted her own spur-of-the-moment proposition, although not for the first time did she notice how much Flo seemed to have aged since their father's death, almost as if the burden of trying to take his place was too much for her.

'She mightn't like it, but I think she'll be bound to agree, once she hears what Neil tried to do. We've got to tell her now. If it hadn't been for her getting so worked up over Henry, we'd have done so before.' More or less unconsciously, May found herself continuing to assume the lead over this particular problem.

'But it's service. *Personal indoor* service, May. Mother always vowed she'd never let any of us do that. Her hopes of Henry one day becoming head gamekeeper on the estate was something quite different.'

'Oh, I know. But it's not as if Katy would be working for just anyone. It's the Fairfax family. They've seen her grow up. Look what Lady Fairfax did when she was little. It's my belief she's got a soft spot for the child.'

'Maybe.' Flo gave a little shrug of resignation. 'But sometimes I wonder . . .' she went on, and then broke off.

Quickly, May took her up. 'What do you wonder?'

'Oh, I don't know. About life . . .' Flo, her mouth set, her little tapestry bag with the tools of her trade dangling over one arm, strode on, purposefully. 'Families,' she continued, tossing her head and throwing the word, as it were, over her shoulder at her sister. 'Mother, in particular. D'you think she's ever been happy? Really happy? I mean, she's always had such a hard time of it. Bringing us all up. I can't imagine how we survived. When you think of all that water round the house. None of us able to swim, yet we had that boat. She can't have known a moment's peace. And then Neil being simple. It's pathetic the way she dotes on him.'

'It often happens, doesn't it? With children who aren't quite right. I suppose a mother feels extra responsible for having brought that kind of baby into the world.' May hurried along, finding it hard to keep up with Flo's longer strides. She was surprised at the weary cynicism that had crept into her elder sister's observations; although she knew, for all Flo's usually sweet and gentle manner, she had never really got over her unhappy love affair in the war. By a kind of silent understanding, they did not talk of Guy Armitage. Nor did they ever walk past The Warren. 'Yes, I realize that,' she now replied. 'But I think Father ought to have left her alone afterwards. It must have been ghastly for her when Katy was on the way, wondering whether she'd be the same.'

May was silent. She remembered how quiet Sarah had been during her final pregnancy and how badly she had gone down after the birth. May had only been eleven at the time. She hadn't understood it. Her mother had seemed so tired and listless. Katy, thank God, had been quite normal – even if she had turned out to be rather delicate to rear – but Sarah had taken so little interest in her, leaving Flo and herself to take care of the baby and the other young ones as best they could. It had never occurred to May to query her mother's malaise too deeply. She had been too young. She had simply accepted it as she had accepted Sarah's eventual return to health. Now, when Flo came out with her next statement, it was as if a whole host of half-forgotten memories came flooding back in sharp relief.

'I always reckoned Lilian Perrick had a lot to do with Mother getting better in the end,' her eldest sister suddenly vouchsafed.

'*Lilian Perrick?*'

'Yes. Or rather Lilian Firman, as she was then, keeping house for her brother up on downside, just before she married. I mean, Mother was in such a bad way, always lying on her bed and leaving you and me to do for Katy and the others, that quite often there just wasn't a meal for Father when he needed it, so he started going up to the Firman house for a bit of comfort. Of course, Lilian always was a bit of a one for the men. Anyway, when Mother got to hear about it, she pulled herself together pretty quick.'

'I see.' The light was fading now and May fastened the collar of her grey flannel coat. She had begun to feel chilly. Her mind had gone back seventeen years. She recalled how she had sometimes wondered where her father was of an evening, why her mother's apathy had all at once turned into something more positive, manifesting itself in overt weeping, red eyes and occasionally a raised voice in the bedroom, and how astonished she had been one night when her father, usually so equable and kind, had become taciturn and short-tempered, so that she had crept into Flo's bed in order to seek comfort, just as Katy, albeit for different reasons, had crept into hers not so very long ago. Was there no peace or respite for a respectable woman, ever? She supposed that money and position helped. Yet had there not been more than one ugly rumour going around the district lately connected with Sir Roger Broadbent and Grace Armitage? Was it possible that both Lady Broadbent and her own mother had, at some time or other in their lives, been sisters in distress?

'Anyway,' Flo continued, 'we'll just have to see what Mother says. I expect you were right to seize the opportunity. We'll all of us miss Katy. For one thing she's become more and more useful, but I know she ought to get out and I can't, for the life of me, think of a better place she could go at the moment.'

They were nearing the head keeper's cottage now and became aware of Fred Ashford, gun under arm and retriever by his side, walking towards them. Usually he would only nod or, at best, give a curt greeting; but on this occasion he actually stopped and passed the time of day.

'I hear young Henry was home a little while back,' he remarked laconically, as an opening gambit, his keen blue eyes looking first at one sister and then the other.

'Yes, Mr Ashford. Just for a week. He's signed on,' Flo answered.

'So I heard. Married, by all accounts.'

'Yes.'

There was an uncertain pause in the conversation. Fred Ashford made a derisory sound, somewhere between a snort and a grunt. Then, beginning to move off again, he said, 'Ah well, 'tis none of my business. Good evening.'

The sisters walked on, for the most part in silence. As they passed the west lodge and went out through the gates, Flo said quietly, 'Now he's lost his only son, I reckon Fred would have liked to have had our Henry under him and trained him on. They say he's disappointed in Percy Hooper's brother. Best not mention our meeting him to Mother. I don't think she'll ever forgive Henry for becoming a regular, and we've got quite enough to tackle her with at the moment.'

It was getting quite dark by the time they walked down River Lane and through the mill gates. The oil-lamp had been lit in the house and, at the still uncurtained window, Katy's slim figure could plainly be seen bending over the table, ironing.

'Poor kid,' said May, softly, suddenly realizing she had gone ahead without making any allowance for the person whom her proposition would most affect. Of all the family, she had always felt that her youngest sister had something about her which set her apart, that she was possibly destined for better things than sewing or ironing, or indeed, becoming nursery maid to Alicia Moreton's first child.

Yet an inherent common sense told her that, although by no means beggars, the Lodges could certainly not afford to be choosers.

8

For the second time in less than three months, Flo stood on Wilhampton station, only now, instead of awaiting two arrivals from the London train, she was saying goodbye to two people who were setting out for the capital: Katy with a third-class, six-and-eleven-pence-halfpenny single ticket; May, who was escorting her, with a twelve-shilling day return.

It was the first week in June and, although it was not yet nine o'clock, the sun had broken through the haze and the three sisters – especially the travellers, wearing straw hats and white gloves and carrying coats over their arms – were feeling the heat.

Katy's trunk – having been trundled up to the station earlier that morning by Herbie with a hand truck – was now safely in the guard's van, packed, as perhaps only the Lodge family could pack, with a neatness which, had the Honourable Alicia Moreton or Nanny Barlow been able to take a look inside, would have more than reassured them – should they have needed reassurance – of the wisdom of taking on such a youthful and untried employee. Indeed, had Katy been older, it might well have made her new employer wonder whether she might have been rather better engaged as a lady's maid.

For, instructed by Flo and May, Katy had meticulously placed all her bulkier accoutrements at the bottom: her winter boots, for instance, her new black indoor shoes, her bedroom slippers, all encased in appropriate bags, speedily run up on Flo's machine from the countless remnants of material stored away in old ottomans in the Mill House attic; then, stacked at each little corner, came such items as bible and prayer book, writing case containing notepad, envelopes and two dozen penny-half-penny stamps, a tin of acid drops (purchased by May from the Perricks' sweet shop), a photograph of the family in a wooden frame, another bag – made from a scrap of the mayoress's latest cream tussore over-blouse – containing brush and comb, and yet another one – this time of jaconet – which held toilet requisites. Somewhat as a *pièce de résistance* was a white wicker sewing basket – a present from Sarah – most beautifully appointed, together with an erstwhile tea caddy full of assorted buttons. Along the whole length of one side of the trunk lay Flo's smart, new, black umbrella. 'After all,' she had said, magnanimously, 'we've got another one between us here.' And making a flat even cover for this miscellany, Katy had spread two dozen, homemade, linen sanitary towels.

Next, swathed in copious sheets of tissue paper, there was a navy-blue winter coat made of West of England cloth and a carefully folded velour hat, cardigan and mittens of the same colour. Above these lay two pairs of woollen combinations, knickers and knicker linings, a couple of liberty bodices, two flannelette nightdresses, a thick plaid dressing gown and two blue serge uniform dresses. Dotted about to fill up convenient spaces were six pairs of neatly rolled-up black woollen stockings.

Further up in the hierarchy came lighter wear for summer: a second uniform dress of navy-blue tobralco – Katy was already wearing the other – a second sea-island cotton vest, cotton knickers and linings and two silk cami-soles trimmed with lace. In the tray of the trunk lay four pristine, white, starched aprons, two strange little white caps of a design particularly favoured by the Fairfax family, a dozen fine lawn hemstitched handkerchiefs embroidered 'K' which were tucked into a pink sateen sachet, together with a larger nightdress case of the same material, two nainsook nightdresses and petticoats, a hair net and an assortment of ribbons. All this was topped by a white, picot-edged, muslin rectangle exactly the size of the trunk which 'you could use,' May had said, hopefully, 'to throw over anything that you might want to keep specially clean. London's a terribly dusty place, by the sound of it.'

The Lodge family might have been forcing its youngest member into personal service, but it was certainly doing so in style. It was doubtful whether any prospective nursery maid had started off better equipped.

The train, belonging to the South-Western Railway Company, had drawn in dead on time. Mr Cutler, the station master, was out on the platform to welcome its arrival and then, having allowed it the statutory four minutes' halt and seen all its passengers, together with their respective luggage, disembark and embark, he waited while the guard lifted his green flag by the last carriage and promptly blew his whistle. Flo stood waving while May, for the fraction of a moment, leaned out of the window, before hastily drawing it up and sitting down in the opposite corner to a somewhat tearful Katy, as the Brunel Belle steamed round the bend and pressed on towards the next stop at Westonbury.

'We'd best both have one of these,' she said, taking a tin of Mothersill's Seasick Remedy out of her handbag. 'It's a long journey and we don't quite know how we shall feel by and by. We'll probably be quite all right, but it's better to be safe than sorry. Nanny Barlow always told me she swore by Mothersill's whenever she and the family went travelling.'

Still half bemused by all that had recently taken place, Katy did as she was bidden and then sat staring out of the window. She had not known what to think when she had first heard about the prospect of becoming a nursery maid in the Moreton household. A little like Sarah, half of her immediately rejected the idea; the other half saw it as opportune. She was not particularly enamoured of babies, but the thing which, as far as she was concerned, tipped the scales was the fact that she would be going to *London*. Here, she differed from her mother, who looked on the capital as, at best, a place of artificiality and temptation — at worst, certain ruination. Sarah Lodge had heard, for instance, about the white-slave traffic, in which young girls were lured by procurers and procuresses into seedy hotels and never seen or heard of again. There was also, she believed, a great deal of vice and gambling which went on in the West End; although exactly where or how Katy might come into this, she had no idea. Then there was the question of what she might do on her half day off each week. Sarah had a remote cousin living in Tooting Bec, but it might be far too long and hazardous a journey for her daughter to undertake.

When the letter had arrived, formally offering Katy the post at an initial salary of seven shillings and sixpence a week, although Sarah knew that in the name of good manners it must be answered as soon as possible, she had nevertheless procrastinated. For several days and nights she had gone about in a state of such mixed feelings that she was to be found, as she often was in times of stress, shaking her head and muttering: 'I don't know. I don't know, I'm sure,' as she bent over her washing or walked down the garden, or climbed the stairs to bed, spending an inordinate length of time on her knees to the Almighty before she actually got into it.

Flo's and May's disclosure about Neil's conduct had, of course, put an entirely different bearing on the situation. Had it not been for that, Sarah knew that she would never have entertained for a moment the idea of her youngest and most delicate daughter going off to London to become a nursery maid in the Moretons' household. It might just have been acceptable, she felt – albeit chiding herself for the unworthy thought – if the Honourable Alicia's father-in-law, old Sir Harry Moreton, had died, and the family was in possession of Bishopsdown, his country seat in Suffolk. But she believed he was quite a sprightly septuagenarian and there was no knowing when his estate would pass to the young people and they would spend more time in safer, healthier surroundings, rather than, as at present, the other way about.

It was on the fourth day of Sarah's tribulation that May had suddenly come back into the living room during the afternoon to fetch a pattern she had forgotten and found her mother sitting at the table, her head resting on her folded arms. Beside her lay pen and ink and writing-pad, on which she had written in immaculate copperplate hand-writing: *The Mill House, Wilhampton, Nr. Westonbury. April 14th, 1919.* She looked up now and stared at her daughter. Almost, there was a defeated look in her eyes. 'She'd best go,' was all she had said. 'How do I start the letter? Dear Mrs Moreton? Dear Madam? Madam?'

May had not been sure and she had gone to fetch Flo. Together, all three had agonized over what they trusted was a satisfactorily grateful, but not ingratiating, reply, and asking what date Katy would be required to take up her position. At the instigation of Flo, a small rider was added that if they could be sent details of the uniform which would be needed, this would be attended to forthwith.

It was not until long afterwards that Flo and May heard the reason for Sarah's final capitulation: that, by a curious coincidence, she had happened to meet Lilian Perrick by the mill gates earlier that day and the latter, although she had not exactly named names, had hinted that these days she felt it necessary to keep Ena under stricter supervision, not knowing who might be about. A twenty-year-old retarded youth had even more to do with Katy going off to the metropolis than she herself ever knew.

Now, as she sat in a third-class compartment of the Brunel Belle, all the traumas of the last-minute farewells over, she felt both scared and relieved: relieved that, what-ever the outcome, there was now no turning back. She was glad of May's company, even though she knew that they were both equally ignorant of the capital. But with this particular sister Katy shared a special kind of empathy, which the episode over Neil had only served to foster. She felt secure in the knowledge that May – who she sensed had had, in some mysterious way, more experience of life than Flo – would invariably understand, that she would make light of Katy's fears, whereas Flo would be apt to ponder over them; and although she knew that both sisters had her ultimate good at heart and that by taking her responsibilities so seriously, Flo's judgement might be the more soundly reasoned, yet she sometimes felt that May's straight-from-the-heart spontaneity caused her often to arrive at equally satisfactory conclusions by happier and less laboured means. Had Flo been with her today, Katy felt sure that she would already have been worrying over the problems of porters and taxi-cabs at Waterloo, whereas May was now obviously viewing the whole business as a great adventure.

Having been lucky in securing window seats opposite each other, more than once her elder sister leant across and caught Katy's arm, pointing out some item of interest; and the latter, however apprehensive she might have been feeling at entering such a strange new world, had had her mind taken off it by being forced to admire some unusual scenery or, as they neared the capital itself, a whole host of enormous buildings, the like of which neither of them had ever seen.

Once on Westminster Bridge – their arrival at the station and the securing of both a porter and a cab having gone surprisingly smoothly – May, whose remarks had been made *sotto voce* in the railway carriage in deference to the other occupants, now burst forth in unrestrained pleasure. 'Oh, chippatoo! Oh, chippatoo! Look, Katy. Just fancy. That'll be the Houses of Parliament and Big Ben. You'll be able to come down here on your half-day, maybe, and look for as long as you like.' Little did either sister know then that Katy would actually be able to see both edifices from her tiny bedroom at 89 Upper Brook Street.

When the cabby was forced to draw up for a while in the centre of the bridge, and the River Thames, sporting innumerable little tugs and barges, lay sparkling in the sun for as far as the eye could see on either side of them, May could hardly contain herself. 'Oh, Katy, it reminds me of a poem we learnt at school. I wish I could remember it. By Wordsworth, I think. Something about "Earth has not anything to show more fair". Isn't London just beautiful? I'm sure you're going to be very happy here.'

Despite her now increasing nervousness, it was hard for Katy not to share, just for a little while, some of her elder sister's enthusiasm, although the grave, forbidding appearance of Mr Walker, the Moretons' butler, as he came – as if by magic – down the steps of Number 89 exactly as the cab drew up at the door, and quickly instructed the driver to go round the corner to a side entrance, soon sent her spirits sinking again. It made her more painfully aware than ever that she was, after all, going into *domestic* service, something to which she knew that her mother, for all her curiously sudden acquiescence, was still most strongly opposed.

Moreover, although she was relieved to find that her trunk, with all its precious possessions, was being efficiently dealt with by a young man in a baize apron and that a plump, pleasant-looking parlourmaid had arrived on the scene to show her and May up to the nursery quarters on the fourth floor, by the time she found herself in the presence of Nanny Barlow, Katy became practically tongue-tied. She had forgotten just how large the woman was and how well known her reputation for sizing people up in a disconcerting fashion, her eyes missing nothing as they travelled up and down, back and forth, all over one, while they seemed to search for an undone button or a stray wisp of hair. Yet, possibly having secretly approved of the slender, immaculately turned-out little figure before her, Nanny Barlow now held out her hand agreeably enough and said, 'My, Katy, and how grown up you are. I'm very glad you've come to help me well before the bairn is due. I hear that you sew and knit well, and there is still much you can be doing. Besides, it will give you good time to get used to the ways of the household.' And then, turning quickly to May, almost as if she felt that she had paid more than enough attention to her new trainee, she added, 'I'm sure we shall get along fine, Miss Lodge, just as long as your sister is conscientious and willing to learn and always remembers who she is working for. There is no better household, other than Lady Fairfax's own, of course, into which she could have come, I'm sure.'

May did not seem to take such words amiss. Katy, in her innermost heart, did. Somewhere, beneath the pale, polite demeanour, lurked the Katy of spirit, the Katy of her great-grandmother, the Katy of the fairground who had sung 'Our Lodger's Such a Nice Young Man'. She did not feel quite right in the nursery of 89 Upper Brook Street and hoped that she would not always be a nursery maid or, at best, a children's nanny.

As the trio sat down to a simple stew and rice pudding, brought up by yet another minion in the Moreton establishment, such feelings were unfortunately only reinforced when Nanny Barlow suddenly said, 'Tomorrow, Katy, you will be able to fetch our meals from the kitchen yourself. But with your young legs that should not be too much for you.' Sadly, what Katy was finding too much for her now was trying to finish the rice pudding which had been heaped on to her plate.

Although she was dreading her sister's departure after the meal was over, it was a relief when Nanny Barlow offered to accompany May 'just for a few steps', as she put it, in order to point out the way to the place she was set on seeing: Bond Street, and how from thence she could easily walk down to Piccadilly and catch a bus to Waterloo. Katy was glad that neither of them could see the tears which fell fast as, miserably, she then began to unpack her trunk in a room which, for all its fine views over London, seemed little more than a cupboard.

9

Alicia Moreton and Marianne Lodge both gave birth to sons within a few weeks of each other, Alicia's child, John William Harry, arriving at the end of August, Marianne's Frank François (the two names bestowed on the infant in an effort at some kind of *rapprochement* with Sarah) being born in the middle of September.

The latter made no comment as to the alleged premature arrival of her new grandchild. The fact that there would now be another Frank in the family was merely acknowledged by a carefully-worded letter to Henry, saying that she trusted the little boy would live up to his deceased uncle's good name. She did not write to her daughter-in-law, nor send any kind of token to the child. Neither did she make any reference to wishing to see Frank François, even though Henry was now much nearer home, having recently been posted to Aldershot. Sarah Lodge had, in fact, with a ruthlessness which often confounded her family, cut Henry off, not with the proverbial shilling – which, in any case, she did not have to give – but with the affection which she might otherwise have accorded him, had he not acquired a foreign wife of dubious status, who had produced a child within less than seven months of marriage. 'There were,' as May and Flo remarked to each other after hearing the news, 'no flies on Mother,' apart, they agreed, from the extraordinary tenderness which she showed towards Neil, invariably turning a blind eye to his unfortunate behaviour, as if by pretending he was not as he was, she could almost bring herself – and, hopefully, others – to think of him as normal.

But that autumn and winter May had many more things on her mind than making conjectures about Sarah's character. What was bothering her was the obvious deterioration in Neil's state of mind, and, though not so obvious but strangely insidious, the deterioration in Flo's state of health. She could not help noticing her elder sister's pallor, the deep shadows under her eyes – especially at certain times of the month – and a lassitude totally alien to her usual hardworking nature. Once or twice on such occasions, May was surprised at being asked to take over the machining for a day or two. Flo was 'flooding', as she put it, and the constant movement of her legs on the treadle made it worse.

'You ought to see Dr Fitzherbert,' May said, one afternoon in early November, when she felt sure that Flo was in more discomfort than she cared to admit. 'He'd give you a tonic.'

'Maybe. I'll see.' The older woman bent to pick up the flat-iron that was heating on a tripod over the grate. 'I don't much care for the thought of him examining me,' she added.

'But I'd be there.' It went without saying that a female member or friend of the Lodge family always accompanied another female patient on a visit to the doctor.

'Oh, I know. But let's just wait a while. Could be, I'm

a bit like Katy. Remember how bad her periods were when they first came on after Father died.'

May was silent. That was different, she felt. Young girls often flooded at the start of menstruation. Many women flooded at the change of life. But Flo was only thirty. That event might well not overtake her until she was fifty or more. Why, Sarah herself, though irregular, hadn't finished yet, although she was always trying to disguise the fact from her children, as if there was something indecent in such a state of affairs in a sober, middle-aged widow. May went on stitching buckram into a collar, listening to the hissing sound of the iron as it made contact with the damp cloth laid over a partially completed broadcloth coat.

Presently Flo said, 'Shall we give over now when I've finished this? We can take the other stuff up to the house to do after tea. There's a lot of hemming and oversewing to get through. I must say I miss our Katy in more ways than one, don't you? She was a better little helpmate than we realized.'

'Yes.' May started gathering up the various bits and pieces around her. It was unlike Flo to want to leave the workroom so early. Usually they kept on until the light had all but faded, but she guessed that today, just standing over the ironing, had probably fatigued her sister enough.

Now, as May came towards the door of the Mill House, it irked her to find Mr Fuller returning the tea-tray which Sarah had taken up to his office earlier that afternoon. There was no need for him to do so. She felt it was slightly *infra dig.* for a manager to perform so menial a task. Yet she knew perfectly well why he did. For although George Fuller was a married man with two children, she was aware that he fancied her and would make any excuse to visit the house on the off-chance of seeing her. She disliked him intensely and, whenever his motorbike could be heard chugging in or out of the mill gates, she was apt to make disparaging remarks. With his scrawny neck and weak blue eyes, he reminded her a little of Ernest Fielding. 'Here comes Duck and Collar,' she would sometimes say, much to her mother's disapproval, or, 'I don't know why his lordship has to make quite such a din, unless it's to make sure we all catch sight of him on his chariot riding by.'

Once, when Sarah had had a bad cold and she herself had felt obliged to take Mr Fuller's tea-tray up to his office at the appointed time of three o'clock, he had tried to get her to sit down and share some of the food with him. 'Your mother makes such delicious cakes, Miss Lodge. I fear I'm fast putting on weight, but I just can't resist them. I am not used to such luxury at home.' And May had inwardly fumed because, although his wife was reputed to be careless and lazy, she felt that it did not absolve him from making veiled references to such failings in the worst possible taste. She had been almost rude as she made a hurried departure, saying that she had too much to do to waste time eating in the middle of the afternoon. But, even so, it had not put the wretched man off. He had said that this must be the reason why she kept so slim a waist and, as she went down the steep wooden steps, she had still heard him muttering obsequiously in the background, 'So good . . . so industrious . . .'

On this particular afternoon she nodded curtly and would have gone into the house without a word, had he not purposely waylaid her. 'Miss Lodge, I was wondering . . . could I speak to you for a moment about your brother?'

'My *brother?*' May stared at him, incredulously, her tiny figure temporarily coming to a halt, while curiosity, even fear, for the moment overcame the desire to shake the man off. Behind her, she could hear Flo locking up the workroom and then, unfortunately, going into the closet before coming up the garden path. 'What about him?' she asked, guardedly.

From the window of the living room in which a lamp had just been lit, she could see the figures of her mother and Neil moving about. It had seemed a relief that afternoon when Sarah had suggested that she should look after her son because he would be able to undertake the small job in which he delighted: that of scooping up into a wheelbarrow the horse's dung left after the carrier's cart had made a delivery to the mill, which it had done just before dinner time. Surely, Mr Fuller wasn't going to make some objection to that, was he? After all, it was good to have the main pathway cleared of manure and sometimes Ernest Fielding asked for a little of it to put in the rain-water-butt by his greenhouse, so that his precious orchids might reap the benefit when they were watered.

At length, George Fuller replied in the kind of Uriah Heep manner with which she had come to associate him, 'I hate to say this, Miss Lodge, but I thought it best to warn you rather than distress your poor mother further.'

'Yes?' Impatiently, her tone demanded that he got on with whatever it was he had to say. He looked so silly, she felt, standing there with the tea-tray in his hands, but she made no attempt to take it from him.

Still the man parried. Bitterly, she resented the way his eyes appraised her, as he at last continued, 'I'm afraid your brother seems not altogether to have stuck to his little task this afternoon. He was found in one of the mill buildings, the one where the women and girls work. That could be dangerous . . .' He coloured slightly. 'The machinery,' he added, with a small embarrassed cough.

'Yes. Yes, of course. I'm sorry. My mother usually keeps a good eye out for him.' May was finding it increasingly hard to remain civil.

'Oh, I know she does, Miss Lodge. She is a wonderful woman, altogether admirable. You all are. But I believe, lately . . . your brother has been a little more difficult to manage?'

May bit her lip. What a long time Flo was being in the closet. After all, she was the eldest, wasn't she? Duck and Collar should have addressed his complaint to her. Then, quickly, May's innate sense of fairness reasserted itself. Flo wasn't well, not that Mr Fuller could have been expected to know that. Yet even so, there was no reason for him not to have approached May herself. She was hardly a child and, besides, she had happened to be around. She could just as well deal with the matter.

'I'll see it doesn't occur again, Mr Fuller,' she replied, coldly, this time taking the tea-tray and disappearing indoors.

She could tell immediately that Sarah was in one of her states or, rather, silent humours. May wondered how Mr Fuller had heard of the incident so quickly. His office window did not look out on the main pathway where Neil had been 'working'. She wondered whether one of the older women had brought Neil back to the house and then, relishing her role of informer in the drama, gone to find Tom Henstridge. Please God it wouldn't have been Cissy Lawes. Cissy had always been the main target for her mother's contempt. Loud-mouthed, forward and 'no better than she should be' was how Sarah invariably referred to her. In the light of hindsight, May realized that such hostility towards the woman and, indeed, all the female members of the staff who had been taken on during the war, probably sprang from her mother's deep feelings of jealousy and resentment due to their close proximity to her late husband – not that she could remember her father being anything other than beyond reproach, in so far as the management of the mill was concerned.

Sarah did not say anything about the afternoon's occurrence when May came in. For one thing, although she would die rather than admit it, she felt she might have been somewhat to blame. Yet she kept telling herself that she had watched Neil just as carefully as usual, firstly from out of the window and then, when he had got up as far as the furthermost building, she had kept popping out of the front door to see how he was getting on. When she thought he was almost finished she had gone inside to take a cake out of the oven, expecting any minute to hear him trundling his wheelbarrow past the house and down the garden path. When he did not, she had gone out to take a further look, surprised to find the barrow still where it was and Neil nowhere to be seen. She had begun to run then, picking up her long black skirt and stumbling in her lace-up boots on the uneven ground.

Her fright had not lasted long. Instinct told her to look in the women's building first and, sure enough, there was Neil with Cissy Lawes and one or two others laughing at him and throwing the loose wool, which they should have been feeding into one of the noisy giant machines, all over

Neil so that he was beginning to look like a snowman. They had stopped at once at the sight of Sarah and, shame-facedly, gone back to their work while, stony-eyed and without a word, she had caught hold of her son's arm and hurried him away.

Now, as the damp, raw, November evening began closing in on the Mill House and its occupants, there was a deep sense of unease in the living room, each member of the family strangely quiet and subdued. After tea, Flo, unsure of exactly what had taken place, but sensing that she would be unlikely to hear until she and May were in bed, picked up her sewing, listlessly. In any case, at the moment she felt almost too drained and tired to bother. Sarah simply knitted in silence, a long grey woollen sock for either Herbie or Neil gradually taking shape as the clicking of her steel needles mingled with the ticking of the grandfather clock in the corner: May worked some buttonholes on the nigger-brown herringbone tweed suit they were making for Mrs Donaldson, the Rector's wife. Neil, still with a few flecks of wool in his hair and on his jacket, sat hunched by the fire opposite his mother, occasionally, under her watchful gaze, prodding it with a poker through the iron bars of the grate.

All of them went to bed early. Sarah had even taken the lantern and locked the mill gates soon after the six o'clock hooter had sounded for the men to stop work. George Fuller's motorbike had been heard chugging by some time before that. His hours were naturally not those of the mill-hands. Nowadays, since Flo and May had ceased to lead the kind of social life they had been used to during the war, Sarah was apt to 'shut up shop' earlier than ever, for although Tom Henstridge had duplicate keys with which he opened the gates each morning, the nightly ritual of locking-up was completely in her hands. It seemed to her daughters that she derived a definite sense of satisfaction, security and even power for this to be so, to know that her flock, albeit diminished in size, was, as her late husband would also have wished, safely indoors, if not actually in bed.

Tonight, after drinking a little soup made from the

stock-pot she invariably kept on the range during winter, everyone was upstairs before nine. Sarah had seen to Neil's undressing and then, with candlestick and matches – carefully never left with him for a moment – had retired to her own room. Overhead, she could hear the girls murmuring, but only for a little while. Presently, all was quiet save for Neil's snores, but she herself was unable to sleep. The clock above the town hall in the market square struck the hours and still she tossed and turned. A kind of nameless panic took hold of her. For all her outward appearance of hardness, adopted for self-preservation's sake, she was much more vulnerable than even any member of her family knew. The previous day's events had upset her stomach and, at five that morning, after only a couple of hours' sleep, she was obliged to take the lantern and go outside to the closet. Nothing, save extreme urgency, would have made her use the commode on such an occasion.

She must have been gone, she supposed afterwards, less than ten minutes. She had returned and climbed back into bed, praying that she might just drop off again for a few moments before the girls' shrill alarm rang out and they came down from the attic and through her own room on their way to wash in the mill.

But sleep still eluded her. Flo and May appeared at six o'clock and then reappeared not long afterwards with the customary dipper of soapy water which they placed by the basin on her washstand. Wearily, Sarah performed her morning ablutions, put in her false teeth and began to dress, lacing up her stays with fingers which she had noticed lately were becoming increasingly stiff. She had just put on her working dress and was pinning up her hair, when the six-thirty hooter sounded, and the men who had been patiently waiting outside the gates now streamed through them and jostled noisily past the house. Sarah sighed, remembering the days when Sidney would have been out to start them all off. With resignation, she picked up her candlestick and went into Neil's bedroom to shake him awake, knowing that no extraneous sounds were usually of any assistance at such times.

His bed was empty. For a moment, open-mouthed, she simply stared at it, the only movement in the room being the flickering of her shadow on the opposite wall. Then, with a small stifled scream, she let the candlestick crash to the ground and heard Flo and May hurrying up the stairs in the dark.

Groping, May managed to find the matches, strike one and bring some light back on the scene, after which she, too, saw the empty bed.

'Oh, my God!' The blasphemous ejaculation, coming instinctively from her lips, very different from her usual, happy-go-lucky 'Oh, chippatoo!', would, at any other time, have elicited a rebuke from her mother. Now, all three women simply looked at each other in horror and bewilderment.

Then, her brain suddenly getting to work again, Sarah said, quickly, 'Find Herbie. Neil can't have gone long. I went to the closet about five, but I was back in ten minutes.'

Yet, even as she spoke, all of them were aware that a lot could have happened since then.

Flo ran up through the now lighted mill, already thrumming with life at the start of a new day. May, clutching a torch, sped towards the mill-race. Sarah took her lantern and hurried, almost involuntarily, towards the Perrick house. Although she realized that Neil had not taken her keys and that it would have been virtually impossible for him to climb over the gates, yet she knew – as she supposed her simpleton son, in his slow, confused mind, probably also knew – that there were other means of exit and entrance to the mill: small, secret and dangerous, a labyrinth of little passages, narrow planks without handrails, spanning swift, sinister streams and mostly known only to those who lived and worked there. The gas lamps were still on in River Lane, shining over the deep, murky, silent water which flowed beside it. Anxiously, Sarah held her lantern on high, the better to light it up, but it picked out little save the grey-green undulating weeds and the Perrick boy's boat, moored on the opposite bank.

No one found Neil until daylight. His body, clad only

in night-shirt and jacket, was spotted by Tom Henstridge, lying against the hatch of one of the tributaries which branched out close to the mill-race. Herbie and Tom brought it back to the house and Dr Fitzherbert was sent for, not, as they all knew, that there was anything he could do – at least, not for Neil. The boy had been in the water some time. But it was imperative that the doctor should come, at once, just as the Reverend Donaldson would be needed a little later on.

It was May who hurried up to the surgery, knowing that she would find Abie Grant, the dispenser, in his starched white coat, already busy amongst his large glass jars of Mist. Pot. Brom., Mist. Gent. Alk., or 'Grey' powder. In his tiny box-like room, Abie could be relied upon to be almost permanently at the ready, checking his supplies and waiting to produce whatever bottle of medicine that Dr Fitzherbert prescribed, meticulously doing up each item in stiff white wrapping paper securely fastened by a blob of red sealing wax, its label proclaiming in his immaculate script the name and dosage for whomsoever it was required.

Today, the place was already filling up as May came through the entrance, hurried over to Abie's small hideout and rapped on the panelled 'window'. It shot up at once and Abie's face, behind its steel spectacles, peered at her cautiously. In many ways, he was not only the doctor's dispenser but also his protector; for Abie was possessed of an uncanny ability to know whether a certain person was crying wolf, or trying to be seen by the doctor ahead of others without due cause. There was not an inhabitant in the whole of Wilhampton or, indeed, most of the surrounding district, whom he did not know and whose character he could not size up to a nicety. Now, his mind immediately went back to the day, just after last Christmas, when it had been Flo Lodge rapping on the panel of his little dispensary when her father was dying. Could it be, he wondered, that this time it was Sarah . . . ? He remembered that she had gone down badly after Sidney's death. He had scarcely seen her in the town all the year.

'Mr Grant.' Conscious that her abrupt and purposeful

entry had aroused more than a little interest and that several pairs of eyes and ears were waiting on her with curiosity, May leaned well forward across the prescription shelf and whispered her message.

Abie, registering both shock and concern, gave a quick, 'Wait here, my dear,' and drew down his little shutter. Almost immediately, he reappeared through another door at the end of the waiting room and summoned May into Dr Fitzherbert's inner sanctum. The good man, who fortunately had not started to see his first patient, was already putting on his coat. 'Your poor mother,' he said, and then, as they hurried back to the Mill House together, 'Your poor, poor mother,' he said again. For so short a distance, he had deemed it quicker to go on foot, much as he was beginning to rely – especially in emergencies – on the twelve-horsepower Doctor's Standard Coupé which he had recently acquired in favour of his old pony and trap; although, even in this, he seldom drove at more than fifteen miles per hour, and still proceeded to lean slightly forward on going up hill and backwards on coming down, just as he had done to help along his one-horsepower former mode of transport.

Herbie and Tom Henstridge were at the door when they arrived, the under-manager keeping a sharp lookout for any would-be ghoulish inquisitors and chivvying on any of the hands who gave the slightest appearance of dawdling past the house as they went about their duties. Inside, upstairs in Neil's room, Sarah was kneeling by the body which, still muddied, soaking wet and reeking of river, had been laid on the bed. Tears were streaming down her face. Beside her, chalk-white and shaking, stood Flo, trying, without success, to get her mother to take a little brandy kept by the family strictly for medicinal purposes only.

Yet, even in her grief, Sarah remembered her manners. She stood up on the doctor's arrival and he, gently hinting that he would like to make his examination in private, suggested to Flo and May that they should take their mother downstairs to lie on the living-room couch. Unwillingly, Sarah allowed herself to be led away and Dr Fitzherbert closed the door.

Presently he, too, came down to join them, doing his best to comfort Sarah and asking that someone should come back to the surgery in half an hour's time to fetch a sedative which he would get Abie to make up. Then, at the front door of the house, while Flo was seeing him out, he said, quietly, 'No need to say anything to your mother now, my dear, but I'm afraid that there will have to be an inquest.'

'An *inquest?*' Flo's eyes opened wide with fear, her nostrils flared. 'Oh, *no!*' She put out a hand and steadied herself at the threshold. She could feel a sudden discharge of blood between her legs. Her forehead broke out in a sweat. Dr Fitzherbert laid one of his own hands on her shoulder.

'You must be brave, my dear.' His keen blue eyes under the bushy eyebrows searched hers. It was hard for him to tell whether her present appearance was all to do with the tragedy which had just taken place. He hoped so, but he did not like the feel of her thin, bony shoulder, the way she seemed to have lost so much weight since he had last seen her. 'It will only be a formality,' he said. 'I'll try to see that Dr Machin makes it as short and painless for you all as possible.'

'But you mean Mother will have to attend?'

'Well, yes. She was the last to see your brother alive. But try not to worry. I will get in touch with the authorities and someone will come to take Neil's body away to the mortuary as soon as possible. And I know that the Rector will be down at once when I send word to tell him what has happened.'

Flo nodded. 'Thank you, Doctor.'

It seemed to her like only yesterday that death had come to the Mill House, that the surrounding waters had, in some mysterious way, claimed another victim; except that in Sidney Lodge's case there had been no question of an inquest.

10

Katy was putting some of John William's nappies through the mangle in the basement of Number 89, when Nanny Barlow came to find her. She was surprised. It was unlike such an august personage to make many sorties below stairs. Katy was fast learning what a tight, enclosed little world it was on the nursery floor of the household to which she now, so unexpectedly, belonged.

'How are you getting on, my dear?' The use of the endearment made Katy even more surprised. Though basically a kind, good woman, Nanny Barlow was quite a hard taskmaster. It was usually 'Katy this' and 'Katy that', and 'Mind you rinse those nappies well, especially the Harringtons. If any soap stays in them, a baby can get nappy rash. None of mine has ever had that.' So far, Katy had hardly been allowed to touch John William herself.

'I've nearly done, Nanny,' she replied, quickly. 'Was there something else you wanted me to do?'

'Presently, my child. But as soon as you've done down here, come straight upstairs. I've something to say to you.'

Katy completed her task, wonderingly. The woman hadn't sounded exactly cross, but the 'something to say to you' seemed ominous. She tried to think of what she might have done wrong. Gathering up the pile of damp nappies, she took them into the drying room, let down the wooden rack from the ceiling, hung them over it and hoisted it back into position again. It was a shame, she thought, that they couldn't go out into the garden and have what her mother would have considered essential: 'a good blow'. But even if Number 89 had a garden into which they could go, it wouldn't have been any good. As May had rightly said, she was finding London, for all the beauty of its parks and splendour of its fashionable West End residences, an incredibly dusty, dirty – and often very lonely – place.

Back upstairs, she found Nanny Barlow sitting beside the heavily-guarded fire, giving John William his bottle.

Although the older woman was far too loyal a servant ever to have voiced such an opinion, Katy sensed that it was a source of regret to her that the baby had been weaned from birth and never offered the breast. But she discovered that this was quite usual in such circumstances, for she had written to May about it, who had explained in her next letter that Mrs Moreton probably had so many engagements to fulfil which would make breast-feeding impossible, 'and besides', she had added, 'the dear thing would want to get her lovely figure back quickly'. Katy had pondered over this for a while, wondering about the importance of both Mrs Moreton's figure and the social round in which she and her husband took such an active part: the almost nightly dinners, dances or theatres which seemed to take place in London's West End. Often, she had lain awake, wishing she might be part of them, vicariously savouring a sudden burst of laughter, the sound of a cab stopping outside the house, the light-hearted exchange of goodnights, footsteps on the stairs. Sometimes, she even caught a faint whiff of cigar smoke.

But today, she simply stood enquiringly at the door of the nursery, a small, upright, fetching little figure in her cap and apron. She had filled out since her arrival and, contrary to what might have been expected, London had put some colour into her cheeks. Even in the few months she had been away from home, Katy Lodge, always a fast learner, had definitely acquired a certain poise.

'You wanted me, Nanny?'

'Yes, Katy. Sit down.'

She walked across the room and took the wicker chair opposite the fireplace.

For a few moments there was silence, except for the sound of the baby sucking and an occasional spluttering noise as a live coal fell from the grate. Then, when John William had finished his bottle, Nanny Barlow sat him up gently to be winded and said, 'I had a letter from your eldest sister this morning, Katy.'

'From Flo?' Terror seized her. Imagination ran riot. Could something have happened? To Mother? To May?

'Don't take on, child. It's probably all for the best. God's will, I daresay.'

'But what . . . ?'

'Your brother, Neil. He was found drowned yesterday morning.'

'Drowned? Oh *no*.' Immediately, her youthful, generous heart went out to Sarah. Hard though she often appeared, and seemingly unfair in her strange, obsessive love for her youngest son, Katy could not bear to think of her mother's suffering. As for herself, she simply found it difficult to take in, to realize that this unfortunate brother of hers, so limited and inarticulate, yet whose presence had been such a constant, positive factor in all their lives, day in and day out, for twenty-one years, was no longer living. What would it be like at home without him?

'The funeral . . . ?' she enquired, tentatively.

'It will not be until a week today. Next Saturday. But it seems . . . your family think it best you should not go. The travelling . . .' Nanny Barlow added, quietly. Both knew that, expense apart, Katy was considered to be on the young side for undertaking such a journey alone. What neither knew was that Flo and May had managed to over-rule their mother in the decision not to drag her youngest daughter home; for, even in the midst of her shock and sorrow, Sarah had nevertheless said that it was only right and proper that all the other members of the family should attend – even Henry.

'I see.' Katy still felt numbed. She could not cry for, since the night when Neil had made his hideous and frightening foray up to her bed in the attic, she had shunned him. Though he was her own kith and kin, he now filled her with revulsion. Whereas, at one time, his cheerful idiot's smile had simply been seen as inoffensive and acceptable – even, at times, a cause for compassion and tenderness – she no longer experienced any such emotion. She looked on him as an alien: an ugly, loose-limbed, ill-co-ordinated predator, demanding and soaking up, like some huge sponge, all the love which Sarah should, by rights, have been giving to the rest of her brood.

Suddenly, she heard Nanny Barlow start to speak again.

'I'll get Clara to take you along to the Grosvenor Chapel in South Audley Street on Saturday afternoon. Maybe you would like to go inside and say a prayer or two while the funeral's taking place. You could be with them in spirit, like?'

Katy looked at her, dumbfounded. Is that what others did? She did not care for the idea at all. She and Nanny Barlow had often passed the chapel on their walks. It was such a grand place. She wouldn't dare to go inside alone. She wondered if Clara, the head parlourmaid, would come in with her. In any case, what could she pray? She could say the Lord's Prayer, she supposed, and ask Him to take care of her mother. When people died, the bereaved sometimes prayed for their souls, didn't they? Would Neil go to heaven? If one was mentally deficient, how much soul did one have? She began to feel guilty at not being able to feel sad at Neil's passing. But wasn't it better for him not to go on living? She sat staring at the fire, lost in thought, thoughts somewhat unusual and mature for one of such tender years and scanty education.

'There now. You'd best be washing John William's bottle, Katy.' Nanny Barlow broke in on her reverie. 'Then put it in the bowl of water on the gas ring and I'll do the boiling-up later. Mind and clean the teat with salt, and rinse it well.' She got up and took the infant back to his crib. She was glad the girl had taken the news so sensibly. She was a good little thing. Well brought up. Came from a reliable family, apart from the poor boy who had just died. She wondered how that had happened. Flo hadn't said much. She'd probably get a letter from Mrs Harwood, the Fairfaxes' housekeeper, in a day or two, telling her more about it. She wondered what John William's mother would say when she returned from the charity bazaar she'd been attending all day. She would be sure to be concerned for, like her own mother, she was a good mistress, always taking an interest in the personal lives of her employees.

Alicia Moreton was, indeed, extremely distressed when she came up to the nursery after tea and heard of the tragedy. Fortunately, Nanny Barlow had been able to have a word with her in private, for Katy had been in her little bedroom busy writing home.

'I'll come back and see her when I've dressed for dinner, Nanny. Best to let her finish her letter now, so that she can run out with it to catch the seven-thirty post. Otherwise I think someone else will have to take it to the special eight o'clock box, as there's a fog coming down fast. I'm sure she's hoping it will be in the Wilhampton Sunday delivery tomorrow. Perhaps you would see she puts an extra half-penny stamp on, in case it has to go into the later collection.'

Charles Moreton was none too pleased when his wife failed to join him in the drawing room before dinner that night. Aperitifs were just coming into fashion and, although at the homes of their respective parents these were never served unless there were guests, Charles had acquired a liking for them each evening, even if Alicia, who was practically teetotal, only sipped a little fruit juice in order to keep him company.

He had scarcely seen her since she had come in. He himself had been at his club all the afternoon, and they had simply exchanged a few remarks in the hall about the pea-souper outside and the time that it had taken Ruther-ford, their chauffeur, to drive her from Belgravia. He recalled her having murmured something about having to go to see the new nursery maid later on who had suffered a bereavement. Sometimes he felt that she overdid her involvement with their servants, especially on the personal side. *Noblesse oblige* was such a motivating force in the Fairfax family, not that his own mother, when she had been alive, hadn't done her bit in that direction. But Lady Fairfax was a kind of queen in the art. He hoped Alicia wasn't going to turn out just like her. She had seemed so happy and carefree when they had been engaged. He supposed that John William coming along so soon after their marriage had somehow sobered her. It would have been nice to get right away now, just the two of them, especially as the nursery arrangements appeared to be working so well, even though he himself found Nanny Barlow a tiresome old battle-axe. She seemed to think she was still as much in charge of his wife as John William. He really must try to put a stop to these long sessions they had together, which he felt sure were having an adverse effect on Alicia. He had a good mind to take her abroad for their first wedding anniversary that was just coming up. His job in the city was not arduous and there was no reason why they should not take advantage of the new commercial airline service which had just opened. They could easily flip over to Paris for a few days. He would mention it when she came down.

Alicia did not arrive until the gong sounded and during the meal it was difficult to say much while Walker, the butler, waited on them. But once back in the drawing room, he brought the subject up.

'Fly to Paris?' She frowned. 'You must be mad.'

'Why?'

'I'm a mother now. You have a son and heir.'

'So?'

'I wouldn't trust myself to one of those machines.'

He was silent in the face of her all too logical objection.

'Besides,' she continued, 'we'll all be going away soon. Christmas isn't far off and Mummy wants us to stay at Wilhampton for at least a month.'

'A *month?*'

'Yes. I mean, you could always come up to town in the week if you've got to, but it'll be nice to get some country air. I think John William could do with it. And Nanny can't wait. Neither, I expect, can Katy.'

'Katy?'

She wished he wouldn't keep repeating her last words in such a stupid, parrot-fashion way. She supposed he had forgotten where their nursery maid had come from.

'Yes, Katy,' she repeated. 'Don't you remember? The girl from the Felt Mills. Her youngest brother was drowned there yesterday. That's why I was up in the nursery talking to her before dinner.'

'Oh, I see. I'm sorry.'

He was standing with his arm on the mantelshelf, one foot on the fender, half turned towards the fire. She was conscious of how strikingly handsome he was, even though

83

his figure did not cut quite the same dash as it had in the uniform which he had worn a year ago. Her mind went back to that time. She had only known him three months before they were married. It had been such a whirlwind romance. The war had still been on; there had been no knowing that he might be killed. Sometimes she had felt unable to wait. She suspected that John William had been conceived on their wedding night.

Presently, he turned, came across to where she was sitting and knelt by her chair.

'Alicia, darling.' He took hold of both her hands and looked at her intently. 'A penny for them.'

She flushed. 'Not for sale, I'm afraid.'

He lowered his head into her lap. They were both the same age but she felt altogether older, as if he needed not only a wife, but someone else: a mother perhaps, even more than John William who, in any case, had an experienced nanny to take care of him.

Suddenly, he looked up. His smile was totally disarming. 'We don't,' he said, 'often have an evening to ourselves. Shall we make it an early one?'

11

'So the long and the short of it is, Ada,' wrote Emily Harwood to Nanny Barlow, 'that there's to be an inquest. I expect,' the letter went on,

> that's why they didn't want Katy back for the funeral. There have been some ugly rumers going around. By all accounts, the boy has been making a proper nuisance of himself lately. Well, I mean, what can you expect? His *age*, you see. And he's very strong. I always said Mrs Lodge ought to have had him committed. It wasn't fair on the others, specially the little young one up with you. It seems as how he's been trying to give the family the slip more than once since she left. Been found in the place where the women work and also

here the word 'loitering' had been misspelt twice and firmly crossed out hanging about up River Lane. At least, that's what Lilian Perrick says, although you can't always be sure with her. She's been hinting he was after Ena. The trouble is that Ena's brother Archie, you know the one who never seems to be able to stay in a job longer than you can say Jack Robinson, is said to have been out and about early the morning Neil got drowned. If you ask me, Archie's a bit of a pocher. I know Fred Ashford thinks he's up to all the tricks. Anyway, with his mother always saying such bad things about Neil, you can't help wondering, can you? I mean, if the two boys met there could have been a bit of funny business. One of the mill men, Bob Harrison, says when he was on his way to work he saw Archie coming out of the little allyway over the footbridge into River Lane just after half past six, Bob being late as usual . . .

Nanny Barlow put down the letter and sighed. She knew all about gossip. She wasn't above wanting to hear a little herself from time to time; but Emmie's letter really had gone a bit far. She could just imagine the talk in Wilhampton. Now that the war, with all its constant excitements and tragedies, was over, any occurrence such as this would be bound to arouse more than usual public interest. The local inhabitants would revel in it. Poor Sarah Lodge. How it would distress her.

Sarah was, indeed, not just distressed. She was anguished. Her family had never known her in quite such a state. True, she had grieved bitterly over her eldest son's death, even more over her husband's. But, however poignant and deeply felt her grief had been, it was within the bounds of normality.

Now, to her daughters, there seemed something altogether alien, even frightening, in her conduct. She withdrew into some private world where it was impossible to reach her. She stared at Flo and May as if they were strangers; and many was the night when, after the men had gone home, they would find her, lantern in hand, going through the mill towards the place where Neil's body had been found, often with the wind cutting across the meadows, loosening her hair and tearing at her skirts, while the sound of the mill-race echoed unceasingly in the background. On one such occasion, May had led her home gently, almost as if she were a child, saying, 'There, there, Mother. 'Tis no good. Father wouldn't want you to take on so. No more would Neil, if he knew.'

And Sarah had looked at her mutely, allowing herself to be taken indoors and sat by the fire, where she suddenly covered her face in her hands and broke into almost silent, yet uncontrollable weeping.

'I don't,' said May to Flo, one evening when they were in bed, 'see how she's going to be well enough to get to Westonbury for the inquest if she carries on like this.' It had been one thing for Sarah, supported by Henry and Herbie on either side of her, to manage the funeral, but the ordeal ahead, so unimaginable, so public, which neither of the men, owing to their respective occupations, would be free to attend, was something dreaded by them all.

'We could ask Dr Fitzherbert about her,' said Flo, suddenly. 'Perhaps I'll go up to the surgery and have a word with him tomorrow.'

'Yes, and then you could ask him about your own trouble.'

'That's better. Besides, we've got enough to be seeing to just now.' The reply was short and definite. May knew better than to persist.

But thanks to Flo's visit, Dr Fitzherbert himself arranged to drive Sarah to Westonbury the following Monday, while Flo, May and Edith took the train. It was against his principles to give lifts to patients, for he well knew the problems, jealousies and accusations which might arise from such involvement. But ever since he had finished his training and decided to take on the Wilhampton practice thirty years ago, he had always been interested in the Lodge family. Its members did not appear to fit into any particular category. They were unusual, especially the mother and the littlest one: Katy. He knew Sarah Lodge to be hard, self-willed and often unreasonable – especially after the birth of Neil, to whom she reacted quite differently – yet he thought he – and perhaps he alone – really understood the underlying reason for this. He had never, as a student, taken a course in psychology, but he had been a lifelong student of human nature. Although he was aware that Sarah suffered from the guilt many a conscientious mother felt on finding that she had brought a simpleton into the world, yet in her case he was fairly certain why she did so to such an unnatural extent.

He could remember a July day towards the end of the last century when, in the company of a female friend, she had come to ask him if she was pregnant. She had been a beautiful young woman, not pretty – her features were too finely chiselled, even aristocratic-looking, for that – but there was something about her that attracted or, rather, commanded, attention. He did not think she seemed too happy when he confirmed her supposition. But she had said, 'Thank you, Doctor,' in a quiet, pleasant enough manner and the two of them had gone away.

It must have been only about a week later when he was summoned to the mill late one evening because the eldest boy, Frank, had fallen out of a willow tree and concussed himself. He remembered how Sidney Lodge, though naturally concerned about the child, had also seemed curiously embarrassed at being the only person present when he made his examination. He had wondered why Sarah had not been around. Then, as he came away from the bedroom, after pronouncing that he did not think that any lasting harm had overtaken Frank, who, though still shaken, was quite conscious again, he had happened to glance through the little glass panel high up on the living-room wall which, presumably, had been inserted at some time or another to give more light to the dangerous stairway he was about to descend. There, lying on the old horsehair sofa, he had caught sight of Sarah.

Puzzled, especially in view of her condition, duty bade him tell Sidney that he would like to see her, and he had pulled back the tapestry curtain which served as the living-room door. She had attempted to stand, but failed. Anxiously, he had hurried across to her and suddenly stopped, noticing her glazed eyes, her breath which smelt of gin.

Claud Fitzherbert had been young and inexperienced, but he realized in a flash what had happened. Sarah Lodge had been trying to abort the child she was carrying. Moreover, knowing her to be usually such a careful and vigilant mother, he had little doubt that had she not been otherwise engaged in her desperate, pitiable attempt, Frank would not have had his accident.

It had been a difficult few minutes. Sidney, Sarah and he were all more or less of the same generation. Not only did Claud Fitzherbert know what had been taking place, but he was acutely aware that Sarah – despite her fuddled state – and Sidney knew that he knew. His whole training, indeed, his whole upbringing, had taught him that human life was sacred; he was passionately dedicated to the ideal of preserving it. Yet, as he looked round the cramped, poorly-furnished living room and saw the two faces before him: the man's a mixture of shame and defiance, the woman's sad and apologetic, he found he could not condemn – only suffer for and with them.

When Neil had been born and Ida Whatley, the midwife, had confirmed his own fears that there was something wrong with the infant, his mind had immediately gone back to that summer night when he had found Sarah, for the one and only time in her life, with 'drink taken'. There was no definite proof, of course; he possessed no medical tract which asserted that what she had done might have harmed the foetus. Yet who could tell? And for all he knew, Sarah had possibly tried other accompanying diabolical tactics to achieve her ends that evening, such as skipping or running on the spot in the silent, empty mill. But as Neil grew larger and seemingly more helpless, many was the time he found himself wondering, as he felt Sarah too must have been wondering, whether her actions had been responsible for the wretched child's abnormality.

Until the boy was about three, she had refused, categorically, to acknowledge that anything was the matter with him at all. Even afterwards, she had kept up the pretence. When, worried about the load she was carrying, Claud Fitzherbert had suggested, gently, that there might be other ways in which Neil could be cared for, his remarks were brushed aside indignantly, even savagely. Over the years he had watched her, while the mask she had adopted became tougher, harder and more impregnable, save for the odd occasion when, just for a while, he had glimpsed the soft-spoken young matron who had visited him in the summer of 1898 when she was three months pregnant.

He never ceased to marvel at the job she was doing, at the standards she demanded, not only from herself but each — save Neil — member of her family. He was both alarmed and distressed when she became pregnant with her seventh child. But there had never been any outward sign of regret or resentment this time, certainly no attempt at trying to avoid her fate. She seemed to have become resigned to motherhood, although there had been a short period after Katy's birth when she had suffered from puerperal depression. But suddenly she appeared to pull out of it. He was never quite sure why. He seemed to recall there having been some gossip going around about Sidney Lodge and Lilian Firman; and Sarah, fighting mad, it was said, had gone up to the house Lilian shared with her brother and hauled her husband home. He wasn't sure, of course. It was difficult, sometimes, to sift out the truth, even if there was a grain or two of it in such a story. But he'd been a medical practitioner in Wilhampton long enough to know that there was usually never smoke without just a spark of fire. But whatever troubles had transpired after Katy's birth, Sarah had triumphed over them.

One Sunday afternoon, when the baby was about four months, he had been delighted to see, from his drawing-room window, the entire Lodge family out together for their customary walk up to Breconbury Woods. They had spread across the whole of East Street: Sidney, with the two eldest boys on either side of him; next, Flo, May and Edith, holding hands; and then Sarah, with Katy in the pram and Neil propped up at the other end. They were more beautifully dressed than ever. He couldn't help wondering whether this particular outing had been purposely 'staged', that Sarah, by presenting such a perfect, united front, was simply showing Wilhampton that there was nothing wrong, nor ever had been. He had continued to watch them, filled with admiration, until they were almost out of sight, comparing them to his own children, who mostly went about like ragamuffins. But then,

Mildred, his wife, had always maintained that she had better things to do than bother about clothes.

It was only years later that he had learned from May Lodge that her mother always reckoned it was a good thing, in times of trouble, to put on what she called 'the ten-pound look'. It was a little maxim, her daughter explained, which she had apparently picked up from somewhere in her youth. He supposed it had come down through the generations since the time of the Reform Bill in 1832, when ten-pound householders were given the vote. But on that particular Sunday afternoon, at the turn of the century, he could only marvel at what he had just seen, wondering how the woman did it, for he imagined her husband's wages would have been not much more than a pound a week.

He supposed that Sarah might have had a bit of a dowry, although he doubted it. He seemed to recall Miss Fielding once having told him that there had been some trouble between Sarah and her parents when she had married Sidney Lodge. He believed she had been a Miss Dufosée, the only daughter of quite wealthy West of England clothiers, whose forebears had come over from France. That was probably where the dress sense came from and why he had always felt the family to be curiously unique, a strange mixture of determination, courage and common sense, yet coupled with charm, sensitivity and nervousness.

Sarah was certainly showing indomitable courage today, he thought, as she sat bolt upright beside him in the car on the way to the inquest: quiet, immaculately turned out as usual and immensely proud. Whatever she was suffering was, for the moment, contained within her mask, although he was aware that her gloved hands were held tightly together, that there were splashes of heightened colour on each cheekbone. But if Flo was worried about her mother's ability to stand up to what lay ahead, he felt fairly certain her fears were groundless. He did not think Sarah would falter in the witness box. She would rise to the occasion.

His assumption proved correct.

She was the first to be called and took oath in a calm, composed manner, having walked up to face the coroner, her head held high, looking neither to right nor left. Her daughters noted, with a mixture of admiration and relief, that the way she comported herself seemed to quell the atmosphere of rising excitement, even hostility, in the packed little courtroom. It would seem that Sarah Lodge, as her grandmother had done more than half a century before, had come 'on stage', totally in command of both herself and her audience.

Dr Machin, as Dr Fitzherbert had predicted, put his questions to her gravely and courteously, his usual somewhat acerbic manner laid aside. He even opened the proceedings by extending his sympathy to her and her family for their sad loss, which she acknowledged with a dignified little bow.

'You were the last to see your son alive, I believe, Mrs Lodge?' he began.

'Yes, sir.' She looked at him very directly, still refraining from glancing for one moment at the sea of faces around her.

'I understand, Mrs Lodge, that because your son suffered certain . . . disabilities, you were obliged to give him special care?'

'Yes, sir. That is correct.'

'Perhaps,' continued Dr Machin, still in the same pleasant manner, 'you could describe exactly what happened on the morning of . . .' he glanced at his notes, 'November the 7th?'

For a fraction, the woman in the box paused. Then, levelly, she replied, 'I did not know anything was amiss, sir, until I went in to wake my son when the half-past-six hooter blew. We had all gone to bed early the night before . . . I'd seen to his undressing . . . he sleeps in a room which leads through from mine . . . I never left my own until I went to . . .' she hesitated again, and then continued, 'the closet, at about five.'

'And how long were you gone, Mrs Lodge?' Dr Machin queried.

'Not more than ten minutes, sir.'

'And then?' her interrogator prompted.

'Well, then, sir, I tried to snatch a little more sleep, but it wasn't to be. I just dressed and went in to Neil, like I always do.' This time there was a slightly longer pause during which there was complete silence, so that her next four words, though quietly spoken, fell with startling impact on the courtroom. 'His bed was empty,' Sarah said.

'And what did you do?' Step by step, albeit kindly, she was being made to relive those hours. Dr Fitzherbert wondered what it was costing her.

'We all went looking, sir. Me and my two daughters,' he heard her reply, at once.

'Which way did you go, Mrs Lodge?'

Sarah frowned a little, but still she answered unwaveringly.

'I went up River Lane, sir.'

There was the faintest murmur in the courtroom, which the coroner silenced with a glance. May caught sight of Lilian Perrick and her family, leaning forward, their gaze fastened intently on the witness box.

'You had no idea where your son might have gone, Mrs Lodge?'

'No, sir.'

'Nor why?'

'No, sir,' repeated Sarah, in the same positive manner.

There was louder murmuring at the back of the courtroom now, which elicited from Dr Machin a definite call for silence.

'Has your son ever done this sort of thing before, Mrs Lodge?' he continued.

'Not at night, I mean, not at that hour, sir.'

'But he has sometimes wandered off in the daytime?'

For the first time, Sarah's composure seemed momentarily to elude her. She put up a hand to her face and then dropped it on to the brass rail at her side. She supposed that Dr Machin must have known that Neil had been on the prowl the day before he drowned. 'Once or twice, sir,' she answered, and this time her voice sank almost to a whisper. 'Being as he was,' she mumbled, ''twasn't always easy to . . . keep an eye on him every minute of the day.'

'Quite, Mrs Lodge. I fully appreciate that. I think that will be all, thank you.'

Flo and May were called next. Each corroborated their mother's statements and how they had all gone off in different directions to look for Neil on finding he had disappeared.

Tom Henstridge then went into the witness box. He confirmed that he had found Neil's body lying against what he called 'Little Hatch' at about eight o'clock on the morning of November 7th.

'There is a small footbridge there, I believe, Mr Henstridge?' Though still framing his questions quite pleasantly, Dr Machin seemed to have reverted to his usual, more cryptic tone in his cross-questioning.

'Yes, zur.' Tom Henstridge's slow, west-country voice reverberated round the courtroom in sharp contrast to the precise speech of his interrogator.

'On which the boy would have been walking?'

'Well, he *could* 'ave been, zur. Or maybe he fell into the race from the big bridge, and that's where the current carried 'im.'

'Would the deceased have had much difficulty in crossing either bridge, Mr Henstridge?'

The under-manager looked at Dr Machin in some surprise. 'Why, yes, zur. Specially in the dark. Stands to reason. And there was no handrail on the little 'un, see.'

'And I believe that was a place which was not often frequented?'

'Hardly ever, zur. Except . . .'

'Except what, Mr Henstridge?' Dr Machin seemed to be chivvying now, as if he were on some scent, professional, probing, eyeing his witness keenly over the top of his pince-nez.

'Well . . .' Tom Henstridge, honest, loyal, none too bright, gripped the rail of the witness box. 'Except when 'twere used as a short cut to River Lane by them wot was in the know, like.'

'Thank you, Mr Henstridge.'

To the Perrick family's obvious consternation, the next person to be called was Bob Harrison. He was a short, fat, shifty-looking man, fond of beer, betting and women, who lived with his married sister on downside. Never a good time-keeper, he admitted, at the start of his evidence, that he had been hurrying down River Lane on his bicycle on the morning of the seventh, just after the six-thirty hooter had gone.

'You were, in fact, late for work, Harrison?' Dr Machin remarked, drily.

'Yes, sir.'

'And you have been telling people that you saw, or thought you saw, Archie Perrick coming out of the alleyway at the top?'

Bob Harrison shuffled his feet uneasily and coughed.

'Well, as I said, sir, I couldn't be sure. I was hurrying, like, and 'twere dark.'

'You had a lamp on your bicycle, I presume, Harrison?'

'Well, yessir, that is . . . no sir. The battery were flat.'

Again, a murmuring ripple of interest rose in the court-room, although how much it was for or against the witness, it was impossible to fathom. This time, Dr Machin simply held up a hand and spoke slightly louder, as he framed his next question.

'What made you think the figure you saw was Archie Perrick, Harrison?'

'Well, sir, I mean . . . I knows as how Archie gets about a bit of an early morning.'

'In other words, you merely guessed?'

'If you put it like that, sir.'

'Are you, in fact, Harrison, quite sure you saw anyone in River Lane that morning?'

Bob Harrison coughed and shuffled his feet once more. Clearly embarrassed, he looked anywhere other than at the coroner. 'Well, sir,' he replied, at length, 'I were goin' lickety-split, like. Fact is, I near as dammit – beg pardon, sir – ran into Mrs Lodge comin' out o' the mill gates, 'cept she 'ad her lantern wi' her.'

'Thank you, Harrison.'

Lilian Perrick sat back, a definite smirk of relief on her sharp little face, watching Bob Harrison step down from the box and her son take his place. Despite a certain similarity in unease which the boy seemed to share with the previous witness, he appeared to have a cast-iron alibi.

He said that he had been nowhere near River Lane after five that morning, for he had left home at that time to cycle ten miles to Tom Sanger's racing stables on the old Barbury turnpike, where he had recently become an employee. This fact was corroborated by none other than Mr Sanger himself, and the smirk on Lilian's face became more pronounced with every minute that the two of them gave evidence.

It only remained for the pathologist and Dr Fitzherbert to be called as final witnesses. Both men were in agreement that it was a case of straightforward drowning, the small cut which had been discovered on Neil's right temple consistent with having knocked his head against Little Hatch in falling. Privately, Dr Fitzherbert felt that Neil, in his confused moronic mind, *had* been trying to get to the Perrick house, that sex was at the bottom of the tragedy, but he thanked God that at least, whatever had been hinted at the inquest, no definite statement to that effect had come out. He was merely annoyed that, because of Bob Harrison's loud mouth, any doubt whatsoever about Neil's death had been introduced into the proceedings, and Sarah Lodge's ordeal had been consequently unnecessarily prolonged. Before stepping down from the box, he took the opportunity, as Dr Machin had also done, of publicly extending his sympathy to the Lodge family in their bereavement and, in particular, to Mrs Lodge, who, as he put it, had been 'a mother in a million'.

So — the inquest was over. Dr Machin brought in a verdict of 'Death by Misadventure'. Claud Fitzherbert drove Sarah back to Wilhampton, trying as far as he was able to steer her thoughts on to more pleasant lines.

'I hear,' he said, 'from Lady Fairfax, that her grandson will be coming to the Hall for Christmas, and Nanny Barlow and Katy with him.'

But from his passenger's next remark, he knew that his observation had fallen on deaf ears.

'If Bob Harrison did see someone coming out of Hatch Alley the morning Neil was drowned and it wasn't Archie Perrick, who do you think it might have been, Doctor?'

12

In the weeks that led up to Christmas, the question of who Bob Harrison might or might not have seen coming out of Hatch Alley on the morning of November 7th became the subject of practically non-stop discussion in Wilhampton's nine public houses, especially The Punch-bowl, the one most favoured by Bob himself. For many years, here was where he was most likely to be found holding court, his graphic anecdotes and vociferous opinions – aided by the help of alcoholic intake usually bought for him by others with the express purpose of being at the receiving end of them – being almost legendary, both in the town and surrounding district.

Now, he was in his element, possessed of a personal mystery story which his audience was finding far more absorbing than his views on Lloyd George and the Government, rising prices, unemployment, or matters closer to home: how Sir Roger Broadbent had managed to pepper one of Lord Fairfax's guns at a recent shooting-party and whether young Dick Swayne, up at Bulbarrow Farm on the outskirts of the town, would ever make half the farmer his elderly, now crippled, father had been.

Even Bob's constant stand-by which could always be relied upon to buy him a few more pints: speculation about Grace Sinca – or Grace Armitage as she now was – was temporarily superfluous to requirements. In any case, since the end of the war, with her father dead and an invalid husband on her hands, there were some people who considered Grace to be more of an object of compassion than anything else. Although, privately, May Lodge did not believe that leopards changed their spots and felt that, whenever Grace had the chance, she was bound to be up to her old tricks again. Indeed, Emily Harwood had often hinted as much to her – though never in Flo's hearing – and only the other day, when they had met in the street, Emily had been on about Grace's having taken to going for long walks by herself, once she had got the Captain to bed of an evening. 'The Lord knows where, May,' she had added, darkly, 'but I suppose it's a question of anything in trousers. Fred Ashford's wife thinks she makes for the shooting lodge on the old Barbury turnpike, and I don't reckon she's alone when she gets there.'

But in the winter of 1919, whatever assignations Grace Armitage might have been keeping, the inquest on Neil Lodge's death and Bob Harrison's stories concerning it were uppermost in the majority of people's minds. 'Who d'you think 'twere, then, Bob?' or 'Come on, you must 'ave seen zummat' were two questions guaranteed to start him off as soon as he stepped inside The Punchbowl, to which his reply almost always began with, 'Well, as I said to the Crowner, 'twere dark . . .' after which his saga would gather momentum, its dramatic qualities more than compensating for its increasing inconsistency.

Fortunately, however, as she made her way towards River Lane on the afternoon of Christmas Eve, Katy Lodge had no idea that she would soon be passing the spot which many people now considered haunted; for it was being put about in the town that Sidney Lodge's ghost had taken to springing out of Hatch Alley to accost anyone who was late for work. Katy merely hurried along, demure and dainty, acknowledging the greetings of several passers-by and ignoring, as far as possible, the curtain-twitching at front windows, which she was well aware always became more pronounced when one of the town's inhabitants returned after a period of absence.

'Katy!' May, with Flo a little way behind her, came running out of the mill gates as soon as she passed the Perricks' shop. 'Oh, chippatoo! My, how good you look.'

She was caught up in first one and then another pair of welcoming arms. And then, at the door of the house, Sarah held out her own, yet almost apprehensively, as if her youngest daughter had become a stranger to her, that since the child had left home, they both had travelled unknown paths.

Katy was quick to recognize the change in her mother. She seemed to have visibly shrunk. Though neat as ever –

there was not a hair out of place, not a crease in the black serge dress with the lace tucker made for mourning after Sidney Lodge's death, and now worn on special occasions only – she appeared old and curiously remote. She said little and when she did speak her voice was flat and detached.

The tea had already been laid, as it was to be eaten early in order for Katy to be back at the Hall by five-thirty, the time specified by Nanny Barlow. On the side of the table, Mr Fuller's tray was waiting to be taken up to his office as soon as the kettle boiled, a duty which today Flo had volunteered to undertake. Presently, Edith and her children arrived and the family proceeded to exchange presents, Katy having brought a hand-stitched lace handkerchief for her mother, a small bottle of lavender water for each of her three sisters and sweets for her nephew and nieces. All the gifts had been carefully wrapped in tissue paper and, much as Katy longed to open those which were handed to her and which she suspected were mostly articles of clothing, she promised faithfully not to do so until Christmas morning.

'When no doubt you'll be busy,' said Flo.

'Yes, but Nanny says I can come to church and maybe she could spare me for an hour or two on Boxing Day.'

'Then we could go to the cemetery,' Sarah broke in, unexpectedly. 'You'll be wanting to see Neil's grave, and your father's, I'm sure.'

Katy started. She had no wish to see either grave. Neither did she want to go to the cemetery. She hated the place, with its heavy wrought-iron gates and dreary-looking caretaker's lodge, the stench of decaying flowers which came from the dump just round the corner, the rows of neat or neglected graves. True, there were many more of the former than the latter, and that of Sidney Lodge seemed the most regularly tended, but Katy could not understand why so many people appeared to take such a ghoulish interest in them, walking up and down the grassy aisles of a Sunday afternoon, shaking their heads and sometimes reading an epitaph out loud to their companions. Even Flo and May were far from averse to going across and inspecting the resting place of some new arrival, made manifest by its covering of wilting floral tributes, which they then proceeded to examine carefully, reading out such words as In Loving Memory or With Deepest Sympathy, and registering approval or disapproval at the choice of phrase which had been used, especially when it came — as it almost always did — from someone whom they knew, or knew of. On these occasions, Katy would merely stand aside, looking across the valley towards Breconbury Woods, longing to run away and hide there, embarrassed and ashamed by the morbid curiosity which seemed to turn a visit to the cemetery into some form of vicarious entertainment. Now, she realized, she would have to go through it all again and, what was more, during her precious time off.

But there was no question of refusal. Katy knew what was expected of her. Already she could see two holly wreaths in one corner of the room which were obviously in the process of being made up. Besides, were they not almost at the anniversary of her father's death? Unhappily aware of dissembling, she replied, dutifully, 'Yes, Mother.'

'Tell us about John William,' May intervened quickly, sensing the uneasiness in the atmosphere.

'Oh, he's lovely. Though I don't really do much for him. Just the ordinary jobs. Washing his nappies and such like.' As soon as she had made the remark, Katy regretted it. There had been no one to do the ordinary jobs for a woman with seven children in a tiny house without even an indoor tap and she wondered whether her unthinking answer had reminded her mother of the fact. But Sarah simply inclined her head, almost approvingly, as though no such comparison had crossed her mind.

The afternoon passed all too quickly and at five o'clock it was decided that May should accompany her youngest sister back to the Hall. As they crossed the market square, Katy said suddenly, 'Mother's very thin, isn't she? So's Flo, for that matter.'

'Yes, but . . . Neil drowning . . . you know, the shock . . .' May saw no point in going into further details. And, in any case, there was nothing specific to say. There was no reason to burden the child with her own nebulous doubts and fears. Katy was still so young. She was looking so well. Yet there was a directness, a maturity about her, which was made only too clear by her next remark.

'I suppose if Neil's death had happened earlier, you'd never have sent me away.'

May hesitated. 'Well, no, my dear. I don't suppose so. But you're happy, aren't you?'

She was surprised at the reply.

'I don't know. It's a difficult thing to be, isn't it? I hope I don't find myself looking after other people's babies for ever.'

May was silent. They had reached the west gates. Away to the left of them they could see the lights of the Hall filtering through the trees. Nearer at hand, Fred Ashford's dogs suddenly set up barking, giving May an excuse for not answering at once.

'I don't see why you should, Katy,' she replied, at length, after they had passed the keeper's cottage. 'You'll probably get married and have children of your own.'

'D'you think so? But I wouldn't want to be like Mother. I'd sooner have someone else to care for my kids.'

'Oh, Katy!' The exclamation was made half in amusement, half in gentle reproach. 'We can't all be the Fairfaxes or Moretons of this world. And there's plenty worse off than we are.'

'Oh, I *know*. But when I think of what it must have been like bringing us all up at the mill and then what goes on where I am now. Mrs Moreton and her husband are out almost every night, that is, when they aren't entertaining at home. Haven't you ever wanted a better life, May? Look how you felt about London and Bond Street that day you came up with me.'

'Yes, but that was only ever a kind of dream, Katy,' came the quiet reply.

After they had said goodnight, May walked home slowly, thinking about her youngest sister's last remarks. There were no flies on Katy. Illness might have made her seem subdued and listless during childhood, but she had come on a lot since then; and being away from home had speeded up the process. There was a big difference in the child May had left in 89 Upper Brook Street six months previously and the young woman whom she had just seen disappear into the side entrance of the Hall. Katy might be only a nursery maid but something – the family she was with, their house, the West End of London, her job – had given her a curious awareness, even a sense of importance, however much she disparaged her position. Of course, May had always known that her youngest sister had aspirations. Yet so had she herself, when she came to think about it. But perhaps Katy's stood more chance of being realized. She had youth and determination on her side. And time. There was not now – nor had there ever been, May realized – the slightest chance of the Misses F and M Lodge setting up in business anywhere other than at the mill. It had been silly of her ever to entertain the idea. They had never had the money; they knew of no one to back them. As it was, they were lucky to have a workroom for which they paid no rent. She might blame the war for initially having made them stay put, but now they had Sarah to think of. Their mother was dependent on them and would never, willingly, leave the mill. That short, sweet, tantalizing vision – prompted by a little lighthearted flattery from Alicia Moreton – of seeing their name above some shop in Bond Street, had been as fanciful as it had been foolish.

Now, as she made her way home, May thought about the time her dreams had been stifled for good and all on her one and only trip to London. After leaving Katy and being shown the way to her objective by Nanny Barlow, she remembered standing in wonderment outside the windows of Asprey's and Cartier's. She had walked up and down, pausing in front of many a clothes' shop, astonished that a simple blouse-dress of cotton crêpe with a vest of cotton georgette could cost as much as twenty-nine shillings and sixpence, that an artificial silk jumper was priced at twelve and elevenpence. And the hats: there had been one covered in pink crêpe de Chine and lace at forty-five and nine, although, on closer study, it had not seemed a patch on her own fine beige straw, the one which she had trimmed with rosettes of ribbons to wear for her ill-fated meeting with Major Walter Perkins.

In fact, although as far as May was concerned, Bond Street might almost have been in some foreign country so great was the contrast to Westonbury's High Parade, she recalled, oddly enough, having felt not altogether out of place there. As she had cast, discreetly, a knowledgeable eye over the fashionable ladies alighting from cabs or chauffeur-driven limousines, savouring every detail of their attire in order to pass on the information to Flo as soon as she returned, she was conscious of the fact that the simple tussore dress she was wearing, though not enhanced by jewellery or other costly accessories, nevertheless compared not unfavourably with the more extravagant ensembles. No one might turn to look at May Lodge twice – for one thing, she had been well aware that to be seen carrying a coat on such a hot day was a handicap – but, on the other hand, she had been pleased to feel she could go home, knowing that the dress sense, with which the distaff side of the family seemed to have been endowed, had certainly not let her down.

She recollected having been more eager to return to Wilhampton than she had been to leave it that morning, experiencing a sense of relief that she was now on her way back to a life which she knew and understood and, once in the train, it seemed as though some unseen umbilical cord grew tighter with every mile it steamed westward. May supposed it was absurd of her, really, to think this; but more than once she had wondered whether there was not some strange magnetism about the place where she had been born. Occasionally, she had felt it had to do with the town itself; more often she connected it with Sarah; even, at times, the mill-race, as if those who lived close to it were caught up in something beyond their control.

Tonight, after saying goodbye to Katy at the Hall, as she recrossed the market square and neared River Lane, she felt it again. She believed her youngest sister might have experienced something of the same sort. There was no doubt that the poor child had wanted to get away from it and spread her wings, to break from that cramping, even

102

cloistered, atmosphere; although not in the way which had been forced upon her.

On reaching Hatch Alley, May was annoyed to find that she had started to hurry. Both she and Flo had heard the rumours which, as yet, had fortunately escaped Sarah's ears. There was nothing in them, of course. How could there be? May did not believe in ghosts – at least, that was what she had always maintained. Besides, good people like her father did not return to this world to scare the daylights out of those they had left behind. Yet, when she arrived at the house, she knew she was flushed and that Flo was aware of her discomposure, even more so when, on the table, she caught sight of a large, rectangular box which looked suspiciously like chocolates, on which the attached label proclaimed in thin, spidery, handwriting: 'For the three good ladies of The Mill House, George Fuller'.

'Duck and Collar brought it,' said Flo, 'just after you'd left with Katy. He seemed most put out you weren't here.'

'That will do, Flo.' Sarah's voice had almost a touch of the old acerbity in it. 'Why should Mr Fuller want to see May? Are you forgetting he is a married man?'

13

'They got damaged when we had a burst pipe over Christmas. That's why they're being sold off cheap.' The young man in the shop near Oxford Street had come across to where Katy was standing just inside the door, studying a trough of dilapidated books marked up at twopence each.

'I see.' She coloured slightly. She had not reckoned on actually buying one, certainly not on being accosted by a salesman. She had simply wanted to look; and it had taken more than a little courage just to step over the threshold of Mason & Son. Moreover, she knew that she should really not have been there at all, but hurrying back to Number 89 with the gripe water she had been sent out to buy at the chemist's next door. But it had seemed too good a chance to miss. She had had her eye on the bookshop for some time.

'What do you fancy?' The young man was of medium height, quite stocky, with dark hair and dark brown eyes, which were now looking at her in a courteous yet amused way. He seemed plainly eager to help.

She hesitated, her colour deepening. 'I don't really know . . . I just wanted to see what there was.'

'Ah, let me think, now. Have you read Emily Brontë?' He began searching through the trough, carefully.

'I . . . no . . . I mean, what is it about?'

He turned to look at her more closely and then continued his search. 'Emily Brontë is the author, or, rather, the authoress. Here.' He pulled out a copy of *Wuthering Heights* and handed it to her. 'I think you'd like this. It's quite a good edition. An absolute bargain at twopence.'

She was blushing furiously now. She had shown her ignorance and made the most terrible mistake – and Katy Lodge did not like making mistakes. Miserably, she hunted in her small pochette and produced the necessary money. She felt that she would have given her entire week's wages to get out of the shop. She waited in agony while he went away to wrap up her purchase.

'I'd like to know what you think of it,' he said, gravely, when he returned and handed it to her. 'I've seen you before, looking in the window. I'm sure you must like reading.'

'Yes,' she mumbled, taking the package quickly and almost running out of the door.

Katy had hoped to have been able to hide it before anyone noticed when she returned to Number 89, but in this she was forestalled. Nanny Barlow was quick to observe that she was carrying two parcels.

'What have you got there, Katy?' she enquired, as she met her on the landing. 'You didn't buy anything else at the chemist's, did you?'

'No. Yes . . . that is . . . I bought a book from the shop next door.'

'A *book*?' Katy felt if she had said she had purchased a fur coat, the woman before her could scarcely have shown more astonishment or disapproval; and the next question not only seemed to confirm this but also to reveal a certain stupidity as well. 'To read?' she added, tartly.

'Yes.' What else did Nanny Barlow think she was going to do with it, for goodness' sake?

'There's no good comes of stuffing your head in books, Katy. Besides, supposing if Master John had had wind and needed the gripe water. When I send you out on an errand, I don't expect you to dilly-dally about in some fancy book-shop. You'd best make up for it by getting down straight away to that pile of sewing on the nursery table. Mrs Moreton's maid is sick and she's sent up a lot of things that want seeing to. I'm sure I don't know what your poor mother would say if she heard you'd been wasting your time and money on *books*.'

'But it was cheap, Nanny. Damaged by water. I only paid twopence.'

'That will do, my girl. Twopence too much. If 'twasn't for the fact that there's so much to do here, and being as how it's sales goods I don't suppose they'd take it back, I'd send you straight up to Masons with it this very minute. As it is, you'd best look sharp and start on them petticoats. Mrs Moreton's having all her clothes shortened now, and this evening she's asked if I can spare you to go down and help her dress before she and Captain Moreton go out.'

Half chastened, half resentful, Katy went into the nursery and did as she was told. She could not understand why it was that people seemed to think there was some-thing disgraceful about her reading; that is, except for the young man in the shop. Of course, she would never go back and tell him what she thought about *Wuthering Heights*. In any case, Nanny Barlow would probably see to it that she got precious little time for reading. She must have welcomed the fact that Amy Robinson, Mrs Moreton's lady's maid, was ill, so that there would be more work than ever to keep her nimble-fingered young nursery maid busy. Of course, this was purely accidental, but more than once lately Katy had noticed that she had been asked to do some extra sewing for her employer, who had even complimented her on it, although not in Amy

Robinson's hearing. As she started to unpick some lace from the bottom of a princess petticoat, she wondered what was wrong with the tall, thin, forbidding-looking woman with whom she had scarcely spoken. She would not altogether mind taking her place once in a while. It would be nice to be able to tell Flo and May that she had seen Mrs Moreton's bedroom and helped her to get dressed.

Later on, when she tapped on the door promptly at a quarter to seven, she was surprised, on entering, to find her employer sitting at her dressing table, wearing a pale blue crêpe de Chine wrap and smoking a cigarette in a long holder.

'Ah, Katy. How nice. Come in.'

She walked across the room, interest quickly dispelling any initial diffidence, conscious of an overall sense of softness cast by the pink-shaded lamps, the large double bed with its cream-coloured drapery, the rich pile of the pink and cream carpet. It was a room in which Katy could imagine spending hours of unmitigated bliss, yet the woman at the dressing table seemed curiously troubled and ill at ease.

'When I've finished this,' she continued, almost impatiently, waving her cigarette in the air, 'perhaps you would give my hair a good brushing. It's been absolutely unmanageable the last few days since Robinson's been ill. I shall be glad when it comes off next week.'

'You're having it bobbed, madam?'

'Yes, it will make life much easier.'

As she began brushing the long tresses, Katy wondered what difficulties there were in a life which seemed, ostensibly, to be so free of them. She also felt a little sad at what she had just heard; for she could not imagine how Alicia Moreton would look without what the Lodge family always called 'woman's crowning glory'. She certainly had no intention of having her own hair cut. She knew her mother would have a fit if she turned into a shorn lamb, which was how most older people dubbed those who had been misguided enough to follow the latest fashion, even if they did keep their switches coiled up in cardboard boxes ready for winding round their heads on special occasions.

Deftly, she continued to help Alicia Moreton with her toilet, mentally noting every little detail so that she could write them all down in her next letter home: a new-type garment called a brassière, specially designed to flatten the bosom in order to produce the modern tube-like figure; the cobweb-thin ninon cami-knickers, trimmed with lace and threaded ribbon; the finest of flesh-coloured silk stockings. Katy was not in any way surprised or overawed by such finery. She had seen much of it – albeit in a somewhat less glamorous and extravagant form – in her sisters' workroom at the mill. Even the pale *eau de nil* satin-covered shoes which exactly matched the low-backed satin dress with its irregular hemline, the diamond brooch and earrings, the long string of pearls and the white kid gloves, did not take her breath away. She was merely glad, after putting the final touches to the coiffure she had arranged so carefully, to see Alicia Moreton finally sweep out of the door and down the circular stairway, an oriental fringed shawl draped gracefully over one arm, looking 'just lovely', as she eventually ended the description in her letter.

Yet, as one of the housemaids came in to make up the fire and she herself started to tidy the bedroom and put away the various pots of face cream, powder, rouge – and even lipstick – on the dressing table, part of her could not help wondering about a state of affairs whereby in order for one woman to go out for an evening's enjoyment, it took another – or many another – to help her to do so.

Although, on further thought, Katy wondered how much Alicia Moreton would enjoy herself this evening. There had been something about John William's mother which she had never encountered before. Her manner had been quick, brittle, over-bright at times. She had even smoked a second cigarette before going downstairs, while she had asked Katy a number of questions about the baby. Did she think he was hardy? Was it not strange that he had failed to gain so much weight last week? London was such an unclean place in which to bring up a child, wasn't it? Full of germs. It would be so easy for him to pick up an infection. It might be better if he were sent to his paternal grandfather's home in Suffolk, where it was bracing, or even back to Wilhampton. She spoke so rapidly, switching from one idea to another, that Katy had not known what to make of it. There was nothing wrong with the child that she could see; and Nanny Barlow seemed to be perfectly happy about him. It was not until a week later that Katy learned that Amy Robinson had left Number 89 because she was suffering from tuberculosis.

There followed a stringent examination of each member of the entire household by the family doctor, particularly John William. His mother seemed forever in and out of the nursery, gazing at the child and asking Nanny Barlow questions, which were not always well received.

'Did he ever come into contact with Robinson, Nanny?'

'Hardly ever, madam. Once or twice on the stairs, maybe, as we were going out or coming in.'

'Did she breathe over him?'

'No, madam. You know I never allow anyone to breathe over my charges, other than those who are doing for them.'

'His milk has always been boiled, hasn't it, Nanny?'

'Of course, madam.' Katy wondered how difficult it had been for the older woman to make the transition from Alicia to Miss Alicia to madam.

One evening, when the interrogation seemed to have gone on for an inordinate length of time, Nanny Barlow reverted to her former role in relation to John William's mother.

'Miss Alicia. If you go on like this you'll make yourself ill, and the bairn, too, I shouldn't wonder. Dr Macleod has given him a clean bill of health. I brought you all up, remember, and we had plenty a scare. Fred Ashford's first wife had it, the one who used to do extra work at the Hall whenever we had company coming. And even the Reverend Donaldson's eldest daughter, who used to come to your birthday parties, had them glands in her neck when she was nigh on eleven. They said it was because Mrs Donaldson would insist on the Swaynes at Bulbarrow letting her have milk from one cow only, instead of doing what Dr Fitzherbert advised your mother: taking it from the best six in the Home Farm herd. But anyway, none of you caught it, thank the Lord. You mustn't fear the worst. Perhaps it would do you good to have a little holiday.'

'Yes, Nanny. Maybe you're right.'

Yet Alicia Moreton did not go away. Until the installation of Edna Mitchell, her new lady's maid, Katy found her services increasingly called upon from the floor below. She did not object, even though it meant longer hours and she was too tired to read much more than a page or two of *Wuthering Heights* each night. But in many ways the work was more interesting. From little snippets of information, she was beginning to get a slightly clearer picture of that tantalizing world outside of which, so far, she knew so little. True, it was still but a blurred negative, but she was quick to retain the name of a restaurant, a theatre, a play, an actor or actress, for mostly Mrs Moreton made no secret of where she was going. Katy was never asked, as Amy Robinson had sometimes been, to wait up to all hours until her employer returned. In any case, it seemed that more often than not Alicia Moreton came home early by herself. She was curious as to what her husband did on these occasions. Sometimes his wife appeared not to accompany him at all, suddenly announcing at the last moment that she would prefer to dine quietly at home, alone. Katy wondered whether he minded such unpredictable behaviour.

Charles Moreton did, in fact, mind very much. Since Christmas, he had become increasingly exasperated with Alicia. Why could she not behave like the wives of their contemporaries, who all seemed to be enjoying themselves? They could both be having a ripping time now, if only she would stop fussing over their child and letting herself get so involved in charity work. There was so much to do, so much to see. There were the various new nightclubs being opened, where they could dance the night away to one of the Dixieland jazz orchestras to which he had become particularly addicted. He was beginning to acquire quite a collection of *His Master's Voice* gramophone records and the strains of a transmogrified 'Swanee' or 'Pasadena' could often be heard floating up from his study on the ground floor. Or there were the pictures and the theatre. He badly wanted to see the latest Charlie Chaplin film and he had actually bought tickets for *Brown Sugar* at the Duke of York's. He hoped Alicia would not say that she did not feel up to going to it when the time came. Sometimes, he felt her contrariness was more than he could stand. Often, he sought refuge in one of his clubs – usually the Cavalry or White's – where he could drink without feeling aware of his wife's disapproval; although, even here, the conversation was occasionally a shade too serious for his liking. He wished some of the older members would shut up about Lloyd George and his handling of the Coalition. As far as he was concerned, he didn't give a damn whether the fellow's methods were devious and disorganized, or that he was failing to live up to his promise of making post-war Britain a country fit for heroes to live in. He was the man who had won the war, wasn't he?

Moreover, he, Charles Moreton, had actually fought in it and now he simply wanted to have some fun. He was not interested in politics, nor those pillars of society who went to church on Sundays and sang Kipling's recessional: 'Lest We Forget'. Personally, he wanted to forget. He'd seen a man with both his legs blown off, rescued him, in fact, for which he had been given an MC. Why shouldn't he have a good time? If unemployment was rising and not only ex-privates but down-at-heel ex-officers were touting hardware from door to door, or sinking their gratuities in dismal little chicken farms, he just did not want to know. One day he would inherit three thousand, five hundred acres of Suffolk and he and his wife and John William – and, presumably, other children – would settle down there, that is, as long as Alicia came to her senses.

If she went on at this rate, he would have to send her to one of those blasted nerve chaps, the kind who had had to be called in on shell-shock cases during the war; although, for his own part, he had no faith in Freud and all that claptrap.

14

When spring came that year and the London parks were splashed with islands of yellow daffodils and the trees began covering themselves with lacy green veils or delicate pink and white rosettes of cherry blossom, Katy was sometimes allowed to take John William for a walk in his perambulator by herself. He was a good-looking child with a mass of fair curls and, now that he was sitting up, many an admiring glance was directed towards the pretty picture the two of them made: the slim young girl with the large, serious eyes, immaculate in her navy-blue uniform; the smiling round-cheeked baby, dressed in a powder-blue woollen jacket trimmed with white fur, occasionally waving a rattle which had been securely fastened with ribbon to the inside of the smart, shining pram.

Since Katy had stood in as lady's maid a little earlier on, she had noticed a certain change in Nanny Barlow's attitude to her. She was less apt to treat her as a child and there had been no further disparaging remarks in connection with the undesirability of reading, although Katy was careful never to be caught doing so. It was simply obvious to her that, because she had been able to undertake her temporary role so satisfactorily and had, in consequence, gained Mrs Moreton's wholehearted approval, this had stood her in good stead with Nanny Barlow as well. That was what made it all the more difficult to do what she was planning to do on her next afternoon off, even though she kept trying to tell herself that it was not exactly she who had made all the arrangements, but the young man in the bookshop.

They had met quite accidentally the previous week, when she had slipped out after tea to post a letter. At least, it had *seemed* accidental although, as there were two pillar boxes both equidistant from the Moretons' house, she was vaguely aware that she invariably found herself choosing the one nearer Oxford Street. Not that she had any intention of visiting Masons again, even though she had at last finished *Wuthering Heights* and thought it quite the most wonderful book she had ever read. For this reason alone, she sometimes felt that she would like to have been able to thank the person who had brought such an opportunity about. But, while being intelligent enough to have appreciated every word, she had become greatly saddened as she reached the end: not entirely by the story itself – much as she grieved for Cathy and Heathcliff – but by the realization of how lacking she herself was, both in experience and education. She vowed that she would do her best to remedy such matters, even if it meant finding another bookshop, or perhaps a library. Never again would she expose her ignorance in the abysmal way which she had done on the day when she had paid twopence for what was now one of her most precious possessions.

After posting her letter, she had at first taken no notice of the voice calling 'Miss' behind her. When hurrying footsteps caught up with her own and she found herself looking into the same searching, dark brown eyes from which she had fled two months previously, she was conscious of the colour coming swiftly to her face, just as it had done before.

'Did you like it?' It was as if there had been no interval of time since their last meeting, no pause in their conversation.

'Oh, *yes* . . . Thank you,' she added, and then became tongue-tied.

'I hoped you'd come back. I had another book I was saving for you at the same price. I've still got it, as a matter of fact. It's Thackeray's *Vanity Fair*. Unless, of course, you've read it?'

'No.' Despite her confusion, she was quick to appreciate his courteousness in not automatically assuming that he would receive a negative answer.

'We've just closed now, but perhaps you'd like to call in? Tomorrow?'

'I . . . well, no. I'm sorry.'

He had looked crestfallen and she feared that she had

been both ungrateful and ungracious. 'I work,' she continued hastily. 'It wouldn't be possible.'

'Are you a nurse?' She saw him looking at her uniform.

'A nursery maid. At 89 Upper Brook Street,' something had made her add.

'When d'you get off in the evening?'

'I don't. I just have an afternoon a week – from two until six-thirty.'

'When's your next one?'

'Thursday,' she replied, doubtfully. 'I'm going to tea with some relations, in Tooting Bec.'

'How d'you go?'

'By bus . . . from Hyde Park Corner.'

'Right. I'll escort you. It's early-closing day.'

As she hurried back to Number 89, she realized that they did not even know each other's names. They had simply arranged to meet again with an almost frightening sense of urgency, so much so that she wasn't sure how it could possibly come about. Would he be at the bus stop? She could never be sure which bus she would actually catch. Nanny Barlow had a nasty habit of finding extra work for her to do on Thursday mornings. He wouldn't, *couldn't*, come to the house, would he? That would be terrible. She had never met anyone with quite such force-fulness. She did not know the word 'hypnotic', but she was certainly aware of a power about him, before which she felt helpless. Suddenly, she thought how nice it would have been to be able to talk to May about it all. Dear May, with her warm, protective, sisterly love. But May was eighty miles away and her letters had been curiously short and uncommunicative lately. She hadn't even said much about Katy's detailed description of Mrs Moreton's clothes, only to vouchsafe the information that she herself was making some handkerchief-lawn nightdresses for the youngest Fitzherbert girl who was getting married in June, and if Katy happened to be passing a shop like Gorringes or Robinson & Cleavers she might just look in the window and see what readymades were selling at, as she was wondering whether to charge three shillings or three shillings and sixpence. 'The doctor being always so good to us,' she had added, 'I'd like to do them as cheap as possible.'

As Katy hurried along to the bus stop on the appointed Thursday afternoon, she half hoped that the young man would not be there. For, although in a way she did not feel she was really committing any crime, for she was still doing exactly what she had said she would be doing, yet she was well aware that had Nanny Barlow known there was a possibility of her nursery maid's being escorted by a young man, she would not only have been horrified, but would have put a stop to her afternoon off completely.

He was there, of course. As they climbed up on to the open top deck of the bus, he told her that he had been waiting since soon after one o'clock, when Masons had closed.

'What's your name?' he said, after they had taken their seats and he had insisted on paying both their fares.

'Katy.'

'Katy what?'

'Katy Lodge. And yours?' she enquired, shyly.

'Philip Mason.'

'*Mason*?'

'Yes. My old man owns the shop.'

'Oh, I see.' Now she came to think about it, he hadn't seemed exactly like an ordinary salesman. She wished she had not shown any initial surprise at his revelation, but he appeared not to mind. There was a determined kind of optimism about him.

'Look,' he said, suddenly, pulling something out of his pocket. 'I've brought that book. The one I was telling you about. I know you'll enjoy it.'

'Oh . . .' Once more, her face grew pink. She had no idea how becoming it made her, how the impulsive young man sitting beside her, noticing the sweep of the long lashes on the blushing cheek – now somewhat carefully averted – and the soft tendrils of brown hair showing beneath the fetching little navy-blue hat, had fallen desperately in love. He was more or less thrusting the package into her hands now, willing her to take it, and she became even more flustered and embarrassed, as she tried to extricate twopence from the little pochette she always carried.

When he realized what she was about, he said, almost angrily, 'But it's a *present.*'

'Oh!' This time she turned towards him, her large grey eyes wide with surprise and pleasure. Katy Lodge had never been given a present by a young man before. That it happened to be a book seemed to make it doubly precious. 'Thank you,' she said, softly. 'Thank you very much indeed. I shall start to read it on my way home tonight.'

He frowned. 'I don't think that's a very good idea.'

'No?' She was puzzled.

'Well, I mean, I'll be with you.'

She was suddenly scared. 'But I can't take you where I'm going.'

'I didn't expect you to. I'll get myself some tea somewhere and then be at the stop whenever you say. I could do with something to eat. I went without dinner so as I wouldn't miss you.'

She began to feel really alarmed now, countless complications chasing in and out of her mind. Her mother's cousin – Aunt Bessie, as she called her – usually saw her on to the bus. Moreover, she would be sure to enquire about the parcel she was carrying. She was a most austere, censorious woman who, while always producing muffins and a freshly-baked cake on such occasions, nevertheless somehow managed to convey the impression that it was a duty which she was only doing for 'poor dear Sarah's sake'. Katy had never really enjoyed a single visit, but, unless she went shopping – or, rather, window-shopping – with Clara, she had nowhere else to go. Haltingly, she started to voice her fears to her companion, but Philip Mason merely brushed them aside.

'I'll keep the book for you in my pocket. As for the bus stop, that's easy. You just pretend you don't know me.'

She nodded. She was not used to subterfuge. Of course, there had been things at home which had had to be kept from Sarah, although she usually found out about them in the end; and then, in Katy's experience, it always made everything ten times worse.

She was beginning to think that it might be best if she did not see Philip Mason again.

15

They went to Putney Heath on the third Thursday in May. Katy had not, as she feared, altogether had to lie about it – at least, not to Aunt Bessie, because it was she herself who had put her off coming. It so happened that luck, or, rather, luck in the shape of Uncle Harold, had played into her hands. Aunt Bessie had written to say that her husband was having 'trouble'. She did not explain what kind, other than that he might have to go into Tooting Bec hospital for an operation. She spelt the last word with a capital 'O' and underlined it heavily. She added that she was very worried about him but felt sure that Katy would understand, although she hoped that she would not be too disappointed.

Katy was not in the slightest bit disappointed, although the news put her in rather a quandary. She felt that it went without saying that Philip Mason would be at the bus stop to meet her on her next afternoon off, for he had done so regularly ever since their first assignation. But she wondered whether she ought to let him know in advance that she would not be making her usual journey. It was now Monday. Should she post him a letter? Somehow, to write seemed so forward. Besides, she did not want to do anything which might, just conceivably, prevent him from coming to meet her, even though she thought that most unlikely. All the same, might he be upset at the cancellation of their customary routine?

In the end, in an agony of indecision, she simply did nothing – relying on one of her mother's favourite maxims: 'When in doubt, don't' – hurrying to meet him on the day in question, flushed and bright-eyed and wearing, because of an unexpected heat wave, a straw boater for which she had daringly paid one and elevenpence-halfpenny in that year's January sales, and which she had trimmed exactly to match the voile dress which had been Flo's and May's present to her the previous Christmas. When Philip Mason saw her coming, his heart gave a sudden lurch. In all his twenty-one years, he felt that he had never seen anyone looking so appealing or beautiful.

When she told him what had happened he stared at her in such amazement and disbelief that, for a moment, she was afraid that perhaps he would just go away again. Then he did a most surprising thing. He threw his own straw hat up into the air, caught it with one hand, grabbed Katy with the other and hustled her away to another bus stop. Before she had had time to know what was happening, they had boarded a bus for Putney.

'The Heath is really country, Katy. Just like where you come from, I shouldn't wonder.'

'Is it?' She was excited and still breathless, for he had made her run quite fast. She felt suddenly reckless, a little as she had done on the day when she had climbed on to the stage at the Wilhampton fair and sung 'Our Lodger's Such a Nice Young Man'. There was about her an unusual combination of decorum, interposed by occasional unexpected wildness. 'Do you go there often?' she asked, after he had bought their tickets.

'Used to, when I was small. Dad had a shop in the High Street in those days. When we moved into the West End, of course, what with Mother getting ill and dying, we never went so much. Come to think of it, I haven't been there for a long time.'

She knew that his mother was dead and that he and his father lived by themselves above the present shop. As he had no brothers and, especially, no sisters, she wondered how they managed the domestic side of their life, but she was still diffident of enquiring.

'Sometimes, I wish we'd never moved,' he continued, 'but I suppose it was a good thing from Dad's point of view. He'd done quite well. Still, I don't mean to spend my own life selling books.'

'Don't you?' She looked at him in surprise. 'But I

thought . . . I mean . . . you know so much about them. You're so interested.'

'Of course I'm interested, Katy. But there's something better I could do.'

'What's that?' She was mystified.

'Write one, of course. One day I'm going to have my name on the cover. I'll be famous. You'll see.'

'Oh *Philip*.' Her eyes shone. She felt as if she were singing inside. 'What will it be about?'

He looked at her very directly. 'A girl called Katy, I shouldn't wonder,' he replied, smiling, and thinking that no girl in the world could blush as promptly and prettily as the one beside him.

As the bus turned south and went over Putney Bridge, he said, 'If I'd known where we were going today, I'd have brought a picnic. Tell you what. I'll buy some cakes in the High Street. I don't know about a cup of tea, though.' He thought for a moment. 'Would a bottle of lemonade do instead?'

'Lemonade would be lovely.'

She realized, with nostalgia, that she had not tasted lemonade since before her father died. She remembered how, on hot summer Sundays, when they walked to Breconbury Woods, he would sometimes secrete a bottle or two in the inside pocket of his best black jacket, which he would produce when they sat down to rest before starting home. She could see him now, releasing the wire-covered top so that the round glass marble stopper went down into the neck of the bottle, and then passing it round, and how Sarah would look disapproving and say that it would spill on their clothes and, in any case, she did not like to see any of her family drinking other than from a cup or a glass, especially, as she put it, 'in public places'. Although it would have been hard to find anywhere less public than where they were sitting at the end of what May, grandly, always called the Camelia Grove – planted by an earlier generation of Fairfaxes – where they only seemed to have the birds for company and Wilhampton was lost in the heat haze far below; while even the usually white-bright chalkpit on the distant high ridge of downs behind Westonbury appeared to have melted into a shimmering blue sky.

Today, as they reached their destination, she was both pleased and surprised to find that Philip had not been altogether wrong in assuming it would remind her of her home ground. There wasn't the view on the outskirts, of course, but it seemed much more of a wood than a heath and she took an almost childish delight in following him through the narrow pathways between the tangled undergrowth, conscious of the sweet smell of brier rose, the springy turf beneath her feet.

'How about this?' he said, at length, when they came to a small clearing, where a giant oak tree towered overhead, so that they might almost have been in some green cave, so dense was the foliage all around them.

He put down their makeshift picnic and took off his jacket, spreading it carefully at the base of the tree for her to sit on. All at once, she became acutely shy. Her previous feelings of elation gave way to overwhelming self-doubt. She knew that she should not be here at all, alone with this strange young man who said he was going to become a famous writer, but whom she had only known such a very little while. Whatever would her mother say? Or Flo and May? Aunt Bessie? Mrs Moreton and Nanny Barlow? She had been wicked and deceitful in allowing the latter to think she was going to Tooting Bec.

'Katy?' Philip, already kneeling on the ground struggling with the top of the lemonade bottle, suddenly looked up. 'Aren't you going to sit down?'

She did so, nervously, carefully arranging the skirt of her voile dress — by no means as short as most of her employer's — over her legs.

When he had at last managed to dislodge the stopper, he handed her the bottle and she took a few mouthfuls.

'Shall we have the cakes now or later?'

'I don't mind . . .' She hesitated. 'Philip, have you the time on you? I . . . mustn't be late back.'

'But we've only just come, Katy. I don't have a watch, but it can't be much more than half-past three. Aren't you enjoying yourself?' He wore the same crestfallen look which he had done at their second meeting, when she had said that she would not be able to come back to the shop for the book he was keeping for her. She was torn between the desire to please, yet the fear of so doing.

Afterwards, she could not quite remember exactly when he had taken hold of her hand or how it came about that his arm was around her, nor how he had somehow removed her straw boater and begun to kiss her, gently at first, but then with increasing urgency. She could only recall that at one point she found herself responding to his advances with the same ardour, of a thrill, a longing, that ran right through her. But suddenly something – possibly the thought of Sarah or even, in some confused, unaccountable way, poor Neil – made her push him aside and struggle to her feet.

There was silence between them. He picked up her hat and waited while she pinned up her hair which had become loosened. The tautness of her dress, straining over her small rounded breasts as she raised her arms, made him turn aside.

'I'm sorry, Katy,' he said, as they made their way back to the bus stop. 'I meant no harm.'

She nodded, still filled with conflicting emotions which she could scarcely understand or control. On the way home, in order to bring some semblance of normality back into their relationship, she asked him, diffidently, when he would start his book.

He continued to look straight ahead. 'I don't know,' he replied, enigmatically. 'It depends on a lot of things.'

She left him in Park Lane, soon after they got out of the bus, horrified to hear the clock above the Grosvenor Chapel chiming seven. As soon as she stepped inside the nursery at Number 89 and saw Nanny Barlow's grave face and heard what she had to say, she became panic-stricken.

'Mrs Moreton would like to see you, Katy. I told her I would send you down to her bedroom as soon as you came in.' There was no reference to her lateness, merely a firm, subdued statement.

Her hand was shaking as she tapped on the door. Her mouth felt dry. She had been found out. Someone had seen her. It had been tempting fate to have thought that she could get away with such outrageous behaviour. In her remorse and anxiety, her imagination became completely out of control. They must have been followed. Someone from the household must have been on the bus, probably peering through the bushes just at the moment when she had put her arms round Philip and kissed him back with an intensity of which she had no idea she was capable. Could a kiss like that make one pregnant? She would then be guilty of that sin of sins. She would bring disgrace on the family. Her mother would cast her out. Whatever happened at the moment, Mrs Moreton would most certainly send her packing from Number 89.

She was so concentrated on what she was expecting to hear that she took little notice of her employer's opening remarks, not really registering anything other than the fact that she must be on the nine o'clock train to Wilhampton in the morning — the matter presumably being so serious that there was no question of her not being able to travel alone.

She was still more or less bemused when Mrs Moreton finally stood up and she caught the words, said with both kindness and concern, 'I am so very sorry, Katy. Let's hope you find things much better than you may think. After all, the telegram only referred to a *temporary* need for your presence at home.'

16

It was Edith who met her. As soon as Katy saw her standing on the Wilhampton platform, she noticed a great difference in her married sister's appearance since they had met last Christmas. Her figure was somehow fatter and dumpier, her blue gingham dress clean but crumpled, her usually smiling face worn and lined, while the mass of auburn hair was flecked with more than a touch of grey. She had, moreover, obviously lost one or two teeth. Of all the family, Edith had always been the most negligent about using a toothbrush, having even said, shortly after marrying Herbie, that it might save trouble if she had the whole lot out. Though younger than both Flo and May, she seemed all at once to have become a middle-aged matron.

'Katy, my dear.' She held out her arms. 'I'm so glad you've come. I didn't think I could leave the children with Herbie and sit up another night at the mill this week.'

'Sit up? Edie, what is it? The telegram didn't say much.'

'No, well, we've been trying to keep it from you, hoping Flo would take a turn for the better, but she's been in bed six weeks now.'

'*Six weeks*?' They began to hurry away from the station, Katy carrying the small suitcase which Nanny Barlow had lent her.

'Yes. It's . . . something internal. She's lost a lot of blood. But she seems to think she's getting better every day, although we can't help being worried. Dr Fitzherbert isn't very forthcoming. But that's not exactly why we sent for you yesterday.'

'What do you mean?' Not for the first time during the past twenty-four hours did panic seize her. 'What *is* it, Edie?' she said again. 'May's all right, isn't she?' May had always come first in her affections.

'Yes, Katy. She's very tired, naturally. But you see . . . well, the long and the short of it is that two days ago Mother . . .' She broke off, uncertain of how best to impart her distressing information, and then continued, hesitatingly, 'Look, lovey, you must be prepared. She's not herself. She's lost her memory.'

'Lost her *memory*?' In spite of her desire to get on, Katy stood stockstill in the middle of the dusty white road. 'But . . . how . . . why?'

'It happened a week or so back, but only for a few hours. Herbie found her wandering about by the mill-race. Dr Fitzherbert says it's quite understandable in a way, when you come to think of it, what with Flo's illness coming on top of all she's been through. It's nature's way out, so to speak. When she came to after the first go, he said we must keep her as quiet as possible, that she ought to get away, but of course you know what she is. And she wouldn't come to me. Besides, poor May needs help. She can't nurse one invalid, let alone two, and carry on dressmaking.'

'Oh, *Edie*!' They had begun to walk on now, taking the short cut across the meadows, which it was only possible to do at this time of the year. The scent of hay was in the air, the hedges on either side of them white with cow parsley, the horse-chestnut tree by the first stile covered with the pink flowering candles which Katy always loved. In the field known as Upper Croft, one of the Bulbarrow farm workers was mowing, his deep gruff voice calling out to his cart-horse to 'Coom up, there, Vi'let', as they turned a corner. Further on, in Lower Croft, in a more inaccessible place near the river which Katy had always called Nomansland, Ted Shergold was cutting some longer grass with a scythe: the slow, rhythmical, swishing sound of his labours mingling with the distant call of a cuckoo and the plop of a trout rising for mayfly, as they crossed over one of the narrow, rickety, wooden bridges.

Summer was everywhere, the countryside alive with new growth. Even Edith began to refer to such things, explaining, a little shyly, the reason for her increase in weight. 'The news isn't all bad, Katy,' she said, 'although I could have wished I hadn't fallen just now. I'm having another baby in October.'

'Another?' Again, Katy was incredulous. She supposed she should say something congratulatory, rejoice with her married sister, but she could only feel dismay.

'Yes. I always wanted a big family, remember? I like to have the little ones around me. Keeps me young.'

'I see.' Although Katy did not really see at all. She felt that Edith's last remark hadn't made sense. Children made you *old*, surely, long before your time, unless you were fortunate enough to be in a position to have them looked after by people like Nanny Barlow or herself. She had only to think of her mother and the pregnant woman beside her to realize that. Suddenly, the morning seemed unreal. She wondered whether any of it was really happening. Only when she heard the old, familiar, relentless sound of the mill-race as they reached the outskirts of the mill itself did the stark actuality of all that she had just been told begin to sink in. As they walked down the main passageway, although the sun was still shining, it seemed as if they had stepped out of the light. She shivered slightly.

'What shall I say, Edie, about why I've come home?'

'I was going to warn you, before we went inside the house. May said she thought it might be best if you pretended to Mother – that is, if she asks, which I doubt – that you've come home early for your holiday. And to Flo too, for that matter. After all, you've been at the Moretons' nearly a year. You're due for your week next month, aren't you?'

She nodded, unhappily. One or two of the mill-hands passed by, touching their caps a little awkwardly and mumbling, 'Good morning.' She caught the whiff of the same curious indefinable smell which she knew, even if she were blindfold, as well as deaf to the sound of the mill-race, would always tell her exactly where she was. It was not unpleasant, simply a 'wet-woollen-clothes-hanging-up-to-dry' smell. She had breathed it, grown up with it. It was somehow there, in her lungs, a part of her. Suddenly it seemed as if she had not been away from home at all. Mayfair, Philip Mason and Putney Heath might never have existed.

Rather to her surprise, her mother was fully dressed and lying on the couch when they entered the front door. May was attending to something on the range, but she quickly put down a saucepan and came to kiss her youngest sister. She said little, but the strength and warmth of her embrace expressed both her relief and pleasure in a way no words could have done. Then she turned to Sarah: 'Look, Mother, who's come home!'

Katy went across to the couch and knelt beside it, doing her best to stifle the fear she felt on looking into the troubled, uncomprehending eyes which stared back at her, and trying not to recoil when she felt a hand come up to touch her cheek.

'Katy.' The voice was curiously laboured and emotionless. 'Shouldn't you be at Miss Maidment's?' Dear God, her mother must have gone back in time over three years o when she had been doing her dressmaking apprentice-ship. Was this really Sarah's way of wiping out all that had happened in the intervening ones? Of letting nature, as Dr Fitzherbert had apparently suggested, help her to escape from all that she had been through during them? She turned uncertainly towards May, wondering how to reply.

'Katy's having a bit of a holiday, Mother,' she heard her say, quickly.

The answer seemed to suffice. Sarah nodded and closed her eyes. Silently, May beckoned her youngest sister out of the room. 'You'd best go up to Flo now. She'll have heard you come,' she whispered. 'She looks different, mind. Try not to show you notice.'

She found Flo lying in the brass-headed double bed in Neil's old room, a thin, white-faced travesty of her old self: her long brown hair loose on the pillows, her emaciated arms resting limply on the counterpane. Yet the fine dark eyes shone with joy at seeing her and she struggled to sit up.

'Katy! What a lovely surprise. Is it really true they've given you your holiday early?'

'Yes.' She bent over and kissed her.

'That must mean you've been a good girl.'

A good girl? The distortion of the truth to which she knew she must adhere seemed somehow doubly distasteful and shameful. She had been anything but a good girl. She had been a wicked one. Perhaps that was why all these troubles had happened. She – or, rather, her family – was paying the price for her sins.

'Just think,' Flo went on, 'we'll have you with us for a whole week. Though I'm sorry you've found Mother and me so poorly. But never mind, we'll both be up and running around again before you go back to London. You mark my words.' Then, as if the effort had been too much for her, Flo lay back and momentarily closed her eyes. There were beads of sweat on her forehead, her faded pink lawn nightdress, trimmed with broderie anglaise, showed signs of damp beneath the arms.

Katy sat down on the bed and held one of her hands,

painfully aware of the difference between the poorly-furnished bedroom she was now in and the luxurious one where, less than twenty-four hours before, she had been told she must return home. She glanced up at the blue and gold embossed text on the wall above Flo's head which Sarah had placed there years ago when Neil had been quite small, embodying the prayer about little children, which ended: 'Suffer me to come unto Thee'. Well, poor Neil had done that, hadn't he? Or so she hoped. But what about Frank lying they knew not where, probably not even buried properly, in foreign soil? She had a sudden desire to get up and tear it down. Although it was prettier and not nearly so harsh and guilt-provoking as the ones which were pinned up each week outside the chapel at the corner of East Street, it seemed so inappropriate, even offensive, with Flo now looking like a death's head, even though she would keep on about feeling better: 'All the more so,' she insisted, 'for seeing you, Katy.'

'Look over there,' she said, suddenly, pointing towards the small whatnot in the corner, on which stood a flagon of Harvest Burgundy and a glass. 'Dr Fitzherbert advised it,' she explained, almost apologetically, as if the presence of alcohol in her room must be excused. 'He says it's excellent for anaemia. It's replacing all the blood I've lost through an early change of life. Mother's put a rusty nail inside, so as to give it more iron. It's done me a power of good already.'

'I'm glad, Flo.' Katy was surprised – even alarmed – at how adept she was becoming in dissembling.

'We couldn't help laughing the other day,' Flo went on, with a little of her old spirit, 'after Edie's eldest had been up to see me. He's such a bright little lad. He went downstairs, looked at Mother's picture of *The Last Supper* hanging over the piano, and asked if it was right for Christ Jesus and his auntie to be drinking burgundy.'

Saddened, Katy left her, marvelling at Flo's implicit and almost childlike faith: presumably in God, in her youngest sister's heaven-sent homecoming and the cheap red wine which she was vaguely aware could be bought at the chemist's in Westonbury.

As soon as she re-entered the living room, May gathered together a mass of black georgette which she had been tacking and stood up. Edith appeared to have gone home. 'Now you're here, Katy,' she said, 'I think I'll go down to the workroom with this. I'm so behind with everything. It's a dress for Lady Fairfax which was promised for yesterday. When she sent down for it I said that, whatever happened, she should have it to wear when they're entertaining at the Hall tomorrow night. Perhaps you'd mind the dinner, lovey, not that Mother or Flo will want very much, I expect.' Then she was gone, pushing out one of her little feet to prop the front door that much further open as she went out, to allow whatever passage of air was possible to pass through the small stuffy house in which, even in the middle of a heat wave, there had to be a fire for cooking purposes.

Katy turned towards the range, anger rising within her that Lady Fairfax's dress had to take priority over so many more grave and urgent considerations. If she – or her daughter, for that matter – really knew the conditions under which May had been struggling to make it, surely they would realize that it was neither possible, nor even necessary, for it to meet the trivial deadline of some purely social occasion? What was that compared to the needs of a seriously ill woman whose mother had lost her memory?

She knew that she was possibly being unfair, that both Lady Fairfax and her daughter were, after their fashion, exceptionally kind-hearted. She had even been sent to Waterloo that morning in her employer's chauffeur-driven Hispano-Suiza. But could they possibly understand the suffering, hardship, comfortlessness and appalling inconvenience of trying to care for the sick in the Mill House? To do that, Katy felt, they would actually have had to be there, performing the task themselves. Whatever tragedies occurred in their own lives they were, materially at least, cushioned against them. The illness of a lady's maid, the sudden lack of Katy's own services, even the indisposition of a member of their own family, were usually but temporary inconveniences. They were not going to have to sit up with an ailing mother or sister or child. Any lack of sleep from which they might suffer during crises would only affect them mentally, never physically as well, as it was all too obvious by their worn and even dishevelled appearance had recently been the case with May and Edith. The lives of Lady Fairfax and her daughter would somehow go on without too much disruption. They might be grieved, at times even shocked, but they would at least be saved any anxiety over their inability to fulfil a dress-making order, the problem of there being only one pair of hands — and overworked ones at that — to bring in the money, where before there had been two.

Sarah still had her eyes closed as, quietly, Katy began seeing to their midday meal, lifting the lid of a saucepan containing a small rabbit stew, another where the potatoes were not quite at the boil. Then she squeezed round the table to the glass-fronted cabinet, extracting a cloth, knives and forks and glasses with which to set the table and lay the only tray she could find — the one she always thought of as Mr Fuller's — before picking up an enamel jug to fetch fresh drinking water from the tap in the mill. As she went towards the front door a shadow fell across the threshold and she suddenly found herself confronted by the figure of a tall, thin, fair-haired young man standing on the step, one who, at first glance, she failed to recognize.

'Miss Lodge? Miss . . . Katy?' He smiled shyly and held out his hand. 'May I come in? I'm Maurice Fitzherbert. I'm living at home again, helping my father with the practice now that I'm qualified. It's been getting so large . . . a bit too much for him to handle by himself lately. He asked if I would call in today to see your mother and sister.'

17

Katy took Lady Fairfax's dress to the Hall the following morning, May having worked far into the night in order to finish it. 'I've put a note inside about why it's late,' she explained, as she handed her the cardboard box, carefully labelled and wrapped in brown paper and string, 'but you might just be able to see her ladyship yourself, if you ask for Emily Harwood when you get there.'

She nodded. There had been little time for a proper talk with May about the situation since her return, but it seemed obvious to Katy that there would be no chance of her going back to London in the foreseeable future. Flo was dying. Without having put it in so many words, May had more or less managed to confirm what Katy felt sure was the case. Even when Maurice Fitzherbert had laughed and joked while visiting her the previous day, a brief glance at the expression on his face – for a second, unmasked – after he came out of the bedroom had left Katy in little doubt as to the seriousness of her sister's illness.

As for Sarah, it was difficult for anyone to predict what might happen. For four days she had been – according to May's brief, whispered account after they had helped her to bed the first evening – in what Claud Fitzherbert had described as another state of shock, possibly because that Tuesday she had asked him, quite directly, whether her eldest daughter had cancer and he had replied, as gently as he could, that he feared it was so; but he had apparently gone on to say that he had known remissions in certain cases and that they must none of them lose hope. One thing which was so much in the patient's favour was her own determination to get better, her firm belief in her recovery – as well, of course, as the loving care of her family. He did not add that if Flo had come to him earlier, he might have advised an operation, not that, in his experience, such a measure often gave other than a few more months' expectation of life.

After his visit, May said that Sarah had disappeared and she had become worried as to where she could have gone. For a moment the thought of the mill-race had unhappily crossed her mind. It had been late in the day, no one was about, and she had rushed straight there, but there had been no sign of her mother. Uneasily, she had returned home. She did not like to go further afield, as she did not want Flo to know of her anxiety; neither did she want to leave her alone. She decided that if Sarah had not returned within another half an hour, she would slip along River

Lane to the Henstridges' cottage, much as she was loath to raise an alarm. Since Neil's death she felt that there had been more than enough talk in Wilhampton about the Lodge family. Although the stories regarding Sidney Lodge's ghost had certainly died down – especially with the advent of the long, light summer days – she was sadly aware that Flo's illness had now taken its place. It had become a much-discussed subject of unwholesome interest, conversations often ceasing abruptly when she entered the shops or passed little groups of people in the street, the tail end of such remarks as 'poor thing', 'a bad business' or 'no age, really' seeming to hang uncertainly in the air.

Then, suddenly, May had continued, just as she was warming some milk that evening to make a junket for the invalid, Sarah had appeared at the front door in the company of the Reverend Donaldson.

'I found your mother in the church, May,' he had said, 'when I went to lock up. I think perhaps she is a little . . . overstrained.' To her daughter's consternation and embarrassment, Sarah had simply walked straight past her without saying a word and gone to lie down on the couch, the total absence of her customary good manners making it plain to them both that, once again, something was very amiss.

Now, as Katy hurried across the market square and was nearing the rectory, she met the rector coming out of his high, wrought-iron front gates. He was a large, hatchet-faced individual, with enormous shaggy eyebrows and a very deep voice, which Katy recalled reverberating throughout St Mark's in a somewhat terrifying manner when he delivered his sermon each Sunday. Hitherto, she had always been scared of him, although she knew that he was a good, sincere man, much respected by her mother and sisters. Once, when she had been about ten or eleven years old and had been passing the selfsame spot where she now found herself, he had happened to be taking some of the doctor's children across to the church in order to let them climb up into the belfry to see the bells. Immediately, he had invited Katy to accompany them. Halfway up the seemingly never-ending, steep, wooden steps, she had begun to feel dizzy but, sandwiched between Maurice Fitzherbert and his sister, Connie, there had been nothing for it but to go on, especially as she did not know any of the children well and stood greatly in awe of them. She had always felt everlastingly grateful to Maurice for telling her, quietly, as they started their descent, to follow him and not look down.

Today, as she began to answer the Reverend Donaldson's solicitous enquiries, she thought how little he had changed compared to the young man whom she had seen yesterday and who was now a fully-fledged doctor. As she went on her way she knew that she too, of course, had altered. She realized that leaving home must have had a great deal to do with it, although it was strange, she reflected, that in some extraordinary way, sooner or later Wilhampton always seemed to pull its sons and daughters back to the fold again. But, be that as it may, she was very conscious that she was now being treated as an adult, whereas twelve months previously she would have been spoken to as a child. The rector had even shaken her hand as they parted, saying gravely, 'I am so very glad to know that you have come, Katy. This is your place now. You're needed at the Mill House so much.'

It was good to have him say this, in spite of the fact that she already knew, only too well, just how much she was needed. Tomorrow, if she found time, she would write Philip Mason a letter and tell him what had happened. She felt sad – albeit a little relieved – that she would probably never see him again. But it was surely right that she should resist temptation, forgo any thought of those moments of delight which had both scared and thrilled her. That was the least she could do. She still could not rid herself of the idea of some just punishment now being meted out for all her misdemeanours, for which she must try to atone.

When she arrived at one of the side entrances to the Hall, she was surprised to find that Ena Perrick answered the door. Katy had not known that Ena – a year younger than she was – had been taken on by the Fairfaxes as under-parlourmaid, although it was hardly surprising that

May had forgotten to mention it. Besides, since all the unfortunate repercussions following Neil's death, she knew that there had been even more of an estrangement between their respective families, although she, personally, bore Ena no ill will and was sorry that because of this and her own departure to London, their friendship appeared to have suffered. She was distressed, now, at the cold way in which Ena greeted her, looking her up and down with a mixture of defensiveness and jealousy in her dark little eyes.

'Hello, Katy. Fancy seeing you.'

'Hello, Ena. How are you?'

'All right. More than can be said for you, by the looks of it. Never seen you so washed out. London town evidently doesn't suit you.'

'I . . . we've sickness at home, Ena. I was up most of last night.'

'Oh.' The girl in the doorway seemed slightly mollified, but not for long. 'I heard something about it,' she mumbled. 'Your mum's wandering, isn't she?'

Katy flushed. 'She's overtired, Ena. May I see Mrs Harwood, please?'

'*Mrs Harwood*?' Ena frowned. 'I'm sure I don't know. She doesn't like being bothered, 'specially on a Saturday morning. She's extra busy because we've company coming. If it's just that parcel you're leaving, couldn't you give it to me?'

'I could, Ena, but I'd like to see Mrs Harwood all the same, if it's possible.'

Katy stood her ground. There was silence between them. Then, resentfully, Ena turned away from the door and disappeared down the dark, flagstoned passage.

Katy waited on the step, feeling that at least Ena might have asked her inside. Surely she would not get very far as a parlourmaid if she treated all her callers in such fashion. It was hot where she was standing, for there was no porch at this entrance and the sun was beating straight down. She wished she had not undertaken her errand without wearing a hat. In London she would automatically have put on her straw boater, however much of a hurry

132

she was in. Could it really be less than forty-eight hours ago when Philip Mason had removed it in the bushes on Putney Heath? In spite of her sorrow and weariness and resolve not to indulge in such speculations, her flush became deeper, the memory of his kisses reawakening that strange, hitherto unknown feeling which she had so unexpectedly experienced. Still clutching her parcel, she closed her eyes and leant against the doorway, the wooden surround warm against her tired body, the scent of wallflowers in a nearby border overpowering in the heavy, noonday heat.

'Why, Katy!' She started, violently, at the sound of Emily Harwood's voice, as she came bustling down the passage to meet her, bright-eyed and red-cheeked, wearing her black nun's veiling uniform dress, her grey hair scraped up into a neat little bun on the top of her head.

'Come into the cool, my dear. You must be fit to faint out there. I can scarce remember it being so hot at this time of the year. Tell me about your mother, and Flo.'

Katy was drawn into a small pantry just inside the door and given a glass of ice-cold water, which she accepted gratefully. She knew Emily Harwood to be a gossip, yet she was also a motherly soul, in fact, more so in many ways than Nanny Barlow. She was not at all the usual forbidding type of housekeeper to be found in such a large establishment. Having been left a widow at a young age with three children on her hands to support, she had been forced to leave them in the care of her own mother and, with great spirit and fortitude, gone into service at the Hall where, over the years, she had risen to her present position. Her treatment of Katy was now certainly very welcome after Ena's sourness, even if it did mean Emily was wanting to hear the latest news from the mill.

'They're neither of them too good, Mrs Harwood,' she replied, slowly, as she drank the water. 'That's why I've come home.' She hesitated and put down the glass. 'May was wondering whether I might see her ladyship. Of course, if it's inconvenient . . .' She broke off, not at all certain that she really wanted to do so, nor that it was a very good idea after all. Surely there was nothing more she could say, other than what was in the note? But she supposed May felt that by seeing Lady Fairfax, Katy would be able to testify to the seriousness of the situation, to justify the sending of a telegram – even if it had been advised by Dr Fitzherbert – which had brought her daughter's nursery maid all the way back from London. Yet there had never been the slightest hesitation on Alicia Moreton's part about the need for Katy to return home at once and it was more than likely that she had by now written to tell her mother exactly what had happened. Katy knew that the two of them kept in very close contact. Her employer had often spoken of how she was looking forward to when a telephone could be installed at the Hall.

It was almost a relief when she heard Emily Harwood say, 'I'm afraid her ladyship isn't here, Katy. She's gone to the Westonbury Show. Lord Fairfax is speaking at the luncheon.'

'Oh, I see. I'd best be getting back then. Thank you for the drink, Mrs Harwood.' She made for the door.

'Right you are, my dear. You run along now. May must be very glad to have your help. Tell her I'll probably look down to see you all one afternoon next week when we're not so busy here.'

'Yes,' she replied, trying not to sound too doubtful. She had a feeling that May might not altogether welcome a visit from Emily Harwood just at the moment, nor anyone else for that matter. It was bad enough having to keep changing the sheets in anticipation of the doctor's visit and seeing that both invalids, besides the house, looked clean and tidy. When Sarah came to again, she would not like to think that her family had not kept up appearances.

18

At first she took him for just another fisherman, when she saw the distant figure casting near the Black Arch one evening towards the middle of June. She knew that there were many people in the neighbourhood to whom the Fairfaxes gave the right to fish the River Willon and the various streams which joined it close by the mill-race. It went without saying, of course, that every tenant on the estate was given a 'day', or sometimes two, during the season, but Katy was well aware that there were many more people besides farmers who received such favours. Sometimes, they would walk home through the mill and, if they happened to know her parents and their creels were full, they would leave a trout or grayling at the Mill House, which Sarah would immediately scrape and clean and then fry in butter the following morning, so that each member of the family could be treated to a taste for breakfast.

Once, when Katy had been about ten or eleven years old, her father himself had been among the lucky ones. Old Mr Swayne up at Bulbarrow had fallen off a rick during haymaking and, as his permit was for a Saturday, he had sent word to Lord Fairfax's agent, asking whether Sidney Lodge – whom he liked and respected – might use it when the mill shut down at 1 p.m. To her great joy, her father had suggested taking her with him. She could remember helping Sarah to cut sandwiches and the two of them setting off, Sidney Lodge with the rod which Mr Swayne had lent him; herself, wearing a red and white spotted cotton sunbonnet, carrying their picnic in a little wicker basket.

She had never forgotten the occasion. It had been so peaceful and trouble free. Her father had seemed altogether different, not the hardworking, often harassed manager of the Felt Mills, but a kinder, gentler, happier person, with time to explain so many things to her: that grayling were not so cunning as trout, that she must keep either close behind him or a good way away, so that she would not get caught herself when he was casting, that if he happened to hook a fish and it was under the limit, he would have to throw it back. She had wondered how he knew so much about the sport, considering she had never seen him engage in it before, other than to help the water-keepers with their annual netting of grayling or sometimes lend a hand with Ernest Fielding's eel stage; but he had told her that he had learnt a lot from his own father – a somewhat shadowy figure in Katy's life – who, until his early death caused by contracting lockjaw, had been a farmer who had come down in the world, gambling away his inheritance many miles west of Wilhampton.

Was it, she wondered, because the memory of that golden afternoon in childhood had always been so special to her that now, whenever she felt she could be spared for a while, she seemed to gravitate towards the meadows? As if mind and body were automatically seeking the place where she knew that quietude dwelled, together with the aptly-named wild heart's-ease and meadow-sweet? Certainly at this particular time of her life a few moments by the banks of the Willon helped to relieve – if only fleetingly – the thought of all the suffering which she had left but a little way behind her at the Mill House.

For although her mother's memory had returned, it seemed but tenuous. Sarah remained both frail and fractious. As for Flo, she appeared to grow weaker daily, railing at the fact that she could no longer get out of bed unaided and that her youngest sister was having to take an extended 'holiday' on her account. This evening, before leaving for her walk, Katy had promised not to be gone long, for it was her turn to sit up during the first part of the night and she knew that May would wish to lock up and go to bed early. When she came to the first stile, she sank down on the grass gratefully and, leaning back against it, closed her eyes and lifted her face to the fast-disappearing sun, unaware that the fisherman whom she had noticed was casting downstream and gradually coming closer. Suddenly, the sound of parting rushes made her start. She turned her head and found herself looking straight into the kind, but somewhat concerned, eyes of Maurice Fitzherbert.

'Good evening, Miss Katy. I'm sorry. I'm afraid I must have startled you.'

'Oh no . . . I was just taking a rest, that's all,' she replied, angry to feel the inevitable blush coming so swiftly to her cheeks.

'A much deserved one, I'm sure.' Carefully, he placed his rod against the stile and then, when he saw her make a move to get up, said quickly, 'Must you go? I'm sure you would have stayed a little longer if I hadn't appeared in such a singularly ungracious fashion. As a matter of fact,' he went on, searching for something in the pocket of his light linen jacket, 'I was intending to stop here for a smoke, before having one final flog below the mill-race. Do you have any objection to a pipe? I know my mother doesn't care for it indoors.'

'Oh no.' She looked at him, nervously. She still felt she should depart. On the other hand, the last thing she wanted was to appear rude. He and his father were doing so much for them all. Yet was he really meaning to linger here with her, alone, in the water meadows, especially at this hour? Supposing they were seen? He was certainly extremely courteous and unassuming, an older, altogether different young man from Philip Mason; but, all the same, she didn't really know him at all. Besides, between his family and hers there had always been that indefinable barrier which made any kind of social intercourse seem — at least, to Katy — not only embarrassing, but somehow wrong. True, it was not such an obvious one as might have been the case had she been, say, Ena Perrick. For the Lodges had always held a rather unique position in the Wilhampton hierarchy, that is, if they held any definable position at all. For they appeared to have no particular niche, belong to no special group. They were neither working class, nor thought of as 'trade', unless one counted Flo's and May's dressmaking business. They were simply the somewhat unusual, closely-knit family who lived at the misleadingly-named Mill House: well-mannered, exceptionally well turned out, mostly well-spoken and immensely proud.

'Do you come here often?' she heard Maurice Fitzherbert ask as, possibly sensing her uneasiness, he sat down, but on the opposite step of the stile, and began to fill his pipe.

'As often as I can.' Shyness had always made her abrupt.

'It's the same with me,' he replied, slowly. 'I've always loved this stretch of water. I think I missed it more than anything when my training and then, of course, a spell in the army combined to keep me away from it. I suppose that's why we've hardly met for such a long time.'

'Yes. Yes, I expect so,' she answered, still agitated. 'And I've been away, too,' she added, shyly, 'in London.'

He nodded and then said, unexpectedly, 'Did you like it there?'

She hesitated. Did she like London? Yes and no, really. The last little bit had certainly been exciting, but she couldn't tell him that. She couldn't tell anyone, not even dear May, although she had felt obliged to explain to her that the letters she kept receiving were from a young man whose father owned a bookshop close to Upper Brook Street, whom she had got to know through the purchase of a marked-down edition of *Wuthering Heights*. Since she had written to Philip Mason soon after she came home to tell him what had happened, he had sent her many letters: strange, impassioned, originally-phrased ones, the last arriving only that morning, demanding to know why she never received any replies.

'I don't think I should want to live there always,' she answered at length, almost primly.

'No. Neither would I. There was a time, when I first started training at Guy's, that I thought maybe I'd try and specialize, have my name up on a plate in Harley Street one day, and then, I don't know . . . I think the war knocked that idea out of my head. I thought it would be more worthwhile to be a country doctor when I qualified. You learn more about individuals. And life. Besides, I'm needed where I am now, a bit as you are, in a way. My father . . .' This time it was he who hesitated, before continuing, 'Well, it isn't common knowledge, but I think he may retire soon. He's always worked so hard. If I were in charge of his case, I'd say he ought to stop at once.'

'Oh, *no*.' Her response was now quite natural and spontaneous, but she hoped that she had not hurt him by it. It was simply that she could not imagine what she and her family would do without the older man. They had always depended on him so much. He had seen them through so many vicissitudes, had taken such infinite trouble over her when she was a child, even to giving her the little dictionary when she had missed almost a whole year's schooling.

'Don't worry,' he laughed, not at all put out. 'He's not going to go just yet. And by the time he does, I'll know a lot more. About all of you,' he added, with a diffident yet almost conspiratorial grin. She started feeling uncomfortable again and rose to go.

He stood up also. 'Good night, Miss Katy.'

'Good night,' she said, wishing he would not address her like that and wondering what on earth she should call him. 'Dr Maurice', as everyone else did, she supposed, as she hurried back through the mill, remembering that the only other occasions when she had actually exchanged more than a few words with him had been the time when he had helped her down from St Mark's belfry after seeing the Reverend Donaldson's bells, and another winter's morning when they had both happened to be buying sweets in the Perricks' shop. She recalled clearly how he had asked for two ounces of gobstoppers, popping one into his mouth as soon as they got outside and, because it was such an enormous sugary marble, before he had had time to suck it so that it became smaller and changed colour, it had somehow shot out of his mouth and rolled all along the gutter of River Lane. Horrified, she had watched him run and pick it up and put it back in his mouth again and, in her innocent anxiety, forgetting both manners and shyness, she had shrieked, 'But it's dirty. You'll catch diphtheria.' And he had replied, 'Don't worry. Abie Grant will have something in his dispensary to save me from that.'

How long ago it now seemed: that time when the very sight of Abie's face, doling out the meticulously wrapped and sealing-waxed remedies from his little square 'window', was enough to make one feel that all would be well, no matter whether the actual preparations were prescribed by Dr Fitzherbert. Even when Katy had been too ill to be taken to the surgery by Sarah and had had to be visited at home, Claud Fitzherbert always magnanimously gave the credit for relief to his dispenser by such remarks as: 'We'll see what Mr Grant can find, my dear, to send away the pain', or 'I believe Abie has the very thing on his shelf for that throat'. It had certainly made her, and most of the other children in Wilhampton, invariably feel that it was the little man in the white coat, living permanently – as they supposed – in his two-by-four, medicinal-smelling box of a room, who was the real miracle worker.

If only Abie could now produce some cure-all for poor Flo, Katy thought, as she went into the front door, noticing May's weary face as she turned away from the range.

'I've made a pot of tea,' she said. 'I hope it's not stewed. I thought you'd be back sooner.' Her voice was not exactly reproachful, but its usual warmth and sweetness were lacking.

'I'm sorry. I met . . . Maurice Fitzherbert. He happened to be fishing and stopped to pass the time of day.' There seemed no point in concealing the fact, at least, certainly not from May.

'Did you now!' May poured out some tea and put the pot back on the hob, thoughtfully. 'There's not many as come like him these days,' she continued, as she started to get out the candlesticks and matches. 'His parents must go down on their knees every night and thank the Lord that when he insisted on interrupting his training to join up, the war didn't take him.'

19

'Earth to earth, ashes to ashes, dust to dust, in the sure and certain hope of the Resurrection to eternal life . . .' The deep resonant voice of the Reverend Donaldson, standing by Flo's grave in his long white surplice, was heard in respectful silence by the little group of mourners. Around them, on the grass, lay a profusion of floral tributes: red roses, white roses, carnations of every hue, arum lilies, love-in-the-mist, marguerites, dahlias and early pale yellow chrysanthemums, the amalgam of colour contrasting starkly, even defiantly, with the sombre setting.

It was very hot in the cemetery. Katy, her face already

blotched and swollen and trying hard to fight back further tears, stared resolutely at the opposite hill, where several little ant-like figures were stooking oats. Had Flo gone to eternal life? Did this devout man really think so? But why should so good and kind a person be singled out for such pain and suffering before she got there?

Katy would like to have asked the rector about the hereafter, but she knew that even to doubt the existence of such a place was blasphemy. She was sure that May and Edith, standing one on either side of her, heads bowed and each clutching a handkerchief, would never have entertained such wicked thoughts. Facing them, flanked by Henry and Herbie on the opposite side of the grave, stood Sarah, a statuesque figure in deep mourning, her expression aloof and enigmatic, as if she were either determined not to break down or was now beyond all feeling. Katy prayed that her mother would not lose her memory again.

Half an hour earlier, St Mark's church had been packed for Flo's funeral. Indeed, Katy could scarcely remember it being so full, not even when her father had died. Wilhampton appeared to have turned out en masse, Lady Fairfax sitting, much to Katy's acute embarrassment, in the pew immediately behind her.

The former had been more than kind during Flo's last agonizing weeks. Almost every other day some little delicacy would arrive from the Hall: grapes, calf's-foot jelly, sponge fingers – not that Flo could eat any of them. She had been too weak, too far gone. Towards the end, May and Katy could only get her to take a few sips of home-made barley water, bathe her parched lips in glycerine and dab her forehead with a handkerchief soaked in eau de Cologne. Yet even then, incredibly, she still talked of 'When I'm better . . .'

On the morning she died, in the middle of August, she appeared to rally a little. Struggling to sit up in bed, she had gazed at her youngest sister very directly and said, 'My Katy, what a beautiful girl you've grown into. You must be careful not to break too many hearts.' And Katy had blushed furiously, wondering whether, by some sixth sense, Flo could possibly have known about Philip Mason. She had looked away but, even as she did so, Flo's hand seemed to become strangely limp in her own. She had turned back and stared at her, sensing at once that there was now only a lifeless body in the bed. Katy had never witnessed actual death before and for a moment she wanted to cry out. But, mercifully, May had suddenly appeared, hurried to the bedside, picked up Flo's wrist, nodded and then said quietly, 'Thank God'.

It had seemed to Katy a bewildering eternity between that morning and the hot sultry afternoon of the funeral. She realized that when her father had died she had been spared all the harrowing details which invariably accompanied such an event, for she had been that much younger and these has been dealt with by her mother and sisters; whereas when Neil had drowned she had simply not been there at all. But now, with Sarah's health so precarious and Edith getting near her time, the whole responsibility devolved, of necessity, on to her and May's shoulders. True, on receiving their telegram, Henry had wired back to say that he would come for the funeral, but this had been quickly followed by a letter in which he stated that he would like to bring his wife and child with him. He added that Marianne would be quite happy to remain at the Mill House while the funeral was taking place, where she could possibly have the tea ready for everyone by the time they returned, besides taking care of Edith's children as well as little Frank. This had upset not only Sarah but – possibly owing to her delicate condition – Edith, who had said that she would not have a moment's peace leaving her offspring in the care of a Froggie. She had seemed to forget that some of her ancestors on her mother's side had come from across the Channel. Katy had been obliged to go up to the post office and send Henry a second wire: 'Owing difficulties please come alone', disliking the slant-eyed look which Mabel Snoad, the postmistress, had given her as she paid the requisite elevenpence-halfpenny.

Yet it had been the flowers on the morning of the funeral which had bothered Katy most. Many of them were sent straight to the house, arriving with a kind of sinister, insistent regularity, heralded by heavy male footsteps. She hadn't known where to put them at first, because May had taken Sarah down to the workroom to make an adjustment to the collar of the new black foulard dress she had made for her. Soon, the Mill House seemed to be full of flowers, their scent sickly and overpowering in the hot, stuffy living room. Wearily, according to May's instructions, she began making a list of their donors in order that they should subsequently be sent a letter of thanks, for the Lodge family did not believe in the impersonal, formal notice which others sometimes inserted in the *Westonbury Journal* on such occasions. Presently, because of the heat and the anguish they were causing her, Katy started taking all the wreaths outside, laying them down in the shadiest part of the garden to await, as Flo's coffin upstairs was awaiting, the arrival of the ancient hearse belonging to Arnold Parker, the local undertaker. Sadly, she knew that when the time came, the coffin would have to be lowered from a bedroom window, there being no other way of transporting it down the narrow, tortuous stairs.

She had been putting out the last tribute of pinks and Michaelmas daisies, when she heard Sarah's voice behind her, enquiring whom it was from. On being told that Archie Perrick had just brought it, her mother simply held out her hand and said, 'Give it to me, child.' Horrified, Katy then watched her disappear with it in the direction of the mill-race, realizing only too well what was to be its fate. She wondered whether, had she mentioned it, the red roses sent by Guy and Grace Armitage with In Remembrance attached to them would have been disposed of in the same way. When Sarah's memory was working properly, Katy thought miserably as she went back indoors, there was no forgetting old scores even in the midst of present grief.

Yet neither, it would seem, did Sarah forget her manners, especially in public places. As they left the graveside that afternoon, she held out her hand to the Reverend Donaldson, thanked him quietly and courteously and asked if he would like to join them for a cup of tea at the

Mill House a little later on. Then, on Henry's arm, she allowed herself to be helped to Arnold Parker's old horse-drawn cab, which was waiting outside the cemetery gates.

May had arranged, despite Sarah's opposition, for one of the more sensible girls at the mill to come into the house and have two kettles on the boil by the time the family came home, but Katy was both surprised and distressed at the number of other people who now quickly appeared, crowding into the small living room or standing, a little uncertainly, just outside the front door. It had seemed bad enough having to bury poor Flo without it being deemed necessary to provide tea and currant cake afterwards. When she felt that she had done her duty as far as she was able, she slipped away to the bottom of the garden, and it was here that Henry came looking for her some three-quarters of an hour later.

'I've come to say goodbye, kid. My train goes at five-fifteen.'

'Oh, I'm sorry. I . . . we all hoped you'd stay longer. Can't you catch a later one?'

'I'm afraid not. I had a devil of a time getting here as it was. It isn't all that long since I had to ask for leave to come to Neil's funeral. Besides, Marianne's expecting me.'

'Yes.' She hesitated. 'Henry, how many people are still up at the house?'

'About nine or ten, I should say. Why?'

'It's just that I don't think I can face going back for a bit. Would you like me to come to the station with you?'

'I'd like that very much. I'll slip up and say goodbye to Mother and May and tell them you'll be coming to see me off. We can take the meadow path.'

As soon as they were on their way, Henry said, suddenly, 'What are you going to do, Katy, now Flo's gone? Go back to London?'

'No,' she answered, quietly, hurrying to keep up with his long strides, 'I'm needed here. I've sent for my things. Even though Mother's better, May needs help with the sewing.'

He looked at her with some concern. There was less of the happy-go-lucky manner about him now. Like Edith,

144

he seemed to Katy to have aged considerably since she had last seen him.

'You won't regret it, will you, kid?'

'No.' She paused and then, as if to reassure herself more than anyone else, repeated, 'Oh, no. Besides, I never particularly wanted to be a nursery maid.'

He nodded, apparently satisfied. Soon, they were obliged to walk single file, hemmed in by a high hedge on either side, the branches of elm and elder intermingling overhead. She was reminded, sharply, of the day, not so very long ago, when the sky had all but been blotted out by the same kind of tracery on Putney Heath. From over her brother's shoulder, she heard him say, 'I suppose it's not the time to ask, really, but I wish you could put in a good word for Marianne with Mother now and then. I'd like to bring her and little Frank to the mill on my next leave. I might be sent to Germany this winter and it doesn't seem right his grandmother's never seen the boy.'

'I'll do my best, Henry. I'd love to see little Frank myself, and I know May would, too.'

He stopped, suddenly, and felt for his wallet, eventually extracting from it a somewhat crumpled photograph which he handed to her, proudly.

'Spitting image, isn't he?' he remarked, as she found herself looking at a woman holding a small boy who did, indeed, look astonishingly like a photograph of his dead uncle taken at about the same age.

'He's lovely, Henry,' she said, wishing she could say the same for his mother, for she could hardly recognize her sister-in-law.

Possibly sensing this, Henry went on quickly, 'Marianne's put on a bit of weight since his birth. She's not looking her best in the photo, I'm afraid. 'Course, it's not been easy for her, Katy, living over here, getting used to another country . . . and people haven't been all that kind. But she's not a bad sort, when you get to know her. She's been very hurt by Mother's attitude.'

'Yes. Yes, I'm sure she has.' She handed him back the photograph and he put it carefully away and walked on. They came to the first stile and he helped her over it. She did not like the thought of his going abroad again. It was good to know that he was in England, even if she rarely saw him. She wished sincerely that there had not been such a rift in family relationships.

On the slope up to the station, she said again, 'I really will do all I can, Henry, about Mother. Although, of course, we can't push anything just now.'

'Oh no. I realize that. But I thought, perhaps . . . you know . . . little Frank looking so like the other one . . . It might help, somehow.'

'Yes. It ought to.'

She stayed on the platform, waving until he was out of sight, her eyes filling with tears as she turned to make her way home. Why couldn't her mother open her heart just a little, instead of locking herself up in that proud, obstinate, private world of hers? She must have had warm, impulsive feelings once, surely? It was common knowledge in the family that she had eventually managed to get her own parents to consent to her marrying Sidney Lodge. But what exactly was it that had made her do so? Had she experienced something of the same kind of feelings which Katy had done earlier that summer on Putney Heath? What else could have made her cleave to the prospective, though impecunious, young manager of the Felt Mills and give birth to Frank nine months after the wedding? Had she ever, Katy wondered now, regretted it? Those six other confinements which followed? Especially the last two: Neil a simpleton, and she, herself, such a sickly child. And then all that had happened since: Frank killed in the war, an early widowhood, Neil drowning and now Flo's death from cancer at the age of only thirty-one.

A little way from home, she sat down for a while on the river bank, watching the water flowing over the weeds, making them wave and undulate like dark green snakes. A family of swans came sedately into view, paddling upstream, the cygnets fussily bringing up the rear. In the distance she could hear the mill-race echoing, as the hymn which the congregation in St Mark's church had sung a few hours earlier still echoed in her mind. Never before had the well-known lines seemed so poignant. She had first learnt them as a small child, standing by Sarah's side when her mother sometimes sang them as she did her washing in the mill. Later on, she had sung them herself at the National School, at the Thanksgiving service at the end of the war, at her father's funeral and today at Flo's – although, after the first verse, tears had forced her to stop.

Katy closed her eyes. Time, like the Willon, was an 'ever-rolling stream' all right, she thought sadly, as she rested her head on her knees, bearing, far too quickly, all its sons – and daughters – away.

20

'So perhaps you would like to come to nursery tea next Sunday,' wrote Nanny Barlow. 'John William and I and the new girl, Ettie, will be staying at the Hall all through September and maybe longer. The matinée jacket you knitted for his birthday fits just right. He can't have too many now, what with there being quite a nip in the air sometimes when we go into Hyde Park . . .'

There was not exactly a nip in the air as Katy walked up River Lane and across Wilhampton market square on the afternoon in question, carrying the small suitcase which Nanny Barlow had lent her when she had come home at such short notice three months earlier. The sun was still hot enough for her to be thankful that she was wearing a black straw hat with a fair-sized brim, instead of being bareheaded as she had been on the last occasion when she had hurried to the Hall with Lady Fairfax's dress. But there was certainly just a hint of autumn in the yellowy tinge of the elm trees in the rector's garden and smoke could be seen spiralling up from one of the allotments on downside, which meant someone had committed the heinous crime of making a bonfire on a Sunday.

Just as before, Katy became aware of the inevitable half-hidden faces peering at her from behind front-room curtains, of the suitcase attracting the interest of more than one passer-by and even prompting prim Miss Whatley, the midwife's sister, to murmur, 'Not leaving us again, Katy,

I hope,' as she shepherded her charges to Sunday School.'
On arriving at the Hall, once again Ena Perrick answered
the door, although this time in a much more civil fashion.

'Sorry about Flo, Katy. But I hear it was a happy release.'

'Yes.'

Ena's eyes strayed towards the suitcase and Katy
explained to whom it belonged.

'Then I should just put it down inside here for the
moment. Nanny Barlow and Master John are out in the
rose garden. She said as how you were to go out there.
Do you think you might come back for good now? I don't
think Ettie's exactly giving satisfaction.'

'No, Ena. I'll be staying home to help May with the
dressmaking. It needs two and Mother still has to take
things quietly.'

'Yes. Yes, I suppose she does.' Ena began to accompany
her a little way down the flagged path. She obviously had
something on her mind. Presently she said, 'Forgive my
asking, Katy, but what happened to the wreath our Archie
brought down to the mill the morning of the funeral?
Mum said that when she went up to the cemetery the next
day to look at the flowers, she couldn't see it. She
wondered whether Arnold Parker left it behind. But if he
had, she thought one of you would have been sure to go
back with it.'

'I . . . I'm sorry, Ena. I really don't know.'

For the second time that afternoon Katy had reason to
be thankful that she was wearing a hat, hoping its brim
was sufficiently broad to hide the colour which now
flooded to her face. She did not like lying. Miss Whatley
had always warned her of the terrible punishment which
would result from such a sin, especially if committed on
the Sabbath. She could remember being terrified as a child
at Sunday School, listening to Miss Whatley warning them
about all the things which would bring down hell-fire if
indulged in on that day, her words supported by a curious
reference to French shopkeepers who had tried to stay
open seven days a week and had all suffered dire conse-
quences. As everyone knew that Miss Whatley had scarcely
ever set foot outside Wilhampton, Katy used to wonder

how she could possibly have come by such unexpected information.

'Oh, well, never mind. Just as long as you let your Mum know one was sent,' Ena went on.

'Yes.' Katy could picture the pink and mauve wreath quite clearly in her mind's eye, much clearer than any other, in fact, including Lady Fairfax's arum lilies. She could even imagine it bobbing about in the mill-race, until it got broken up and carried away, along with so many other things which the Willon seemed to dispose of in its impassive omnipotence.

They were now in sight on the high box hedge which surrounded the rose garden and Ena turned to go. 'See you again, then, Katy, before you go home, I expect. There's not all that much to do today, thank the Lord, none of the family being in residence.'

'Isn't Mrs Moreton here?'

Ena stared at her. 'No. Didn't you know? She's in a sanatorium. Her ladyship's gone to visit her.'

'*Sanatorium*?' Immediately, Katy's mind went back to the previous winter and the hurried departure of Amy Robinson.

'You mean . . . she's got tuberculosis?'

'Lawks, no.' Ena gave a quick glance towards the hedge in front of them, obviously anxious not to be caught gossiping by Nanny Barlow. Then, in a mysterious, almost conspiratorial manner, she tapped her forehead. 'I overheard them saying in the servants' hall it's a nervous collapse. Seems as how she got in such a state no one could do anything with her. Perhaps I could pop down to the mill on my next half-day and tell you more . . .'

Ena turned back to the house. Slowly, Katy walked on to the rose garden, hardly knowing what to think, other than it wouldn't do to have Ena coming to the mill and that, whatever happened, their friendship could never be the same again.

'Why, Katy.' She found Nanny Barlow sitting on a cushion on one of the old stone seats. Beside her was a pram in which John William's mother had once sat and

149

where now her son, wearing a white cotton sunbonnet and showing four new teeth, smiled broadly at the visitor.

'I do believe he remembers you, Katy.' Nanny Barlow gazed fondly at the infant. 'He's very forward for his age, aren't you, little man?'

Katy bent over the pram and held out a finger, which the child clutched firmly before becoming distracted by a bumblebee droning nearby.

'Perhaps you'd like to hold him for a while before we go indoors for tea. I told Ettie to have it ready by half-past four.' She undid the baby's harness and lifted him up. 'There, John William. Who's a pretty boy, then?'

Katy sat down on the seat and took the child in her arms, astonished at how much larger and heavier he had become since she had last seen him.

'He's pulling himself up now,' Nanny Barlow continued proudly. 'But I'm not encouraging that. Children who walk too soon get bandy legs. Best keep them babies as long as you can. Now, how's your mother, my dear? And May?'

'As well as can be expected, Nanny.' She was surprised as the ease with which they seemed to have slipped into an altogether different relationship: no longer nanny and nursery maid. Suddenly, it came to Katy that, for all its limitations, she was now a person in her own right. She might not be independent of her family, but she was no longer in domestic service, that state of life about which Sarah had always held such contemptuous views. Coming home had certain compensations, even if it did mean that she would never see Philip Mason again. Only the previous week she had written to tell him this and said that she thought it would be best it he did not write to her any more.

Katy was surprised that Nanny Barlow did not refer to Alicia Moreton's illness until the end of her visit, although she was aware that she was of a far more taciturn nature than Emily Harwood and, owing to her unique position in the household, much more likely to respect any confidences. Only as she got up to leave and a somewhat timorous Ettie had been sent to prepare the baby's bath, did the older woman say, 'You must come again, Katy. I think we shall be staying here even longer than I first thought. I'm afraid John William's mother has been ordered a complete rest, so it seems best for us to stop with his grandmother for the time being.'

'Thank you,' she replied, 'I'd like that very much,' while realizing that the only means of hearing more about what had happened to Alicia Moreton was through Ena Perrick, and that possibility was probably best avoided.

Fred Ashford's dogs set up barking as she neared the west gates and the man himself came out of his cottage and wished her a gruff 'Good evening'. She hurried on, not altogether liking the expression in his eyes, an expression which she could not help having noticed on many another man's face since she had come home. She was aware that all the Lodge girls were reputed to be good-lookers; what she did not know was that the youngest, for all her delicacy as a child, was turning out to be the best.

She became worried when she saw May standing by the mill gates, obviously watching out for her as she came down River Lane and, on drawing nearer, a look on her elder sister's face which she couldn't quite make out. For a moment she wondered whether Sarah had lost her memory again, yet somehow May seemed more excited than anxious.

'Oh chippattoo, Katy! You'd best get up there quickly.'

'Up where, May?' She paused, and then said, incredulously, 'You don't mean . . . Edith's baby's arrived?'

'No, lovey. But someone else has. I've sent him up the meadows. It's your young man from London. It seems as how he's come to spend his holiday in Wilhampton. He's got lodgings at the Snoads'. He's on about doing temporary work, maybe helping with the harvest if we know of a farmer who wants some casual labour, so all I said was . . .'

But Katy did not stop to hear what May had said. She was gone, rushing up through the mill, pulling off her hat as she did so, face flushed, eyes dancing, her hair a little dishevelled as she almost threw herself over the first stile.

She saw him standing by the Black Arch, just where Maurice Fitzherbert had stood not so very long ago. When she came within hailing distance, she shouted, 'Philip'. He turned and began running towards her, so that when they at last met it was almost a collision. He swung her up in his arms. Then he put her down again.

'Fancy writing like that, Katy,' he said, looking at her in that strange compelling way she remembered so well, 'as if you'd never see me again.'

21

Much to Sarah's displeasure, Philip Mason lodged at the Snoads' for a week. Had it not been for May's intervention, Katy might well not have been allowed to see him at all during that time. Her mother accused her of having been brazen, deceitful and wicked in keeping his existence so secret. In consequence, he was offered no hospitality at the Mill House, but in the evenings, after he had knocked off work – having shown commendable initiative in obtaining some straight away at Bulbarrow Farm – he was allowed to take Katy for a short walk, 'providing you're back before it gets dark, my girl', Sarah would say as she went out of the door.

Once alone, she and Philip would link arms and, on reaching that secluded corner of the meadows which Katy called Nomansland, he would stop to kiss her. But possibly because he realized how much he had scared her on Putney Heath, possibly because he himself was more than a little scared of Sarah, he was gentler with Katy now, exercising – albeit not without difficulty – a restraint which made her feel safer with him. She no longer resisted his advances. Although her acquisition of a young man was sadly frowned upon, it was at least now out in the open and much of her previous guilt about their relationship disappeared. In fact, sometimes as they started home in order to comply with her mother's curfew, she felt frustrated and disappointed with Philip for reminding her that the light was fading fast.

Only on the final day of his holiday were the two of them able to spend longer alone, both acutely aware of the impending parting. He had ceased his labours at Bulbarrow now, for the harvest was over and preparations were going on that very Saturday afternoon for the harvest supper which was to take place in the big tithe barn later that night. They had therefore set out earlier and gone further afield, crossing the Willon by the Black Arch and then taking the steep short cut up the downs to Breconbury Woods. At the top, as if by mutual consent, they had stopped and turned round, gazing silently down on the whole of Wilhampton, spread out like some tiny toy town below them.

'It's a lovely place, where you live, Katy,' Philip said, at length, with his arm still round her. 'Shouldn't mind having a place in the country myself one of these days.'

She looked at him shyly. He was very tanned now. His work on Bulbarrow, though but short, seemed to have suited him. She had been surprised at the way he had enjoyed – and apparently become quite skilful at – pitching sheaves.

'I know your mother's taken against me, Katy,' he continued. 'I wish she hadn't. I don't like to think of her and me not getting on, when we're married.'

'*Married*!' She was astonished, exultant.

'Why, yes.' It was he who now showed surprise that she should ever have doubted the fact. 'Of course we're going to be married. I'd hoped to have been able to fix everything up this week. But I can see your mother's got to get used to the idea, not being well and all that. I'll come again, Katy, as soon as I can. Meanwhile, see if you and your sister can't put in a good word for me.'

His arm tightened around her and she leant against him, inwardly almost laughing with joy, wondering whether any girl had ever had such a strange, self-assured proposal – if she could actually call it that. Even though it might take a little time to get Sarah's consent, even if she had to go on helping May for a year or so first and she and Philip could only be together sometimes, they could surely become unofficially, and then officially, *engaged*. She would be a young woman with a 'bottom drawer', waiting to marry the man she loved.

He began to kiss her. Without quite knowing how it had come about, she found herself lying stretched out beside him on the warm, springy turf. She was aware of different scents, the ones which belonged to down and woodland: gorse, bracken and wild thyme. Those of the meadow and mill seemed far away. She closed her eyes. His body felt very strong and hard against her own.

'Katy.' The urgency which both had experienced on Putney Heath overcame them again but now, with her eager and willing participation, it reached a far greater intensity. 'Katy,' he kept murmuring and, whenever he gave her breathing space, she heard her own voice replying, 'Philip, oh Philip.' Through her thin voile dress and petticoat, she felt his hand caress her breasts and then gradually move lower until it seemed as if it was half-hesitantly, yet half-purposely, pushing between her legs. She began to tremble, conscious of a very different sensation from any she had hitherto known. Then, all at once, he took his hand away and guided one of her own to the same place in his own body. 'Please,' she heard him say, 'Please, Katy'. Suddenly a deep shudder seemed to go through him and he called out. After that they both lay still and silent, while a lone plover circled overhead.

Presently, he touched her face very gently. 'You didn't . . . mind, did you, my love?'

'No.' Did she mind? She was confused, unsure.

'I mean . . . it's not as if . . . anything happened.'

'No.' She buried her head in his shoulder, anxious that he should not see that her eyes were bright with tears. Even if, as Philip had said, nothing had really taken place, yet, in her heart of hearts, she felt as if it had. If he had not 'come' – which she supposed, to use May's word, he must have done – when he had, would their lovemaking have progressed further? Would he have gone on to seduce her totally? Would she have allowed him to? To her shame, she was afraid that the answer would have been yes. Even though she still had no clear idea of what exactly happened, she knew that, just for a moment, she had wanted whatever it was desperately. She had been ready not only to give in to Philip's desires, but her own. Scared though she was, she had not been shocked or disgusted. A naturally passionate nature meant that there had been no lasting scars after her unfortunate experience when Neil had crept up to her attic bed. Neither, today, had she pushed Philip aside, as she had done on Putney Heath. She had been prepared to abandon common sense, propriety, a lifetime of the strictest moral indoctrination for the sake of a hitherto unknown but overwhelming urge which she could not explain. There, high on the downs above Wilhampton, on a sunny September evening in 1920, she had been willing to risk the near-certainty – as she now saw it – of pregnancy, her mother's wrath, the door of the Mill House being closed to her for ever.

To Katy, a miss had never been as good as a mile. Her guilt returned, this time to a far greater degree. An overactive imagination started making fact out of fantasy. She had turned into one of those members of society whom Sarah had always held up as a terrible example to all her daughters from the moment they were old enough to understand. She was 'no better than she should be', a 'fallen woman', someone who 'had to get married', like Nancy Shergold, Cissy Lawes and, so rumour had it, Lilian Perrick (except that Ena was reputedly such a tiny baby that she had been able to be more or less successfully passed off as premature, on arriving eight months after the wedding).

The sun had disappeared behind the woods when they got up to go and began walking home through the darkening evening. In the distance Katy could see a figure coming towards them which, as it drew closer, to her consternation she recognized as that of an even worse type of female than the ones who had recently come so swiftly and unhappily to her mind. Grace Armitage, her blonde hair Eton-cropped, a jersey coat slung carelessly over her shoulders and the hem of her short purple tunic dress riding high above her knees, gave Katy a sideways look as she passed and muttered a scarcely audible greeting.

'Who on earth was that?' asked Philip, half turning to stare after her.

'Oh, someone I hardly know. She got hold of the man

my sister, Flo, was once hoping to marry,' she answered, defensively.

'*Did* she, now.' Philip raised his eyebrows, gave a soft whistle and said no more.

As they came down the lane by Bulbarrow Farm, old Mr Swayne's daughter-in-law crossed over to the barn carrying a huge piece of cold boiled gammon. 'Why, if it isn't young Philip Mason,' she said, smiling; for although he had only worked for them for so short a time, she had not been able to help noticing the strong, thickset, dark-eyed 'young chap from Lunnon', as he was good-humouredly referred to, each time she had taken tea out to the harvesters. 'I reckon we shouldn't have got that last field ricked but for you. And, of course, the weather, thank the Lord,' she went on, cheerfully. 'You should be a-joining in the fun tonight, but I daresay you've got better things to do, eh?' She darted a quick, mischievous, yet friendly glance at an increasingly dismayed and embarrassed Katy.

'Do they always have this kind of celebration at this time of the year?' Philip asked, as they walked on.

'Oh, yes. I believe the Swaynes fixed it up for tonight thinking their harvest would have been finished much sooner, but we had a lot of rain the week before last. That's why they were anxious to get all the help they could the last few days. Otherwise, I suppose it would have had to be postponed.'

'What happens? At this supper, I mean?'

'Well, I don't know much because women never go, of course,' she answered, absently, her mind still preoccupied with what had taken place on Breconbury Down and Dorothy Swayne's innocent but unfortunate remark.

'But you must know a bit. I'm curious.'

She wondered how he could possibly be – amazed and somewhat resentful at how quickly he could switch to other matters, even to showing interest in Grace Armitage.

'Well, I suppose it's . . . almost like a private harvest festival . . . everyone at Bulbarrow being glad that all's safely gathered in. And it's a way for Mr Swayne and his family to say thank you to all the men who have worked for them through the year. They have speeches and toasts. And songs,' she added, as an afterthought.

'What sort of songs?'

'Oh, I don't know. You've probably never heard of them.' She was still offhand, unwilling to engage in a conversation in which temporarily, at least, she felt so little concern. "Buttercup Joe," she threw out, curtly, 'and "Dick Turpin". I believe the head carter does an accompaniment on the accordion. And they sing "God Save the King" at the end.'

Philip Mason was silent for a while, taking in all she had said. Presently, he asked, 'Does anyone else go? Besides the farmer and the farm workers?'

'Oh, yes. A few visitors get asked. The rector and the schoolmaster. And Bill Lawes, the blacksmith. And of course, Fred Ashford, the Fairfaxes' head keeper.'

'Nothing like that happens in London,' he said wistfully, almost to himself.

'No, I don't suppose it does. But then . . . it's different in the country.' Her simple words were, perhaps, more profound and of much more significance to their present situation than she could possibly have realized.

She wished him goodbye at the mill gates, holding out her hand almost formally.

'You'll come to the station to see me off tomorrow, won't you, Katy?' He looked at her anxiously. 'My train goes at midday.'

'I . . . I think perhaps it would be better if I didn't. Mother's been worried . . . that there must have been talk. Especially with you stopping at the Snoads'.'

'Talk?' He frowned, scuffing one of his feet on a stone.

'Yes. I can't explain, Philip. But your coming from London . . . us being seen together . . .' She looked away, uncertainly.

'Then your mum should have been more reasonable. Asked me in. You told me how it was between her and her own parents. Katy, we needn't wait. I want to marry you. We could run away.' He caught hold of her shoulders, forcing her to look at him, his dark eyes staring at her, willing her to agree. She was aware of footsteps in the lane and shook herself free.

'No, Philip. Please . . . wait a little.' She turned and made for the gates, her thoughts in confusion as she ran the short distance to the house.

May was sitting on the sofa sewing, as she came in. She glanced up quickly and put a finger to her lips. 'Best be quiet, lovey. Mother's got a headache so I've sent her on up to bed. Did you have a nice walk?'

'Yes . . . thank you. Oh, May . . .' She went across the room and threw herself down at her elder sister's feet, burying her head in her lap, the tears which she had long been fighting back now spilling over, her shoulders shaking with a sobbing she could not control.

'Hush, lovey. We don't want Mother to hear. I know Philip's got to go tomorrow, but you mustn't take on so.' May stroked Katy's head gently, somewhat perturbed and more than a little curious, waiting for her to become less distraught. Then, when it seemed as if no further information was likely to be forthcoming, she went on, quietly, 'Lots of couples have to have partings – and sometimes quarrels. Perhaps that's what happened tonight? But never mind. Philip Mason may be your first young man, but that doesn't mean he'll be the last.'

Even in her distress, Katy sat up and stared at her.

'How d'you mean?'

'What I say, lovey. There's plenty of fish in the sea. After all, you've got another fine one already, right here in home waters.'

Still Katy stared, in utter bewilderment, so that May was forced to say, at length, 'Oh, come now, lovey. You must know Maurice Fitzherbert's been sweet on you from the moment you first came back from London.'

22

'You're very quiet, Katy.'

It was a fortnight later. She and May were in the work-room, busy putting the finishing touches on, of all things, a tweed, heather-coloured coat-dress for Alicia Moreton.

'I want it to be a surprise, Miss Lodge,' Lady Fairfax had said to May on a totally unannounced visit. 'Now that the poor darling is having to stay longer in the nursing home and so missing John William — and, of course, her husband,' she added, hastily, 'I felt she needed a little present. There's nothing like new clothes for cheering a woman up when she's depressed, is there? So I bought this length of material when I was last in London, knowing full well that you were the only person in the world who could do justice to it, and be able to make it up without needing a fitting. You have all my daughter's measurements in that little red book of yours. You know her figure to a "T".'

Lady Fairfax had then gesticulated rather vaguely and turned to Katy, who was still standing hesitantly by the workroom door, having previously risen to answer their visitor's imperious knocking. 'And how Nanny Barlow misses *you*, my dear,' her ladyship went on, 'poor Ettie being not quite . . .' But what poor Ettie was 'not quite' had somehow then been carefully lost in a flurry of good-byes, possible delivery dates and the information that 'Next Tuesday, my dear Miss Lodge, believe it or not, the Hall will be on the *telephone*,' as if May might be going to ring up to confirm that the dress was ready.

Katy had not made any reply to May's observation about her quietness. She had simply persevered with the oversewing she was doing, trying not to worry about the fact that the period she had been expecting five days earlier had not yet arrived. She thought that May had probably guessed what was troubling her, for it was impossible, living at such close and inconvenient quarters, to keep their respective times of the month secret from one another, even though her elder sister was now sleeping in Flo's room and Katy herself was alone in the attic.

She wondered whether to confide in May, but dearly as she loved her, and however sure she was that that love was reciprocated, she did not quite know what to say. The logical, sensible side of her told her to stop being a fool. She knew that she had nothing really to worry about. She had not been seduced. She was still a virgin. Yet the wilder, passionate, imaginative side of her nature kept superimposing itself on the other, guilt lending it momentum, making her believe that, in some mysterious way, what she had feared could have easily happened had actually come about. Otherwise, why was she not 'so', as her older sisters always referred to it.

After tea that day it was May who decided to take Alicia Moreton's dress up to the Hall herself. The evenings were closing in fast and rumours of Sidney Lodge's ghost coming out of Hatch Alley had unfortunately started up again. She knew that Katy had heard some of them and she did not want the girl to become more distressed than she already seemed. Now that the dress was finished she was determined to have a long talk with her the following day about whatever it was she had on her mind.

Some time after she had gone, Katy took a candle and went up to the attic. Here, she knelt down by one of the old ottomans, lifted the chintz-covered lid and ran her hand down its sides until she came upon what she was looking for. Then, carefully hiding it beneath a bundle of dirty clothes, she went downstairs again. Fortunately, Sarah appeared to be busily occupied, crocheting an elaborate new shawl for Edith's baby, which was due any day now and, on the pretext that she wanted to do a little washing, Katy picked up a lantern and went into the mill, choosing the furthermost building for her proposed action. Here, behind the big hammer which, throughout the day, resounded with a dull regular thud as it beat the crude, half-made felt into hard, manageable strips, she began to skip, the familiar tune which she had sung at school coming swiftly back to mind: 'Here we go looby-loo, here we go looby-light, here we go looby-loo, all on a Saturday night.' Every so often she did a little twirl with the skipping rope, first to the right, then to the left. Occasionally, she did some fast double-skipping. She had forgotten just how good she had once been at it. The exercise, if nothing else, relieved her tension. 'Here we go looby-loo,' she sang more loudly, oblivious for some time of the shadow cast up on the opposite whitewashed wall, the shadow of Sarah standing silently watching her.

'And what, my girl, do you think you're up to?' Her mother moved closer, her shadow looking larger and infinitely more menacing as she did so.

'I'm . . . skipping . . .' Katy's voice faltered.

'I can see that. Why?'

Before she had time to reply, Sarah came round by the big hammer and caught her arm. 'I can tell you why, my girl. It's that young good-for-nothing from London, isn't it? He's got you in the family way, hasn't he? I always said to May that we should never have let you go out with him. Coming down here to stay as bold as brass and then making himself scarce as soon as he'd got what he wanted . . .'

'No.' Katy pulled her arm free. Anguished, she managed to break into her mother's tirade. 'No. It wasn't like that.'

'No? Then what are you skipping for? I reckoned you were late some days back. I may have been ill and not known what was going on for a while, but there's not much gets by me now.'

'Mother, I promise you. I'm not . . . pregnant. It's just that . . .' To her overwhelming relief, she heard footsteps and May appeared.

'Whatever's going on?' She was still in her outdoor clothes, breathless and anxious at having found the Mill House empty.

There was a kind of triumphant anger in the way Sarah now rounded on her elder daughter. 'Well may you ask. I told you so, didn't I? But oh no. You with your fine romantic notions. You knew better. You've always given in to the child. And now look where it's landed us.'

For a moment the three women stood motionless in the

dim silent mill, for after the men knocked off work each night, no gas lights could be lit until the following morning. Then, as the tears started to stream down Katy's face, May went across to her, put an arm round her shoulders and said, 'Come, lovey. We'd all best get back to the warm now.'

Once inside the living room, Sarah sat stiffly upright by the range, her hands folded in her lap, her eyes fixed on the sofa where her two daughters also sat, the elder still with a protective arm around the younger.

'Are you . . . ?' May began quietly, suddenly remembering with painful clarity the afternoon at the White Lion when Major Walter Perkins had taken her virginity. For a moment she found herself sending up a little prayer. Then, when Katy shook her head so vehemently, she felt it had been answered, for she did not believe that her youngest sister would lie to her. 'You've been scared, perhaps, lovey?' she went on, gently.

A muffled 'I suppose so' came out between the sobs.

May looked across at their mother and then back to the girl beside her. For all her own warm-hearted spontaneity, she was well aware that she did not possess Katy's vivid uncontrollable imagination. Yet she could remember many a previous love affair and knew that it was perfectly possible for an impressionable young woman to become fanciful, to succumb to irrational ideas which, in consequence, might act adversely on her physical well-being, even to delaying the onset of a period, or actually producing a phantom pregnancy. She seemed to remember something of the sort having happened to one of the Donaldson sisters, who had mysteriously left Wilhampton for a time, although how she had come across such private and personal information, she had no idea. She only knew that Katy's basic good sense and honesty was making her speak the truth.

'She's had a bit of an upset with her young man, Mother,' May continued. 'Katy's not quite herself. I think we should leave her be for a while.'

Grim-faced and grudgingly, Sarah turned and stared into the fire. The very next day, Katy's period appeared.

It was, perhaps, fortunate at this juncture, that Edith's baby — another boy — was born. The event took Sarah's mind off her youngest daughter and, each day, she walked up to downside to see how mother and child were progressing. Katy herself, having spent a year under Nanny Barlow's tuition and therefore considered by her family to be highly trained in child care, found herself actually sleeping in her married sister's home for at least a fortnight. She did not particularly enjoy it, but it was preferable just then to remaining at the Mill House. She found her other nephew and nieces, together with the new baby, exhausting to deal with and wondered how Edith could possibly be pleased at the prospect of a non-stop round-the-clock working life for what looked like countless years to come. The constant crying of Norman Sidney Ernest — as his proud parents were intending to have him christened — got on her nerves and when May received a sudden order for several new outfits from the mayoress elect of Wilhampton, she was glad of the excuse to return home.

'I'd never have thought,' her sister said, as they sat huddled over the workroom fire one raw November morning, tacking and stitching an unusual voluminous black cloak, 'that Miss Fortescue would have wanted to be mayoress. I mean, not having a husband and all that, and being so busy with her writing.'

'No.' Katy rethreaded her needle. She could visualize Miss Fortescue clearly: a clever, beady-eyed lady who lived at the Moat House and who had both scared and fascinated her during her childhood. She was reputed to have had many a celebrity staying with her from time to time: authors and artists and poets. Many of them came, so Mabel Snoad said, from some place called Bloomsbury which had always made Katy want to laugh, as she couldn't help connecting it with bloomers. They were somehow strange-looking people, the men with beards and longish hair and the ladies often wearing cloaks like the one she and May were making now. Miss Fortescue could be seen taking them for walks on Sunday afternoons, although she herself always seemed to dance rather than walk, waving her little hands about in an airy-fairy way as she acknowledged the greetings of all and sundry. But despite her eccentricity, she was well-liked in the little town, even if her visitors would keep going into the post office and pestering Mabel to send unintelligible telegrams back to London or sometimes even foreign parts. Next to the Hall, the Moat House, with its curious comings and goings, was a constant source of interest to the local residents.

Presently, Katy said quietly, 'I think Miss Fortescue won't make a bad mayoress, when you come to think of it. She's fond of Wilhampton. Didn't she write that history of the place some time back?'

'Yes, I think so.' Unlike Katy, May was not much interested in history or books. Her mind dwelt much more on the here and now, and the lighter reading matter which was to be obtained from the new women's monthly magazine, *Eve*. 'Anyway, she's going to cut quite a dash in this, isn't she,' she continued. 'She's even sent down some of the buttons and facings from her father's old naval cloak for us to use on it. Now, where did I put that bit of buckram for the collar?' She got up to look for it glancing, as she did so, out of the window and exclaiming, 'Why, there's Mabel's brother coming through the gates with the second post. D'you want to see if you've got a letter, lovey?' She knew that Katy was still eating her heart out because she had not heard from Philip Mason since he had left. Her natural compassion went out to her, even though privately she had come to the same conclusion about the young man as her mother. Somehow he was an alien, unused to Wilhampton ways, not good enough for her youngest sister. May wished the girl would cast her mind in other directions.

Katy needed no second bidding to go and see what Bill Snoad had brought. She put down her sewing and ran up to the house where her mother handed her a letter with obvious curiosity. 'It's not from that there Philip, my girl, if that's what you're thinking. It's a Wilhampton postmark.'

Acutely disappointed, Katy took the envelope and tore it open, pulling out a sheet of thick, heavily-embossed writing paper. With growing astonishment and even apprehension, she read:

East Lodge
Wilhampton,
Nr. Westonbury,
November 4th, 1920

Dear Miss Katy,

There is a dance in aid of the Red Cross to be held at the Town Hall on Friday, November 26th. It would give me great pleasure if, by any chance, you could come to it with me. There will be others in the party, and my mother is arranging a small buffet supper at home beforehand. She will be attending the dance herself. If convenient, I could call for you at, say, six-thirty, and would escort you home at 11 p.m.

I do hope you may be able to manage it. I look forward to hearing.

Yours sincerely,
Maurice Fitzherbert

'It's an invitation, Mother,' she said, at length, uncomfortably aware that Sarah's eyes were still watching her. 'You'd best see for yourself.' She passed the letter over, dismayed at the expression of satisfaction which seemed to creep over Sarah's face as she, too, read it.

There was even exultation in her mother's eyes when she finally looked up at Katy again. 'Well, there, Miss. The sooner you forget about that young varmint from London, the better,' was all she said.

23

'Taffeta,' May said. 'Midnight-blue taffeta, Katy. You'd look lovely in that.'

'Would I?' She was still confused and had yet to reply to Maurice Fitzherbert's invitation. The thought, not only of going to a dance with him but of having to have supper in his parents' home first, was tantalizing but at the same time daunting. Mrs Fitzherbert was such a remote, forbidding kind of woman: tall and thin, with sparse grey hair scraped back from a vaguely disapproving face. If Katy had known how difficult it had been for Maurice to persuade his mother to include her in the party at all, and that she had finally left it to him to issue the invitation rather than write to Mrs Lodge herself, she would definitely have refused.

'Oh, chippatoo! Just think. Your first long dress, Katy.' For once, her elder sister's enthusiasm somehow jarred.

'They're not wearing full-length dresses so much in the evening now, May.'

'Not in London, maybe. But you'll find they'll all be in long ones at the town hall. I wonder what Mildred Fitzherbert will wear herself? She's never been a one for clothes. They say she buys them off the peg in Burts in Westonbury. Anyway, I bet you'll be the best-dressed girl in the room that night.'

'That's if I go.'

May stared at her. 'Katy, love, you're surely not going to throw dirt in that young man's face, are you? Why, there's a lot of girls round here who'd give their ears to be asked to a dance by Maurice Fitzherbert.'

'Perhaps. But anyway, I expect they all know the latest steps.'

May banged the iron down on one of her own skirts which she happened to be pressing. There followed an angry hiss of steam as it met the damp cloth which she had placed carefully over the hem. 'That's easily remedied. You'd best have a couple of hours with Annie White.'

'*Annie White*?' Katy seemed to remember that at the beginning of the war both Flo and May had gone into Westonbury for dancing lessons with a woman called Annie, who lived next to the asylum. 'You can look out of her upstairs room and see the inmates running round in the courtyard below,' Flo had said. 'I recognized Arnold Parker's brother, the one with that funny grin and the streak of yellow in his hair. I suppose that's where poor Neil might have ended up if it hadn't been for Mother.' Her words had made Katy feel quite frightened at the time.

'Yes, I'll drop Annie a line,' May continued, putting the iron back on the trivet in the grate and draping her skirt over the back of a chair. 'She's still going strong, as far as I know. I'll make you a present of a lesson or two. Annie would probably be only too glad of a little extra money, what with that old barracks of a house to keep up and having to look after her crippled mother. Proper old witch, Mrs White is. Poor Annie. I believe her fiancé was killed just before the armistice.'

With so much pressure put upon her, Katy wrote a formal note of acceptance to Maurice Fitzherbert and found herself walking the three miles into Westonbury early one Saturday morning to visit Annie and buy material for her dress. 'See you get the *best* taffeta, Katy,' May had said. 'Nothing tawdry, mind. Give it a good feel. You want to find something that's going to stand out in the room, without it being too shiny or showy. And you could look around for some dancing slippers while you're about it. Silver, I think. I'd like to come with you, but I've simply got to get on with the Snoad girl's wedding dress.'

Katy had set off apprehensively. She would have liked to take the old-fashioned lady's bicycle which was kept in the lean-to by the closet, but Sarah had never really approved of any of her daughters riding a bicycle, especially into Westonbury, and consequently, over the years, it had seldom been used.

She was lucky in straight away finding in Burt and Burt exactly what she was looking for and, having purchased a pair of evening shoes for three shillings and ninepence and a length of deep blue taffeta at two and elevenpence-halfpenny a yard, she made her way to Annie's house. Here, in a long upstairs room which, as Flo had said, overlooked the grounds of Latimer's Folly – as the asylum was called – she was instructed for almost two hours in such dances as the waltz, the quick and slow fox-trot, the one-step, the Boston two-step, the veleta and the polka, while an old Sonora gramophone was constantly wound up to play the appropriate tunes. Even the scandalous and much-frowned-upon tango appeared not to be beyond Annie's expertise. 'Although,' she remarked, drily, 'we'd best not waste any time on that kind of caper. I can't see the Wilhampton Conservative matrons allowing any cheek-to-cheek hanky-panky to go on in the town hall. Nor the ones in Westonbury, for that matter.'

When it was nearing one o'clock, Annie said, 'There. We'd best give over now. I've got Mother's dinner to see to. You've done very well, kid. I shouldn't think you'd need to come again, although you'd always be welcome. You're a natural, like your sisters. How are they, by the way?'

'Flo . . . died, Miss White.'

'*Did* she now? I'm very sorry. Must have missed it in the *Journal*. Call me Annie, will you? Everyone else always does.'

As Katy put on her coat and picked up her shopping basket containing her purchases, her purse and the sandwiches she had brought to eat in the shelter in the war memorial gardens before starting home, Annie continued, 'Funny thing. I somehow had a presentiment about Flo. I saw a halo round her head once. They say as how I've got second sight. She was a good young woman. Too good, for this wicked world.'

Katy's eyes widened. She was glad that Annie thought her proficient enough not to come to her again. For all the pleasure the dancing had given her that morning, she felt there was something eerie about the place she was in. She did not know how much it had to do with the proximity of Latimer's Folly and the remembrance of Flo's words, the nearness of the unseen and supposedly witch-like Mrs White, the drabness of the decor in Annie's house or possibly, more than anything else, her final strange revelations combined with her unprepossessing manner and appearance. She was the last person whom Katy would have suspected of being a dancing teacher. For one thing, she was so large and muscular, and there had been a definite smell of sweat about her as their session had progressed. It was obvious that she did not go in for twice-daily washing and the use of Burow's solution under the arms, as the Lodge girls had always done. It was hard to believe that Annie had ever had a fiancé. But perhaps she had let herself go – as May would have said – since his unfortunate death. Katy paid her the two shillings and sixpence for which she asked, and hurried gratefully away.

As November 26th drew nearer and her dress was almost completed, despite having still heard nothing from Philip Mason, Katy found it hard not to feel a certain excitement, even if it was more often than not overshadowed by trepidation. Sometimes, of an evening, she and May would go into the deserted mill and, humming some of their favourite songs, do a little dancing together, May being careful to take the man's part.

'I wish you were coming, May,' Katy said at the end of one such session. 'You used to lead such a gay life once. Don't you miss all that?'

'Yes and no. I suppose you could say that I had my fling while the war was on. There's no one in Wilhampton I fancy now. Besides, there's not a lot of choice. So many of them were taken, poor things. You don't know how lucky you are, Katy, to have had this invitation from such a fine young man.'

Katy was silent. She supposed that she was. There were, she knew, very few possible suitors in the locality, especially of Maurice's age and background. In fact, she could think of hardly any and wondered who the other young men in the Fitzherbert party would be. There was definitely no one around nowadays for May, as she had rightly said. Apart from Mr Fuller, who continued to cast sheep's eyes at her whenever he had the chance, her elder sister seemed to have no beaux now.

'Why didn't you marry, May, in the war?' Katy asked, at length, when they were back indoors again. 'I mean, you must have had plenty of chances.' She had never put quite such a direct question to her before, but Flo's death had thrown them closer together, even though both still held back from certain confidences.

For a moment, May hesitated, wondering whether to tell Katy about what had happened to her at the White Lion, but then decided against it.

'I kept thinking there were plenty more fish in the sea, I suppose,' she answered, slowly. 'But Mr Right just didn't seem to come along.' She had no wish to disillusion her youngest sister about men, particularly at this moment. She felt that it was a mercy that no permanent damage appeared to have been done to the girl after the Neil episode. It must have been God's will that she had gone up to the attic just when she had that night. Katy still evidently had a normal interest in the opposite sex. She wondered what exactly had taken place between her and the young man from London; but whatever it was she obviously hadn't been completely put off his advances. She couldn't have had quite the kind of experience that she herself had undergone with Walter Perkins. The girl, unfortunately, was still hankering after Philip Mason. It was a pity that since he had come into her life she no longer seemed to have the high matrimonial aspirations which May knew she had harboured a year or so ago.

They were alone in the living room now, for Sarah had gone up to bed. She watched Katy covertly as they sat, one on either side of the fire, drinking a final mug of soup together. Her little sister had certainly grown up a lot lately, May thought. She had a sweet face, a beautiful one, but there was rather too much sadness in it now. True, she was still young, but to May she seemed to be cut out for marriage – as long as it was to the right man, of course. Maurice Fitzherbert was better than she or Sarah – or Katy, if she did but know it – could possibly have hoped for. He would look after her and she needed looking after. May couldn't quite explain it, even to herself, but she sensed that Katy was more passionate than she had ever been. Perhaps that was what was troubling the girl. Whereas she herself had enjoyed many a flirtation and had often played the coquette, she had never really wanted things to go further. She suspected that Katy was different. She was single-minded. She would only be interested in a deep and lasting relationship. She might want – even need – a physical union with some man, although her upbringing would surely see to it that she wore a wedding ring first.

May continued her musings long after they had gone to bed. She supposed things had got a little out of hand with Philip Mason. But that would never happen with Maurice

Fitzherbert. He would always behave impeccably. Nevertheless, he was obviously very smitten. Otherwise he wouldn't have stuck his neck out as much as he had already done. To be seen dancing with her youngest sister in public, even if it was in a party chaperoned by his mother, was bound to cause tittle-tattle. He must mean business. May wished she could get Katy to see it. Maurice would never let her down, not like some men she could think of – Walter Perkins and Guy Armitage springing instantly to mind. And even sober, old-fashioned Cyril Butt, the auctioneer, who lived in Mulberry Cottage at the corner of the market square and who May had always thought was devoted to Flo – not that she had ever given him any encouragement – had never come near the Mill House once he heard that she had cancer.

The clock above the town hall struck midnight and still. May was unable to sleep. If only Katy could forget Philip Mason. He was no good to her. Perhaps the dance would alter things. She hoped so. She would love to be a fly on the wall that night. Without realizing it she had, for some time, been living vicariously through her little sister, transferring all her own half-wise, half-foolish, romantic ideals on to her slender young shoulders. Now that Flo was gone, she would, she knew, miss Katy sadly when she married, but if it was to Maurice Fitzherbert the girl would not be much more than a stone's throw away. As for help with the sewing, she would try to find some school leaver whose mother might be only too pleased for her daughter to gain some experience in return for her services. Of course, it would mean having to do a lot more work herself. Her apprentice would have to be watched. Even Katy, despite a short period at Miss Maidment's, had taken quite a time to do a flawless buttonhole. But it would be worth it, just to know her sister had made such a fine match and was happily settled. It somehow did not occur to May that Katy would be anything other than that, once the knot had been tied. Moreover, there would be no need to worry over Sarah quite so much. Their mother seemed almost to have taken on a new lease of life since Maurice's invitation.

On the evening of the 26th, May closed up the workroom early and prepared a hip bath for Katy in front of the range in the living room. 'But I shall want to clear it well away by half-past five,' she warned her. 'We must have everything nice and shipshape by the time Maurice calls for you, even if he doesn't stop to come in. I suppose you'd best dress in the attic.' Thoughtfully, she had left a paraffin stove burning there throughout the day, for the weather was freezing. 'But it's better than rain,' May went on, cheerfully. 'I wouldn't like to think of that blue taffeta getting wet round the bottom. Whatever happens, mind and pick it up when you're walking through the streets.'

'Yes.' In spite of herself, Katy's eyes were bright, her cheeks already more than a little flushed. Naked in the hip bath, with her thick brown hair piled high on top of her head and wielding a back brush, she looked, in the lamplight, like some desirable nymph, half innocent, half beguiling — a combination of attributes which, had she known, had firstly tormented Philip Mason and was fast ensnaring Maurice Fitzherbert.

The scent of Floris's malmaison soap soon filled the living room. By the time Katy had stepped out of the bath, dried herself in the big white towel which had been put to warm by the range, dabbed Burow's solution under her arms and applied a fine cloud of malmaison dusting powder, it was all-pervading. Back in the attic, May helped her to dress, her everyday warm woollen underwear being, for once, discarded in favour of Jap silk. 'Though I hope you won't catch your death, love. It's shramming outside,' she said, unconsciously lapsing into West Country dialect. She had lent Katy a blue fringed shawl, appliquéd with kingfishers of a deeper blue, as well as her old fox fur jacket. 'I should keep the shawl on at supper,' she continued. 'They say the Fitzherbert house is on the cold side. Still, the town hall usually warms up quite quickly once the dancing starts, as long as Arnold Parker's boy gets the big stove going in time.' It was somewhat of a joke in Wilhampton that the more Willy Parker neglected his duties, the better it was for his father's undertaking business.

There was no long mirror in the attic, so Katy went

down to survey herself in the one on the front of the wardrobe in what was now May's bedroom. There was no doubt that her elder sister had done a wonderful job on her dress. She had reckoned that Katy was young and attractive enough not to have to follow the latest fashions completely which, in any case, May considered ugly; she had therefore decided to go in for more classical lines. 'With an evening dress, that's always permissible, Miss Lodge,' Lady Fairfax had once said to May, 'just as long as it is *well-made*, from *good* material.' So, having pored over various pattern books, May had opted for a simple V-shaped neckline, a definite waist and a full skirt. With Katy's hair now done up in a chignon, the minimum of Icilma cream and Tokalon powder on her cheeks, May's amethyst pendant hanging just above the contours of her small rounded breasts, her Dorothy bag containing comb, handkerchief and *papier poudre* slung over one slender white-gloved arm and her feet encased in her new silver slippers, there was something almost princess-like about the little figure – or so Maurice Fitzherbert thought – when she opened the door to him on the stroke of six-thirty. Rather as Philip Mason's heart had done when she had run to meet him at the London bus stop, he found his own beginning to beat much more quickly.

He came inside the house just long enough to shake both Sarah's and May's hands; then, helping Katy on with the fur jacket, they left to walk – shyly and almost in silence – the short distance to East Lodge. On arrival, an elderly maid called Nellie Harwood – a cousin, Katy believed, of Emily's – came forward from the dim recesses of the hall and ushered her upstairs to a large spare bedroom. Now that she was actually in the Fitzherbert house, any previous anticipation immediately gave way to panic. For one awful moment, she wondered whether she would simply say that she was not feeling well and ask to go home. The sound of voices and laughter floating up from somewhere below was, indeed, making her feel slightly sick. She felt that Nellie's eyes were upon her, disapproving and resentful. She should never have accepted the invitation. She was out of place in such society; and she had forgotten to practise slipping her hand through the vent of her glove as May had told her she must do when she ate. Besides, no one would want to speak to her. She would be unable to make any conversation herself. Those notions which she had once entertained in Upper Brook Street about leading a grander life were as wrong as they were ridiculous. It had sometimes been bad enough having to talk to Maurice's father professionally, but it would be ten times worse at a party in his own home.

Miserably, she followed the dour parlourmaid along the passage and down the stairs to where Maurice was waiting for her at the bottom. As if sensing that she perhaps needed more than mere physical support, he held out his hand to her long before she came to the last few steps. Then, after Nellie had disappeared once more into the nether regions, he led her to the drawing-room door, pausing just long enough before he opened it to say, quietly, 'I've never seen a prettier dress.'

She flushed. The compliment, coming as it did so unexpectedly but at just the right moment, sent her into the room looking suddenly radiant. Even Miss Fortescue's nephew, a sophisticated young solicitor from London, who was standing in the furthermost corner, found himself quite unable to remember what he had been saying to the eldest Donaldson girl after he had been introduced. Only Mrs Fitzherbert failed to seem impressed. 'Well, now we are all here,' she said, calmly, 'perhaps we should go into the dining room and have some refreshment.'

It proved to be not quite the ordeal that Katy had feared. Maurice's father went out of his way to ply her with things to eat. Elizabeth Donaldson, though used to such company, nevertheless still appeared gauche and self-conscious, standing stiffly in an unsuitable dress of pink tulle and constantly dabbing a perspiring nose with her handkerchief. Her young brother, Benjamin, who had just left school, and a girl called Mary Tottenham from Westonbury whom Katy did not know were both extremely polite and friendly. Maurice and Gilbert Fortescue always seemed to be hovering close at hand. It was just the hostess who somehow appeared disconcertingly unaware of Katy's presence, as she passed vaguely by carrying a plate of sausage rolls or some rather thick ham sandwiches.

At the dance itself, to which her husband did not accompany her, she sat on a seat in the corner of the room in the same detached kind of fashion, a lonely shapeless figure in an ill-fitting dress of beetroot-coloured velvet. Katy could not help noticing that it had about it a combined whiff of mothballs and stale perspiration, which became ever more pungent as the evening progressed, and reminded her of poor Annie White. Having danced the first dance with her son – a slow fox-trot to the tune, somewhat inappropriately, of 'If You Were The Only Girl In The World' – although some of the older generation came across the room to talk to her, she did not take to the floor again throughout the entire evening, an evening which Katy herself soon found she was enjoying tremendously. Both Maurice and Gilbert turned out to be surprisingly good dancers. She seemed to be dancing non-stop. Even young Ben Donaldson proved to be adept at the Tato polka. When 'God Save The King' was suddenly struck up at 11 p.m., she felt that she could have gone on all night.

In contrast, Mrs Fitzherbert, with obvious relief, made a quick dart towards the cloakroom, marshalling her three young ladies behind her like some officious mother hen. On the steps of the town hall their little party broke up. The Donaldsons made for the Rectory, together with Gilbert Fortescue, who was staying the night at the Moat House with his aunt. A car and chauffeur were waiting for Mary Tottenham. Maurice and his mother both accompanied her home.

It was freezing very hard now and the moon, shining on the river by the mill gates, seemed to flood the whole of River Lane with ethereal white-bright light. As they passed Hatch Alley, Katy shivered slightly, but not altogether with cold. It was, she knew, ridiculous, and even wrong, to think that her father, of all people, would haunt the place; yet on a night like this it was impossible to forget the stories which she knew were going around.

She was aware of Maurice glancing at her curiously. She supposed that none of the Fitzherberts would have heard the rumours, although one could never be sure. Dr Fitzherbert and the Reverend Donaldson had a disconcerting way of knowing a surprising amount about what was going on in Wilhampton.

At the end of the lane she held out her hand gravely to both her escorts and thanked them. Then, as Maurice bent to help her through the trap door in the big gates, she heard him say, quietly, 'I'm so glad you could come, Katy. Let's hope there will be more occasions.'

Once inside, she locked up quickly with the key which had been hidden in its usual place beneath a brick and ran the last few steps to the house. She was not altogether surprised to find that May was waiting up for her, a saucepan of milk keeping warm at the side of the range. Her elder sister did not need to ask whether she had enjoyed herself. As soon as she entered the living room, eyes shining, a feathery paper squeaker sticking out of her Dorothy bag and carrying a small parcel which May suspected was probably a prize, it was all too obvious that the evening had been a success.

'Tell me who was there, lovey,' she said, as she began pouring the milk into a glass.

'Oh, anyone and everyone. I do wish you'd been there, May. And you were quite right. They were all in long frocks, except Grace Armitage.'

'You don't mean she put in an appearance? Whoever with?'

'Some man she said was a cousin, I believe. But they didn't *seem* like cousins, not the way they danced. And you should just have seen her dress. It was scarlet satin with one of those dipping hemlines. It was so short in front and the back was cut so low that Arnold Parker's eyes were nearly popping out of his head. And, oh May, just look . . .' She thrust the parcel she was carrying into her sister's hands. 'This is for you. It's a box of chocolates Maurice and I won doing the veleta.'

Only when she came to the end of her detailed account of the evening and mentioned that not only Maurice but also his mother had accompanied her home, did May purse her lips slightly. She hoped that there was not going to be trouble with 'Old Mother Mothballs', as she privately thought of the doctor's wife.

24

Shortly before Christmas, there occurred three things of more than a little interest to the Lodge family, particularly its youngest member. Katy heard from Philip Mason; Alicia Moreton, together with John William, Nanny Barlow and Ettie's replacement, was reported to be staying at the Hall for an indefinite period, while the most incredible rumours were going round Wilhampton about a *divorce* between her and her husband. Lastly, the cold weather at the end of November, after a brief respite, returned with greater intensity, so much so that Lord Fairfax asked his agent to ask the Swaynes who, in turn, immediately instructed Ted Shergold to 'flood Lower Croft', in order that it could become a skating rink for all the local inhabitants.

Maurice Fitzherbert was one of the first to avail himself of this gratuitous amenity whenever he could safely spare the time; and soon he was knocking on the Mill House door asking if Katy would accompany him.

'But I can't,' she said, flustered, 'skate.'

'That's no problem. I'll teach you.'

'But I haven't any skates.'

'You can borrow my sister's. Connie left a pair behind when she married. I'm sure they'd fit. They're screw-ons.'

Flattered, tempted, yet still doubtful, Katy agreed to cycle the short distance to Lower Croft with him at two o'clock that Saturday afternoon. For once, Sarah made no objection to such a hitherto disapproved-of form of transport for one of her daughters.

The number of people already whirling and twirling and suddenly sitting down amongst shouts of laughter which, she saw as soon as they arrived, both surprised and delighted her, even though the letter from Philip Mason was still uppermost in her mind. But soon she found it necessary to concentrate so completely on keeping her balance, even that took second place. Maurice had fastened on her skates while she perched on one of the wooden planks which Ted Shergold had thoughtfully placed near the edge of the ice. Then, helping her to stand, she had staggered forth beside her companion, floundering, falling and picking herself up again or, rather, being picked up.

Maurice proved to be an excellent teacher: good-humoured, patient and immensely strong and steady, qualities which she began to appreciate more and more as the afternoon wore on. With his arm constantly round her, his quiet voice giving her both instruction and encouragement, she became aware of a well-being and happiness which she rarely experienced. Once, when he left her to rest for a few moments on an old willow stump while he went off to do a few quick turns by himself before resuming their lesson, she was reminded of another Saturday afternoon, long ago, spent in these selfsame water meadows when her father had taken her fishing. Just for a while she had known then a kind of peace which, despite all the excitement of the present setting, she knew today. If only, she thought suddenly, as she watched Maurice heading back towards her, Philip Mason had not written again.

They stayed on the ice until after three-thirty, by which time it seemed as if half Wilhampton — especially the older generation — had taken to skating. To her astonishment, at one point she caught sight of Lord Fairfax himself doing a very neat figure of eight. Occasionally, Arnold Parker flashed by, shouting, much to Maurice's amusement, 'Watcher, Katy'. Even Mabel Snoad (all fourteen stone of her) and retiring Miss Whatley, the Sunday-school teacher, had ventured forth; while towards the end of the afternoon Miss Fortescue appeared, dressed in a most fetching scarlet and black outfit and black velvet toque, in the company of a strange bearded gentleman with a cushion strapped firmly round his bottom. Katy began to wonder how she could have come to miss such occasions in previous cold winters, but supposed that her own delicate health as a child, followed by the war and her two brothers' disappearance into the army, had probably had a lot to do with it.

As a red ball of sun started to sink over Breconbury Woods, Maurice and Katy glided, with considerably more aplomb than when they had first started out, towards the planks at the side of the ice. Here, Maurice repeated his self-appointed task at her feet, this time removing her skates which he then tied together and slung, along with his own, over the handlebars of his bicycle.

'Tomorrow? Will you come again tomorrow, Katy?' he asked, shyly, as they neared River Lane. 'I think my father and mother want to have an hour on the ice themselves, probably after church. Say we make it two o'clock, like today?'

'Yes. That would be lovely.' She looked at him gratefully, albeit privately amazed that anyone as seemingly staid and sober as Mildred Fitzherbert could skate. Maurice seemed to be constantly surprising her now with little things he said or did, presenting her with vignettes of an entirely new world. It was not the world of the Moretons of Upper Brook Street which, in any case, she had only glimpsed from behind invisible but nevertheless impenetrable barriers; it was not the world of an unpredictable, headstrong son of a London bookseller, who fancied himself an embryo author; nor was it the world of two very different homes in the locality: the Hall, with its remote, timeless, well-ordered way of going about things, or the Mill House itself which, after all the vicissitudes which had recently overtaken the family who dwelt in it, was somehow, Katy felt, a sad place, especially since her mother, far from mellowing with age, had turned into such a querulous martinet. Maurice Fitzherbert had shown her, albeit briefly, a world in which, despite her previous misgivings, she thought she might nevertheless be at home. His free and easy manner, the way he was so obviously liked and respected by all and sundry, was very gratifying. She felt both proud of him and proud that he had made it so plain he wanted her as a companion.

As they cycled home the following Sunday afternoon,

now much more at ease in each other's company, he suddenly said, 'You know, Katy, there's something I've been wanting to tell you ever since that night of the dance when we came back down River Lane. Those rumours . . .' he hesitated and gave her a quick smile. 'I think you should know,' he went on, 'that I am the so-called "ghost" of River Lane.'

'*You* . . . ?' She was so startled that for a moment she took her eyes off the road, allowing the front wheel of her bicycle to wobble alarmingly.

'Steady,' he said, waiting for her to right herself before continuing. 'Yes, I've been feeling awfully guilty about it ever since I first heard the stories that were going round this winter. I thought back to the November of last year and realized that the incident must have coincided with a couple of nights I'd spent at home. On that particular Friday morning I'm afraid I'd been up to some of my old tricks. You know how our garden runs down to the Willon. Well, I've baited eel hooks there for as long as I can remember. I don't suppose Ernest Fielding would have approved, what with his precious eel stage, but I don't think he ever knew. And it seemed a fairly harmless peccadillo. In fact, so far as I know I think our family has always had the riparian rights along the East Lodge bank, although I suppose eel baiting might have been considered a bit over the odds.'

'I *see*.' She, too, was smiling now, even though she was a little disconcerted about his use of 'peccadillo' and 'riparian' and would have to look the words up in the little dictionary his father had given her as soon as she got back to the Mill House. 'Thank you very much for telling me.'

'Well, I felt I just had to. I was absolutely mortified when I saw you shiver as we passed Hatch Alley. You see, that was where I came out after baiting the hooks. I remember this figure on a bicycle suddenly swerving – a little as you did just now. I never thought much about it at the time. I'd decided to go straight on and pick up the gun Fred Ashford had promised to lend me. The Fairfaxes were having a tenants' shoot and because they had happened to learn that I was at home, they'd sent word to ask if I would join them. They were a gun short because old Mr Swayne up at Bulbarrow wasn't well enough to make it, and apparently his son doesn't shoot. Oddly enough, I never knew about your poor brother until Mother wrote to me about the tragedy after I got back to London. And naturally Father would never have said anything.'

'I *see*,' she said again.

'Anyway, I'm terribly sorry for all the distress I must have caused you and your family. You will let your mother and sister know, won't you?'

'Of course.'

They were nearing the mill gates now. As they parted, he said, 'I'm afraid, being a weekday, I shan't be able to spend quite so long at Lower Croft tomorrow, although Father and I aren't exactly overworked at the moment, thank goodness. It's healthy weather. Much better than the floods. Say, all being well, I call for you at about a quarter to three? We could put in perhaps half an hour?'

'Yes, that would be best for me, too,' she replied, adding, a little hesitantly, 'I have work to do also,' although she knew perfectly well that May would be only too willing to let her off.

'Of course. I was forgetting.' He smiled, helped her through the small door with her bicycle – the big gates being closed for the weekend – lifted his cap and was gone.

They were quite the last to leave the ice that Monday afternoon. Katy had by now progressed so well that, rather like the night of the dance, she felt she could have gone on skating for ever. When, eventually, they finished their final round, Maurice seemed to take an extra long time to remove her skates, as if he, too, was unwilling for the afternoon to come to an end. She watched him as he knelt at her feet: noted the fine golden hair curling out from beneath his check tweed cap, the sweep of his long, equally golden eyelashes, the glowing cheeks and the firm jaw, the thin, delicate, yet capable fingers which were slowly and carefully dealing with her skates, as she supposed they must, at other times, deal with far more serious and complicated operations.

'Will 'ee shut the gate, zur?' Ted Shergold's voice suddenly called to them from the roadway and Maurice looked up quickly.

'Yes, Ted. I'll see to it.'

'Thank 'ee. Good night, then.'

'Good night, Ted.'

The man rode away on his bicycle, confident that if there was one person who could safely be entrusted with such a task, it was Dr Maurice, who he had been quick to notice was in no particular hurry. But he was also well aware that he himself was in charge of Lower Croft and the temporary function it was fulfilling. There might not be any danger of escaping cattle, but it was necessary for him to see that all the skaters had left the ice and the place was properly closed up each evening. Now, well content, he reckoned he had done his duty, besides having given Dr Maurice and that pretty little Lodge filly a bit of a bonus into the bargain. He was no spoilsport and he thought the world of the Fitzherberts: father and son. The young doctor had done a good job when his wife, Nancy, had had a miscarriage back in the summer. Of course, he hadn't been able to save the baby, but that was probably just as well. There were already quite enough mouths to feed in the Shergold household.

It was very quiet in Lower Croft now. Over the still evening air Katy could even discern, quite plainly, the sound of the mill-race echoing in the distance. A homing pigeon swooped low overhead and once or twice there came the faint barking of a dog, belonging to the dairyman in one of the Bulbarrow farm cottages on the opposite side of the valley. Otherwise, there was only the crackle of footsteps on frosty grass as they walked slowly up to the roadway and Maurice carefully shut the gate.

She was surprised when, as she started to take hold of the handlebars of her bicycle, preparatory to turning it round for the homeward journey, Maurice suddenly restrained her and she found both her hands caught in his.

'Katy,' he said, simply. 'Will you marry me?'

She was dumbfounded. She stared at him, mutely, appealingly, as if he had presented her with too great a problem, much more difficult than a mere proposal of marriage.

'You don't,' he went on, quickly, sensing her embarrassment, 'have to say now. I know it must seem awfully precipitant. But just think about it. I wasn't, in any case, contemplating getting married until after Father retires, probably at the end of next summer, but . . .' and here he gave her a look of such adoration and trust that, for a moment, she turned away, 'I think I've been in love with you, Katy, perhaps without knowing it, ever since we climbed up the Wilhampton church tower to see old Donaldson's bells.'

He stooped to kiss her then. It was a very tender kiss, altogether different from the kind she had experienced with Philip. She could not quite explain it but when he let her go, as gently as when he had taken her in his arms, she felt in some way disappointed, as if the afternoon had suddenly been spoilt, that it was a pity for lovemaking to have to come into their particular relationship.

There was a certain constraint between them now, as they cycled home, even though Maurice was as charming as ever and asked her, in the same diffident but hopeful way, if she could bear to come with him again on the morrow. 'Not that you really need any more *lessons*, Katy. Just practice. You're well able to take care of yourself now.'

She laughed. 'I'm glad you think so. But I don't believe I'd fancy going up to Lower Croft alone, somehow.' Yet even as she accepted his invitation, she knew that, whatever happened, things could never be quite the same between them again and that, more than ever, it was necessary to do something which she had been putting off: answer Philip's letter.

As soon as she got indoors, she went straight up to the attic and took it out of the drawer in which she had hidden it. So far, she had kept its content to herself, although she knew that May had known of its arrival and was longing for Katy to confide in her. Now, seated on one of the old ottomans, she spread it out once more and, in the fading light from the window, aided by one of the gas lamps which had just come on at the mill gates, she began to reread it, astonished that after so long a spell of silence, Philip was able to start off in such a cheerful, optimistic and self-confident manner:

Dearest Katy Mine,
   I haven't written before because after you never came to see me off at the station, I thought maybe I should try to forget you. But I haven't been able to, Katy. I wonder if it has been like that with you? Something tells me that it has.
   I want to come and see you again because I have some very good news, which I think will make a lot of difference to our situation, especially as far as your mother is concerned. I shall have to work late in the shop on Christmas Eve, it being one of our busiest times, but I shall catch a train from Waterloo on Christmas morning. I've booked to stay until Boxing night at the Holmwood Guesthouse in Westonbury. Oh Katy, I can't wait. I'm sure everything will come right for us now.
                                    Ever your own,
                                        Philip.

Still in her hat and coat, she remained seated by the window, outwardly calm and expressionless, inwardly distressed and confused. It was thus May found her some twenty minutes later.

'Katy, love. What is it?'

She turned to her silently and then, after a pause, said quietly, 'He's asked to marry me.'

'Who? Philip Mason?'

'No, well . . . not exactly. I mean, Maurice Fitzherbert.'

'Oh, chippatoo! But you're not really surprised, are you, love? It's been sticking out a mile, although I must say I didn't think as how he would come round to it quite so quick.' As always, when excited or under stress, May's grammar, as with other members of the family at such times, temporarily failed her. 'What did you say?' she went on, eagerly.

'I didn't say anything. I mean, there's no hurry. He said

so himself. He . . . won't be free to marry until after his father retires at the end of next summer.'

'No. But naturally he wants to become engaged. Have it announced. I mean, in his position, Katy, he can't afford for there to be talk, not that there hasn't been some already. And the dear thing doesn't want to compromise *you*. My word, next summer will come round in no time. A lot of couples have a much longer engagement. Why, his sister Connie was engaged to that farmer for well over three years. Oh, lovey, I'll see you get a much better trousseau than either she or even Alicia Moreton ever had. September would be just the month for a cream satin wedding dress and perhaps a pale gold shantung going-away outfit. I expect he wants to come and speak to Mother, doesn't he?'

'We didn't get that far, May.'

'But you'll let him know, my dear, won't you? Poor young man. He's so in love. And just think: you'll be the doctor's wife, one day mistress of East Lodge. It's like a dream come . . .'

Katy cut her short. 'Don't say that, May. Please. I don't know. That's the trouble. I'm in a muddle. I just don't know.'

'Don't *know*?' May looked at her, uncomprehendingly.

For answer, Katy passed her Philip's letter. She was surprised at her elder sister's quick and uncharacteristically harsh reaction.

'You'd best write to that young jackanapes at once, my child. He spells trouble. You know that as well as I do. I thought at first that maybe he was a help to you, what with all the sadness over Flo dying, especially as he was so keen on books, like you. But then, I don't know. He was too cocky, somehow. We can't have him poking his nose in now. You'll get a bad name. You've been seen out and about this winter with one of the finest and straightest young men in the district. How d'you think Maurice Fitzherbert's going to feel if he catches sight of Philip Mason hanging around River Lane, out for what he can get?'

'But he says he has good news, May.'

Her elder sister made a sound she had seldom heard her use before: a most derisory, unladylike snort.

'And what d'you suppose that might be? Has he written a book or something? You said he fancied himself as a writer. You must get a letter off to him first thing tomorrow. Come along down now. It's perishing up here. I'm shrammed. We've got the place to ourselves. Mother's gone up to mind Edith's kids while she has the rest of her teeth pulled. Herbie's going to fetch her when he knocks off work, because she felt a bit queer after the gas last time.'

Katy did as she was bidden, sitting lost in thought while May made a pot of tea and toasted some bread on the end of a long fork before the open range. Sensing, perhaps, that she had said enough for the moment, she then got on with her sewing and remained quiet for the rest of the evening, merely reminding Katy before Sarah returned that, whatever happened, she must stop Philip Mason coming to Westonbury at Christmas and that she would have to tell her mother about Maurice's proposal. 'Although it might be as well,' she added, thoughtfully, 'not to say anything until tomorrow. She's always tired when she's been up to Edith's. Those kids are a bit too much for her. But when you do speak, for the Lord's sake don't mention your other young man.'

Katy slept fitfully that night, pondering on the strange sequence of events which had recently overtaken her. If it had not been for the cold weather, she would never have been out with Maurice three days running, for in their particular circumstances there were so few opportunities to get to know each other better. She knew that it was unlikely that Mildred Fitzherbert would welcome her as a casual visitor at East Lodge. It was unthinkable that she could ever entertain Maurice in the Mill House. Other than an occasional visit to the pictures in Westonbury – to which he had made a tentative suggestion the previous afternoon – she could think of no other eventuality which could have given them such a splendid chance of enjoying each other's company – and such *close* company – as skating on Lower Croft. She knew that if it had not been for that, she would never have listened to May for a moment about putting Philip Mason off, however much his visit would upset Sarah. As it was, she had yet to write the letter. She still badly wanted to see him. She wanted to hear about his good news. She wanted – and here she found herself going all hot and actually blushing under the bedclothes – to feel his arms around her, his hands . . . This time, she made a conscious effort to think about something else.

Katy was startled when, having dozed off for an hour or so, she suddenly awoke to find her head and neck arched backwards, a fierce, rhythmical, semi-frightening yet strangely pleasurable throbbing taking place in the lower half of her body. She had no idea what was happening to her. She only knew that whatever it was it had something to do with Philip and that she had been dreaming of him just beforehand.

She did not sleep again that night. Miserably, she listened to the dull roar of the mill-race, punctuated at regular intervals by the town hall clock as it struck the hours. The moonlight was still filtering through the thin curtains when, at six o'clock, she heard May's alarm go off and then her sister get up and go down into the mill to wash. For once, she did not join her. Presently, she heard her return and take the usual dipper of soapy water into Sarah's room. Just before six-thirty, there were footsteps in River Lane and the scraping noise of a key in a lock, as Tom Henstridge came through the gates and passed under her window. Gradually, as the day gathered momentum, other sounds became apparent: more footsteps trooping down River Lane, bicycles being leant against a wall, the coughing, spitting and clearing of throats in the raw December morning, snatches of conversation, a short burst of raucous laughter, as the men congregated outside, waiting for the shrill blast from the hooter which governed their lives to summon not only them, but countless other inhabitants of Wilhampton, to work.

25

When Maurice Fitzherbert failed to call for Katy at a quarter to three that Tuesday, both she and May supposed that a patient must have detained him. It seemed unlikely that he would let her down without good reason.

'He's probably been called out to Arnold Parker's daughter,' said May, somewhat uncharitably, Katy felt. 'You know, Ethel, the one who had to get married to Percy Hooper's brother. I remember when I was fitting her for her wedding dress last June, I reckoned she was about three months gone and her time would be around Christmas. She was already a twenty-seven-inch waist.' (She kindly did not add that only the previous week Emily Harwood had mentioned that her cousin Nellie, at East Lodge, knew for a fact that Grace Armitage was forever sending for the doctor nowadays on one artful pretext or another, and it was 'as plain as a pikestaff which one she hopes will call at The Warren'.)

Katy merely nodded. She had been in the same class at school as Ethel Parker, a doe-eyed, loose-lipped girl about whom, on more than one occasion, she had heard the familiar defamatory remark: 'no better than she should be'. All the same, it hardly seemed fair or even reasonable immediately to pick on Ethel as the sole cause of Maurice's non-appearance at the mill gates. Although he had said it was healthy weather, there must surely be plenty of others in the district who might suddenly require the urgent attention of either Dr Fitzherbert or his son.

In many ways, Katy felt relieved that she would not be going skating today. For one thing, her bad night had made her feel heavy and listless. For another, having been late in rising she had, in consequence, only had time to make do with some sketchy ablutions at Sarah's washstand. Moreover, she had still said nothing to her mother about Maurice's proposal; nor had she written her letter to Philip.

Surprisingly, it was not until seven o'clock that evening before the news came to the inhabitants of the Mill House, explaining just why Maurice had not called for Katy earlier on. Even then, the information did not come through him but, of all unlikely people, Edith's husband. Herbie stood at the door, anxious and breathless, asking whether one of them could come up to downside because Edith had been taken bad again. After the previous evening's extraction, she had apparently had a lot of bleeding from her gums and as soon as he had got home he had hurried — so far as his heart would let him — back to the surgery to get something to stop it. Here, he told them, he had been confronted by a strange locum because Dr Fitzherbert, 'the old one,' as he went on, 'had a fall on the ice at midday. He's in Westonbury Infirmary. A bad business, by all accounts. Straight over on the back of his head.'

'Oh, *no*!' Sarah clapped a hand over her mouth. Katy simply stared at her brother-in-law. May, with admirable presence of mind, immediately started taking charge of the situation, electing this time to go up to Edith's home herself. 'You'd best stop here with Mother, Katy. I expect Maurice will send word himself as soon as he can,' she said, as she hurriedly packed a few night things and put on her hat and coat. Then, sensing that it might be as well to give her youngest sister plenty to do, she added, 'I'd be glad if you'd get on with that oversewing on Mrs Donald-son's afternoon frock, and if I'm not back by tomorrow morning, there's all those sequins to be sewn on Miss Fortescue's velvet coatee.'

It seemed to Katy a long, depressing evening after she had gone. Sarah, sitting by the range, upright in her high ladder-backed chair, was silent other than occasionally murmuring, with a shake of her head, 'Poor man. I don't know. I don't know, I'm sure.'

Hunched over Mrs Donaldson's dress, Katy kept blinking back tears, remembering how good Maurice's father had been to her as a child, his daily — sometimes twice-daily — visits when she had had diphtheria and meningitis, the little dictionary which he had given her, the courtesy he had shown her when she had come to his home as a guest but a few weeks ago.

When, at half-past eight, there were footsteps and a gentle knock at the door, both women looked at each other apprehensively. Katy put down her sewing and went to answer it. As she expected, Maurice Fitzherbert was standing outside.

'Please . . . will you come in? I'm . . . so sorry. We have heard the news.'

The young man accepted gratefully, stooping to enter the small, clean but cluttered living room, where Sarah at once rose from her chair and held out her hand. 'Good evening, Dr Maurice,' she said, quietly. 'May I get you a cup of tea or . . .' and here, to her youngest daughter's astonishment, her mother added, 'perhaps a little brandy?' So far as Katy knew, there was only a thimbleful left in the 'medicinal' bottle, which had last been brought out when Flo died. It was therefore somewhat of a relief to her when Maurice – albeit not altogether unexpectedly – chose to have tea.

'I thought,' he said, slowly, as he sat drinking it, 'you would have been bound to hear about the accident sooner, but I'm sorry I couldn't let you know myself. My father hadn't intended to skate at all today, but he was called out to see one of the dairyman's children in the cottages not far from Lower Croft. As he had his skates in the back of the car, he thought he would have a quick turn or two before coming home to lunch.' There was a pause and Maurice passed a hand wearily over his face before continuing, 'He just fell . . . backwards. He's still unconscious. My mother is spending the night at the hospital. I'm afraid I can't say . . . what the outcome will be.'

Katy could not help but respect and admire the calm and dignified way her own mother now spoke, as if, however sad and distressing Maurice's words had been, she knew instinctively how to respond to them. 'We shall all pray for your father, Dr Maurice. Not just myself and my family, but all Wilhampton. He is a good man. Everyone owes him so much.'

She watched Maurice put down his cup and look at her

mother very directly. 'Thank you, Mrs Lodge,' he answered, simply. 'Thank you very much indeed.' It was almost, Katy felt, as though, for the moment, she herself was excluded, that Sarah and Maurice had some strange, indefinable, silent rapport. Presently, he stood up. 'There will be a bulletin posted outside East Lodge each day, but I will do my best to keep you informed personally. Thank you very much for the tea, Mrs Lodge.'

'Thank you for coming, Doctor.' Sarah rose also, reached up for the bundle of keys hanging by the mantelshelf and handed them to Katy. 'My daughter will see you out and lock the gates.' She held out her hand gravely and wished him good night. When it came to a time like this, Katy thought, as she returned to the house, as long as her mother was well, one could hardly fault her behaviour.

In the days that followed, an undisguised gloom seemed to settle on Wilhampton. True, most of its inhabitants invariably took a morbid interest in tragedy, almost seeming to relish the misfortunes of others; but there was not a soul who did not wish Dr Fitzherbert a speedy recovery and truly grieve for him and his family, anxiously waiting on the bulletins pinned up on East Lodge gate and passing on any fresh information to others. Special prayers were said for him in St Mark's by the Reverend Donaldson. Small gifts were constantly being left with Abie Grant at the surgery. Even though Mildred Fitzherbert was not as popular as the rest of her family, people watched out for her, murmuring, 'Poor woman, poor woman,' as they saw her being driven to and from Westonbury by her son who, himself looking tired and drawn, carried on with the practice. No one, other than a few strangers, felt like going to Lower Croft to skate any more. In any case, the cold snap was showing signs of coming to an end.

Although the situation, distressing as it was, made it easier for Katy to reach a decision about putting Philip Mason off coming to Westonbury – for it was unthinkable now that she could possibly see him – nevertheless, the letter which she eventually sent to London took her several hours to compose. 'Dear Philip,' it began,

Thank you for writing as you did. I am very sorry but owing to unforeseen circumstances I'm afraid I would be unable to see you if you came here, so it would be best if you made other plans for Christmas. I trust you will understand. It is difficult for me to explain. I send you every good wish for the future and am glad about your good news, whatever it might be.

Yours sincerely,
Katy.

She was not at all satisfied with her final effort, even as she put it into the posting box, and still had misgivings about the bald, matter-of-fact way she had phrased it. She only knew that it was imperative, not only to put Philip off coming anywhere near the district, but also to put him right out of her mind altogether. At the moment, the latter was not as difficult as it might have been, for all her time seemed to be taken up with concern for Maurice and his father, and most evenings the former either called or sent word to the Mill House so that, as he had promised, the Lodge family was kept informed of the very latest developments. For a few days, she still held back from telling her mother of Maurice's proposal, but soon his attentiveness, the way he seemed to derive a certain comfort from his brief visits, the look in his eyes as he wished her goodnight, made it almost incumbent on her to say something.

'I am no fool, my child,' said Sarah, soberly, in response to her halting statement, one evening when they happened to be alone, May having gone to pay a quick visit to Edith, who was still feeling shaky and depressed after the loss of all her teeth. 'When this crisis has passed – and please God, it will be for the better – and Dr Maurice feels free to speak to me, I shall be pleased to give you both my blessing.'

Katy bent lower over the stocking she was darning, experiencing, not for the first time, a sudden suppressed anger that her mother and May took so much for granted, and that she herself was trapped, a victim of events over which she seemed, perforce, powerless.

It was well after nine o'clock on Christmas Eve when

Maurice arrived with some small packages for them all – 'definitely not,' he said, with a disarming smile, 'to be opened until tomorrow' – and told them that there had been a slight improvement in his father's condition. 'Although it is still only early days,' he continued, as he sat down to drink his customary cup of tea. 'But, at any rate, he opened his eyes this afternoon and my mother knew that he had recognized her. I'm driving straight into Westonbury to fetch her home when I leave here. She's hoping to attend midnight mass at St Mark's as usual.'

Sarah inclined her head. 'We shall all be going, too, Dr Maurice. I'm sure your father will be uppermost in everyone's prayers.'

At that moment – no carol singing having preceded it – some swift footsteps, followed by a loud banging on the door, startled them all. It was loud and positive, as if the caller was determined to brook no denial and that whatever he or she had to say was unquestionably urgent. It was May who rose, pushed back the tapestry curtain and answered it. Philip Mason, where all could see him, was standing on the threshold.

There was a short electrified silence and then, striding into the living room, he went straight towards Sarah and held out his hand.

She did not rise. An expression of undisguised hostility came over her face. Yet, conscious that it was important to maintain some semblance of manners in front of her other and infinitely preferred visitor, she allowed him to shake her hand and said, coolly, 'Good evening, Mr Mason.'

'Good evening, ma'am.' He smiled, pleasantly. There was something more mature, even more likeable, May felt, about the young man to whom, in the late summer, her mother had practically shown the door. Eager-eyed, fresh-faced and dressed in a smart, velvet-collared, navy over-coat, he had about him a quieter, less brash self-confidence, an air of success which was not altogether unattractive. She felt that he had his feet firmly on the ground now, knew exactly what he wanted and how to go about it.

He turned next to Katy and, diving into the pocket

of his coat, produced, as Maurice Fitzherbert had also produced shortly before, three parcels, gaily wrapped, which she guessed, instinctively, must be books. Completely betraying her supposed ignorance of the slightest possibility of such a meeting, she said, 'I thought you couldn't get away until Christmas morning.'

'That's right. When I wrote, I didn't think I could. But I've just taken on a good new salesman. Three days ago I reckoned I could leave him to it tonight.' The reference to 'I' and the fact that Philip himself seemed to be so very much in charge escaped no one.

Quietly, Maurice Fitzherbert rose. 'I must go, I'm afraid, Mrs Lodge. Thank you for the tea. A very happy Christmas to you all.'

Sarah had by now also risen. 'Good night, Dr Maurice,' she said, this time making a point of very courteously holding out her hand. 'Let us hope that tomorrow you will have even better news for us.'

After he had gone, she turned and looked Philip Mason straight in the face. 'And I would thank you to leave also, Mr Mason. There is no reason for you to come to this house again. My daughter, with whom you appear to have communicated lately, is otherwise committed.'

Philip frowned. 'Committed? What do you mean, ma'am? How? Who to?'

'To the gentleman who has just left.'

'What? The *doctor*?'

'Yes, Mr Mason. If it were not for his father's serious accident, their engagement would have been announced by now.'

For the first time, Philip's confidence seemed to desert him. He rounded on Katy, a desperate, almost haunted look in his eyes. 'It's not true. You can't tell me it's true.'

Miserably, she stayed silent, while hearing her mother reply, levelly, 'It's quite true, Mr Mason.'

He turned back to Sarah. 'But it's me, Mrs Lodge, she's going to marry. I can give her a good home now. My father has left the shop and passed all the running over to me. He's just married again himself. Married *well*, you understand, ma'am. He's gone away to live in Wales. There is nothing to stand in the way of Katy and me . . .'

She cut him short. 'I am sorry, Mr Mason. It is too late. I must ask you to leave.'

Helplessly, hopelessly, Katy watched him fling himself out of the house. For a moment, she remained quite motionless, as if no longer in command of her own fate or fortunes. Then, before either Sarah or May could stop her, she dashed out of the door after him, coatless, feet flying, her voice calling, 'Philip, Philip,' as she caught sight of his figure fast disappearing into the night.

Halfway up River Lane, he stopped and turned. In the light of the gas-lamp, she saw a look of incredulous joy come over his face as she drew closer. He opened his arms and she ran into them, the sound of the mill-race not even the faintest echo in her ears.

26

On Friday, February 18th, 1921, there appeared in the *Westonbury Journal* three items of news which May Lodge carefully cut out and took up to her bedroom that night. Here, she placed them in her rosewood box with its pretty mother-of-pearl inlay on the lid, which always stood on her dressing-table and where, over the years, she had safely tucked away many a keepsake.

The first of these items, printed on the front page of the paper, was headed SON TO CARRY ON, and read:

We are happy to report that Dr Claud Fitzherbert, of East Lodge, Wilhampton, who suffered a serious accident while skating on the ice at Lower Croft, Bulbarrow, last December, has now returned home from hospital. While still confined to a wheelchair, Dr Fitzherbert is nevertheless making a slow but steady recovery. Though originally not due to retire until the end of the summer, he has now completely passed over the practice to his son, Dr Maurice Fitzherbert, who interrupted his medical training to serve in HM Forces during the latter part of the war.

Later this year, the mayoress, Miss Fortescue, is hoping

to arrange a presentation party for Dr Fitzherbert in the town hall, in gratitude for his long, selfless and devoted service to all those countless patients whom he has attended in Wilhampton and its surrounding district since 1889.

The second item, which appeared on one of the centre pages of the *Journal*, could almost have had the same caption as the first, but was instead entitled, somewhat baldly, DEATH OF BARONET, after which came the words:

> The death occurred on Friday last of Sir Harry Moreton, Bt, of Bishopsdown House, Suffolk. Sir Harry, who was seventy-five, is succeeded by his son, Captain Sir Charles Moreton, MC, who, with his wife, the former Honourable Alicia Fairfax, of the Hall, Wilhampton, will be taking over his late father's country estate. Sir Charles and Lady Moreton have one son, John William Harry, now heir to the baronetcy.

The last item, though the shortest, was the one May looked at longest before closing up her little treasure chest. It consisted of four lines only, halfway down the MARRIAGES column on the back page:

> MASON–LODGE. On February 12th, 1921, at St Mark's Church, Wilhampton, by the Reverend Donaldson, PHILIP GORDON, only son of MR FRANCIS MASON and the late MRS MASON, of 51 Davies St, London, W1, to KATHERINE VERA EVELYN, youngest daughter of MRS SARAH LODGE and the late MR SIDNEY LODGE, of the Mill House, Wilhampton.

It had not been at all the kind of wedding May had envisaged. There had been no cream satin dress or pale gold shantung going-away outfit. Yet, when she took into consideration everything that had happened to the Lodge family during recent years, it had seemed entirely appropriate for Katy now to be married very simply and very quietly, wearing a sober, beige alpaca coat and a small feather-trimmed velvet toque of the same colour. Moreover, she had still been married in St Mark's, once May had finally managed to overcome her mother's opposition to the match and persuade her to bow to the inevitable. It had been either that or having the girl run away, and she knew that the last thing Sarah wanted was the remotest possibility of anyone in Wilhampton suggesting that her youngest daughter had had to get married.

Even though the wedding had been hastily arranged, so far as she knew, May reflected, as she took the pins out of her hair, there had not been any gossip of that kind – only great astonishment and regret that the groom was not Dr Fitzherbert's son. Since those few tense traumatic moments on Christmas Eve, when May had run up River Lane after Katy, somehow decorum had been re-established, convention upheld. The door of the Mill House was opened to Philip Mason – however grudgingly at first – but the more May saw of him the more she had come to like him. Naturally, her tender heart grieved deeply for poor Dr Maurice; and she and Katy had sat down and had a good cry the night after he had called with a wedding present: a painting of Wilhampton done from the top of Breconbury Downs by a most distinguished artist, a friend of Miss Fortescue, who often stayed at the Moat House. May hoped that it would not be too long before the young man married someone else, for she had always believed that a doctor needed a wife. She prayed that he would find some nice girl who would make him a good one; although she felt that it would have to be someone placid and forbearing. It certainly wouldn't be easy being a daughter-in-law in the Fitzherbert household now, she mused, not the way it was; for it did not look as if the older couple would be moving to a smaller home, as had originally been expected. Katy, with her passionate, imaginative nature, might have found it more than a little frustrating and circumscribed.

After brushing her hair, May knelt down to say her prayers before she undressed, as the room was cold and so were her feet, which she was looking forward to warming on the stone hot water bottle which Sarah had earlier placed in her bed. Then, methodically folding up each garment as she took it off, she put on her long-sleeved flanelette nightgown and climbed into bed, her thoughts quickly returning to her youngest sister, as she blew out her candle.

She found it impossible not to wonder how Katy was

getting on. Soon she would be back from her brief honeymoon in Brighton. Somehow May felt sure that it would have been a success. It was a love match, all right. Although, sadly, she seemed to recall having once said that about Alicia Moreton's betrothal. Still, one could never tell. All those scandalous rumours about a divorce had evidently been untrue. Of course, there was never smoke without fire and – although it seemed wicked even to think it – May supposed that it was always possible . . .

She tried to remember how much time the Moretons had spent in Wilhampton since Katy had first referred to her employer's indisposition. Not a lot, on the whole. Certainly, apart from the Christmas before last, when they had stayed at the Hall for quite a while, she had not caught sight of Sir Charles – as she must remember to call him – in church, looking, as she invariably thought, rather bored. On the other hand, Emily Harwood had told her that during the last year Grace Armitage – for whom she appeared to have an especial loathing – had often left her husband in the care of Cissy Lawes' mother and gone waltzing off to London to do goodness knows what. But surely . . . no, it was inconceivable . . . Besides, the Captain had saved Guy Armitage's life, hadn't he? It was amazing how long it had taken for that to become known. Charles Moreton had been commendably modest about winning an MC. She would say that for him. He was a most courageous, well-bred young man, not at all the sort to carry on with Guy's wife. Particularly when he had such a beautiful one of his own. It was good to know that she was now Lady Moreton and would soon be settled in Suffolk. Dear Miss Alicia . . . Somehow it would always be difficult to think of her as anything other than that. And a little while ago she had really looked quite bonny, thank goodness, when she had summoned May to the Hall to discuss three crêpe de Chine rest gowns for summer wear, which she wanted her to make up. The particular choice of garment, for use some months ahead, had made May wonder whether perhaps she was going to have another child. As she was showing her out, Nanny Barlow had somehow hinted that it never did to have all one's eggs in one basket and that it would be nice if a brother or sister came along to stop John William from becoming spoilt. It was funny to think that, but for a few strange twists of fate, Katy might still have been a nursery maid helping to look after him in Suffolk, instead of the wife of a young, go-ahead, London bookseller.

May closed her eyes, trying to switch her mind on to all the things she must remember to do in the morning. It was a pity, she felt, that she had to spend so much time supervising her new apprentice. She couldn't yet trust Arnold Parker's youngest daughter with even the simplest hemming, but she supposed that would come. The girl was cheerful and willing. She would say that for her. Fortunately, she appeared to have inherited her father's optimistic attitude to life, despite his lugubrious profession.

The clock above the town hall struck eleven and still May lay awake, acutely conscious of the familiar sounds of the night in the overall stillness. She could hear Sarah snoring rhythmically in the next room; occasionally, a small breeze rattled the catch of her window. From somewhere over Bulbarrow way an owl hooted. Once or twice there were halting footsteps in River Lane – probably Lilian Perrick's husband returning from The Punchbowl. And in the background, as always, came the relentless, insistent roar of the mill-race. Somehow, May felt, it seemed louder than usual tonight. Of course she realized that there had been a lot of rain lately and the Willon was running high. Duck and Collar, silly man, had remarked on this all-too-obvious fact when he had waylaid her at teatime as she came up from the workroom. She knew that it wouldn't take many more downpours before she might hear those other sinister sounds, the ones they had all come to dread each winter: the slapping, gurgling and rising of water beneath the downstair floorboards. After all, it was February. February filldike. The floods could still come . . .

May pulled the bedclothes up a little higher and pushed her feet further down the feather mattress, searching for the hot water bottle. She told herself that it was no good worrying. It was always best, like Arnold Parker, to look on the bright side of life. And if the floods did come, she thought, as she drifted off to sleep, at least Katy, her youngest sister, would now be spared them.

The Way
of the River

1

'When will you make Greta's dress, Aunt Chip?'

May Lodge momentarily laid down the crêpe de Chine camisole that she was hem-stitching and regarded her seven-year-old niece, gravely.

'When I've finished Lady Fairfax's order, Emily. If you like, you can fetch that old rag-bag in the corner and see if you can find something pretty you would like her to wear.'

Eagerly, the small girl got up and did as she was bidden. Then she sat down on the floor of the workroom again and, extracting a mass of material of all shapes, sizes and colours, she proceeded, oblivious of her aunt, to address herself to her doll, holding up this and that against the stiff, pink, scantily-clad form, as if she were a couturier advising some particularly important client.

May watched her covertly as she resumed her sewing. She thought her a beautiful child, not nearly so thin and frail-looking as her mother had been at the same age. With her dark curly hair, enormous brown eyes and rosy cheeks, Emily disproved all her grandmother's forebodings about London not being a proper place in which to bring up children. If only Sarah would admit that she might be wrong; but then, May reflected, she had never done that in all her life. Besides, with Emily's mother now so ill in hospital, and all the other tribulations which had recently overtaken the small family, May felt that perhaps some of Sarah's condemnation of the capital seemed almost justified.

'This is nice, Aunt Chip.' Suddenly the child held up a piece of midnight blue taffeta. 'Greta would look lovely in blue.'

'Let me see.' May held out her hand. 'Why, I do believe

that's a scrap from the very first dance dress I ever made your mother.'

'Is there enough?' Emily was standing now, looking at May anxiously, one hand still clutching the doll, the other placed, almost in supplication, on her aunt's knee.

'I think so, my dear. We might put a few lace frills and flounces round the bottom, just to help out.'

'Oh, *yes*. Thank you. Will it be like the ones Mummy used to wear when she danced at the theatre?'

This time May's response was a little more reserved, but Emily appeared not to notice as, with her imagination roused, she produced a sudden spate of further questions.

'Where was I, Aunt Chip, when you made Mummy's first dance dress?'

'You?' May could not help smiling now. 'Why, you weren't born, Emily. It was just before your mother married. Let me see, over eight years ago. The end of 1920.'

'Where was the dance? In London?'

'Oh, dear me no. It was here, in Wilhampton. In the town hall.'

The child looked puzzled. 'Did Daddy come all the way from the bookshop to take her?'

'No, dear. Now, put all those other scraps back where they belong, will you.' May felt that the conversation was getting a little out of hand, and that it would be as well to steer her niece's thoughts in other directions. But she had reckoned without Emily's persistence. Although the little girl obediently began to refill the rag-bag, she obviously had something on her mind and did not intend to let the matter rest.

'Who did Mummy go to the dance with, Aunt Chip, if she didn't go with Daddy?'

May broke off some silk thread, removed her spectacles and began putting her sewing things away methodically in the work-basket at her side. 'What a lot of things you want to know, Miss. Your mother was very pretty. Indeed, she still is. She happened to have more than one young man in those days. She went to the dance with the doctor who called to see your grandmother yesterday about her rheumatism.'

'The *doctor*? But . . . I heard you and Granny talking about his wife after he'd gone, Aunt Chip.'

'Did you? Well, little pitchers shouldn't have such long ears. Dr Fitzherbert and your Mummy went to the dance before *either* of them was married. Now, that's enough chattering. How about showing me those steps you were on about.'

This time the child's attention was immediately diverted.

'Oh, *yes*! Have you got a comb and a piece of tissue paper, Aunt Chip? Then you could blow a tune for me through it like Mummy does. Play "Bye, Bye, Blackbird", extra fast. Do.'

May searched in her handbag for a comb and then got up to fetch some clean tissue paper from the store which she kept in the bottom drawer of the big deal chest of drawers. She felt that it did not really seem right to be going in for such frivolity at a time like this, yet Katy had expressly said in the letter she had written to her sister asking if she thought Sarah would agree to having Emily at the Mill House while she went into hospital: 'Whatever happens, May, if she does come, don't tell her too much. She picks things up so quickly. I want her to be happy. Don't let Mother talk about the operation in front of her. I'll be thinking of you, imagining you dancing with her and singing "Here We Go Looby-Loo", like you used to do with me, once.'

Apart from a few unfortunate remarks which had slipped out, May felt that, on the whole, they had complied with Katy's request, even if it had meant Sarah constantly reiterating her doubts and fears as soon as the child was in bed, forcing May to listen, night after night, to a tirade about how they should never have allowed Katy to marry Philip Mason, that she should never have gone to London and that, certainly, she should never, ever, have got in with all those shameless, wicked, stage folk.

With the latter sentiment, May could not but agree. It had definitely been a shock when, three years ago, just after the General Strike, Katy had written to say that a certain Mr Marcus Kreiger, a distinguished and regular customer of Philip's, had offered her the chance of appearing in a musical he was backing in the West End. The letter had not mentioned that it so happened Mr Kreiger, a rich and successful entrepreneur, had also offered to lend Philip a considerable amount of money in order to help him over the financial difficulties in which Mason and Son, the booksellers, like many another business at that time, found themselves.

'When are you going to begin, Aunt Chip?' Emily's voice broke into May's reveries, somewhat plaintively.

'I'm sorry, dear.' May sat down again and, with comb and tissue paper poised, added, 'I don't expect that I shall be as good at this as your Mummy is.'

'Never mind. You can just start me off.'

After a few moments, May did, in fact, find to her relief that there was little need for her continued and somewhat breathless accompaniment. Emily was well away, humming to herself and now kicking her heels up sideways in a most spirited execution of the Charleston. The whole performance was so accomplished, yet so natural, that May could only sit back in fascination and wonder until, suddenly, the door of the workroom was thrown open and Sarah Lodge stood on the threshold.

'May I ask what is going on?' Her mother, in her long black moiré dress with the customary tucker of snow-white lace at the throat, made an imposing, intimidating figure. May, although thirty-eight and used to Sarah's vagaries, seemed far more embarrassed than her niece who, although awed by her grandmother, was, as yet, more perplexed by, than actually frightened of her.

'Emily was showing me how she does the Charleston, Mother.'

'The *Charleston*!' No Sarah Bernhardt could have invested the word with more meaningful odium. Although Sarah Lodge had never witnessed the dance since the craze for it had swept the country a few years earlier, she knew enough – through reading the papers and listening to 2LO on their crystal wireless set – to have formed her own uncompromising opinion on the subject. As far as she was concerned, even if the Prince of Wales did dance it, the Charleston was not suitable for *ladies*. It made them look vulgar and corrupt. It was far worse, in fact, than the cancan. As for her own grand-daughter doing it, that was not to be countenanced.

A flash of memory suddenly jerked May back ten years to the time when Sarah's intense displeasure had been incurred over a vaguely similar incident: how she had mercilessly dressed them all down after hearing that Katy had got up on the stage at the local fair and sung 'Our Lodger's Such a Nice Young Man' to the whole of Wilhampton. May could see the scene quite clearly in her mind's eye: the lamplight flickering over the five faces round the tea-table in the living room of the Mill House. Even poor dear simple Neil had seemed to register his mother's anger and indignation. As for Katy, she had been in tears while Flo, quite gently and kindly, had tried to find out exactly what had happened. Of course, what had made it seem so much more deplorable to Sarah was the fact that she herself was then still in mourning for her late husband. Sidney Lodge, the manager of the Felt Mills for thirty-two years, had scarcely been dead three months. And today, although her youngest daughter was not dead, she had undergone a serious operation and therefore, in Sarah's eyes, it did not behove any member of the family to be seen enjoying themselves, even a small seven-year-old child.

'You will not dance the charleston again, Emily, here or, I trust, anywhere else.' Her pronouncement was made with the same compelling sepulchral intonation that May remembered so well and against which no member of the Lodge family had ever dared to argue. 'I came to tell you both that tea is ready.' With that, Sarah turned and left the workroom as abruptly as she had arrived.

'Hurry up, dear. Best pop round into the closet before we go.' May gave Emily a gentle push and busied herself collecting up the various items she would need in order to continue working in the Mill House that evening. Then, when the child still seemed to dawdle, she began chivvying her. 'There, run along. We don't want to keep your grand-mother waiting.'

'But Aunt Chip . . .' The bottom lip had turned down. Emily was not exactly crying, but she had begun to look very near it. 'Can't I dance the charleston again, ever?'

'Well, dear. You heard what your grandmother said. She doesn't like it.'

'Why not? Mummy and Daddy do it. They used to dance it ever such a lot, once. I used to hear them. They put the gramophone on down in the shop after it shut and they charlestoned all up and down the rows of books. One night I crept downstairs and watched them. I couldn't understand what they were doing at first. I thought they looked rather silly. Then, when they saw me, they laughed and taught me to do it, too.'

'Did they? Well, your Mummy and Daddy are much younger than Granny. And me, for that matter. And . . . well . . . I expect it's all a bit different in London.'

May was aware that she had made an inadequate excuse. With anyone less intelligent than Emily it might have sufficed. But this was a child who thought things through. She needed sensible answers, careful handling. Even after May had got her to go to the closet and locked up the workroom for the night, she knew that Emily was still mulling over the problem as they made their way through the garden in the fading sunlight of the early April evening. As it was a Saturday, the Felt Mills had shut down at one o'clock and there was no mill hooter to mark the passing of the hours; but, away to the right May could hear, as always, the roar of the mill-race: insistent, relentless, immutable, a sound which had formed the background to her existence for as long as she could remember. She looked down at the small form beside her, clutching her doll and the remnant of blue taffeta. She wondered what, if anything, the mill-race meant to Emily. Certainly, she liked to be taken to see it, to stand holding May's hand as they watched the water flowing swiftly along and then cascading down into a bubbling white whirlpool, to feel the occasional spray that was sent up and to ask pertinent questions as to whether anyone had ever fallen into it, and to speculate about what would have happened to him or her if they had. But she supposed that Emily, quite naturally, was growing up with different memories, different values. Although the mill-race might be May's particular constant, her niece would hold other things dearer to her heart. Yet, for the life of her, May could not imagine how an only child doing the charleston with her parents in a London bookshop could compare with the pleasure derived by a large family of brothers and sisters, holding hands of a Saturday night, as they danced round in a circle singing 'Here We Go Looby-Loo', while the mill-race played its timeless hypnotic accompaniment in the background.

How long ago that all seemed. There had been seven of them once, and now only four were still alive: Henry away in the army, Edith struggling to raise her own family up on downside, Katy in London and she herself the only one unmarried — her once-lovely cheerful face more lined of late — still living at home, supporting and caring for an increasingly irascible old lady. She prayed that this evening was not going to prove too difficult, that Sarah would not remain in one of her silent humours. It was bad enough having to wait until half-past eight, the time May had arranged to be at the Snoads' ready for a telephone call from Katy's husband to let them know the latest news.

As May entered the Mill House and pushed aside the tapestry curtain which had always served as a door between the tiny hallway and the living room, she caught sight of something else beside the usual plate of bread and butter and homemade buns laid out on the white embroidered tablecloth. 'Oh, chippatoo,' she exclaimed, using that curious pet expression of hers, which invariably came out quite spontaneously whenever she was particularly pleased, and which her small niece had been quick to shorten into a nickname for her favourite aunt.

'Just look, Emily,' she went on, appreciatively, feeling that there was now hope of some kind of rapprochement with Sarah, 'I do believe your grandmother has bought you a Wilhampton lardy cake for tea.' It was a little extravagance in which she knew her mother occasionally indulged, and May could only suppose that she must have decided on the treat when she had gone out shopping that morning.

The child's face brightened. Then, in that strangely dignified, old-fashioned way which she had noticed Emily adopt on more than one occasion, she watched her go round the table to where Sarah was sitting, lay a hand on her knee and say, quite simply, 'Thank you very much, Granny.'

Sarah Lodge looked down at her grandchild. For a moment, the stern grey eyes softened. Something approaching a smile seemed to wipe away the impenetrable mask which had hardened over the years.

Whatever else Emily's mother had or had not done, May said to herself as she squeezed into her usual place directly in front of the upright piano, Katy had certainly taught her daughter manners.

2

The bus came slowly over Westminster Bridge. At the back, a youngish thickset man with dark hair and dark brown eyes stared unseeingly out of the window. He seemed quite oblivious of the scene before him: the bright bobbing lights on and around the Thames, the Houses of Parliament and Big Ben proclaiming the time – a quarter past eight. The conductor had to ask him twice where he wanted to go and waited, with ill-concealed impatience, until he eventually said, 'Dover Street' and handed up a penny-halfpenny.

Half an hour ago, the Sister on the ward where he had watched his wife steadily deteriorating ever since they had cut her stomach open five days ago, had told Philip Mason that unless there was some sign of improvement within the next twenty-four hours, they would have to operate again first thing on Monday morning. With her reserved austere expression – about as unbending, Philip thought, as the stiff starched apron she was wearing – she had even produced a form for him to sign, giving his consent. He had wanted to tear it up and throw it in her face, but he knew that that would have been throwing away the only hope. Somehow he had seen it coming, had sensed, from the very first evening that he had visited Katy, still smelling of ether after she had come round from the anaesthetic in such obvious discomfort, that the operation had been bungled. When she had subsequently kept nothing down for three days, not even water, he had asked to see the surgeon, but the same Sister had looked at him askance. In any case, he had learned from her tonight that the man who had operated on his wife was now out of the country and, should another operation be necessary, it would have to be performed by his assistant, a Mr Reeves.

'Bloody man's probably gone on holiday,' Philip found himself muttering out loud, so that a woman in the seat in front of him turned round in indignation.

When the bus reached Dover Street, the conductor, who had been keeping an eye on him, tapped his shoulder and, not without a certain amount of relief, reminded him that this was his destination. Wearily, Philip Mason dragged himself to his feet and stepped down into Piccadilly. As he attempted to cross it, the driver of a cab sounded his horn angrily and he was forced to step back on to the kerb, watching with a kind of grim resignation the party of laughing, smartly dressed men and women inside. They would, he supposed, be off to a theatre – the place where Katy would have been a year or so ago.

He knew now, of course, only too well, that he should never have agreed to her dancing in that Musical which Kreiger had been backing. It had all been a most terrible mistake. They must have been mad, both of them. True, he had had certain reservations at the beginning, but his wife had been so keen and it was wonderful to see her completely lifted out of the depression from which she had suffered, intermittently, ever since Emily's birth. When comfortable, middle-aged Ellen from the shop had turned out to be such a splendid part-time nurse for the child, he'd given in. Besides, there was the financial aspect. It had nothing to do with anything Katy might earn – the last thing he had ever wanted or envisaged was a working wife — but Marcus Kreiger had generously offered to help him over the difficulties in which he had found himself, chiefly through rashly trying to branch out into the antiquarian book trade.

Philip Mason was well aware now that he had been just as foolish over this as he had been in letting Katy go on the stage, but rare books were something which had always appealed to him. He had also got the idea into his head that if only he could acquire some extra capital, he might be able to sit back and do something which appealed to him even more: write a book himself.

Initially, things had gone well. He was personable and gregarious and enjoyed visiting the homes of wealthy connoisseurs and patrons of the arts. That was how he first encountered his ostensible benefactor. But lacking specialized knowledge and with the world recession getting worse all the time, he soon realized he was in for trouble. Kreiger's offer couldn't have come at a more opportune moment. The man appeared so genuine, so anxious for Philip's enterprise to succeed. Having no wife or children of his own, he seemed set on taking the little Mason family under his wing. Both Katy and Philip had come to regard him more as a father figure than anything else. Neither had suspected that all those dinners at Boulestin's for the three of them, those trips to the country at weekends in his large Bugatti, the chauffeur to drive Katy home after the theatre, was just a way of leading up to what he was really after — and that was to get her into bed.

Philip would never forget the night she had been so late back. He had not worried at first, because she had telephoned, excitedly, to say that Kreiger wanted her to stop off for half an hour at his flat in Eaton Square, where he was entertaining an impresario whom he felt might help in furthering her career. When it got to well past midnight, Philip had become uneasy. Katy was not strong and usually wanted to get to bed as early as she could. He tried to ring Kreiger's number, but was told by the operator that it appeared to be out of order. He couldn't take himself round there because he couldn't leave Emily; for unless it was a very special occasion, Ellen did not sleep at Davies

Street. By two o'clock, he was almost demented. When, eventually, he heard a cab stopping outside the shop, he had run downstairs to open the side door and Katy had flung herself into his arms, sobbing.

There had been no further communication from Marcus Kreiger since then, other than a prompt, curt, business letter requesting the repayment of five hundred pounds. Philip hadn't known what to do, where to turn. His father was now dead but, in desperation, he had travelled to Wales to see his stepmother. Belle had certainly surprised him. He knew little about her other than that she was rich in her own right and, during the few years she and Francis Mason had been married, she had appeared to make him very happy. To Philip, the only scrap of comfort in the whole situation was the fact that his father, having finally passed the shop over to him completely, had never lived to witness what a mess his son had made of things. After talking to Belle, it occurred to him that possibly she had always had a shrewder idea of what was going on in the Davies Street establishment than her husband. He remembered her sitting there during his visit: a handsome well-preserved woman, with thick black hair drawn back into a tight bun and straight penetrating blue eyes; how she had listened to his halting confession in silence and, at the end of it, remarked, 'I wouldn't have thought you would have been quite such a fool, Philip. It seems to me that both you and Katy need your heads seeing to. I don't believe in lending money any more than I believe in borrowing it. You know the old adage: "Neither a borrower nor a lender be . . . "?'

Philip had found himself breaking out into a sweat and then, quite suddenly, Belle had gone across to her desk and picked up a pen. 'Here,' she had said, handing him a cheque for five hundred pounds. 'Take it. This is a gift. There will be no more forthcoming, mind. I advise you to go home and *work*. You must put your house in order. It seems to me that you and your pretty little wife have been burning the candle at both ends. Bright young things, eh? Poor dear Francis would turn in his grave. In a quiet way, he built up Mason and Son into one of the best small bookshops in the West End before he retired. You've let the side down. Oh, I know there's a depression on, but with all your advantages you should have been able to weather it. Incidentally, how is the child?'

'Emily? She's fine, thank God.'

'Good. You have a lot to be thankful for, Philip. Next time I come to London, I'll look in. By then, I'll probably have quite a fair-sized Christmas order.'

When he had tried to thank her for her generosity, she had cut him short. 'I don't want *words* of gratitude. I want *actions*. The best thanks you can give me would be if, by the time I come, I find things looking up.'

Philip Mason had gone back to London and taken his stepmother's advice to heart. With Katy now permanently at home and Ellen therefore able to resume her former full-time duties as a saleswoman, he had dispensed with two of his other assistants, sold off the remaining stock of rare books and spent all his own time in the shop. He knew he had been lucky, luckier than he deserved. He had been in a tight corner and Belle Mason had got him out of it. He did not intend to make the same mistakes again. Soon, his spirits rose. His natural optimism reasserted itself. With Katy by his side, he was confident that everything would come right. The country's economic problems couldn't, surely, go on indefinitely. Why, in a little while he might still be able to branch out again. Meanwhile, he would pay off Kreiger and keep to rigid accounting. He would go very carefully. He would economize in every way, not take any risks. There would be no more dining out. Indeed, how could there be, now that Kreiger was no longer picking up the bills. Katy and he would definitely not have another child – although this was something they had more or less decided on some time ago.

Philip had always been rather surprised that his wife who, after all, had once been a nursery maid to Lady Fairfax's grandson, did not seem to take more naturally to motherhood. It went without saying, of course, that they both adored Emily, but he sensed that the mental troubles which had afflicted Katy on and off since giving birth had much to do with feeling trapped by the demands

214

of a small infant. He supposed that was why Kreiger's offer had meant so much to her. A chance of escape. Katy, when she was not overburdened by responsibilities, was so different, so vivacious, so frivolous, even. She could be such a splendid companion, such fun to be with. And such a wonderful bedmate. He had always felt, during their courtship, that that would be the case once they were married. He hadn't been disappointed. He had rejoiced in the way she had given herself to him with such abandonment on their wedding night. He felt sure that Emily had been conceived there and then. He had never ceased to marvel at that side of her. Presumably, that bloody old goat, Kreiger, had sensed it, too.

Somehow, the memory of the man's treachery kept haunting him when he left the bus that night after leaving Katy in such distress, looking so white and drawn in St Thomas's Hospital. Possibly the difference between that and the sight of the carefree glamorous party in the taxi-cab had triggered it off. Of course, Kreiger had never actually *had* his wife. Katy, bless her, had seen to that, even if she had been forced to undergo such a strenuous, ignominious struggle with the brute before getting away. But, all the same, she had never been quite her old self, since. She had never attained those periods of light-hearted gaiety which, however fleeting, had so delighted him, had never – now he came to think of it – been quite such a passionate lover. She had become altogether quieter, more preoccupied. The bouts of depression which had sometimes attacked her seemed to have turned into a more permanent, lack-lustre malaise.

It had been some time before she mentioned any physical pain. He wondered now how long she would have kept it from him, had it not been for the fact that one Saturday evening, after he had finished doing the weekly accounts and had been pleased with the result, he had come up to bed earlier than usual and attempted to make love to her. For the first time that he could ever remember, she had resisted his advances, had caught hold of the hand which had begun to caress her breasts and buried her face in his chest with a muffled, 'Don't, please. Not tonight, Philip.'

215

Puzzled, he had waited a little while and then turned on the light. Nervously, she began to tell him. She had pointed to a place somewhere in the middle of her diaphragm which she said had been hurting for some time. At first, it had apparently only been an occasional niggle but, lately, it had become more constant, more acute. Tonight it was at its worst. In an effort to allay his fears, she had remarked that it was probably only indigestion – perhaps the herrings which she had bought that morning in Shepherd Market and cooked for their supper had not agreed with her.

Their doctor did not seem to take much notice when, on Philip's insistence, they had visited him the following day. He was a dour, elderly Scot, who had always made it rather obvious that he looked on Katy as a *malade imaginaire*. Some time ago, he had scribbled 'Neurasthenia' across her notes, a word which he had been apt to use, disparagingly, when confronted by overstrained or shellshock cases in the last war. It was only when, a few weeks later, Philip had found his wife doubled up with pain after bathing Emily, that Dr McGraw had made a domiciliary visit to Davies Street and agreed that perhaps some X-rays were called for.

The first results had been inconclusive; but, after a second, more thorough investigation, necessitating a twenty-four-hour stay in hospital, he had informed Katy's husband that the specialist at St Thomas's had advised 'bypassing the duodenum'. Philip knew little about such jargon, but had managed to enquire, 'You mean, because she has a duodenal ulcer?' Dr McGraw had then become evasive. 'Possibly,' he had replied, 'or . . . some kind of kink.' '*Kink?* What are you getting at?' In an agony of worry and suspicion, Philip became truculent. Was the doctor trying to tell him that Katy was dying from cancer, just as Flo, her eldest sister – the one he had never met – had done during the summer of 1920? It had not really helped when Dr McGraw had replied, coldly, 'I am simply trying to say, Mr Mason, that your wife has a very slight physique. She has always been thin. Lately she appears to have become thinner. Possibly some unusual exertion might have caused an . . . abnormality in the gut.'

The thought had not come to Philip straight away. When it did, the sheer horror of it had made him feel sick. 'Undue exertion', Dr McGraw had said. Of course, it *could* have been all that dancing . . . or the need to make some much more unnatural and frantic efforts. How about the night Kreiger had inveigled her into his flat, in which there had been no impresario – only the man himself, with his ageing execrable lust?

Philip had never mentioned such a supposition to his wife. He had discovered that 'bypassing the duodenum' was quite a commonplace operation at the time, almost fashionable, in fact. It seemed as well to let her and her family think that a gastric ulcer was the trouble. And for all he really knew, so it was.

Even tonight, as he hurried up Dover Street, down Hay Hill and into Berkeley Square, he still didn't know what was really the matter with his wife. Suddenly he realized that it was getting on for nine o'clock, and he had promised to telephone May at eight-thirty. He wondered what he should say when he got through to her. So far, he had managed to keep the seriousness of Katy's condition – especially since the operation – to himself. It was no good getting anyone else into a state, particularly his mother-in-law. The old lady might have one of her turns again, even lose her memory as she had apparently done once or twice before he had ever married her youngest daughter. Besides, she had never really liked him. She would be bound to think that Katy's illness was somehow his fault. Maybe it was, but that didn't make it any better. And once Sarah Lodge got an idea into her head, he knew from past experience that nothing would remove it. She would go on and on and then Emily would be bound to overhear her. Still, he'd have to say something about Katy's condition now – at least, to May. It seemed pretty certain that his wife would go under the knife again on Monday morning.

Once inside the shop, he went into his office at the back, sat down at his desk and stared at the instrument standing on it: tall, black and impersonal, like a candlestick. Eventually, with reluctance, he unhooked the receiver.

3

'Hello?' May Lodge did not like using the telephone. The long wait that evening at Mabel Snoad's had increased both her natural fear of the instrument and the dread of the news it might bring.

'I'm sorry I'm late.' Despite his weariness, Philip Mason made an effort to do his best. He liked his sister-in-law. She was a good sort – devoted to Katy and, it would seem, the child.

'How are . . . things?' May asked, warily. Philip's voice sounded faint and she pushed the hand which held the receiver close to her ear. She pictured him, eighty miles away in that strange, suspect, teeming metropolis, where she had only been once in her life – the time she had taken Katy to Upper Brook Street to begin her duties as nursery maid to Lady Fairfax's grandson. It was not that May hadn't wanted to see London again, nor that she hadn't been asked to go there. Katy and Philip had repeatedly suggested that she and her mother should spend a holiday with them. But unfortunately Sarah had been horror-stricken at the idea; for although she had occasionally travelled the three miles to Westonbury by train, she considered any longer rail journey to be far too hazardous. Therefore, because Sarah refused to leave Wilhampton for even a few days, May was obliged to remain there also.

. She did not think that she could have heard Philip aright when his next words came all the way down the line: unreal, unbelievable and, somehow, wholly shocking.

'I'm afraid . . . they're probably going to have to operate again, May.'

'*Again?*'

There was silence, and then Philip's voice sounded in her ear once more, 'Something's gone wrong. She can't keep anything down. A sort of complete blockage, I think.'

She could sense Mabel Snoad hovering, waiting on her words in the next room. As postmistress of Wilhampton there was little she was unable to ascertain through one means or another. It was common knowledge that steaming open envelopes had at one time been her forte. The advent of the telephone had but given her extra scope for such detective work.

'When will you know?' May drew the mouthpiece nearer to her face.

'Monday. I'll ring again Monday night.'

'Thank you, Philip.'

'How's Emily?'

'She's very well.'

'Good. Give her my love . . . and May?'

'Yes, Philip.'

'Keep all this from her, won't you?'

'Of course, my dear.'

After they had rung off, May Lodge sat for a while trying to grasp the full implications of what she had just been told. *Two* operations within a week. No nourishment of any kind in between. Dear God. How could any human being survive that? Especially Katy. She was far too delicate, as it was.

'Worse, is she?' She had not noticed Mabel come into the room until a shadow fell across the table where she was sitting and her moon-like face with the pebble glasses peered at her, curiously.

May stood up. 'I'm afraid the news . . . isn't too good. Perhaps you wouldn't mind if I came in again to wait for another call on Monday evening, Mabel?'

'No, of course not. Anything I can do to help. Would you like a cup of tea, dearie?'

'No thanks. I must be getting back. I'm late enough as it is. Mother will be so anxious.' She picked up her handbag.

'Yes . . . yes. Your poor Mother.' Mabel came with her to the door, obviously disappointed that no further titbits of information were forthcoming.

It was quite dark now – and cold. Instead of the hot clamminess which May had experienced while telephoning, she began to feel shivery. As she hurried along East Street and was about to turn into River Lane, she caught sight of a tall thin figure coming towards her. When it passed beneath a gas lamp, she recognized it as none other than Maurice Fitzherbert.

'Good evening, May.' He removed his dark stiff-brimmed trilby. Like the good doctor he was, his manners and appearance could never be faulted, something which May had invariably noted and appreciated. 'Have you heard about Katy, today?' he went on, his keen blue eyes searching hers, anxiously.

'Yes. I've just been speaking to Philip on the telephone.' She paused. She could feel the tears beginning to well up, uncontrollably. Then, without exactly meaning to, she burst out, 'There might have to be another operation, Maurice.' She did not often address him by his Christian name only, but tonight he was not merely 'the doctor'. He was the man who had wanted to marry her youngest sister and who she had a feeling was, even now, still in love with her.

'Oh, *May!*' He seemed stunned. 'Did Philip . . . say anything else?'

'Not very much. I gather . . . things didn't go right. Nothing's getting through. There's a sort of stoppage . . .'

Without replying, he began accompanying her back to the Mill House in silence. He knew that there could be post-operative strictures after any abdominal operation and presumably that was what had now happened. But from all he had heard of the case, he could not help wondering whether Katy had been opened up unnecessarily. If she had an ulcer he was of the opinion – although aware that he was very much in a minority – that it could be treated by rest and diet; whereas this diagnosis of a possible 'kink in the gut' – recently hailed with such enthusiasm by the medical profession – seemed to him a complete fallacy. The only kink as far as he was concerned was in the mind of the eminent surgeon who had first propounded it.

When they reached the gates, he waited and held out his hand. 'Katy has great courage, May,' he said. 'She may not be strong, but she's overcome a lot of illness in the past. I remember my father telling me how she pulled through from diphtheria and meningitis as a child. Don't lose hope. Perhaps . . . I might call on you and your mother on Monday evening?'

'Oh, yes. Thank you, Maurice. We should like that very much.'

We should like that *whatever happens*, she found herself thinking, as she passed through the smaller gate and locked up for the night. *Whatever happens* it would be good to have Maurice Fitzherbert around. He was such a tower of strength. If only Katy could have fallen for him as he had for her. She would be here, now, in Wilhampton, probably fit and well, the *doctor*'s wife. But it wasn't to be. She'd been set on Philip. You could see that in her eyes whenever he came to the mill. She had never looked at Maurice that way, even though she liked and respected him so much. He would never have settled down at East Lodge. And, of course, while his parents had still been living in part of the house, it wouldn't have been easy. Maurice's poor crippled father would never have made trouble, but his wife – 'Old Mother Mothballs', as May had always privately thought of her – would have been a trial for any daughter-in-law. It was said that there had been no love lost between her and Maurice's wife right from the start, even though the girl had come from a good family. And May was well aware that Mrs Fitzherbert senior had never thought Katy good enough for her son. In her eyes, a daughter of the late manager of the Felt Mills was not at all suitable, especially with an elder sister who had actually married one of the mill hands.

She could see Sarah standing at the open door of the Mill House before she ever reached it. On coming closer, she noticed the strain on her face and the way she was clasping and unclasping her hands in that curious 'washing' movement which she adopted whenever she was particularly distressed.

'She's worse, isn't she? Don't try to hide it from me, May. I knew, when you were gone so long.'

'Yes, Mother.' She realized that it was no good trying to keep it from Sarah now. She would have to know.

'What is it? What's happened?'

'They might have to do a second operation.'

'Oh, my God.' It was only in extreme mental agony that such an ejaculation ever escaped Sarah's lips. Now, as she went back into the living room and sat down in her usual chair, she repeated it twice, rocking her body to and fro while covering her face with her hands.

May fetched some milk from the stone slab by the tiny window at the back of the hallway, poured some into a saucepan and set it on the range. Then she went across to the glass-fronted cabinet and extracted a small bottle of cheap cooking brandy that was kept there strictly for medicinal purposes. It was possible, she thought, that such measures might be even more necessary within the next forty-eight hours, but she hadn't liked what she had seen in Sarah's face tonight, that strange, stricken, wild-eyed look that had sometimes preceded one of her 'turns'.

'Drink this, Mother,' she said, at length, handing her a glass. For a moment, she thought Sarah was going to refuse to take it, but then, suddenly, she seemed to capitulate and held out her hand.

'You've laced it, haven't you, my girl,' she said, after taking a sip or two.

'Only a little, Mother. It'll help you to sleep.'

'And what good is sleep to me? It can't help Katy.'

'No, but we must all . . . do our best to keep calm. After all, there's Emily to consider.'

At the mention of the child's name, Sarah said no more.

On Sunday morning May did not take Emily to church as she had intended, because she was fairly certain that Maurice Fitzherbert would have been in touch with the Reverend Donaldson and prayers would be said for Katy. The child would then be bound to ask questions. She therefore suggested that Sarah might go to matins and that she and Emily should stay home, cook the dinner and start to make the doll's dress.

It seemed a sensible arrangement and one with which her mother could scarcely disagree. When the bells of St Mark's began to ring out at quarter to eleven, Sarah Lodge walked slowly up River Lane, a tall, still handsome woman, proudly erect – despite her rheumatism – wearing her best black serge coat and velour hat with the pearl hat pin, black leather gloves, and carrying her prayer book and large black leather handbag which, like her black leather lace-up boots, had been carefully polished that morning.

Inside the Mill House, May covered Emily's Sunday dress with a makeshift apron, put some flour in a basin and broke two eggs into the well which she had made in the centre. Then, with some milk in a jug ready to be gradually poured into the mixture, she began instructing her niece into the art of making batter. She did not herself feel much like eating roast beef and Yorkshire pudding today and she doubted that Sarah would either. But they had a guest, a little thing with a good appetite who seemed to enjoy what she called the 'smoky' food cooked on her grandmother's open range. Besides, whatever the circumstances, such fare was almost a ritual observance in Wilhampton on the Sabbath, even if, throughout the years, Sarah had been forced to buy only the cheaper cuts, such as flank or buttock, sometimes remarking, with satisfaction, after returning from her Saturday morning shopping, that she had made a 'good buy' or had purchased a 'pretty piece of meat'.

While the meal was cooking, May set to work cutting out the dress she had promised, while Emily watched her every movement, explaining the necessity for a very pretty one so that Greta would look either like her own mother or the film star, Greta Garbo, after whom the doll had apparently been named.

'When you've finished, Aunt Chip, I'll draw a picture of her to send to Mummy. She'd like that, wouldn't she?'

'Yes, dear.'

'When do you think she'll come home from the hospital?'

'I'm not . . . sure, Emily.' May spoke slowly, choosing her words with care. 'She may have to stay there quite a while.'

'Is she ill like she was when she was a little girl?'

'Something like that.'

'Did you look after her then?'

'Well, I suppose we all helped.'

The child became pensive. Presently, she said, 'It must have been nice having brothers and sisters. Where are they all now, Aunt Chip?'

Dear God, what a little cross-questioner she was. A veritable sea-lawyer, May felt. It wouldn't do to go into the family history, not at this moment, with Katy at death's door. In any case, how could one ever explain death to a seven-year-old? How did one tell her that her Uncle Frank was killed in the Great War? Emily didn't know what war was. That her aunt Flo had died in agony from cancer when she was only thirty-one. That Sergeant Henry Lodge hardly ever came home because he had had a shotgun marriage to a Frenchwoman who had given birth seven months after the wedding and Sarah had never forgiven him. That Neil . . . There was no way she could tell Emily that Uncle Neil had not been quite right in the head, that sex had finally destroyed him at the age of twenty-one, when, having failed to violate his sister, Katy, he had gone after young Ena Perrick at the top of River Lane and, in the process, fallen into the Willon and drowned.

May laid down the half-made doll's dress and took off her spectacles. 'Your aunt and two of your uncles are in heaven, Emily,' she said quietly. 'I'm sure you will come to know your Uncle Henry one of these days, and some-time soon we'll go up to downside and visit Aunt Edith and your cousins again.'

'This afternoon?'

May hesitated. 'Not this afternoon, I think, Emily. But we might take a short walk up through the meadows while your grandmother is resting.'

Somehow, May did not want to leave Sarah alone too long. Besides, Edith and her family would not be exactly ideal company at this particular time. There would be no chance of talking to her sister and brother-in-law by themselves, not with all the children milling around. There were six of them now: noisy, out of hand, not a bit like Emily. May felt that it might be as well if Katy's child did not mix too much with them. She chided herself for disloyalty, but she felt that Emily seemed to be cast in an altogether different mould, a different class. She had already noted the wondering, almost perplexed, look in the child's eyes when Edith had brought all her brood down to the Mill House a few days ago, how Emily had failed to understand much of what they were talking about because of the broadness of their accents, how surprised and even shocked she had been at some of their table manners, and how Edith herself had been obviously embarrassed, so marked was the difference between the cousins.

It was strange, May reflected, that considering her own upbringing, Edith had let herself go so much, how her appearance, at times, though not exactly slatternly, was careless, how she seemed to lack the willpower or energy to discipline herself or her children. May was aware that her lot was not easy, that her husband's weak heart was a constant source of anxiety to her. But Edith had so many advantages which her own mother had never had: an indoor tap, for instance, a front and a back room, a wash house and a pull-the-chain privy, both within a stone's throw of the back door.

'What are you thinking about, Aunt Chip?' Emily's voice brought May's reveries to an end.

'I'm sorry, my dear.' What was she thinking about? She looked at the child, fondly. 'I was wool-gathering, I expect.'

'Wool-gathering?'

'Yes, bless you. Thinking about the past — and the present. Now, how about us seeing whether the potatoes have turned a nice brown. Your grandmother will soon be back from church.'

4

Contrary to all fears and misgivings on the part of her family and friends — and even the medical staff who attended her — Katy Mason pulled through her second operation. For five days, while she was still on the danger list, her young husband travelled backwards and forwards

225

to St Thomas's Hospital in silent despair. At Wilhampton, May found it increasingly difficult to keep up a pretence of normality in front of Emily. Often, she sent the child out for a walk with Dora Parker, the undertaker's youngest daughter, whom she employed to help with the sewing. As for Sarah Lodge, she became more and more withdrawn, her face only showing signs of emotion when she stood at the door of the Mill House each evening, waiting for May to return from the Snoads' with the latest news.

It was not until the following Saturday that she saw her eldest daughter actually running through the gates, waving. For a moment, Sarah hesitated: unsure, half incredulous, half fearful of she knew not what. Then she, too, began to run forward awkwardly, holding out her hands. May caught them in both her own; her eyes had tears in them, but they were not unhappy ones.

'Oh, chippatoo, Mother! Katy's sat up and eaten some fish. She's out of danger. It's early days ... but they think ... everything will be all right now.' Suddenly, aware that even such good news was too much for Sarah, May put an arm round her and helped her back into the Mill House where, not long afterwards, there was a gentle tap on the door and they were joined by Maurice Fitzherbert. He had called on them every evening that week.

His whole being, May noticed, seemed to alter when they told him what had happened. It was impossible not to sense his cautious relief, his deep interest and concern as to the best way of caring for Katy after she came out of hospital.

'Perhaps, ... when she is strong enough for the journey ... she might recuperate here? With summer coming on, I can't think of a better place, nor two people who would look after her so well.'

May and her mother exchanged glances. 'Yes, Dr Maurice,' Sarah replied, quietly. 'We've hardly liked to discuss it before, but there's nowhere like home, is there, especially when you've been ill.' The fact that Katy already had a husband and home of her own in London seemed to be forgotten.

'There is, of course, Emily to consider,' May broke in.

'It's holiday time now, but her schooling . . . I'm not sure what her parents will want to do about that.' Of the three of them in the room, she seemed to be the most aware of the nuances, the uncertainties and possible complications of the situation. It was not that she wanted to prevent her sister from coming. Far from it. She knew how unsuitable London was for any convalescent. Moreover, in Davies Street who would look after both Katy and Emily? Ellen was wanted full-time in the shop and Philip could not possibly afford a nurse. Yet she was troubled. By the time Katy was allowed out of hospital her husband would have been on his own for some little while. He still seemed very much in love with his wife and, although a spell at the Mill House might be necessary and desirable, he probably would not take kindly to a further enforced parting, especially one where there was eighty miles between them. Besides, was there not someone else now sitting in this very room who, however impeccably he would always behave, was also still in love with her youngest sister? Much as May did not want to admit it to herself, she was beginning to feel, more than ever, that this was the case. Maurice Fitzherbert had never given her the impression that he was particularly happily married; and on the few occasions she had met Clare, his wife, she could understand why.

Yet from Sarah's next remark, it was obvious that she, at least, either could not or would not see that there were any problems in connection with Katy's being nursed back to health in her old home. 'Emily's bright enough as it is, May,' she said. 'And, if need be, she could always do a few morning lessons with Ethel Sharman round in St John's Green.'

So it came about that a month later Philip Mason brought a painfully thin, fragile young wife to stay for an unspecified length of time in Wilhampton. May arranged for a car to be at the station to meet them, and at four o'clock on the appointed day, she and Emily set out across the water meadows on foot, also in order to await the London train. Summer by now seemed to have settled itself in like a long-staying guest. The field known as Lower

Croft was bathed in sunlight and buttercups; the willow trees all appeared to have donned mantles of the palest green lace; a cuckoo called incessantly from somewhere over by Bulbarrow Farm. Emily, wearing a new mauve voile dress which her aunt had made specially for the occasion, skipped along with the same kind of *joie de vivre* that May remembered the child's mother had been apt to display from time to time. She hurried after her, a small trim figure – not quite as slim as she used to be – but, as always, faultlessly turned out, in a tussore navy-blue and white polka-dot two-piece, her fine fair hair now fashionably shingled, her clear blue eyes in the carefully powdered face almost as eager with anticipation as those of the little girl she was accompanying.

'Will the train blow its whistle over the Black Arch, Aunt Chip?' The railway bridge, so named because an engine had once caught fire thereon and consequently blackened the brickwork, seemed to hold a curious fascination for her niece.

'Not while your Mummy and Daddy are in it, Emily. They will be getting off before it reaches there.'

'Oh.' The child slowed down and kept at May's side for a while. 'Wouldn't Mummy sooner come back through the meadows like you said she loved to do when she was a little girl?'

'Not today, my dear. Your Mummy won't be able to walk very far yet. You must remember, she has had an operation.'

'Why did she have an operation, Aunt Chip?'

Why did Katy have an operation? Why, indeed. Philip had said that the doctors had been singularly evasive on the question; and no wonder, May felt, considering they had bungled everything so badly. From what she could gather they had merely referred to 'a little trouble' in something called the duodenum, which had now been successfully by-passed and Katy would, in time, be completely restored to health. At least, thank God, it was nothing like what had happened to poor Flo.

'Your Mummy had a sore spot in her tummy, Emily. She had to have an operation to make it well again,' May replied, and quickly changed the subject. 'Now, mind how you get over that stile. You don't want to catch the hem of your nice new dress.'

She took hold of her niece's hand as the London train, dead on time, steamed in to Wilhampton station. But as soon as Emily caught sight of her father alighting from one of the carriages, she broke away and hurled herself towards him. But when, after embracing her, Philip turned and held up his arms to lift the travesty of his once-pretty young wife down on to the platform, his small daughter looked back towards her aunt, half in puzzlement, half in fright.

We should have warned her, May said to herself. Even she had not imagined that her youngest sister would be quite so emaciated, quite so weak.

On the way back from the station in the old Buick six tourer belonging to Dora Parker's brother who had set himself up as the local taxi driver, May rode in front while Emily sat between her parents on the back seat. Although Katy had put an arm round her daughter, May sensed that even this was an effort, that she was utterly exhausted by the journey and that the child was both shocked and bewildered by the change in her mother.

It had been arranged that Philip should stay the night at the Mill House where, perforce, he would have to sleep in the front bedroom with his sick wife in the double bed which, under ordinary circumstances, was occupied by May and, during earlier times, had been given over to poor Flo and, before her, the hapless Neil. Today, as soon as the little carload arrived at the mill, Katy was immediately tucked up in it, after which there followed a not altogether companionable evening. Philip took his daughter for a walk. Sarah, meanwhile, kept muttering to May that her son-in-law had no business to have let things come to such a 'pretty pass'. Katy, upstairs, mercifully slept.

It was not until Philip Mason returned to London on Sunday evening that Sarah began to relax a little, exhibiting some of the careful, sacrificial attention to the needs of her youngest daughter as she had done many years ago. Often, of a morning, when May had taken Emily round to Ethel Sharman's to join in the lessons she gave to a few local children, Sarah would start to see about Katy's toilet. She would begin by bringing up a dipper of warm soapy water from the mill, pouring it into the blue and white china basin on the stand in the corner of the bedroom, after which, while her daughter was washing, she would turn and pummel the intractable feather mattress. Then, as soon as an ethereal but steadily improving Katy came down into the living room, she would insist on her drinking an egg flip before sending her out to lie in a long basket-work chair in the garden. The weather was glorious, that summer of 1929, and it was here where Maurice Fitzherbert invariably found her, as he stopped by for a few minutes each day after his morning surgery. From their separate vantage points in the workroom and the Mill House, May and her mother noted his visits but, because they were professional and undertaken in full view of all concerned, they did not always make it their business to be present, as they would automatically have done for any member of the family had they taken place in a bedroom or even a living room. Besides, since Katy's arrival, they had come to treat Maurice more and more as a greatly valued, long-standing friend.

One Saturday morning in the middle of June when Katy, with Emily helping her, was sitting in the sun shelling peas, she began to wonder whether it was not now time for her to return to London. She was feeling a great deal stronger and the enforced absence from her husband was beginning to worry her. Although, so far, Philip had managed to spend every Saturday night at the mill, he had written earlier that week to tell her that his stepmother would be in London on this particular one and had asked him to dinner at her hotel followed by a visit to the theatre to see a Cochran revue. He had gone on to say that he hoped she would not mind but, as Belle had been so good to him, he hardly liked to refuse. Katy knew that it was silly, even mean of her to mind – especially as travelling cost money and times were still so hard – yet she found herself minding very much. The thought of dinner and the theatre had reawakened some of the old longing for the life she had once known. She had no intention of ever going on the stage again. It was just that it would have been nice to dress up, go out and — here, she tried, but failed, to push the thought away — have her husband make love to her afterwards, not simply share the same bed in the careful, almost afraid-to-touch way he had done during his all-too-fleeting visits to the Mill House. Now that she was so much better she had begun to chide herself for not realizing how he must have been missing that side of their life together. Selfishly, she had felt too ill to care. Now, it was very much on her mind. If Philip had been coming to spend this Saturday night at Wilhampton as usual, she had been planning to surprise him, determined to make him resume their marital relations, whatever the doctors had warned him.

'You've stopped shelling, Mummy.' Emily's direct piping treble broke into her thoughts. 'And there's a big car drawn up at the gates,' the child continued, with a small frown on her face.

Katy started, and looked up to see a chauffeur opening a car door, out of which a tall elegant woman emerged, followed by a golden-haired boy slightly older than her own daughter. Then, as the two figures came towards them, she put the colander of peas down by her side, brushed some empty pods from the skirt of her dress and rose to greet her former employer and the child whom she had once helped to care for when she had been a nursery maid in Mayfair.

'Lady Moreton!' Katy held out her hand. 'And John William,' she added, turning and holding out her hand a second time. She did not say 'Master John'. Somehow, after all that had happened to her and with her own child standing by her side, it did not seem appropriate. Whatever the circumstances, there had always been a curious sense of decorum, even dignity, about each member of the Lodge family, no doubt initiated and instilled by Sarah, but never carried out to greater perfection than by her youngest daughter.

'Katy! What a lovely surprise. My mother said that you had been home ill, but I had no idea that you would still be here. I haven't seen you since we moved to Suffolk and sold 89 Upper Brook Street. I'm afraid we've only rather a dull flat in town nowadays. And can this really be Emily?' She, too, then shook hands with Katy's daughter, before remarking, 'John, take off your cap, for goodness' sake. Sometimes I wonder whether you've lost all your manners since going to that horrid prep school.'

Lady Fairfax's grandson removed his cap gravely and held out his hand to Emily, who took it with equal gravity. The two women, so different in their respective circumstances, nevertheless watched the little performance with the same kind of fond motherly indulgence, although Katy kept finding it hard to believe that she had once changed the nappies on both of them.

'We're staying at the Hall,' Alicia Moreton went on, 'because it's John William's half-term and as his school is so much nearer to Wilhampton than Bishopsdown his grandparents thought it would be such a splendid opportunity to see him. Something tells me that we shall often be this way now. And I'm afraid that I can't help being pleased about this for another purely selfish reason of my own, the one which has brought me here today.' She paused and gave Katy an almost conspiratorial grin. 'I was wondering whether your dear sister would be prepared to make me a . . . Oh, *good*, here she is.' Alicia broke off, as May came walking towards them, her face filled with pleasure at the sight of such unexpected visitors.

There followed further exchanges of news. Katy learned that John William's sister, Phoebe, had been left behind in Suffolk because she had just had her tonsils and adenoids out; that Nanny Barlow, though not quite so active, nevertheless still tried to rule the roost over the little girl and her young governess, insisting on constant doses of Parrish's Food and Virol; that on no account was Lady Moreton going to allow Phoebe ever to go to boarding school and that if she had been able to have her way, John would never have been sent away either. 'But, as he's down for Eton, his father thought . . .' Alicia flushed, letting her remark trail away, uncertainly.

When the two older women had disappeared inside the

workroom, Katy took the children over to the mill-race. For a while, they stood in silence, one on either side of her. Presently, the boy said, 'What is it for?'

She looked down at him and smiled, registering the handsome intelligent face. 'Well, at one time, it used to drive the big wheel that made the Felt Mills work. But nowadays electricity has taken care of all that.'

'So the mill-race isn't really necessary any more,' he continued, studying the swiftly-flowing water before it suddenly dropped into the frothy turbulence below him.

Katy hesitated. 'Not . . . exactly, I suppose.'

'Could you stop it, do you think?'

'Stop the mill-race?' This time she answered promptly, almost as if he had said something shocking. 'Oh no. One couldn't stop it. Besides, I can't imagine that anyone would want to. I think it will go on . . . for ever.'

She had a sudden startling feeling that she was taking part in a scene which had happened before. She was not acquainted with the expression *déjà vu* – she only knew that she was caught up in something immutable, beyond her control, as all-powerful as the race itself. She remembered how she had sat by it after her sister Flo's funeral, and how the words of the hymn they had sung at the service kept haunting her: *Time like an ever-rolling stream* . . . In spite of the heat of the day, she shivered slightly.

'I think we should go back and find your mother now, John,' she said, and the two children raced ahead of her through the garden.

'You look tired, lovey,' May remarked, as they stood at the mill gates, watching the huge Rolls slowly disappearing up River Lane on its way back to the Hall.

'Do I? It's nothing.' Katy turned and started walking back to the house. 'But I suppose . . . well . . . seeing John William and Alicia Moreton again after all these years . . . it takes one back, doesn't it?'

5

'If you went to the baker's at the Four Corners, Emily, and bought seven cakes for sixpence, how many would you get for a shilling?'

'Fourteen, Miss Sharman.'

'And if you went to Miss Clutterbuck's shop in the market square and asked her for a yard of ribbon at a penny-halfpenny a yard and then decided you wanted another yard, how much would you have to spend?'

'Threepence, Miss Sharman.'

'Quite right, Emily.' Ethel stood up, aware that four pairs of eyes were gazing at her expectantly. 'I think that will be all for this morning. You may get down now.'

Ethel Sharman had been giving private lessons in Wilhampton for twenty years, ever since she had left the teachers' training college in Westonbury at the age of twenty-two. She had been a pretty young woman with a wealth of light brown hair, large blue eyes and a creamy-coloured complexion. If anything, her teeth were too prominent – the result, so it was said, of having fallen down as a child and knocked her front ones loose. An ingenious dentist had fixed them back in again, but it had unfortunately left her with a slight speech impediment so that, already possessed of a shy, retiring nature, it was not perhaps surprising that she had remained a confirmed spinster. She had found teaching any large class of children altogether too nerve-racking. Indeed, on the few occasions she had attempted it, the perspiration running down from her armpits had ruined several woollen dresses. Therefore, when her father had died of consumption during the war – quickly followed to the grave by his grieving widow – Ethel, an only child, had eked out her inheritance in the family home by taking in the daughters of parents in the district willing to pay for her admirable, if old-fashioned, tuition. She did not go in for teaching little boys. For one thing, she was frightened of them. For another, she felt that they would have to be segregated from her little girls, which would have meant their coming in the afternoons when at least twice a week, if the weather was fine, she liked to take her various charges on nature walks.

Today, Ethel was rather hoping to have been able to have a private word with May Lodge when she came to collect her niece. Emily was still being escorted to and from the Mill House each day, although May had intimated that she did not think it would be necessary much longer, something with which Ethel entirely agreed. Emily was more than capable of walking the short distance alone. In fact, Emily was more than capable of a lot of things. That was the trouble. She was far and away the brightest pupil Ethel had ever taught and that was what she wanted to speak to May about.

Glancing out of the window, Ethel was rather pleased to see that the child's aunt had been waylaid on the green by the garrulous Mrs Betts, who no doubt wanted yet another outfit made for her. With any luck, she would be able to see the others off before May arrived at the front door. The Lamberts, the new people at Edenbury, the village just south of Wilhampton, were already waiting for Elsie Jane in their Model T Ford. Likewise, she could see Dick Swayne, from Bulbarrow Farm, nosing his lorry along the lane towards her house to pick up his youngest child. Ethel invariably worried about taking any money at all from him for teaching Helen, because she knew what a hard time of it he was having in the present agricultural depression. But when she had once demurred, he had said, like the good father he was, 'Money on education's well spent, Miss Sharman. A year or two with you will always stand Helen in good stead. I'd as soon sell another cow as see her go to the National School.'

As for Ethel's fourth pupil, the Reverend Donaldson's grand-daughter, there used to be a time when his gardener, old Harry Ford, would stump over the green with little Daphne Chadwick, who was being brought up at the Rectory because her parents were in India. But ever since last Christmas the child had been allowed to go to and fro by herself. Ethel was sorry to see her departing today looking a little glum, and was afraid that it was because Emily had given such an astonishingly good performance over her arithmetic. If it had not been for the fact that Ethel had a rather important cousin who worked in the Air Ministry coming to lunch and Bessie, her daily maid, had already laid the table in the dining room, she would like to have put Emily through her paces there, leaving the others by themselves to get on with various tasks in the sitting room. As it was, she realized that she had made Daphne jealous and, with her sensitive compassionate nature, Ethel did not like to see any of her pupils upset; even though, she had to admit to herself, it would have been nice if Emily's prowess could galvanize Elsie Jane into a little more effort.

When Ethel had eventually said goodbye to her three other charges and May was on the doorstep, she asked her if she would mind stepping inside the hall for a moment. Then, turning to Emily, she suggested that she might like to run into the garden and look for Jumbo, her tortoise. The child needed no second bidding, albeit well aware that Miss Sharman obviously wanted to 'talk secrets' with her aunt. She suspected that it must be something to do with her but, much as she would have liked to hear what it was, she would never have dreamt of not immediately acquiescing to Miss Sharman's wishes. Besides, Jumbo was really the greater attraction. He might, Emily knew, be *anywhere*: by the cucumber frame, under the crab-apple tree, hiding in the herbaceous border. He was very old, much older than Grandmother Lodge, and apparently he only moved about in the summer. Emily had never seen a tortoise before – London did not seem to have any – and Jumbo was therefore a constant source of interest and wonder. She ran off down the grassy path to the wall at the far end, on the other side of which she knew that there was a very important mysterious place: the Hall, where Lady Fairfax lived and where the golden-haired boy and his mother had been staying the time when they came to call at the mill. Emily would like to have taken a peep over the top of the wall, but it was far too high and there was such a forest of yew trees behind it that she doubted she would be able to see very much; she knew she would simply have to wait until Aunt Chip took her there one day, as she had promised to do.

Back in the house, as soon as Emily was out of earshot, Ethel Sharman said quickly, 'As there might not be many more opportunities, Miss Lodge, I thought I should just like to tell you that I consider your niece to be an exceptionally clever child. Academically, I would say that she is at least a year in advance of her age.'

'A *year*!' Flattered, May stored up Ethel's words verbatim, anxious to relay them to Sarah once Emily had gone to bed that night. 'We always felt she was bright,' she continued, 'but . . . well . . . a whole year! You do surprise me, Miss Sharman.'

'Yes, and it's not only over certain subjects, you understand. She is as good at sums as she is at composition. Sometimes I feel, if it were not for the unusual circumstances, she is almost wasting her time here. The others are keeping her back, although it isn't necessarily a good thing for a bright child to be brought on too quickly. Of course, it is never easy for one person, trying to deal with different ages and levels of intelligence. But I feel I am in charge of a little girl with great originality of thought and I naturally don't want to go wrong. Have you any idea what plans her parents have for her schooling?'

'No. I must ask my sister. At present she goes to a small Church of England school near where they live in London.'

'And she will be resuming her classes there after this summer?'

'Yes, Miss Sharman. Her parents will both be coming down to Wilhampton in August to fetch her home again. I'm sure we're all very grateful to you for agreeing to coach Emily for the time being.'

'It's been a pleasure, I assure you.' Ethel's eyes strayed towards the end of the garden where Emily was still running up and down, obviously unable to locate the tortoise. 'I suppose,' she continued quietly, and here a certain wistfulness seemed to creep into her voice, 'that it comes but once in a governess's life – indeed, sometimes never at all – to have the privilege of a gifted child in her hands. Sometimes I feel that my nature walks with Emily, the ones we have taken alone, are my best way of helping her. Living in London as she does, she seems so anxious to learn all about the flora and fauna. It is almost as if she is . . . how shall I put it? . . . starved of the countryside. Do you know what she said to me the other day? "Miss Sharman, wouldn't it be nice if the River Willon and Grandmother's house and the mill-race were all in Hyde Park, instead of the silly old Serpentine? I don't suppose I shall ever find meadow-sweet and heart's-ease there." Ah, look, she seems to have found Jumbo at last. I must be keeping you, Miss Lodge. Forgive me.'

On the way home, Emily chattered away happily, informing her aunt that Helen Swayne had asked her and Daphne and Elsie Jane to tea on the following Saturday. With Ethel Sharman's words still very much in her mind, May could not help noticing – not for the first time – how well the child had settled down and how comparatively little she missed her parents and her London home. Although she had shed a few tears at the station on the day they had waved goodbye to Katy some weeks previously, Emily had soon begun looking for wild flowers as they walked back to the Mill House through the meadows, remarking, excitedly, that Miss Sharman had promised to take her up to Breconbury Woods on their next nature walk to look for a very special kind of orchid. 'Although if we find it, I shan't be able to tell you exactly where it is, Aunt Chip,' she had said. 'Miss Sharman says we must keep it a secret, because if other people got to know, they might go and pick it and then there wouldn't be any more.' Almost, May had felt a stab of jealousy.

It was as if Emily had somehow come to regard the whole locality as her spiritual home. Although she was a naturally healthy happy child, it seemed Ethel was right in sensing that living at the Mill House satisfied something important which she lacked in London. May wondered what would happen when she returned there. She knew that she herself would miss her niece profoundly. She had never consciously thought about it before, but she realized now that Emily, in turn, supplied her with something which she, too, needed: the fulfilment of her maternal instinct which, since her youngest sister had married and left home, had been sadly frustrated. Wryly, she reflected that in this connection she and Ethel Sharman were probably sisters in distress.

May hoped that everything was going well for Katy now. She had doubted that she had been fit enough to return to Davies Street and Sarah had been openly hostile about it. Yet they had been unable to prevent her. Katy had suddenly behaved almost as she had done on the night when she had dashed out of the Mill House after Philip, just before their marriage, desperately afraid that she was going to lose him. As for the fact that she now had a child to consider, she had obviously been only too relieved to leave Emily behind at Wilhampton. It was undoubtedly the most sensible solution and May suspected that the child's mother was well aware that she was not yet capable of caring for a home, a husband and an energetic small daughter. Moreover, the summer was so exceptionally fine, with day upon day of glorious sunshine, that it seemed virtually cruel to condemn Emily to the confines of a flat over a London shop when there was such a splendid alternative eighty miles away.

All the same, although May was overjoyed at still being able to look after Emily at the mill, she was uneasy about the situation. She noted the letters which Katy wrote regularly to her daughter — simple, sensible and cheerful — saying how much both she and her father were looking forward to seeing her again in August. Equally regularly, she supervised the child's replies in immature yet — considering her age — well-formed script, illustrated by copious annotated and amazingly graphic drawings of her grandmother, her aunt, Miss Sharman, Jumbo and the other children with whom she had become friends. (There were also, May was interested to see, frequent pictures of the mill-race which, although looking more like a burst water main than anything else, nevertheless obviously meant something in Emily's young life.)

Yet in the letters which May and Sarah received, the former noticed a curious restraint, a lack of her sister's usual spontaneity, a feeling that Katy was, perhaps, hiding something, doing her best under difficult circumstances. May hoped that her doubts and fears were groundless and that Sarah had not detected any underlying distress, but even as she hoped she knew that Sarah, with her almost uncanny perception, would have suspected something.

One evening, when the two of them were sitting on upright chairs outside the front door of the Mill House, because the heat of the day had made the interior of the living room – with its open range for cooking – almost unbearable, Sarah said, 'Katy's not happy, is she? Something's wrong.'

'Wrong, Mother?' May replied, procrastinating.

'Oh, come off it, my girl. For goodness' sake, you can't fool me. You must surely have read between the lines. It's my belief the trouble's more in the mind than the body this time. Illness always puts a strain on any marriage, particularly if it's the wife who's the invalid.'

May noted that her mother appeared to have conveniently forgotten how much she herself had been instrumental in aiding and abetting Katy and Philip's separation and thus possibly accentuating whatever was the present problem.

6

Katy had been back in London for several weeks before suspicion became certainty. It happened one day when she was going out through the shop and the postman handed her the twelve o'clock delivery. Philip was busy at the time, talking to Ellen about the 'window' he wanted her to do after closing that evening for a new novel, *The Man Within*, by a young writer called Graham Greene. Katy took the letters back into the inner office to place on her husband's desk, glancing through them as she did so to see if there was one with a Wilhampton postmark, especially one written in Emily's large but increasingly well-formed script.

Today, however, there appeared to be nothing for her;

240

yet there was a thickish envelope addressed to Philip in mauve flamboyant writing which had evidently been posted in New York some ten days previously. She knew that he occasionally received business communications from America, but these were always typed. This particular letter had something very personal about it and was obviously written in a female hand.

For the rest of the day her imagination took hold of her to such an extent that she went about in anguish, attempting – but failing – to come up with any satisfactory explanation for such a curious missive. Neither she nor Philip had any personal connections overseas, unless she counted her only surviving brother's intermittent postings to Germany or Belle's trips to Monte Carlo in the winter. But she happened to know that both these individuals were at present in England and, besides, the handwriting on the envelope was completely unknown to her.

Usually, if anything of interest occurred during the day, Philip seemed only too anxious to talk to his wife about it in the evening; but on this occasion, when supper was over and he had still not referred to the letter at all, Katy could hardly contain herself any longer. When he suggested a short walk across Hyde Park she acquiesced readily, hoping against hope that this would give him the opportunity of saying something to her which would allay her fears. Yet, when they had sat by the Serpentine for at least a quarter of an hour and still he had only spoken of purely mundane matters, she suddenly turned to him and said, 'I saw you had a letter from New York this morning.'

'New York?' He remained staring out across the water.

'Yes. As it was hand-written, I couldn't help wondering who it was from.'

He was silent for so long that she knew her instinct had not let her down. Presently, with an effort at casualness, he went on, 'Oh, it was just from someone I met . . . with Belle, as a matter of fact.'

'With *Belle*! You mean that time she took you out?'

'Yes. It was quite accidental. She didn't plan it or anything. But some American professor she happened to know was staying at her hotel and joined us for dinner.'

'Oh.' For a moment relief swept over her. 'I hope he wants you to send him a nice lot of books.'

Again there was silence. When his reply eventually came, the words seemed to eat into her. For the first time since she had recovered from her illness, she began to feel sick. 'Well, no . . . Actually, it was his daughter who wrote.'

'*Daughter*?' She sat bolt upright on the green wooden bench, her hands clenching and unclenching. There was almost a look of her mother about Katy now. Two bright spots of unnatural colour appeared on either cheekbone. 'Is that the reason,' she continued, slowly, 'that you have not made love to me since I came home, Philip?'

This time he turned to face her and held out his hand – but she did not take it.

'Yes, Katy,' he replied, huskily.

She stood up then and began to run, blindly, hopelessly, in the direction of Park Lane. Quickly, he caught up with her and, slipping an arm firmly round her waist, forced her to slow down and walk beside him. 'Listen, my love,' he said, 'you haven't given me a chance to explain.'

'There isn't any need. There is nothing to explain.' She tried to break away, her large grey eyes full of resentment and hostility, but he managed to pull her down beside him on to another seat.

'But there is, Katy. There is.' He spoke urgently, the words tumbling out, disjointed yet forceful, willing her to accept them. 'I'm never going to see Jessie McCutcheon again. I don't want to. It was . . . something which happened . . . quite by chance. It had nothing to do . . . with love. On either side. *Please* understand that. I love you, Katy. I always shall. But . . . well . . . it had been a long time since . . . I mean, the doctors warned me. Those weekends when I came to the mill were pretty good torture really, having to share the bed and not being able to . . . When I stayed in London because of Belle, it was a relief in a way. Oh, I'm *sorry*, my love. But you must see. I mean, this girl made it quite plain that she was prepared to . . . fulfil a certain need.'

She was crying now and he took out a handkerchief and passed it to her.

'Where . . . did it take place? Not . . . in Davies Street?'

'Good God, no. What do you take me for? You don't think I'd be such a cad as to . . .' He broke off and looked at her miserably, unable to think of a less offensive expression than 'foul the nest'. Presently he went on more quietly, 'Belle went back to Wales that Sunday and the Professor pushed off to Scotland. Jessie suddenly rang me up and said she hadn't seen enough of London. That might have been an excuse, of course, but apparently she'd never been here before, even though she'd "done", as she put it, most of the other European capitals. She simply stayed on by herself for a few days in a private suite of rooms.'

Blinking back tears, she asked him, 'Was she pretty?'

This time he almost laughed with relief at her simple, typically feminine question. 'No. Not at all. To me, there's never been anyone prettier than you, Katy, and you know it. Jessie was smart, certainly, and like all Americans pretty experienced. But if you really want to know, she had a rather long horse-like face. I should say she was probably quite a few years older than either of us.'

'But why was she writing to you, if you're never going to see her again?'

'I think it was simply her way of saying goodbye. Tidying things up. I suppose it was silly of her. She should have guessed you might be home again. For all her sophistication, I don't think she was maybe all that bright. You can read her letter if you like.'

Katy shook her head. The fact that he had offered to show it to her suddenly made it seem unnecessary, even distasteful. She knew that he was speaking the truth, that he was somehow glad that the affair was out in the open. Of course, things could never be quite the same again. Their marriage had suffered a crisis and she was not sure how their life together would take shape from now on. But Philip had told her that he still loved her and she would – indeed, she must – hang on to that. She was aware that, despite all that she had been told, she still loved him, and she sensed that he had been just as haunted during the past few weeks as she had. Thank God that at least the uncertainty and unaccustomed wariness of each other was at an end. She was still too shaken and upset to think quite clearly, but somewhere, in the back of consciousness, something told her that in future she must pay more attention to that curious sixth sense which had suddenly sent her back to London, albeit this time too late. After all, she was the seventh child of a seventh child, wasn't she? May always kept reminding her of that.

When Philip suggested that it was time to start home, she did not demur, but walked silently beside him, still pondering over the events of the past few months and how much easier it seemed to be for men to be led astray than women. No matter how ill Philip might be, she did not think she could ever be unfaithful to him. This business about Jessie 'fulfilling a need', was that only a male prerogative or necessity, the gratification of which had to be expected and accepted – or, at least, tolerated – by a wife, especially a sick or absentee one? Certainly, if the boot had been on the other foot, she doubted that Philip would have behaved as submissively as she was now doing. She recalled how demented he had been the evening when she had returned from Kreiger's flat. She wished she knew more about men, that she was not still, at the age of twenty-seven, so hopelessly naïve. Probably being the youngest, frailest and most cosseted member of the family hadn't helped. Nor, she supposed, had marrying so young and becoming wrapped up in her husband stood her in any better stead – at least, from that point of view. If she hadn't been so shielded all her life, she would probably have become aware much earlier, firstly of her poor simple brother's designs on her and, later, that bounder, Kreiger.

Katy had never consciously given sex a great deal of thought, other than it was something which, with her husband, she wanted and enjoyed very much. After Emily's birth she had left it to Philip to take all the necessary precautions against having another child. Indeed, in the early years of their marriage she felt that there seemed little else she could do. Only back-street pharmacies sold contraceptives for women and these were not always reliable. She could not possibly have afforded to go to the strange gynaecologist who had set up in London and fitted intra-uterine rings. But she was certainly not unacquainted with the influence which Dr Marie Stopes was having in the country and had read her book *Married Love*, Philip having acquired a few copies which he kept 'under the counter'. Suddenly she found herself wondering whether she should not have taken more of the responsibility for birth control — as it was now called — upon herself. Was this what her husband had meant when he had described Jessie McCutcheon as having 'experience'?

They paused for a moment outside the shop and she waited while he checked Ellen's window display and nodded approvingly. Then, as he got out his key and opened the side door, standing back to let her enter first, he said, gently, 'A penny for them, my love.'

She managed a small smile. It was not natural for her to remain withdrawn or to keep any secrets from him for long. 'I was thinking about men and women . . . and sex,' she added, simply.

'Really?' He closed and locked the door. There was a look in his eyes which she had not seen for a very long time. Then he gathered her in his arms and carried her upstairs to bed.

7

'They won't move you up, will they, now you've been away so long?' 'My mum said you'd been very ill.' 'We've learnt to subtract pounds, shillings and pence.'

Emily Mason stood in the girls' playground of St Nicholas's Church of England school at the start of the autumn term. She looked very brown compared to the other children surrounding her, most of whom had never been away from London in their lives. Few of her contemporaries' parents could afford a seaside holiday, especially in the present economic depression, although Patsy Milward had apparently spent a week at Clacton and Mary Gaunt had been taken to a boarding house in Bournemouth for a whole fortnight because her father — who worked in the post office – had won a fifty-pound prize for writing a clever 'bullet' in one of *John Bull*'s weekly competitions.

Emily did not mind the various remarks directed at her. She had hitherto always been a popular child and she realized that her friends could hardly be expected to know what had happened to her. Without precocity yet with an appealing old-fashioned dignity, she now proceeded to tell them.

'I've been staying with my Granny and my Aunt Chip – well, Aunt May, really, but that's what I call her – because it was my mother who was ill. Not me. She had to have an *operation*.'

There was a chorus of suitably impressed 'Ohs'.

'So I had private lessons. In the country.'

'Private?' Her audience looked a little out of its depth. Someone said, 'You mean, just you and the teacher?'

'Well, there were three others. And she wasn't a teacher. She was a governess. We went to her house for lessons every morning. She had a tortoise.'

'A *tortoise*?' Several pairs of eyes regarded Emily with increased interest.

'Where did she keep it?' It was Mary Gaunt speaking. 'In her back yard?'

'No. In her garden. She had a big garden, like my Granny.'

'Oh.' The pupils of St Nicholas's knew what gardens were but to have had the run, so to speak, of *two* large ones all the summer was a little difficult for them to envisage.

'Was there grass, like in the parks?' asked Patsy Milward.

'Yes. Lots and lots of grass. And at my Granny's there was a river. A big river and lots of little rivers. There was a place in the big river called a mill-race, where it went extra fast and then dropped down into a kind of whirlpool. And there were flowers. Ever so many of them. Roses and honeysuckle. My Granny's closet was covered with honeysuckle.'

'Closet?'

For the first time Emily hesitated a little. 'She didn't have a lavatory indoors,' she explained, guardedly. She did not add, 'nor a tap either,' and was a little relieved when the bell sounded for morning prayers.

At the end of the day, Miss Jamieson, who had been teaching Emily for every lesson – the child having been automatically moved up on the strength of her natural intelligence and the fact that she had had private tuition – tapped on the headmistress's door and asked if she might have a word with her about 'the Mason child'.

'Emily Mason, Miss Jamieson? What about her?' asked Mrs Bailey, removing her spectacles and giving all her attention to her young but, as she sometimes felt, rather too intense assistant.

'She's been brought on, Mrs Bailey. Too fast for her own good, if you ask me. Of course she always was forward, but if she stays in Lower II for another year, she'll simply be marking time.'

Mrs Bailey gave a small frown. She was a good woman, in some ways not unlike Ethel Sharman, except that she possessed the confidence and capacity to accept responsibility for many children whereas Ethel could only manage a few. She had lost her young husband in the war and, with great fortitude, resumed her teachers' training, after which she had quickly risen to her present position. The study of character absorbed her, be it that of her pupils, her teachers or her friends and neighbours. The only person with whom she did not get on was Mr Corbett, her opposite number in St Nicholas's Boys' school. There appeared to be some personal feud between them, the origin of which was something of a mystery. This afternoon, when Frances Jamieson tapped on her door, she had rather been hoping to indulge in what she sometimes jokingly referred to as her 'secret vice': her second Kensitas cigarette of the day. But with Maud Bailey duty always came before pleasure. She asked Frances to sit down and picked up her fountain pen, turning it over in her hands in much the same way as she began turning the problem of Emily Mason over in her mind.

'If we move her up into Lower III, Miss Jamieson,' she said, thoughtfully, 'I am a little concerned about the effect it might have on her from the point of view of the friends she will leave behind. As a matter of fact Emily's parents came to see me before term started. I realize we may have scholarship material on our hands. Mr Mason feels he is now in a position to send Emily to Court House School next year and her name has been put down there. I shall be sorry to see her leave but I know it will be for the best. In the meantime, I don't want . . .' Maud Bailey searched around for a suitable way of expressing herself and then continued, 'Emily to become too aware of her potential. She is at present such a friendly, natural, outgoing child. It would be a pity to do anything that might change her.'

'Oh, I appreciate that, Mrs Bailey. I wouldn't like to see her . . .' This time it was Frances Jamieson who was temporarily at a loss for words. 'Puffed up,' she eventually added.

'No.' 'Conceited' was the word which Maud Bailey felt she might have used herself. She had a sudden vivid mental picture of Emily and her mother, walking across the small square at the back of the school, and how impressed she had always been by the way both of them were turned out. Mrs Mason was a cut above the usual mother who escorted her child to and from St Nicholas's. Maud knew that she had been very ill lately. She also knew that if it had not been for the hard time Mr Mason had been through, financially and emotionally, Emily would probably have been sent to Court House before now. The question of whether to make further changes in the life of a child who had already suffered considerable upheaval of one sort or another during the course of the year was something she felt she wanted a little time to think about. With that rare insight and common sense which had so swiftly secured her the post she now held, Maud Bailey said, 'Miss Jamieson, I was wondering whether perhaps it might be a good idea if, tomorrow, in your composition class, you asked the pupils of Lower II to write about what they had most enjoyed last summer. I should like to see Emily Mason's effort. Then I might be better able to judge what to do for the best.'

The following evening, having dealt with a complicated letter about the leasehold of St Nicholas's, and a curt missive from Mr Corbett asking how many girl pupils would be taking part in the nativity play at Christmas, Mrs Bailey sat in the small home she had been assigned next to the school, lit a cigarette and picked up a piece of lined paper, headed in clear bold handwriting: *Last Summer* by Emily Mason. 'Last summer,' she read,

I went to stay with my Grandmother and my Aunt May. [She noted that the word 'Chip' had been carefully crossed out.] They live at the Mill House, Wilhampton. Granny did not like my dancing the Charelstone. But she was kind at other times. My Aunt May looked after me most. She is nice and makes dolls dresses and says O Chip-patoo when she is happy. I went to lessons with Miss Sharman. At first Aunt May took me but then I was aloud to go by myself. Miss Sharman has a tortuss. His name is Jumbo.

At the mill they make felt. There are lots of black cats who sleep on the bags of wool. There is also a big river and lots of little rivers. The big river goes fast and has something called a mill-race. Sumtimes I went into the mill and watched my granny doing her washing in a big tub while she sang hyms. All round about there are meadows. They are bright green and smell riverry. They have fethery flowers in them called Meddow Sweet. They also have lots of cows who flick there tails to keep off the flys. Miss Sharman sumtimes took me to the woods on the hill to look for orkids. There was one all yellow with purpil spots. It grows in a very secret place that only Miss Sharman and me know about.

I am looking forward to going back soon. The mill is a lovely place and my Granny cooks lovely dinners and sumtimes she buys lardy cakes for tea. My Mummy says the mill-race will go on for ever and ever and ever so I should like to live there for ever and ever and ever too.

Maud Bailey took off her spectacles, which she was a little disconcerted to find had become misted over. Emily's simple description had brought back memories of her own youth. She also knew all about rivers and mill-races and meadows, for she had been the daughter of that special breed of agricultural worker, a drowner. Like Emily, she had been bright and, instead of ending her education at fourteen, she had won a scholarship at the age of eleven which had enabled her to go to a Grammar School. Every summer she still went back to the Somerset village where she had been brought up and listened to her elderly father, now crippled with rheumatism, recalling the days when it seemed that he and he alone controlled all the waters for miles around. When she thought about the children now under her care it saddened her that none of them knew the benefit and delight of a country upbringing. Although it had taken serious illness on the part of Emily's mother for her daughter to be sent to Wilhampton during the most glorious summer since 1921, Maud felt that the child had been given something beyond price. She decided that she would move Emily up to Lower III but keep a careful watch on her development. It would be a pity to force so promising and original a pupil. She must remember to tell Cora Peters, who would be directly in charge of her, to see that she had every opportunity to learn to spell, especially when it came to the words 'tortoise' and 'orchids'.

Emily herself took her elevated status with comparative equanimity. She was sorry not to be working alongside Patsy Milward and Mary Gaunt, but she still mixed with them in the playground. They themselves regarded her not so much with jealousy as awe. Emily Mason appeared to be 'different'. She knew things about which they were totally ignorant, like the fact that the milk which came in bottles to their parents' doorsteps each morning actually came from a cow; and that a little girl called Helen Swayne had a father who knew how to get milk out of something called a cow's 'udders'. Their curiosity was intense. Their little friend seemed a source of the most amazing and interesting information.

It was perhaps at home in Davies Street where Emily did not fare quite so well. It was not that she regretted being back with her parents again, nor that she did not delight in having one or the other of them read to her each evening – Katy had just started *The Secret Garden* which held her spellbound – but many was the time when she found herself thinking of the Mill House and its occupants, particularly Aunt Chip, and wishing that they could all go back to Wilhampton to live.

As the winter drew on, she became puzzled and alarmed by several things which she either overheard being talked about by grown-ups, or read herself on the newsvendors' placards when her mother fetched her home from school. WALL STREET CRASH was one of them, but when she asked Katy what it meant, she was told that it was nothing to worry about because Wall Street was a long way away in America and that it had not really fallen down – just a lot of people in it had lost all their money. But at the beginning of December there was something which was not quite so easy to dismiss. THAMES OVERFLOWS – HOUSES AT CHISWICK UNDER WATER, ran the headlines by Bert's stand at the corner of Berkeley Square. Emily waited silently while her mother stopped and bought an evening paper.

'What does it mean, Mummy? What's happened to the houses?' she asked, as they hurried along.

'There's been a lot of rain, darling. It's usually the way, after a fine summer. Then the floods come.'

'Oh.' Emily sneezed and Katy looked at her anxiously. 'You haven't got another cold, have you?'

'I don't know. Mummy, will the Mill House be flooded?'

'I . . . hope not.'

The child was quick to sense the hesitancy in her mother's voice. 'But if the floods did get in, what would happen to Granny and Aunt Chip?' she persisted.

'Oh, I expect . . . they'd go up to Aunt Edith's on downside.'

Even as she spoke, Katy knew perfectly well that the rising Willon had never yet forced Sarah to leave her own home. 'Come hell or high water' seemed more than an appropriate expression to describe her mother's stoicism in the face of floods. Besides, Edith's house was already far too small to accommodate her large unruly family. Moreover, Katy feared that there were other difficulties, an added cause for anxiety this winter. In May's last letter she had mentioned Sarah's increasing stiffness, that Maurice Fitzherbert did not seem too happy about her and that, privately, she felt her mother was 'failing'.

'Can Aunt Chip swim, Mummy?' Emily broke in on Katy's train of thought. She smiled down at her daughter affectionately, her fingers tightening on the small hand she was holding.

'No, my love. But I'm sure that won't be necessary.'

Katy did her best to be reassuring, to push aside the memory of a December eleven years ago, just after the war ended, when the floods had risen, insidiously at first and then with sinister urgency, how she had been sent up to Ted Shergold, the drowner, with a note from her father – bedridden with acute bronchitis – to ask him to look to the hatches by Bulbarrow Sluice, and how Nancy Shergold – a termagant of a wife if ever there was one – had more or less shown her the door. Then, three days after Christmas, with the water slapping, gurgling and still rising in the living room below him, Sidney Lodge had given his last agonizing gasp for breath. Katy had never known another winter like that for, a few months later, she had become a nursery maid in Mayfair and, within two years, the wife of a young bookseller in the same area. Emily, please God, would never know one. What a blessing it was that the child had only had to be sent away during the summer, that she simply knew the lighter, sweeter side of life at the Mill House, not the dark wet winter by the Willon, with its ever-present threat of destruction and disruption lurking in the background.

Yet, over this reflection, Katy discovered that she was guilty of having reckoned without her daughter's quick intelligence and vivid imagination. In the middle of the night Emily awoke, screaming. On rushing into her room, Katy found that she had apparently had a nightmare in which 'Aunt Chip was walking about with only her head above the water'. Nothing her mother could say seemed to comfort the child so she eventually brought her, still trembling, back to spend the rest of the night in her and Philip's double bed.

Unfortunately, the trouble did not end there. Emily's disturbed sleep continued. Many was the time when her parents found her still wide awake when they came to bed. Katy took to leaving both doors open between their respective bedrooms and a nightlight on the landing. To satisfy herself, she would lie awake until she felt that the child had at last dropped off and then creep into her bedroom to make sure, usually finding the small body curled up in a tight ball with Greta clutched in her arms.

Quite often, Philip decided to make good use of this waiting period and one night Emily, who had not yet fallen into a deep enough sleep, awoke to hear strange sounds coming from her parents' room which she could not make out at all. It was sometimes a comfort to hear them carrying on a conversation. It made her feel less frightened. But tonight they did not appear to be talking to each other. It was almost as if they were engaged in some kind of friendly yet energetic tussle. She heard the creaking of bed-springs, a muffled laugh, her father repeating the word 'Darling' at least three times, after which there was a curious, low, breathless moaning. Terrified of she knew not what, she began to shout until Katy appeared at her bedside, flushed and anxious, tugging at the shoulder straps of one of the pretty celanese nightdresses trimmed with lace, which May always made for her and which had fallen from her shoulders, partly exposing her small rounded breasts.

Emily began sobbing now and her mother did her best to persuade her to come back to her own bedroom for the rest of the night, just as she had done before. But this time the child defiantly shook her head. Distressed and confused, she felt that there had been something going on there which, in its way, was as frightening as the floods, that her parents shared some horrible secret from which they wished her to be totally excluded.

8

A week before Christmas, May Lodge closed and locked her workroom door soon after three o'clock in the afternoon. The light was fading fast and she realized that she could just as well busy herself in the warmth of the Mill House living room. She was about to tack in the collar and cuffs on an ensemble that she was making for Lady Fairfax, besides trying to deal with one of the new-fangled zip fasteners which her ladyship had brought from London; as this latter task was one which May had never undertaken before, she knew it would need time and patience to get it right. Moreover, by working in the house she would be keeping Sarah company. She was aware that her mother was fretting about the rising waters and that this winter she seemed more than usually troubled. She would either remain silent for hours on end or go about muttering and shaking her head. Once or twice, after dark, May had caught her going up through the mill, shining her big torch – which now replaced her lantern – on to the fast-flowing Willon and repeating, agitatedly, 'It's just like it was before Sidney died.'

May was annoyed to find George Fuller – the manager of the Felt Mills – standing at the Mill House door where he had come to collect his tea tray. She knew that he had a perfect right to be there and that, owing to Sarah's increasing infirmity, it was good of him not to expect her mother any longer to climb the stairs to his office. But, possibly because of her long-standing antipathy towards the man, the imposition of producing tea for him five days a week – which the owners of the mill had placed upon Sarah as part of the agreement whereby she could remain in the house for her lifetime – irritated May beyond measure. George Fuller, as far as she was concerned, was a ridiculous, obsequious boor. He had a long-suffering wife and two children, but she was well aware that he 'fancied' her. He would make any excuse to stop and pass the time of day and sometimes it was all she could do to treat him civilly, especially when she thought of how she had early on christened him 'Duck and Collar', because of his long neck and weak blue eyes. Today, she saw those eyes light up at the sight of her. His opening gambit did nothing to dispel her feeling of utter distaste.

'Ah, good afternoon, Miss May. Or should I say "Good evening"? It is uncommonly dark, is it not?'

'Yes, Mr Fuller.' *Uncommonly dark*, May noted

contemptuously. No one in his right mind would talk like that.

'It would seem that we are in for more rain. I fear the Willon is riding high.'

'Yes.'

At that moment Sarah appeared at the door with the tea-tray and May tried to end the conversation by going inside; but still the man lingered.

'I gather from Ted Shergold,' he went on, 'that Lord Fairfax reckons on having some extensive repairs done to the gates of Bulbarrow sluice next summer, as well as many of the hatches round about.'

'Next summer's a while away, Mr Fuller,' Sarah suddenly said, tartly. 'The work should have been done last summer. We had a hundred and forty-six days without rain.'

'Yes . . . but . . . I mean, no one was to know.' It was well known that when confronted by any awkwardness, George Fuller always took to compromising. 'I've told Tom Henstridge to see that the planks and sandbags are put out ready. We must just hope . . .'

'Hope's not going to keep the water out, Mr Fuller. It'll be in this house by Christmas. Or before. You mark my words.'

May had seldom known her mother address anyone in such fashion other than the members of her own family. In fact, she had certainly never before heard her make the slightest derogatory remark about the Fairfaxes. For one thing, Lady Fairfax had been responsible over the years for a considerable amount of the Lodges' income and perquisites. For another, she belonged to the 'gentry' and, with few exceptions, the gentry in Sarah's eyes could do no wrong. Any bad hats which a county family might happen to spawn generally had excuses made for them. Her mother must be deeply disturbed to have spoken her mind so plainly to a man to whom, whatever she privately thought about him, she nevertheless usually accorded the respect which she considered to be his due as manager of the Felt Mills in her late husband's place.

Mr Fuller also seemed surprised by Sarah's unaccustomed acerbity. With a hasty 'We must look on the bright side, Mrs Lodge,' he retreated with his tea-tray.

Inside the living room Sarah lit the oil lamp and sat down by the range to resume her knitting, while May placed her sewing things carefully on the horsehair sofa, the legs of which had been raised up by bricks some days ago as a precaution in case of flooding. It would be another hour or so before they themselves had tea and, to ease the tension in the atmosphere, May switched on the battery-operated valve wireless, which now replaced their old crystal set with its awkward unsociable earphones. Unfortunately, however, this only seemed to make matters worse, for she tuned straight in to 'Happy Days Are Here Again' being played by Jack Payne's dance orchestra at Savoy Hill.

'Turn that thing off, May.' Sarah's voice was still sharp and scolding.

'But, Mother . . .' May tried to remonstrate with her. Personally, she could think of nothing better than a little of Jack Payne's light-hearted playing. Why, the broadcast was taking place probably not more than a couple of miles away from where Katy lived, and this she tried to explain to Sarah. The wireless had given May's life an extra dimension and it saddened her to be asked to forgo so simple and, as she felt, innocent a pleasure. She could visualize well-dressed ladies and gentlemen doing the fox-trot, possibly at some West End tea dance, and how the ladies' longer skirts would be swirling gracefully about their silk-stockinged legs. (May always read the fashion news in *Britannia and Eve* and knew that 'hemlines were coming down as fast as the stock market'.) The thought that some of those far-away sophisticated beings might be dressed by Coco Chanel or Edward Molyneux gave her a vicarious kind of thrill. It seemed such a pity that, to Sarah, such goings-on seemed to have the reverse effect.

'Turn it off, I say,' her mother now repeated. 'It's wicked for tunes like that to be played when you think of all the troubles in the country just now. Where are the happy days? You know as well as I do, my girl, there aren't any, not for the likes of you and me.'

With resignation, May turned off the bakelite knob and began taking a mass of purple velvet out of the clean white linen bolster case in which she always kept her current sewing. There was silence in the room now, save for the clicking of Sarah's steel knitting needles and the occasional noise of a cinder falling into the hearth.

Just before five-thirty Duck and Collar returned his tea-tray, after which his motor bike could be heard chugging away from the mill. At six, the hooter sounded for the men to clock off. There was the customary heavy tramping of feet and a few raucous salutations as they filed past the house and then, once again, silence, save for the rain which had begun pattering on the windows and an occasional squally gust of wind which tore at the catches.

With difficulty, May restrained her mother from going outside to look at the river and, having placed a stone hot-water bottle in each of their beds, suggested that she should have an early night.

'Although how a body is expected to sleep,' Sarah muttered as she eventually picked up her candlestick, 'I'm sure I don't know. Edith's husband's taken all the light stuff upstairs, but for goodness' sake don't leave anything else lying about. We don't know what we might find come morning.'

Once she was alone, May switched on the wireless again very quietly and began to listen to the news, thankful that Sarah could not hear Stuart Hibberd's voice saying, 'This is London . . . The unceasing rain of the past few weeks has given cause for grave concern. Flood water all over the country is rising. The situation along the Thames embankment is crucial. Aerial photographs taken over the home counties reveal that the actual course of the rivers – particularly the Wey – is impossible to define. In the west country there is such widespread flooding that there are growing fears for the safety of both people and livestock, particularly in isolated districts. The Minister for Agriculture, Mr Noel Buxton, is to make an extensive tour of the area . . .'

There was a suitable pause and then came the words: 'Speaking at a dinner in London last night, the Prime

Minister said that although the figures for unemployment were still rising, living standards – outside the worst-hit regions – were creeping up. Mr Ramsay MacDonald went on to point out that . . .' But here, May switched off and pursed her lips. She had heard all she wanted to know. In Wilhampton they were in for trouble, one which was quite different from being out of work. They were in for the kind which her favourite announcer had described at the beginning of the News. They were up against the rising Willon, not the rising number of jobless in the country. Sadly, she reflected that, however much she had enjoyed the advent of wireless, although it certainly brought Jack Payne's 'Happy Days' into the living room, it also brought the bad ones right home as well. Perhaps it was a mercy that there had been none of it during the war. But that, thank God, was a war to end all wars. Had not her eldest brother, Frank, given his life to ensure that this was so?

By ten-thirty, after a small cup of soup, May herself went up to bed. As she passed through her mother's room on the way to her own she found Sarah still wide awake, with that fixed staring expression which she invariably wore in times of stress.

'Have you shut and locked the gates, May?' Although her mother's voice was still peremptory, May could not help noticing how nervously her hands plucked at the coarse sheet.

For the first time that she could ever remember, May told Sarah a direct lie.

'Yes, Mother.' It seemed wrong to add to her anxiety, to explain that after the news on the wireless she had decided that, even though Tom Henstridge had the spare keys with which he let the men in every morning, it would be better just now that they should not barricade themselves so completely during the hours of darkness.

At midnight the wind rose to gale force. May had known previous storms of such magnitude. She had seen many a winter flood come and go; yet she could not recall ever having been imbued with the same kind of foreboding which she suspected she now shared with Sarah.

Just before one o'clock there was a sudden strange noise

from the direction of Bulbarrow which May had never heard before. It was like a distant cracking or splintering which momentarily drowned the shrieking of the wind and the roar of the mill-race. In the next room Sarah cried out and May rushed in to find her sitting bolt upright, every muscle tensed, the expression on her face one of frozen terror.

'Mother!' May sat down and cradled the rigid body in her arms, doing her best to stifle her own fear; for she knew that the sound which she had heard was the presage of no ordinary catastrophe, any more than Sarah's present condition was the symptom of any hitherto known affliction. Within seconds, they heard the first rush of water pounding down the mill. As it hurled itself against the side of the Mill House, Sarah's eyes seemed to roll upwards and then glaze over. A minute later she fell back, lifeless, against the pillows.

At first, May was too stunned to do other than stay beside Sarah's body, her left arm more or less pinioned beneath it. She was dimly aware of water heaving and gurgling in the living room below, while an icy draught of air came straight up the staircase. When she was at last able to move, the fingers of her right hand searched in vain for her mother's pulse, even though she knew that she would not find it. May had seen death before: her father, Neil and Flo. After ten more minutes, very gently, she drew the sheet over Sarah's face. Then, picking up a torch, she went to the window and watched its faint gleam shining down on to a wilderness of water which seemed to be pouring out of the downstairs windows into some turbulent black lake.

May had no idea of the depth of the flood, but she knew that it was impossible to get help. There was no one near enough at hand to whom she could call out. She was desperately conscious that Sarah needed the last offices but that she lacked the skill to perform them herself. It was this, rather than any danger she might be in, which was uppermost in her mind. Her mother, so proud, so impeccably clean and neat throughout her life, must be decently laid out as soon as possible. With every hour that went by the task would become more difficult.

Just before dawn, May heard the sound of a voice calling her. She went again to the window and leaned out, shining her torch as before on to the water below. From the direction of River Lane she could see a boat approaching in which there were two figures. As they drew nearer the house, she recognized them as none other than Maurice Fitzherbert and his gardener, Fred Musselwhite.

'May, are you all right?' Maurice, his voice quick and anxious, put out a hand and grasped the top of the porch. Then, steadying both himself and the boat, he stood up, his head little more than six inches below her own. 'May, if I help, do you think you and your mother could get out of this window?'

'Mother is dead, Maurice,' she replied, quietly.

'*Dead*?' He looked at her incredulously, his face white and drawn in the flickering torchlight.

'Yes. She had a stroke when the first rush of water from Bulbarrow hit the house.'

'Oh, my God. May, my dear. I am so very sorry. Look, I'm coming up.'

With extraordinary dexterity, he swung himself out of the boat and, within seconds, had squeezed through the window and was standing beside her in the room. A quick examination of Sarah's body confirmed May's words and he turned to look at her, imploringly.

'May, you must come away. Now.'

Although she had the greatest respect for him, she looked at Maurice Fitzherbert askance.

'I cannot leave Sarah *alone*, Maurice . . . not properly laid out, uncoffined . . . But thank you for coming,' she added, hastily, feeling that perhaps she was being ungrateful.

'But May . . .' He hesitated for a moment. He had guessed what her reply might be, but he felt that there was something else which had to be said. 'May . . . there's a nasty gap in the side of the house. I'm afraid . . . of the foundations . . . There could be some subsidence.'

She looked at him levelly. 'I understand, Maurice. But, all the same, I could not leave.'

He did not argue. He knew the Lodges. They were like some of the men he had fought with in the war. They did not quit. They might be highly strung and nervous, but in times of trouble they stood their ground, closed ranks and went on with some kind of innate courage and a sense of what was right and proper. He realized that May Lodge would sooner die than cease her vigil. Out of one of his inner pockets, he produced a small flask of brandy which he pressed into her hands with the words, 'I'll send help as soon as I can.' Then he let himself out of the window and down into the boat.

As Fred Musselwhite picked up the oars and drew away into River Lane, there came into Maurice's mind some words which he remembered the Reverend Donaldson having used many years ago as a text for one of his sermons. It had been when he was hoping to marry Katy Lodge and he had never forgotten them: *Many waters cannot quench love, neither can the floods drown it*. The love which Sarah Lodge had given to the members of her family must sometimes have seemed of a curious kind: harsh, protective, tyrannical and demanding. Yet in times of real crisis she would never fail them any more than her eldest living daughter would fail her now.

Back at the wreck of the Mill House, calm with the dignity of love and grief, May Lodge waited for morning.

9

One Saturday morning towards the end of January, a small neatly-dressed woman and a pretty, though serious-eyed, little girl wearing a scarlet coat and smart, leather, buttoned-up gaiters, could be seen feeding the pigeons in Grosvenor Square. When the bag of stale crusts which they had brought with them was empty, Emily Mason turned to May Lodge and said, 'Why must you go away tomorrow, Aunt Chip? Why can't you stay and live with us in London?'

May looked down at her niece, fondly. 'Because I have work to do, Emily, back in the country.'

'But Mummy said you wouldn't be able to work at the mill any more.'

'No, dear. But I'm very lucky. I'm going to have this new little home I told you about, where I shall be able to do all my sewing.'

'But why can't you do it up here? I heard Mummy telling Daddy that there were lots of people in Mayfair who could give . . .' The child hesitated a little, before adding 'their ears for one of your creations.'

'*Did* you, then?' May smiled. 'Well, there are a lot of people in Wilhampton who also seem to need my creations, as you call them. And somehow I must hurry up and see about making them, as well as putting to right all the things that got damaged by the floods.'

There. She hadn't wanted to mention the word but it had somehow slipped out. Emily became silent and May felt that, one way or another, the child had probably heard more than was good for her about the recent disaster, however much she and Katy and Philip had tried to keep it from her. May sensed that a change had come over her niece since she had last seen her. She was no longer the happy, carefree, eager young thing she had been back in the summer, rushing home to the Mill House from Miss Sharman's, breathlessly reporting on some latest piece of learning or the stealthy movements of Jumbo. She seemed to have become suddenly older, altogether quieter; and May did not think it was entirely to do with the fact that her grandmother had died and the Mill House was to be pulled down, much as she knew that the news had saddened her.

For a while, May's mind was jolted back to that terrible night before Christmas and the following morning when Sarah's body, wrapped in a sheet, had had to be lowered from the bedroom window into a boat, this time under the direction of Arnold Parker, the undertaker, after which, a little later on, he had returned for May. She recalled how, before clambering out herself into the strong waiting arms of Arnold's son, she had managed to hand him down a few of her possessions, such as her rosewood treasure chest, some necessary items of personal clothing and two bolster cases containing half-made orders, including Lady Fairfax's purple velvet ensemble. And then, as she was rowed to safety, she had turned to look at the full devastation of the scene behind her: the huge gaping hole where one side of the living room had been, the upended horsehair sofa, her mother's favourite picture of *The Last Supper* hanging incongruously in space and the old tapestry door curtain floating like some magic carpet by the partially submerged piano.

Up until then, May had remained steadfast and composed. Now, the full shock of all that had taken place began to sink in. She could not remember very much about the subsequent sequence of events, except how kind people had been and that, although Edith had wanted her to go up to downside, Maurice Fitzherbert had insisted that she must stay at East Lodge – even though May later suspected that his wife had been far from pleased, especially when Katy appeared. She was vaguely aware that her youngest sister seemed to come and go and then return again with Philip for Sarah's funeral, to which both Henry and Marianne had come. She thought it must have been the evening before that, when she had been sitting quietly by herself in one of Maurice's spare bedrooms – still in a state of semi-shock – Lady Fairfax called to see her. There had been a light tap on her door and she recalled Maurice taking her down to the drawing room, where he left them alone. She had an impression of being embraced, but that Lady Fairfax's manner was somehow different – there appeared to be a certain nervousness about her, even an air of contrition. When she spoke, her sentences were disjointed, a little difficult to follow.

'May, my *dear* . . .' There had been a long pause and then she had continued, all in a rush, 'What can I say? Words seem so useless . . . As I told Jimmy last night . . . there must be actions – *now*. I . . . that is, we . . . would like you to have old Mrs Hardiman's cottage. You know, Number Three, Cob Lane.'

For a moment May had been too taken aback to speak.

Then, with the realization of all that she was being offered, she murmured gratefully, 'It's so very kind . . .' Yet there was something bothering her, a thought which seemed to jostle for attention among the many others in her still confused mind. 'But your ladyship,' she at last managed to say, 'isn't Number Three earmarked for Percy Hooper when he marries the Roper girl next April?'

There had then been such a long pause that May began to worry that she had said something offensive. It was with obvious effort that her visitor eventually started to tell her that, sadly, Sarah had not been the only casualty in the floods. Percy Hooper had attempted to carry his aunt, Mabel Snoad, to safety on his shoulders but had slipped; although Mabel had survived, Percy had been knocked out and carried away by the current.

May remembered that it had seemed very quiet in the Fitzherbert drawing room then. She knew Percy well. She had watched him grow up. She could see him as a lad on his red bicycle and how, in the war, he had brought the telegram with the news of her eldest brother's death on the Somme; and then, early in 1919, a second one telling of Henry's marriage to Marianne. He had always been polite and willing and, if still alive, would have taken charge of the post office when Mabel retired. That poor girl he was to have married. Why, May had promised to make her wedding dress. It did not seem right that Dolly Roper's loss should be her gain and she said as much to her visitor. But her remark was gently but firmly dismissed.

May had then raised another point which was troubling her. There was the question of rent. She and Sarah had accumulated a few savings between them and she knew that, as the only unmarried child, her mother's share would now come to her. But it would be very little. She would no longer be able to afford much help with her sewing. She would have to work hard, very hard. But she would not, could not, accept charity. It was finally agreed that Luke Ridley, the Fairfaxes' agent, would come to see May about this and at last her visitor rose, the word 'pepper-corn' coming from her lips more than once before she left the room. It was not until much later, when May had had time to mull over the conversation, that she kept thinking about Lady Fairfax's curious unease, how she had never looked her straight in the eye during her entire visit and that perhaps Sarah – as so often before – had been right when she had told George Fuller that the repair work in the meadows should have been done the previous summer.

May had been staying with Katy in London for quite a while before a semblance of her old self became apparent. It was possibly the company of her niece rather than that of her sister and brother-in-law which helped to restore her natural outgoing responsiveness to the world around her. Gradually, May became increasingly aware that the child needed her in some way which was hard to define. This was confirmed more than ever on the morning when they were walking back to Davies Street after feeding the pigeons.

'You'll have me to stay in your new home, won't you, Aunt Chip, often?' Emily said, slipping a small hand in hers.

'Why yes, my dear. As often as Mummy and Daddy can spare you in the holidays.' Sensing that perhaps they were getting on to a delicate subject, May continued, 'Now, let's think. We've still got a little time before we're expected home. Suppose you take me along to Bond Street so that I can look in the windows and see what all the fashionable ladies are wearing. Then I'll be able to make the same sort of things when I get back to Wilhampton.'

How long ago it seemed, May thought, as they made their way, since the day when she had brought a timorous Katy up to London to begin her duties as nursery maid in the Moreton establishment and, before going home, had walked the length of Bond Street because she had once cherished a dream that she and Flo could have set up shop there. And now, here was Katy's child, living within a stone's throw of the place, leading her towards it with a hop and a skip and the words, 'Oh, *yes*, Aunt Chip. We'll go to Asprey's first and then Madame de Rosa's. Mummy says she has the best ready-made coats and skirts in London, but that we must never call them *costumes*.' May smiled again at the subtle niceties of speech with which

Katy was evidently imbuing her daughter. She was glad to think that, if only for a few moments, she had been able to bring back the Emily of last summer before she had become subdued and hurt by May knew not what.

Once she had returned to her home town, the mass of work which awaited her, combined with the support of countless friends and neighbours, all helped to ensure that the benefit which she had derived from her stay in London was by no means wasted. To her astonishment and gratitude, she found that her new home had been scrubbed out from top to bottom by two of the girls who worked at the mill; that Edith, despite the constant demands of her family, had managed to fit and hang curtains in every window; that a brand-new carpet – a present from Edwina and Ernest Fielding, the owners of the mill – had been laid in her sitting room and that as much furniture as could be salvaged from the Mill House had been installed, albeit somewhat incongruously, in her tiny rooms. To her great joy she also found that Arnold Parker's son had rescued, stripped and reassembled her treadle sewing machine so that it gleamed as new. Only one little gesture of goodwill seemed to jar. On the sitting-room table there was a large box to which was attached a label reading: 'To a brave little lady'. She knew the writing. With a mixture of dismay yet – to her mortification – growing excitement, she opened it to find that Duck and Collar had sent her a brand new wireless set.

It was not until the end of March that May was able to bring herself to go anywhere near the mill again. She had written George Fuller what she hoped was a suitably appreciative letter of thanks, while praying that they would not actually meet – at least for some time. She therefore chose a Saturday afternoon for her visit when, with luck, she hoped that there would be no one about. She was relieved to find that the gates were unlocked and that there was no need to ask Tom Henstridge for the keys. But once inside she was brought up short, unable to orientate herself, so great was the shock she received.

Where the Mill House had stood there was now only a pile of rubble. It was as if, suddenly, her bearings had been swept from under her, her roots cut off, the whole of her past life but an illusion. She found herself clenching and unclenching her fingers rather as Sarah had done in times of great distress. For a while she even wondered if she were dreaming. She had known no other home for nearly forty years, save the tiny one to which she was now endeavouring to become accustomed. The Mill House had been a stronghold, a refuge, a ship which had seemed incapable of capsizing. It had been commanded by a woman, hard yet vulnerable, fearful yet courageous. With no indoor sanitation of any kind, one living room, desperately inadequate sleeping space and little money, she had reared seven children to know love and anger, gaiety and sadness. In a word, she had given and maintained *life* – good life. And now there was no life. There was not even death. There was – desolation. Only a few daffodils tossing bravely in the breeze by the garden gate seemed to give any indication that here was once vital human habitation. Even her workroom, May noticed, was being transformed into a red-brick eyesore, for whose erection a willow tree had been slain and slaughtered.

Then she heard it. She supposed that she would have done so before had she not been so grieved and distracted by the scene around her. Slowly, May walked towards the mill-race. She did not know how long she stood beside it. She only knew that it seemed to be giving her back something she had lost. It was just the same. The floods had not altered it one whit. It was the guarantor of the past, the present and the future. She waited while the shadows lengthened, watching the water flowing, falling and bubbling up again before it swirled around and then drifted away quite calmly, even serenely, towards the sea. It would go on like this for ever. She must remember to tell Emily that in her next letter.

May Lodge opened her handbag, took out a clean white linen handkerchief and quietly blew her nose.

10

'I want to see *Anna Christie* at the Empire,' ran Belle Mason's letter at the beginning of April, 'and I've been sent these two tickets for the Private View at the Royal Academy on Friday, May 2nd, so I've decided to come up to town for that weekend. I thought perhaps both of you would like to see Garbo's first talking picture and Katy might care to accompany me to the RA.'

'*Accompany Belle to the Private View*?' Katy stared at her husband in astonishment, as he read the letter out loud at the breakfast table. 'But . . . how . . . I mean, I didn't know Belle ever went to things like *that*. Who would have sent her the tickets?'

'Search me. But I think, in a quiet way, old Belle has quite a few influential friends through her first husband. She's always been interested in the arts. I'm delighted she's asked you. I'll write back and say you'd love to come, shall I?'

'No. Please don't. I can't possibly accept.'

This time it was Philip who looked at his wife in disbelief, as he asked, quickly, 'Why on earth not?'

'I . . . It would mean a new outfit. I could make a dress, of course, but it's not just that. It's everything — shoes, hat, bag . . . even gloves. We can't possibly afford it.'

Philip Mason was silent for a while. Then he said, quietly, 'It's time you had a new outfit, my love. We're going to afford it. You can't say we've been exactly extravagant the last few years. We've lived pretty quietly since . . .' he hesitated a little, hardly wanting to refer to the event, before continuing, 'since Belle helped me out of that hole I was in. Besides,' he went on, more cheerfully, 'look how much you've done for me behind the scenes since you got better. I know things are still pretty tight, but the business seems to be holding its own, in spite of the recession. Between you and me, I think Belle's been quite favourably impressed. Otherwise, she'd never have made the suggestion. You'd better start doing some window-shopping straight away.'

To Emily's acute embarrassment, she watched her mother suddenly get up, throw her arms round her husband and give him a long affectionate kiss. Since that night during the last winter when the child had overheard their secret, puzzling, yet obviously pleasurable activities, any overt demonstration of love between her parents seemed somehow unacceptable. Many was the time – however guilty it made her feel – when she could not help wishing that her mother was more like dear dependable Aunt Chip.

Katy herself was not unaware of her small daughter's changed attitude towards her nor, greatly to her chagrin, the reason for it. Nowadays, she made a conscious effort to appear correct – even rather prudish – in her presence. She was resolved that never again would Emily hear any sounds of physical intimacy taking place between herself and Philip, however much she longed to give in to his far from infrequent desires, the delaying of which often proved frustrating and inhibiting to them both. Today's spontaneous loving response to his magnanimous suggestion was, she felt, an unfortunate lapse on her part. With a 'Hurry up and get ready for school, darling,' she chivvied the child out of the room.

But on the way back from escorting Emily by bus to Court House, Katy's mind reverted swiftly to the exciting prospect ahead. It had, as Philip said, been a long time since they had indulged in anything but the most prudent expenditure. Now, suddenly, that mercurial temperament which occasionally transported her from a dutiful, conscientious wife and mother into a carefree young girl again took hold to such an extent that Katy told the conductor she wished to be put down at Queen's Road. After all, there was no time like the present. She was so near Whiteleys and she would only be *looking*, giving their materials a little pinch between finger and thumb – just as she had been taught to do – to make sure of their quality.

Something in black and white, she wondered, as she made her way along the pavement. One could never go wrong with that. It was always smart. Of course, the Private View took place at an unpredictable time of the year. Printed chiffon would be nice, but the beginning of next month could still be cold. She could not possibly run to a dress *and* a coat, whatever Philip said and however many gorgeous revolutionary proofed materials were now appearing in the shops. Perhaps a simple lightweight silk or wool suit would be best, worn with a little pillbox or a broad-brimmed deep-crowned Garbo hat? She fancied the latter, although would that be right with a *suit*? She wished that her bobbed hair had had time to grow a little longer and that she could have a permanent wave, in keeping with the current trend. What a pity May was not with her. Dear May. Even if she did not live in London, she always seemed to know best. Her youngest sister supposed that being responsible over the years for making so many of Lady Fairfax's clothes probably had a great deal to do with it – that, and her assiduous study of the latest fashion news.

Katy was almost at the main doors of Whiteleys when she saw in their window something which caused her to stop and stand quite still for several minutes. Cunningly draped over a garden seat was a quantity of black and white printed chiffon at three and elevenpence halfpenny a yard. Laid nonchalantly beside it, almost as if its owner had forgotten to pick it up, was a large – unpriced – black straw hat, trimmed with the same material.

Katy did some mental arithmetic. She knew that the hat would be out of the question. It could be anything from three guineas upwards – and she still had to get shoes, bag and gloves. But surely, with a bit of ingenuity, she could buy a straw crown and trim it herself? Of course, there was still the problem of the weather, but it wasn't as if the Academy was out of doors. She'd always heard that the glass in the roof at Burlington House tended to attract the heat and, after all, she only had to get there and back. She hesitated for only a fraction longer and then went inside to make her purchase.

Katy was well aware that, if she asked, her eldest sister would have been only too willing and eager to make the dress for her; but she desisted for several reasons. For one thing, she knew that May — fortunately, as usual — had more than enough work on her hands. (In her last letter she had mentioned that she was already starting on Lady Fairfax's Ascot clothes.) For another, May would never allow any of her family to pay her. But apart from these considerations, Katy was anxious to see what she could create on her own. It would be, as she wrote to May that night, a challenge; and as the time went by she became increasingly absorbed in her efforts. When the date of the Private View drew nearer, she began — much to Philip's amusement — listening carefully to the weather forecasts on the wireless, even though she knew they were mostly unreliable and, as little as twelve hours beforehand, could be totally wrong.

Three days before the actual event, a large box arrived at Davies Street bearing a Wilhampton postmark. Mystified, Katy opened it to discover, meticulously packed between layer upon layer of clean tissue paper, a black garment which, on lifting it out, proved to be a lightweight proofed cloak made from just the kind of material she might have bought if she could have afforded it. In May's immaculate script there was a short letter which read: 'You said you had taken a gamble on it being fine for the 2nd, but I thought the enclosed wouldn't come amiss if it isn't. Anyway, whatever happens, this sort of thing never dates and will last a lifetime. I've made it on the long side and only tacked the hem in case it needs adjusting.'

Almost in tears, Katy put down the note and tried the cloak on. How *did* May do it? What must the material have cost? Even allowing for some small dividends from her savings in the Co-operative Society, her income was probably not much more than four pounds a week. Katy was well aware that she invariably undercharged her customers — even Lady Fairfax. It seemed so sad to think that her eldest sister rarely went to any of the occasions for which she so assiduously decked out others. Yet she never seemed to mind. She was nearly always cheerful. Presumably, in doing her work behind the scenes, she reaped her own particular reward.

Belle Mason was certainly unprepared for the vision which arrived in the foyer of Brown's Hotel three days later. She had always known that her stepson's wife was attractive and had flair, but this extremely chic young woman, with almost a Parisian look about her, seemed scarcely recognizable. With her large black hat, classic black accessories, and what appeared to be a black and white swirling chiffon dress beneath a smart black cloak, Belle noticed several heads turn as Katy walked towards her.

'My dear! How ... charming you look.' The older woman rose, wondering for a moment whether Philip's wife had taken up acting again. Where on earth had she acquired her ensemble? It must have cost a pretty penny. She hoped that the young couple were not heading for further financial difficulties.

As if reading her thoughts, Katy said quickly, 'I'm glad you think so. I made the dress and hat and my sister, May, made the cloak.'

'*Really*?' Never having been exactly good with her needle, Belle Mason could not refrain from staring at her guest in silent admiration.

'Well, yes. Perhaps you forget. All my sisters and I learnt sewing.'

Having decided – albeit a little sadly – to leave the cloak at the hotel owing to the day's increasing warmth and brightness, Belle was not surprised to find even more heads turned in their direction when they arrived at Burlington House. She felt that her young protégée could easily have been an artist's model. At one point, while they were studying Laura Knight's *Ballet Girl and Dressmaker*, a voice behind them said, 'Why, Katy, how lovely to see you. It *is* you, isn't it, hiding under that gorgeous hat?' On turning round, rather to her surprise, Belle found herself being shyly introduced to someone called Lady Moreton. On the way back to Brown's for lunch, Katy explained that she had once worked for the Moretons when they had lived in Upper Brook Street, adding quietly, 'That's how I came to meet Philip.'

'I *see*.' Belle glanced at her curiously. Katy had certainly come on a lot since the diffident little thing she remembered marrying her stepson nine years previously. 'I know so little about you, my dear,' she continued. 'I shall try to make amends.'

During the rest of her visit, Belle Mason's interest in the members of the small family she had so surprisingly acquired through remarriage in later life increased with each time she saw them. She was particularly impressed by the solemn, well-mannered little girl. Having never had any children of her own, she had hitherto considered them a drawback. Now, she was not so sure. There was something to be said, as one grew older, for taking an interest in the younger generation, or generations. Emily Mason seemed an unusual child. With those long-lashed, enormous brown eyes and expressive face, she could be a beauty in ten years' time. With guidance, Belle felt that she might well be able to revolutionize Emily's life. Her mother was pretty and she definitely had a certain something about her; but she was obviously a mercurial type, delicate and on the nervy side. The daughter would appear to be made of more sober, sterner stuff – so long as she was brought up aright. Emily Mason was the young girl she herself might have been had she not been born with rather too large a nose and thickish ankles so that, only in her late twenties – aided by a natural vitality and enquiring mind – had she managed to achieve an assurance and poise which overcame such handicaps.

Now, at the age of fifty-five, it suddenly came to Belle Mason that, through her step-grand-daughter, she might live again. When Emily was a little older she would have her to stay. She could even take her travelling. It would be nice to have a healthy young companion, even if, later on, it was necessary to watch out for and ward off undesirable suitors. She was pleased that the child was going to a better school. She was glad that she had come to her stepson's rescue when he had been in difficulties some years ago. He was not the first person to whom she had given money in times of trouble and so far her generosity had never been misplaced. It was obvious that Philip had buckled to and taken her advice, which could hardly have been easy with a seriously ill wife on his hands. She felt that she would like to do more for him now, possibly take steps to ensure that his little daughter soon received even better tuition. Emily was clever, apparently, and there was talk of a scholarship but, if this did not come to pass, there were other ways of seeing that she received a first-class education, especially when it came to finishing schools.

Belle Mason found herself looking forward to many things as the train taking her home steamed out of Paddington station. She might be once again alone in life, but she knew that she had a lot to be thankful for, not the least, financial security – that is, so far as anyone could have that in such uncertain times. She decided that she would definitely buy the new Austin car she was constantly seeing advertised and take up driving. It would be as well to start in the summer months and she would see about it as soon as she got back.

Well content, Belle Mason settled herself into the corner of a first-class carriage and, turning her mind to more immediate pleasures, opened a small attaché case at her side. Here, she took out *The Good Companions*, one of the half a dozen new books which she had purchased from her stepson. There was nothing like a good read and she did not think she would be disappointed in the latest J. B. Priestley. She knew that it was a mutual love of books which had brought about her surprising but – except for its shortness – extremely satisfying second marriage.

What Belle Mason did not know was that it was exactly the same thing which had started Philip's and Katy's romance when, in the spring of 1920, he had sold her a copy of *Wuthering Heights* and why, nine months after their wedding, they christened their baby daughter Emily, after its author.

11

Since May Lodge had moved into Cob Lane, she and Ethel Sharman had become more and more friendly, for they found they had much in common. They now lived but a minute's walk away from each other, both were spinsters of about the same age, both had above average intelligence and both were of a sensitive, caring disposition. But the main bond between them was undoubtedly their mutual interest in Emily Mason who, during the summer holidays, had spent a whole fortnight with her aunt in her new home.

Far from any longer harbouring feelings of jealousy over Ethel's fondness for Emily, May was now only too glad to have her niece taken for nature walks once again by her neighbour, as it enabled her to get on with her sewing. Besides, she realized that her small back yard was no substitute for the old-fashioned spacious garden at the mill and that it was wrong to have such a young thing cooped up with her for too long at a stretch. Neither did she feel that it was suitable to let Emily spend too much time in her sister Edith's overcrowded and distressingly disordered household. Sad as it seemed, the difference between Katy's only child and Edith's six unruly ones became increasingly apparent whenever the cousins met.

Although May remained loyal to a degree and would never breathe a word of such innermost thoughts to anyone, many was the time that she silently shook her head over Edith's lack of discipline, both in connection with the way she brought up her family and the way she had let herself go so much in recent years. May did her best to make excuses for Edith, knowing that tiredness, depression after losing all her teeth, shortage of money and a none-too-strong husband had much to do with such a sorry state of affairs. She was constantly trying to help out, running up a pair of small boy's trousers on her machine or a pinafore frock for a little girl. Nevertheless, it was impossible not to deplore the fact that Edith's children seemed so coarse, that they all spoke with such broad west-country accents, that the eldest, Donald, had become an agricultural labourer and the twin girls, Della and Debbie, were apparently hoping to get jobs as usherettes at the picture-house in Westonbury. Yet May had to admit to herself that Katy, whom she had once more or less forced into becoming a mere nursery maid in order to get her away from the attentions of a simpleton brother, had actually this year gone to the Private View at the Royal Academy. One could never tell what might transpire in life. It was such a lottery.

Once Emily had returned home at the end of August and the nights began drawing in, Ethel Sharman and May Lodge often spent the evening together. Mostly, this took place in May's little sitting room, where they could talk while she carried on with her sewing. Although much of their conversation inevitably turned on Emily or local matters, they also took a lively interest in current affairs, Ethel providing the more serious background knowledge, May, with her increasing penchant for the wireless, often making pertinent and humorous remarks about the foibles of public figures or her disagreement with the Labour Government.

Sometimes, May felt quite guilty about the pleasure she derived from George Fuller's present to her and once, when she had accidentally met him in the street, she had asked him if he would like to bring his wife and children to tea. But this half-innocent, half-clever suggestion had had the effect which, in previous years, she would have given anything to bring about. Duck and Collar had backed away as if thunderstruck. With a 'It's most kind of you, Miss Lodge, but . . . I fear . . . my wife being delicate . . .' he had disappeared in the direction of the mill and May realized that, whereas George Fuller would have been more than happy to visit Cob Lane by himself, nothing would induce him to bring his family with him.

So May remained in her little home, listening to George's wireless set and hoping that he was not now regretting his generosity. Sometimes, as she cut, tacked, machined or stitched some garment, she reflected on how much her job – or profession, as Sarah would have called it – brought her into the stream of things, giving her experience of so many aspects of life and the hopes and fears of such a cross-section of the community. When she was asked to make a wedding dress, May thought about love – even if sometimes she suspected the bride was pregnant and the bridegroom marrying under a certain duress, or what the

276

local inhabitants called 'force put'. Later on, when she was asked to make maternity clothes, she thought about the strange miracle of birth. Usually young mothers made their own layettes, but May was often requested by those of better means to make little girls' party frocks or bridesmaids' dresses, for which she did the most intricate smocking. On these occasions she thought about Emily and the pain and joy of growing up. Then there were the purely social events: the parties and receptions for which all women wanted to look their best. 'A tuck here, perhaps, Miss Lodge, do you think?' someone might say during a fitting, or, 'Possibly a little deeper armhole... Unfortunately ... perspiration, although I have bought the latest brassière with the rubber *shields* ...' And if May knew her client well, she might reply, 'I believe the new Odorono is quite effective,' which remark was sometimes countered with, 'Oh, I *know*, Miss Lodge, but I believe it is apt to rot the material and my mother feels it is dangerous to use ... against nature ... one does not know what one might be damming up.'

Lastly, of course, there was the mourning, and that was always a sad task. Just now, at the beginning of October, May was making mourning for the niece, by marriage, of Miss Fortescue, who had died quite peacefully in her sleep at the Moat House.

'Such a nice woman,' Ethel Sharman said, when she called one Sunday evening and noticed the half-made black coat hanging up behind the sitting-room door. (May never worked for remuneration on the Sabbath, although she was busy making Edith a new woollen skirt). 'I was so sorry when I heard she'd passed on. She was so fond of Wilhampton. In a way, she put us on the map with all those books she wrote about the west country. She'll be greatly missed. I wonder who will take the Moat.'

'Yes. I hope it will be someone she would have approved of. I've always thought it such a pleasant home. A good atmosphere. One can always tell. Poor dear Mother used to say that personality got into the woodwork. Would you like me to turn on the wireless, Ethel?' Although May would never dream of admitting it, she always found herself keener to indulge in her favourite pastime on a Sunday, possibly because, however moral and high-minded the programmes, none of them started — apart from the religious ones — until three o'clock in the afternoon.

But, whatever the day, one thing May never liked missing was the news. By no means a vain woman, it always gave her a kind of personal satisfaction — even thrill — to hear the chimes of Big Ben and the words: 'This is London', and to know that her youngest sister was living there, right in the heart of things. It was almost as if Katy was alongside the announcer. Although the latter never actually divulged his name, May had come to know them all through their photographs in the Radio Times and putting two and two together, and tonight, even before John Snagge had uttered the word 'disaster', she knew from the gravity of his voice that some terrible calamity had occurred. Silently, the two women sat staring at each other as, sentence by sentence, the full horror of the R 101's crash in Northern France was gradually revealed to them. When, finally, the words 'It is not yet known whether there are any survivors from the fifty-four people on board' May leaned forward and switched off the set. She felt, rather as she had done during another disaster nearer home the previous winter, that just for the moment, she had heard enough.

There was now complete silence for a while in the little sitting-room. Presently Ethel said, 'My cousin, Edwin, the one at the Air Ministry, told me a bit about that airship. He said it was known to be too heavy compared to the R 100, but there was too much pressure from the politicians to go ahead with the maiden flight. He said it hadn't had enough proper trials. I believe someone at the top wanted to prove that State enterprise was best. There's been a lot of bad feeling. He never thought personally that it would reach India.'

'Oh.' May was still stunned and Ethel's inside information was a little difficult for her to follow. She was thinking of the fire and all the poor souls who couldn't get out. 'Recrimination's not going to bring them back,' she said slowly, almost to herself.

'Oh, I know, May. Nothing can do that.' Again there was silence before Ethel continued, quietly, 'Although you can't help wondering, can you, about air travel? I've never been too sure. I suppose it's the thing of the future. It stands to reason, but I wouldn't want to leave *terra firma* myself. Last August, when Emily and I were walking along the top of the old Barbury turnpike, I remember there was a tiny aeroplane flying across the valley and at one point it looked as if it was dead level and coming straight at us. I don't mind telling you, May, I was scared, but I tried not to let Emily notice. When it was only a little distance away, it rose and just hopped over us, so to speak, and we could see the pilot waving. I daresay she told you all about it.'

'Yes. She said that if it hadn't been for you she would have run away. She had one of her nightmares afterwards. But perhaps it was just as well she felt like that. After all, we don't want another Amy Johnson on our hands in a few years' time.'

'No, although by then . . .' Ethel broke off, uncertainly, before going on, 'Edwin seems to think that anything could happen. Now that there's this man called Hitler getting more and more power in Germany, he says there might be another war and if there is, as like as not, most of it will be fought in the air.'

May looked at her visitor incredulously. 'Oh no, Ethel. You must have got it wrong. There won't be another war. The last one made quite sure of that.'

'Please God, you're right, my dear.' Ethel stood up. 'I must be going. I've some letters to write and I want to see the books are all set out ready for tomorrow's lessons. Perhaps I could call in again during the evening. We shall have further news by then.'

After May had wished her visitor goodnight, she sat quite still for a while staring into the fire. Today's tragedy and Ethel's words had brought back memories of the last war, many of which she would have preferred to forget. Her brother Frank's death, for instance, and her own and Flo's disillusionment with two particular men who had danced attendance on them before leaving for the front.

She recalled the terrible Sunday when, due to her naïveté, believing the major with whom she was in love was ill and needed help, she had been tricked into going to his suite where, despite a struggle, she had been forced to fulfil quite a different kind of need from any she had had in mind. She remembered how she and Flo had agonized together for eighteen days afterwards, until she knew she was not pregnant and then how, the following year, she had had to act as helpmate and comforter to her eldest sister. Poor Flo. The whole family had thought it was a foregone conclusion that she would marry Captain Guy Armitage and then he had been suddenly snapped up by Grace Sinca, the strange newcomer at The Warren, a woman whom the whole of Wilhampton considered 'no better than she should be'. The first intimation that Flo had of Guy's faithlessness was when she had read the announcement of his marriage in the *Westonbury Journal*. She had rushed off and shut herself in the closet where May, managing to get in and sit beside her on the wide wooden seat, had done her best to reassure her that she was 'well out of it'. When, not long afterwards, Guy Armitage had returned from Passchendaele with both his legs blown off, she had kept quiet. She was not a vindictive woman. Whatever hurt the man had done to her sister, she did not think in terms of retribution. It was only Sarah who, one night when the two of them happened to be alone, mentioned the word 'come-uppance'.

It seemed such a very long time ago. Katy had been but a child. She hardly knew what war was about. She and Flo had made her a kilt and May could see the little thing now, gaily swinging along the pavement in it, keeping time with the troops as they marched through Wilhampton singing 'Colonel Bogey' and 'Pack Up Your Troubles'. It was silly of Ethel to talk about anything like that happening again, even if she felt that it would never be *quite* like that. The trouble with Ethel was that she was a little too full of theories, apt to pay too much attention to that cousin of hers in the Air Ministry.

The cat, Tommy, which May had acquired since coming to Cob Lane, suddenly jumped up into her lap, purring.

She stroked him absently, still lost in reverie, thinking that although she had never moved very far away from her home ground, she had experienced quite a bit of life, one way or another. She would be forty next birthday. She was aware that she no longer possessed the slim waistline for which she had once had such a reputation. She was middle-aged now and she was alone; but if the good Lord granted her health and strength she hoped she would be able to carry on working for many years to come. Her greatest fear was the thought of becoming dependent on anyone. Her dearest wish was that she would live to see Emily grow up. She would so like to be able to make her wedding dress. However much she herself might be disillusioned by men, she was still an incurable romantic at heart. Emily would look lovely in cream satin with a veil of Brussels lace . . .

12

'Mrs Mason was in no way to blame for the accident, you understand, Mr Mason. She had taken to driving very well. This man in the Lagonda simply came round the corner on the wrong side. She didn't stand a chance.'

'I see.' Philip sat in the offices of a firm of solicitors in Monmouth and stared at its senior partner, a Mr Thomas Morgan. He had travelled to Wales from London after receiving a letter from the latter informing him of his stepmother's death and the date of her funeral.

Philip had still been unable to believe it, even as he had watched Belle's coffin lowered into the grave that morning. It was impossible to think he would never see her again. She had seemed so very much alive, so vital, so altogether charming on her last visit, back in May, when she had taken Katy to the Private View. He had felt it quite easy to understand her attraction for men, even though he had never ceased to be surprised that, being a woman of the world, she had fallen for his quiet unassuming father. But perhaps, their very differences — apart from the interest in books which they had in common — had all helped to account for what had seemed to him to be a strange union. He wished now that he had taken the trouble to get to know his stepmother better. She had certainly been kind to him, much kinder than he deserved. But it had never occurred to him that her magnanimity would stretch beyond the grave. He had always supposed that she had many other relatives and commitments.

'Mrs Mason made certain specific bequests,' he heard Mr Morgan continue, in a high sing-song Welsh accent, 'such as to her housekeeper, Mrs Williams, for instance, and to one or two friends, but her residual estate is to be divided: half outright to yourself and half in trust for your daughter.'

'I see,' Philip said again. He wondered vaguely what this would amount to: one thousand, two? He had no idea. Mr Morgan did not seem in any particular hurry to enlighten him and he naturally did not like to ask.

'Mrs Mason remade her will, Mr Mason, just after returning from London last summer. I helped her to draw it up. She happened to mention how pleased she was with the way you were now managing your late father's business. She was particularly taken with your little daughter — Emily, as I believe she is called. I shall always remember . . .' He broke off before continuing with a smile, 'I'm sure you won't mind my telling you this, but when she got up from the chair where you are now sitting, she said, "My stepson has come on quite a bit, Mr Morgan, during the last few years. I think he would have a better idea of knowing how to handle an inheritance . . . well, that is to say, in a few years' time. Naturally I hope it won't be coming to him just yet". She looked so bonny as she went out. We were all so sorry when we heard about the accident. It seems, indeed, quite tragic.'

'Yes. Yes, it does.' Philip felt his responses to be totally inadequate, but Mr Morgan appeared not to notice.

'I was wondering whether you would like to visit the house, Mr Mason? Mrs Williams is still living there. A valuation for probate was done yesterday. As I mentioned before, my wife and I would be happy to put you up for the night if you should wish.'

'I . . . well, it's very kind of you but . . .' Philip hesitated, unsure, confused. He had brought no overnight bag and had told Katy he would be returning that evening.

As if reading his thoughts, Mr Morgan continued. 'There is a late train which would get you back to London about eleven-thirty, if that would suit you better. We could take a quick look at the Hollies and then you might wish to bring your wife another time?'

'I . . . yes.' Would Katy want to see it? Was Mr Morgan expecting them to live in it? Surely not.

Once again, the man before him seemed to know what was going through his mind. 'I was thinking perhaps, that there might be certain things belonging to Mrs Mason which you would like to have in your London house. I believe you have a flat above the bookshop?' Then, quite suddenly, as if his next statement was a mere formality and would come as no surprise, Mr Morgan went on, 'If the house and its contents are to be sold, I should say that after the very generous provision which Mrs Mason has made for Mrs Williams and the other small bequests, something in the region of ten thousand pounds would be coming to you outright and ten thousand to your daughter in trust, as I said, to be administered by myself and one of my colleagues. I believe that Mrs Mason was extremely anxious that Emily should have the benefit of a first-class education and it was something she was meaning to discuss with you on her next visit to London, possibly making some provision for this during her lifetime.'

Philip was silent. Twenty thousand between himself and Emily. It seemed a fortune. 'I had no idea,' he said, at length, 'that my stepmother was so wealthy.'

'No? Her first husband . . .' Mr Morgan hesitated and then went on, 'Well, I don't suppose I would be betraying any confidences if I say he made quite a bit of money towards the end of his life dealing in art. He was very knowledgeable. Mrs Mason had some fine pictures.'

Philip tried to think back to the few occasions when he had visited the Hollies. He had always been vaguely aware that it was a pleasant, well-appointed, comfortable home, but he had never been there for very long and mostly such times had been taken up with other considerations: his father's funeral, for instance, and the day when he had gone to ask his stepmother for help and had been too agitated to retain anything other than a mental picture of Belle herself, immaculate, poised, sitting at her desk as she wrote him a cheque.

On the way back to London that night, after Mr Morgan had shown him round the house, he still hadn't been able to recall many details other than, as the solicitor had said, his stepmother had one or two fine pictures and he had been surprised by the sumptuousness of her bedroom which, presumably, his father had once shared. He had found himself staring at the large mahogany four-poster and wondering about the sexual side of their marriage. He had always imagined that, after his mother's death, his father had ceased to be interested in that kind of thing. He had seemed so wrapped up in the shop, too old for such activities. Yet he had only been fifty-five when he died – much younger, in fact, than that brute, Kreiger, who had tried to seduce Katy. He would certainly have to bring her down to see the Hollies soon. He wondered what she would say to the news. He wondered what they would do.

The idea did not really take hold of him until the train was well past Reading, although he was aware that it had been there: flitting in and out of consciousness throughout most of the journey. He was fairly sure that Katy would not want to live in Wales. On the other hand, there would be no need to remain in their small flat above the shop, would there? Why not get a manager to live in it? There was somewhere else where he and Katy and Emily could go which might suit them all very much better. Should he suggest it at once, or perhaps wait a little while? Perhaps the latter course would be more prudent, although plans for the future of the Mason family were presenting themselves thick and fast. Belle's legacy would perhaps enable him to do something which he had not thought possible since his marriage. Yet had he not told Katy during their courtship that he had an ambition other than bookselling? Somehow, the advent of Emily, the decline in his fortunes, his unwise foray into the antiquarian trade and then Katy's illness had pushed it into the background.

As the train neared Paddington, it slowed down to a crawl. A thick peasouper lay over the capital. It was almost one o'clock before he alighted on to the platform and realized that the quickest way of getting to Davies Street was on foot. Hunching his shoulders and tucking up the collar of his overcoat, he set off, ignoring more than one entreaty from some shivering, ghostly, female figure as it loomed up at him out of the fog with such words as, 'Wouldn't you like a bit of home comfort on a night like this, dearie?'

He hurried on, longing for the home comfort which he knew would be awaiting him a little further away. He guessed that Katy would be waiting up and was afraid that she would be worried which, indeed, she was. Clad in a warm pink woollen dressing gown, she was half-way down the stairs before he had time to close the side door to the street. Her eyes, as always on such occasions, seemed enormous, the blue shadows beneath them, which had never wholly disappeared since her illness, very much darker than usual.

'Darling!' She wound her arms round him, tightly. Suddenly, he realized that she had never before been left alone so late at night. She seemed all at once a child again, in desperate need of protection, in desperate need of love.

'There.' He held her closely and kissed her several times. 'There, my love. I'm sorry I'm so late. The fog's terrible.'

'Yes, I know. I couldn't help thinking of . . . well, accidents,' she added, softly, smiling now, as she started back ahead of him up the stairs. 'I've been keeping your supper warm in the oven. I hope it's not ruined.'

He began to tell her whilst he ate it and she sat opposite, staring at him intently, her elbows resting on the table, her small face cupped in her hands. When he got to the actual figure which would be coming their way, her eyes widened and she looked almost fearful.

'But . . . darling . . . I mean, what will you *do*?'

'I've been thinking, love, all the way home. I've got one

or two ideas up my sleeve, but perhaps now isn't the time to talk about them. You're tired. So am I. Let's go to bed.'

They tiptoed quietly past Emily's room. Although the child was sleeping better, there were still nights when she awoke and needed comforting. When he at last had Katy in his arms, Philip hoped that this would not be one of them. In spite of having talked about tiredness, he found himself making love to his wife who, to his joy, responded with something akin to her former ardour. Afterwards, as they lay intertwined, he murmured, softly, 'Katy, love, d'you remember that afternoon on Putney Heath, way back the year we first met?'

'Yes, Philip, of course,' she replied, equally softly.

'And I said there was something else I might do besides selling books?'

'Yes.'

'Well, I've never got around to it, have I?'

'No.'

'Well, I was wondering whether now mightn't be the time to try, once we've moved.'

'Moved? But where . . . ?'

'Katy, don't you remember that other day, a bit later on at the end of the summer, when I'd come to see you at your home and we went up on Breconbury Down?'

'I remember it very well.' Indeed, she thought, it was etched on memory, bitter-sweet, the afternoon when she might so easily have lost her virginity.

'Well, I've never forgotten either. You were so lovely, Katy. I just didn't know how to . . .'

She tightened her arms around him. 'And there was something else you said was lovely that day, too, Philip.'

'Yes. I think I said that it was a lovely place where you lived and that I wouldn't mind living there myself one day.'

13

'So how much do you think the Moat House might fetch, Cyril?' May Lodge had led up to the question cautiously, doing her best to bring it into the conversation simply as a matter for general discussion. The last thing she wanted was for it to get around Wilhampton that Katy and her husband were interested in buying the place. But after her youngest sister's last letter, May had been hoping that she might come across Cyril Butt, the retired auctioneer – quite by accident, of course – as he went out for his daily constitutional.

She had been lucky. On her way to Miss Clutterbuck's to purchase a few yards of dimity for re-covering her old feather mattress, she had caught sight of Cyril coming down East Street towards Mulberry Cottage, his home in a corner of the market place. He was always easily recognizable for, with his fawn whipcord breeches, shiny brown leather gaiters, check coat and cap and long stout thumb-stick, he was a typical John Bull figure, invariably accompanied by Lion, his aged golden retriever. As casually as she could, May slackened pace and slightly altered her course so that, by the time she reached the war memorial in the centre of the square, Cyril was courteously raising his cap and wishing her good morning.

Ever since Flo's last illness, May had never felt altogether kindly disposed towards Cyril because, for many years prior to that, it was obvious that he was 'sweet' on her eldest sister – not that Flo had given him the slightest encouragement. All the same, many people thought that, as the dutiful only son of a tyrannical mother, when the latter died Cyril would be sure to 'pop the question'. Yet, after Mrs Butt eventually passed on round about the time when it became public knowledge that Flo had cancer, Cyril's attentions had been noticeable only for their absence. 'You'd think,' Sarah had remarked on more than one occasion, 'that he'd send word or call to enquire now and then,' to which sentiment May had been forced to agree, albeit sometimes adding, 'I suppose he's one of those who are scared of the disease, always being so healthy himself.'

Now, on this particular morning, Cyril did, indeed, still look amazingly robust. Puffing out his red cheeks against the cold, he had observed cheerfully that it looked as if they might be in for a hard winter. 'Never seen so many berries as there are along the Barbury turnpike, May. Incidentally, talking of that, would you care to come in and have a glass of sloe gin? Just the thing on a day like this.'

May had been torn between desire to do so but fear of what people would think. For a comely middle-aged spinster to be seen going into the home of an elderly bachelor was something which some busybody would be sure to notice, even though Cyril had a living-in housekeeper. But over the latter state of affairs there had never been any gossip, simply because, May supposed, prim Phyllis Hopkins was a good few years older than Cyril and had been housekeeper at Mulberry Cottage throughout his mother's day.

Possibly because he had sensed May's hesitation and the reason for it, Cyril had suddenly and somewhat ostentatiously pulled out his watch on its gold chain – even though he could perfectly well have glanced up at the town hall clock – and continued pleasantly, 'Edgar Swanton said he'd probably call in round about now after he's been to see Dick Swayne up at Bulbarrow. Did you know that Dick's decided to grass down the whole of his farm and go in for this new method of open-air machine milking? Wise fellow. Farmers can't make money out of arable land these days, not with the government importing so much cheap wheat.'

The information that Cyril was expecting another caller helped May to accept his invitation. To have the chance of chatting with *two* knowledgeable auctioneers – even if one of them *was* more interested in land than houses – was too good to miss. She had therefore found herself crossing the threshold of Mulberry Cottage for the first time for over ten years and that sipping sloe gin in Cyril's sitting room in front of his open log fire was a very welcome change from her usual hard-working routine.

After Edgar Swanton had joined them, she had been quite happy to remain the least talkative of the three, surreptitiously appraising Cyril's antiques – she felt she had to hand it to Phyllis Hopkins for the shine on them – while listening to the men's remarks concerning the agricultural depression and their admiration for the way Dick Swayne was attempting to help himself out of it. Somehow it had then seemed entirely natural for the conversation to progress from land to houses and this was where May had been able to ask their opinion about the Moat.

'Twelve? Maybe fifteen hundred, wouldn't you say, Edgar,' Cyril remarked, relighting his pipe.

'Yes. Thereabouts, I suppose. Depends if there's anyone who particularly wants it. I believe it's been let go a bit lately since Maggie started failing. But it's a sound buy. A compact little property. I should say that that's the kind of reserve Maggie's heirs are intending to put on the place when it comes up for auction next month.'

May found herself colouring slightly. Edgar's reference to 'anyone particular' had made her wonder whether he could possibly have heard about Katy; but she decided that that would have been impossible. She had told no one, not even Ethel Sharman, about the correspondence she had been having with her youngest sister.

When May had first realized why Katy was so interested in the Moat House, her reaction had been one of total confusion. The possibility that the girl – as she still thought of her – might be mistress of such an establishment was too astonishing to envisage. It went without saying that it would be wonderful to have her favourite sister and niece living in Wilhampton. But would Katy be able to adjust to what would be a very different way of life from that which she had hitherto known in her home town? And could Philip really afford to leave the bookshop to a manager? Or would it mean him travelling up and down to London each week? And Emily's schooling? Might it not be difficult to get her into Wickfield House without her name having been put down years ago? It was a fine public school on the outskirts of Westonbury, taking boarders and day girls, but May believed that there was a long waiting list for both. There seemed so many imponderables about the whole scheme. It was such a big step to take. She felt scared and excited. She wished the young couple had some older man to advise them, someone perhaps a little more worldly-wise than either of the two before her, who had now got on to the subject of Ramsay MacDonald and whether his government could last much longer.

Moreover, there was another vague niggle of doubt in the back of May's mind which simply would not go away. She knew that it was one which Katy and Philip, in their love for each other, would probably never stop to consider. Yet, as she made her way back to Cob Lane that morning and saw Maurice Fitzherbert driving out of the Hall gates, she found herself worrying about it more than ever. She was convinced that, for all the outwardly calm and pleasant manner which he showed to the world, he was, at heart, a deeply unhappy man. It would have helped, she felt, if he had had children, but he and his wife had been married for several years now and still there was no sign of a family. Many was the time she had noticed the fond way he had looked at Emily when the child had been staying with her, and how he never seemed to miss an opportunity of enquiring after Katy.

On entering her front door, May found yet another letter from her youngest sister which had arrived by the second post. It was, perhaps, not quite so enthusiastic as the others and she sensed that Katy herself had now begun to have certain misgivings, even if none of them included the close proximity of a long-standing admirer. Nevertheless, it appeared that she and Philip were planning to leave Emily in the care of Ellen and come down to Wilhampton for a day the following week in order to look over the Moat House – after which visit, May thought grimly, it will be all over the town. She wondered whether it would be possible to have a word with her youngest sister in private when the time came.

On the day before the proposed visit, May prepared a dish which she knew to be Katy and Philip's favourite:

jugged hare. Fortunately, Ted Pretty, the new head keeper on the Fairfax estate, had been asked to leave a hare with her a few days previously and this she now skinned and cut up, frying the pieces until brown before putting them in a stew jar with a little salt, an onion stuck with cloves, lemon juice, peppercorns, parsley, thyme and a small glass of port from the bottle which Ethel Sharman – somewhat surprisingly – had given her on her last birthday. Then, covering all the ingredients with stock from the stock-pot she invariably kept going throughout the winter, she stood the jar in a saucepan of water to simmer for several hours on her small gas stove. During this time, she set about making forcemeat – which she shaped into small quenelles ready for frying – and peeled some potatoes and carrots. She felt it was important not to be overburdened by too many tasks the following morning, even though there would be no need to go to the station to welcome her visitors, as they were apparently stopping off at Weston-bury and being driven out to the Moat by one of Edgar Swanton's colleagues in the firm in which Cyril's name still took precedence, Butt and Swanton.

As on previous occasions of late, May was once again struck by her youngest sister's appearance when Katy and Philip eventually arrived at Cob Lane. There was, May felt, a stamp of the big city about the fine-drawn young lady who came through the door. Katy could well have been a model. The fur-trimmed coat she was wearing – made, so she afterwards explained, by herself – fitted her slim figure to perfection. The little fur hat to match was perched at just the right angle on the soft brown hair which – much to Sarah's disapproval – had been bobbed a few years ago but recently allowed to grow again so that it could be marcel waved. Katy's complexion – always flawless – was, even so, now definitely enhanced by the most skilful use of make-up. She looked fragile, almost ethereally beautiful. Would she, May wondered, take to country life again if she and Philip really did buy the Moat? It would, admittedly, be a vastly more comfortable home than the one in which she now lived. But, all the same, May could not help feeling that, as the three of them settled down to eat, it was her brother-in-law who was the most enthusiastic about the whole idea.

'It would be marvellous for Emily,' Philip was now saying. 'Of course, we haven't liked to say too much in front of her. But I mean, just think, May, if she went to Wickfield House. That's what Belle would have wanted, I'm sure. And the child seems to have an almost uncanny affinity with Wilhampton. You've mentioned it yourself.'

'Yes. There's no doubt that she's uncommonly at home here, Philip.' And she would be but a stone's throw away, May thought, just as Katy would have been if she'd married Maurice Fitzherbert. Almost, it would be like a dream come true . . . Surely, she could not, would not, raise any nebulous fears in the face of so much youthful optimism. She was a silly old spinster who was now, quite fortuitously, being offered a second chance in life: that of living for and through her youngest sister and niece. Even so, Philip's next suggestion was one she had never for one moment contemplated.

'We were wondering, May, just supposing we did get the Moat, whether you'd come and live with us. You know the house. There would be plenty of room.'

'Oh, *Philip*.' She was caught off guard, completely flabbergasted.

'Just think, though,' her brother-in-law went on. 'You could have the big west bedroom all to yourself, which I believe Maggie Fortescue's companion used to have.'

'I . . .' May was still at a loss. To have been asked was so very gratifying and yet . . .

'We'd so love you to come,' Katy broke in, her eyes bright and entreating. 'And it's not entirely disinterested, mind. Philip might have to be away quite a bit. I'd want some company then.'

May looked across at her youngest sister, registering, despite the optimism and genuine warmth of feeling, a certain nervousness, almost helplessness, in her manner, as if she were in need of much more support than her husband could possibly give her. Even so, May held back. A sixth sense or, perhaps, simply a basic common sense, told her that the proposition would not work. However much she might wish to be involved in the young people's lives, her own was — and always would be — altogether different. She had her independence now. True, she paid but a peppercorn rent for it, but Number Three, Cob Lane, was hers for as long as she wanted to live there. She was a dressmaker — a much respected one — of Wilhampton. For as long as she could, she intended to go on being one. How could she possibly carry on with such an occupation if she lived with Katy and Philip at the Moat House? How would her brother-in-law like clients such as Arnold Parker's wife walking up the drive to be fitted? Or did they imagine that she would merely become a lady of leisure living off their charity? But, whichever way she looked at it, she knew that it was not — as her mother used to say — feasible. Levelly, she met the gaze of the two eager faces across the table as she laid down her knife and fork.

'Thank you, my dears, for asking me,' she said, simply. 'I appreciate it more than I can say, but . . . I believe it would be best for me to remain where I am. Although,' and here May smiled slightly before adding, 'if ever you needed me, well, I shouldn't be far away, should I?'

14

'Just a shade longer, I think, May, don't you? Skirts really do seem to have come down a lot lately, thank goodness. I always thought the short style a few years ago was quite abominable, even for women with pretty legs.'

'Yes. I couldn't agree more, your ladyship.' May knelt on the floor in front of the coal fire in Lady Fairfax's boudoir and adjusted some pins on the hem of a wool romaine afternoon frock. 'There.' She stood up and took a few steps backwards, while her client surveyed herself in a long gilt mirror and nodded, approvingly.

'Excellent, May. Quite excellent. I really don't know how you do it. And you must have had so many demands on your time lately, with Katy moving into the Moat.'

May helped Lady Fairfax out of the partially made

garment before replying, quietly, 'Yes, it's been a busy few months, but I've tried not to let it interfere too much with my work. And Katy is quite capable, even though I sometimes think she looks as though a puff of wind might blow her away.'

'Dear thing. Do give her my love. I shall call on her later on, when she's had more time to settle in. You must let me know when it would be convenient. How's Emily, by the way? I'm sure she must be thrilled to be living in Wilhampton, isn't she?'

'Oh, yes, your ladyship.' May fastened some hooks and eyes on the placket of the tweed skirt which Lady Fairfax had now put on again and continued, 'We're just a little concerned about her schooling, though. My brother-in-law hoped to have got her into Wickfield House next September term, but unfortunately she may have to wait at least another year or more.'

'What's happening to her meanwhile?'

May could not but appreciate the directness, the quickness of mind which had always been able to grasp the essence of a difficult situation and which had made Lady Fairfax, if not exactly loved, certainly greatly revered throughout the neighbourhood.

'Ethel Sharman is teaching her again for the moment,' May replied, 'as she did the summer before last when my sister was so ill. But I fear that Emily is really too far advanced now for the kind of tuition Ethel is able to offer.'

There was a pause. May carefully folded up the dress and placed it, along with her other bits and pieces, in the small suitcase which she had brought with her.

Presently, Lady Fairfax said, 'I can't promise anything, mind, but you do know I'm on the governing board of Wickfield, don't you, May? We've got a meeting coming up next week. I'll see if I can have a word or two afterwards with Miss Lawrence, the headmistress.'

'Oh.' May coloured. 'I . . .' She did, indeed, know that Lady Fairfax was on the board of governors because Philip had shown her the school's brochure, but the last thing she would have dreamt of doing was to try to take advantage of the situation. 'I do hope you did not think that I . . .' she continued, hesitantly.

Lady Fairfax cut her short. 'Of course not, May. I know you better than that. But in certain instances I see no harm in seeing whether I can do anything to help. I understand Emily is a very bright little girl. Let's hope that whatever happens she will do well at Wickfield when she gets there.'

On her way back to Cob Lane, May called in at the Moat. Although it was mid-March there had been freak snowstorms throughout the country and, as she crossed over the small bridge leading up to the front door, she found Emily, Helen Swayne and Daphne Chadwick attempting to make a snowman in the garden. Immediately, her niece disengaged herself from the others and came running towards her.

'Aunt Chip! Aunt Chip! Have you come to tea?' Emily threw her arms round May and looked up at her, expectantly.

'No, dear. I've just called to see Mummy for a few minutes. Is she in?'

'Yes. She and Rose are making curtains. Daddy's in London, but he'll be back tonight. Do stop to tea. We've got indigestibles.'

'*What*, my dear?'

Emily went off into peals of laughter. 'That's what Daddy calls them. You know, the baker's seven cakes for sixpence that Miss Sharman is always making us do sums about.'

May smiled. 'I think I'd better leave those to you and your friends, Emily. Besides, I have to think of my figure these days.'

'Well, you could still have a biscuit or something. Perhaps Mummy will make you change your mind.'

Katy did, in fact, persuade May to stop for an early cup of tea with her alone. 'I'll be glad of a break,' she said, a little wearily. 'Making all the upstairs curtains is more of a job than I bargained for. I suppose I should have got Burt and Burt to do them like the downstairs ones, but it seemed such a wicked extravagance.'

It was the first time May had heard Katy refer directly

to the cost of moving house. She hoped that her sister and brother-in-law had not underestimated their total commitment. Belle's legacy had seemed almost beyond belief, yet, nevertheless, May kept thinking of all the outgoings there must be just now: two young living-in maids, Rose and Miriam, for instance – not that either of them was getting more than five shillings a week. But then there was the Morris Cowley Philip had bought and all the furniture that was needed. True, the Moat was a comparatively small country residence and Katy had managed to pick up some excellent bargains at the local auctions. Philip had given her a book on antiques which she had put to good use, so much so that Mr Motcombe, the auctioneer's clerk in the furniture department of Butt and Swanton, had complimented her on the acquisition of a particularly fine Queen Anne walnut bureau bookcase. Even so, May thought, as she sat drinking tea in the small sitting room overlooking the lawn where the three children were still playing, there was the garden to keep up and once Abel Firman, Maggie Fortescue's ancient gardener, could no longer manage it, some new man might want more than the thirty-two and sixpence which she believed old Abel to be getting.

'You look worried, May.' Katy held out her hand for her sister's cup and refilled it. 'Is anything wrong?'

'Oh no, my dear,' May replied quickly, embarrassed at having to dissemble a little. 'In fact, I may have some good news. Mind you, don't let on to anyone but Philip, but Lady Fairfax says that after the next governors' meeting she's going to have a word with Miss Lawrence about the possibility of getting Emily into Wickfield House a little earlier.'

'*What?*'

'Yes. I happened to mention the difficulty, quite by chance after she'd asked about the child. She simply volunteered to see what she could do.'

'Oh, *May*! It would be wonderful if Emily could start there this September. Helen and Daphne are both going then. Of course, they've had their names down for ages. God knows how Dick Swayne's going to afford the fees, but apparently he's determined to do it somehow. Emily's bound to feel so left out if she can't start with them. And Ethel, naturally, will be taking on some younger pupils this autumn, so the poor kid will be worse off than ever. Philip and I have been racking our brains to know what to do for the best.'

'Well, don't get too excited, my dear. Perhaps I shouldn't have said anything to you yet, but I've just come from the Hall and I couldn't help wanting to let you know. It's almost like history repeating itself, isn't it? Lady Fairfax seems to be taking as much interest in Emily as she did in you when you were a little girl. Incidentally, she wants to call on you when you're straight.'

'Oh.' Katy flushed and turned away for a moment. When at last she spoke, her eyes had lost their temporary look of hopefulness which had been so apparent while May had been talking about Wickfield House. 'It's complicated, isn't it?' she said, slowly.

'Complicated?'

'Well, yes. I mean, me, here, mistress of the Moat, a daughter down for Wickfield . . . You know. There's people in Wilhampton who give me a funny look sometimes. Even Edith, the other day . . . I'm sure she was trying to avoid me.'

'Oh no, my dear. You must be mistaken. Edie loves you.'

'Yes, I *know*. But she feels awkward. We both do. And her kids. They and Emily have nothing in common. I don't suppose I thought about all that sufficiently when Philip first proposed the idea. I felt I'd had enough of London and it would be lovely to come back here again. It's only really now that we've arrived that it's becoming so difficult. And this business about Lady Fairfax calling. Strictly speaking, I'm meant to call back – anyway, on people I don't know. Leave cards. All that sort of thing. Philip's made me get some. But May, I can't see myself doing that, can you?' Quite suddenly, Katy covered her face with her hands and burst into tears.

May went back to Cob Lane more troubled than she cared to admit. Her little sister was up against problems far more demanding and confusing than the making of new curtains. She was a stranger on her home ground. She was out of her depth: neither mill manager's daughter nor wife of a local inhabitant, as she would have been had she married Maurice Fitzherbert. May was well aware that becoming wife and mistress of East Lodge would have necessitated plenty of adjustment; but with Maurice beside her, she felt, Katy would have found it so much easier. He was thought the world of in the district, just as his father had been. With his support and gentle encouragement, he would have helped his young wife over many a hurdle. He knew what to do; he had the right touch with all and sundry. He was unfailingly reliable and full of common sense unless, perhaps, one counted falling in love with Katy as a deviation from his customary conventional way of life. But surely he couldn't be blamed for that? She had been so lovely and appealing that summer of 1920, when she had come home to help nurse Flo and Maurice had had to make regular visits to the Mill House. She was just as lovely today – more so, perhaps. But though her appearance might now be that of a desirable woman, she was still very much a child at heart. That wilful mercurial temperament needed some kind of sheet anchor. Suddenly, there crept into May's mind an old adage of her mother's which she had not thought about in ten years: 'The ivy needs the oak'.

Once inside her front door, she was pleased to find that her carefully guarded fire was still glowing. She was also rather relieved to feel that Ethel would not be calling that evening, as she was going to a concert in the Assembly Rooms in Westonbury. May had declined to accompany her because, besides having so much work to do, she knew that a string quartet would not play the kind of music which appealed to her. She much preferred what she called a 'proper tune', one to which she could dance, or hum, or – at least nowadays – simply listen to on the wireless.

With her customary efficiency, May swiftly lit the gas mantle, made up the fire, washed her hands in her tiny scullery and went back into the sitting room, where she switched on Duck and Collar's present, delighted to find that she was still in time for the 'Thé Dansant' immediately preceding Children's Hour, which had been advertised in the *Radio Times*.

There was nothing better to take one's mind off one's troubles, May reflected, as she settled down to work on Lady Fairfax's dress, than a little dance music, especially when it was Henry Hall and his orchestra playing 'A Room with a View' and 'My Blue Heaven'.

15

Philip Mason sat in his small study at the Moat – the one which Maggie Fortescue had always used – and tore up twelve sheets of foolscap. It was the middle of July and he had written four chapters of a novel. The fifth was now in the waste-paper basket.

Out of the window he could see Katy talking to Abel. They seemed to be in earnest consultation about something or other. He knew that they got on well together and he was pleased. Abel was not one of those people about whom Katy sometimes complained, the ones who looked at her 'sideways'. Abel called her 'Ma'am' and was obviously impressed by her knowledge of gardening. Philip also sometimes expressed surprise at her aptitude in this connection; then she would remind him, gaily, that he had forgotten she was the daughter of a man who had regularly won first prize at the annual Westonbury Show, for growing roses as well as onions.

Yet it was not often that her light-heartedness broke through these days. He sensed that she was finding their new way of life far more trying than she cared to let him know. He was annoyed that he seemed to be able to do so little about it. Surely there was nothing wrong in a local girl coming back with a comparatively affluent husband to live in the place where she was born? He found himself becoming angry at the small-mindedness, the illogical and, as he felt, totally unreasonable attitudes adopted by so many Wilhampton residents and all the petty gossip that went on. He only heard about it, of course, from Katy;

299

and half the time he felt – and, indeed, hoped – that, with her vivid imagination, she was probably fantasizing. On the other hand, he supposed that there must be a few grains of truth in what she said. Otherwise, he would not catch her looking so strained when she was off guard.

Philip had never lived in a community before – especially a country one. His early upbringing in Putney could scarcely be counted because, even then, the Masons had kept themselves very much to themselves: his father seemingly content to devote his life to his books, his mother delicate and increasingly withdrawn. When they had moved to the West End and his mother's health began to fail, they seemed to have fewer friends, their old ones dropping away when it became no longer possible to visit or entertain. He had never realized until now how lonely his father must have been and what the advent of Belle must have meant to him. He supposed that, in a way, meeting Katy had had something of the same sort of effect on him.

If only he could make her see now that she had nothing to worry about, that they had taken a big step forward together and that everything would come right. Perhaps if the book which he had set himself to write proved to be a winner, she would be able to laugh away the feeling that people thought she was giving herself airs. In any case, she would have enough to give herself airs about. If money did not mean all that much to the people of Wilhampton, surely being the wife of a successful author did? The trouble was that he was finding writing so much more difficult than he had anticipated. When he had shown Katy his initial chapters, although she had obviously been very interested, he had been a shade disappointed that she had not been more enthusiastic about them. She was a voracious reader and he valued her opinion. He decided that he would not show her any more of his work until someone else had seen it. That was why he was going up to London the following day to see an agent. He was also due for a visit to the shop and was intending to combine the two engagements, spending a night in their old flat, the use of this being one of the conditions laid down when he had installed Jack Lumley, his manager, in it.

Presently, he got up to join Katy in the garden. There seemed no point in starting to rewrite Chapter Five until he had had a personal talk with someone from A. J. Smythe's and received a report on the first four. Meanwhile, he would try to forget about his fictional *Sun in the Morning* and try to enjoy some of the real stuff which happened to be all too rare that summer.

Katy was bending over one of the borders, weeding, by the time he reached her. Abel was nowhere to be seen. He caught her by the waist and attempted to kiss the nape of her neck, but she straightened up quickly and disengaged herself from his embrace.

'Philip, please. Abel's somewhere around.'

'So what?'

'Well, I mean . . .' She backed a few steps away from him. There was a small smudge of earth on one of her cheeks. Her eyes had that discouraging look in them that he had come to resent.

'We're married, aren't we. It's not as if I was trying to play fast and loose with your local adulteress, as I gather Grace Armitage up at The Warren is, or was, called.'

'No. Don't be silly. But I think this sort of thing ought to be reserved for when we're quite alone. Besides, Emily will soon be coming back from Bulbarrow and probably bringing Helen with her. I expect she'll have been up on the Swaynes' old pony again. Apparently, she's longing to learn to ride.'

'So I gather. Well, that's all right by me if you can arrange it.'

Katy was silent. 'I suppose she could go to Joan Cory's riding school,' she said after a while, 'although I must say I'm not all that keen.'

'Why on earth not?'

Again she was silent before eventually replying, 'I daresay I'm just nervous about it all. And when little girls first get bitten with riding, as I believe Emily will, then there's no stopping them. She'll want a pony of her own and goodness knows what.'

It was Philip who now did not answer immediately. Then, as they began walking over to the summerhouse together, he said, 'Hadn't we better meet that one when the time comes, darling? Besides, now that Emily's going to Wickfield House this autumn, there won't be all that opportunity for riding. I must say your sister did a damn good job over that.'

'Oh, *Philip*.' She wished he would not talk in this way. It seemed crass, insensitive. 'You *know* May acted quite unconsciously.'

'Of course I do, silly. All the same, I believe your eldest sister's *unconscious* often works a great deal better than most people's conscious.'

They went inside the summerhouse. She could not help smiling at his last remark and he took her hand. This time she did not remove it.

Katy knew that Philip was right about May. There was a curious artlessness about her which somehow achieved the most amazing results. Totally without guile, she went on her way, free from almost all the adverse emotions which destroyed, or at least hampered, the rest of mankind. True, she worried, but her worries were all for others and even these she tried not to show. She was not a particularly religious woman but she seemed to have a blind faith that by doing her best, the best would automatically follow. Everyone liked her and – with the possible exception of George Fuller, Cyril Butt and Grace Armitage – she liked everyone. What was more, May adored Wilhampton. To her there was no place on earth to compare with it, not that she really knew any other place to compare it with. All the same, as she grew older, she was often apt to remark that certain things in her home town were infinitely superior to those to be found in Westonbury: the Wilhampton vegetables, for instance, which mostly came from the Hall nurseries; the water in the reservoir half-way up Breconbury Down, which was pumped by Ikey Shepherd in his shining immaculately kept pumping house; the doctor, who was the kindest and cleverest on earth. Even the unpredictability of the Willon, which had, in turn, carried away her father, her youngest brother, her mother and, in the end, the family home, was somehow put down to 'the way of the river' – albeit now mercifully under stricter control, since the completion of the work which the Fairfaxes had put in hand on Bulbarrow sluice and the surrounding hatches after the catastrophic floods in the winter of 1929.

One could say, Katy reflected wryly, that May was altogether too good, too trusting. And yet, she was no fool when it came to the question of human relationships. She was acutely aware of atmosphere, of problems which had not even been voiced. Katy knew that her sister completely understood, far more than her husband, the sense of insecurity from which she now suffered.

There was the sound of children's voices on the bridge over the front driveway and presently Emily and Helen came into view, Emily with a bandaged arm. Katy stood up and went towards her daughter quickly.

'Darling! Whatever's happened to you?'

It was Helen Swayne who answered. 'I'm so sorry, Mrs Mason, but she had a fall. Beauty slipped on the cobble stones in the yard. My mother bathed Emily's arm at once and put on iodine. She says that she doesn't think there's anything to worry about.'

'But . . . how deep are the cuts?' Katy did not want to doubt the efficacy of her neighbour's first-aid treatment, especially in the presence of Dorothy's daughter yet, all the same, she had a particular fear of such mishaps, remembering how her own grandfather had died from lockjaw. If Emily had fallen in the yard, there would bound to have been horse manure about.

'It's only a graze, Mummy, I promise you. It really doesn't hurt at all now,' Emily said, quickly.

Katy let the matter drop, but with misgiving. As soon as Helen had gone home after tea, she decided to undo the bandage and take a look. Certainly, the area above Emily's elbow looked clean but definitely red and swollen.

'I think,' she said, thoughtfully, 'perhaps we'll just let the doctor see it.' Ignoring Emily's protests, she went downstairs and telephoned Maurice Fitzherbert.

Fortunately, she found him in. 'If you bring her round straight away, Katy,' he informed her, 'I can see her before evening surgery.' Chivvying a still-protesting daughter, they set off for East Lodge.

The days had passed when Katy would have automatically gone to the surgery entrance at the doctor's house, along with the majority of local inhabitants who were 'on the panel'. She and Philip had become paying patients – not that as yet they had had to bother Maurice much; but nevertheless they were now entitled to knock on his front door through which, this evening, they were ushered into the hall and along to the drawing room by a rather scared young woman whom Katy did not know, but could only assume to be one of the innumerable domestics who seemed to come and go in rapid succession at East Lodge, ever since Maurice's wife had been in charge of it.

It was the same room into which Katy had first gone eleven years ago when, shaking with apprehension, she had come to a buffet party before being escorted by Maurice to her very first dance. Now, during the few moments she and Emily waited there, she thought how little it had changed. There was the same heavy Victorian furniture which she remembered in his parents' day, the enormous ebony-framed pictures of highland cattle; even the antimacassars on the chairbacks looked as if, apart from possibly one or two washings, they might have been placed there by 'Old Mother Mothballs', as she happened to know May had called Maurice's mother. She wondered why the present mistress of East Lodge had done so little to the room and found herself thinking about how she would set about improving it: pale walls, flowers, a little chintz, she felt, would have worked wonders.

And then Maurice was with them. Gravely and courteously, he took them along to his small consulting room in between the surgery and the rest of the house. With infinite care and gentleness, he examined Emily's wound and re-dressed it. Then he sent her back to the drawing room so that he might have a few words with Katy alone.

'You're thinking about lockjaw, aren't you?' he said, closing the door and coming straight to the point.

'Yes, Maurice.'

'Look, Katy. There have been certain adverse reactions

304

to the anti-tetanus serum. The treatment is still in its infancy. Dorothy Swayne did a good job and what is more she did it immediately. I don't think you need worry. I see plenty of worse injuries daily – and there must be even more I never see. Just keep an eye on it. There shouldn't be any problems.' He smiled and changed the subject. 'How's the Moat coming along?'

'Oh, fine, Maurice. I . . . we . . . were hoping perhaps you and Clare would come to a meal with us sometime, perhaps Sunday lunch?'

For a fleeting moment a look of distress, almost hope-lessness, seemed to cross his face and then it was quickly masked. His normal pleasant manner reasserted itself and he said, quietly, 'It's very kind of you, Katy. Perhaps a little later on. Clare . . . hasn't been feeling too good lately.'

She knew that it was an excuse and that he knew that she knew. She stood up. 'I mustn't keep you, Maurice. Thank you so very much for seeing Emily.'

He stood also. She noticed how grey his hair had become at the temples, how he stooped much more these days, how incredibly like his father he was becoming. She had made no attempt at dressing up to see the doctor, as many people in her position were apt to do. She was still wearing what she thought of as her gardening clothes: a simple but well-fitting brown linen dress and old brogue shoes. Her hair was slightly tousled. Although she had made up her face carefully that morning, this was no longer so apparent, for that teatime she had simply rubbed the smudge of earth from her cheek and dabbed some powder on a rather shiny nose.

Yet, after Maurice Fitzherbert had shown Katy Mason and her daughter out, he had gone back to his consulting room and sat quite still for several minutes, lost in thought. He supposed that Katy must have been about ten years old when she had first seemed to need his help, coming down the steep wooden steps of St Mark's steeple when the Reverend Donaldson had taken them up to see his bells. She would have been about eleven when, forgetting her shyness for once, she had warned him that he might catch diphtheria if he put the gobstopper he had been sucking back into his mouth after it had rolled in the gutter. He could remember quite clearly trying to allay her fears by telling her that Abie Grant, his father's dispenser, would be certain to have something to save him from that. Then there had been a gap when they had not met for some time. Apart from brief visits, his medical training and army service had kept him away from Wilhampton. She must have been eighteen, that evening when he had surprised her in the meadows while she was taking a rest from the heartbreaking task of helping to nurse her dying sister. He could visualize her quite distinctly, as if it were yesterday: the way she had put up her hair, the slimness of her waist, the simple blue cotton frock she was wearing and how its bodice strained a little over her small rounded breasts, her large eyes which seemed unconsciously to be asking for love and protection and the way her colour seemed to come and go. And then – Philip Mason, damn him, had stepped in and shattered all his hopes and dreams.

Gradually, the murmuring from the other side of his consulting-room wall grew louder. He pulled out his watch. It was two minutes past six. He had never, unless he had been called out in an emergency, been late for surgery before. Wearily, he stood up and opened a door. The hum of conversation ceased abruptly and Maurice Fitzherbert called for his first patient.

16

'I'll do my best to let you have a report on these as quickly as possible, Mr Mason.'

The young woman sitting behind the desk at A. J. Smythe's held up the four chapters of *Sun in the Morning* and flashed Philip a brilliant smile. In fact, she seemed to have been smiling at him most of the time since he had first entered her office, which had been encouraging. She had glanced briefly at the synopsis which he had attached to his slim folder and said, 'Hmm, sounds interesting, almost like a love affair between town and country. And I approve your title.'

Philip had felt even more hopeful. It was good to have found someone so positive and optimistic. He had been expecting to consult a Mr Burgess and had been initially rather annoyed at being told that Miss Woodley would see him as Mr Burgess had been unexpectedly called away. But he had soon come round to thinking that possibly a female agent was exactly what he wanted. After all, he knew enough about the book trade to know that it was mostly ladies who bought books, ladies who liked novels, ladies for whom he was presumably trying to write. He found himself wondering why Miss Woodley was not married and how she had come to be doing her present job. He could not say that she was exactly pretty. Her features wcre too bold, her figure too flat and her whole appearance really rather mannish. She seemed to be still adhering to the fashions of a few years ago: her dark hair was Eton cropped and she wore a curiously shapeless black sleeveless dress that contrasted sharply with her bare white arms, which she waved about rather dramatically – especially the one holding a long cigarette holder. Yet she definitely exuded some kind of sex appeal which Philip could not quite define. He felt that she bore a slight resemblance to a cross between Belle and Grace Armitage.

'When do you go back to the country, Mr Mason?' she continued. 'Incidentally, may I call you Philip? I'm Barbara. I always like to get on Christian name terms with my authors as soon as I can. It's so much easier when it comes to discussing their books.'

'Of course.' Philip found her friendliness disarming. And she had actually called him an author. All the same, he did not think he could quite bring himself to say Barbara just yet. 'I shall be leaving London tomorrow at midday,' he informed her, 'after I have seen to some business at the shop.'

'Ah.' She looked at him thoughtfully, the elbow of one white arm now resting on her desk as it held up a well-manicured hand to support her chin. 'You don't know how lucky you aré, Philip,' she said, at length, 'to have such *intimate* knowledge of the book world. I really can't wait to start reading this.' She glanced down momentarily at his manuscript and then raised her greeny-grey eyes once more to his. 'If I can,' she went on, 'I'll see what I can do tonight and give you a ring first thing in the morning.'

'Really?' It was more than he had dared to hope for.

'Where will you be staying?'

'At my flat. I mean, at my former home. Above Masons. I let my manager have it on the understanding that there would be a bed for me there whenever I wanted it.'

'Ah, I *see*.' Barbara Woodley had a low husky voice which often laid great emphasis on certain words, somehow making them seem extremely meaningful – if only to her. It occurred to him that perhaps she had a sore throat and was smoking so much today in order to soothe it, as the cigarette advertisements were constantly advocating.

Philip rose to go and she stood also, coming round the desk to accompany him to the door. He was aware of her heavy musky scent – not the pleasant summery kind that Katy used – which he did not care for at all. In fact, on the way back to Davies Street, he thought how much more attractive Barbara Woodley could have made herself if she had wanted to; although perhaps she did not really care for men, except as business propositions. For all he knew, she might be one of those incomprehensible women like those in Radclyffe Hall's *Well of Loneliness*. He remembered all the fuss there had been about the book three years before, how the judge had condemned it outright at the obscenity trial. Philip had managed to get hold of a copy, but he had not let Katy read it. Still, there was no point in making conjectures about Barbara Woodley's private life. It had nothing to do with him. The great thing was that she seemed interested in his work and that was all that mattered.

For the rest of the day Philip was kept busy going through certain accounts and discussing various problems with Jack Lumley, so much so that when, at eight o'clock, Jack's wife suggested sending them both down some cold supper on a tray, it seemed the most sensible thing to accept her kind offer. Philip had not been up to town for a fortnight and was surprised at what a lot of tricky questions had arisen in his absence to which only he could provide an answer.

He was also surprised next morning when, before the shop opened, Jack came to tell him that he was wanted on the telephone. Surely . . . no . . . it wasn't possible that Barbara Woodley would be ringing him so soon. It must be Katy. He hoped there was nothing wrong and that she was telephoning, as she was sometimes apt to do, merely to ask him to bring back something or other which she was unable to buy in Westonbury.

'Philip?' The voice seemed even more husky than it had yesterday. 'I thought those chapters quite fascinating.'

He found himself swallowing hard. His heart began to thump as if he had been running.

'I'm glad,' he managed to say at last.

'Look, we *must* talk about them. There's certain things I'd like to suggest. I mean, I don't want to interfere in any way, but . . . you know, just one or two tiny points. I think it would be helpful to meet again before you go and bury yourself in all that cow parsley or whatever it is you do down in Wilhampton. I was wondering . . . You couldn't have lunch with me today, could you?'

'I . . .' He had told Katy he would catch the midday train. She and Emily were going to the Westonbury Show and he had promised to look for them in the tea tent at four o'clock and drive them home. 'I could,' he went on, quickly. 'I shall just have to alter some arrangements in the country.' Katy would surely understand. This was so much more important.

'Oh, *good*. It *does* seem such an opportunity, Philip. Can you meet me at one o'clock at the Casa Mara?' She gave him the address and rang off immediately.

Katy was actually none too pleased when he got through to her a few minutes later, but on hearing how impressed A. J. Smythe's appeared to be with what he had shown them, she gave in with a good grace. As he put down the receiver, he realized that he had omitted to mention that it was a lady who was taking him out to lunch; but then he reflected that it would be much easier to explain about all that when he got back to Wilhampton.

During the morning Philip found his thoughts straying more and more to his forthcoming engagement with Barbara Woodley. For one thing, apart from his step-mother, he had never been taken out to lunch by a female before. Even if this was a business affair, surely he should pay? Would Barbara want to go over his manuscript with him at the table? Or were her 'one or two points' simply something she wished to discuss in more general terms? Then he was surprised at her choice of restaurant, for the Casa Mara was nowhere near A. J. Smythe's. It was in Kensington – a long way from the Strand. But he supposed that there was probably some very good explanation and he would soon find out.

He arrived a little before one and waited in the small foyer which, after the glare outside, seemed incredibly dark. At one point he began to wonder whether Barbara might also be lurking in one of the dim alcoves and took the precaution of wandering round to make sure. Then, to his relief, he saw her coming through the door. With the light behind her she made rather a striking silhouette. It could almost have been that of a young boy, except that she was wearing a straight, thin, yet rather revealing dress – a kind which he believed Katy would describe as 'button-through' – long pear-shaped earrings and, on the hand which she raised in greeting, he noticed several bangles around the wrist. To his dismay, he also noticed that she did not appear to be carrying his manuscript. He had a copy, of course, but could she possibly have left it in a taxi? Surely she wasn't intending to *keep* his initial chapters?

'Hello, there!' At least Barbara did not seem to be worried about anything.

'Hello.'

'Would you like a drink here or shall we go straight through and have one while we're ordering? I've booked a table right at the end where we shall be least disturbed. There's so much to-ing and fro-ing here.'

He was annoyed with himself for not asking her first

310

about a drink. Feeling that it was expected of him to comply with her latter suggestion, he answered, 'Yes, perhaps it would be best to have drinks at the table, you must let me . . .'

With a quick, 'This is on the firm, Philip,' she brushed his remark aside and they followed a waiter down a dark passageway between separate little cubicles resembling, he felt, horses' loose-boxes, each seemingly lit by scarcely more than a nightlight. When they had eventually squeezed themselves side by side behind their table, he became uncomfortably aware of two things: the overpowering musky scent she had worn yesterday and the fact that it was more or less impossible for their thighs not to touch.

'You'd like a Martini, wouldn't you? They make rather good ones here.' She had turned to face him and her lips, when she spoke, seemed less than two or three inches from his.

'Thank you. A Martini sounds . . . fine.'

Then, when the waiter placed the drinks in front of them, she raised her own and, looking him once again full in the face, said solemnly, 'To *Sun in the Morning*,' before giving a low little laugh.

Philip glowed. His amazing luck at having been taken on by Barbara Woodley instead of Mr Burgess, her obvious admiration for his work, the exceptionally strong Martini to which he was not accustomed – especially at midday – were all combining to make him feel on top of the world. His book was going to be a winner. He'd had an expert's opinion about that. It had been silly of Katy not to have recognized the quality of his first four chapters at once, silly of him to have ever let her lack of enthusiasm depress him. After all, his wife was still very much a provincial little thing at heart. She did not *know* what went to make a bestseller. This woman beside him did. Barbara was reading manuscripts every day. But, incredibly, it would seem that she had not read anything as good as *Sun in the Morning* for a long time.

'It's so . . . refreshing, Philip,' she was now saying. 'Of course, you'll be *expanding* the characters all the time.'

'Expanding?'

'Yes, well, developing. I mean, so far we've only got Elspeth in her . . . how shall I put it . . . *unawakened* days.'

Again he noticed, just as he had done yesterday, the slightly mysterious allusive way in which she spoke. She had somehow managed to make the word 'unawakened' sound infinitely exciting.

'Is that one of the points you mentioned that you wanted to talk to me about?' he asked, becoming more at ease with her.

'Did I?' She laughed again. 'Maybe. But as a matter of fact, Philip, I've really no criticism. I *long* to read more. I'm *dying* to know when Howard . . .' She stopped, suddenly.

'When Howard what?'

This time she gave him a look of mock disapproval. 'Oh, come now, Philip. You know perfectly well what I'm waiting for. I'm always interested to know how my authors deal with the subject. Personally, I should think you'd do it rather well.'

All his growing confidence deserted him. He found himself becoming hot all over. Fortunately, their food arrived at that point and Barbara appeared not to notice his discomfiture as she began to eat.

It was not until the end of the meal, after they had talked — mostly about himself and his life in Wilhampton — that he began to wonder what the time was. He had told Katy he would catch either the three-thirty or the five-thirty train. He was sure that the first one was now out of the question. Even so, he felt that some sort of move should be made. For one thing, surely Barbara would have to get back to A. J. Smythe's. Surreptitiously, he looked at his watch.

She was quick to notice. Dropping a hand lightly on his, she said, 'Philip, I'm so sorry. You must have been wondering what on earth I've done with your manuscript. It's quite safe, but it's at my flat. I left it there when I went to the office this morning meaning to pick it up on my way here, but I got held up by an incredibly dull man who's writing a book about the Andes. So I came straight on as I didn't want to be late. But I only live a few steps away. Would you care to come along and get it with me?'

'Yes. Yes, of course.' He felt tremendously relieved.

After reassuring him about lunch being on the firm, she signed the bill and then, allowing him to leave the tip, they made their way outside.

It was very hot on the pavement and he was glad when she led him down a side street into a small shady square. At a tall Victorian dilapidated-looking house in one corner, she stopped and got out her keys. 'It's rather a sad façade, don't you think,' she said, half apologetically, 'I believe it belonged to some American who came to grief in the Wall Street crash. Then some entrepreneur snapped it up for a song. He was meant to be converting it into separate flats but so far nothing much has happened. I've just got a bed-sitting room on the first floor and the use of a bathroom. But at least my room's large. When I'm feeling depressed I like to imagine all the receptions that must once have taken place in it. Although sometimes, I must admit, that makes me feel even more sorry for myself.'

He had not thought of Barbara Woodley as ever feeling sorry for herself. She did not appear to be that kind of person, although he was still uncertain as to what kind of person she really was. He could have kicked himself for not asking more about her at lunch.

As soon as he followed her into her room, Philip could see what she meant about it. It was certainly large and the ceiling was high and ornate; yet the paintwork was peeling and there was an overall look of neglect about the place. Heavy worn curtains, assisted by the plane trees now in full leaf in the square, shut out much of the light. For a while, the green murkiness prevented him from seeing into the corners, but presently he became aware of a screen in one of them, round which he could just discern a small gas ring and a wash bowl; in another, to his astonishment, there was a bed made up on the floor. There appeared to be little other furniture, but a vast quantity of books and pile upon pile of papers and manuscripts. He wondered where his own was.

'It's not quite what you were expecting, is it, Philip?' Barbara had made no move to look for *Sun in the Morning*, but was standing watching him, almost defiantly.

'I . . . well, I don't know what I was expecting, exactly.' He smiled, but he felt uneasy and wished to goodness that he had not been obliged to visit the place where she lived.

'No?' This time she gave another of her low little laughs. He saw that she seemed to be deliberately fiddling with one of the buttons at the top of her dress. He watched her silently as she undid it and her fingers dropped to the one below. It was very quiet in the room now, except for the occasional distant muffled sound of traffic from the Kensington Road. He tried to tell himself that he did not know what she was about, that all he wanted was to find his manuscript and get out. Yet somehow he could only stand and stare at her as she revealed more and more of her slim boyish body.

'You asked me at the beginning of lunch, Philip,' Barbara went on slowly, in that strange hypnotic husky voice, 'about those one or two little points I mentioned. Well, as I said, I've really no criticisms – only that at this stage of the book I honestly believe I could help you *expand* Elspeth, if only you would stop looking so frightened and come here.'

17

'Emily dear, stand still, do. I can't possibly fit you for your school overalls if you keep jigging that silly yo-yo up and down.'

'Sorry, Aunt Chip.'

It was the end of August and Katy was ill in bed with summer 'flu. May had volunteered to finish making the remainder of the uniform which the pupils of Wickfield House were requested to wear. Personally, she thought much of it quite unnecessary, especially the items listed for a day-girl. How could Emily possibly need three long-sleeved red tobralco overalls? Or five long-sleeved winceyette navy and white striped blouses with ten detachable white piqué collars?

Katy had bought most of the basic requirements from Burt and Burt in Westonbury: her daughter's navy West of England overcoat, for instance; a smart navy serge skirt and pleated gym tunic; and such necessities as Emily's 'board', the straw boater with the navy ribbon and red badge on the front, which all the Wickfield young ladies took a pride in wearing as long, so Emily informed May, as it did not look too new. 'No one wants to look like a *new* girl, Aunt Chip. Helen and Daphne and I are determined to make our boards look positively ancient as soon as possible.'

All the same, Emily looked very much like a new girl, May thought, as she accompanied her and her mother to Wickfield House on the first day of the September term in 1931. Her face had that apprehensive vulnerable look of which May had been so aware when she had stayed in Davies Street getting on for two years ago now. Since Emily had come to live in Wilhampton May thought that the child had seemed to recover her usual *joie de vivre*; but just lately there had been times when she was not so sure. She wondered if it had something to do with Katy, whether perhaps Emily overreacted to her mother's recent unaccountable fits of depression, however much May knew that her sister tried to disguise them.

There was no doubt that both Katy and Emily had, understandably, been disappointed that Philip had had to be in London on this particular day, even though Katy had learned to drive the family car and delivering a daughter to school on such an occasion was not exactly a father's responsibility. Indeed, it was an exclusively female gathering, May noted, which milled about in the hall of Wickfield's junior house, as more and more small girls arrived with their escorts, including Helen Swayne and her mother. There appeared to be no sign of Daphne Chadwick, but May supposed that the little thing must have already been taken care of as, owing to her grandfather's imminent retirement and the fact that her parents were still in India, Daphne had been obliged to become a boarder and, consequently, taken to the school the previous evening.

Always interested in whatever was going on around her – especially in a situation such as today's which she had not hitherto experienced – May was delighted to see that

Emily's uniform fitted a great deal better than most of the other children's; also that her niece was one of the prettiest amongst them. Presently, there was a call for silence and then, one by one, each new girl was put in the charge of a companion: a child who had already been at the school for at least two terms. In the case of Emily, a diminutive ginger-haired little boarder called Charlotte Blakeley suddenly whisked her away through an inner door and Katy and May were left, rather sadly, to make their way outside and back to the car.

'It was good of you to come, May. I must say I felt in need of a bit of support. Wickfield's so vast. I didn't like seeing Emily swallowed up like that, did you?' Katy opened the near side door of the Morris for her sister and then went round and slid into the driving seat.

'No. But it isn't as if she's a boarder like Daphne Chadwick and that other poor mite who led her away. You'll be fetching her home again at half-past three.'

'Yes. Silly of me to mind,' Katy replied, drawing away from the kerb. 'But with Philip having to go to London so much these days, Emily's a good little companion.'

May was silent for a while. She knew what Katy meant. She had been aware of Philip's increasing absences from home for some time and wondered whether all was well with the shop. She did not like to probe but occasionally, as now, it seemed as if her sister might almost welcome some kind of friendly enquiry.

'How's Philip getting on with his book?' May asked at length. 'I suppose having to be in town rather holds him up.'

'Yes, in a way, although . . .' Katy waited for a policeman to wave them over a crossroads and then went on, 'It's really often the book which takes him to London.'

'How do you mean?'

'Well, he's got these agents. Apparently there's someone there who's advising him as he goes along. A mannish young woman, as he calls her, who is very enthusiastic about it.'

'Oh.' May had not come across any mannish young women. In Wilhampton, even if a girl was as 'plain as a yard of pump water', as her mother was apt to put it, she was never described as mannish. She felt her brother-in-law's statement to be rather odd.

'I hope she knows what she's talking about,' Katy continued, expertly double-declutching as she negotiated some of Westonbury's narrow old streets. May was surprised at what a good, careful driver her youngest sister had become — an even better one, she felt, than Philip, who was apt to jerk the gears and get annoyed when he was overtaken.

'I suppose she wouldn't be in her job if she didn't, would she?' May answered, trying to be comforting in a conversation which was somewhat beyond her. She found it hard to imagine how anyone wrote a book and had been astonished when she had heard that her brother-in-law was attempting it.

'No. All the same, I should have thought it would have been far better for Philip to get on and finish it now. I know I wouldn't want anybody breathing down my neck if I were trying to create something or other.'

May could not help noticing the tone of exasperation which had crept into Katy's voice and she kept thinking about their conversation long after her sister had dropped her in Cob Lane. Often that day she laid down her sewing and sat staring into the fire, allowing the cat to jump up into her lap. Katy wasn't happy. She had not really been happy since coming back to Wilhampton. Apart from all the other difficulties her sister was up against, May felt that it was possible she had been away too long. Katy had severed — or almost severed — that strange hold which May always vowed her home ground seemed to exercise over its inhabitants; although, when she came to think about it, she had to admit that it was not necessarily those who were born and bred there who seemed to come under its spell. Had not Philip himself been the prime motivator in moving his wife and child back to the place? Ever since he had spent his holiday working on the Swaynes' farm during the summer when he was courting Katy, May knew that he had hankered after living in the district. Nevertheless, what, ostensibly, had seemed a good idea did not

317

now appear to be working out. May wondered whether it would ever do so. She was still convinced that she had been right to maintain her own independence and decline to live at the Moat as she had been asked, but, all the same, she wished that she was able to give her youngest sister more positive support. It had been good to have been needed this morning, even if it was not for very long. She was looking forward to hearing how Emily had got on when the child paid her a promised visit at the weekend.

May was by no means the only one waiting on such news. That evening, Ethel Sharman called in soon after tea. She, too, had just started out on a new term's lessons. It was often a difficult time for her and this September she had felt particularly bereft. For several years she had known and taught the same three little girls – Emily, perhaps, not so long as the others, yet Ethel felt that she knew her better. Emily had certainly been her favourite, although she had done her best not to show it. She wondered so much what would happen to them all now that they had left her care. It was hard having to adjust to new faces, different levels of intelligence. She was therefore all the more grateful for the unexpected compensation that had just come her way and about which, after listening to May's description of all that had taken place that morning, she proceeded to give her neighbour the details.

'I've got another new pupil arriving next week, May. You'll never guess who. Not in a month of Sundays.'

'Then tell me, Ethel, do.' May looked up from the buttonhole she was working on a blouse for the mayoress elect: Arnold Parker's daughter-in-law.

'Phoebe Moreton,' replied Ethel, watching intently to see the effect the name would have on her listener.

'*Phoebe Moreton?* Oh, chippatoo! You don't mean it, Ethel.'

'Yes I do. Lady Fairfax asked me to go round to the Hall this afternoon and it's all fixed up. Apparently her daughter and her husband are off to the States for a couple of months. The boy, John William, is at boarding school, as you know. But Lady Moreton is insistent that the girl must always be taught privately. It seems, however, that she finds it difficult to keep a governess.' Though not given to gossip, Ethel's voice now dropped to a confidential whisper. She was obviously excited. 'It seems to me,' she went on, 'Phoebe's a bit wild. But there's another draw-back. The governesses don't like old Nanny Barlow forever interfering and telling them how to care for the child. Lady Fairfax didn't *say* that exactly . . . I mean, not in so many words. But one could sense that there's a difficult situation going on in Suffolk. Anyway, the long and the short of it is that while Sir Charles and Lady Moreton are abroad, Phoebe and Nanny Barlow and some young helper called Daisy from their local village are all coming to Wilhampton, and Phoebe will be brought to me each day for lessons.'

'Well I never did. But you'll like that, won't you, Ethel?' May resumed her sewing, conscious that she had let herself get behindhand with it that day.

'Yes, I suppose so. It's a challenge, so to speak. But mind you, I don't want a subversive influence disrupting my classes. I don't quite know *how* wild Phoebe is. I've still got Elsie Jane, remember, until her parents move after Christmas, and she's so easily led astray.'

'I'm sure you'll manage, Ethel. And besides, I shouldn't think Lady Fairfax would stand any nonsense from her grand-daughter. It will probably do the child a power of good to have a spell at the Hall.'

Ethel's news certainly took May's mind off her more personal concerns and, later on when she was in bed that night, she found herself speculating as to which side of the family Phoebe's wildness came from. She would never have described dear Miss Alicia – as she always thought of her – as *wild*. On the other hand, she was obviously highly strung. There was that bad breakdown she had had the year after John William had been born. There had been a lot of speculation about that, although no one in Wilhampton had really heard much. The Fairfaxes had hushed it up pretty effectively, simply letting it be known that their daughter had been overdoing things and ordered to have a complete rest. But May had been well aware of the rumours which had gone round, how some people hinted that it was a case of delayed puerperal depression. Personally, she had never thought that. She had felt it probably had much more to do with husband trouble. Besides, the word *divorce* had actually crept into certain conversations, as well as the name of Grace Armitage. May, like Ethel Sharman, did not hold with gossip but, all the same, she had not been able to help *wondering*. The Moretons had not spent a great deal of time in Wilhampton that year, but it was well known that Grace, according to the Fairfaxes' housekeeper, was forever 'waltzing off to London'. May supposed that it was just possible that Charles Moreton had fallen victim to whatever strange alchemy Grace seemed to have for the opposite sex. Men were so fickle, as she knew to her cost. They could so easily be led astray.

Was that, she hazarded, as her mind reverted to her own kith and kin, what had happened to Philip? Why Katy was so on edge these days? Unable to settle down? That derisory reference she had made this morning to some 'mannish young woman . . .' The more May thought about it, the more she came to realize that Grace Armitage could hardly be called the fluffy feminine type.

18

'There's my bus, Aunt Chip.'

Emily's rendering of 'Over the Waves' came to an abrupt halt. The lid of May's piano suddenly shut with a bang, after which she heard her niece dash out of the front door and across the green into Wilhampton market square.

From her bedroom window in Cob Lane, May stood watching the flying figure, waited for several minutes until it was joined by Helen Swayne and an older Wickfield pupil and then, after seeing all three board the Westonbury bus, she went back to making her bed.

It had been like that for several weeks now. Ever since their respective mothers had mutually agreed that, at least in the mornings, Emily and Helen could be trusted to take this form of transport to school as long as Hazel Betts could escort them, May had become accustomed to the front door of her cottage opening unceremoniously, often as early as seven forty-five, and straight away finding herself listening to some of her niece's latest musical accomplishments.

Although she was pleased to have this fleeting daily contact with the child, May was becoming increasingly perturbed by Emily's almost obsessional fear of being late for school through missing her bus. However much she pointed out that the driver always waited at least ten minutes in the market square and, if the worst came to the worst, there was always a second bus which followed on in a quarter of an hour, Emily was invariably out of the door as soon as the big red double-decker came into sight before it slowly turned round and halted in its customary place, while the driver and conductor sauntered off to the local café for a cup of coffee.

May had actually brought up the subject of the child's unnatural agitation with Katy, only to receive the rather despairing reply, 'Oh, I *know*. I've even mentioned it to Maurice because Emily won't sit still long enough to eat a proper breakfast, but all he says is that she'll probably come out of it and meanwhile I'd better give her a piece of toast to eat as she runs down the drive.' To which May had said, 'Or let her have breakfast with me rather than playing the piano.'

Emily was completely oblivious of the fact that her mother and aunt were so concerned about her behaviour. For the moment, Wickfield House was the most important thing in her life, that is, apart from some incomprehensible incidents at home which made her wonder whether other day-girls ever suffered from the same tribulations. Surely Helen Swayne's mother never lay on the bed in the daytime with the curtains drawn? Or started weeping for no apparent reason? In any case, grown-ups were not meant to weep. Only people of her own age were allowed that privilege, such as yesterday when it had been quite understandable for Helen to cry in the cloakroom after gym.

Emily had done her best to console her friend by calling Miss Burrows 'preposterous' and 'a monster', but she knew that Helen was still desperately hurt and embarrassed by what had happened that morning when her mother arrived to drive them both home in the afternoon. For after Helen had climbed right to the top of one of the ropes in the junior section of the gym, Miss Burrows had told her to stay there. Then she had asked the rest of the class to look up and say what was wrong with the small figure, miserably clutching on several feet above them. There had been a few feeble sniggers and then Janie Crossman, a pert sharp-featured girl, had piped up, 'She's got smiles, Miss Burrows.' And Miss Burrows had said, "Quite right, Janie. You may come down now, Helen, but please ask your mother to buy you some longer black stockings.'

Much as Emily adored being at Wickfield, she had been appalled at Miss Burrows's mean behaviour. Although she knew that no one was meant to show gaps of flesh between the tops of her stockings and the bottoms of her knickers and that sometimes culprits were teased for having so-called 'smiles', it seemed quite unjustifiable for poor Helen to have been singled out by a mistress in such a shockingly unkind way.

Today, as they sat together on top of the bus, Emily noticed that Helen was still very subdued. Only when Hazel Betts had disappeared into the senior school and they themselves were alone together in the junior cloak-room did Helen suddenly pull Emily into the corner behind the hot-water tank, lift her skirt and say, 'Look, Mummy sewed some black stuff round the tops. You see, these stockings are new ones. She couldn't afford to buy me any more just now.'

'Oh, I see.' Emily did not know what else to say, even though she did not really see why Helen's mother could not buy her another pair of stockings. She was vaguely aware that her own parents occasionally talked about something called a depression and referred to the Swaynes as being badly hit by it and very hard up; yet to Emily they always seemed to have so much: a large rambling farmhouse, countless buildings and outhouses, acres and acres of green fields, cows and chickens galore and a *pony*.

True, Black Beauty somewhat belied her name. No one could describe her as exactly beautiful today. For many years past she had patiently borne Helen's two older brothers on her broad back. Now she was old and fat and lazy, not a bit like the smart shining pony which Emily had seen Phoebe Moreton riding in the company of the Fairfaxes' groom. All the same, Helen had something she longed for and it distressed Emily that her mother kept procrastinating about letting her have proper riding lessons with Miss Cory.

When half-term came and there was a meet of the local hounds at the Hall, Emily inveigled Katy into taking her to it. Almost at once, she caught sight of Phoebe Moreton astride the same pony, both of them looking even more dashing than ever. Then suddenly, she saw Phoebe's brother, the golden-haired boy whom she remembered meeting at the mill. Incredibly, he seemed to notice her just at the same moment and came sauntering over to where she and her mother were standing.

'Good morning,' he said, raising his cap and smiling first at one and then the other of them. He wore long fawn corduroy trousers and a smart check sports jacket which exactly matched his cap. She wondered why he was not mounted like his sister. She smiled, shyly, relieved that her mother was able to do the talking for them both.

'How nice to see you, John. It must be your half-term, too.'

'Yes. I'm here until Monday night.'

'You're not riding then, like Phoebe?'

He frowned slightly. 'No,' he said and then, after a slight hesitation, added, 'as a matter of fact, I don't much care for it. Ridiculous animals, horses.'

Emily found herself staring at him in astonishment. It seemed an extraordinary attitude to adopt. Here was a boy with every opportunity at his command, who could have ridden whenever he came home to his parents or grandparents – and yet he spurned the idea. She felt that there must be something very odd about him. Almost as if he sensed her silent disapproval, he suddenly continued, defensively, 'Phoebe and I are going to see Charlie Chaplin at the picture house in Westonbury on Monday afternoon. Would you like to come?'

Again her mother came to the rescue. 'I expect your grandmother has arranged the treat just for the two of you, John. I don't think . . .' But at that point, Lady Fairfax came up to them all and her grandson wasted no time in asking if Emily could accompany them.

'But, of course.' Was there, Katy wondered, a faint flicker of irritation in the ageing blue eyes, a slight forcedness in her usual spontaneity? 'I will get Johnson to drive us all round to the Moat so that we can pick Emily up and drop her again when we come back. I would have suggested her coming to the Hall for tea, but I'm afraid that will have to be rather a rushed affair, as we have to get John William back to school by 7 p.m.'

'Yes, I quite understand. But it will be lovely for Emily to see the film. Thank you so much.'

Lady Fairfax's attention was claimed elsewhere and in that seemingly vague yet skilful way which Katy remembered so well, she watched her drift away towards a top-hatted, pink-coated gentleman, who leaned down from his mount and began saying something to her about the new national government. But soon their conversation was drowned by the sound of a hunting horn and the hounds moving off in the charge of Colonel Egremont, the master, Tim Cutler, his huntsman, and an amateur whipper-in called Major Freddie Waring. Emily stood spellbound as the field came after them, Phoebe Moreton, although at the back and on a leading rein, looking extremely self-confident and disdainful and obviously not taking kindly to the admonishment from Tom Bartlett, the Fairfaxes' groom, to 'Hold back there, Miss. There's no hurry. They're only going to draw Home Farm cover first.'

With a sudden surge of uncustomary hatred and jealousy, Emily watched her pass, noted the black velvet peaked cap, the beautifully-fitting jacket and jodhpurs, the yellow string gloves and the way she kept tossing her head, a little in keeping with the pony she was riding.

Although Emily had never been taken to the pictures, she said to her mother on the way home, 'I don't want to

324

go to that Charlie Chaplin film with John William and his sister on Monday. I think he's soppy and Phoebe's quite *preposterous*.' The last newly acquired adjective was one which Emily was apt to use these days as often as she could, particularly in connection with the Wickfield gym mistress.

Katy Mason looked at her daughter in some concern. 'I don't think we can refuse now, darling. You'll probably enjoy it when you get there. Besides, you heard what Lady Fairfax said. You don't have to go back to the Hall for tea with them.'

'No, I suppose not.'

Nevertheless, when Monday afternoon arrived, Emily felt very much in the same frame of mind as, just before two o'clock, she waited for her escorts by a downstairs window, wearing a pretty blue tweed dress and coat – made by her aunt, a blue velour hat, brown hand-knitted gloves and stockings – made by her mother – and smart brown leather shoes with a bar and buckle. As soon as the Fairfaxes' car could be seen approaching, Katy opened the front door, watched while the chauffeur stopped, got out and carefully helped Emily into the back seat, where Lady Fairfax was just visible giving a small wave as the little party drove off again.

'And I wonder,' said Philip, suddenly coming out of his study at that moment, 'what our young daughter will have to tell us about *that* little outing when she gets back.'

Katy shrugged and began to walk away. It had been like that between them for some time now whenever they had been alone.

'Katy.' He called after her as she began to mount the stairs. 'I think you should know something.' She halted, but still remained with her back towards him, one hand on the banisters. 'I no longer have an agent,' he continued, quietly.

This time she turned and stared at him. 'Have you finished *Sun in the Morning*, then?'

'No.'

'But . . . I don't understand.'

'I decided that . . . I might be better off alone . . . I mean, an agent seemed to interfere . . .'

'In more ways than one,' she answered, bitterly.

'If you put it like that.'

There was silence in the hall then. A wintry sunlight filtered through the window on the stairs. Her small figure seemed fragile and defenceless as it waited motionless, caught in its rays. He took a step towards her, conscious of how perfectly dressed she was, as always, of the way she now wore her hair so that it fell in soft brown waves round her pale face, of the wary look in her large grey eyes. He had been a fool. He felt he could have killed himself for the hurt he had caused her.

Instead, he held out his arms.

19

'And then he carried her upstairs.'

'Why? Was she took bad?'

'No, silly. He just carried her on into their bedroom and *locked the door*.'

'But . . . whatever for?'

Rose put down her iron and burst out laughing. It was the following day. Emily was back at school. Philip and Katy had gone to London together and May was due at the Moat at four o'clock in order to take charge during their absence. It was the first time that Rose had had an opportunity of telling Miriam what she had witnessed the previous afternoon from behind a crack in the baize door, while her friend had been allowed out to visit her sick mother. She now looked at Miriam with a mixture of knowing indulgence, suddenly aware of the gap in their ages – Rose was just seventeen and Miriam two years younger – and wondering how best to enlighten her on such matters.

'Well,' she said, at length, picking up the iron and holding it to her face to test the heat before banging it down again on a pillow case, 'it isn't as if they're not married, is it? I expect he just wanted to . . .' Rose dropped her voice, even though they were alone in the house, 'well, *you know*,' she whispered.

Miriam did not know. She sat on one of the wooden kitchen chairs and stared at Rose in bewilderment. She was a short, thickset girl with a pale moon-like face, straight dark hair and round, steel-framed spectacles. She was not one of a family, for her mother had been widowed at the end of the war while she was still a baby. She had no idea what Rose was talking about, nor could she appreciate the significance of her next remark, which did not seem to bear much relation to the earlier ones.

'They didn't come downstairs until just before Miss Emily come back from the pictures, about five o'clock.'

'Oh.'

'I suppose they could have 'ad a bit of a sleep afterwards.'

'After what?'

This time Rose frowned a little in exasperation. Miriam was being singularly stupid. Was she really unable to grasp what was being said to her? Of course, with looks like hers it was perhaps natural for not to have much interest in the opposite sex, nor they in her. She did not have a young man like Rose's Archie Carter, who would keep putting his hands where he shouldn't while they said good-night in the shrubbery, when he brought her back to the Moat at nine-thirty after her half-day off. Still, it was time Miriam was acquainted with the facts of life. Perhaps she could jolt her slow intelligence by a perfectly simple straightforward statement, something which she could not fail to understand.

'She might have another baby because of what they did yesterday.'

Miriam's eyes behind her spectacles seemed to grow twice their size.

'You don't mean they . . . ?' Her words trailed off, uncertainly. She was vaguely aware that a baby could not be produced except through some kind of secret and shameful goings-on between a man and a woman; but exactly what form such goings-on took she had no idea, other than that she believed they happened at night.

'Of course I do,' Rose answered, smugly.

'But in the *afternoon?*'

Suddenly, the memory of her last half-day off came vividly into Rose's mind. She knew that it wasn't going to be easy fending off Archie Carter much longer, especially if they were still walking out next spring when the lighter evenings came and they went up to Breconbury Woods. 'There's no set time for that sort of thing, Miriam,' she now replied, as one with experience.

'Oh.'

'Anyway, I can tell you that whatever happened made Mrs Mason ever so pleased. Madam's been such a down-in-the-mouth lately, but yesterday evening, when I was clearing away the tea things, she was all smiles. She and Mr Mason were laughing away while Miss Emily was pretending to be Charlie Chaplin and then, this morning, when she came to tell me they was going to London, she asked me if I'd iron that pretty new nightdress Miss Lodge made her a little while ago so's she could take it with her.'

May, too, had certainly noticed a dramatic change in her youngest sister when Katy had suddenly burst in on her early that morning, asking if she would spend the night at the Moat because she and Philip wanted to go to London unexpectedly. 'He's taking me to Noel Coward's *Cavalcade*, May. It's a miracle he got tickets. It's only been on a few weeks, but he rang up and there were two cancellations, so then he asked Jack Lumley to send someone straight down to Drury Lane to buy them.' She seemed all at once a girl again, the one May remembered just before her marriage: elated, flushed, her whole being excited as a child's at the thought of a promised treat. It was difficult to credit that she was the mother of a little one who would be ten years old in a few weeks' time.

In fact, May reflected, as she locked up Number Three Cob Lane that afternoon and started to walk towards the Moat, the child in Katy was never far from the surface, for all her seeming air of sophistication which she did her best to show to the world. Only perhaps those close to her knew the fearful, immature, despondent side of her nature and even they did not always understand it. May

328

had had a shrewd idea of the present trouble, but she had never been directly confided in. However, thank goodness whatever it was had presumably now been resolved; yet she wondered for how long. All the old reservations she had had about Philip before Katy had married him kept coming back, but to a greater degree. He wasn't stable enough, he was too impulsive, too full of impractical ideas. This business of writing a book, for instance . . . Not for the first time did six little words keep repeating themselves in her mind: *Katy should have married Maurice Fitzherbert.*

May had not been long at the Moat before she saw the Swaynes' car coming up the drive. She knew that when it was their turn to collect Emily and Helen from Wickfield it usually just stopped at the gate. But today it turned in and from where she was standing at the drawing-room window she watched Dick Swayne get out and accompany her niece up the steps. She went to the front door anxiously, wondering whether something was wrong with the child, and was relieved when Emily simply threw her arms around her as usual and skipped into the house. All the same, she thought that Dick looked unnaturally grave, as he took off his cap.

'I wondered if you'd heard the news, May.'

'News . . . ?' She stared at him, blankly.

'About Lord Fairfax. He died today.'

'*No!*'

'Yes. I had to call at the estate office on my way into Westonbury and they told me there. Apparently he had a stroke this morning.'

'Oh, *Dick* . . .' May was well aware that James Fairfax had never been an exactly strong character; he had never had the same force of personality as his wife, nor commanded the same respect. Many people in Wilhampton still held him and his *laisser faire* attitude responsible for the floods in 1929; but all the same, he had been lord of the manor for as long as May could remember. Within his limits, he was kind and meant well. It was just that his nature was too easy-going, too lacka-daisical for the duties demanded of it. But his wife seemed to have more than compensated for such defects. In fact, when May came to think about it, they had always gone well in double-harness, as Sarah would have put it. She could not imagine what the Hall would be like without them. For Lady Fairfax would almost certainly move out and their eldest son, Edmund, and his wife, take over; and Edmund, so it was rumoured – the owner of a small estate in the next county – was hardly ever at home. At least Lord Fairfax had usually been around somewhere, even if it was mostly with a gun under his arm during the winter and a fishing-rod in his hand in the summer.

After May had said goodbye to Dick Swayne, she found it hard to concentrate on Emily's excited chatter throughout the rest of the evening. She realized that it was only to be expected that the death of Lord Fairfax meant little to the child, even if she had gone to the pictures with his grandson and grand-daughter the day before. She knew well that grandparents were often shadowy figures to the younger generation, becoming more and more so as the latter grew up. She herself had extremely dim memories of her own. But now, in middle age, it made her feel sad to think how the old, who were coming to the end of their days, had so much more interest in the young who, with hardly a backward glance, imagined life would go on for ever. For May, although the passing of Lord Fairfax evoked no personal grief, nevertheless it emphasized the end of an era, rather as her mother's death had done two years previously; but then, with her habitual way of trying to make the best of things, she reminded herself that at least he and Sarah had had a reasonable innings.

She was not altogether surprised when, after seeing Emily on to the school bus the following morning, she returned home to find an envelope addressed to her in Lady Fairfax's handwriting lying on the front mat. She had already wondered about mourning, for although she knew that the wardrobe of her most distinguished client invariably contained plenty of black, the death of her *husband* would almost certainly necessitate more. Therefore later that day, a little before the requested hour of 3 p.m., May set off, discreetly, for the Hall.

When she arrived and was shown up to Lady Fairfax's boudoir, she found her, as she had anticipated, perfectly calm and composed. Her face was pale and there were deep lines beneath the eyes which showed signs of having recently shed tears, yet tears which May felt certain would have been shed in private. Her voice, when she spoke, was quieter than usual, yet it still had the same clear authoritarian ring about it.

'The funeral won't be for well over a week, May,' she said, after the latter had proffered some simple condolences. 'I've had a cable from Alicia. She and her husband are sailing from New York on the *Mauretania* tomorrow, but one has to allow for the weather in the Atlantic at this time of the year. It could take up to eight days, so as there's time, I thought perhaps you could possibly make me a two-piece with this length of black bouclé I bought in London only last month.' She went over to a chaise longue and picked up the material. 'You know the style I like, May,' she continued, handing it to her, 'and you've got all my measurements. I don't think my figure's altered since last time, except that I would like you now to make the skirt a good three inches longer.'

There was a knock on the door and a parlourmaid appeared to tell her that she was wanted by her son on the telephone. With a hasty, 'Perhaps you'd have a word with Nanny before you go, my dear. I'm afraid the news has been a terrible shock to her,' she hurried away.

Although May had heard from Ethel Sharman how much Nanny Barlow had aged, she was unprepared for such a pathetic sight when the same young parlourmaid showed her along several passages and into a small room near the nursery quarters. The old lady sat hunched in a wicker chair by the fire, her face blotched, her eyes puffed and swollen. She wore a black knitted shawl over her shoulders and her whole body seemed to have shrunk to half its former size. It seemed impossible to believe that this was the upright, well-preserved woman under whose jurisdiction and care May had once put Katy over twelve years ago. For a moment, she did not appear to recognize her visitor and then, when she did, she said, querulously.

'Ah, it's May, isn't it? May Lodge. Come about the mourning, have you?'

'Yes, Nanny.'

'A bad business. A very bad business. And Miss Alicia on the other side of the world. She'd no call to go waltzing off like that and leaving Phoebe with this silly girl, Daisy.'

'But Phoebe's had you, Nanny. And Lady Fairfax, and even Ethel Sharman in the mornings to keep an eye on her.' May did her best to be placatory. 'And it's probably been good for her coming to . . .' May almost said grandparents, but corrected herself in time. 'The Hall,' she added, quickly.

Nanny Barlow seemed not to pay the slightest attention to her words. 'Her mother ought to be here,' she said, 'especially at a time like this.' The voice had become fiercer now. 'Phoebe's headstrong,' she went on. 'With my arthritis, I can't be with her every minute of the day and she needs a firm hand. What do you think happened this afternoon? She was gallivanting down the back stairs all dressed up for her daily ride. I was only just in time to stop her. The Lord knows where Daisy was. Of course, Tom Bartlett would never have taken her once she'd got to the stables, but just think of the child running across the forecourt in her riding clothes with her grandfather hardly cold. Why, when Miss Alicia and her brother were small and Lady Fairfax's mother died, I had black armbands on 'em within the hour *and* I never took them into Wilhampton for three months afterwards.'

May was silent. From the direction of the day nursery she could hear a few faltering notes being played on the piano and then a child's voice raised in argument. She remembered her own mother's attitude to death. But time had gone on since then. Things had changed; although obviously Nanny Barlow had not changed with them. Suddenly, the piano-playing started up again, louder than before. Despite all her infirmities, May realized that the old lady before her was not exactly deaf. Nanny Barlow rose, with difficulty, and walked towards the door, shaking her head. ' "Little Brown Jug",' May heard her mutter, as she left the room. 'I ask you. Playing "Little Brown Jug" with death in the house.'

Almost it could have been Sarah speaking, in the spring of 1919, after Katy had won a prize for doing an impromptu turn at the fair: 'And how do you think I shall look? It will be all over Wilhampton tomorrow. My youngest daughter singing "Our Lodger's Such a Nice Young Man" and her father not dead three months.'

20

The telephone rang on an afternoon when Katy had gone into Westonbury to do some shopping and fetch Emily and Helen home from school. Philip got up and went into the hall to answer it, not without a certain amount of relief. He felt that he could do with a respite. He had been working on another chapter of *Sun in the Morning* but, although Barbara Woodley was no longer interfering with the plot, he was finding it heavy going.

'Philip.' He had forgotten just how deep and husky her voice was.

He found himself staring at the tall black mouthpiece clutched in his right hand as if it had turned into something venomous, an instrument of torture. Fear and fury welled up inside him. The woman had no business to be ringing. Thank God Katy was out of the house.

'I have nothing else to say, Barbara.'

'Perhaps *you* haven't, my sweet. But I'm afraid *I* have. Are you alone?'

'For the moment.' He dropped his voice, suddenly conscious that Rose or Miriam might be listening from behind the baize door. Rose, particularly, had been altogether too full of herself lately and he had not liked the way she had sometimes glanced at him. He wished he had not spoken Barbara's name. 'I have to go now,' he added, curtly.

'Just a minute, darling. I don't think you quite understand. It isn't as easy as all that. You must realize. I

333

wouldn't have rung otherwise. I have to see you. It's very important.'

'That's impossible.' He was careful not to mention her name again. He found he was actually shaking now. 'Goodbye,' he said, flatly, and was about to hook up the receiver when her next words made him pause.

'Philip, wait. Please. I'm desperate. I'm . . . pregnant.'

He could feel a tightness in his chest. He was sweating profusely although it was freezing in the hall. Out of the corner of his eye he suddenly noticed the Morris turning in at the gate.

'I'll write,' he replied, quickly. 'Someone is coming. Don't ring again.'

He was still standing by the telephone when Katy and Emily came through the front door, their arms full of parcels. He watched them from what seemed like a great distance, as if his wife and child were on the other side of some thick glass barrier, one which he could not and, indeed, had no right to break through. He knew that he had to get away for a while.

'I want to take the car to the garage for some more oil,' he mumbled, and almost bolted from the house.

It was getting quite dark as he drove up to Breconbury Woods, turned round and switched off both the lights and the engine. There were high scudding clouds in the sky from behind which, every so often, a moon shone down on the scene before him. He was bitterly cold now, for he had come out without an overcoat, but it did not seem to matter. Nothing mattered. He had failed the two people who meant more to him than anything else in the world. He lit a cigarette with hands that still shook and remained staring down into the valley below, while the lights of Wilhampton appeared one by one. God, what a mess. He had allowed Barbara Woodley to trick him as if he were some kind of greenhorn. He had believed what he supposed he had wanted to believe. With what had appeared to be the most touching sincerity she had told him, on that first afternoon when she had inveigled him into her home and her bed, that much as she adored children she would never be able to have any because a doctor had diagnosed a twisted fallopian tube. How *could* he have been so gullible? Anyway, what exactly was a fallopian tube and how, when and why had it been diagnosed? But just then, as far as he was concerned, Barbara's handicap had seemed highly convenient. He had made love to her almost savagely; in fact, there had always been a curious element of reckless animosity in their relationship, as if it were an unwelcome necessity. As the weeks went by he came to suspect she was a nymphomaniac. It angered him that he never wholly seemed able to satisfy her. At the end of their sessions together, when he was about to leave her room which, for all its size, was beginning to give him claustrophobia, she would sit up in her bed on the floor, looking like some Lorelei in the greeny half light, her naked torso with its small flat breasts somehow half appealing, half repellent, as she held out her arms and whispered, huskily, 'Please, Philip. Please.' And he would find himself becoming ensnared once more by her strange magnetism and fall back into bed with her, while hating himself for so doing.

She had become almost hysterical when, with all the determination he could muster, he had called to tell her that their affair must cease and their business association as well. She had accused him of every felony she could think of, including a final taunt of being bourgeois. 'All writers have mistresses, Philip,' she had said. 'That's what gives inspiration to their writing. I'm not harming your cosy country domestic set-up. I'm helping it. That precious little wife of yours will have only me to thank, if she did but know it, when *Sun in the Morning* hits the headlines. *She'll* be the one who will bask in all the reflected glory. Not me. But I'm prepared for that . . . just as long as you . . .' And here she had burst into wild, uncontrollable sobs.

It was the disparaging reference to Katy which had made him fighting mad and helped to strengthen his resolve; for even while Barbara had been hurling abuse at him he could feel his sensuality being aroused, knew that he had only to take a step or two towards her and he would be able to quieten her tirade in a way which would have been pleasurable to them both. When he had managed to make it quite clear that he meant what he said, that he was not going to make love to her that day or any other day and, apart from anything else, it was he who was writing *Sun in the Morning* and he did not want an agent continually imposing her own ideas on it, she had given him a cold hard look and thrown the offending manuscript across the floor. He could recall her standing, clad only in a black silk kimono – the garb she usually received him in – as he gathered it up and hurried out of the door, how she had shrieked after him, regardless of any other tenants in the house, 'You'll pay for this, Philip Mason, in more ways than one.'

Well, she had been right on that score. His whole life was in ruins now. He had failed as a husband, a father, a writer and even an antiquarian bookseller. The only thing he had ever been any good at – and even that was merely in a mediocre way – was taking on Mason & Son; and he was not at all sure that he was not now falling down over this. Jack Lumley was a nice enough, conscientious man, but his management left a lot to be desired. Even the possession of something which Philip knew that he did not deserve – Katy's love – was now in jeopardy. How could she possibly go on loving him if she knew the truth? He could never bring himself to tell her, but she would be bound to find out sooner or later. It would be better if he were dead.

He realized that she would already have started to worry about him now, wondering what had kept him. She always worried when he was late, bless her. He remembered the night he had come back from Wales in the fog and how she had thrown her arms around him with relief when he had finally walked through the door, how he made love to her a little later on after telling her about Belle's legacy. Under the circumstances, it probably hadn't been an exactly fitting thing to do, but somehow he hadn't been able to help it. He had been so full of plans for their future. And she had been just as excited, too. He had thought, by bringing her back to Wilhampton into such a much better home, that everything would be just about perfect. But it hadn't worked out like that. People said money didn't bring happiness and they were right. Although it wasn't the money, really, that was the trouble. It was he who was to blame. If only he'd had the sense not to fool around, Katy would have come to make the necessary adjustments and enjoy her role as mistress of the Moat House. In fact, on the evening of that fatal day when he had first gone to Barbara's home and let his wife and child down over the Westonbury Show, Katy had been so taken up with the roses she intended to grow and exhibit the following year that she appeared not to have noticed his own preoccupation. Why on earth, when he had had so much, had he gone and fouled it all up? They could have had a good life, watching Emily grow into a young woman, giving her the education of which Belle would have approved. How could he ever have thought that Barbara Woodley had anything which his wife did not? Why, Katy was a princess compared to her.

He knew now what he had to do and the sooner the better. So great was his anguish, it never occurred to him that Barbara Woodley might have had other lovers, that he was not necessarily the father of her child. In the moonlight he noticed, lying in the pocket of the car's dashboard, a small notepad on which Katy sometimes made a shopping list. He pulled it towards him and took out his fountain pen. Tearing off the first scribbled-on sheet, he wrote 'May' at the top of the next blank one. He scrawled a few more words and put it on the front passenger seat. Then he got out of the car and began to walk.

It took him about three-quarters of an hour. At one point he knew he must be passing within a few feet of the spot where he and Katy had lain together on that never-to-be-forgotten evening during their courting days when, but for the grace of God, he might have taken her virginity. A little lower down he recognized the place where they had met Grace Armitage on their homeward journey and he had been given some inkling of the nature of the woman – undoubtedly another Barbara Woodley, he now thought, bitterly. Then he came in sight of Bulbarrow Farmhouse and buildings, remembering how Dorothy Swayne had given them a cheerful greeting as she crossed over to the barn carrying something for the harvest supper to be held later on. She could well have been pregnant with Helen at the time, he supposed, knowing that Emily's little friend was the elder by several months. His walk tonight seemed to bring the past back in painfully sharp relief, as if he were now engaged on its inevitable sequence or conclusion, as though he were being called to account, his actions predetermined, foredoomed. The only deviation he made in the route was when he turned off at the outskirts of the town, for he knew that the mill gates would be shut and locked at this hour and in order to reach his destination he would have to go by the meadow path.

He heard it now, becoming louder with every step he took. It was about a mile away, then half, then a quarter. He crossed over the stile by the place which Katy always called Nomansland and here it sounded very close. Not much longer now. His mind was made up. And once he had done what he had to do, he would be close to Katy for ever. She would understand why he had chosen the mill-race. She had great perception.

He walked on, something telling him that this was the way, the only way, the way of the river.

21

May was listening to some dance music on the wireless when the knock came on her door, loud and insistent. Slightly annoyed at having to switch off Roy Fox's rendering of 'Whispering', she got up to answer it, wondering who her caller could possibly be at this hour, for Ethel had long since come and gone.

She was confronted by the small dumpy figure of Miriam, her face anxious and whiter than usual, her eyes blinking rapidly behind her steel spectacles, as she burst out, breathlessly, 'Please Miss Lodge, Mrs Mason says can you come at once. It's something about Mr Mason.'

'What about him?' May's voice was sharp, alarm sweeping away all its usual warmth and sweetness.

'Well, ma'am, it seems as how he went out in the car at tea time and . . .' The girl before her took another deep breath before adding, 'He's not come home.'

'All right, Miriam. You run straight back and tell Mrs Mason I'll be on my way. I expect Mr Mason's car has broken down or he's just had a puncture,' May replied quickly, doing her best to allay what seemed like rising hysteria. She knew well what any drama of this sort could do to young girls like Miriam, how they tended to exaggerate and work themselves up, while deep down revelling in the importance of being the harbinger of disaster. All the same, she thought it unlikely that a breakdown or a simple puncture would have prevented Philip from sending word by now. It was getting on for nine o'clock. She wished that Katy had asked for her sooner. Where could her brother-in-law possibly have gone? Whatever he might or might not do in London, he had behaved most circumspectly in Wilhampton. It was uncharacteristic of him to leave his wife guessing as to his whereabouts. As May went back into her sitting room and hastily began damping down the fire, something warned her to put a few overnight things into a bag.

She was just locking her front door when she heard the sound of heavy male footsteps at the end of Cob Lane. She looked up and, in the light of one of the street lamps, saw George Burbage, the Wilhampton policeman, coming towards her.

'Miss Lodge . . . ?'

'Yes, George.' This time she knew real fear: all-consuming, paralysing, the kind she had experienced on a few other occasions in her life, but always hoped she would never experience again. She remained motionless, the key still in her hand.

'You'll be going to the Moat, ma'am, I daresay.' He was plainly distressed. 'I have bad news, I'm afraid. Could we go back inside your house for a while?'

She led him in and relit the gas mantle. Awkwardly, he removed his helmet and then pulled a piece of paper from one of his pockets. 'This'll be for you, Miss Lodge, I reckon,' he said, handing it to her.

May took the note and stared at it in bewilderment, although it was short and painfully explicit. The words seemed to bounce back at her, clear, challenging, yet somehow curiously simple and trusting: 'May. Tell Katy I'm sorry. I love her and Emily so much. Please take care of them for me. Philip.'

There was silence in the little room. She put out a hand and steadied herself on the back of a chair, but she did not sit down.

'Have you . . . found him yet?' she asked, at length.

'No ma'am. We didn't know anything was amiss until a little while ago when Mrs Mason telephoned. And then, just after, this note was brought into the station.'

'Who by?'

'Ted Pretty, the Fairfaxes' new keeper. He happened to be out after poachers up at Breconbury Woods and came on Mr Mason's car parked with no lights on. So he took a look inside.'

'Then . . . there's still hope . . . ?'

George Burbage hesitated. 'I suppose so, ma'am. We wondered . . . if you might have any idea where . . .' He coughed, unable to go on.

It came into her mind with curious inevitability. She looked straight into George's troubled eyes. 'The race,' she said, quietly. 'Have you tried the mill-race?'

'I think the keeper's down there now,' he answered gruffly, 'although being night-time and the moon gone . . .'

She nodded. 'I see. Thank you for coming, George.'

He asked for the note, explaining that she would be given a typed copy. She handed it back to him and, as soon as he had left her, she set out once again for the Moat. Of all the things which she had had to face in her life, May knew that this would be the worst. Until there was definite news, she would have to keep up some form of pretence – and May Lodge was not good at any kind of subterfuge.

As soon as she turned into the driveway, she saw Katy's figure silhouetted in one of the lighted hall windows; then, quickly, it moved away. Almost immediately, the front door opened and her sister came flying down the steps.

'Oh, May, I thought you were never coming. What can have happened? He said he was going to Parker's for some oil for the car, but that was hours ago. It's so unlike him. And it isn't as if . . .' she continued, and then broke off as they went into the house.

'As if what, my dear?' May put down her small case and took off her coat, feeling that it might be as well to keep Katy talking, especially as by so doing she might glean some useful information.

'Well, I mean . . . you must have guessed. We've had a bad patch, but it was all over. We've been so happy these last few weeks . . . ever since we went to *Calvalcade*, you remember? It's been like another honeymoon lately, May.'

'I'm glad, Katy,' She *was* glad, too. Whatever happened, whatever the future held in store for her sister, at least Katy would have that to remember and hold on to. She had always had such great capacity for happiness, however short-lived it might sometimes have been. When May managed to persuade her to come away from the hall window and into the warmth of the drawing room, she asked her whether she had eaten anything that evening, and was hardly surprised to receive the swift reply, 'Of course not. How could I?'

'What about Emily?'

'She's had her supper and is in bed asleep, thank God. If it hadn't been for her, I suppose I might have raised the alarm earlier, but I tried not to show I was worried. I managed to pass off Philip's absence by saying he'd probably called in for a chat with Dick Swayne or someone. But I didn't think it was very likely. As soon as she was upstairs, I telephoned Dorothy . . . and when she said they hadn't seen him, I rang the police.'

May was silent. She watched her sister light a cigarette, her hands making several attempts at striking a match. She knew that Katy was drawing on all the resources at her command in order to remain calm, yet with every moment that passed she was finding it more difficult. Presently, she got up and went into the hall where May heard her telephoning the police station again, after which she returned with two stiff brandies and sodas. May took one with misgiving, remembering their mother's 'medicinal' bottle which she used to keep for emergencies. The amount of alcohol which Katy had poured out tonight would just about have filled poor Sarah's flask to the top. She also felt that the effect on her sister's empty stomach might be disastrous, yet she noticed that after taking a few sips, Katy certainly seemed to brighten a little. 'They say at the station there's no further news, May, but Philip *could* just walk in,' she said, with a pathetic attempt at optimism. 'You don't know,' she went on, 'there might be an explanation. Funny things happen. I mean, he could have lost his memory, like Mother did, remember?'

'Yes, dear,' May replied, while hating herself for lying. She felt fairly certain that, distraught and confused as her brother-in-law might have been, he had not actually suffered any loss of memory. There must be a deeper, more complicated reason for the situation although, after Katy's patently honest revelation of their recent happiness, she could not, for the life of her, think what it was.

Neither sister went to bed that night. Each remained, fully clothed, sitting one on either side of the fireplace waiting for news, mostly in silence. Once or twice May tried to get Katy to lie down on the sofa, but any such suggestion was met with fierce resistance. When, around midnight, May made a tentative suggestion that she could ring Maurice Fitzherbert, this also received a negative response. 'There's nothing he could do,' Katy replied, and May knew that, for the moment, she was right. As the night wore on, one or the other of them threw another log on the fire; occasionally May went into the kitchen to make some tea, glad that Katy had shown no attempt to replenish their glasses.

When morning approached, they mutually agreed that, if possible, it would be best to get Emily off to school as usual, that they would simply tell her that her father was unwell and, if it became necessary, that he had had to go to hospital – which wouldn't be far wrong, May thought grimly. For whatever happened, that was where, in all probability, Philip would be taken, just as Neil had been taken all those years ago, after he had accidentally fallen into the Willon.

Rather to her relief and astonishment, her niece accepted the situation without too many awkward questions and, as May hurried her down to the market square at a quarter to eight, she was more than thankful to be able to say, 'Why, I do believe that for once Helen is ahead of you,' and to see Emily's flying figure running to catch up with her friend.

May had taken the precaution of telephoning the Swaynes half an hour earlier. They had already heard the news that Philip was missing, but Dorothy assured her that nothing had been said in front of their small daughter. The possibility that someone else could make an unfortunate remark which Emily might overhear that day was a chance which May felt simply had to be taken. It was preferable to having the child hanging about at the Moat, where she might possibly be subjected to something far worse.

The sight of Maurice Fitzherbert's car on the gravel outside the house as she returned to it made May send up a small prayer of thanks that she had got Emily away in time. Although she knew that Maurice was more than likely to make a courtesy call if he heard any patient of his was in trouble, she somehow had a feeling that he had now called to see Katy for a very specific purpose. She was not proved wrong. She found him standing by the fireplace in the drawing room while her sister sat staring straight in front of her, in the same chair in which she had kept her vigil throughout the night. She did not look up as May came in. She did not seem to be aware of either of them. Her eyes were quite blank, her mind obviously far away.

Then, quite suddenly, the sound of the eight o'clock mill hooter seemed to galvanize her into action. With a swift movement, she stood up and rushed towards Maurice. He put out one of his hands, but she shook it away angrily. 'You must take me to him,' she said. 'Where is he? What have you done with him?' She seemed to be beside herself now, flailing at him with her fists, forcing him to catch hold of both her arms tightly.

343

'Steady, Katy, my dear. Steady. Not now. It wouldn't be . . . right.'

'Right?' May heard her voice rise. 'Right?' she repeated. 'It's my right, isn't it? Someone's got to identify him. I'm his wife, aren't I? Besides, just because he's dead doesn't mean he wouldn't want me to be with him now.'

All at once she seemed to crumple, so that he had to hold her up. 'Please,' she whispered. 'Please, Maurice.' Her eyes were luminous, pleading. May knew that he could not refuse.

He helped her gently from the room and across the hall. Then, with a quiet, 'Her coat, please, May,' Maurice Fitzherbert carried Katy Mason down the steps of the Moat and into his car.

22

Half a mile to the south-east of Wilhampton, just off the main road leading to Westonbury and nestling in a bend of the River Willon, lay a small hamlet called Netherford. It boasted scarcely more than two dozen habitations, ranging from one large eighteenth-century house – Netherford Grange – to a farmstead by the name of Sweetacres and then to a variety of smaller dwellings, mostly tied cottages occupied by agricultural labourers but interspersed with a few slightly bigger homes of a residential kind, one of which was called the White Hermitage. In the spring of 1932 this, together with Netherford Grange, came up for sale.

The Dowager Lady Fairfax bought the Grange. May Lodge, on behalf of her sister and with the help of estate agents and solicitors, acquired the Hermitage.

May had had a sad, difficult and perplexing time. As was to be expected, she had not fallen down on the charge laid upon her by her late brother-in-law, but it had worried and aged her considerably. Her hair had suddenly turned quite white; her gentle, usually cheerful face was now lined and worn. Nor had her youngest sister's looks fared any better. Katy Mason had become – just as she had after her operations – thin to the point of emaciation.

The young widow had been too shocked to be of any assistance in the winding up of her husband's estate. Her overwhelming distress and melancholy meant that she was unable to make decisions or express any wishes, other than that she did not want to remain at the Moat. May, with no previous experience of legal, business or even money matters, nevertheless found herself discussing all three with both country and London solicitors – for there was the question of the sale of the bookshop – as well as having to deal with curious unexpected problems which daily presented themselves. Every night she went down on her knees to give thanks for the never-failing support and advice of Maurice Fitzherbert who, on realizing that Katy's condition was becoming worse rather than better, suggested May should be given a full power of attorney. Another form of help, for which she was more than grateful, came from the Swaynes who, from the time of the tragedy, had immediately swept Emily up and taken her into their rambling, loving, happy home at Bulbarrow, insisting that she must remain with them for however long it was necessary and especially over Christmas.

May had also derived further comfort from a third and completely unexpected source: Edith. Hitherto, her middle sister had kept well away from the Moat. Katy's new lifestyle, though never having made Edith envious – for that was not her nature – had certainly overawed and inhibited her, particularly in front of Philip. She had there-fore rarely visited the house but now, knowing that May and Katy were in trouble and living there alone, she often popped in for half an hour or so when she could spare the time from the demands of her family; but, tactfully, she refrained from suggesting that Emily might sometimes visit her cousins on downside.

The child had taken the news of her father's death far better than May had expected. Although at the inquest a verdict was brought in of 'suicide while the balance of his mind was disturbed', Emily had been given to believe that Philip had been taken ill and drowned accidentally while trying to walk home after his car had broken down. The note he had left — thanks to Maurice Fitzherbert — was never read out in court and when the coroner asked May if she knew of any trouble or difficulties her brother-in-law might have had which would have forced him to take his life, she had replied in clear definite tones, 'No' — even qualifying this by adding that she understood her sister and her husband to have been extremely happy at the time of his unfortunate death.

And that was true, May remembered thinking, as she had stood in the box. It had been quite embarrassing the way Katy and Philip seemed only to have had eyes for each other during those last few weeks. It had hardly seemed right to her that a couple who had been married getting on for eleven years should make the mutual physical attraction between them quite so obvious. It made May sorry for Emily, who she sensed felt both distressed and shut out. Still, she was glad now to think that her sister and brother-in-law had had that brief seemingly idyllic period and no power on earth was ever going to drag from May Lodge the fact that, some days after Philip's body had been found half a mile downstream from the mill-race, she had answered the telephone at the Moat and a deep husky female voice had asked to speak to Mr Mason. When May had said, 'I'm sorry, I'm afraid Mr Mason passed away last Tuesday,' there had been a click and the line had gone dead. Naturally, she had said nothing to Katy and, fortunately, there had been no further communications of that sort. May did not suppose that anyone would ever know the full story. She had simply sensed that it was a long-distance call and it was highly likely she had been talking to the 'mannish' lady agent in London, to whom her sister had once referred so disparagingly. The more she reflected on it the more May felt that her brother-in-law must have got himself into a mess from which the desperate course he had chosen seemed, sadly, the only way out.

It was Cyril Butt who had actually started her thinking in earnest about Katy's future home, when she had met him one cold January day on her way to post yet another of the interminable complicated documents on which her signature was constantly required.

'Katy will be selling the Moat, I suppose, May,' he had remarked, soberly.

'Why, yes, Cyril. She's no call to stay there now,' she had replied, rather surprised that he should have brought the subject up at all.

'Quite so.' May could recall how Cyril had then puffed out his cheeks, moved his thumb stick a little closer and, leaning forward confidentially, had continued, 'This isn't common knowledge, May, but there's a small place at Netherford coming up for sale. Pretty. Compact. In good condition. Might suit her down to the ground.'

'Really?' At once May had become interested. She knew that a tip from Cyril was not to be ignored. He had then proceeded to tell her all about the White Hermitage, advising her that if they wanted to know more it would be worth while quickly getting in touch with Gordon Brewer, who saw to all the house property at Butt and Swanton.

Tentatively, that same night, May had broached the subject with Katy. She found her sitting, as she so often did of late, smoking the inevitable cigarette and staring into the fire.

'It's for you to say, May,' she had replied, indifferently, after hearing what Cyril had said.

'But, my dear, it would be *your* home, yours and Emily's.'

'And yours.'

For the first time since Philip's death, May felt an exasperation which was difficult to hide. Surely Katy could 'take on' a little now, if only for Emily's sake.

'You mean you want me to live with you?' she had queried, somewhat tartly.

May was quick to note a flicker of astonishment in the large grey eyes as Katy answered, simply, 'But of course.'

Although it had never been mooted before, May had suspected that this was what had been in Katy's mind all along, so far as she had anything in mind these days, other than Philip; but the calm assumption that May would automatically give up Number Three, Cob Lane, together with her independence, and take care of Katy and Emily for as long as she was required was a little hard to take. May knew that she *would* do it and part of her would find great happiness in living in the same house as her much-loved niece. But it would have been nice to have been *asked*. Besides, one never knew; one day her youngest sister might marry again and where would she be then, with no Cob Lane to which she could retreat?

Doing her best to ignore Katy's last remark, she had said, quietly, 'The White Hermitage would be very convenient from the point of view of Emily's schooling. She could still catch the same bus as Helen at the Netherford stop.'

'I suppose so . . . although it might be best if she became a boarder.'

'A *boarder*?' May had been genuinely shocked. 'But I thought you and Philip always vowed you'd never let her do that.'

'But Philip . . . isn't here any more. And I'm no good to her now, am I?'

This time May had not been able to refrain from speaking out. 'Look Katy, you'll have to pull yourself together. Emily needs you now more than ever. She's been at the Swaynes' long enough. Besides, it's wrong of us to go on imposing on Dick and Dorothy's good nature. Oh, I know they're kindness itself and it was all I could do to get them to take anything for Emily's keep, but the child asked only last Sunday when she was coming home.'

May had watched Katy stub out her cigarette and light yet another one. She could remember the stillness in the room, alleviated only by a cinder or two falling from the grate and the wind getting up outside. In order to relieve the tension, she had picked up some knitting. Other than managing to execute her outstanding orders, May had done no sewing of late. She wished Katy would answer her but apart from remarking, 'I expect the Hermitage would be as good a place as any,' her sister had lapsed into silence and withdrawn into that private world of hers for the rest of the evening.

In the ensuing months, while Gordon Brewer negotiated the sale of the Moat and the purchase of the White Hermitage, May often thought about her little dressmaking business and how it would be bound to suffer. She was not so concerned about the financial aspect for, by going to live with a sister who had been left comfortably off, this did not in itself present a problem, other than the very real emotional one concerning May's abhorrence of becoming dependent. She supposed she would still do work for a privileged few such as Lady Fairfax and some long-standing clients which, with the dividends from her small savings, would bring her in a little income. But the thing which really bothered her was feeling that the special link which, through her work, she had forged with the life of Wilhampton would be, if not exactly broken, certainly weakened. She was so much a part of the little town; she had been the recipient of so many confidences as, discreetly, she had slipped a tape measure round a waist or, pins in mouth, knelt to adjust a hemline. Ever sensitive to the feelings of others, she had shared in their sorrows, rejoiced in their happiness. True, the market square was but twenty minutes' walking distance from Netherford and it had even crossed her mind that she might learn to drive. But in her new life there would not be the daily contact, the constant exchange of news. She would still be on home ground, as it were, yet on its periphery. May Lodge who, for over twenty years, had sent out bills, written in her immaculate script, firstly from *The Mill House* and latterly from *Number Three, Cob Lane, Wilhampton*, felt in some inexplicable way that, by going to Netherford, she was letting the side down.

The move took place one late April day, when patches of primroses bloomed in the hedgerows and clumps of daffodils flowered gaily in all the gardens of the little hamlet, while the chestnut trees were in full bud on either side of the high wrought-iron gates to the Grange. All around, the countryside was bright with the promise of new growth, the water-meadows by the Willon lush with early grass, the fields of corn a rippling sea of silvery green – for Robert Farley at Sweetacres had not, like Dick Swayne, been forced to give up arable farming.

With the eagerness and optimism of youth, Emily, carrying a basket containing May's cat, hurried up the path of the Hermitage ahead of her mother and aunt, thrilled at the prospect of living in what she called a fairy-tale house. And, with its thatch and whitewashed walls, May could not help thinking that their new home did have that quality about it. She hoped Katy would start to pick up a bit now that she was in different surroundings. May knew it would be uphill work but she was determined to do all she could to help her. After all, life had to go on. They had Emily to care for. Whatever happened, the child mustn't be allowed to suffer.

'Why, look, Katy,' she said, as they approached the front door. 'That honeysuckle over the porch is going to look lovely in a month or so's time.'

Her sister simply nodded and went quickly inside.

23

After Maud Fairfax and May Lodge had been living in Netherford for a year or more, a subtle change became noticeable in their relationship. The older woman was now ageing fast. She no longer needed the clothes which she had been accustomed to ordering when her husband had been alive, having become far less active both in her public and private life. Though she had by no means taken to widowhood as hard as Katy Mason, she nevertheless concentrated on interests of a much more personal kind: her grandchildren – especially John William – the upkeep of her new home, and a few close friends and associates of long standing, amongst whom she regarded May with particular affection.

Sometimes, if they happened to meet of an afternoon while she was taking an increasingly leisurely stroll with her equally slow and ancient spaniel, she would suggest that May might like to come back for tea at the Grange and, on one of these occasions, the subject of Katy's almost total withdrawal from life came up – as it so often did – in their conversation.

'Could you not get her to *join* something, May? It's so unnatural for a beautiful young widow to remain quite such a recluse at this stage. I don't necessarily mean going in for "good works", as Alicia's husband puts it so disparagingly, but Katy was very fond of the theatre once, wasn't she? I believe Westonbury has a very flourishing dramatic society nowadays.'

'I've suggested something of the sort many times, Lady Fairfax' – May no longer said 'Your ladyship' – 'but she simply doesn't appear interested . . . in anything.'

'Not even Emily?'

'Well . . .' May hesitated. 'I suppose, to a certain extent. Sad as it seems, the fact that the child has become slightly short-sighted has possibly helped to take her out of herself a little. She's agreed to her riding more. In fact, I've just about persuaded her to let Emily have a pony of her own. I'm sure Robert Farley up at Sweetacres would let us some grazing. And it's not as if there would be any question of stabling because it could sleep rough all the winter. A pony would only need a little hay and a daily inspection. I'm sure there would be no problem.'

'What a very good idea, May. You *must* pursue it. With the long summer holidays coming along, Emily could be out riding every day, especially with Helen Swayne for company. I hate to think of the child's eyes suffering from too much close study.' The Dowager Lady Fairfax knew little about defective vision. Her own and that of her family had always been perfect. It was true that she had taken to using her lorgnettes more frequently of late, but the idea of a pretty little girl of Emily's age having to wear glasses was hardly to be countenanced. It was bad enough seeing them on the face of poor unfortunate Miriam, who was now working as kitchenmaid at the Grange; although her employer could not help reflecting that there was certainly one advantage in this case. Miriam was living proof of Dorothy Parker's 'men seldom make passes'. She was not likely to attract 'followers'.

It therefore came about that a few days later, Katy –

having been given a detailed account of her sister's recent tête-à-tête with the Dowager – set off to call on the Farleys. Because of her dislike of meeting people, she was apt to take the car on the shortest journey, but this evening she elected to walk. It had been a glorious June day and the scent of hay in the air remained almost overpowering, even though it was long past sundown. Katy had been well aware that Robert Farley would have been working so hard that she could not expect to find him at home until nightfall – one of her chief reasons for deciding to go on foot – but, as she walked up the driveway to Sweetacres, she hoped that she had also left it late enough for him to have had his supper.

'He's just finished, Mrs Mason. Do come in,' His wife, Frances, replied in answer to Katy's initial question, as she ushered her into a dark, heavily furnished sitting room, not unlike the Swaynes'. Had it been May paying the visit, Katy knew that her sister and Robert's wife would have been on Christian name terms, for May had an extraordinary capacity for getting to know all and sundry with a friendliness which neither overstepped nor fell short of the required mark. She sat down and waited anxiously while Frances went away to fetch her husband.

When Robert Farley came through from the kitchen – his wife excusing herself on the grounds of having to shut up the hens – Katy was struck by this big burly man's aura of utter dependability and kindliness. In manner, he reminded her of Dick Swayne and Maurice Fitzherbert. In their separate ways they were all as different from Philip as chalk from cheese, yet each had about him something for which part of her longed, even though neither possessed that particular quality in his make-up for which, over eighteen months after her husband's death, she still felt a physical ache. She looked across at the man opposite her, his strong weather-beaten face illuminated by a single oil lamp – for Netherford, as yet, boasted no mains gas or electricity – and listened with gratitude as he responded with such wholehearted enthusiasm to the proposal she had put before him.

'But *of course*, Mrs Mason. I'd be only too pleased to

help. You could have the grazing in the paddock at the back of the White Hermitage where I keep my own mare for most of the year, and then we could put the pony into the Daisy Field at other times. I usually keep a bit of hay in the nearby skilling and maybe Emily would like to put her tackle in the shed at the end and use the place for saddling up.'

'It's very kind of you . . . Please, you must let me know whatever you feel it is worth . . . I am so grateful.'

For the first time, Robert Farley seemed embarrassed. He did not reply at once, and then he said, 'Oh, hardly anything . . . I mean, it'll be nice to have a child with a pony around again, now all our youngsters are grown up.'

'But I insist, Mr Farley. You don't know what it will mean to us . . . to Emily.'

Again he paused before answering. She knew that the Farleys were not as up against it as the Swaynes but, all the same, times were still hard for farmers. Presently, he said, quietly, 'Well, would half a crown a week be acceptable? That's with the hay thrown in, of course.'

'But that's far too cheap.' Katy might have been brought up at the Felt Mills, but she knew enough about farming to know that such a bargain was overwhelmingly to her advantage. Yet he shook his head at her reply.

'No, it'll be a pleasure, I assure you. It was a sad day when we had to sell the children's pony. Have you anyone in mind you're thinking of buying from?'

'No . . . I wondered if you could give me a little advice about that.'

'Shorty,' he answered, promptly. 'Shorty Miller over at Little Meysey. He's a bit of a rogue but if you mention my name and how the pony will be kept at Sweetacres, he won't do you down. Tell him you want a safe little mount, about thirteen hands, I should say. Emily's getting tall now, isn't she? A bonny lass. Tell you what, would you like me to have a word with Shorty?'

'Oh, *would* you?' Almost, he was beginning to infect her with his own enthusiasm. 'Thank you *very* much.'

She rose and Robert Farley stood also: tall, infinitely reassuring and wise, not in any scholarly way, but in a much more important one. It was impossible to define. She only knew that the man before her was what her father would have described as 'a good 'un'. He possessed a countryman's innate common sense which had been handed down to him through a long line of forebears. As he accompanied her to the gate of Sweetacres, they met his wife coming across the yard from the chicken house. Katy shook hands with them both, envying them – though not in any jealous way – their completeness, their mutual satisfaction in their life together.

The moon had risen as she started to walk the quarter of a mile home. Already squares of dim orange light showed in the upstairs windows of most of the cottages. It was a busy time and Katy knew that most of the farming fraternity would soon be asleep. She also knew that even a little later on in the year, in that traditional lull between haymaking and harvest, they would still be going to bed by nine or nine-thirty. After all, she reflected a little wryly, that was what was known as 'honeymoon time'.

An owl swooped low across her path and disappeared into the grounds of the Grange. Once or twice a moth fluttered close to her face or some small animal made a rustling noise in the hedgerow. The only house which showed a glimmer of light downstairs was Greenways, the home of Gordon Hillier, a somewhat unaccountable figure who she believed had left London and settled in the neighbourhood some years ago. As she came almost level with the front door, she noticed him sitting in his porch, smoking a cigarette.

'Good evening, Katy.' His voice was soft yet it had a curious vibrance. She was surprised that he had addressed her by her Christian name, for she had scarcely spoken to him since coming to Netherford.

'Good evening, Mr Hillier.' To her dismay, she saw him get up and amble towards his gate, so that she was obliged to pause.

'A lovely day it's been,' he remarked, casually, by way of an opening gambit. He was quite close to her now and she was aware of his short, thickset body and bald head and the way his eyes under their shaggy eyebrows stared at her, intently. She had never given him much thought before, other than that he appeared to be rather an ugly man who, according to May, did not mix much in the local community. 'He goes in for those Bloomsbury types,' her sister had said, scornfully. 'You know, the ones who used to visit Maggie Fortescue at the Moat. Only his friends aren't so nice as hers were. It's my belief half of them pretend to be married for the look of the thing, but I swear that the whole boiling are no better than they should be.'

Remembering May's words, Katy answered almost grimly, 'Yes, it's certainly wonderful haymaking weather.' She felt suddenly uncomfortable and wished that she had not allowed him to waylay her so that she had been forced to exchange pleasantries. She started to move away but he said, quickly, 'You wouldn't care to join me in a glass of mead, would you? It's what I happened to be drinking when you came along.'

She was astonished. Did he really think that she would go, alone, into his house – or, at any rate, his porch – at this hour? What did he take her for? May was right. Probably all his friends were no better than they should be.

'Oh, no,' she replied, curtly, just remembering to add 'thank you' before continuing, 'I . . . have to be getting back. My sister will be expecting me.'

Did he give a slightly sardonic smile after saying, 'Another time, maybe?' She wasn't sure. She only knew as she left him that whenever she had occasion to walk to Sweetacres again, she would take another route.

It was only later, much later that night, when she woke from a troubled sleep, her body throbbing, and Philip's name on her lips, that she realized, to her horror, that the person who had been making love to her in her dream was not her late husband, but Gordon Hillier.

'When are you going to have Toby clipped?' Phoebe Moreton, immaculately turned out, as usual, in a heather-coloured tweed coat and beret to match, was surveying Emily's pony over the top of the paddock gate.

'He's not going to be clipped. He's got to sleep rough.' Emily slipped another lump of sugar into Toby's mouth and coloured slightly. It was mid-October and Phoebe, together with a new French governess, had been sent to convalesce at the Grange after a recent attack of scarlet fever. She turned her small, proud, sharp-featured face towards her companion, a mixture of astonishment and condescension in the pale blue eyes.

'But what about the opening meet?'

'I . . . I don't hunt. So far I just have lessons with Miss Cory or go for rides with Helen Swayne or Mr Farley.'

'Oh.' Phoebe plucked a blade of grass from the nearby hedgerow and sucked it, thoughtfully.

Emily had been wondering whether she would have to offer Phoebe a ride on Toby and was relieved when her guest had not arrived in jodhpurs. She felt sure now that such a thing was not desirable from either of their points of view, especially after Phoebe's next remark.

'I'm going to the Hall tomorrow to ride with my cousins. You know, Belinda and Gillian.'

Emily did not know – at least, only of them. This time it was her turn simply to say, 'Oh.' She was beginning to wish very much that her mother and aunt had not insisted that Phoebe must be asked back to the White Hermitage, in return for a rather tedious tea party which she had been obliged to attend at the Grange the previous weekend. She also wished sincerely that Helen Swayne was not in bed with a bad cold today and therefore not available to give her some moral support. The nights were drawing in fast and she could not imagine how she could entertain Phoebe until Mademoiselle Hervouët came to take her away at six o'clock.

But fortunately her guest settled the problem herself by asking after tea whether she could look at a new book of Lionel Edwards's drawings, which she had noticed lying on a side table.

'I believe he lives round these parts, doesn't he, Mrs Mason?' she said, for all the world as if she were forty-five instead of twelve years old.

'Yes, Phoebe,' Katy replied, wondering if the child always behaved like this. She said as much to May, as they retired to the latter's small workroom, leaving the two children to get on as best as they could. But if Emily was dismayed by their departure, Phoebe appeared totally indifferent. She sat herself down on the mat in front of the fire and studied the book silently.

After a while, she said, 'Did you know that John is going to be an artist when he leaves school?'

'No.' Although Emily's dislike of Phoebe Moreton was growing stronger every minute, she was aware that she had little time for her brother also. She supposed he was just the sort of boy who *would* prefer to go out with a sketchbook rather than with the hounds.

'Well, that's what he *says*,' Phoebe went on, in the same condescending grown-up fashion, 'but Daddy's sure Eton will knock that out of him.' Suddenly bored, she shut the book and said, peremptorily, 'Do you like school?'

'Yes, very much.'

'Sometimes I think I'd like to go but . . . I don't know. It would interfere with hunting so much. And I wouldn't want to wear glasses. Ma'amzelle says girls often do when they go to school. I suppose that's what happened to you. Do you wear them riding?'

'No.' Emily's eyes strayed towards the clock on the mantelpiece. There were seven minutes to go.

'Does John like Eton?' she asked, desperately trying to be as polite as possible.

'No. He hates it. But Daddy says it'll get better as he gets older. He's still at the fagging stage.'

'Fagging?' Emily was at a loss. She noticed Phoebe frown

and the look of astonishment and condescension creep into her eyes again.

'Yes, you know. The younger boys have to run about doing errands for the bigger ones. I must say I shouldn't like that sort of thing myself. It sounds perfectly ghastly.'

'Oh.' With relief, Emily heard the click of the garden gate and then, mercifully, her mother coming downstairs to answer the knock at the front door.

'Ah, ma chérie! T'es-tu bien amusée?' Mademoiselle Hervouët seemed to fill the whole sitting-room with her bulk and excited volubility.

After Phoebe had given an almost inaudible, 'Oui merci, Ma'amzelle,' Emily shook hands and wished them both goodbye.

'Please, Mummy,' she said, after the front door closed, 'not again,' to which she was glad to see that, for once, Katy actually smiled.

Later on, when she came to think about it, Emily realized that her mother had been altogether less sad and serious during the past few months. She could not help wondering whether Toby had something to do with it, for ever since his arrival Katy had certainly been out and about more, coming down to the paddock, helping her to saddle up and chatting to Robert Farley if he happened to be around; and one night, she had even gone out alone somewhere, although when Emily had asked Aunt Chip where, she had been rather surprised to receive a short and somewhat evasive reply, which she knew better than to pursue.

Some two or three weeks after Phoebe's visit, Emily was further surprised to be told that there was a party taking place at Greenways that Saturday evening to which her mother had been invited and, a little before seven o'clock, Katy came downstairs in a smart black crêpe tiered dress which neither her sister nor her daughter had seen her wearing for a very long time. She had obviously had her hair professionally set that day and, with just the right amount of jewellery — some small pearl-drop earrings and a necklace to match — there was something mysterious, almost magical, about her as she went out of the door, wrapped in the black cloak which May had made her many years ago.

'Mummy looked lovely, didn't she, Aunt Chip?' Emily said, as they heard the sound of her high heels receding down the garden path.

'Yes, dear.'

'She looked just like she used to when she went off to dance at the theatre. What time will she be back?'

'I really don't know.'

'Can I stay up and hear all about the party?'

'Oh, no,' May said quickly. 'You'll be asleep long before it's over.'

'Who else will be there?'

May paused. 'Hard to say. No one from these parts, I should think. I believe Mr Hillier has guests from London staying at Greenways. Now, Miss, it's time you stopped asking so many questions and also put away that book. You know you aren't meant to use your eyes too much in artificial light.'

'Is lamplight artificial, Aunt Chip?'

'Yes, of course. Anything that the good Lord doesn't give us is artificial.'

When May had seen to Emily's supper and at last chivvied her, reluctantly, to bed, she wondered whether she herself would now do exactly what her niece had wanted to: stay up until Katy returned. But soon she decided against it. Her sister was a married woman – or, rather, widow – of thirty-one. She was not the young girl of eighteen whom May had waited up for at the Mill House back in the November of 1920 when Maurice Fitzherbert had taken her to her first dance. May's reasons for staying up then were both natural and understandable. It had been simply a pleasurable duty combined with a genuine desire to know that her youngest sister had enjoyed herself. She had had no fears of Katy not returning safely as soon as the dance ended. She knew Maurice Fitzherbert and his family far too well for that. But tonight it was different. She was worried on more than one score. Ever since Gordon Hillier had suddenly rung up a few weeks back and asked to take Katy to the pictures in Westonbury to see Fred Astaire and Ginger Rogers – an invitation which, to May's surprise, her sister had accepted – she had noticed a subtle change in her. And while ordinarily she would have welcomed almost anything and anybody who brought this about, Gordon Hillier was the exception to such sentiments.

To try to take her mind off her anxiety, May picked up some sewing and turned on the wireless; but even that well-known reassuring voice ordering London to 'Stop' for 'In Town Tonight' failed to hold her attention. Presently, she got up and made herself a little soup from the stockpot which was still kept in exactly the same way as it had always been in Sarah' days, and then, after drinking this and filling two hot-water bottles, she went upstairs, placed one in Katy's bed and one in her own and retired for the night.

Yet sleep eluded her. Very faintly, over the cold clear air, she heard the clock above the Wilhampton town hall strike eleven, twelve and then one. 'She's having a good time,' she kept saying to herself. 'And so she should. She's beginning to pull out of it. It's nice to see her getting out, meeting people. Philip would have wanted her to. She's been leading the life of a nun too long.' Yet at the thought of nun, May's uneasiness increased. Gordon Hillier was no monk. She felt certain of that. Neither would she have thought that he was a marrying man. Did Katy not realize what she might be letting herself in for?

At last, just after 2 a.m., she heard the sound she had been waiting for: footsteps along the lane. They grew louder slowly, not one person's but two. Again she tried to tell herself that that was only to be expected. No gentleman would allow a lady to return home alone at this hour. All the same, May felt that there seemed to be silence for an inordinate length of time at the garden gate until, at last, she heard Katy's footsteps alone coming up the path and her key turning in the lock. Suddenly, she was unable to refrain from putting on a dressing gown and going down to greet her.

'Oh, May! You're not asleep. You haven't been worried, have you?' Katy said apologetically, blinking in the light of the lamp which her sister had turned up high and dismayed to see the anxious face, shiny with cold cream, its features slightly distorted by a tightly-fitting lace and crêpe de Chine boudoir cap.

'Well . . . a little. You know how it is. I thought it was getting rather late.'

'I'm sorry . . . But it was *such* a good party. Wasn't it a coincidence? Gordon had some people staying with him who I'd actually once met in London when . . . I was in that revue.'

'Really?' May noted the flushed cheeks, the bright eyes, the way her sister's whole being seemed to have come alive again, as she threw off her cloak with a casual graceful movement. She herself felt a spoilsport, a silly old Mother Grundy or 'Mother Mothballs', as she used to call Maurice Fitzherbert's mother, well aware how anxious she had been that her son should not marry Katy Lodge.

'I'm glad you had a good time, my dear,' she said, quickly. 'Would you like a hot drink before you go up?'

'Oh, no thanks. Gordon gave us all some mead to finish up with. I must say it was very good.'

Without saying more, they went upstairs quietly, careful not to wake Emily, and parted on the landing. May got into bed again and pushed her feet down the feather mattress to where her hot-water bottle was still warm. But it was quite a while before she drifted off to sleep; and when she did so she found herself thinking the same thought which so often came to mind: if Katy had married Maurice Fitzherbert, none of this sort of thing would ever have happened.

25

'There's been talk, May.' Edith picked up the teapot from her kitchen table and poured out a second cup for her sister and herself. 'No sugar today, then?' she enquired, as an afterthought.

'No thanks, Edie. I went on the scales in the chemist's only an hour or so ago.'

It was a few weeks after Christmas and May, who had now learnt to drive, was visiting Edith after doing some shopping in Wilhampton. She was by no means as expert at the wheel as Katy, but Arnold Parker's son, who had given her lessons over a year ago, had pronounced her perfectly safe to go out alone, even if reversing into small spaces was not exactly her forte. As with the wireless, driving a car had given May's life another extra dimension. She was delighted to be able to transport herself hither and thither in such an independent way. She went slowly and carefully, gave all the correct hand signals, could double-declutch and did not feel at a disadvantage because she found it easier to negotiate the Wilhampton streets rather than the Westonbury ones; for, as far as May was concerned, her home town was almost always where she wanted to go. In her eyes there was and never would be anywhere quite like it even though, with her customary cheerful resourcefulness, she found Netherford and its inhabitants a pleasant place in which to live – that is, if it were not for Gordon Hillier.

'Where did you hear it, Edie?' she now asked, stirring her tea from force of habit, even though there was no sugar in it.

'Where do you think? In Lilian Perrick's shop. She was serving Phyllis Hopkins when I went in to buy our Georgie some sherbert.' Here, Edith broke off and told her youngest son to run round the back and go and play next door. As soon as he had departed, she continued, 'It was the words "merry widow nowadays" which caught my attention and the way they stopped talking suddenly when I appeared. As soon as Phyllis had gone out – I must say she's a dour one if ever there was one – I asked Lilian if it was Katy they'd been discussing.'

'And what did she say?'

'Well, she hedged a bit and went rather red. You know what Lilian is. I know for a fact she gossips about our Della. Calls her a honeypot for the boys. I must say myself that I wish Della was like her twin sister. Debbie's much more serious-minded. But that's by the way. To get back to Katy. There was Lilian smirking behind the counter and eventually she came out with, "Well, Edie, your youngest sister's always been a bit on the flighty side, hasn't she?" "Flighty?" I asked her. "How dare you talk like that, Lilian. Just because she's pretty and has lived in the West End of London doesn't mean she's flighty. She's been through a lot lately, poor girl." And then Lilian gave one of those shifty looks of hers and said, "Oh, I *know*, but she's making up for lost time now, by all accounts. I'm not saying there's anything wrong in it, mind, but you'd think she might take up with someone, well . . . more her own age. Besides, folks say a lot of funny things go on at Greenways." '

May was silent. She knew that she would have to have a really serious talk with Katy when she got back. It wouldn't be the first time. But whenever she had tried to broach the subject, her youngest sister had simply opened those enormous grey eyes of hers and said, 'But May, where's the harm? Gordon's got such an original mind. More like Philip's. He makes me laugh. I'm not hurting anyone by seeing him sometimes.'

When May had pointed out that she did not know what effect it might have on Emily, Katy had replied that her daughter seemed happier now that she was happier. In a way, May knew this to be true, but she wondered how long it would last. Emily, at the moment, for all her intelligence, was extremely immature and naïve. She was what the Dowager was apt to refer to as: 'A typically nice English girl – late in growing up'. But one day not too far ahead, they were going to have to tell her about the start of menstruation and the facts of life. It wasn't like it had been in May's day. Not a word of enlightenment had ever come from Sarah; only, oddly enough, from Lilian Perrick, who had lent her a curious book called *The Cradle Ship*. May had been thirteen at the time and, with its allusive prose and whimsical drawings of some mother-to-be going around in long floating gowns with her husband always hovering anxiously in the background, the whole subject had seemed somehow more shameful and shrouded in mystery than ever. Of course, now that Emily was so often riding or running about on at least two farms in the neighbourhood, May felt that she had probably assimilated quite a lot of knowledge concerning procreation; moreover she supposed that there were certain girls at school willing to impart some extra clumsy and inaccurate information. But it would be so much better if her mother, at the appropriate time, could talk to her naturally and sensibly about the subject. Yet would Katy be able to do that at the rate things were going? It was even possible that Emily would soon start asking awkward questions about her mother and Mr Hillier.

'She's always been different, hasn't she?' Edith went on, breaking in on May's thoughts. 'I mean, Katy's had grand ideas. She's never been quite one of us. No more than Philip.'

'Yes, I know what you mean.'

'I often feel sad she couldn't have fallen for Maurice Fitzherbert like he did for her. I know you do, too. D'you see much of him these days?'

'Not a lot. Although, as a matter of fact, I'm going to call in at East Lodge on my way home.'

'Oh, *May*. Nothing serious, I hope?' Edith looked concerned. Her eldest sister was the mainstay of the family. She hated to think of her ill.

'No. Probably just the change of life. But I keep getting a rash come up on my face and neck.' May could actually feel it now beginning to trouble her. 'I'd best be getting along, Edie. I want to have a look in on Ethel Sharman, too, if I can. She's a bit lonely since I left Cob Lane.'

On Katy's insistence, May was no longer a panel patient of Maurice's and therefore, just before five-thirty, she drew up at the front door of East Lodge, got out of the car and rang the bell. Gone were the days when no female patient would dream of visiting the doctor without some other female to accompany her. To May's surprise the door was answered by Clare Fitzherbert herself who explained, none too graciously, that owing to certain temporary domestic changes, she was having to act as parlourmaid.

What a strange choice of wife, May reflected, as she sat in Maurice's sombre old-fashioned drawing room. Of course, he had been caught on the rebound. No doubt about that. And if one did not look too closely at Clare's face, her actual physique was vaguely similar to Katy's. She was small and thin, with a mass of the same light brown hair. But after that, the likeness stopped. May believed that Maurice's wife had been a little more charming and attractive during their courtship, but something must have gone seriously wrong soon after the wedding. Was it, May wondered – albeit feeling guilty for even harbouring such a thought – a problem of sex? After all, there had never been any children. Presumably the marriage bed wasn't happy.

'May?' Maurice had come into the room so quietly and she had been thinking so hard that she had not heard the door open. She stood up, flustered. The rash was quite evident now and there was little need to explain why she had come, when she found herself seated in his small consulting room at the back of the house.

After he had examined her carefully and asked a few questions, he pulled a piece of headed notepaper towards him and started to write out a prescription. 'This ointment should help, May,' he said, handing it to her. 'But I can't guarantee it. You see, I think . . . the trouble is probably . . . well, of nervous origin. You've been carrying quite a load the last few years, haven't you, my dear.'

To her mortification, she found tears beginning to well up in her eyes. Embarrassed, she opened her handbag and fumbled for a handkerchief. It was ridiculous. She ought not to be crying like this. True, she had cried once before in front of him, when she had first heard how ill Katy was and that she would probably have to undergo a second operation. But there was nothing like that now. Katy was, on the whole, very much better than she had been for some time. Emily might have had to take to wearing glasses but she was getting on well at school and, with a pony of her own, she was in seventh heaven. Compared to many people, they were not worried financially. And being able to drive a car had given May so much more freedom. There was nothing to cry about.

Yet she was aware of the deep concern in Maurice Fitzherbert's eyes; how he almost, but not quite, put out a hand to comfort her; that of all the people in the world – even before any blood ties – she felt much more kinship with this gentle, compassionate man who so easily might, many long years ago, have become her brother-in-law.

'You couldn't get away for a while, could you, May?' she heard him say, quietly. 'A little holiday would do you good.'

'Away?' She looked at him, askance. 'Oh no, Maurice.' How could she possibly go away? Anyway, where could she go? There was, she supposed, her brother up in Catterick, but she saw him so seldom that they had grown apart. She knew that Henry would be only too pleased to have her, but she was not so sure about his wife. Poor Marianne had been given the cold shoulder by Sarah, all right, back in 1919, when she had given birth to Frank François only seven months after the marriage. No, it wouldn't be any good going to visit Sergeant Henry Lodge and his wife. Besides, she was very much needed where she was just now, although she couldn't tell Maurice why. He evidently had not heard anything or surely he wouldn't have suggested her leaving Netherford? Or had he? Maybe he thought her absence might make Katy behave more responsibly. One never knew how much a doctor, or a rector, for that matter, was aware of what was going on. The Reverend Donaldson and Maurice's father had had an uncanny knack of keeping their fingers on the corporate pulse of the neighbourhood. She suspected that Maurice had inherited the same ability. All the same, whatever he felt, she wasn't going to risk any kind of holiday. There was Emily to consider. She came first.

'If you won't go away, May,' he said, as she got up to go, 'try to take things a little easier. I hope the ointment helps but, in any case, come and see me again in a couple of weeks. How's Emily, by the way?'

She had recovered her composure now and was able to answer him quite cheerfully. 'Oh, she's fine, thank you Maurice. And of course she positively worships that pony of hers.'

He smiled and wished her goodbye. Only as she was

driving home did it suddenly occur to her that for the first time she could ever remember, he had not actually asked after Katy.

26

There was no harm in it, as she kept telling May. Her involvement with Gordon Hillier really only amounted to a visit to the pictures and dinner at the White Lion in Westonbury about once a week, or possibly supper at Greenways, when there were always others present. Gordon had behaved quite decorously – apart from one or two occasions when Katy felt that he had been on the verge of doing or saying something just a fraction more intimate, such as on the evenings when he had walked her home or the time when she had looked up suddenly from where she had been sitting on his sofa, listening to his friends discussing the theatre, and found him watching her, carefully. But she was no longer apprehensive about him. The leisurely pace at which he seemed prepared to let their relationship develop had allayed any initial fears. She knew that he admired her and enjoyed her company and for this she was grateful. It was so long, so very long, since a man had made this quite so obvious. But that was as far as the whole thing went or was going to go. She wished that she could get May to see this.

One evening towards the end of April, Katy was in her bedroom getting ready for a slightly different kind of outing with him. It had been a cold late spring but, during the past few days, one of those quick-change acts which only the English climate seemed able to perform success-fully pushed summer on to the forefront of the stage. Robert Farley's arable fields, which had hitherto worn only the thinnest of green sheets over the brown earth, suddenly appeared to be covered by a thick emerald quilt; the foliage of the trees, which had been but flimsy lace mantles, was now dense and luxuriant; the blackthorn might still be in the hedges, but the sun was warm and Emily's pony occasionally kicked up his heels and tore around the paddock for sheer joy of living.

Gordon had said that it seemed a shame to waste such lovely weather by sitting in a stuffy picture house and proposed taking a picnic and driving Katy some twenty miles over to Great Ridgeford. It seemed an admirable suggestion and, having got him to agree to her at least providing the food, she found herself very much looking forward to the expedition. She had never been to the Ridgeford villages, but she had heard that on a clear day from the downs above them it was perfectly possible to see the English Channel.

Now, having put on a cream tussore blouse and a light-weight grey flannel skirt, she sat at her dressing table, carefully applying vanishing cream and powder and just a touch of lipstick and rouge. Katy had no desire – nor, she knew, would it be suitable – to emulate those fashionable ladies, the photographs of whom she had just begun to study again in the popular press, particularly the two she had noticed in the latest edition of May's *Britannia and Eve*: Barbara Hutton and some woman called Mrs Simpson. With their almost black lipstick and heavy eye-shadow, they seemed to her to have turned themselves into clowns. All the same, she did not believe in leaving her looks entirely to nature, as did Frances Farley and Dorothy Swayne. Even May approved of a little make-up, although lately she had had to refrain from using any at all owing to her unfortunate rash. Poor May. Katy knew that she had given her a bad time the last few years. It seemed so ironical that just when she herself was beginning to pick up the threads of life once more, she had burdened her sister with a different kind of anxiety altogether. It often made her feel guilty, yet she was loath to give up her new friendship. If only she could get May to approve of Gordon Hillier. She would like to have asked him to the White Hermitage. After all, it was *her* home, but she did not want to incur further trouble – something which she felt he understood – and therefore, so far, he had not set foot inside the door.

Presently Katy got up, took out a grey swagger coat

from the wardrobe, collected her handbag and went down into the garden to find Emily putting Toby through his paces in the paddock, while May was watching from over the fence. The child had erected some sticks, through which she was preparing her pony for the bending race at the Wilhampton gymkhana later in the summer. Emily, flushed with triumph at Toby's last effort, pulled up and shouted, 'Did you see that, Mummy? He's coming along beautifully. We could even *win*. Toby could get a red rosette.'

Katy laughed. 'That would be wonderful, darling. But isn't it time you gave over now?' She would like to have seen her daughter safely dismounted before leaving.

'Shan't be long. Just another few tries.' Emily waved gaily and trotted the pony to her improvised starting line, while the sisters exchanged quiet goodnights. Both knew that it would be doubtful if Katy returned much before eleven.

The drive to Great Ridgeway gave Katy not only pleasure but a great deal of interest, making her realize how comparatively little she knew of her home ground other than within a five- or six-mile radius. She had dim recollections of being taken further afield by train when she was a child in order to visit both her maternal and paternal grandparents; but such occasions were rare and, through going to work in London at so young an age and then living there immediately after she married, there had been little opportunity to explore the west country. True, the advent of buses and motorcars had made travelling a great deal easier during the few times she had stayed at the Mill House, but it was not really until she and Philip had come to live at the Moat, and sometimes of a Sunday afternoon he would take her and Emily out in the Morris, that she began to appreciate their all-too-brief journeys into the New Forest or the Blackmore Vale. Since her husband's death she had only used the car for purely practical purposes.

This evening, as Gordon drove her up over the Dorset Downs and stopped by an old barn situated on what seemed like the top of the world, she drew in her breath and then gazed silently at the scene all around her for quite a while.

'It's like a . . . sort of glory, isn't it?' she said, turning to him at length.

He smiled at her choice of phrase. 'Yes, I thought you'd like it. Shall we take our picnic over to those trees? That's where we should just be able to see the Channel.'

She nodded and got out of the car, waiting while he extracted the hamper and a rug from the boot. Slowly, they made their way over to a small clump of beeches, where he spread out the rug at the base of one of the largest and they sat down facing due south. In the distance, where the greeny-blue horizon dipped slightly, there was a patch of deeper blue. It seemed perfectly natural for him to pick up her hand as he pointed it out to her. 'The sea, Katy,' he said, softly.

She had never thought about it very much before but now, still looking ahead, she replied, 'Do you know, Gordon, I've only been to the seaside once.' She did not add 'on my honeymoon'.

'Really?' He did not seem altogether surprised. He simply continued, 'Well, perhaps we could put that right this summer . . . Besides a lot of other things.'

She was in his arms then. She kept telling herself that she hadn't meant it to happen, that she hadn't expected it to, but soon she was being given little time to think. She was being pushed backwards, gently but expertly, until she finally found herself stretched out full length on the rug and responding eagerly to something of which she had long been starved. In between his kisses, she was vaguely aware of the leafy tracery above her. She could have been once again on Putney Heath or Breconbury Down with Philip. She might not feel for Gordon Hillier in the same way as she had for her husband, yet his love-making was something she understood, wanted and needed. She felt his hands start to unbutton her tussore blouse and she did not restrain him.

'I always suspected,' she heard him say, 'that you might be rather good at this sort of thing, Katy.' His voice was lazy, bantering.

She blushed and turned her head away.

Katy never knew exactly when or how she managed to stop what had seemed like the inevitable taking place. One minute she was prepared to give in to an overwhelming physical urge, the next it was as if some bell in her inner consciousness was ringing loudly, insistently; and as if in some inexplicable way it was unmistakably connected with Emily. She sat up quickly, so quickly, in fact, that Gordon Hillier was left lying beside her, bewildered and frowning.

'What is it, Katy?'

Agitatedly, she buttoned up her blouse. 'I'm sorry . . . I shouldn't have let you . . . Forgive me.'

'But you were enjoying it, my dear, just as much as I.'

'Yes . . . No. I mean, it was wrong of me.'

He propped himself up on one elbow. 'Hardly fair, was it?' he said. 'After all, it isn't as if you're . . . inexperienced. Is it your habit to lead men on and then hold out on them? There's a word for that kind of woman, you know.'

'Yes . . . I know. I've said I'm sorry. I can't explain.'

'Is it because you weren't . . . prepared? I'd have taken care of all that, you know.'

'Yes. I'm sure.'

'Well then . . .' He attempted to pull her down beside him again, but she struggled free.

With a shrug, he sat up also, opened the picnic basket and began looking inside. Presently, he handed her a glass of white wine. 'I have never,' he said, as he slowly sipped one himself, 'entirely understood women. Possibly you take more understanding than most.'

It was not even ten o'clock when they came over the Barbury turnpike and dropped down into Netherford. Katy was surprised to see a car parked outside the Hermitage. As they drew closer, she recognized it as Maurice Fitzherbert's.

'Oh, my God!' She clenched her fists together, staring at it in horror.

'Don't worry, Katy. It may be nothing.' He dropped a hand on to her knee, but it was a purely avuncular gesture.

Angrily, she brushed it aside. 'How can it be nothing,

Gordon. Maurice wouldn't call at the Hermitage at this hour for *nothing*.'

Her voice had risen, hysterically. He stopped at the gate. Before he had had time to reach across and open the door, she was out and flying up the garden path.

27

For over a fortnight, May and Katy between them kept an almost round-the-clock vigil by Emily's bedside in Weston-bury Infirmary, where she was taken after being thrown from her pony. One evening, towards the end of that time, the child opened her eyes and asked for her mother. Ever afterwards, Katy thanked God that she had been the one who was there. Yet it was but the beginning of a long, slow and painful recovery. Even at the end of it, Maurice Fitzherbert warned Katy that it was possible Emily might always walk with a slight limp.

During those first agonizing two weeks, Katy did something which she had not done for a long time: she prayed. In their separate ways, both sisters felt responsible for the accident: May, because she had been the prime motivator in Emily's having a pony; Katy, not only because of her absence from home at the time of the fall but because of what she had been doing during that absence. The memory haunted her, tortured her. That early, harsh indoctrination concerning good and evil from which she felt she had managed to escape now seemed to re-establish itself more firmly than ever. Her parents' warnings and strict conventional attitudes – especially Sarah's condemnation of any woman who, in her eyes, was no better than she should be – kept repeating themselves in her tired brain; while she was constantly reminded of those terrifying, doom-laden texts which were even now still pinned up outside the chapel on the corner of East Street and to which, in her youth, her eyes had been inescapably drawn: *Be sure your sin will find you out, Enter not into temptation* and *The sins of the fathers* . . . Only in this case, she thought grimly, it was not an errant father who had visited his sins upon his children but a wanton mother. Her personal castigation knew no bounds. Whatever had *induced* her to go on a picnic with Gordon Hillier? She had known deep down, hadn't she, that it was asking for trouble?

In the long hours of watching and waiting, Katy recalled that other picnic with Philip on Putney Heath soon after they had met which, though of a more innocent nature, had nevertheless been followed by retribution. In many ways, she felt that there was a definite similarity between that which had taken place in the early summer of 1920 and that which had so nearly happened in the spring of 1934. Because even then, there had been the same initial abandonment, the sudden halt she had put to proceedings and the shock of her return when she was told that she was wanted immediately at the Mill House, because her mother and her eldest sister were seriously ill. Did one's life path always follow the same pattern, she wondered? Was a person conditioned to make the same kind of mistakes over and over again which gave rise to the same sort of tragedy and remorse? She supposed that she was being morbid; for, in the light of experience, she knew, logically, that her actions could not possibly have caused her mother's or Flo's or Emily's misfortunes; yet she was unable to rid herself of the idea. There were, as Sarah used to shake her head and mutter, 'More things in heaven and earth . . .'

Emily did not return to the Hermitage until the end of July and when she did, there was a very great change in her. Physically, she was pale, weak and a little uncertain on her feet. Moreover, during the time she had spent in bed she seemed to have grown several inches and was now taller than either her mother or her aunt. But it was mentally that the alteration was most apparent. There had fortunately been no brain damage, even though she had suffered a fractured skull; yet the child had been through a lot and this manifested itself in a quiet, curiously detached attitude to the world around her.

It had been agreed by May and Katy that Toby should be sent temporarily, and in all probability, permanently, to one of Frances Farley's nieces; and this Emily appeared to accept quite naturally. She did not refer to what had happened. For one thing, mercifully, she could remember nothing of the fall, how, in her excitement, she had turned the pony too short and he had gone down, throwing her between him and the side of the skilling on which she had hit her head. That scene was imprinted, indelibly, on May's mind only. She could recall the sudden fear, the bundle of yellow jersey and fawn jodhpurs lying on the ground, running towards it and kneeling down, the miraculous arrival of Robert Farley and how he had taken off his jacket and placed it gently over the inert form, while warning May not to attempt to move the child until the doctor came; and then there had been the waiting until, suddenly, she was aware of Maurice Fitzherbert's quiet voice and the ambulance backing into the paddock. Once they had settled Emily inside it, May had been allowed to accompany her niece on that slow harrowing drive to the Infirmary, where she found Maurice already standing at the entrance to receive them, after which he promised to return to Netherford in order to bring Katy to the hospital as soon as possible.

Naturally, neither sister spoke very much of all that had taken place that night, and the fact that Emily herself never enquired made it that much easier. What was soon to prove more of a problem, however, was the child's education. Maurice Fitzherbert did not consider Emily fit enough to return to Wickfield House for some time and the services of Ethel Sharman were therefore called upon once more. While doubtful that she was up to the teaching standard required, Ethel was only too pleased at the thought of being in contact with her favourite pupil again and it was agreed that, with the help of all the books listed by the school which Emily would have been studying had she been there, Ethel would come to Netherford three afternoons each week, transported to and fro by either May or Katy. As the nights drew in, the little ménage at the White Hermitage settled down into a different, calmer and, in many ways, less troubled routine than it had for some time. It might have been a house of women, but at least they were all in accord and the simple, if cloistered, atmosphere seemed to give each one of them a necessary period of reparation.

Gordon Hillier had written Katy a kind and sympathetic letter soon after the accident to which, in due course, she replied. He did not attempt to ask her out again and she naturally had no wish to go. By mutual tacit agreement, their affair – if such it could be called – was over. May, with commendable restraint, never mentioned it. The rash on her face and neck, like Emily's condition, slowly improved, as she set about making her sister, her niece and herself new winter dresses. Such an undertaking was not without forethought because, on the advice of Maurice Fitzherbert, Katy had booked up to take the three of them for a week's holiday at the end of October to a hotel on the south coast and the thought of this began to rekindle some of Emily's former animation.

'Will I stay up to supper with you and Mummy, Aunt Chip?'

'It depends,' May answered, guardedly. 'And anyway, Miss, it's called dinner at the Boscombe Towers.'

'Oh. I bet that's why you're making me a new dress, though.'

'Perhaps. But a nice blue velvet frock will always come in useful. I believe Phoebe Moreton and her brother will be spending Christmas at the Grange and there could well be a party.'

Emily became pensive. She had not seen Phoebe since she had come to tea at the White Hermitage the previous year, when she had found her precocity appalling. To meet her again would probably mean being asked awkward questions about Toby and riding, something which Emily preferred to forget. 'I'd rather stay up to dinner than go to a party at the Grange,' she said. And there the matter rested.

Although the visit to the seaside was taken out of season, it proved to be an unqualified success. May, having never spent a night in a hotel before, took particular pleasure in studying the other guests, casting a discreet but knowledge-able eye over every detail of their apparel. 'I haven't seen anything that's a patch on Emily's velvet or our wool georgettes,' she would say to her sister, with satisfaction. 'And as for that old crone in the corner. Did you ever see such an ill-fitting reach-me-down?' And Katy, pleased that the week was going so well, would smile and agree.

As for Emily – although her wish to remain up for dinner was granted – she found her chief source of delight at teatime, during which an orchestra played Viennese waltzes and some of the latest Cole Porter and Noel Coward hits, 'Night and Day' and 'I'll Follow my Secret Heart' being her two favourites. She would sit entranced, absentmindedly stuffing herself with cucumber sandwiches and chocolate éclairs until, to her regret, the musicians packed up and went away at five-thirty. When, on the last night of the holiday, May and Katy took her to a production of Dodie Smith's *Autumn Crocus*, she decided then and there to become a playwright, especially when she heard that this particular play was written by a shop assistant. It must be quite easy, she felt, and went back to Netherford with her imagination fired and her head full of promising ideas.

In a sudden burst of confidence, she said as much to John Moreton one afternoon during the Christmas holidays, when they cycled over the Barbury turnpike together while Phoebe had gone riding with her cousins. Emily no longer found he was quite the object of scorn which she had once considered him to be. He had shown her, diffidently, some of his drawings, and she could not help feeling that they were rather good. He was so totally unlike Phoebe that it was hard to think of them as brother and sister; certainly, he was much easier to talk to.

'Do you,' he said, on the way home, 'ever ride now?'

'No. I had this accident, you know.'

'Yes, my grandmother told me. Do you . . . mind? About not riding, I mean?'

'Not really. I . . .' She hesitated. Colour flooded her face and she hoped he would not notice. 'I'm rather scared of horses now,' she went on, with a rush.

She was relieved at his matter-of-fact reply.

'Quite understandable. I've always thought them stupid animals, as I believe I once told you. I wish my sister wasn't so mad about them. She doesn't think of anything else and there are so many other things to do with one's time.'

She wondered whether to risk her next question and decided that, as he himself had switched the conversation on to such personal lines, he would not mind.

'Do you like Eton better now?' she asked.

'It's not so bad. I enjoy cricket. And art. And I've just taken up photography. Incidentally, doesn't one get a marvellous view of the valley from here.'

By mutual consent, they slowed down and dismounted, studying the scene before them and the silvery course of the Willon, so much easier to discern now that the trees were bare.

'It's a bit like being in an aeroplane up here, isn't it?' he continued. 'It reminds me of something one of our English masters said the other day: when you look down on a river from a great height, instead of just sitting by its banks, it's as if you can see the past and the present and the future all at once.'

'Yes, I . . . suppose it is.'

'Look,' he said, suddenly pointing. 'There's the Felt Mills. Do you remember that time I first met you when you were staying there with your mother and she took us to see the mill-race? D'you ever go there now?'

She looked away and he could have kicked himself. That was where her father had drowned, hadn't he? He seemed to recall there having been some sort of mystery.

'I'm sorry,' he went on, quickly. 'I . . . was forgetting.'

This time she turned to face him. 'It's quite all right,' she replied, quickly. 'It was a long time ago.'

And so it was, she thought, as they remounted and free-wheeled practically the whole way home. Her memory of the tragedy had always been shadowy and confused. She had never known much about what had happened, other than that neither her mother nor her aunt wished to talk about it. Gradually, she had begun to sense that there was something not quite straightforward – even shameful – connected with her father's death. In some curious way it became linked in her mind with those puzzling, secretive, nocturnal goings-on from which she had been excluded as a child. Once or twice, as she grew older, she had been on the point of asking May a few questions, but at the last moment she had refrained. Perhaps, after all, it was better not to know. She liked things the way they were: just her mother, herself and Aunt Chip. She would never have breathed a word to anyone about it, not even Helen Swayne, her best friend, but somehow life seemed easier without her father about the place.

At the gate of the Hermitage, John raised his cap and wished her goodbye, remarking that he was looking forward to seeing her at the tea-party his grandmother was giving the following afternoon. 'She's hiding clues,' he added, with a smile. 'That's why she and Phoebe's new governess wanted us all out of the way today. As far as I can make out, Granny has been organizing treasure hunts all her life. I don't know how she still does it now she's confined to a wheelchair.'

Emily went indoors, any sense of embarrassment which had overcome her a little while ago having been completely swept aside by his gentle apology. Now that she had got to know John Moreton better, she felt as if she would have some ally at the forthcoming party at the Grange. She had ceased to dread it. She would be quite interested to take part in a treasure hunt. She wondered whether she would need to wear her spectacles for it. She certainly wasn't going to keep them on at tea. It was perfectly possible, by dint of a few little tricks such as screwing up her eyes, to get by without them when she wanted to, even if the world did seem rather on the hazy side.

28

'I'm glad Doctor Fitzherbert thinks Emily can start again at Wickfield House in the summer term,' said Ethel Sharman, one late March evening the following year when May was driving her home. 'Not that I won't miss my visits to the Hermitage more than I can say. But the child needs companionship of her own age now, May. She's been with grown-ups too long.'

'Yes. Yes, I daresay you're right, Ethel.' May drove slowly, keeping her eyes on the narrow Netherford lane. She never, in fact, went very fast and rarely got up to even thirty miles an hour, the speed limit recently imposed in built-up areas by the young go-ahead Minister of Transport, Mr Hore-Belisha. Tonight she was taking extra care, because a mist had formed in the water-meadows by the Willon and she would be thankful to reach the main road where she always found the new cat's eyes such a blessing after dark. It was a relief when her passenger, possibly sensing her need for concentration, lapsed into silence.

But just before they reached Cob Lane Ethel suddenly clapped a hand on her forehead and burst out, 'Oh May, I quite forgot. I meant to mention it before. Would it make any difference, do you think, if I made my final session with Emily next Tuesday instead of Monday? I've got Edwin coming to lunch that day. You remember, my cousin at the Air Ministry.'

'No, of course not, Ethel. How is he, by the way?' May knew that Ethel had a high regard for Edwin, who appeared to be her only relative.

'Well, he's worked off his feet, poor thing.' Ethel's voice became subdued. 'And you know, May, from what he says in his letters, you can't help *wondering*.'

May negotiated the tricky turning into Cob Lane and drew up outside Number 7 before answering. 'Wondering what, Ethel?'

'About this conscription that's been introduced in Germany. This man Hitler . . . You don't know what to think. He's got such a shifty face. I mean, what's he re-arming *for*? That's what I should like to know.'

'Not another war, Ethel. That's for certain. And anyway, there couldn't be. The League of Nations will see to that.'

'Please God you're right, my dear. But I just don't like it somehow. You should have seen the photographs in the last issue of the *Illustrated London News*. Edwin sent it to me. I'll bring it along next time I come.'

After she had wished Ethel goodnight, May backed the car and turned round – not without a little difficulty – and then, glancing somewhat wistfully at her old home, drove back to the Hermitage. The trouble with Ethel, she reflected later on that night when she was in bed, was that she would keep reading the more serious papers and magazines. They were all right in their way, but it didn't do to dwell quite so much on the possibility of wars or the blunders of politicians. It was so much better to look on the bright side and, personally, May felt she had a lot to be thankful for just now: Emily's return to health (her niece hardly ever limped except when she was very tired); Katy's less self-absorbed and altogether more mature attitude to life, which she was forced to admit was thanks – agonizing as it had been – to the child's accident; then there was the miraculous disappearance of her own distressing rash and, what was more, a very special summer to which they could all look forward.

To May's surprise and delight the Dowager Lady Fairfax, unable to take any active part in proceedings herself, had put forward May's name as a suitable candidate to sit on a committee to organize the forthcoming Jubilee celebrations and, after her election, it would have been hard to find a more energetic and enthusiastic member. Along with the Dowager's daughter-in-law and various other lady parishioners, including Dorothy Swayne, May found herself discussing a variety of ideas with the Reverend Morgan – the new young rector of Wilhampton – Maurice Fitzherbert, Cyril Butt and Robert Farley; for Netherford, being so close to the small town, always joined forces with it at times like these. The proposals most favoured to do justice to the occasion ranged from a pageant, a tree-planting, a children's tea party, a torchlight procession, an ox-roasting in the market square and a concert by the Wilhampton brass band.

'You can't have them all, May,' Maud Fairfax had said with a smile, one evening when she had gone to the Grange to report proceedings. 'Personally, I should think a children's tea party, a tree-planting and a torchlight procession would be best. A nice Jubilee oak on Breconbury Down at the top of Dick Swayne's farm would seem most appropriate. I feel a pageant would be too much of a problem. I remember the one poor Maggie Fortescue arranged at the time of the Coronation. Such *bickering*, May. You've no idea. They wanted poor Dick Swayne's father and mother to dress up as George III and Queen Charlotte, but Mrs Swayne, bless her soul, said that nothing would induce her to do that because, although George III was known as the farmer king, he was also as mad as a hatter and her husband was the sanest person she knew!'

May had not been able to refrain from rocking with laughter and saying, 'Oh, chippatoo!' until the Dowager had gone on a little more seriously. 'If only Alicia were here instead of Rachel, it would all be so much easier, but I'm afraid my daughter-in-law isn't quite up to . . . well . . . taking charge of a *pageant*.'

It was not often that Maud Fairfax went as far as to voice the slightest regret that the young woman who had stepped into her shoes was in any way a disappointment to her. But May had known long ago, without being told, that the Dowager was more than a little unhappy at the way things were run at the Hall these days and the fact that her son was so often abroad. The uncertainty as to whether he would even be at home on the sixth of May had already precluded his being asked to chair the Jubilee Committee, which duty was now being undertaken, well-meaningly but ineffectually, by his wife.

The next morning May decided to pay one of her visits to the Grange, not so much this time to tell the Dowager what progress was being made as to elicit further advice from her before the next committee meeting, which was due to take place that Friday. Although May was not without her own ideas and opinions and was now quite able to put them forward to good effect, she well knew that Maud Fairfax had a lifetime's experience behind her and that, whatever pronouncement she made on such matters, it was not only sound and sensible but in some curious way she was still in remote control. She might be confined to a wheelchair but there was not much of importance that escaped the former chatelaine of the Hall.

She might never have had, like the Reverend Donaldson and Maurice's father, quite such close day-to-day contact with the local inhabitants, but she had always had her own particular ways of finding out about them and showing concern for their well-being. Even now, handicapped as she was, while she obviously enjoyed May's visits for their own sake, the latter was not unaware that her hostess put them to good use from the point of view of keeping in touch with all that was going on in the neighbourhood.

Yet, on her arrival that day, May soon discovered that there was something which had pushed the Jubilee committee – at least, temporarily – right into the background.

'I've sad news, I'm afraid, May. Nanny Barlow died last night. Of course, we've all expected it for a long time, but, nevertheless, when death finally comes . . .' The Dowager sat very erect in her wheelchair and for once she did not end her sentence. Her eyes had an unusually faraway look in them and May knew at once what she was thinking. The woman before her was older than Nanny Barlow. She must know that she could not have many more years ahead of her. Then, after a little while, she seemed to return to the present and her customary efficient and practical way of dealing with things.

'Nanny expressed a wish to be buried in Wilhampton, May. So Alicia is making arrangements her end. I should think the funeral would be some time in the middle of next week. Not many relatives to inform. A niece and her husband – but I think they were rather a disappointment to her. Other than them, well . . . we seemed to be her life.' She paused and then went on, 'I suppose, in these days, some people might consider that wrong. But . . . I don't know. I believe Nanny wouldn't have had it otherwise. There'll be an announcement in *The Times* and the *Telegraph* tomorrow. I've already telephoned the *Westonbury Journal*. And I'm getting on to the Reverend Donaldson. I'm sure he'd be only too glad to come back and give the address. And we must sing "All Things Bright and Beautiful" at the service. It was her favourite hymn.'

May felt the tears beginning to come. Hastily, she pulled out a handkerchief. She knew that people like the Dowager hardly ever cried in front of others, although she suspected that they probably cared just as much in their controlled, dignified way.

'I'm sure Nanny Barlow would like that,' was all she managed to say.

As she left the Grange, the Reverend Morgan, young, fresh-faced, eager to please, was coming up the steps. May knew he would do his best. But how could he possibly *know*: about the Fairfaxes, their Nanny, their children and their grandchildren, and the curious inter-relationship between their family and that of the Lodges from the one-time Mill House, Wilhampton? It would take a lifetime to explain that − if it was possible to explain, which she doubted. One had to live in a place, love it, cherish it, even. It had to become part of one so that one's life was inextricably bound up with it, just as the River Willon threaded together all those little towns and hamlets through which it passed on its omnipotent way to the sea. Quietly, May wished the Reverend Morgan 'Good morning', and hurried back to the Hermitage.

After much deliberation, especially on Katy's part, it was agreed that Emily should attend the funeral the following week. 'I think she's old enough,' May had said. 'And it isn't as if she was all that close to the old soul, as you were once. That's all to the good, really. And I expect Phoebe and John William will be there, especially as he's likely to be home for the Easter holidays.'

May felt her opinion in the matter to be justified when the three of them sat halfway up the front aisle of St Mark's the following Thursday afternoon. She watched both the Moreton children walk up to the front pew beside their parents − John in his Eton uniform and Phoebe in a smart navy coat and beret − where the Dowager was already waiting in her wheelchair, with her daughter-in-law beside her. There was no sign of the present Lord Fairfax.

'I don't like it,' May said to her sister that night when Emily was in bed. 'His poor wife. She does her best. It isn't her fault. They say he's in Monte Carlo. Perhaps you couldn't expect him to come back for his old Nanny's funeral but I hope to God he'll be here for his mother's.'

Katy looked at her sister in some surprise. It was so unlike her to speak so vehemently, although she knew that May was becoming a force to be reckoned with. She felt that she might even end up on the local council at the rate she was going.

29

Although, despite her long absence from Wickfield House, Emily found that she was put in the same advanced form when she returned there that summer, she decided of her own volition to do a few extra studies in English Literature during the forthcoming holidays. As long as such an undertaking was done in daylight and not carried to excess, Katy felt there was no harm in it, especially as no deterioration in her daughter's short sight had been found during a recent eye test. She was glad that Emily shared her love of reading and therefore, while she herself was enjoying Scott Fitzgerald's latest novel, *Tender is the Night*, which she had just borrowed from Boots' library in Westonbury, Emily was becoming enthralled by *Wuthering Heights*.

At first, Katy had been reluctant to let the child read this particular book, which she always kept in a drawer by her bed, but when Emily explained that it had been listed by the English mistress at Wickfield as 'recommended reading', she had given in and handed it to her.

'You'll take great care of it, won't you, darling. If it hadn't been for *Wuthering Heights*, I might never have met your father and you wouldn't have come into the world.' Katy had just begun to talk about Philip quite naturally, something which May noted with pleasure and relief.

'Yes, Mummy. Of course.'

Emily took the book eagerly. She already knew the story of how her mother, as a young nursery maid in London, had been looking at some good, albeit damaged, editions which were for sale in a trough in Masons' doorway, and how her father had practically forced his future wife into buying one because he desperately wanted to get to know her better. Emily had considered it highly romantic and the knowledge that when she had been born her parents had decided to call her after the authoress of *Wuthering Heights* had naturally only increased her interest in it. It had always been a disappointment to her that, until now, she had not been considered old enough to read it.

She could think of nothing better, she decided, when, on a second sunny August day running, she settled down with the book, leaning back against her favourite willow tree at the end of the overgrown lane leading from the Hermitage to the river. To her right, she was aware of the thrumming of Robert Farley's tractor and binder as it circled a field of golden wheat; on the opposite bank of the Willon she could see his herd of shorthorns moving slowly towards the gateway of the meadow where, with a gentle 'Coop . . . Coop', his dairyman, Fred Cutler, called them for the afternoon's milking; while halfway up the downs in the distance, she could just discern a small group of ant-like figures stooking oats. But soon her surroundings were lost to her. Emily was back in time at another farm owned by another man, where it was winter, not summer, and the heroine was returning from a different Grange from the one she knew at Netherford. Emily had just got to the place where Cathy, still dressed in all her finery, rushed to embrace Heathcliff when, to her extreme annoyance, she was brought rudely back to the present century by several shrill 'Cooees' coming from somewhere close at hand. There was then the sound of parting rushes and Mavis, Edith's youngest daughter, stood before her.

'Hullo, Em.' The girl spoke half defiantly, half mockingly.

Mavis was a month younger than Emily, but she looked older in every way. There was a curious provocative maturity about her. She had a pale pert freckled face, albeit somewhat redeemed by a wealth of auburn hair, similar to her mother's at the same age. Her body was short but shapely and now, with both hands held firmly behind her back, she looked almost as if she wished to draw attention to it and the way her thin blue cotton dress strained over her small thrusting breasts.

'Hullo, Mavis.' Emily blinked a little behind her glasses and kept a thumb on the page she had been reading. She knew that her Aunt Edith was expected to tea but had imagined that she would come, as usual, alone.

'I was going to stop home and mind Georgie,' Mavis volunteered, 'but when he got asked next door I decided to come along. It's not a bad walk, is it? In summer, that is.'

'No.' Emily was always at a loss to know how to deal with her cousins and she knew that they knew this. She often pictured them giggling behind her back and, although she had no desire to be like them, she wished that she could behave more spontaneously in their presence instead of so often being, as now, tongue-tied.

Certainly no such problem ever bothered Mavis. Suddenly, she flung herself down on the grass beside Emily and burst out, 'Mum's in a terrible way. I'm not meant to know. That's why I've been sent down here to find you. She wants to talk things over privately with your Mum and Aunt May.'

'Oh.' Emily could not think what was the matter unless, perhaps, it had to do with her Uncle Herbert's health. Many was the time she had overheard whispers to the effect that he was unlikely to 'make old bones'.

'Don't you want to know what it's all about?' Mavis enquired, obviously slightly put out that her initial information had not elicited a more forthcoming response.

'Yes . . . But . . . I mean, you said you weren't meant to know.'

Mavis's pale blue eyes opened wide in astonishment. If her cousin was that much of a prig, she felt it was time to shock her well and truly out of it.

'Della's in the family way,' she announced, loudly. 'She's *three months gone*.'

Emily remained staring straight in front of her. The sun had momentarily passed behind a cloud and it seemed as if all the enchantment of the afternoon had gone with it.

She knew what Mavis meant, even though it was knowledge which had scarcely been assimilated. As far as she was concerned, it was a subject which one simply never thought – and certainly never talked – about. It was disgraceful, frightening and had to be hushed up. Della had done something wicked, which was connected with a man. Just what, Emily had no idea, except that it resulted in a baby. How this came about when one was not married was a complete mystery. In her mind, giving birth was synonymous with marriage. After all, her mother had implied as much when she had given her a little talk on the subject not long ago. And whatever it was that men and women did together which resulted in a baby, while it was shameful if they were not man and wife, it was apparently perfectly acceptable – even creditable – if they were.

Or was it? Into her mind, unwilling and unbidden, came the recollection of those nights in Davies Street long ago, when she had been suffering from nightmares and occasionally overheard something which she did not understand taking place in her parents' bedroom. Even if it were not shameful or wicked, it had definitely seemed very frightening and was obviously something which had embarrassed her mother, who had tried to pretend it hadn't happened. Emily had done her best to forget about it, as well as the guilty knowledge that when, after her father's death, she had suddenly realized that nothing like that could happen again, she had felt immensely relieved. It had never occurred to her that her mother might ever remarry. She supposed that Katy's friendship with Gordon Hillier, owing to his age, had simply come about through a mutual interest in the arts, although she had sometimes wondered why they now saw so little of each other.

'It was the torchlight procession on Jubilee night that was at the bottom of it.' Still aggrieved and aggressive, Mavis broke into her thoughts. 'I could have told Mum all along,' she continued. 'We lost Della towards the end. Debbie thought she'd gone with the Pearsons next door, but I knew better. I saw her slip away with . . . well, p'raps I'd best not say who I thought she was with.' Even Mavis seemed to have some sense of obligation at this point. 'Anyway, whoever it was, I knew what she'd probably be up to. You see, she's not the same as Debbie. I know what Della likes.'

Part of Emily wanted to scream and ask Mavis to stop, yet part of her wanted to know more. *What* did Della like? What was Mavis getting at? She did not have to ask. Her cousin, obviously enjoying herself, seemed to be in full spate now.

'You see, my brother David . . . well, when they were growing up . . . I used to watch them through this little hole in the bedroom wall . . . when Mum and Dad were out. That wasn't often, mind you, but just sometimes they used to go to the pictures when Dad felt they could afford it and p'raps there was a Laurel and Hardy film on. Donald and Della used to take off all their clothes then. Of course, I mean, he never *did* anything. After all, she was his sister. But, you know, he . . . mucked her about.'

Emily felt as if she were going to be sick. She wished Mavis would go away. For some unknown reason, she found her glasses misting up and she tried to fight back the tears. This, surely, wasn't what happened? The way grown-up people went on? The way her own mother and father behaved? The way she herself had been brought into the world? There must be some mistake. Mavis, after all, was just a silly and not particularly intelligent girl who had got hold of the wrong end of the stick. Yet she seemed so assured, more enlightened, it would seem, than Aunt Edith if, as she maintained, she knew what her sister had been up to on the night the Jubilee oak was planted.

Presently, conscious that she had made her point, Mavis sat up and, slightly changing her tactics, said, 'Have you started yet?'

'Started?' Emily was confused, still miserable.

'Oh, Em. You know what I mean. I had the curse two years ago, but I had a feeling you hadn't.'

'No,' Emily answered, this time quite calmly. 'And I do wish you wouldn't go on about these sort of things, Mavis.'

'All right.' Suddenly and quite naturally, the girl beside

her put out a hand in a friendly gesture. 'I know you're different from us,' she continued. 'Mum always said that. Just like your own Mum was. Reckon you'll make a good match one of these days. Nothing like what's happened to our Della will happen to you. D'you know what Dad said a little while ago? He said, "Katy and her kid have class". Funny, i'nt it, when you come to think of it. Here's you staying on at school for quite a while yet, I suppose. But I'll be leaving after Christmas. I think Mum's hoping to get me a domestic job over Baverchalke way where I'll live in. It'll make things easier at home. A bit more room for Della and her brat, that's if Bob Swayne don't marry her.' Hastily, Mavis clapped a hand over her mouth and then added, apologetically, 'Sorry, Em. I've properly let the cat out of the bag now, haven't I?'

'*Bob Swayne?*' Emily turned, white-faced, and stared at her cousin. 'Bob Swayne,' she repeated in a whisper. 'Oh no, Mavis . . . you can't mean it. He's Helen's brother. It's not . . . possible.'

'It's possible all right, Em, even though . . . well . . . he's several cuts above us, so to speak. Mind you, I'm not saying for sure it was him. Della likes the boys, as I said. And they like her. There's been plenty after her lately.' She stood up. 'I wonder if they've stopped threshing out what's going to happen to her back at the Hermitage. P'raps I'll go and see.'

After she had left her, Emily remained by the willow tree, *Wuthering Heights* still open in her lap. But she did not read again that afternoon. She sat, unsure, bewildered and feeling somehow besmirched. It crossed her mind that her Aunt Edith would soon have not six but seven young things to care for in that small, hopelessly inconvenient house on downside, that is, if she did not get Mavis away to Baverchalke. Or would whoever it was who had done this terrible thing to Della marry her and make whatever was so disgraceful altogether respectable again. It would be nice to think so. Emily did not particularly care for any of her cousins, but she did not wish them any harm.

Still she sat on, reluctant to go up to the house, watching the Willon flowing gently along in front of her. Presently,

the cows started meandering back into the opposite
meadow, the afternoon's milking over. After a while, a
fisherman came into view, leisurely casting downstream.
Gradually, the unhurried peace of her surroundings began
to soothe her shattered senses.

It was, perhaps, an unusual thought for one so young
but when, at last, she walked slowly back up the narrow
pathway and climbed over the little stile into the Hermitage
garden, she was comforted by a feeling that whatever
happened, she would always have herself, that as long as
she remained alone and never married she would be all
right.

30

During the rest of the holidays, for the first time since she
had known her, Emily was reluctant to remain very long
in Helen Swayne's company. But gradually, with relief, she
came to realize that whoever had got Della into trouble,
it was certainly not Bob Swayne. Whenever she went to
Bulbarrow there was just the same easy friendly atmos-
phere as there had always been. Helen's parents were their
usual charming selves and Bob, who she had to admit was
strikingly good-looking, did not behave as if some cloud
was hanging over him. Besides, Emily was conscious
enough of class distinction to know that it was most
unlikely that he would have anything to do with a girl
living on downside. Dorothy and Dick Swayne had made
tremendous sacrifices to send him and his younger brother
Tim away to a minor public school catering specially for
the sons of farmers, and now Bob was destined – at least,
for a year or two – to help his father at home on the farm.
As for Helen, she appeared to be perfectly happy, full of
plans for something she called landscape gardening;
making a rockery and pool in a small corner of Bulbarrow
garden which had been given over to her.

Yet the stigma hanging over Emily's own family was,
she knew, still there and becoming more oppressive and
threatening every day. She could see the worried preoccu-

pied look on her mother's and aunt's faces, however much they tried to appear normal in her presence. She occasionally overheard snatches of conversation which were hastily broken off whenever she entered the room, such as 'Pity Edie wasn't stricter . . .' 'Needed Sarah's hand . . .' or 'D'you think Henry might . . . ?' But whatever her Uncle Henry might or might not do was something about which she could only make private conjectures. Mostly, such remarks came from May, Katy's remembrance of the recent far from creditable occasion in her own life possibly inhibiting her from being quite so openly censorious.

Emily was angered that everyone seemed to imagine that she herself knew nothing of the situation and, in consequence, she was obliged to keep up some kind of pretence. But one day, just before the start of the Wickfield autumn term, there was an incident which was so bewildering that it made her conscious of how very little, in fact, she did know. She had gone to Westonbury alone by bus to collect her school satchel which was being mended at the saddlers. While she was waiting at the stop outside the White Lion for the return journey, two women came along and stood behind her. She had no idea who they were, other than that from their conversation it appeared they were going to visit some family living on downside, 'Next door,' said the elder of two, 'to that poor Edith Lench, the one whose daughter's up the spout.'

Emily had felt the same sudden surge of nausea which she had experienced in the meadows on the day when Mavis had launched forth on her hideous outburst of enlightenment. Now, once again repelled but riveted with curiosity – especially by the crude expression which, though totally inexplicable, seemed nevertheless suggestive of something horrible – she heard the other woman reply even more incomprehensibly, 'I gather it's a married man, isn't it? Lilian Perrick's son, Archie, by all accounts. He always was a bit of no good. Poor Sarah Lodge. I should think it would make her turn in her grave.'

After that the bus had arrived and Emily heard no more. But all the way back to Netherford her mind had been in a turmoil. She was dimly aware that Lilian Perrick, at the Wilhampton sweet-shop, had a married son who was constantly on the dole. She was not sure, but she believed that he, his wife and several children lived in one of the new council houses which, sadly, had recently been put up on what was once known as the buttercup field belonging to Bulbarrow Farm. She had not seen him for some time, but her recollection was that of a thin ferret-faced man whom Dick Swayne occasionally employed during haymaking and harvest. She looked upon him as quite middle-aged, at least thirty-five. It was just as impossible to think he was the cause of Della's downfall as it was Bob Swayne. Even more, in fact. For Archie Perrick was *married*. The two old gossips at the bus stop were obviously being just as foolish, in their way, as Mavis had been. Surely everyone knew that once a man was married he could only be the father of his wife's children?

Emily had been back at Wickfield for about a week when she came home one day to find a visitor at the Hermitage. As she entered the small drawing room, her mother introduced her to her Uncle Henry, whom she had never seen.

She took to him at once. In his khaki uniform with his sergeant major's stripes on his arm he stood up and courteously held out his hand.

'So this is Emily, my youngest sister's child.' His weather-beaten face creased into a friendly smile. 'I've been looking forward to meeting you.'

Solemnly, she shook hands and took off her school board and coat.

'Uncle Henry is staying the night, Emily,' May said, quickly. 'Run and wash your hands and then we can all have tea.'

She sensed immediately why he had come and what they had been talking about before she arrived, although the conversation was now carefully steered into other directions. Henry Lodge began referring, quite naturally, to his present life at Catterick, to his wife, Marianne, who was 'getting on a bit like we all are', and to their son, Frank François, who had 'sensibly decided not to follow in his father's footsteps'. 'He's a bit like you, Emily, I shouldn't wonder,' Henry Lodge went on. 'He's not leaving school till next year and then, if we can somehow manage it, he wants to go into the printing trade, Although,' and here she saw her uncle's face cloud over as he continued, 'God knows if he won't end up in uniform, after all, the way things are going.'

May remained silent. It was Katy who said, 'How d'you mean, Henry?'

'Mean? Well, I don't like it. Baldwin got in at the last election in June because the Conservatives never said anything about the need for rearmament. But, by God, we need to. I've been through one war and I can't see what's to stop another in a few years' time.'

'Oh, *Henry*!' Rather as she had remonstrated with Ethel Sharman not long ago, May started reaffirming her belief in the League of Nations but her brother cut her short.

'Don't let yourself be fooled, my dear. Germany left the League two years ago. It's about as much use at stopping a war as . . .' Here Henry seemed to search around for a suitable comparison which would not offend feminine susceptibilities and suddenly came up with, 'Well, a mothers' meeting. And you forget,' he continued, 'I've been out in Germany quite a bit. Our battalion was one of the last to leave at the end of the occupation in 1930. This man Hitler means business. Maybe we've only got ourselves to blame. The Treaty of Versailles wasn't just. Although . . . I don't know . . . when you've lost a brother in the fighting . . .' Henry's voice, so certain, so authoritative, suddenly became husky and altogether different.

The conversation was above Emily's head. She had never heard of the Treaty of Versailles. Her form at Wickfield was doing the French Revolution and she was longing for the *Scarlet Pimpernel*, with Leslie Howard and Merle Oberon, to come to the Odeon in Westonbury.

Presently, May drove Henry off to downside and, apart from a brief meeting the following morning, Emily did not see him again. By the time she returned from school that afternoon he had gone. She did not learn until almost a fortnight later – and then only by a short statement from her mother which brooked no further enquiries – that he had taken Della with him. She never knew until a long time afterwards that, because of her grandmother's hostile attitude over the so-called premature arrival of Henry's son, he was determined — despite his wife's natural reluctance — to do his best for his sister's child. As it turned out, his good nature was rewarded. Early the following year, just before she gave birth to a daughter, Della — greatly to her family's surprise and relief — married a young lance corporal in Henry's regiment. The news was imparted to Emily in a slightly more forthcoming manner yet, even so, she knew that the subject was not one upon which her mother and aunt wished to dwell — at least, not in front of her.

But in any case, news on a national scale was now occupying their thoughts, so much so that even the pupils of Wickfield House were made to feel its import. On January 20th they were all summoned into the big hall, where Miss Lawrence told them that King George V was dying. Throughout the day the usual clatter and hubbub of school life was subdued. No games were played and when Emily returned to the Hermitage she found Katy and May listening intently to the voice of Stuart Hibberd as he gave out hourly bulletins on the wireless: 'The King's life is drawing peacefully to a close'. All other programmes ceased and the intervening silence was broken only by a ticking clock, distressingly similar to the sound of a beating heart. At breakfast next morning, Emily was surprised to find how sad her mother and aunt seemed and it was obvious that May had actually been crying. The king had been but a shadowy figure in Emily's own life and the Prince of Wales, so far as she thought of him at all, a much more interesting and romantic one. She wondered whom he would make his queen and hoped it would be some beautiful girl such as those she was constantly drawing in her private sketchbook: tall and willowy, with a dreamy expression and masses of lovely long wavy hair.

May, too, evidently hoped vaguely for something of the same sort. When, during Ascot week, she noticed photographs of Edward VIII in the company of a dark, sophisticated-looking and much older woman than she would have expected, she was clearly upset. May always made a point of carefully studying the Ascot fashions and would come out with many a quick and, on the whole, remarkably shrewd observation on the merits or otherwise of a certain person's attire. In her eyes, Mrs Simpson was 'smart, but too *hard*'. She would have done better, May felt, to be dressed by Molyneux, as Princess Marina was; but her chief crime was the fact that she was a remarried divorcée, 'not at all the kind of woman with whom the king should be consorting'.

As the year progressed, although the British press was singularly restrained on the subject, any little item of information which May could glean only served to increase her consternation. She could not understand what had come over the new king, 'gallivanting', as she put it, here, there and everywhere, especially on board the yacht *Nahlin*, in the Adriatic, in the company of what she called a 'fast set', in which 'that woman' appeared to be a fixture. It would never do for Mrs Simpson to become queen of England. Surely Mr Baldwin would put a stop to that.

When, in fact, that December, Stanley Baldwin came up to May's expectations and managed to prevent such an occurrence, May was infinitely relieved. The Duke of York might be shy and stuttering and totally lacking in that rather doubtful aura of glamour which had surrounded his elder brother, but the new Queen Elizabeth looked charming. As for the pretty well-dressed little princesses, all those shocking rumours about Margaret Rose being deaf and dumb were now proved to be clearly without foundation. She felt that the monarchy, as never before, was an institution with which the whole nation could identify. Rather as May's own family problems had been solved earlier that year, she was delighted to think that those of the throne had now been so satisfactorily straightened out.

31

'My grandmother is asking for you, Miss Lodge. I . . . we . . . wondered if you could come.'

It was February 1938. John William Moreton, now up at Cambridge, stood on the doorstep of the Hermitage: tall, thin and incredibly handsome. There was something about him, May felt, which was at the same time assured yet vulnerable. With his fair wavy hair and disarming smile, he reminded her a little of a young Maurice Fitzherbert.

'Of course,' she said. 'Come in one moment while I get my coat.'

He had to stoop to enter the front door, rather as she remembered Maurice had once had to do at the Mill House. She saw him look round as if he was expecting to see Emily. Quickly, she explained that her niece was at school, rehearsing in a play she had written for which she had won a prize and, as it meant staying late that night, her mother had driven into Westonbury to fetch her.

'Ah, I see. Is Emily leaving Wickfield at the end of the summer?'

'Yes, John.'

'But not to go to university, I hope?'

'No. She's decided to attend the local art school.'

'Oh, good. I can't help feeling that at Cambridge girls don't seem . . . well . . . quite right, somehow.'

He helped May into his small sports car and they did not talk again until they were on their way. As he turned into the gates of the Grange, she said, gently, 'Your grandmother is worse, John?'

'Yes. That's why I drove my mother down yesterday. It's pleurisy as well as pneumonia, I'm afraid.'

'I'm so very sorry.' May knew what that augured, especially for an octogenarian. To say more seemed somehow superfluous.

As if sensing her thoughts, the young man beside her

said, 'She's eighty-two, you know. I suppose . . . I mean . . .
it's a good age, isn't it? But it's difficult to imagine . . .'
He broke off awkwardly, obviously embarrassed at having
said more than he intended. May had always known that
there had been an unusually close link between the old
lady and her grandson.

She could see a light now in one of the bedrooms of the
Grange which she knew belonged to the Dowager and, as
they came to a halt by the front door, another car came
swiftly up the drive and pulled up beside them. Maurice
Fitzherbert got out and together they all three went into
the house.

While Maurice was shown upstairs, Alicia Moreton
came into the drawing room to talk to May. Her appear-
ance gave the older woman a shock. Alicia's hair was quite
grey and there were deep lines under her eyes, which May
felt had been there for some time and were not just due
to the present situation. She could not help wondering
about her marriage. How happy had she ever been? Was
Charles Moreton still philandering, chasing after women
such as Grace Armitage, the Wilhampton *femme fatale*,
with whom it had long been recognized that he had had
some kind of liaison when John William had been a baby?

'It's good of you to come, May.' Nervously, Alicia
picked up a silver cigarette box, held it out to her visitor
and then, when the offer was declined, took a cigarette
herself, lit it and inhaled deeply. 'I don't think Mummy's
going to pull through,' she went on. 'But she's wonderfully
brave, as you might expect. She's even on about having
some new nightdress made.'

When May was eventually shown up to the Dowager's
room, Alicia's words proved correct. It appeared that the
old lady did, in fact, want a new nightdress, but one for
a very specific purpose.

'That silly girl, Miriam, has ruined all my others,
May . . . These days they don't understand about washing
properly . . . Not a decent one left to be laid out in.' Maud
Fairfax closed her eyes for a moment. She seemed to be
saving her breath for her next startling announcement.
'Over there,' she said, suddenly, with a touch of her old

imperiousness, pointing to a chintz-covered ottoman in the corner. 'There's a length of white crêpe de Chine . . . If you slip your hand down the side . . . a muslin bag. Lace,' she said, and stopped again.

May went across the room and did as she was bidden, soon returning with both items. The voice from the bed was more feeble now. 'The lace . . . is from my first dance dress, May. When I met Jimmy. We weren't . . . well off. Indian civil service . . . But my mother's cousin had this fichu . . . It was given to her by the old Duchess of Roxburghe . . . I know you'll do your best . . .'

A nurse came silently into the room with a small glass of medicine and, equally unobtrusively, May withdrew.

John Moreton was waiting for her in the hall when she came down the stairway.

'I'll drive you home, Miss Lodge.'

'It's kind of you, John, but it's only a little way. There's really no need.'

'But it's the least I can do.' He glanced at May's packages. 'I believe my grandmother has been putting you to work.' She was struck again by his extraordinary charm.

She saw lights in the window of the Hermitage as soon as they swung into the lane, which meant that Katy and Emily were back. 'Would you,' May asked, when he drew up at the gate, 'care to come in?'

He accepted with alacrity. There was, she supposed, little to occupy him in Netherford at the moment, with a dying grandmother and a mother who seemed so preoccupied and tense.

Emily was standing in the small hallway when they entered, surveying herself in an antique looking glass which Katy had recently bought in one of Butt and Swanton's furniture sales. She was adjusting an old-fashioned wig with ringlets. Her face still bore traces of the make-up she had worn for the dress rehearsal of her play, *The Princess in Waiting*. As she turned towards them, May felt she was being confronted by a side of her niece that she did not know. She looked beautiful, much more mature, but infinitely lonely.

'Hullo,' Emily said, clearly so preoccupied with theatrical problems that her surprise visitor appeared scarcely to register. 'I don't think the costumiers have done very well with this.' She held out the wig to May. 'It's too mousy. My princess was meant to be blonde.'

'But I thought you looked most becoming in it.' Gallantly, John Moreton did his best. The young girl before him seemed all at once to become aware of his presence and her face brightened.

'Oh, do you think so?'

Katy had by now come out of the sitting room and May, having explained that she wanted to get on with some sewing, went straight up to her workroom. She knew that there was some urgency about her allotted task. By the time she heard John Moreton leave, she had already cut out his grandmother's nightdress. By ten o'clock the next morning she was on her way back to the Grange with it. But she did not see her client again. Later in the day the Dowager went into a coma and that evening she died.

To May, her passing marked not only the end of an era but the loss of a relationship which had meant more to her than she had ever realized. Often, she would walk past the Grange and wonder what was to happen to it. She knew that Alicia was staying there temporarily, engaged in some necessary clearing-up operations. But, apart from the funeral, she saw nothing of Charles Moreton, nor the present Lord Fairfax. Rumour had it that the latter, having arrived an hour before his mother died, had left for the continent again as soon as she was buried.

When, a few months later, May received a thick white envelope with a London postmark, she was astonished to find, on opening it, that it was from a firm of solicitors, informing her that, under the terms of the late Dowager Lady Fairfax's Will, she had been left five hundred pounds and a cameo brooch 'in gratitude for a valued friendship and loyal assistance over a great number of years'.

Quietly, she passed the letter over to Katy and pulled out a handkerchief. '1909, it was,' she said, 'when Flo and I were first summoned to the Hall. You were only seven. I can remember it as if it were yesterday. It was a Wednesday in April, the weather a bit like it is now. Mother made us both wear grey flannel costumes and white blouses. We sat up half the night getting them finished. Maud Fairfax was in her prime then. She wanted some dresses made for Ascot. I was so nervous writing down the measurements when Flo called them out, that when we got back to the mill we weren't sure whether I'd written a thirty-two- or a thirty-three-inch bust. We had to do the cutting out making allowances and put things right at the first fitting. But she seemed pleased with the result. I mean . . . we always had her custom from then on.'

'Yes.' Though Katy was not in tears, she was very near them.

'She was a good woman,' May went on. 'She did a lot for you when you were young. Always sending down things from the Hall when you were poorly. She's going to be missed. There aren't many like her these days. I believe she had quite a hand in keeping the estate together these last few years. Cyril Butt said the agent used to go and see her at least once a fortnight. But now . . . the Lord knows what'll happen. I mean, her daughter-in-law's not much use, although I can't help feeling sorry for her. I suppose, if John William were of age . . . well, there's no male heir, is there?'

'No. But presumably one day John will inherit Bishops-down from his own father.'

There was suddenly silence between the sisters, both wrapped in private thoughts which, had they wished to exchange them, might not have proved so very dissimilar, except that May's had gone as far as to contemplate a cream satin wedding dress and a veil of Brussels lace.

Later that night, when she was in bed, Katy found herself still mulling over their conversation, the past and the present jostling for supremacy in her mind. She could see Sarah and the Mill House with startling clarity. Having been so young at the time, she could not recall the incident of the white blouses and grey costumes to which May had referred, but her sister's reminiscences had certainly brought back her mother's extraordinary power over her family, the way she had almost always been able to make her children jump to do her bidding. Katy could not help feeling that, tragic though the circumstances had been surrounding Sarah's death, it was a blessing that she had been spared the knowledge of Philip's. It was not that she would have exactly grieved over her son-in-law – only for the wayward daughter who had gone against her wishes in marrying him.

Katy was grateful that she could now, at last, look back a little more calmly and rationally on her husband's suicide. The thing which had invariably upset her most was the fact that, whatever the trouble had been, he had not felt able to confide in her. She knew she would have forgiven him, whatever it was. She had soon realized that it must have been connected with Barbara Woodley yet, equally, she had known that he was speaking the truth when he had said that his affair with her was over. Not until she had eventually started to let her mind open up to all the possible reasons he might have had for throwing himself in the mill-race, did the real one enter into it. If only Philip had not been so impetuous, although, in moments of brutal honesty – such as tonight – she was well aware that this was what had originally attracted her to him. She had never felt the same way about any other man, that is, unless she counted her temporary lapse from convention with Gordon Hillier; and that little episode was, thank goodness, over and done with. At the moment she was glad to be leading a perfectly innocuous existence, yet somehow she knew it was not good enough, especially with Emily growing up. She should be making more of an effort; she should have got to know some of the parents of her school friends. Apart from Dorothy and Dick Swayne she was really only on nodding terms with the rest. Emily needed to move in a wider social circle; even though the child seemed to have attracted the attention of an eminently suitable young man, she was still only sixteen and, for more than one reason, it was difficult to think that anything would come of that particular relationship.

In the distance, she heard the faint sound of the Wilhampton town clock striking 1 a.m. She turned over, restlessly, reflecting on how she had failed, miserably, whichever way she looked at it. She had withdrawn from life. Unlike May, who appeared to have an inborn facility for getting on with everyone, she was aware that she only seemed able to come alive and respond in the presence of certain people, presumably the kind like Gordon, who were few and far between in and around Wilhampton.

Almost involuntarily, she stretched out a hand to the empty space beside her, wondering if this was to be her lot for the rest of her life. She felt immeasurably grateful to May for all her support, yet just now she would have given almost anything to have had a man about the house, or even one who would simply advise her about Emily's future. The child had become difficult of late. She knew she was talented, more intelligent than clever and that, when she left off her glasses, she was – or would be – beautiful. Her headmistress had been so anxious for her to go to university. She had passed her School Certificate at such a ridiculously young age. But, in consequence, Emily now seemed determined to leave Wickfield as soon as possible and attend the local art school, this desire having apparently superseded any previous ones. Had her daughter, perhaps, inherited her father's impetuosity? Should she, as her mother, have given in to what were possibly no more than youthful capricious demands of the moment?

The obvious person to consult was, Katy knew, Maurice Fitzherbert. He was the one man in whom she could, and probably should, confide. But lately she had begun to hold back more and more from asking anything of him other than of a strictly medical kind. She had always imagined that, as the years went by, he would come to regard her simply as a friend. Certainly, while Philip had been alive she had scarcely given the matter a thought, one way or the other; but nowadays, despite his impeccably correct and courteous manner, she had sensed that his feelings for her remained constant. It would have been so easy, sometimes, to turn one of his professional visits into more of a social occasion: offer him tea or a drink – not that she thought he would ever accept the latter. But whenever he had said, a little reluctantly, that he must be getting on, she had always stood up at once and, almost formally, held out her hand.

She recalled the last occasion when, after showing him out, she had spent the evening wondering why so nice a man who did so much public good was destined for such private sadness, regretting bitterly that she seemed to be the cause. It would have been so much better if she and Philip had never returned to Wilhampton or, after his death, she had moved right away again. But then she had reminded herself that she had been in no position to make such a decision. Besides, May would have hated it and there had been Emily's schooling to consider.

She turned over yet again. As, at last, she drifted off to sleep, a thought which had so often assailed her over the years seemed to float in and out of consciousness: that she was bound, irrevocably, to the banks of the Willon and the place where she had been born and bred.

32

'How much do you think Emily ought to have as a dress allowance now she's left school?'

Katy and May were sitting in the little workroom at the Hermitage while the latter put some finishing touches to an outfit for Ethel Sharman, whose cousin at the Air Ministry was at last — at the age of fifty — getting married to a lady who worked as a secretary in the Foreign Office. Emily had gone to supper with the Swaynes. Although it was a sultry August evening, both sisters had come indoors early, for there had been nine consecutive days of thunderstorms and it looked as if yet another was looming up.

'I should have thought six pounds a quarter, or thereabouts,' replied May, snipping off a thread and standing up to put Ethel's simple, beige, wool georgette two-piece on to a hanger. 'She should be able to manage on twenty-four pounds a year and it will teach her the value of money before she comes into her own when she's twenty-one. After all, you've promised her a new winter coat for her seventeenth birthday and her underwear is well up together.'

The room was suddenly lit by a flash of lightning and for a while May remained looking out of the window.

'Do you remember,' she went on, as she sat down again, 'when poor dear Mother was alive, how she always came up to the attic if we had a storm in the night and draped a sheet over the looking glass on the dressing table?'

'Yes. And then Father would go downstairs and make us all a cup of tea.'

'She used to say that the lightning was the devil's writing in the sky and the thunder was God telling us not to look at it. When something nasty happened, even if it was a long time afterwards, she always maintained it was because we hadn't paid enough attention to His warning.'

A violent clap of thunder brought their conversation to an end and throughout the rest of the storm they said little. Both knew that just now there was enough potential danger in the world around them for Sarah to have had plenty of reason for justifying her predictions.

Presently, May switched on the wireless, shaking her head as the evening's news appeared to be even worse. She had never been much of a student of history or geography and had, in fact, had to turn up an old atlas to ascertain the exact position of the country whose name was currently on everybody's lips: Czechoslovakia. It seemed so far away and remote somehow, even though she had recently noticed several advertisements in the press for a fifteen-day holiday there for only twenty-two guineas. These had been accompanied by drawings of young women with plaited hair wearing dirndl skirts and wooden clogs. She felt it must be such a pleasant, quiet, old-fashioned place. If only Germany could let well alone. She could not think why this wretched man Hitler had to keep meddling in other people's affairs, nor why law-abiding people like the British had to be drawn in to keep the peace. It seemed such a pity that her favourite politician, Mr Eden, hadn't been able to do better with his League of Nations. Her belief in it had been sadly undermined now that Germany and Japan and Italy were no longer members. There was so much going on that she did not understand – and most certainly did not like. Only that morning she had received a letter from Henry, informing her that he was being sent down to Salisbury Plain immediately – as an instructor on some training exercises – and, although she was pleased to think that this might mean an opportunity of seeing him, she felt sure his posting had something sinister to do with what was happening on the continent. Almost everything these days, including the weather, seemed to be conspiring to make her restless and on edge – much more so, she realized, than Katy who, possibly because of her age, had never been quite so conscious of the evils of war as any of her elder sisters.

'I think I'll drive over to Bulbarrow and fetch Emily home now,' May said, suddenly. 'I don't know about you, but I could do with an early night.'

In one way it was a relief to listen to her niece's cheerful unconcerned chatter on the way back: to hear of Helen's intention of taking a Domestic Science training now that she, too – a year later than her best friend – had passed School Certificate; to agree with Emily that it seemed unfair that she should be subjected to a driving test after she obtained her provisional licence at the end of November, whereas her aunt had been spared such an imposition; to discuss the possibility of buying a new car after Christmas.

For a few moments, May found herself quietly looking forward to the coming months. But as soon as she was in bed that night the fear returned. Unable to sleep, she could not help thinking how the future hopes of everyone could so easily be shattered. What might they all have to face, especially the young men she knew? John William, for instance; Bob Swayne and his brother, Tim; Edith's two eldest boys, Donald and Ernest, and the lance corporal who had so surprisingly and providentially married a pregnant Della; then there was Robert Farley's son, a fully-fledged solicitor yet, as May well knew, also a territorial. And what about her other nephew, Frank François, and even her own brother? Please God Henry would be too old for active service. But *surely*, no one in his right mind would let war happen again. The government would do *something*. Reason would prevail. Or would it?

Oddly – or perhaps not so oddly – enough, it was John William who was uppermost in her mind, rather than her own kith and kin. To May, he was such a splendid example of English manhood. She was aware that she was probably just a silly old spinster, but in her eyes he seemed well-nigh perfect: a kind of golden boy, with his dazzling good looks, irreproachable manners and irresistible charm. She had never dared to say as much to her sister, let alone her niece; but it always touched her that he came to call on them whenever he was in Netherford. This was more often than she had ever dared to hope for, because his grand-mother had left him the Grange in trust until he came of age. Throughout much of that summer it had been closed up, but now a resident caretaker had been installed and, at the end of July, John had spent a fortnight there, toge-ther with a friend from Cambridge.

It went without saying that Emily could never visit the place unchaperoned when he was in residence, but one evening, while his guest had gone off somewhere or other by himself, they had entertained John to supper at the Hermitage and he and Emily had gone down to the river by themselves afterwards. May had watched them covertly for a little while from her workroom window: the boy, so tall and thin and graceful; the girl – her glasses temporarily abandoned – a little shorter, her figure somewhat given to puppy fat yet still beautifully proportioned, her rounded limbs bare and brown, her dark wavy hair falling thick and loose in the fashionable page-boy bob. For all the difference in their ages and background, May sensed that they found pleasure in each other's company. The very fact that her niece had been so reticent about the occasion afterwards somehow made her even more sure that this was the case. But, of course, she must remember that Emily was still so young, little more than a child, really. It was no good building castles in the air. She was behaving just as she had done over Katy and Maurice Fitzherbert and where had that got them all? One could not legislate for romance. Just because it had slipped through her own fingers was no reason for trying to resurrect it vicariously through others. Besides, love almost seemed to be something best avoided with the world in the state it was today.

When, nearly three weeks later, the European crisis deepened, May was never far from her wireless set. Throughout the Prime Minister's three visits to Germany, firstly to Berchtesgaden, then Godesburg and finally Munich, she and Katy waited with mounting anxiety. Knowing that there was an unbroken intercession for peace round the Unknown Warrior's tomb in Westminster Abbey, they often slipped into St Mark's and said a prayer or two when they went to Wilhampton, where they would find others doing the same thing. One day they ran into Edith hurrying out of a side entrance, her face white and tense. On the last day of September, when Neville Chamberlain returned to England with his 'Peace with Honour' message, May wept.

Summer seemed loath to leave this year. Though the trees were tinged with yellow and there was definitely a nip in the misty early morning air, the heat of the sun soon broke through, dispersing the tiny sparkling cobwebs on the dew-drenched grass and bathing the Willon valley in calm, golden light. Sometimes, all three inhabitants of the Hermitage would rise early before Emily left for art school and go mushrooming at Sweetacres, a pursuit for which Robert Farley had long given them permission.

Once, a little later on in the day, May went alone to pick blackberries along the Barbury turnpike. When she had gathered enough to make one of her specialities – blackberry and apple jelly – she sat down on the grass and contemplated the scene spread out below her, sharp and clear like a child's model toy. She knew and loved every inch of it: the Felt Mills with its tall black chimney, Bulbarrow away to the west, the grey spire of St Mark's, the dark mass of yew trees almost, but not quite, hiding the Hall, the cluster of mostly thatched dwellings which made up Netherford, the distant town of Westonbury with its white-bright chalk-pit high on the downs behind; and then, as if it were somehow threading the whole tapestry together, lay the River Willon, peacefully shining in the autumn sun.

She was so lost in appreciation of all that she could see that she did not notice Robert Farley coming along the hedge until he was almost beside her. Gun under arm and Sweep, his black labrador, at heel, he smiled and wished her good day. Then he, too, stood looking down on the view before them. She knew that he was a man who did not find it easy to express himself, but who probably felt a little as she did about the countryside where they were both born and bred.

'It's . . . beautiful, isn't it?' she said, simply. 'It's days such as these that make one feel so grateful to Mr Chamberlain.'

When he did not reply, she glanced up towards him and was astonished to find his previously genial expression gone, his eyes now hard, his jaw set. He remained silent for so long that she realized she must have upset him in some way.

At length, he said, quietly, 'We let the Czechs down, May. You can't get away from it. It might be peace in our time, though I doubt it. But one thing I do know is that there's precious little honour attached to it.'

This time it was she who remained silent. Sweep flopped down beside her and, absently, she stroked his ears. After a while Robert went on, almost as if he was talking to himself, 'Besides, it wasn't right . . . a British Prime Minister flying *three* times, cap in hand. Chamberlain's never made a journey by air before. He's an old man. Sixty-nine. Hitler's twenty years younger. The boot should have been on the other foot.'

33

'Telephone, Emily.'

May laid down the receiver and watched her niece come hurrying across the garden. She had fined down since the previous summer – not without some careful avoidance of certain items in her diet, such as Wilhampton lardy cake, of which she was particularly fond. There seemed now to be a radiance about her — especially when she left off her glasses — not dissimilar, May felt, to Katy's during the year when she had first fallen in love with Philip.

Yet with Emily, there was a difference. May found it difficult to explain. Though more socially aware and certainly far better educated than her mother, she had a strangely disconcerting innocence about her. While she obviously attracted the opposite sex, she treated all the young men she knew in an artless, almost sisterly, manner, accepting their attentions with surprised pleasure which held them bewitched, but at arm's length.

There was Bob Swayne, for instance, who had twice taken her to the pictures, firstly to see Merle Oberon and Laurence Olivier in *Wuthering Heights* — which Katy and May had subsequently gone to by themselves — and secondly, Vivien Leigh and Clark Gable in *Gone With the Wind*. On both these occasions Helen, though older but still very much a schoolgirl, had kept tactfully in the background. One or two male students from the art school had also asked Emily out, Katy making it a rule, however, that she could not go anywhere with anyone unless they had first come to the Hermitage. Such stringent vetting — usually accompanied by a small glass of sherry — was something which the sisters enjoyed discussing afterwards. So far, each young man Emily had brought home had been perfectly presentable, although May sometimes wondered how her mother would have handled the situation if one had arrived of whom she did not approve.

May noticed that the responsibility for her daughter seemed to weigh more and more heavily on Katy's shoulders these days. Considering how emotional and highly strung her sister had been, she never ceased to be surprised at the way she appeared lately to have settled down. May loved her dearly, but she often felt that she did not altogether know her. Katy was well-informed, read assiduously, had become an active member of the local Red Cross Society — into which she had roped both Emily and herself — and had agreed to help organize, as well as exhibit in, the forthcoming Westonbury Show. But the word which invariably came into May's mind whenever she thought of her was: wasted.

Now, in order to leave her niece alone at the telephone, May went out to join her sister, who was carefully tying up a new clematis which she was training to grow against the thatched cob wall behind the herbaceous border.

'It's John William,' she said.

'I thought it probably was.'

'That's three times in the last fortnight.'

'Yes.'

'He's in love with her, Katy.'

'But she's not in love with him. Or anyone, for that matter.'

Katy turned round and pushed back a strand of hair which had escaped from the neat bun she wore nowadays, a style which May did not think exactly suited her. All at once, she realized her youngest sister was middle-aged. She was quite grey at the temples and her once-slim figure had definitely thickened round the waist.

'They're still children,' Katy went on. 'Far too young for anything serious.'

'You and Philip weren't much older.'

'Yes ... but Emily's not really physically ... well, mature. She's still very much at the romantic stage. They both are.'

May was silent. They walked across the lawn and sat down on the old wooden seat which had once graced the garden of the Mill House. She knew her sister was right. The trouble was that she herself was a romantic. She had been one all her life. But since her unfortunate experience in the last war, she had always shied away from the thought of that ugly act in which romance presumably culminated.

'Besides,' Katy continued, 'however suitable it might seem from our point of view, the Moretons would never approve. They've probably got very definite ideas about the sort of background any future daughter-in-law of theirs would have to come from.'

Suddenly a door slammed and Emily came running out of the house.

'John wants to take me to Lord's, Mummy.'

'Lord's?'

'Yes. You know, the Eton and Harrow match. He adores cricket. His family always takes a box. Two days. In July.'

'Is he waiting for an answer?'

'No. Apparently Lady Moreton has written to you about it. Her invitation's in the post.'

There was a pause. Katy wondered how much difficulty John had probably encountered in getting his mother to do so. She supposed that, with his persuasive charm, he had managed to overrule any objection. 'It would mean us staying in London,' she said, at length.

'Couldn't we?'

It was May who, in not much more than a murmur, seemed to settle the question. 'I could make her outfits . . . Sprigged muslin . . . would look lovely at this time of the year.'

Her niece pulled her to her feet and, after a few protesting 'chippatoos', waltzed her round the garden.

Early the following Saturday morning, Emily drove both her mother and aunt to Bournemouth. She had passed her driving test the previous winter at her first attempt and, although May and Katy occasionally remonstrated with her for going too fast, they knew that she was basically the best driver of the three. Having spent several hours in their favourite shop, they came away with everything they wanted. As such unanticipated requirements were quite beyond Emily's dress allowance, the cost was borne mostly by Katy, although May insisted on paying for various trimmings, including some artificial flowers with which to adorn her niece's two hats.

During the next fortnight she could scarcely have worked harder, or with more enthusiasm, had she been preparing for a wedding. Crisp white muslin billowed around her small sedate figure, as she sat threading black ribbon through neck, wrist and waistline. A white straw hat with a single red rose in the front lay perched on top of her tailor's dummy. Then came the turn of some printed lilac-coloured chiffon on which, at her niece's request, she had promised to sew deep purple bows. 'Like the tune,'

Emily said, as she herself began sewing imitation violets on to a lilac-coloured crown. 'They're playing "Deep Purple" all the time on the wireless these days.'

'Do you remember, Aunt Chip,' she said, one evening after Katy had driven into Wilhampton on Red Cross business, 'when I was a little girl staying at the mill, how you made a dress for my doll out of a remnant from the first dance dress you ever made Mummy?'

'I remember, Emily.'

'And now you're making clothes for me to go to a . . . well, not a dance, but something almost more exciting.'

'Yes.'

'Aunt Chip. Why did you never marry?'

May took off her spectacles and laid down her sewing. She had not expected quite such a direct question, although she could recall Emily's mother having asked her the self-same thing at round about the same age. But now, just as then, it was something she did not want to talk about. Why had she never married? She couldn't tell Emily – any more than she could have told Katy – about Major Walter Perkins . . . how, ever afterwards, she had known that she could never face the physical side of such a union.

'It's hard to say, my dear.'

'But you'd have made a marvellous wife. Always doing things for others. It doesn't seem . . . right, somehow.'

'It depends,' May answered, guardedly, 'how you look at it. I shall get a lot of pleasure seeing you go off to Lord's. I think you'll find even Lady Moreton won't be better turned out.'

On the following Thursday, the three of them travelled up to London by train to stay at Brown's Hotel. After the heat of the journey, its foyer seemed refreshingly cool and dark. Suddenly, Katy had a vivid recollection of the day when she had come there to meet Belle before going to the Private View at the Royal Academy. How long ago was it? Eight . . . no, nine years. So much had happened since then. Yet Brown's appeared just the same: solid, quiet and comfortable. Even the head porter's face was vaguely familiar. The only difference seemed to be that last time it was she who had been arriving so eagerly, 'dressed up to kill', as Philip used to say; and today – or, rather, tomorrow – it was the turn of her daughter. May had even made the child a smart lightweight cloak, just as she had done for her, in case the weather turned cold or wet.

But fortunately, it did not. She noticed John William give a start and then a look of admiration – even awe – come into his face when he called to collect Emily, arrayed almost entirely in white, the next morning. Then, as he shook hands with them all, he said something which once again jerked her back, not nine years but nineteen. He used the selfsame words which Maurice Fitzherbert had used when he had taken her to her first dance in Wilhampton town hall: 'I've never seen a prettier dress.' She watched Emily flush, saw the delight in May's eyes and, as the two young people went out of the door, hoped no one had noticed that she had been fighting to keep the tears from her own.

The sisters saw little of Emily that day or the next, for Sir Charles and Lady Moreton were taking a large party out to dinner on the Friday evening, in which she had naturally been included. Left to themselves, they mostly looked round the shops together, although on Saturday morning Katy slipped away for an hour or so and walked up through Berkeley Square and into Davies Street. She was surprised to find on reaching Number 51 that it was no longer a bookshop. Its window was filled with flowers. Somehow, she felt pleased. Mason and Son had ceased to exist rather as that part of her life had ended also. Just occasionally, as now, a few little bright hurting memories thrust themselves forward and played havoc with her determination to suppress them. She knew it was no use looking back, even though nowadays it was sometimes difficult, even scaring, to look forward. Only the previous evening, she and May had gone into Hyde Park and seen all the air-raid shelters. She was aware that many of them had been there since the previous year, but it was obvious that fresh ones were being dug. She had walked back to Brown's, grateful that she was the mother of a daughter, not a son.

Late on Saturday night, when they were on their way

home in the train, she listened to Emily's graphic account of all she had done. It was rewarding to realize how much the visit had meant to her and how well she had acquitted herself. Alicia Moreton had apparently complimented her on her clothes remarking, on being told how much May was responsible for them, that she had always known her aunt had genius. Even Phoebe had admired her hats.

'It was all so beautiful,' her daughter prattled on. 'Of course, I'm sorry Eton lost. It was the first time they'd done so for ages. I really don't understand much about cricket and, as I'd left off my glasses, it was difficult to see what was going on most of the time. But when the intervals came and everyone strolled out on to the ground, the colours were unbelievable. I'd love to have painted it. The only really sad thing was when some very old man came into the Moretons' box and started telling Sir Charles that there was bound to be a war. There won't be, will there?'

'I hope not, darling.'

'If there is, John says he's going to leave Cambridge and join the RAF.'

'The *RAF*?'

'Yes.'

The train was drawing into a station now and a news boy ran along the platform shouting 'Late Night Extra', but the rest of his words were drowned in the sound of slamming doors and people greeting each other or shouting goodbye. A whistle blew, there was a hiss of steam, and slowly they started moving westwards again.

As their carriage drew level with the lighted entrance to the station, May noticed the news boy, this time standing beside a placard. The train had begun to gather speed but she could still read the headlines. They were large and clear: BRITISH PLEDGE TO POLAND.

34

Emily sat behind the wheel of the car at Wilhampton station. On its windscreen was a sticker denoting the number and sex of the evacuee children whom her mother

– now out on the platform with a contingent of Red Cross helpers – had volunteered to house at the Hermitage. May had remained behind there, busy with last-minute preparations. 'Girls,' Emily remembered her aunt saying, a few days earlier. 'Best ask for girls. You can come into my room, my dear, and we can put up two camp beds in your own.' Dutifully, Emily had removed all her precious belongings, including books and drawings, from the bedroom which she had recently helped to redecorate in her favourite colour: pale mauve – the same shade as that of the dress she had worn on the second day at Lord's.

It was a warm evening – the first of September. Presently, having wound down all the windows of the new Ford Katy had bought soon after Emily passed her test, she decided to get out. But she did not move more than a few steps away. Drivers had been specially requested to stay by their vehicles. She had never seen so many people and cars milling about the station. It seemed as if the whole of Wilhampton had turned out in force. Helen and Bob Swayne waved to her from the other side of the yard, Helen in her mother's second-hand Baby Austin, Bob in the family milk van. It appeared that Dick and Dorothy were expecting, with their typical generosity, to care for at least four children, besides a mother and baby.

Away to her left, Emily caught sight of Frances Farley and Luke Ridley, the Fairfaxes' agent, as well as Mrs Morgan, the rector's wife, all parked next to each other. Presently, a cheer went up as old Mr Butt arrived, nosing his ancient Singer through the crowd, its windscreen proclaiming that he was willing to accommodate two boys over five years of age. Emily hoped that his housekeeper – prim Phyllis, as she was known – would be able to manage them. Ethel Sharman, not being a driver but having elected to house two evacuee schoolmistresses, was to be seen in a small group – including Edith, who had valiantly offered to have a child of either sex – standing anxiously beside one of the Parkers' taxis, which seemed to have a variety of stickers all over it. Every so often, Emily noticed the rector and Dr Fitzherbert going in and out of the station doors, yet there was no sign of Clare.

Idly, she wondered whether, in spite of war appearing imminent, his wife was the only person in the whole of the little community who was being unco-operative or if a doctor's household was, perhaps, in some way sacrosanct. She felt rather excited, albeit slightly shamefaced, about this. She was not sure how much it had to do with the strange unprecedented situation or the fact that John William was coming to the Grange in two days' time.

Suddenly, a bell rang. There was an instant hush while the stationmaster's voice gave out: 'The train from Portsmouth is now arriving.' She scanned the railway line through her glasses, on to which she had clipped the dark lenses she had lately taken to wearing for vanity's sake. Soon, she heard the familiar roar and stood watching while puffs of steam above the treetops came closer and closer, as the engine rounded the last bend and drew slowly to a halt.

After what seemed a very long wait, she saw her mother coming towards her with three little girls, wearing identification labels and gas masks slung over their skinny bodies. They were dirty, dishevelled and in tears. Any previous feeling of excitement gave way to overwhelming pity.

'This,' said Katy, 'is Susan, and Shirle and Pearl. Susan is seven and Shirley is six. They are sisters. Pearl is five and she has come all alone.' The youngest child looked at Emily and held out her arms. She picked her up and in that one small moment it seemed as if she had left her own childhood behind her for ever. She helped them all into the car and drove away, Maurice Fitzherbert raising a hand in friendly salute as they passed. It was only now she was older that she had come to realize, with sadness, the extent of his carefully masked devotion to her mother. She felt he would have made a wonderful stepfather.

There followed a busy thirty-six hours. The children, tired and disorientated, woke crying both on Friday and Saturday night. Rather to her amazement, Emily found that it was to her they seemed to turn. They kept asking for 'Miss' and she got little sleep. On Sunday morning, she devised a way of keeping them quiet with paper and crayons while she waited with her mother and aunt for the Prime Minister's broadcast at eleven o'clock. There was a little light music being played on the wireless – an unusual occurrence for the Sabbath – and then silence, after which came Neville Chamberlain's voice: grave, regretful and final. Having received no reply to his ultimatum to Hitler to withdraw his troops from Poland, he informed the listening nation that he had no other option but to declare: 'This country is at war with Germany.'

Almost immediately, they heard the Felt Mills chimney let out an air-raid warning siren. It rose and fell in a hideous distant wail. Then, after a while, when no expected aircraft appeared in the sky, the all-clear sounded.

'Thank God,' said May, 'that Mother isn't alive.'

At the mention of 'Mother', the little girl called Pearl rushed towards Emily and began to scream. The two others followed suit. Sunday lunch was not an easy meal. All the inhabitants of the Hermitage were exhausted but fortunately, about two o'clock, the children were coaxed to sleep.

'Why don't you go and lie down too, my dear,' May suggested to Emily. 'You were up most of last night.'

'I think . . . I'd sooner sit by the river,' she replied. 'It's as good a place to rest as any.'

It was very quiet underneath her favourite willow tree, save for the sound of Fred Cutler calling the Sweetacres cows for their afternoon milking, and the occasional 'plop' as a trout or grayling rose to the surface of the Willon and then, as quickly, disappeared beneath the dark green undulating weeds. She leaned back, conscious of that special rivery fragrance she had come to love. She took off her glasses and closed her eyes. Soon, she too, was asleep.

He arrived so quietly that she had no idea how long he had been watching her when she awoke. She was vaguely aware that the shadows had lengthened and the cows had returned to the opposite meadow. He was lying sideways on the bank a little way away from her, his head propped up on one elbow.

'John!'

'Emily!' He smiled, got up and sat down beside her.

417

'When did you come here?'

'About an hour ago.'

'An *hour*?'

'Yes, but I didn't want to wake you. Your aunt said you'd had a rough night. I thought the sleep would do you good.'

'That was . . . very kind.'

'You seem to have your hands full at the Hermitage.'

'Yes.'

'I'd like to have evacuees at the Grange, but I don't quite know who would look after them and I'm afraid the authorities have other plans for the place.'

'Oh. What kind?'

'An army HQ. I've got to see some general in Southern Command about it tomorrow.'

'Will you,' she asked, shyly, 'be staying long?'

'I'm afraid not. You remember what I said at Lord's. I have an interview in London next Wednesday.'

She turned to face him, suddenly apprehensive. 'What kind of an interview?'

'You know. For the Air Force. They may not call me up just yet, but I don't want to hang around.'

'I see,' she answered slowly, and they lapsed into silence.

It was a good ten minutes before, diffidently, he took her hand.

'I like to think of you being in Netherford,' he said, 'whenever I'm away. Although I suppose . . . I mean, you might want to do other things now.'

'I . . . really don't know.' She hadn't thought. It had all happened so quickly. She still could not envisage a war, especially here, in these peaceful surroundings. But she supposed he was right. Somehow, painting pictures seemed quite out of the question at the moment.

'Emily.' His hand on hers tightened. 'There's something else I'd like to think. This war . . . it can't go on for ever. I'll be twenty-one next August. Will you marry me then, war or no war?'

She did not answer at once. She suddenly realized that she had known, all along, that one day he would ask her, but she had not expected it would be quite so soon. She

418

would like to have gone on as they were. She felt that she was in love with him. It was wonderful to have him near her. She liked the feel of his hand holding hers. She was frightened for his safety and wished that he was not so set on joining the RAF. She longed for him to kiss her and had been disappointed that he had not done so on the night he had brought her back to Brown's after Lord's. But marriage was different. Marriage meant something else. If she did marry him, would he, perhaps, leave out that frightening part of it, at least until after the honeymoon?

When she still had not replied, he continued, 'I thought . . . well, I hoped . . . that we could become unofficially engaged. In fact . . .' Here he broke off and searched in one of his pockets, suddenly producing a small, blue, jeweller's box. 'It was my grandmother's,' he explained, opening it. 'I felt you might like to wear this little eternity ring.'

She stared at it, almost uncomprehendingly. Then she said, softly, 'Will you put it on, John?'

Carefully, he lifted up her right hand and slipped it over the third finger. It fitted beautifully. At last, he gathered her in his arms and kissed her, very gently, on the lips.

Then they remained, without speaking, watching the river flowing serenely past them, on and on through the golden September afternoon.

Many Waters

1

The trains kept coming.

There had been over twenty of them passing through Westonbury station during the night – one roughly every half-hour. All their carriages and corridors were packed with soldiers in varying degrees of exhaustion. In the dimness of the blackout it had just been possible for the volunteer helpers to discern their dishevelled bodies, some stretched out, dead to the world, lying half on top of each other on the floor; some without boots, their feet so swollen that they were incapable of struggling to the windows for the cups of hot sweet tea and sandwiches being handed to their more fortunate companions, who did their best to pass them back inside. Occasionally, an excited French voice could be heard above the deeper gruff chorus of 'Bless you, lady', 'Thank you, ma'am'.

It was now eight o'clock on the morning of Saturday, June 1st, 1940. A bright summer sun was just beginning to break through the early morning mist covering the valleys of southern England. The survivors of the British Expeditionary Force were coming back from Dunkirk.

When fresh volunteers arrived at the station to relieve those who had been on night shift, Katy Mason and her sister, May Lodge, drove back to Netherford to snatch a few hours' sleep – although not before they had dealt with the various messages which had been thrust into their hands by men desperate to let their families know they were safe. Scrawled on the back of cigarette packets or odd scraps of paper, Katy and May had sent off quite a collection of these since they had offered their services at the beginning of the week. Where possible, they telephoned relatives. If not, they posted the missives, made all the more poignant by their brevity: 'I'm OK, Mum . . .', 'Be seeing you, Ginger'.

As Katy turned down the lane towards their home, the signpost saying NETHERFORD ¼ MILE had already disappeared and they could see anti-tank traps being erected a little further on towards Wilhampton. Nazi invasion was feared imminent and both women knew that the Government had given orders that anything which gave an indication of the name, direction or distance to any place must be obliterated.

'I do wish,' said Katy, as they walked up the garden path to the White Hermitage, 'that Emily wasn't billeted in Westonbury. I'd sooner she slept in the nurses' home when she comes off duty at the Emergency Hospital, rather than cycling into the town.'

May was silent. She was just as worried about her niece as she knew the girl's mother was, but she hadn't liked to bring the subject up. She was all too well aware that the English Channel was only forty miles away. If the Germans came on over . . .

'Emily said something about going on night duty the last time we saw her, didn't she?' she answered, at length. 'I believe Matron always makes the VADs sleep in hospital quarters then.' She tried to sound hopeful, but there seemed so little to be hopeful about.

Katy shrugged. 'I suppose that might happen. But I can't help being sorry she didn't decide to stay home like Helen Swayne and work on the land. I'm sure Helen's father at Bulbarrow or Robert Farley up at Sweetacres would have given her a job.'

'I'm not sure, Katy. Land work's hard. Emily's never been too strong since that riding accident.'

'No. But nursing's not exactly easy, is it?'

This time May said nothing. They were both tired. It was no time for arguing.

Like most of their friends and neighbours, the evacuation from Dunkirk had taken them completely by surprise. Even now, witnessing but an infinitesimal part of it with their own eyes and listening to snatches of servicemen's conversation, it was hard to take in that it was really happening. Official news was, of necessity, negligible. It did not seem possible that the British Army was withdrawing, defeated, from the continent, that some of the men to whom they had ministered that morning had been ferried across the Straits of Dover by the Margate lifeboat – others, by a small Thamesside tug. The situation was unthinkable, unprecedented, a nightmare from which they would awake.

Yet, as May lay on her bed a little later on, unable to sleep, she knew well enough that she was not suffering from any nightmare. This was war, real war, not the 'phoney' kind they had experienced during the past winter. This was what her brother Henry, and her friend, Ethel Sharman, had been hinting at for many years, long before she herself had given up hope of the League of Nations. She realized that she should never have let that curious absence of open conflict since the previous September mislead her into thinking that Germany did not mean business. When, just before Christmas, the parents of the little evacuee children whom she and Katy had been housing at the Hermitage arrived demanding to take their offspring home, she regretted bitterly that she had not urged them to wait a while. Poor little Susan, Shirley and Pearl, now back in Portsmouth, a front line town if ever there was one. She wondered how they were faring.

Her thoughts, confused, disillusioned and weary, began turning towards all those other people she knew who might be in particular danger, especially the young men. John William Moreton, to whom Emily was unofficially engaged, immediately sprang to mind. He was still training to be a pilot somewhere in the north of England, but any day now they expected to hear he had got his wings. Then there were her nephews: her poor sister Edith's two sons, as well as Edith's son-in-law, the Corporal who had so providentially married a pregnant Della. May knew that Private Donald Lench was with the BEF, but as yet they had had no news. With an irrational hope she had wondered whether she might see him passing through Westonbury station and be able to rush back to Wilhampton to tell Edith. And then what about her own brother, Sergeant Major Henry Lodge, a veteran of the First World War? She had hoped and prayed that he was

at least too old for active service, but his son, her othe
nephew, Frank François, was just the right age. So wer
Helen Swayne's two brothers. But, in any case, activ
service was perhaps no longer something which took plac
overseas. It might mean here, at home, in England. Ir
Westonbury. In Wilhampton. Dear God, there could be
Germans goose-stepping down the lane to Netherford.

Back on the station that night, May went about he
duties with a heavy heart, albeit doing her best to smile
through the gloom at the indistinct khaki-clad figure
jostling for attention at the train doors. A little Frenchman
with tears in his eyes, pressed a few francs into her hand
Once, an ambulance train crawled through without stop-
ping. From behind the blacked-out windows there was jus
a glimpse or two of a Red Cross nurse, but the condition
of the occupants in the carriages could only be guessed at

About 2 a.m., when there was a slightly longer pause ir
proceedings, she and Katy went into the waiting room and
lay down on one of the long narrow benches. May closed
her eyes, vaguely aware of that unmistakable railway
smell: stale, smoky, unventilated. She was forty-eight years
of age now; she had known Westonbury station all her
life but never, in her wildest dreams, had she ever imagined
that she would spend the night on it, doling out refresh-
ment to the defeated British Army.

Even after the official evacuation from Dunkirk was
over on June 4th, May and her sister still drove in from
Netherford each evening to continue their ministrations.
Being close to Salisbury Plain, Westonbury had always
been very much a centre for army personnel and now troop
movement was intense. Soldiers seemed to be everywhere,
anywhere, their officers valiantly attempting to bring order
out of unparalleled chaos. But at least one thing was clear-
cut and certain. To the astonishment – and admiration –
of the whole world, Great Britain, responding to Winston
Churchill's speech in the House of Commons, was going
to fight on *alone*: 'on the beaches, . . . on the landing-
grounds, . . . in the fields, . . . in the streets, . . . in the
hills . . . ,we shall *never* surrender . . .'

In Wilhampton and the little hamlet of Netherford, the

inhabitants seemed to close ranks as they watched, prayed and went about their work. Two platoons of Local Defence Volunteers, commanded respectively by Dick Swayne and Robert Farley, carried out nightly vigils on the surrounding downland. Leaflets were put through letter boxes headed: IF THE INVADER COMES. WHAT TO DO AND HOW TO DO IT. There was an atmosphere of tense readiness, yet somehow combined with overall calm. Each day the sun shone with a rare brilliance. In the water meadows at the end of the Hermitage garden, the River Willon flowed serenely along while the Sweetacres herd of shorthorns awaited, with their customary impassivity, Fred Cutler's call of 'Coop Coop' to bring them in for their twice-daily milking. The dairyman was getting on in years now, but he had been one of the first round at the police station to join up after Anthony Eden, back in the middle of May, had made his wireless appeal for volunteers for Local Defence. When it had been explained to Fred that rifles were in such short supply that he could not, as yet, be issued with one, he had merely nodded and turned up for drill with a pitchfork.

Gradually, a semblance of near-normality crept into everyday life, if only for an hour or so. Emily Mason, back at the Hermitage on forty-eight hours' leave, changed out of her grey cotton nurse's uniform, put on the radiogram and went out into the garden in a bathing costume to listen, through the open windows, to some of her favourite dance music: Ambrose and his orchestra playing 'Just One of Those Things' and Glen Miller's rendering of 'In the Mood'.

The girl was tired and had lost weight lately, but her aunt thought her even more beautiful than she had been a year ago. There was something almost madonna-like about her oval face with its large, serious, brown eyes, framed by a dark shining page-boy bob, the fashionable style into which her hair fell quite naturally when she was not obliged to roll it up under a nurse's cap. Her present slimness suited her. Her long legs — now stretched out hopefully to acquire a sun tan — were just about perfect, despite the serious injury to one of them which she had suffered after falling from her pony as a child. Moreover, May was glad to feel that she could scarcely be looked upon as 'a girl who wore glasses'; for although Emily needed to rely on them at work or when driving a car or going to the pictures, she seemed to have developed such a technique for whipping them on and off that it was rare for anyone to catch sight of them perched on her nose for any length of time.

'Nice to have you back, my dear,' May said, as she came out into the garden to sit with her for a moment.

'Lovely to be here, Aunt Chip.'

Presently, May enquired, gently, 'How's John?' Emily's romance had always been of paramount importance in her mind. It was something precious, apart, to be cherished and fostered, until the time when, please God, it would culminate in matrimony – although, sadly, her hopes of seeing her niece going down the aisle of Wilhampton church wearing a train of Brussels lace and a cream satin wedding dress which May, herself, had made, now seemed very remote. The brides of today appeared mostly to marry in register offices, dressed in ordinary coats and skirts or even uniform.

'He's fine,' Emily answered. 'I had a letter from him only this morning.' She had never resented her aunt's interest in her personal affairs. She had always been well aware how May's mind worked and she knew that Aunt Chip – as she had dubbed her since quite a little girl because of her habit of saying 'Oh Chippatoo' whenever she was particularly pleased – was invariably on her side. She often felt quite guilty that she seemed to be fonder of May than she was of her own mother. 'He's hoping to get down here in a fortnight's time,' she went on. 'The trouble is I don't know if I'll be able to get off duty then, Matron's such a ghastly old battle-axe.'

May was distressed. This was terrible. And the poor boy would just about have got his wings, wouldn't he? 'But surely, . . .' she began, 'I mean she'll give you special dispensation. After all, you are *engaged*.'

A small frown passed over Emily's face. 'Only *unof-*

ficially, Aunt Chip,' she replied. 'It isn't as if it's been announced. I don't have an engagement ring.'

May glanced down towards the third finger of her niece's right hand where she always wore the small eternity ring which John had given her on the day war was declared. May had never altogether approved of their being unofficially engaged. To her, it was something or nothing. It did not seem quite fair, somehow, although she knew perfectly well how and why it had come about. They were both so young. John William Moreton would not be twenty-one until the coming August. Emily was still only eighteen and a half.

But it was not just their extreme youth which was against them, May realized. John was the only son of Lady Moreton, the daughter of the late Dowager Lady Fairfax of Netherford Grange. May had once made clothes for both women. Although the fortunes of her and her youngest sister − despite Katy's widowhood − had improved over the years, there was no getting away from the fact that Alicia Moreton would want her son to marry someone who came from the same background as his own − a far more elevated one than Emily Mason's. But for the war, the Moretons would always have taken it as a matter of course that any future daughter-in-law of theirs would have been presented at Court and done a London season. However well Emily had been educated, however much the young couple were in love, May understood perfectly why there had been no official engagement. Sir Charles and Lady Moreton were playing a waiting game. Of course, when John William came of age and inherited outright all that his grandmother had left him in trust, including Netherford Grange, it would be a different matter. Although even the Grange, May reflected, would hardly be available for John this August. It would still be occupied by the British Army, that is, unless it fell into far worse hands.

Inside the Hermitage, she became aware of another record dropping down on to the radiogram's turntable. The mellifluous strains of Carroll Gibbons at the piano playing 'A Nightingale Sang in Berkeley Square' floated

out of the window. May stood up. She did not want t
spoil Emily's precious time off by showing undue concer
With a brief, 'I expect you'll find Matron will relent, m
dear,' she excused herself on the grounds of having t
cook the lunch.

But as she busied herself in the kitchen, questions kep
pouring into her mind for which there seemed no answer
What could one say? What could one do for this youn
girl whom she had watched grow into womanhood an
loved as if she were her own child? Dunkirk and the Battl
of France might be over, but they were all still awaitin
the unknown.

It was the last day of June. Had not Churchill warne
the country less than two weeks ago that the Battle o
Britain was about to begin?

2

'Nurse Mason. I want you to special Corporal Long.'

'Special, Sister?'

'Yes. Screens must be put round his bed. You will no
be required to look after any other patient. Only th
Corporal, you understand. You must wash your hand
before and after every time you attend him. Is that clear?

'Yes, Sister.'

'We are not . . . exactly sure what is wrong with him
Tomorrow morning, Dr Martin is going to perform
lumbar puncture.'

'A lumbar puncture, Sister?' Emily was aware that sh
was probably sounding singularly obtuse, but she ha
never heard the word 'special' used in this particula
context. She supposed it was feared that the patient migh
possibly be suffering from something infectious o
contagious; although, if so, she was surprised that he ha
been sent to a general ward. As for a lumbar puncture
she knew nothing about that either. She made a menta
note to look up the latter in her small medical dictionary
when she got back to her billet in Canon and Mr
Fawcett's house that night.

She felt sorry for Corporal Long, whom she had admitted to the ward earlier that afternoon when both the Sister and the Staff Nurse had been off duty. As the senior VAD in charge, she had written down his name, rank, number, religion and address of his next of kin. Afterwards, because he had looked so pale and drawn and there appeared to be little indication as to why he had been sent to Ashmore Emergency Hospital, she had returned to his bedside and enquired, 'Is there anything particular troubling you at the moment, Corporal?'

The poor young man had looked at her miserably and then, in a strong cockney accent, still staring her straight in the face, had replied, 'There is something wrong with my penis, Nurse.'

To her everlasting credit, Emily had replied calmly, 'I see'.

But she did not see at all. It was another word which she had never heard. She might be considered the most conscientious and responsible VAD on the ward – and, in consequence, had been made the senior one in charge – but when it came to the ways of the world, she realized she was hopelessly naïve and inexperienced.

When she had gone along to the kitchen, where Bunty Carrington and Liz Brewer were spreading margarine on to thick slices of bread, spurred on by the afternoon session of 'Music While You Work' on the wireless, she had wondered whether she would ask them to enlighten her. But then she had decided against it. She had a shrewd idea that the Corporal's trouble was connected with those unmentionable parts of a man's anatomy which, having been brought up in an all-female household since the untimely death of her father when she was a small child, were still a complete mystery to her. Even though she had, by now, blanket-bathed many a male patient, none of them had been too ill not to have taken hold of the flannel at the crucial moment, while she had tactfully looked the other way. If she now revealed her ignorance to Bunty and Liz they would, in all probability, laugh at her. Although they were of a rather different class, they reminded her of her cousins, her Aunt Edith's children. They were knowing and sexually aware, despite the fact that neither – so far as she knew – had an unofficial fiancé, as she had. She rather thought Bunty was carrying on with some captain in the Tank Corps whom she actually *slept* with; although how she could possibly bring herself to do this and why she was not terrified of becoming pregnant, Emily could not imagine – unless she relied on some mysterious substance called ergot, about which Bunty had tried, unsuccessfully, to engage her in conversation one day, when they had been cleaning bedpans together in the sluice.

When the time came for Corporal Long's lumbar puncture the following morning, Emily was surprised to learn that it was not, after all, going to be performed by the civilian medical practitioner from Westonbury who usually attended the ward. Apparently, Dr Martin was ill and Dr Fitzherbert from Wilhampton had been called in.

Emily had known Dr Maurice – as she always thought of him – for almost as long as she could remember. He had seen her through countless childhood ailments, as well as her much more serious riding accident. In keeping with everyone else in the district, she thought the world of him. He was so kind and patient and invariably stopped his car to have a word or two, if he caught sight of her when he happened to be passing through Netherford. Although this was his custom with many of his patients, young and old, she had begun to sense, as the years went by, that he took rather a special interest in her and her family. She was not, even now, sure of the whole story, because Aunt Chip had been so evasive about it when she had first started asking questions; but one night, when she was getting on for seventeen and they happened to be alone together, they had got on to the subject of love and marriage.

She could remember May putting down her sewing and saying, 'Never play fast and loose with the love of a good man, Emily. That sort don't grow on trees.' When she had asked, innocently, 'Who would you say was the *goodest* one you know, Aunt Chip?' May, without a moment's hesitation, had suddenly burst out with, 'Why, Maurice Fitzherbert, of course. Apart from Dick Swayne and Robert Farley, there's no one to hold a candle to him round these parts.' And then, as if it was a relief to be able to unburden her feelings for once, she had gone on, 'I swear he's as in love with your mother as he was when he took her to her first dance back in 1920, not that he hasn't been a past master at keeping it to himself. But it's a thousand pities he married that little sourpuss, Clare Mallieu, on the rebound.'

Emily had remained silent for a while. When, at length, she had suggested how splendid it would be if Dr Maurice got a divorce and married her mother, May had looked at her, askance. Obviously regretting her rash disclosure, she had quickly put an end to the conversation with, 'That would be out of the question, Emily. Maurice is a *doctor*. He would never get divorced. It would ruin him. Besides, who's to say your mother would have him, even if he were free?'

May's words came back to Emily with startling clarity when she saw Maurice Fitzherbert talking to Sister Matthews at the entrance to the ward that morning. He was so tall and handsome and reliable-looking with it. She felt that John William could easily look like that in twenty years' time. She could not understand why her mother — or, for that matter, any woman of her age — would not 'have him', as May had put it. When he walked towards Corporal Long's bed and came round the screens, his eyes seemed to light up and his face crease into a more than usually friendly smile as he saw her standing there. But, quickly, his innate professionalism took over. Giving due recognition to her new status, he said, quietly, 'Good morning, Nurse', and she, understanding and responding to the necessity for formality, replied, gravely, 'Good morning, Doctor'.

She did not play much part in the following proceedings. Sister Matthews herself stood by the surgical trolley, passing instruments to Maurice Fitzherbert as and when he required them. Only after the small operation was over was she left with instructions not to move the Corporal in any way unless she called for assistance. Throughout the rest of the day, the young man became more and more morose and uncommunicative. Time hung heavily for both of them for, until there was a report on the sample of spinal fluid which had been taken, she was still unable to join in the customary bustling activity of the ward. In one way, Emily was relieved, as she was suffering from a particularly heavy period and would have liked nothing better than to sit down. Once, for a few moments, she perched on the end of Corporal Long's bed, doing her best to cheer him up with a little light-hearted conversation. Unfortunately, it was exactly at this juncture that Sister Matthews suddenly put her head over the top of the screen.

Never before could Emily recall having been the target for such wrath.

'Nurse Mason!' Sister Matthews's voice seemed to reverberate round the entire ward. 'What *do* you think you're doing?'

Emily was on her feet now, trembling. 'I . . . I'm sorry, Sister.'

'Sorry is not enough for such a total breach of discipline. Come to my office at once.'

There, Emily was subjected to a tirade which lasted twenty minutes. The woman seemed to be almost crazed with anger. Two splashes of heightened colour appeared on each cheek-bone. Her small dark eyes glittered. She charged Emily with having brought disgrace on the whole nursing profession, of being guilty of indecent behaviour, of deception and falling down on her trust.

Emily knew that it was no good trying to defend herself. She knew she had broken the rules. No nurse was ever allowed to sit down while on duty, especially on a patient's bed. It was pointless to say that she had a pain in her stomach and was finding it hard to stand up doing nothing. When, at last, Sister Matthews ran out of both accusations and breath, Emily was sent to fetch Nurse Brewer, who she was told would now become senior VAD in her place and take over the special care of Corporal Long.

All the nurses and patients in Ward E were aware of what had happened and many a sympathetic glance was directed at Emily, who was fighting back tears. No one liked Sister Matthews. She was well known for her spitefulness, even though most of the other sisters at Ashmore seemed to have more than their share. Middle-aged, unmarried and power-conscious, they one and all possessed the diabolical ability to terrify almost every young nurse who came under their authority.

The hours dragged on. Emily was due for an early evening: that is, her statutory two hours off duty each day were to come at the end of it, so that she could leave the ward at six o'clock instead of eight. She wondered whether Sister Matthews would put a stop to this. Whatever happened, she would be sent to Matron.

The dreaded summons did not come until five-thirty. She walked up to the main building where Miss Butler's office was situated, feeling sick. She supposed she would be sent home, made to come before some sort of court martial, like a soldier who had defected on duty. She waited outside the door for a few moments, doing her best to summon up courage. At last, she took a deep breath and tapped.

'Come in.'

She knew the voice so well: low, sepulchral and surprisingly aristocratic. She understood Miss Butler's father had been a General, as well as titled, and that she herself had been a VAD in the First World War who had taken the unusual step – considering her upbringing – of subsequently embarking on a full nurse's training.

As soon as she opened the door, she could see her small upright figure sitting behind her desk, an enigmatic expression on her face. Emily was so busy concentrating on it that she was not at first aware that there was anyone else in the room, until she heard the sound of a chair being pushed back in the corner behind her. She spun round, as John William said, cheerfully, 'Hello, darling.'

'You did not tell me, Nurse Mason,' Miss Butler remarked, while Emily looked first at one and then the other in total confusion, 'that you were *engaged*.' Her voice somehow did not sound quite so threatening as usual. In fact, Emily reflected later, if she herself had not been in such a state of anxiety, she might have noticed it was quite pleasant, even benign.

'I . . . that is . . .' Helplessly, she turned back to John, standing there in his officer's uniform, his newly-acquired wings resplendent above his left-hand breast pocket. She was astounded at his lack of embarrassment, at the way he seemed so utterly at ease in this terrifying sanctum, as if Miss Gertrude Butler might be some maiden aunt of his with whom he had a particularly close relationship. She noticed that there was a cup and saucer on a table by his chair. He must have been given *tea* . . .

'Pilot Officer Moreton tells me he has got three days' leave, Nurse, which he intends to spend at his home in Netherford. Now, let me see. Today is Wednesday. I have ascertained from Sister Matthews that you are due for an early evening tonight. I propose that you go off duty at once. We shall not expect you back at Ashmore until Sunday morning at eleven o'clock, when you will report to Sister Bond at the night nurses' quarters for duty that same night.'

She stared at Miss Butler, incredulously. It was all she could do to bring out a whispered, 'Thank you, Matron'.

'Nice old thing,' said John, as they walked down the corridor together, hand in hand. 'Apparently, her mother knew my Grandmother Fairfax in the year dot.'

She wondered whether she would ever achieve a fraction of his calm self-assurance. At the moment she was still too shocked from the day's events to say very much. Not until they were leaving Westonbury – John having waited in his car while she hastily collected up her belongings at the Fawcetts', who had been forewarned of her departure – did she begin to relax. He had the roof of his little MG down and her hair, no longer pinned up according to regulations while on duty, fell loosely on to her shoulders and lifted in the breeze as he gathered speed. Suddenly, the hospital, Sister Matthews, Corporal Long and Miss Butler seemed very far away.

John drove back by the longer route which took them over the old Barbury turnpike. At the top, he turned off down a grassy track and halted above a perfect view of her home ground, stretched out below them in the golden evening sunlight. It was the same view they had often stopped to look at as children when they had been out for a bicycle ride, where they could see the River Willon threading its way past all the old familiar landmarks: Wilhampton church with its lovely grey spire, the tall black chimney of the Felt Mills where her mother's family had come from, the dark mass of yew trees which she knew hid the Hall where John's own mother had been born, while to the west lay the house and buildings belonging to Bulbarrow Farm, the home of Helen Swayne, her best friend. Then, in the foreground, nestled the little hamlet of Netherford. It was just possible to catch a glimpse of the Hermitage and the gates leading to the Grange which John's grandmother, the Dowager Lady Fairfax, had left him and where, although it was now occupied by the army, he would be sleeping while on leave. Closer still, she could see the fields of ripening corn bordering the track leading down to Sweetacres.

'I'm glad,' said John, slowly, as he put his arm round her, 'that your war work only takes you as far as Weston-bury. I believe I told you before that I always like to think of you around these parts whenever I'm away. It's a funny thing, but although I've been brought up in Suffolk, I'm much more fond of this place and I feel you seem to belong to it, somehow.'

She rested her head on his shoulder, just where his new wings had been sewn. 'Where will you be sent?' she asked.

'I'm afraid I'm not allowed to tell you . . . exactly. But I'll write. Every day, if possible.'

His arm around her tightened. 'And I will, too,' she replied, as she lifted her face to be kissed.

3

August came.

The warm summer had brought about an early harvest and self-binders were busy all over the south of England. At Sweetacres, Robert Farley's winter-sown oats had been cut and stooked in mid-July. At Bulbarrow, although Dick Swayne had turned to dairying during the farming depression of the later 1920s, the War Agricultural

Committee had requested him to plough up several fields after war was declared, with the result that, thanks to the underlying fertility of the soil, he was now about to reap some of the best barley for miles around. With both his sons away in the army, Helen had virtually become his 'right-hand man', finding herself fully occupied all the hours of daylight, as she drove a tractor, transported temporary labour to and fro, or took teas to the harvest field, which her mother had prepared in the farmhouse kitchen.

The enemy had made no attempt at invasion – yet. But the LDV – recently renamed the Home Guard – kept an increasingly disciplined and active vigil. On every hill top, from dusk until dawn, four ill-assorted, poorly equipped volunteers took it in turns to do their duty: farmers, farm workers, businessmen, retired soldiers, the butcher, the baker and even the local poacher, were all represented.

At the Hermitage, Katy Mason and May Lodge – as members of the Red Cross – were becoming more and more involved in preparations for turning the Hall at Wilhampton into a convalescent home. Lord and Lady Fairfax now occupied the flat above the stables; most of their staff had disappeared into the forces, while the older employees remained to cook and clean once the place filled up with patients.

It was rare for anyone to catch sight of Edmund Fairfax. Having escaped from Deauville in the nick of time before Dunkirk fell, he appeared to take little interest in the war, his estate, his home or his family. Deprived of his continental pleasure grounds, he spent much of his time in London, ostensibly staying at one of his clubs: Brooks's or White's. His wife, Rachel – 'to give her her due', as May was apt to say – did her best. She was constantly waylaying both sisters to talk about plans for the conversion of the Hall, genuinely anxious that the project should be a success. But May could well remember the dowager once inadvertently letting slip that her daughter-in-law had little organizing capacity. Certainly, these days, Rachel seemed to go about with a vaguely harassed expression on her face, making remarks such as: '*Ten* beds, you think in here, Miss Lodge?' or 'How clever of you, Mrs Mason, to suggest we need a larger hatchway between the kitchen and the patients' dining room.'

Rachel had, however, put forward a slightly different but quite positive proposal at their last meeting. 'Surely,' she had said, 'it's time we all used Christian names. I'm sure we're going to be seeing a lot of each other. And we have so much in common. Not just the new Home. I believe my nephew, John William . . .' and here she had hesitated and coloured slightly, before going on, 'is often at the Hermitage. I understand he and Emily . . .' But this time she had broken off altogether, relapsing into her more habitual state of uncertainty before starting to change the subject.

As for Emily herself, she was still on night duty at Ashmore and finding it harder and harder to sleep during the daytime. Often, she would come off duty and cycle down into Westonbury with a friend for hot chocolate at the Cherry Tea tearooms, but making quite sure to be back at the night nurses' quarters by 11 a.m., the time at which, theoretically, the VADs were expected to go to bed for the day. But although they might be incarcerated by that hour, few of them actually went to sleep much before one or two. In the small partitioned room in which Emily had a cubicle, she was often subjected to the sound of two cousins playing dance records – albeit muted – on their gramophone, or being forced to listen – in spite of doing her best to plug her ears with cotton wool – to idle chatter about their respective boyfriends, who all appeared to be Guards officers. Sometimes, in her less charitable moments as she lay tossing and turning, Emily suspected that their calm indifference to or unawareness of others was due to the fact that they were both Honourables. But then she had chided herself for the thought, remembering how John William came from the same sort of background, and surely no one possessed greater sensitivity than he did.

One morning, towards the middle of the month, she came off duty at 8 a.m. and went, as usual, to see if the post had arrived with a letter from John. A few days before, she had bought him a present for his twenty-first birthday: a small gold pen. She was wondering whether she should send it to him or whether, by the remotest chance, she would hear that he was coming on leave.

She was feeling particularly weary that morning for, during the night, she had had another of her 'attacks'. They had been happening quite frequently lately and she had been given to understand that they were what was known as 'night nurses' paralysis'. They occurred at the end of her two hours' rest period, which all VADs were allowed to take, either between 11 p.m. and 1 a.m. or between one and three. At these times, owing to her lack of sleep during the day, she would disappear gratefully into some quiet part of the long makeshift hut – usually the linen cupboard – where she would avail herself of some blankets and quickly fall into a kind of stupor. When her allotted two hours were up, one of the other nurses would come along to wake her but, although she could hear a voice urging her into action, it took several minutes for her to regain full consciousness. Meanwhile, she was aware of her limbs thrashing about frantically, waiting for her mind to get the upper hand over her body. It was a horrible experience and she had begun to dread it. Sometimes, she wondered whether she was altogether cut out for nursing.

To her disappointment, there was no letter from John that morning and after breakfast, as she felt too tired to cycle down into Westonbury, she went straight back to the night nurses' quarters, undressed and got into bed, thankful that there was no sign of the Honourables and their disturbing presence.

Yet sleep still eluded her, even though she pulled down the black-out curtains and tried to make her mind a blank. There was, she knew, an additional anxiety bothering her which did not help matters. It was connected, yet unconnected, with the more obvious one: the war, her fiancé's safety, her own inadequacy. It was the fact that time was running out. Gently and persistently, John kept reminding her that he still wanted to get married once he came of age. Just before saying goodbye on his last leave, he had taken her in his arms and said, 'Remember darling, what

I asked you when we were sitting by the Willon almost a year ago now: Will you marry me, war or no war, when I'm twenty-one?' True, he had often qualified this by adding that he hoped he was not being selfish, that she must realize that she might be tying herself to a man who, if not killed, could well become maimed and disabled for life. But she had assured him that that would never make any difference to her feelings for him. And this was true. She still loved him in just the same way as she had when, on the day war broke out, he had placed the little eternity ring belonging to his grandmother on the third finger of her right hand. But it was the thought of actually *marrying* which made her panic. Lately, she had begun to despair. In every letter she had received, he appeared so confident, so full of plans: perhaps they could marry in St Mark's at Wilhampton – quite informally, of course. Or they could get a special licence and have a register office wedding in London and spend whatever leave he had left at the Dorchester or the Ritz. Her mother and aunt would come up for the occasion, naturally, as well as his own parents . . .

Even though they were not the root cause of her trouble, the reference to Sir Charles and Lady Moreton only added to her doubts and fears. She knew that they did not have anything against her personally, but nevertheless they did not approve the match. By marrying her, John's relationship with his parents would be bound to suffer, not that she was blind to the fact that it had already become strained. For him to have spent his last leave almost entirely in her company must surely have been a source of regret, if not reproach.

But there was something else: something deeper, something which she found far more difficult to think about calmly and logically, a problem which was impossible to discuss with anyone, certainly not her mother or John or even dear understanding Aunt Chip. It was simply that she did not think she could face the physical side of marriage. The whole idea of it upset her. She was still unsure as to what exactly happened, but she had never forgotten the strange isolated incidents as a small child, when she had overheard those bewildering, frightening sounds coming from her parents' bedroom: the breathless energetic tussle which seemed to be going on, the creaking of bedsprings, the muffled laughter, her father's repeated whispers of 'darling', and then, finally, most horrendous of all, her mother's low moaning. It was something etched on her memory, vivid, indelible, which, however hard she tried, would not go away.

Somewhere a clock struck eleven. The Honourable Jane and the Honourable Monica came crashing through the door, presumably laden with parcels, for Emily could hear them being unwrapped. 'Not bad, are they,' Jane was saying. 'It's so difficult to get a pair of black silk stockings these days, especially in a dump like Westonbury. But if I've got to wear my uniform to go to that tea-dance with Billy on Saturday because there won't be time to change for duty when I get back, I'm damned if I'm going to let him see me wearing lisle ones.'

'What are you going to do?' enquired Monica. 'Shove a pillow down the bed to make it look like a corpse in case Sister Bandy-legs comes snooping around? I hope you won't get caught sneaking out of the top gate.' 'Hardly likely,' came the reply. 'Old Fred won't be gardening on a Saturday afternoon and I overheard Bandy-legs saying she was going to the pictures with that toad of a Sister Matthews.'

Their conversation droned on. It was impossible to ignore it, even though it was silly, superficial and boring. Emily learned that Jane thought Billy 'meant business', that Mummy was 'awfully keen about him', that if Jane did marry him, it would compensate Lady Lesley for not having been able to give her daughter a season because of the 'too, too beastly war'. Miserably, Emily supposed that both Jane and Monica were exactly the kind of girls whom John's mother would have wished him to marry. They might not possess his particular sensitivity, but they certainly shared with him a *savoir faire*, an innate confidence in themselves, which Emily would have given anything to possess.

At last, about one o'clock, the room became quiet and

she dozed fitfully until it was time to dress at six-thirty. When she arrived for supper at the main building, she was cheered to find that there was a letter from John which had come by the second post. She tucked it into a pocket, wanting to be alone when she read it. It was not until eleven that night, when she went off to the airing cupboard for her two hours' rest, that she brought it out and, in the dim blue light from the corridor, began to read:

Darling,
    How I wish we could be together on my twenty-first, but there doesn't seem a chance. Things are hotting up and I'm being posted again. But whatever happens, I'll be thinking of you all the time, Jerry permitting. And you might just warn that nice Matron of yours that whenever I *do* next get a spot of leave, you'd like some too, so that, if you still feel the same way about me, you could become Mrs J. W. Moreton . . .

Her eyes blurred. It was very quiet in the hut now. Somewhere overhead there was the sound of a plane – 'one of ours', as people said. She wondered just where John would be sent. It was sure to be the south-east. She did not like the reference to 'hotting up'. He would probably be risking his life daily, hourly. He was such an expert at the understatement. He said so little about the war and the wireless was just about as cagey. It was so difficult to know what was happening, so hard to know what to do for the best. She seemed to be making such a poor attempt at being a nurse, especially now that she was becoming increasingly inefficient through lack of sleep. Might it not at least be better to make one brave young man happy by marrying him on his next leave and giving him what he obviously so desperately wanted? That is, if she could.

4

On the afternoon of Saturday, September 7th, 1940, something occurred which had been dreaded – albeit awaited with mounting certainty – ever since the fall of Dunkirk.

The Luftwaffe, presumably as a preliminary to invasion, set out to destroy London.

Shortly after 3 p.m., Edmund Fairfax left his club in St James's and took a diagonal short cut through Green Park to a flat in Mayfair. He was just letting himself into the front door when the air-raid siren sounded. He was not particularly worried. There had been plenty of similar warnings lately, although he could wish that Chloe Ford, his mistress, did not get quite so worked up about them. He found her standing at the doorway of her bedroom, having heard his key in the lock.

'Edmund? Thank God you're back. We must go down to the basement at once.' She was wearing a pink crêpe de Chine négligé trimmed with swansdown, hardly the garb, he would have thought, for appearing in front of the caretaker or, for that matter, any of the other residents in this particular block of flats in Curzon Street. He suspected that she had little on underneath.

'Don't be silly, darling.' Edmund felt vaguely irritated. Chloe was a pretty, dark, voluptuous young woman whom he had met the previous winter at a party given by, of all people, his highly conventional sister, Alicia Moreton, on one of the rare occasions when she and her husband had been staying at their London home. Chloe had been so noticeably not only the most attractive but also the most inexplicable guest to find at such a gathering, that Edmund had become immediately intrigued. He had also noticed that the attention of his brother-in-law, Charles, often strayed in her direction. It had not taken Edmund long to discover that she had not been invited, but had simply been brought along by some colonel who appeared to be more interested in Sir Charles Moreton's whisky than his lady companion. It had seemed perfectly natural – and quite in order, considering the colonel's increasing inebriation – for Edmund and Chloe to leave the party together.

Soon, along with many other things, he was paying all the expenses connected with the running of her West End flat. He discovered that she had been a model who was now, owing to the nature of her employment, rather at a loose end. He had assured her that she had no need to worry. As far as he was concerned, Chloe Ford was a find. She was able to alleviate the excruciating boredom of his life at Wilhampton, particularly since he and Rachel had removed to what he called 'the stableboy's quarters'.

Having spent so much time abroad, Edmund found that he now had few friends in the country and certainly nothing in common with those of his wife. Rachel seemed to go in for hobnobbing with the most astonishing collection of people. It was strange, he felt, considering she had been the daughter of Sir Roger and Lady Broadbent of Westonbury House, that she appeared to be more in her element amongst such ordinary – and, to his mind, dreary – types. Lately, she had become increasingly involved with two women in the Red Cross who were constantly at the Hall, helping with its conversion into a convalescent home. They were pleasant enough in their way, he supposed. Katy Mason was certainly attractive and had good legs. He also understood that she was the mother of the girl whom his nephew, John William, wanted to marry; he had therefore been obliged to be vaguely polite on the few occasions he had met her. But he wished the boy would not be such a fool. Alicia's son could do so much better. Perhaps the RAF would knock some sense into him, that is, if he didn't get killed. Prior to the war, Edmund had been considering whether to make the estate over to him in his will. Having no male heir himself, once Rachel and the girls were provided for, it seemed like a good idea, rather than letting it all be broken up and sold on his death. He had been meaning to talk to Alicia and his solicitors about it but, as it was not a subject on which he wished to dwell, he had kept putting it off.

Purposefully but gently, he now propelled a trembling Chloe backwards into the bedroom and on to the bed. He felt he knew what was needed. It would take her mind off things. Skilfully, he slid a hand through the opening of her négligé and, for a few moments, she seemed ready to acquiesce to his advances. He had seldom known a woman who so obviously enjoyed the sexual act. He could feel himself becoming aroused. Quickly, he withdrew his hand and started to undress.

It was just at this second that they heard the heavy crump of enemy bombs – not just one or two high incendiaries, but what seemed like hundreds: thunderous, ominous, coupled with the staccato sound of ack-ack guns retaliating.

Frantically, Chloe flung herself off the bed. She was almost out of the door before Edmund was able to pull her back and make her put on a siren suit. When both of them were reasonably clad, he accompanied her down into the basement.

Apart from a rather dour caretaker and his wife, two elderly maiden ladies and a middle-aged businessman, they were the only others taking shelter there. Chloe lived in what had once been a private house now divided into comparatively few flats whose inhabitants, on this warm sunny Saturday afternoon, were probably out or away. Conversation was at first desultory but, as time went on, a certain camaraderie developed, even though they were such an ill-assorted group and it was evident that the two spinsters viewed Chloe and himself with suspicion.

After the all-clear sounded around six-thirty and they were once more back in the flat, they stood at the windows looking out on to what appeared to be two sunsets: a natural one to the west, a terrifying man-made copper-orange one to the east. It was as if the whole of London was on fire. As daylight faded, from the direction of the City a fierce molten glow dominated the entire scene, the dome of St Paul's and the rest of the London skyline silhouetted against it, while further away columns of smoke spiralled upwards somewhere near Woolwich and the docks.

Edmund had been intending to take Chloe to the theatre that night to see Celia Johnson in *Rebecca*, but his assurances that the Luftwaffe would hardly be likely to return and it would therefore be quite safe were instantly rebuffed. It was all he could do to persuade her to come out to dinner at Grosvenor House. When, while they were walking back to Curzon Street, the air-raid siren sounded again, he was forced – grudgingly – to admit that maybe she had been right. But the idea of spending any more time in the basement alongside the Misses Tetley – as they had introduced themselves – appalled him. While Chloe, once more clad in a siren suit, disappeared below, he himself spent practically the whole night alone in her large double bed.

Not that he was able to sleep very much. Until 3 a.m. the noise of bombing seemed to intensify. Edmund had been meaning to stay up in town for at least another night or two. Now, he was not so sure. It might be more advisable to go home. With Chloe so agitated and likely to keep to the basement if there were further raids, it would hardly be much fun. When daylight came, he made the excuse of having to get back to Wilhampton to be ready for a meeting with his agent the first thing on Monday morning.

'But what about me?' She stared at him, incredulously. When he did not immediately reply, she said, 'I can't stay here, Edmund. I must move out to the country at once.'

'But where to, my dear?'

'Anywhere. A hotel . . . until I can find a more permanent home and sell the lease of this place.'

'I think that would be very foolish. You won't get much for it, as things are at the moment. Besides, you'd be so bored. You hate the country almost as much as I do. And it would be much more difficult for me to visit you.'

'I don't see why.'

'Ask yourself. For one thing, we shouldn't have the privacy. For another, in London I have an alibi – my clubs. Even if I don't sleep in them much, I call in each day. Rachel might just ring up, once in a while. Anyway, I don't know how much longer I'm going to be able to wangle petrol for driving. I'll probably have to travel by train. How could I get to you if you take yourself off into the back of beyond?'

She found his crass selfishness not only unbelievable but somehow frightening. Of all her lovers, she had always suspected that Edmund Fairfax might turn out to be the meanest in every way. Now, shaken by the events of the previous night and with no one else to turn to, she began to cry.

If there was one thing Edmund could not stand it was

the sight of a weeping woman. He went into the bathroom and started to shave. Presently, he came back into the bedroom and began dressing, while she watched him mutely, her eyes still red-rimmed, her face blotched and puffy. As he finally made his way to the door, she became hysterical, clinging to him so that he had to prise her arms away from his body.

'I'll ring,' he said, a little more kindly. 'But I can't say when. You know how difficult it is.' As he got into the lift to go downstairs, Edmund Fairfax felt the time had come to sever their relationship.

There were road blocks all the way back to Wilhampton. Once out of London he was stopped by either regular soldiers or Home Guard at almost every bend of the road. At one point, as he handed up his identity card to a sergeant in the RA, he asked the reason for such vigilance, only to receive the reply, 'I don't rightly know, sir. But there's one hell of a rumpus on. We've been stood to all night. You'd best go careful.'

Between Westonbury and Wilhampton he was halted once again by a member of the Home Guard whose face seemed vaguely familiar. He believed he was a shepherd on one of the estate farms, and it seemed obvious that the man knew who he was perfectly well. Tired and disgruntled, he merely gave his name. There was surely no need to show his identity card for the umpteenth time, when he was within so short a distance of his own home. But the man insisted. Edmund could feel his temper rising. Attempting to brush aside the gnarled outstretched hand, he started to let in the clutch, but suddenly became aware of another figure in shapeless uniform standing by the front of the Daimler with a rifle at the ready. Enraged but out-manœuvred, he put his hand in his pocket and pulled out the necessary document.

'They were only doing their duty, Edmund,' Rachel said, when he told her of the incident over lunch. 'They've got orders to shoot, you know, if anyone refuses to hand up an identity card. And there is this big scare going on. I've heard it started when someone rang the church bells over at Great Ridgeway.'

He was silent. She was so infuriatingly reasonable. So well-meaning. He tried to remember why he had married her. She had never been remotely pretty, but he had sensed that she would not be the kind of wife to make any trouble. And there had been the financial aspect, of course. The Broadbents had come into money and his own family had been short at the time.

5

October arrived, raw and rough. The lane down to Netherford was covered with wet brown leaves, as Maurice Fitzherbert drove down it on a certain Tuesday afternoon at the beginning of the month. He was on his way to visit May Lodge who had broken her wrist the previous afternoon, having tripped over some rubble which workmen had left lying about at the Hall.

The door of the Hermitage was opened by Katy and he could see at once that there was something far more serious troubling her than May's accident, nasty though that had been. Her face wore the same wide-eyed, stricken look that he remembered seeing nine years ago on the morning when he had been obliged to tell her that her husband's body had been found drowned in the Willon.

'Oh, *Maurice*. Please come in.' He noticed she was actually trembling.

He stooped beneath the low lintel and followed her into the sitting room, where she sat down quickly and motioned him to do the same. There was no sign of May.

'What is it, Katy?' he asked, gently.

'It's John William,' she replied, and covered her face with her hands.

His whole being wanted to get up and hold her in his arms. Instead, he leaned forward and asked quietly, 'When did you hear?'

'Half an hour ago. Alicia Moreton telephoned. They've no other news. Just . . . missing.'

'Oh, my dear . . . And Emily?'

'She doesn't know yet. She's coming off night duty

tomorrow morning. I'm fetching her home for two days' leave. I thought . . . well, perhaps it might be best for her to get a little sleep before saying anything to her. She's been looking so wretched lately.'

'Yes. Yes, of course. I'm sure . . . that would be best,' he answered, in not much more than a whisper.

Never before had he felt so totally inadequate. His calling had given him plenty of experience in dealing with loss and suffering. He had always hoped and prayed that perhaps his presence or a few chosen words might have helped a little at the time. But this was different. This was something deeply personal. Unconsciously, he had looked on Emily as the child he had never had, the daughter of the woman he had wanted to marry and whom he had long known he would always love.

'There might still be . . . a chance,' he went on. 'If he was shot down over the sea, he could . . . have been picked up.'

She looked at him now through her tears. 'I suppose so. But . . . it's such a very slender one, isn't it, Maurice?'

There were sounds of footsteps on the stairs and May came into the room, her arm in a sling. He had been going to ask if she was in any pain, for he had not been too happy about the orthopaedic department in Westonbury Infirmary, since the somewhat elderly surgeon had come out of retirement to take the place of the young doctor who had disappeared into the army. But, confronted now with so much greater distress, such a query seemed almost out of place. Suddenly he realized, as never before, how both he and May, in their separate vicarious ways, had come to look on Emily as their own.

Presently, he leaned down and opened his bag. What he was about to do was, he knew, a poor remedy to fall back on, one which, at best, could possibly only offer four or five hours' oblivion, if that. The agony would still have to be faced once morning came. Nevertheless, perhaps both sisters might be better able to do so if they did not have a completely sleepless night. He did not approve of such measures in the ordinary course of his work; but this was an emergency. He shook out four pills from a bottle and handed them two each.

'Would you,' he asked, as he at last got up to go, 'like me to come along before evening surgery tomorrow to see Emily?'

'Oh, *would* you, Maurice?' Katy's eyes, as always when in distress, seemed to haunt him all the way home. What could she say to her daughter after the girl – hopefully – had had a little sleep? What could *he* say?

His mind went back to the last war: the appalling conditions in the trenches, the mud, the sickening smell, the corporal with both his legs blown off who kept cursing God, the other mutilated dead and dying bodies lying all around. He recalled Emily's young man as he had caught sight of him on his last leave: so handsome, so full of life, driving his little MG out of the gates of the Grange, presumably on his way to the Hermitage. He thought of the boy's grandparents, especially the Dowager. It was a mercy that they were both dead. They had been so much a part of Wilhampton that when the new Lord Fairfax and his wife had inherited the estate he had found it hard to adjust to such a very different patronage.

Maurice had never been a bitter man – even though he had loved and lost – but something very near bitterness came over him now. Why should John William have given his life in this way, just as so many of Maurice's contemporaries had given theirs? Then, suddenly, he checked himself. He must not automatically think of the young man as dead. Not yet. There was, as he had said to Katy, just a chance. John William could have been rescued, even now on his way to a German prisoner-of-war camp, although, please God, not seriously wounded. Would it be right to give that poor girl hope? It was all so unbelievable. He could not envisage aerial combat, even though he knew it was taking place daily, hourly, not so very far away. He had never flown himself. He knew so little about it. He only knew that every war was the same – but different; that this time the lives of people such as himself depended on what Churchill had described as a handful of pink-cheeked young pilots, or 'the few' to whom so many owed so much.

His mind was still in turmoil as he let himself into the front door of East Lodge. Clare met him in the hall, her manner, as so often, aloof and vaguely hostile.

'You're late,' she remarked. 'Ethel Sharman has just been through looking for you. The surgery's full.'

'Yes, I'm sorry, but I'm afraid that there's been bad news . . .' The words slipped out. Normally, he would never have dreamt of discussing his daily rounds, but this was hardly a medical matter. He felt obliged to continue. 'John Moreton is missing,' he said, flatly.

'Oh, I'm sorry.' Her reaction was immediate but somehow automatic and perfunctory. It was, perhaps, no more than he would have expected as, indeed, were her two questions which quickly followed it.

'Where did you hear? Have you been to the Hermitage?'

'Yes. I went to visit May. She broke her wrist yesterday.'

'I *see*.' His wife's emphasis on the last word did not escape him.

Wearily, he went into his small consulting room at the back of the house which led to both the surgery and a tiny extension which, in his father's day, had been a dispensary but which now, since Wilhampton boasted a chemist's shop, had been turned into an office for his secretary-cum-receptionist. The girl who had previously held this post had left to join the ATS and Maurice was now being assisted by two very dissimilar types: Marlene Parker, the local garage proprietor's daughter, and Ethel Sharman, the middle-aged teacher who gave private lessons to children of the more affluent parents in the district who could afford to pay for her good, if old-fashioned, tuition.

Because of Ethel's principal occupation, she was only able to manage evening work at East Lodge and so far, rather to Maurice's consternation, had refused to take any remuneration for it, saying that since the two evacuee schoolmistresses whom she had been housing had returned home with the majority of their charges, she felt any help she could give Maurice was her personal contribution to the war effort. Certainly, he found her useful. With his ever-growing practice, his involvement with the prospective convalescent home and his undertaking to act as stand-by for emergency work in Westonbury, he had come to rely on her more and more. She was careful and conscientious, kept all his records and files meticulously – so far little Marlene Parker had not been allowed to touch them – and, what was more, Ethel knew the local inhabitants almost as well as he did.

'Herbert Lench is your first, Doctor,' she said to him now, as she popped her head round the door and handed him a file as soon as she heard him arrive. 'His wife made him come. He never complains himself, but she told me the other day she was worried because his heart pains are getting worse.'

'Thank you, Ethel. Give me a minute to look at this and then show him in.' He took the file and, with an effort, did his best to switch his mind to the problems of the Lench family. Yet it was far from easy. Herbert was the husband of Katy's middle sister, Edith.

Later that night, when he was alone in bed – for he and Clare had long since ceased to share a bedroom – his thoughts returned to the Hermitage. He hoped that its two inhabitants were getting some sleep. He wondered just how Katy would break the news to her daughter. There was no doubt that Emily would take it bravely, possibly too bravely. The girl would withdraw. Hide her grief. Presumably carry on at Ashmore Emergency Hospital, waiting for further news, praying that by some miracle John William was still alive.

The clock above the Wilhampton town hall struck twelve. Although Maurice might, in an emergency such as today's, prescribe sleeping pills for his patients, he never took one himself. It was an unbroken rule. Whatever the circumstances, he could usually get a few hours' sleep. He had trained himself to do so, rather like a general in battle. Besides, there was no knowing when he might be called out and it would be disastrous to be in any way sedated. He often found himself on the road at night. Gone were the days when people thought more than once before calling on the doctor in the small hours. In many ways, the advent of the telephone had not made life any easier.

Yet, as he tossed and turned and listened to the town hall clock striking one, two and then three, he could never remember a night when he had so longed for the sleep which now eluded him. His mind kept revolving in kaleidoscope fashion, the past and the present jostling for attention. He could recall Katy at just about Emily's age, looking ethereally lovely when he had taken her to her first dance: her slim figure in a blue taffeta dress, her soft brown hair done up in a chignon, the scent of malmaison . . . He remembered how nervous she had been, as she had descended the stairs at East Lodge, and how he had tried to give her confidence by telling her how pretty she looked, before taking her through to the drawing room where his parents and the other guests were waiting. She had always been so vulnerable; he had ached to protect her. And he could have done it, too, if a certain thrusting young bookseller from London hadn't stepped in and shattered all his dreams. He had tried to forget, but it had been so difficult with her mother and sister still living close by at the Mill House. When Clare had come along, he had foolishly tried to endow her with what he felt to be all the attributes of his former love. No wonder that his fiancée had more than once remarked during their engagement: 'I don't know if I shall be able to live up to your ideal, Maurice.' Sadly, all too soon after the marriage, both knew she could not. The wedding night had been a disaster. Like most girls of that era, she had no knowledge of sex and he had been a virgin also. No intercourse had taken place during their honeymoon and very soon afterwards she had left him in no doubt that she found the idea of copulation – at least, with him – repugnant. He never ceased to blame himself. Clare must have realized that he could not get Katy out of his mind, that it was she whom he wanted in his arms. In less than six months his wife had gone into Westonbury and bought single beds. A year later she had taken herself off into a separate bedroom.

Nothing like that, Maurice felt sure, had happened in Katy's own marriage. He had always been painfully aware of the very strong physical attraction there had been between her and her husband. He had despaired when he had heard they were coming back to Wilhampton to live because Philip had come into some money. He did not want to witness their mutual happiness in each other, even though, when it had become obvious that something was wrong, he felt he could have killed Philip for making her unhappy. He had always known that his suicide had had to do with another woman. But how any man could fool around when he was married to Katy was something beyond his comprehension.

Four a.m. struck. In a few hours' time she would be driving into Westonbury to fetch Emily. In just over twelve he would be at the Hermitage again. Please God he would be equal to the task.

6

Edmund Fairfax sat in his agent's car outside Westonbury station waiting for the arrival of the London train. His sister had telephoned from Suffolk the previous day saying that she wished to make a brief visit to Wilhampton and could she spend the night with them.

Edmund had never had a close relationship with Alicia, any more than he had ever had a close relationship with anyone. Moreover, he found her far too conventional, her do-gooding activities as tiresome as those of his late mother's and his own wife. But the news, over three weeks ago, that John William was missing, had shocked him more than he cared to admit, making him realize that perhaps it was as well, after all, that he and Rachel had only managed to produce daughters. The war was taking a heavy toll now. The situation was damnable. He hadn't been to London since the last time he had seen Chloe, back at the beginning of September. She had written from some hotel in, of all places, North Wales. He had sent her a carefully-worded reply, together with what he felt to be a not ungenerous cheque, saying that it was possibly as well that she remained out of town while the bombing continued. So far, there seemed to have been no let-up. Presumably, that was why Alicia's train was so late today.

When, at last, the bell rang heralding its arrival, he got out and strolled towards the station entrance. For a few moments he failed to recognize the sad, grey-haired, shrunken figure coming through the ticket barrier. He had been vaguely aware for some time that Alicia had not worn well, that middle age had crept up on her sooner than most women and, so far as he thought about her at all, her husband probably had something to do with it. But he knew that he was hardly in a position to criticize his brother-in-law. He himself was no paragon, although certainly Rachel seemed to have accepted the role she had been obliged to play much more easily than his sister. He supposed the fact that his wife was neither pretty nor passionate and had never been physically in love with him must have helped. Alicia was a different type altogether. She was highly strung. He remembered her as being beautiful and even rather flirtatious – a long time ago.

When she finally emerged from the throng, he held out his hand and took the overnight bag she was carrying; but they did not kiss. As they walked across the station yard, he said, 'I hope you don't mind Luke Ridley's old barouche. I feel it's . . . advisable these days, not to be seen using the Daimler too much.' It was a relief to find some mundane topic with which to start the conversation.

'Yes. No. Of course.' Alicia seemed to be answering at random, her words hardly making sense. All the way back to Wilhampton she sat stiffly beside him, her hands clasped tightly in her lap. When they drew up in the stable yard, she said, suddenly, 'This is an impulse visit, Edmund. I felt I should like to see Emily.'

'Emily?' He frowned. Why should Alicia come all this way to see Emily Mason? There had never been an official engagement. Just a youthful romance. His nephew would surely have found someone more suitable – given time. Best leave the girl alone now. She would get over it.

'Yes.' Alicia became all at once quite coherent. 'John was more in love with her than I think any of us realized. In the very last letter I had from him . . .' She paused and then continued, quietly, 'It was *serious*, Edmund. He was determined to marry her. If he had had any leave after his twenty-first, they would have been man and wife by now.'

He found himself thinking: thank God he didn't. Aloud, he simply said, 'They were far too young, Alicia.'

Her reply startled him in its swift uncharacteristic bitterness. 'We were all young once, Edmund.'

At lunch he remained silent, leaving the conversation to the two women. Though so dissimilar in temperament, today they obviously shared a deep mutual unspoken understanding. Hearing them making plans for the afternoon, he made an excuse as quickly as he could and left them alone.

Emily was lying down in the small dark back bedroom of the Fawcetts' house, when a tap came at the door. Wearily, she got up to answer it. Now that she was once again on day duty, she spent most of her free time in such fashion, although Helen Swayne, no longer working quite so hard since the arrival of the dark evenings, often cycled into Westonbury, either to keep her company or beg her to come to the pictures. At this hour, however, she knew that it was unlikely to be Helen and, on opening the door, she found Mrs Fawcett standing uncertainly outside, her usually severe expression replaced by one of flushed agitation.

'There is someone to see you in the drawing room, Emily . . . A Lady Moreton.'

'*Lady Moreton?*'

'Yes, dear.'

'Thank you, Mrs Fawcett. I'll be down at once.' She went back into the bedroom, hastily put on her regulation black lace-up shoes and ran a comb through her hair.

John's mother was standing by the empty fireplace when Emily came in. Awkwardly, the older woman moved a step forward. Suddenly, the girl before her took the initiative. She went across and kissed her visitor. Then, almost as if she were helping some patient, she pushed Alicia Moreton gently into an armchair.

'You loved him, too. I wanted you to know . . . I understand.' John's mother spoke quite calmly, if a little disjointedly, at first. 'I thought it was . . . important that we should meet . . . That it would help us both, somehow.'

'Yes. Thank you.'

'I'm afraid, I forgot . . . how long you'd known each other. I mean, when you were both quite small . . . we used to stay at the Hall. I remember we called once at the Mill House, when you and your mother happened to be there.'

'Yes. I was seven. That was the first time we met.'

'So long ago . . . John used to love coming to Wilhampton. He seemed to have a kind . . . well, affinity with the neighbourhood. And he was very close to his grandmother. But, of course, I realize now . . . there was always you.'

Involuntarily, Emily glanced down at the Dowager's eternity ring on her right hand and then back at her visitor.

'I'm sorry . . . the engagement was never announced, my dear,' Alicia said, obviously noticing the gesture.

'It doesn't matter, now.'

'Will you keep in touch? Come and stay with us in Suffolk? Perhaps on your next leave? We should like that so much.'

'Thank you. Yes. I should love to.'

'Around Christmas, maybe?'

'We don't get any leave then . . . but I think I may have a few days in the New Year.'

'Yes, I see. How stupid of me. Nursing must be very arduous.'

'In some ways.'

A silence descended on them, but it was not an awkward one, although Alicia Moreton, still in her fur coat, shivered slightly. There was no heating in the Fawcetts' drawing room. Outside the window, the small front garden lay wet and dripping in the advancing twilight.

'My sister-in-law is waiting for me in the car. Could we drive you back to the hospital? I understood from Matron that you have to be on duty at four-thirty. I gather they are very busy just now.'

'Yes, but I have my bicycle, thank you all the same.'

'What time do you finish tonight?'

'Eight o'clock.'

'And then you cycle back here?'

'After supper. Yes.'

Alicia Moreton looked away. 'John's sister was talking of becoming a VAD, but she's just decided to join the FANYs. I think, perhaps, it's as well. Phoebe isn't exactly cut out for nursing.'

For the first time, Emily managed a small smile. 'I often think I'm not either, Lady Moreton.'

The meeting lasted barely a quarter of an hour, yet on parting both the older and younger woman felt better for it having taken place.

It was well into November before the letter arrived. May happened to meet the postman as he cycled down the Netherford lane, stopped and searched for it in his bag. It was the only one for the Hermitage that morning and she thought Bill Musselwhite gave her rather a curious look as he handed it over. She thanked him and went back indoors to find Katy. Addressed to Miss Emily Mason in John William's pencilled but unmistakable handwriting was a flimsy foreign-looking letter-card, declaring the sender: Vor und Zuname: Pilot Officer J. W. Moreton 2977/35. There was no date on the outside, simply Kriegsgef-Offizierlager VA Deutschland (Allemagne).

The sisters looked at each other. It was May who first broke the silence. 'I think . . . as it is unsealed . . . we should . . . perhaps just . . .'

Katy pulled open the flap gently. She read no more than two lines before carefully closing the missive up again. 'John is a prisoner of war,' she said. 'Emily must have this at once.'

7

In June 1941, during the same week that Hitler attacked Russia, there appeared in *The Times* and the *Telegraph* a small item of news of a strictly personal kind. It ran:

Pilot Officer John William Moreton and
Miss Emily Mason

The engagement is announced between Pilot Officer John William Moreton, only son of Sir Charles and Lady Moreton of Bishopsdown House, Suffolk, and Emily, only daughter of Mrs Mason and the late Mr Philip Mason, of The White Hermitage, Wilhampton, Wiltshire.

This public confirmation of Emily's betrothal was the result of a great deal of thought, deliberation and protracted communication on the part of all concerned. The circumstances were unusual. John William was still a prisoner of war. Moreover, in his very first letter to Emily he had intimated that it would be unfair on his part to ask her to wait for him and, although he naturally longed to hear from her, he did not want her to feel in any way tied. Emily, in the first flush of overwhelming relief and quick to sense his underlying despair and desperate need – however carefully camouflaged – for hope, had written back at once saying that she was prepared to wait for ever.

Apart from the War Office's subsequent official notification of John's capture, there had then followed a long period when neither Emily nor Alicia received any letters at all until, sometime in February, several of them arrived all at once.

Alicia had then made another journey to Wilhampton and had a long talk with both Katy and Emily. She, also, was only too well aware of the need to give her only son something definite to hold on to and she could not help feeling that, at this stage, it was important for her and her husband to show their whole-hearted approval of the match by making a public announcement, however long the two young people might have to wait before they could be married. She now had nothing but praise for her prospective daughter-in-law, conferring upon her – in a somewhat bewildering and neurotic fashion – almost saviour-like qualities. She appeared to be not the slightest bit jealous that the one letter per week which her son was allowed to write was mostly addressed to the White Hermitage. She kept in constant touch with Emily and, as next of kin, spent infinite time and care in getting off as many Red Cross parcels as she could to Oflag VA. When, at long last, both women received the necessary agreement from John to publicizing the engagement, she saw to it that it appeared in the papers the following day.

Having been so long an unofficial fiancée, Emily was astonished by the reaction when she became an official one. The Matron at Ashmore sent for her to express congratulations. Friends at the hospital kept waylaying her to do the same. A party was arranged and even the attitude of the two Honourables – both still unattached – changed dramatically overnight. With a mixture of curiously naïve admiration and envy, they asked to see her ring – an antique cluster of diamonds belonging to John's mother, which she had apparently always intended giving him for such an event – and which Emily, while on duty, now wore on a gold chain round her neck. She also received countless letters, amongst them a particularly warm-hearted and encouraging one from Maurice Fitzherbert; while many of John's friends whom she did not know but who obviously could not write to him, sent her messages to pass on. Life, in spite of all its vicissitudes, suddenly seemed to take a turn for the better.

Not everyone who saw the announcement, however, reacted in quite so forthcoming a fashion. One such person was Chloe Ford. It was not that she had anything against the young couple – she had never met them. She merely noted their betrothal with a detached and cynical interest, as she sat in the bar of the Green Dragon at Colwyn Bay while her companion had gone to buy her another gin and tonic. She had not heard from Edmund Fairfax for some time; she did not even know that his nephew was missing. The family meant little to her now. Never a woman to be long without a male escort, she had let a certain major into her life. He had a wife, naturally. All her gentlemen friends were invariably married. She had few illusions left, although that did not stop her from assiduously studying the engagement and marriages columns in the papers in a vicarious kind of way. She was thirty now and did not suppose that her own name would ever figure amongst them, even though she knew she still had the power to attract a certain kind of man with a view to a less permanent relationship. As she herself liked variety, such a liaison, while it lasted, was not without its compensations. Her present lover, Thornton Fairclough, now wending his way back towards her with a drink in each hand, was in many ways an improvement on Edmund Fairfax. While he did not possess that impregnable aura of sophisticated assurance which seemed to be the special perquisite of the aristocracy, he was so much *easier*. He had none of Edmund's coldness. Sometimes, she felt Thornton really cared. He had a worried bloodhound look about him that she took to be guilt and evoked in her almost a latent maternal instinct – something which definitely Edmund had never done.

When he sat down beside her again, Chloe did not refer to what she had just read. She realized it would hardly have been politic. Besides, it was irrelevant, something connected with her past. She merely put her glass down right on top of the particular lines which had caught her attention and gave Thornton an encouraging smile. He was due to go home that night for the remaining thirty-six hours of his leave, having told his wife that was all he would be getting. But Chloe was not thinking that far ahead. There was still the afternoon.

By three o'clock, when they were safely ensconced in her bedroom, the barmaid at the Green Dragon started to tidy up and gather together any newspapers which had been lying around, before going back to the small cottage in which she lived. Betsy Morgan, however carefree and cheerful she might have appeared in front of her customers a little while previously, now assumed a rather different mien. Only a few of the regulars at the Green Dragon were aware of the front she was constantly putting up, that she had a husband in the merchant navy whose ship was probably, at this very moment, battling its way across the Atlantic, and that for some time she had been caring, single-handed, for a relative who was a casualty from the London blitz.

That afternoon, Betsy found her elder sister huddled, as usual, by the small kitchen range, her damaged right arm hanging limply over the side of the chair, her face devoid of all expression. Betsy had never had a lot of time for Barbara in the past. They had scarcely anything in common, but, being of a compassionate nature, she now felt extremely sorry for her. She was also more than a little worried on her own account because, unless Barbara soon started to pick up, both mentally and physically, she couldn't see what was going to happen. Barbara had always been so independent before. She was the bright ambitious one of the family. As a child, she had won more than one scholarship and had virtually paid for her own education. On leaving school, she had taken a secretarial course – at which she had come out on top – whereupon, much against her parents' wishes, she had gone to London and very quickly obtained a post in a publisher's office. Her family had been forced to admit, grudgingly, that she had done quite well for herself. After a few years, they learned she had joined a literary agency and were suitably impressed, even if not altogether sure exactly what that meant. She rarely came back to Wales and her letters became fewer and fewer. Then, suddenly, they ceased altogether. Her mother, naturally, was anxious and eventually, one Saturday, she packed her husband off to the metropolis to find out just what had happened. On arrival at the address last given them – a small flat in Battersea – poor Sidney Woodley was confronted by his daughter, her infant son of around six months and a young woman who, apparently being an impecunious writer, looked after the child while Barbara carried on with her job.

Sidney had gone back to Colwyn Bay wondering how best he could break the news to his wife. Apart from the shaming and inescapable fact that Barbara was an unmarried mother and that the father of her infant son was dead, he had learned little else. His daughter had been irritated, impatient and defensive. She had told him that, as she knew her situation would distress both him and her mother, she had kept it from them. She said she was perfectly capable of managing her own life. She was earning a reasonable salary and saving as hard as she could in order to be able to send the child away to school as soon as he was old enough. She was not in need of either help or sympathy.

And until recently, Betsy realized, Barbara had been as good as her word. At the age of seven, young Paul – whose mother had adopted a wedding ring and called herself Mrs Woodley – had been sent to a small boarding school in the home counties. When the bombing started, she had paid extra so that he could remain there during the Christmas holidays where, for four days, she had stayed at a nearby hotel in order to see him. But soon afterwards, she had written to Betsy asking whether, if anything happened to her, she would mind being named as next of kin. Such a request had been difficult to refuse. Their parents were in failing health. It was the first time that Barbara had asked anything of the family, but it was quite obvious what had prompted her to do so. Her writer friend had apparently married. If Barbara became incapacitated or died, who would look after the child?

Betsy, generous to a fault, and having no children of her own – something for which she longed – had immediately agreed. Nevertheless, it had been a great relief when, earlier that year, the Luftwaffe had given London almost six weeks of raid-free nights. When she had read in the Sunday papers of March 9th that the Café de Paris had had a direct hit, it never occurred to her that her elder sister might have been in it.

It was not until a week later that she received a communication from Charing Cross Hospital. She had stared at it disbelievingly. The next day she had travelled to London to fetch Barbara – still in a state of shock – back to Colwyn Bay. Not only had her sister been injured in the Café de Paris. She was unable to return home because she had none to go to. That, too, had been reduced to a pile of rubble the same night.

Betsy had hoped, as time went by, that Barbara would pull out of it; but so far, she had been disappointed. Today, as she handed her a copy of *The Times*, with a cheerful, 'Here you are, love. I know this is your cup of tea,' she was met with the same mumbled, even grudging, 'Thank you'.

Yet, as the evening wore on, Betsy was surprised at how often she found Barbara picking up the paper again and studying the same page. She was glad that something appeared to have caught her attention at last, although she refrained from asking any questions. Long ago, she had learnt they would only be met with silence. Her elder sister had always been a dark horse.

8

May was laying out teacups on a table in the garden of the White Hermitage one Saturday in early July. Although she and Katy spent most of their time at the Hall during the week — May in charge of housekeeping and Rachel Fairfax and Katy being mainly responsible for administrative work for which, with admirable foresight, the latter had taught herself to type — neither of them went there at weekends. Both on Saturday and Sunday afternoons they kept open house at the Hermitage for any other-rank patients wishing and mobile enough to make the short journey from Wilhampton. Clad in their bright hospital blue uniforms with white shirts and red ties, they would come, in twos and threes, sauntering down the Netherford lane, grateful to spend a few hours in what all of them longed for: a home atmosphere.

The success of such hospitality soon became very apparent. The sisters were apt to find the place crowded out, especially when the weather was poor and everyone was forced to remain indoors. But they were equal to the task. Although neither of them knew it, they had been affectionately dubbed Martha and Mary: May, the ebullient practical one of the partnership, Katy the more serious-minded, often to be found sitting quietly in a corner while some distraught and temporarily disordered individual poured out his heart to her.

When May heard a car draw up at the gate on this particular afternoon, she wondered whether it was one ordered privately by Corporal Watts, a casualty from Dunkirk who, although physically restored to health, had not been able to forget his ordeal: the unearthly scream of the Luftwaffe strafing the overcrowded beaches, the black pall of smoke covering the entire town, the piers which jutted into the sea – *human* piers, the front ranks up to their necks in chill grey water, patiently waiting for boats from England. May doubted that he would ever now erase the memory – or, at least, learn to live with it – and happened to know that, prompted by Maurice Fitzherbert and a visiting army psychiatrist, his discharge from the Royal Engineers was shortly to take place.

She was surprised, therefore, to see that the person getting out of what appeared to be a station taxi was a woman. She watched her say something to the driver, turn and unlatch the gate and then slowly, very slowly, walk up the garden path. She was middle-aged, thin and gaunt, with closely-cropped grey hair and a marked limp. But, as she drew closer, it was the visitor's eyes which held May's attention more than anything else: dark, heavily fringed and somehow desperate-looking. All at once, she experienced a strange nebulous fear.

'Were you looking for someone?' May asked the question in an unnaturally high-pitched manner and the woman halted, a slightly puzzled expression now coming over her face.

'Yes. I wanted to see Mrs Mason. Mrs Katherine Mason. I believe this is her home?' The voice was low and husky, almost mannish. May knew that she had heard it before, once, and once only, on the telephone, shortly after Katy's husband had committed suicide.

'Mrs Mason is very busy this afternoon,' she answered, defensively, 'as you can see. We are entertaining . . . patients from the local convalescent home.'

'But they are not here yet.' It was more of a flat statement than a query.

'No.'

'Then perhaps I could see Mrs Mason for just a few moments. I promise not to take up too much of her time.'

Reluctantly, May motioned the woman to a garden seat and went indoors to look for Katy. She found her just putting the finishing touches to her appearance and not for the first time was she struck by her youngest sister's curious mixture of detachment and vulnerability, as if she both fought shy of, yet manifestly needed, a husband to protect her. Today she was wearing a smart – if several years old – black and white silk dress, her slightly greying brown hair swept up into a chignon, her figure, for all its thirty-nine years, still shapely and supple. Recent events had perhaps given her an added poise. Her successful efforts at the Hall and Emily's engagement obviously had something to do with it. Yet, as May watched from a window while Katy went out to greet their visitor, she prayed that the stranger now rising from the seat – with obvious difficulty – was not going to take such new-found confidence away.

'You wanted to see me?' Katy stared at the woman, quickly becoming aware, as May had done, that she was being threatened by something which she could not, for the moment, quite understand.

'Yes. I hear you are expecting guests. It should not take long. Possibly you have guessed who I am?'

For a fraction, Katy hesitated. Then she answered, slowly, 'You are Barbara Woodley.'

'Yes.'

There was silence broken, suddenly, by the sound of distant voices and footsteps in the lane.

'I think perhaps we should go indoors,' Katy said, and led the way to May's small upstairs workroom at the back of the house. As soon as she had closed the door and they were seated, she continued, abruptly, 'Why have you come to see me after all these years? What do you want?'

'Nothing for myself, I assure you. After I learned that your husband had . . . died, I naturally never thought to distress you further.'

'Then why . . . ? Why *now*, for God's sake?'

'I have come to see you on account of my son.'

'Your *son*?'

'Yes.'

There was a click of the garden gate, the sound of May greeting the first arrivals. Katy felt suddenly very cold, although it was a warm day and outside she could see the

Willon glinting in the sunlight, the same river into which, on a November night getting on for ten years ago now, Philip had thrown himself because of his involvement with the woman in front of her. Afterwards, she had gradually come to realize that a pregnancy must surely have been the reason for the drastic step he had taken, but she had never known for sure – neither had she wanted to. Besides, she had always imagined that his mistress would never actually have borne his child. From the little she had gathered about her she did not sound the type. Surely Barbara Woodley had been too worldly-wise not to have known what to do, however difficult, in such circumstances. Or was that wishful thinking? The fact that she had allowed herself to become pregnant showed a certain foolhardiness, unless it had been deliberate on her part in the hope that it would bind Philip to her in some way. But surely, after his death, she would have taken herself off to one of those hush-hush nursing homes, which Katy had a vague idea existed on the south coast and where secret abortions were carried out by doctors of doubtful reputation – unless, of course, Barbara had left it too late.

But over and above all these considerations, there was another reason why Katy had eventually tried to close her mind to the situation, one which she supposed Philip, in his hopeless desperation, had never stopped to think about. If there had been a baby, who was to say if it was his or not?

'Where . . . is your son?' she asked, at length.

'Paul's away at boarding school. That is to say, just for this term.'

'How do you mean?'

For answer, Barbara lifted her right arm and let it drop limply by her side. 'I can no longer work, as you see. In any case, the publishing trade is in a bad way. Lack of paper. I doubt I could get my job back, even if my health improved. So – he'll have to leave.'

Again there was silence. Down in the garden, the sound of more voices mingled with the clink of teacups. As if from a long way off, Katy heard Corporal Watts asking, 'Is Mrs Mason not here today?' She had begun to feel quite sick now. If only May would come. She needed help. She couldn't handle this alone. It was a confrontation for which she was totally unprepared. Her whole being wanted to get the woman out of the house as quickly as possible, tell her that she had no right to be there, that she must never, ever, come near her again. Yet, as she looked at the haggard face with its sad haunted eyes, she knew that was impossible. Whatever Barbara Woodley had or had not done, she was paying for it now. Besides, there was the child, Philip's child, if all she said was to be believed.

As if reading her mind, Barbara suddenly started searching for something in her handbag. Presently, she pulled out not just one but three photographs, all of the same little boy and all bearing an uncanny unmistakable likeness to one which Katy possessed of Philip taken at round about the same age.

'Spitting image, isn't he?' Barbara's voice cut into her thoughts, deep and curiously unfeminine. 'I haven't lied to you.'

Katy knew she was speaking the truth. 'What . . . exactly . . . do you want?' she asked, even though she also knew the answer.

'I told you, nothing on my own account. I can hardly expect you to worry about me. I'm just a casualty of the blitz. I was in the Café de Paris back last March the night it was hit. But when they tried to send me home because the hospitals were so full, I hadn't got a home to go to. Jerry had scored a direct hit on that as well.'

'Then . . . where are you living now?'

'With my sister, in Wales. Paul's still at boarding school. I managed to pay the fees for this term, but after that . . .' Barbara broke off, looked out of the window for a moment and then, still with her eyes averted, continued, 'I happened to see the announcement of your daughter's engagement. I couldn't help feeling she'd done rather well for herself. You must be pleased. I don't suppose you want her or the family she's marrying into to know that there's a half-brother somewhere around.'

The word formed in Katy's mind, hideous and unacceptable. She was being blackmailed. The whole afternoon had taken on a macabre unreal quality. If only May was with her or, better still, the one man in the world on whom she could always rely: Maurice Fitzherbert. Yet, oddly enough, it was not really Barbara's ostensible threat that was worrying her. The existence of Paul, now that it had come to light, would have to be accepted, just as the existence of her impoverished overburdened sister, Edith — the wife of a mill hand — would have to be accepted. She could not seriously believe that either would really jeopardize Emily's future marriage, whenever that might be. It was much more the photographs still in her hand which were causing her to think, and think hard. She had the power to help this child, Philip's son. It was as if the eyes now looking straight at her were those of her late husband's, beseeching her to do so.

'You are asking me,' she said to Barbara, and she was conscious of her words coming out, precise and separate, like the tiny pebbles which she used to drop into the mill pool when she was a little girl, 'to pay for Paul's education?'

Barbara Woodley inclined her head slightly. 'That was why I came,' she replied. 'I can assure you that the money wouldn't be wasted. He is, so the school tell me, an unusually bright child.'

9

In the small and once sadly overcrowded house on downside, where Edith Lench had brought up her large family — as well as for the past two years looking after an evacuee boy from Portsmouth — her husband had just suffered another attack of angina. It was a far more serious one than any she had hitherto known. The pain had come on acutely as he was climbing the stairs to bed, but although he had quickly used one of the little amyl nitrite tablets that Dr Fitzherbert insisted he must always carry with him, this time it had had little or no effect. Edith had loosened his collar and eventually managed to get him into the bedroom, where he now lay on their narrow brass-railed bedstead with his eyes closed and his face as white as the pillows she had propped behind him.

After a little while, she crept out on to the landing and went into another room at the back of the house, now shared by her youngest son of twelve and the lad to whom she had so generously given a home and whom she had come to love as much as – and possibly even more than – any of her own offspring.

'Porty.' Gently, she shook the small form in the nearest bed. 'Porty!' she said, again, a little louder.

Suddenly, a fair tousle-haired head emerged from beneath the blankets and two sleepy eyes peered at her in the flickering light of the candle she was carrying.

'Porty, I want you to dress as quick as you can and run down to East Lodge and ask the doctor to come. Say Mrs Lench sent you because her husband has been taken very ill.'

'Yes, ma'am.' Porty – as he had affectionately been nicknamed by the Lench family – had always called Edith 'ma'am', even though he thought of her as a mother and a far better one than his own, whom he had left behind in Portsmouth and who, unlike the majority of his friends', had never once shown the slightest desire to have him back with her again. But that suited Porty well. He liked living with the Lenches and he loved the country. He was delighted to have left school and be working for Mr Swayne at Bulbarrow Farm. As far as he was concerned, he hoped the war would go on for ever; although he supposed that when he was eighteen it would mean joining the army like Mrs Lench's two eldest boys. But that was four years hence. For the moment, helping to look after a couple of carthorses and learning how to manage them behind a plough or harrow – as well as many another exciting task – kept him happy all the hours of daylight. And in the evenings, now that the nights were drawing in, he was glad to be of use to the kind woman who housed him, chopping up firewood and doing various odd jobs because her husband never seemed well enough to help her.

It took him no more than a couple of minutes to put on his clothes and start off down the rough uneven road into Wilhampton. There was not a glimmer of light behind the blacked-out windows – Bill Musselwhite, the chief air-raid warden, saw to that – yet the outlines of the houses showed up starkly beneath a brilliant hunter's moon and he found that he had no need to use the little torch which he had bought for sixpence out of his first week's wages, before handing over the remaining five shillings to his surrogate mother.

Porty was a good lad and well aware of the urgency of his errand. He knew that Mrs Lench never made a fuss for nothing and he suspected that Mr Lench was going to die. He had a vague recollection of his paternal grandmother 'passing on', as grown-ups always seemed to refer to death. He could recall his mother pouring out a glass of stout and saying, 'Thank Gawd', because she had bitterly resented having the old woman to live with them. But he was sure Mrs Lench would never say anything like that. She was such a nice comfortable person and she had looked so anxious when she had woken him up.

Porty was breathless by the time he got to the front door of East Lodge. On any other occasion, he would automatically have gone to one of the other entrances, but at this time of night he knew that they were behind high locked gates, so that it was the front or nothing. He felt slightly nervous as he tugged at the big brass bell and heard it reverberating loudly all over the house. Presently, there was the sound of a bolt being pushed back, a light being carefully switched off because of the black-out and then the doctor himself stood before him in his slippered feet.

'Please, sir . . .' Porty brought out his message in between short sharp gasps and it took Maurice Fitzherbert scarcely more than a second to sum up the situation, get the boy into the hall, tell him to wait while he collected his things and that he would then drive up to downside with him immediately.

Porty sat on a high-back mahogany chair and looked round him wonderingly. He had never been inside what he thought of as a 'posh' house before. He was fascinated by the huge staircase with its heavy oak banisters and red carpet, held in place by gleaming rods, so much so that he almost jumped out of his skin when a figure wearing a boudoir cap and a blue dressing gown appeared at the top. It suddenly dawned on him that it must be Mrs Fitzherbert, but he was surprised at how cross she sounded when she called out, just as her husband came back into the hall carrying his bag, 'Who is it this time?' The doctor simply replied, 'Herbert Lench,' but he did not answer at all when his wife, sounding even more cross, remarked, 'Oh, Katy's brother-in-law again.' Porty could not help feeling that there was something a little odd about their brief conversation, although he realized it was none of his business and, besides, this was no time for bothering about it. He simply helped Dr Fitzherbert unlock his gates and had no idea that, as they drove off to downside, the tall kindly man beside him was reflecting that never before, in spite of all the family's tribulations, had the Lenches called him out at this hour of the night.

When they arrived at Number 32, Porty hung round inside the kitchen while the doctor went straight upstairs. He did not think it seemed quite right for him to be feeling hungry with so much trouble in the house, but nevertheless he did. He wondered whether Mrs Lench would mind if he ate a biscuit from the tin with the picture of kittens on which she kept in the larder. But he decided it would be best to wait and ask. After a while, he curled up on the old horsehair sofa and fell fast asleep.

She was crying when he woke. She was sitting in the chair on the other side of the fireplace and her small body appeared to be racked by great, yet almost silent, sobs. He looked at her wonderingly and for a moment she scarcely seemed to register his presence. When she did, she said, 'Oh, Porty,' and he got up and went over to her. She put her arms round him tightly and he knew at once she was a widow and, instinctively, that she was now looking to him as the man of the house.

Then suddenly, in spite of her grief, she said, 'You must

get to bed again. It won't do to have you late at Bulbarrow in the morning.'

'But, ma'am . . . What about you?'

'I'll be all right, Porty. The doctor has gone home to telephone my sisters. I dare say they'll be along in their car soon. You need to get your sleep.'

He climbed the stairs with misgivings and tiptoed past the door behind which lay what his father would have called 'a goner'. He wondered what Mr Lench looked like now and whether his soul was already up in heaven, watching to see how they were all getting on.

Downstairs in the kitchen, Edith Lench was beginning to think a little along the same lines. How would she manage? She would have a widow's pension and it was true that lately, with Herbie off work and so much on the panel, it had been difficult enough to make ends meet. Of course, Mavis, her youngest daughter, who lodged at a friend's home during the week in order to work in a nearby munitions factory where they paid good wages, gave her ten shillings when she came home for the odd weekend; and Porty, bless him, handed over almost all he earned, although it was not as much as the regular allowance she had drawn from the post office when he had still been the government's responsibility. It would be another two years before Georgie, her youngest son, went to work and as for her other children who had left the nest, she neither wanted nor expected any assistance from them. In any case, her two eldest boys, Donald and Ernest, were both somewhere in North Africa and Della, who had mercifully married a corporal when she was already pregnant by another man, now had a second child on the way and had turned out to be a hopeless manager.

Edith was well aware that Della's twin, Debbie – already a sergeant in the ATS and quite a different character – would now almost certainly insist on helping, as would May and Katy and her brother, Henry. But she would so much rather not accept anything from anybody unless she could give a fair return. She would like to go out to work herself now. The trouble was that, throughout her married life, Herbie had been so against it. It was a question of pride and she knew that her sisters were equally appalled at the idea. She supposed they felt it reflected badly on all of them. How odd it was to think that the clever courteous man who had just left her house might actually have been her brother-in-law if his mother hadn't, for obvious reasons, been so against the match and Katy so stuck on that unreliable young bookseller from London.

Presently, she heard the sound of a car winding its way up the road to downside. She rose slowly and put a kettle on the small gas-stove. She knew that life had to go on somehow and Katy and May would be sure to like a cup of tea when they arrived.

10

One evening shortly before Christmas, Helen Swayne hurried down the lane from Bulbarrow to catch the bus into Westonbury. As she reached the railway arch, she caught sight of a diminutive figure about to turn up the road towards downside.

'Why, Porty! You're late getting home tonight.'

'That's all right, miss. I had to take Blossom to the blacksmith's and I gave her a bit of a groomin' afterwards. She likes attention, that one.'

Helen laughed. Porty's devotion to her father's two carthorses had become well known; however much they might or might not have liked attention, there was no doubt that the small boy from Portsmouth enjoyed giving it to them. She wished him a friendly good night, and called out, 'Remember me to Mrs Lench,' as he disappeared into the darkness.

Once on the bus *en route* to meet Edith's niece, Helen reflected how strange it was that Emily's life had always been so different from that of her cousins on downside, and would be even more so when, please God, the war ended and John William came safely back from Germany. Everyone, of course, was much more hopeful about the ultimate outcome since the Sunday at the beginning of the month when, horrendous as the news had been, most of the United States Pacific fleet was destroyed in one fatal attack on a place which Helen had never heard of: Pearl Harbor. Even when, a few days later, more bad news had come through concerning the sinking off Malaya of two of Britain's biggest and best battleships, the *Repulse* and the *Prince of Wales*, it had still been a tremendous relief to know that the Americans were definitely in the war now and that, despite the German/Italian/Japanese alliance, 'Four fifths of the world,' as Churchill put it, 'are with us.'

So many unexpected and unimaginable things seemed to be taking place far away from the tiny area in which she lived, that Helen had begun to feel restless. Lately, when bad weather precluded her from doing very much out of doors and she had remained inside the farmhouse, helping her mother to churn a little extra butter or writing letters to her two brothers in the forces, she wished that she could take a more active part in the war. Although she was ostensibly a land girl working on her father's farm, she had never officially become a member of the Land Army. She realized that she had been invaluable during the last two summers, but now that Charlie Harper – a reservist – had suddenly and surprisingly been sent back to Bulbarrow as a key agricultural worker, she felt her presence not nearly so necessary, particularly since little Porty was shaping up so nicely. With thousands of others losing their lives daily, it did not seem quite right that her own was so easy, that she could get time off whenever she wanted and obviously had preferential treatment because she was living at home. It had occurred to her that she might join the ATS and it was this which she wanted to talk to Emily about tonight before going to the pictures.

It was very cold in the little back bedroom which Canon and Mrs Fawcett made available for a VAD on day duty at Ashmore Emergency Hospital. Both girls now sat huddled in their outdoor clothes, Emily in her navy uniform coat, Helen in a thick plaid cloak which she had bought on leaving school and which she liked to feel hid her rather dumpy figure. She was by no means a pretty girl, although she had one redeeming feature: very fine, clear and direct blue eyes. But her face was round and freckled and her fair hair still unbecomingly short. Uncertain how to make the best of herself, it was not surprising that so far she had attracted no young man. While she did not stand in awe of Emily – theirs was a friendship far too deep and loyal for that – she was nevertheless conscious that her best friend, now engaged to the only son of a baronet, had already travelled – metaphorically, at least – along paths quite unknown to her. Yet tonight, as they sat side by side on Mrs Fawcett's high uncomfortable single bed, however dissimilar their appearance and status, basically they remained the same two somewhat ingenuous young girls who had been brought up in a small country community and who, at a singularly unfortunate time of their lives, had found themselves caught up in circumstances which made any planning for their futures so uncertain and confusing.

'Your parents will miss you terribly, Helen, if you leave home. And it goes without saying, of course, that I will, too.' Emily had been completely taken aback by her friend's disclosure. It was hard to think of Helen not being at Bulbarrow.

'Oh, I *know*. That's what makes it all so difficult. I don't want to be selfish, especially with Bob and Tim both away. But . . . well . . . do you know, Em, I haven't spent a night outside Wilhampton since I was born and I'd love to see a bit more of the world . . . that is, England. And nowadays I simply don't feel I'm contributing to the war effort sufficiently. Daddy's got enough staff and it isn't as if Mummy needs me. I mean, Mrs Sherston from Portsmouth is still living in the old nursery quarters with her kid. What with the raids being so bad and her husband being called up, she's decided to stay with us for the duration. She's awfully good about helping.'

'Yes, I see.' For a while there was silence and then Emily continued, 'I do understand, Helen. I've often felt I'd like to get right away, too. I've even considered going to London and taking a proper nurse's training at one of the teaching hospitals as our Matron, Miss Butler, did in the last war. But . . . well . . . it's difficult to explain . . . John likes to think of me sticking around these parts. I believe he'd even prefer me to be working at the Hall rather than Ashmore.'

'Would you want to do that? With your mother and aunt already so involved in the place?'

'No. And besides, it's mostly psychiatric nursing there. Trying to keep the patients' minds off what they've been through. I believe Dr Maurice is awfully good with them. That is, when he can spare the time.'

'I'm told your mother's not bad at that either. I gather those afternoon tea parties at the Hermitage are a great success.' Helen hesitated for a moment and then went on, 'Em, I hope you don't mind my saying this, but don't you wish she and Maurice Fitzherbert could have married?'

'Yes, often.' Suddenly, Emily thought how preoccupied her mother had appeared lately as if, rather like the men she was trying to help, there was something on her own mind. Sometimes it seemed as if she was about to confide in her daughter but then, at the last moment, had decided to keep whatever it was to herself.

'It seems such a shame,' Helen continued. 'I believe his wife gives him a terrible time. With all he has to do I don't know how he stands it. But I suppose . . . having to be out so much is a relief. It's better to keep busy. That's why I'd like to get my teeth into a really proper war job.'

Emily nodded. She thought of John William and how frustrated he must feel, playing endless games of bridge in below-zero temperatures, although in his last letter he had mentioned briefly that he was taking the female lead in a show the prisoners were putting on for Christmas and that people's ingenuity was quite remarkable when it came to creating ladies' dresses. Presently, she said, 'I don't blame you, Helen. And anyway, I believe you've already made up your mind. When were you thinking of going?'

'In the New Year. I thought I wouldn't say anything to the family until after Christmas. We're rather hoping Bob may get forty-eight hours' leave round about then. Mummy's going to arrange a party. You'll just have to get off and come to it. He's longing to see you again.' She flushed, regretting the last words which had somehow slipped out. She had long known that her eldest brother was much more keen on Emily than he would have anyone believe.

As they left for the pictures, Mrs Fawcett waylaid them in the hall, her expression, as always, a mixture of annoyance and anxiety. Emily had already told her where she was going and what time she would be back, but her reluctant hostess invariably required confirmation. She had never had a child of her own and the unaccustomed responsibility for any young lady from Ashmore weighed heavily with her.

'You will be sure to be back by nine, won't you, Emily? The canon and I like to lock up then, as you know.'

'Yes, Mrs Fawcett. The film ends at a quarter to.'

After they had gone out of the front door and were walking along the street, Helen said, 'Do you mind her fussing so? I mean, you might be a kid of twelve rather than an engaged girl of twenty.'

'Not really. She can't help it. Although I must say it was a bit embarrassing a little while ago when one of John's Cambridge friends came to see me. He was early, but she wouldn't ask him into the house. I found him walking up and down outside in the cold waiting for me to get back from the hospital. When I told her that he wanted to take me out to dinner at the White Lion she nearly threw a fit. In fact, she wasn't going to let me go at all until somehow or other it transpired his father was a bishop. That seemed to make everything all right.'

They had reached the Gaumont Palace by now. Once inside, they began to feel warm again for the first time that evening. Ironically, the film they were going to see was *When Tomorrow Comes* starring Charles Boyer and Irene Dunn. Quickly paying their one and sixpences, they hurried up the stairs just as the last strains of 'We'll Meet Again' were being played on the organ.

As the music faded away and the screen lit up, Helen whispered, 'I hope it'll be soon for you and John, Em.'

11

On the 26th of January 1942, Lieutenant Vernon Keeler
– one of the first in a batch of two thousand American
servicemen – came down the gangplank of a troopship
and stepped ashore at Belfast. By early February he and
his unit were transferred to the north of England and, later
that month, sent south. Here, he found himself in what he
referred to as 'a real beautiful part of the old country' and
considered that he was extremely lucky to be billeted at
the White Hermitage on 'two little landladies who were
kinda quaint'.

May and Katy were not altogether surprised when,
earlier that month, a courteous American colonel had
appeared on their doorstep enquiring if they would be
willing to take a lodger. 'No meals, of course, ma'am. Just
a bed. But we're so hard put to it getting our boys fixed
up until things are a bit better organized.'

Everyone in the district had been watching with curiosity
and admiration the speed and efficiency with which, ever
since Pearl Harbor, a camp had begun to take shape at
the side of the Barbury turnpike, strips of concrete and
Nissen huts sprawling out like a spider's web in every
direction. Though from the air it was camouflaged by trees
it was nevertheless an eyesore to local inhabitants, but an
important and necessary one. The Yanks were coming and
that was what counted. No matter if bulldozers and jeeps
were, as Fred Cutler, the Sweetacres dairyman, said, 'all
over the auction', no matter if Singapore had fallen, the
Eighth Army in retreat in Egypt and the Germans at the
gates of Moscow; England, with the whole might of the
United States now behind her, would not only survive but
she would, perhaps, not too long hence, seize the initiative
again. Winston Churchill and the new Chief of the
Imperial General Staff, General Alan Brooke, might be
facing what looked like the most appalling problems and
reverses, yet the very presence of so many jaunty, square-

shouldered, optimistic, gum-chewing GIs seemed to give –
at least to the ordinary man and woman – a feeling of
both relief and hope.

At the end of Colonel Beatty's visit to the White Hermi-
tage, Katy had agreed to letting her daughter's bedroom
to a billetee, rather in the same way as it had been appro-
priated by three little evacuee children at the beginning of
the war. She was sorry that it would once again mean
Emily doubling up with May when she came home on
leave from Ashmore, but it was the least they could do.
Moreover, someone requiring a bed only would be no
trouble and not interfere with their other war work.

All the same, both sisters received something of a shock
when Lieutenant Keeler arrived: rather older than
expected, dark-haired, powerfully-built, devastatingly
smart and with what they were later to discover appeared
to be a limitless supply of Lucky Strike cigarettes – Katy
had never lost the habit of smoking since Philip's death –
candies, soap and something hitherto unknown to them:
nylon stockings.

'He's an unusual young man,' May remarked, one
evening after he had been with them for a few weeks. 'I
understand he's a sort of singer. He seems to be always
out in the evenings performing at impromptu concerts.'

'Yes. Although I can't quite make out if that has been
his main occupation in civilian life. He talks vaguely about
his "folks", as he calls them, in Ohio and that he's never
been able to see much of them because he's had to travel
a good deal. Somehow I get the feeling that the singing is
a sideline. I suppose we shall find out in due course.'

But as time went by the sisters were given little oppor-
tunity for discovering more about their agreeable energetic
billetee. Vernon Keeler rose at six-thirty and left the
Hermitage before May came downstairs to make the early
morning tea. He was sometimes apt to appear again round
about seven in the evening – having ascertained that at
this hour it would be quite convenient for him to take a
bath – after which he would be gone again before eight.
His return in the night was so silent that it was rare for
either May or Katy to hear his key in the lock or a footstep

on the stairs. Sometimes, he did not appear to have returned at all and occasionally, at short notice, he informed them that he was going to London for the weekend.

It was hardly surprising, therefore, that Emily did not encounter him until well into April. She came home on the bus one evening and arrived at the Hermitage just as he was walking down the garden path *en route* for his now taken-for-granted nightly social activities. Faced by his immaculate appearance, she became acutely aware that she was not looking her best. She had had a hard day, her feet were hurting and she had not bothered to let down her thick dark hair, so that it was still pinned up in the unattractive style which she was obliged to adopt under a nurse's cap. Although she was grateful to be having forty-eight hours away from Ashmore, she was not looking forward to them quite as much as usual, since she was no longer able to enjoy the privacy of her own bedroom. Now that she was older, as well as engaged, she found that, much as she loved her aunt, she did not want to share a bedroom with her; although, naturally, she would never have dreamt of complaining. She knew that it was only a small inconvenience and well aware that others were enduring far greater hardships every day.

'Good evening. You must be Emily. The nurse.' Vernon Keeler stopped, drew himself up and saluted, smartly. There was an interested, slightly amused expression on his face.

'Yes.' She found herself colouring and was annoyed. It was a nervous habit which she hoped she had almost overcome.

'I guess you must hate my guts. It's too bad my turning you out of your bedroom. Though it's sure nice for me. And I admire your choice of books tremendously. I hope you don't mind, but I've read *Wuthering Heights* and last night I finished *Vanity Fair*.'

'Really? I hope you liked them.' His smile and direct approach were somehow disarming.

'Sure. Especially *Wuthering Heights*. That really got me.' She hesitated, wondering whether to tell him that her parents had named her after its author, but decided against it. After all, they had only just met and such a revelation could mean but little to him. She was entirely taken aback when he suddenly said, 'Would you care to come to the White Lion dancing hall tonight?'

'Oh no, thank you.' She recoiled from the suggestion instinctively. Then, feeling her refusal might have sounded rather rude and abrupt, she added, 'We've been having rather a busy week at the hospital. I'm hoping to catch up on a bit of sleep.' She felt it was a poor excuse, one which Lieutenant Keeler would never use, nor need to use.

'Too bad. Some other time, maybe?' He gave her another smart salute and disappeared towards his bicycle, which she had noticed leaning against the garden fence.

Did he, she wondered after she was in bed that night, kept awake by her aunt's snores, know that she was engaged? That her fiancé was a prisoner of war? That did not, of course, preclude her from occasionally accepting invitations to a dance or party. But somehow she never enjoyed them very much. The ring on her finger certainly kept men at a distance. Not that she would have had it otherwise. She had no wish to encourage the opposite sex, although she regretted that being, as it were, bespoke, she was probably rather dull company. Long before the end of such evenings, she often found herself impatient to get back to the Fawcetts' and into bed. She was unaware of the expression – and would scarcely have understood it if she had – but cruder members of society might have said that Emily Mason had 'shut up shop'.

Both her mother and aunt sensed the girl's predicament and had become increasingly concerned about it. It had been one thing to feel overwhelming relief when they had learnt that John William was alive and, subsequently, to share all the excitement of his and Emily's official betrothal; but time had gone on now. Whereas most of Emily's contemporaries, while working hard, nevertheless enjoyed an exhilarating social life – far more so, in fact, than they might otherwise have experienced in peace-time – she herself remained rather a lonely figure. Now that Helen Swayne was away in the ATS, she spent most of her off duty engaged in solitary pursuits: reading, drawing or writing small articles or verses which occasionally — very occasionally — saw print.

The period which had given her most pleasure of late had been when her cousin, Frank François, whom she scarcely knew, had been sent to Salisbury Plain on an officers' training course and had come into Westonbury as often as he could to see her. She had found him an interesting companion — quite unlike any previous idea she had formed about him — and was sorry when, as a fully-fledged second lieutenant, he had been posted back north, not far from where his sergeant-major father had been training raw recruits since the beginning of the war. 'I'm glad to have got to know you, Emily,' he had said, on leaving. 'Do write, won't you? I wish . . . well . . . my mother wasn't so against you all down here. But I suppose it's understandable in a way. I mean, I gather our Grandmother Lodge gave her the cold shoulder, all right, back in 1919.'

Emily knew the story. Not only had Marianne been *French*, but she had given birth a little too soon after the marriage. But that was all so long ago now. She knew that her mother and aunts would be only too willing to extend the hand of friendship, as her Uncle Henry would, too. After all, she remembered how he had turned up trumps when one of her Aunt Edith's daughters had got herself in the family way, how he had taken a pregnant Della back to Catterick with him, where she had subsequently and miraculously married a lance corporal in his regiment. It seemed such a shame that, until recently, Frank François had remained almost a stranger to her. She liked him so much. Only the previous day she had received a most amusing letter from him. She hoped that he would be posted back to the area again at some time or other. He had been such a charming escort, one with whom, as he was a cousin and she an engaged girl, she had felt able to relax.

She had been thinking about all this as she stood at the Netherford bus stop on the Sunday evening, prior to returning to the Fawcetts'. Since basic civilian petrol rationing had been extinguished in March it was no longer possible for Katy or May to drive her to Westonbury. Suddenly, her train of thought was interrupted by a jeep full of Americans screeching to a halt beside her and a voice calling out, 'Hi, Emily! Back to duty? Hop in.'

Without hardly knowing how it had happened she found herself being hustled inside, where she sat squashed between Vernon Keeler and another lieutenant whom he introduced as 'My buddy, Holden Fearon'.

Just as they reached the outskirts of the town, the driver slowed down and began pulling up at a small public house called the Black Horse. She turned to Vernon in alarm.

'Please, I must get back,' she said, quickly, as the others all started to get out.

He smiled and took her arm, preparatory to helping her down also. 'We shan't be long here, Emily. But anyway, what's the hurry? You're already ahead of the bus. It's only a quarter to nine.'

'But you don't understand. Canon and Mrs Fawcett, the people I'm billeted on, lock up at nine. They're expecting me.'

'*Lock up at nine?*' He stared at her, incredulously. 'Jeeze. They must be gaolers. How the hell do you enjoy yourself?'

'I . . . don't go out a lot. And when I do . . . well, I come to some arrangement with them.'

They were alone now, the rest of the party having gone inside the inn. She was still sitting in the jeep with Vernon standing on the pavement beside her. She noticed that his previous devil-may-care attitude seemed to change. There was something almost like awe, even pity, in his eyes.

'Wait a minute,' he said. 'I'll just let the others know what's happening.' He disappeared and returned almost immediately, sliding quickly into the driving seat.

As they started off, he dropped a hand lightly on her knee. 'Where to, ma'am?' he enquired. 'I sure don't want the canon and his wife to lose their beauty sleep.'

12

Katy Mason sat at her small antique bureau writing out cheques. Over the years she had become most methodical about accounting and, with May's assistance, had kept to a sensible and satisfactory form of budgeting. Of late, however, there had been two items which had not exactly come into her calculations, particularly the first. This was the matter of some sixty pounds a term to cover Paul Woodley's education and school uniform. The second — more likely to have been expected sooner or later — was the subsidizing of her now widowed sister, however difficult it had been to get Edith to accept anything at all.

So far, Katy had told no one except May about the arrangement she had come to with Barbara Woodley and, to her great relief, so far there had been no unfortunate repercussions. No letters had passed between them. Barbara merely sent the account and Katy posted her a cheque by return. Yet now, as for the third time she studied the flimsy printed sheet headed *Westwood Preparatory School for Boys*, and noted that there was a little extra for cricket coaching during the forthcoming summer term, she was overcome by a sudden desire to see the child. He would be ten years old soon. She wondered how he fared during the holidays, how his mother was and whether she had been able to work again. According to the postmark on the latest envelope, Barbara was presumably still in Wales. Katy supposed that some time she ought to tell Emily that she had a half-brother, but somehow she shrank from it. Life wasn't easy for the girl at the moment and she had an uneasy feeling that their new billetee had something to do with it. She still found Vernon Keeler extremely polite and pleasant whenever they happened to meet, but there was about him a self-assurance, a sophistication, which was disconcerting. He was so very much a man of the world and although she was glad to think that her daughter occasionally had a little fun, she was sorry when she learned that he had asked to take her to the pictures.

Emily herself had actually been none too happy about the invitation either; but he had been so persuasive and had been so kind about getting her back to the Fawcetts' on her last leave that she had eventually agreed, provided that they went on an evening when she came off duty early. Even so, it had meant asking Mrs Fawcett for permission to stay out slightly later and the subsequent interrogation which went on almost made the outing seem hardly worth it.

'Who will you be going with, Emily?' Agnes Fawcett looked at her out of faded reproachful eyes, her whole manner somehow suggesting that there was something wrong, even sinful, in what she was proposing to do.

'A Lieutenant Keeler, Mrs Fawcett. He's an American officer.'

'An *American* officer?' While sharing her husband's relief that so many US troops had arrived in the country, she was nevertheless scared of them, despite the fact that a nice friendly corporal had offered to carry her shopping basket back from the market a day or so previously. 'Is it someone your mother knows?'

'Yes, Mrs Fawcett. He's billeted at home.'

'Oh, I *see*.' Although the information put a slightly different complexion on things, Emily still heard her muttering to herself as she went away, a habit which was becoming increasingly apparent every time she was upset.

'You've sure got problems,' Vernon said that evening when, after knocking, Agnes had asked him to wait on the pavement until Emily came out of the front door. 'Can't you find a more reasonable landlady?'

She laughed. 'I'm afraid not. It's all worked out by the hospital authorities.'

Summer seemed all at once to have arrived that week and she had changed into a light frock, letting her hair fall loosely on her shoulders in the way she usually wore it when not in uniform. Over her left arm she carried a cardigan and, as they walked along side by side, she noticed him glance at the ring on her third finger.

'Who's the lucky guy, Emily?'

She flushed. 'His name is John Moreton. He's a prisoner of war. He was shot down in 1940 and picked up in the Channel by some Germans.'

'Say! That's too bad. Had you known him long before that?'

'Since I was a child.' Her reply was abrupt, somewhat defensive. She decided that she did not really want to discuss John with this strange American, although she was at a loss to know why.

He took her to an officers' club before the film started and seemed surprised when she only asked for a soft drink with her sandwich. He himself ordered a Scotch. She supposed he was probably finding her as dull a companion as she feared most other young men did these days and was relieved when they were at last inside the Gaumont Palace, where she became completely enthralled watching Greer Garson in *Mrs Miniver*. Afterwards, with great courtesy, he escorted her back to the Fawcetts', gave her a smart salute outside the front door and disappeared into the dusk. He will not, she said to herself as she climbed into bed, ask me out again. As she drifted off to sleep, she thought she would prefer it if he didn't. It was hard to explain but there was something about him which, for all his charming spontaneity, was a little perplexing and overwhelming.

Emily Mason was not the only person in the district who found that the presence of some individual American in their lives created curious and unexpected situations. The Fairfaxes, for instance, had accommodated Colonel Beatty in their small newly converted stable flat. As far as Edmund was concerned, the fact that their billetee often produced a bottle of whisky more than compensated for having to live at such close quarters with him. He found the Colonel good company. Rachel, on the other hand, though usually kindly disposed towards all and sundry, took a poor view of the two men's drinking sessions, although she had to admit to herself that a third party about the place helped to alleviate her husband's boredom and discontent, which he was apt to make so apparent whenever they spent an evening alone together. She had been almost relieved when, after Hitler had ceased his aerial bombardment of the country and turned his attentions towards Russia the previous June, Edmund had begun to go to London again. His absences were not now quite so frequent, but she could not help wondering whether Chloe Ford – of whom she had always been well aware – had come back into the picture again, or whether he had taken another less demanding mistress. It did not greatly bother her. She had never been very interested in sex. She had made her own life now. She kept in constant touch with her two daughters – Gillian still at school and Belinda, who had just joined the FANYs – she had the pleasure of seeing the successful conversion of the Hall into a convalescent home and the gradual feeling that the people of Wilhampton, if not exactly regarding her in the same light as her revered mother-in-law, nevertheless liked her and appreciated her well-meaning efforts on behalf of the war and the local community as a whole.

Certainly, this kind of satisfaction did not apply in the case of one of her neighbours, the wife of the man who was giving so much of his time helping to care for the disturbed patients in Rachel Fairfax's former home. Clare Fitzherbert had become more and more disliked in later years. Since the war, it was rare for anyone to hear a good word said about her. She had taken in no evacuee children at the beginning and now, incredible as it seemed, it was being put about that she had become a little too friendly with a middle-aged American captain to whom she and Maurice had let a bedroom. No one quite knew how the rumour had started, but it seemed to have something to do with one of the mill-hands having seen her and Captain Bradley Butler sitting close together on a seat by the Willon which ran along the bottom of East Lodge garden.

For Maurice's sake, Ethel Sharman had done her best to stop the tittle-tattle. 'It's a wicked shame,' she said to May, one teatime when the latter had called in to see her on her way back from the Hall. 'With him so good, one just doesn't want to hear that his household isn't anything but ... well ... as clean and straight as he is. She may not have made him much of a wife but we can't have people saying that she's no better than she should be. Besides, at her time of life it's ridiculous. Although I suppose that might have something to do with it. I mean . . . some women do act a little strange then. But she's always been such a buttoned-up little thing. Not the type to go fooling around. Personally, I don't believe there's a word of truth in it. It's all the fault of that loud-mouth, Lilian Perrick's grandson, who's too weak in the head to get into the army.'

But despite Ethel's loyal efforts, the rumours proliferated. Clare was said to have been seen one night putting up the black-out herself at the Captain's windows, while he hovered in the background; she was reported to have spent twenty-four clothing coupons – half a year's ration – on a new outfit and, in keeping with many another Wilhampton housewife, when not bare-legged in the warmer weather, she now wore nylons.

Maurice Fitzherbert had at first been pleased when his wife seemed altogether more agreeable. Even when it dawned on him that the proximity of Captain Butler was the cause, he had not really minded. As with the Fairfaxes' marriage, a third party in the ménage, even if he was out a great deal of the time, somehow relieved the tension. Clare had ceased to nag. Having never been able to make her happy himself, his nature was such that he did not resent anyone who could. Working the clock round as he was doing, it seemed all to the good that she had some agreeable company of an evening. It never occurred to him that her relationship with Brad – as they had come to call him – could or would be anything other than platonic. After all, Clare had made it abundantly clear on their honeymoon that she found the sexual act abhorrent.

He was called out one night in July to attend a woman in labour on downside. It was 4 a.m. before he returned. As he climbed the stairs he noticed a dim light showing beneath his wife's door. She had said something about a headache the previous evening and he wondered whether she might be unwell. He gave a gentle tap. When there was no reply, he quietly turned the handle.

He closed the door again so silently that, as he went on to his own room, he did not think they could possibly have heard him. He did not undress. He simply lay down on his bed wondering how it was that a middle-aged and not particularly attractive-looking American, whom his wife had only known a few months, had succeeded where he himself, twenty years ago, had so lamentably failed.

13

'Squa . . . ad, abaaht turn! Quick march. *Squa . . . ad*, Halt! Right turn. Mark time . . . Come on now, pick 'em up, ladies, pick 'em up. Squ . . . ad, Halt! Stand easy.'

Helen Swayne often wanted to giggle when RSM Franks drilled them on the parade ground at Guildford. It seemed so ridiculous for a whole lot of women to be doing a kind of 'knees up' as this extraordinary little man – who had naturally been nicknamed Frankenstein – roared orders to them. It was a far cry from the life she had known at Bulbarrow. On the other hand, she was enjoying it and, just before being sent on a pre-OCTU course, she had met a young Lieutenant named Colin Mackay with whom she was now conducting a regular correspondence.

Earlier that summer she had been singled out to go before War Office Selection Board – Wosbies, as they were called – with a view to becoming an ATS officer. She had spent the best part of three days being tested for qualities of leadership, intelligence, stability and practicality. She had come through the ordeal well. Her experiences while helping her father on the farm had stood her in good stead when it came to such things as seeing the best way of lifting a dummy casualty over a gate, or working out a pay-sheet, or organizing the evacuation of a building because of a mock bomb scare. She had been involved in plenty of crises at Bulbarrow, known the value of corporate effort and the necessity for someone to take charge in an emergency in a prompt unflustered way. At the end of her testing period not one of her superiors was in any doubt that Helen Swayne was officer material. Now, incarcerated with all the other cadets in a Nissen hut by 9 p.m. each night, she would sit on her hard camp bed writing letters to Colin, her parents, her two brothers – Bob now with the Eighth Army in North Africa – and Emily.

'Can you imagine, Em,' ran her latest one to her best friend, 'marching up and down three times a day, with this ferocious chap bellowing at us and saying he's never seen such a lot of slouchers! Mind you, it's good for the figure. I've got quite a *waist* now in spite of so much potato pie. If ever I get to my passing-out parade and acquire a Sam Browne you won't know me . . .'

Emily sat reading the letter on her equally hard bed at the Fawcetts', and smiled. She was glad Helen seemed to be doing so well and liking the life she had chosen. It was good, also, to know that she had a young man, whom she was apparently hoping to bring home to meet her parents when they could synchronize their respective leaves. She herself was missing John William very much these days. Since taking her to *Mrs Miniver*, Vernon Keeler had asked her out several times but she had accepted only once, when it was unavoidable. She had happened to be at home and he had suggested taking her to a party in a neighbouring village, given by a woman who seemed to specialize in entertaining American officers. It had been quite an interesting experience in the beginning and she had listened with surprise and pleasure while Vernon sang 'Ave Maria', realizing that he had a remarkably good voice. But, later on, she had begun to feel out of things, especially when most of the others – now slightly inebriated – clustered round a piano singing 'Deep in the Heart of Texas', 'Praise the Lord and Pass the Ammunition' and 'Chattanooga Choo-Choo, Won't You Choo-Choo Me Home'.

It was well into autumn before Vernon telephoned to ask her out again, suggesting that they should go to see Leslie Howard in *49th Parallel* when it came to Weston-bury the following week. Before she could reply, he had continued, quickly, 'It won't be like last time, Emily. I mean, I know you didn't enjoy all that sing-song stuff.' She had become acutely embarrassed, particularly as she knew that Agnes Fawcett was hovering disapprovingly on the other side of the baize door leading to the kitchen. 'I just can't, Vernon,' she managed to break in at last. 'You see, I'm going to Suffolk then to stay with my fiancé's parents.' There had been quite a pause before he had said, quietly, 'Ah, I *see*.' For some unknown reason she found that she was trembling when they rang off.

She travelled up to Waterloo on a grey misty morning at the beginning of November. It would be her third visit to Bishopsdown and although she found staying with Alicia and Charles Moreton a little nerve-racking, she was looking forward to it – especially since the advent of Vernon Keeler into the ménage at home had not only deprived her of her bedroom, but the very fact that he was there at all somehow disturbed her. She had been hoping he might be posted soon, but May had just informed her that he had been promoted to captain and appeared to be taking on more and more responsibility in the camp on Barbury. It was not, she supposed, surprising, for he was obviously an extremely able and unusual young man, infinitely superior to some of the other American officers she had met, the ones, for instance, who had clustered round the piano, crooning the night away.

Katy had been a little worried about her daughter's journey to Suffolk – not, this time, through fear of airraids on London, for these had mercifully ceased – but because on previous occasions Alicia had always come there to meet her. Now, however, owing to various commitments in the country, she had asked if Emily could get herself to Liverpool Street and catch a train for Ipswich. 'You'll take a taxi, darling, won't you?' her mother had said. And she had replied, shortly, 'All right.'

Emily knew that she had sounded ungracious, but she was becoming increasingly annoyed at the way she was so often treated like a child by her elders. After all, she would be twenty-one in a month's time. She could look after herself. She had been nursing for the best part of three years. She might not have had much experience of the opposite sex from the emotional point of view, but there was little that she did not know about men when she thought of all the bodies she had had to care for daily.

Moreover, she was *engaged*, wasn't she? She looked down at the ring on her finger. One day, surely, it would come right. There had been talk of a Second Front for quite a while. The English and Americans would cross the Channel, sweep across Europe and John William would be liberated and return home. They would be married at St Mark's in Wilhampton and Aunt Chip, bless her, would make the wedding dress.

But on her arrival at Bishopsdown, Charles Moreton did little but talk about the gravity of the situation in the Middle East and the battle being waged by General Montgomery round El Alamein. The first attack had gone badly. 'We've had enough reverses,' he kept saying, as he sat close to his wireless set, listening for whatever scraps of news were allowed to be given out to the listening nation. 'We've got to win this one. What happened at Tobruk last summer was a disgrace.'

When, on the night of November 4th, a programme was interrupted warning people not to switch off their sets because an important announcement would be made at midnight, the man's voice was obviously charged with excitement. A few hours later a communiqué from Cairo revealed that the Germans were in full retreat. Charles Moreton went down to the cellar and brought up a bottle of champagne.

Throughout the rest of Emily's visit, the atmosphere at Bishopsdown was more light-hearted than she had ever known it. Alicia's habitual tenseness seemed to disappear. She and her prospective daughter-in-law went for long walks together, when Emily learned more and more about John's early years.

'He was always so different from his sister,' Alicia said one afternoon. 'I often think they should have changed places – or, rather, sexes. John was awfully brave to join up at once. He must have hated the RAF deep down. As a little boy, he loathed seeing anything killed, even a wasp. I expect you remember what he thought about horses and hunting. Later on his father was furious when he found out he felt the same about shooting and fishing. I can remember the head keeper once bringing John home in tears after a rabbit shoot.'

They were on their way back to Bishopsdown now and in the bare flat Suffolk landscape Emily could see the house in the distance: grey, gaunt and somehow forbidding-looking. Would she really be one day mistress of the place? Somehow, because John William so adored the west country and had been left Netherford Grange by his maternal grandmother, she had always imagined living there – that is, so far as she had imagined anything at all. One hardly dared look into the future too much. But the news of the recent victory in the Middle East, and the fact that she was staying in John's family home when it had taken place, had started her thinking. His parents would, she hoped, live to a good old age and there was no knowing what he might do if and when, please God, the war was over. It could be many years before she might be required to become responsible for such a formidable establishment.

Suddenly, as she and Alicia walked up the long tree-lined drive, a couple of golden retrievers at their heels, the memory of her last conversation with Vernon Keeler came unaccountably into her mind. She could hear again that curious 'I *see*' at the end of it. What, for goodness' sake, did he see? He might be an ally but he was an alien. He knew nothing about England and the English and the way in which, for all the difference in social distinctions, she and her fiancé had been brought up. Vernon was an inter-loper, a looker-on who could not possibly understand and appreciate the codes and customs of what he referred to as 'the old country'. Or could he? He was unusually intelli-gent and perceptive, more so, she suspected – while hating herself for such a disloyal thought – than John William.

At the end of the week she travelled back to Westonbury and was surprised to find her mother waiting for her at the station. Petrol for private motoring being non-existent, it had been arranged that Emily would simply walk straight back to the Fawcetts', ready to go on duty the following morning. After all, her small suitcase would be fractionally lighter without the little present – an edition of Mrs Duer Miller's *The White Cliffs* – which she had bought for Alicia, and the rations she had also taken with her. She was well aware that, whoever one stayed with, a few ounces of butter, cheese, tea and sugar were not only acceptable but expected, as well as a bar of soap.

As she came along the cold windswept platform, she could tell from Katy's face that something was wrong. She put down her case as her mother leaned forward to kiss her.

'What is it, Mummy?'

'I thought I would come, darling,' Katy said slowly, and hesitated, unsure whether to say more or wait a while.

Quickly, Emily made the decision for her. 'Please, what is it?' she asked again. 'You've bad news, haven't you?'

'Yes. We only heard today. Bob Swayne was killed at Alamein. Helen will be coming home on forty-eight hours' compassionate leave tomorrow. I thought . . . well . . . you should know. I expect you may want to see each other.'

Emily stood quite still, staring at Katy disbelievingly. Passengers jostled past them, yet they seemed unreal. The noise of people shouting greetings to each other came as if from a long way off. 'Oh, no,' she said, and then again, 'Oh, *no!*'

They were the last two to come through the ticket barrier. Katy had one of the Parkers' taxis waiting for them outside and in less than ten minutes it pulled up outside the Fawcetts'. Without saying more, Emily kissed her mother goodnight and went indoors.

It was freezing in her bedroom, and Agnes Fawcett was not a woman to think of putting a hot-water bottle in a billetee's bed. But it did not matter. Not now. Bob Swayne, her best friend's brother, had lost his life fighting in the desert, while she had been celebrating the victory he had helped to ensure. He was always so cheerful and gallant and, in a way, just as handsome as John William. She had sensed that, kind as he had been in sending congratulations on her engagement, he had been secretly disappointed. She knew he admired her and she had hoped that it might not be too long before he, too, acquired a fiancée. But now he never would. That lively energetic figure, so loved by all who knew him, would never come bounding up the drive at Bulbarrow, calling out a friendly greeting to anyone within earshot. Poor Dick and Dorothy. And Helen and Tim. What would they do? It didn't bear thinking of. What *was* the war all about? God, why couldn't it *end*?

She was unable to cry. She simply lay in bed numbly, hearing the Fawcetts' grandfather clock in the hall strike the hours. Only when, some days later, the church bells rang out all over Britain, not to announce an invasion but to mark a victory, did she lock herself in one of the lavatories at Ashmore and burst into tears.

14

It was not often that Maurice Fitzherbert could pay courtesy calls these days, but one afternoon in the early part of the New Year he happened to be driving down the Bulbarrow lane and realized that he just had time to visit the Swaynes. He had done so whenever he could since their bereavement, invariably coming away marvelling at Dick and Dorothy's fortitude and lack of bitterness. It was true that both seemed to have aged considerably in the last two months and, although they received him with the same obvious warmth and pleasure, there was a certain quietness about them, a look – when caught off guard – of sadness which he knew would always remain.

'Oh, Maurice. How nice. Do come in.' Dorothy opened the front door in answer to his knock. She was even thinner than he remembered her at Christmas and her greying hair was now almost completely white. 'Dick will be back shortly,' she continued. 'He went up to see how Porty and Charlie Harper were getting on opening up the potato clamp. Let me get you a cup of tea.'

Ignoring his protests that he did not really need it, she ushered him straight into their large, warm and welcoming kitchen and set the kettle on the range. There was something about the Swaynes, Maurice felt, that no amount of evil or adversity could warp or destroy. They were like that other farming couple at Netherford, the Farleys of

Sweetacres. Was it, he wondered, the daily involvement with all living things – humans, animals and plants – and the knowledge and acceptance of their ultimate death which set them apart? As a doctor, he was only concerned with the first category. But the Swaynes and Farleys went further. They were caught up in something much more basic. He knew, of course, that not every marriage in the farming fraternity was as blessed as those of the two he knew best, but of all his patients, the ones who lived in close contact with the land seemed by far the easiest and least demanding to deal with.

'I gather Porty is shaping up well,' he said, as she handed him a cup of tea.

'Oh, yes. He's a miracle, that child. Dick's just given him a rise. He's still only fourteen, but he's as good as a grown man at many jobs. What's more, he's such company for Edith Lench, since she's been a widow and most of her family have left the nest.'

'Yes, so I understand.' At the mention of Edith, he made a mental note that she was another person on whom he must call when next he was on downside, not as a doctor but as a friend.

'We had a letter from Helen this morning,' Dorothy went on, as she sat down opposite him in an old basket chair. 'Her passing-out parade is in a week's time and I'm going up to Windsor for it. D'you know, Maurice, I haven't spent a day away since the war began. I must say I'm looking forward to it. Poor child. I think she feels since Bob was killed . . . well, guilty for ever having joined up. She tells me she's put in for a compassionate posting to Southern Command when she's commissioned, so that she'll be able to get home more easily.'

'I'm glad.' He was glad, also, at the simple and direct way both Dorothy and her husband always brought Bob's name into their conversation. 'What news of Tim?' he asked.

'Oh, he's fine. Still up near Chester. He got his second pip last week. He insists that his sister will have to salute *him* first when next they meet.'

There was the sound of footsteps on the gravel outside

and soon Dick Swayne joined them. They talked mostly of farming matters for another quarter of an hour and then Maurice got up to go.

His own home seemed singularly cheerless as he let himself in that evening. Clare appeared to be out, but he had no idea where. Since conscription of unmarried women had come into force just over a year ago and all married women were obliged to undertake some form of national service, Clare had become a member of the WVS, but she was extremely uncommunicative about what she did or where she went. Had theirs been a different marriage, he realized that she might well have taken Ethel Sharman's place and been thereby exempt from other war work, rather like Dorothy Swayne who did so much to help Dick, both indoors and out. But Clare had always seemed to resent being a doctor's wife, so much so that even when her presence was expected at some medical dinner or dance, he had often found himself attending such functions alone.

It occurred to him that her present absence might have something to do with Bradley Butler, who had been sent on a three-weeks' course twenty-five miles away on Salisbury Plain. But he did not greatly care. Since that fatal night when he had found her in bed with the man, he had felt too weary, too old and far too busy to tackle her about it. They had lived for so long as strangers in this over-large house, which she had made no attempt to turn into a more attractive home, that the present situation only grieved him from the point of view of gossip. When, eventually, he heard her return shortly before ten, he was already in bed. He switched off the light, the same picture coming into his mind as it so often did at such times: that of Katy Mason, wearing a blue taffeta frock in the winter of 1920, when he had taken her to her first dance.

Possibly, because of the sense of togetherness which he had witnessed that afternoon between Dick and Dorothy Swayne, he thought of her more than ever that night. He had not actually seen Katy for some weeks now, but only the previous day he had caught a brief glimpse of Emily when he had had to make an emergency call at Ashmore.

He had not thought she looked at all well. There were deep shadows under her eyes, an almost haunted expression on her face. He knew that she could hardly be finding life easy these days. John William had been a prisoner almost two and a half years now. The situation distressed him. He could not help wondering whether perhaps it had been altogether wise for the young couple to have become officially engaged. Emily was far too conscientious and serious-minded to be able to enjoy herself under such circumstances and, in consequence, was obviously leading an unnatural life for a girl of her age. He wondered if she realized it herself.

Emily did, in fact, realize it only too well. As she went about taking temperatures and pulses, making beds, cleaning bedpans and cycling backwards and forwards between Ashmore and the Fawcetts', she had begun to wonder how much longer she could keep up the pretence. For some time now, ever since, in fact, she had last stayed with the Moretons, she had known that she was not in love with John William. But that was by no means all. She knew that she was hopelessly in love with Vernon Keeler.

Such a possibility was something she had fought shy of admitting to herself long before that. But now, since Boxing Day, it had been impossible to close her mind to it. She had happened to come home that afternoon, surprised to find that Vernon was there and also appeared to have a few hours free. He had suggested going for a bicycle ride and they had gone up to Barbury, and then pushed their bicycles along the track until they reached the old keeper's cottage belonging to the Fairfaxes. It was semi-derelict, the only temporary occupants being members of the Home Guard who sometimes used it as a shelter at night. It had been a very cold clear day, the sky a pale icy blue, dotted about here and there with small white clouds like soapsuds. For a while, they had leant against the porch looking down on the Willon Valley in silence. All at once, she had shivered and, without quite knowing how it had happened, she had allowed herself to be drawn inside. In a shaft of winter sunlight, filtering through one of the latticed windows, she had noticed an old primus stove, a kettle, a couple of tin mugs and a broken-down bunk.

Vernon wasted no time. Leading her across the room, he pushed her gently down on the bunk and began kissing her firmly in a way she had never before experienced. When she had made an attempt to stop him, he had put a finger on her lips and said, with mock severity, 'Come now, Emily, you know perfectly well it's what you've been waiting for.' And, as he began kissing her again, she had known that he was right.

That night, back in her cold uncomfortable bed, she had felt, both mentally and physically, in a turmoil. She was aware that it had been Vernon, not she, who had finally and abruptly broken off their dalliance. Pulling her almost roughly to her feet, he had said, 'Come on. We must go. Girls like you are too much of a good thing to be alone with in a place like this.'

She had known, without wanting to know, what he meant. She had known that she wanted to be alone with him, that she would have liked him to go on kissing her, that she would have liked . . . And here, clutching a pillow to her body more tightly, she had suddenly started trembling again, just as she had done when he had said, 'I *see*,' at the end of his telephone call before she had gone to Bishopsdown. She knew, at last, what it was to be in love, physically, to want what she had never wanted – and had, indeed, been frightened of – with John William.

But, as the days went by, she did not know what to do about it. There was no one – except, perhaps, Helen Swayne if she had been around – in whom she could confide. She could not tell her mother or her aunt, although she feared that they must certainly have suspected something. She could never tell John's mother. Far less could she ever tell John, incarcerated as he was in the most appalling conditions in a German prisoner-of-war camp – especially when his last letter, written in November and which had only just come through, ran: 'I shall be thinking about you on Christmas Day. I hope to be home next August . . . We shall have to discover each other again. I wonder if you will have changed. Something tells me that

501

you won't. Is England much the same? Are all the young people getting married? Time is dragging along here. There is snow on the surrounding hills and it is pretty cold. Unfortunately, our Red Cross parcel issue has been cut to one a fortnight . . .'

When a man was living on little other than hope, she could not, would not, deprive him of that. John William believed in her, trusted her. It was all the more unthinkable when, in one of his earlier letters, he had said, 'Some of the others here have been receiving what we call their "rejection slips" – you know, girls not wanting to wait. Somehow, I don't feel you'll ever send me one of those. At least, I pray you won't . . .'

Moreover, she kept saying to herself, it wasn't as if Vernon Keeler had asked to marry her. He was still rather a mystery. She knew so little about his background. And she realized that she was not by any means his only girl-friend, however painful it was to accept. Kissing her in the keeper's cottage on Barbury was probably incidental to him. Or was it? She believed – or liked to believe – that he enjoyed her company. Certainly, they had begun to have longer and longer discussions on the arts, philosophy and the world conflict in which they were caught up. He had intimated that it was good to find a girl who 'kinda thought'.

At last, with infinite regret, she decided that the only thing to do would be to write to him, tell him that she had behaved wrongly on Boxing Day, that she would not be able to go out with him again and that their association must cease. It would be a difficult letter to word, but she would have to do it and the sooner the better. She would address it to the camp, as her mother or aunt would be sure to notice her handwriting if she sent it to the White Hermitage.

Having made up her mind on this course of action, she was cycling up to Ashmore the following day at a quarter past seven, with the letter – as yet unsealed – still in her pocket. Having spent many cold and agonizing hours over its composition the previous night, she wanted to have one final check before consigning it to the pillar-box. As she neared the hospital gates, a figure stepped down from a stationary jeep and a voice said, 'Hi, Emily. I didn't know how else to contact you, what with the life you seem to lead between two prisons. I'm afraid it's short notice but we've got quite an important do on. I've only just heard. There's some brass hat coming down to inspect the camp and I've been asked to sing after dinner tonight. I'm allowed one guest. Will you come?'

She hesitated, acutely aware of the unposted letter — lying like some self-imposed stumbling-block — in her pocket, of her resolve, of the fact that it would, in any case, be difficult to swap evening duties, let alone obtain Agnes Fawcett's permission. All she had to do was to hand over the envelope and run.

Instead, she stood there silently in the half-light of the cold January morning. The look in his eyes left her in no doubt that her acceptance was important to him. She would manage it somehow. She *had* to manage it.

'Thank you, Vernon,' she said, quietly. 'I should love to come.'

15

'You didn't actually . . . ?'

'No, of course not, Mummy.' Impatiently, Emily cut her mother short.

'Thank God.'

Katy had not been able to refrain from expressing her overwhelming relief out loud. There was silence then between them. She went across to the window and stood looking down on the garden and the river beyond. Everywhere there were signs of approaching summer. The fallen blossom from the fruit trees lay thick and white on the grass and the Sweetacres herd of shorthorns had been turned out in the water-meadows again for their early bite. Inside the Hermitage, Emily lay in bed, once more in her own room since Vernon Keeler had been posted a few weeks earlier.

Katy had returned from the Hall early that afternoon in

order to have a talk with her daughter in complete privacy. She had been distressed when Miss Butler had telephoned from Ashmore the previous day to say that she was sending Emily home on a fortnight's sick leave, as the doctor in charge of the nurses' health considered that she needed a complete rest. She had been having fainting fits, her periods were irregular, she was extremely anaemic and he would be glad if Dr Fitzherbert could attend her meanwhile. Maurice was due to call later on, either before or after evening surgery.

Katy knew that her daughter would never lie to her. The worst had not happened. Emily had not been seduced. She was not pregnant. On the other hand, it was alarming to see her looking so wretched. Katy had long suspected that there was some trouble connected with Vernon Keeler, but she had never thought it was quite so serious. She had relied on Emily's good sense. Now, she could have kicked herself for not stepping in sooner. When it came to affairs of the heart, she should have known that sense was nowhere in it. The day that Vernon suddenly announced he would be leaving and going to London, she had merely given a sigh of relief and trusted that that would put an end to the problem. She had been totally unprepared for Emily to have subsequently broken down over it. Gently, she tried a little further probing.

'When did you first realize you were . . . well, quite so attracted to him?' Katy could not bring herself to say 'in love'.

'Ages ago.'

'And Vernon?'

'I'm . . . not sure.'

'Has he said anything to you about marriage?'

'Yes. Soon after Christmas.'

'What exactly did he say?'

'That he probably had no right to ask, but if I wasn't sure about . . . John, would I consider becoming his wife.'

'And what did you say?'

'What *could* I say?' Emily began to sob, uncontrollably.

Katy came across to the bed and tried to put her arms round her, but she was instantly rebuffed. I'm handling

504

this badly, she thought. I ought to be able to help. I've comforted plenty of other people in distress lately, but now that it's my own daughter in need, I don't know what to do. It isn't as if I can't remember my own youth, what it was like when I was so desperately in love with Philip and Sarah was so set on my marrying Maurice. God, it's like history repeating itself, except that Emily's plight is so much worse. There's that poor young man out in Germany. I, at least, was a little more free to follow my heart, even if I suppose it did mean breaking Maurice's. But at least he wasn't in a prisoner-of-war camp at the time. I suppose Emily feels she *has* to remain true to John. She can't just run off with Vernon. I wonder if it would have been better if, in the end, I hadn't been so headstrong, if I'd settled down with Maurice? Marriages based on strong physical attraction aren't always necessarily the ones which last. Vernon Keeler, for all his good qualities, doesn't strike me as being altogether the faithful type. He's got the same fatal magnetism about him that Philip had. And if he's really set on a singing career, Emily might have a terrible life if she married him. And we wouldn't even know. She would go off to the States when the war was over and we'd hardly ever see her. It doesn't bear thinking about.

Her daughter seemed to have ceased crying now and Katy fell back on that simple, mundane, but – as she had come to find – often surprisingly efficacious form of comfort. 'I'll go down and make us both a cup of tea, darling,' she said.

Emily shut her eyes, her thoughts going back, as they invariably did whenever she was alone, to the last time she had seen Vernon. She had been on night duty and he had written to ask if she could meet him that Sunday morning at the Black Horse before she had to report back to the nurses' quarters by eleven o'clock. She had been surprised at his request. Since the time when she had thrown caution to the winds and accompanied him to the dinner at Barbury camp at the beginning of the year, they had taken much more care not to be seen together. For both had known, that night, that their love affair was rather more serious than 'Just One of Those Things', as the popular song of the moment put it. They had therefore met, secretly, whenever possible. The coming of the lighter evenings — until she went on night duty — had given them more opportunity for cycling into the countryside together. Such assignations had often, Emily felt, been tempting fate. But their lovemaking, mostly thanks to Vernon, had always stopped just short of what she supposed was the point of no return. Whenever she had come home to the Hermitage, he had been careful to absent himself so that they hardly met. Sometimes she had lain awake agonizing over where he was or with whom he might be. Every time she received a little note — he no longer telephoned her at the Fawcetts' — suggesting a rendezvous, she felt powerless to refuse. Her whole being had felt on fire as she went to meet him. She had not stopped to think where their relationship was leading. She only knew that she had to see him, that she lived to see him. If he now wanted to see her at the Black Horse — the place where he had tried to take her the first time they had met — then to the Black Horse she would go.

He had been sitting on an old wooden seat in front of the inn when she arrived, a little breathless, on her bicycle. He had suggested going round to the back and walking down to where the Willon ran along at the bottom of the garden. The sun had not quite broken through the early morning mist, which still hung over the meadows. She remembered thinking, with intense bitterness, that in a few hours she would have to return to her hot, cramped cubicle for what would probably be another almost sleepless day.

She recalled sitting down on a different seat and Vernon saying 'Emily' in such a curious way that she had at once been put on her guard. 'I've something to say to you,' he had continued. Then, when she did not reply, he had told her, quite simply, that he was going away. 'As a matter of fact, I've already left the Hermitage,' he said. 'I stayed here last night.'

She had not been able to take it in at first.

'Where?' she managed to ask, at last.

'London. I'm being posted. I'm to be a sort of liaison officer at the War Office.'

She had stared at him, incredulously. 'When . . . ?' Her voice was no more than a whisper now.

'I'm leaving Westonbury on the midday train.'

She could recall looking down at her hands, slightly red and roughened by her work, now lying clasped tightly together in her lap. She saw a stain on her uniform dress, which she had not had a chance to change since coming off duty; she noticed that her black lace-up shoes were badly in need of a clean. Somewhere, quite near at hand, a cuckoo kept calling, persistently. She felt as if time, for her, had stopped, and yet she was acutely aware of life going on round about as if nothing had happened, that the Willon, now sparkling in the May sunshine, was meandering along in its usual purposeful, yet unhurried, way. She thought how strange it was that all the important episodes in her life seemed to have taken place near or beside it.

Presently, he picked up one of her hands and said, 'Look, darling. When I asked you to marry me after Christmas I didn't feel it was very likely you'd accept. I shouldn't have done so, really, knowing how you were placed. This guy in Germany . . . he's obviously a good chap, poor devil. Anyway, I believe you'll at least have to wait and see him again. You'd never be happy if you let him down now. You're too fine a person. And, who knows, we may not be getting a Second Front this year, but it'll come next. That's for sure.'

She had known he was right, but it hadn't made the situation any better. It had never occurred to her in her misery that he had probably put in for a posting, that, under the circumstances, he was behaving extremely well. She only knew that if he had suddenly whipped out a special licence so that they could have married immediately, she would have done so without question. She had also known something else. If he had asked her, then and there, to come up to his room, she would have gone.

They had taken the less frequented route back to Ashmore. He had pushed her bicycle and, at a point where she could take a short cut through some trees, he had stopped and leant it against a giant oak. Taking her in his arms he had said, 'I'll never forget you, Emily. But . . . try to forget me.'

That night, while standing at a patient's bedside, she had fainted.

16

'I understand she's ill.'

'Yes.'

'Have you any idea exactly what's the matter? Her mother sounded rather vague, I thought, when I rang last week.'

'Not really. I think the girl's just been overdoing things.'

'And, of course, missing darling John.'

Rachel Fairfax changed the subject. She had some first-hand evidence of Emily's trouble, but she was not going to tell anybody about it. She would never breathe a word about the day, a month or so ago, when she had been going to see a Red Cross commandant in a neighbouring county. Because her visit was of a semi-official kind, she had been able to use her car. She had driven through Westonbury and on up towards Ashmore, where she had branched off on to a seldom-used minor road, overtaking, in the process, a young nurse on a bicycle. Only after she had passed did she realize it was Emily. Normally, she would have stopped, but she was late and she realized that the girl seemed to be slowing down and dismounting. Her attention was then suddenly taken up by another figure on a bicycle – an American officer pedalling towards her at a furious rate. Before she rounded another bend, she could see, in her driving mirror, that the two of them were evidently meeting.

Rachel Fairfax, for all her apparent naïveté and self-deprecation, was no fool. In that one fleeting glimpse she had sized up the situation completely. Being of a kind, compassionate nature, she felt extremely sorry for the girl, for she knew enough about her character to realize that she would never indulge in any light-hearted love affair, especially with a fiancé in a German prisoner-of-war camp. In many ways, Rachel thought her sister-in-law's last remark singularly insensitive. Might not Alicia appreciate that, after all this time, Emily would not necessarily be missing John William quite as much as missing love itself? Surely she must realize that a girl of her age needed a relationship with a member of the opposite sex?

Maurice Fitzherbert said much the same to Katy one evening after Emily had been home for a fortnight and showed no signs of improvement.

'Couldn't you get her away somewhere, Katy? A complete change of scene might help.'

'Yes. I've thought of that. Alicia Moreton badly wants her to go up to Suffolk but, under the circumstances, I hardly feel that's wise.'

'No. How about you and her going away for a break together – that's if they can spare you from the Hall.'

'We could do that, I suppose, Maurice. Although . . . well, I'm not sure I'm the right person for Emily to be with just now. It might be better if May went.'

'Well, one or the other of you, then. A patient was telling me only the other day of a guest house near Oxford which, in spite of the times, he could well recommend.'

Katy felt unable to tell him that there was another reason why she would welcome a little time to herself, much as she would have liked his advice. Only the previous day she had had a letter from Barbara Woodley's sister, Betsy Morgan. Barbara was in hospital and, it would appear, dying. It was a curious letter in that the writer made it plain that unexpected circumstances had arisen which she would like to discuss with Katy, if it was at all possible. May, who despite her usual charitableness to all and sundry had from the very beginning strongly disapproved of her sister becoming involved in the situation, was decidedly against any such meeting. 'It'll only mean further trouble,' she said, on finally agreeing to take Emily away. 'Trouble and money,' she had added, shortly. 'You've got enough problems on hand as it is.'

All the same, having seen her and Emily off to Oxford,

Katy went to Wales. She chose a time when she hoped that she would not be too greatly missed at the Hall and wrote to ask Betsy Morgan to reserve her a room one Saturday night at some convenient small hotel. Naturally, Betsy booked her up at the place where she worked, the Green Dragon.

'It's the best I could do,' she said, rather apologetically, as she showed Katy up to an attic bedroom. 'The others on the first floor are mostly occupied by regulars. But at least this is a bit more comfortable than my own home. It's good of you to come.'

Katy was relieved at her manner. Betsy did not strike her as a troublemaker who was out for all she could get. She appeared to be an eminently sensible, genuine and warm-hearted person and her subsequent remark seemed to confirm this.

'You must have had a tiring journey. I expect you'd like a bite to eat now and perhaps we should talk in the morning. Anyway, I'm on duty until 10.30 p.m. Suppose I come early tomorrow before the bar opens. I don't know if you were thinking of seeing Barbara?'

'Well, yes, if she would like me to.'

'I think so. That is, if she recognizes you. Some days she's well . . . pretty far gone. I don't think I'll be able to go with you, as I can't get away from here till three and you said your train left Colwyn round about three-thirty.'

'That's right. Where is her hospital?'

'Not far from the station. I'll order you a taxi, shall I, at whatever time you say?'

'Thank you.'

Betsy stood, a little uncertainly, at the door. 'It's sad about Bar,' she said. 'But I don't know. Maybe it's for the best. She's been so depressed since her injuries. But it's cancer that's taking her away.'

'I see.'

'She's too ill to be consulted about the boy. That's why I wanted to talk to you. You see, I've got a few plans in mind and . . . well . . . I'd like your approval.'

Again, Katy was struck by Betsy's artlessness and sincerity. At dinner that night she kept wondering what plans Barbara's sister could possibly have in mind. She knew so little about her. She did not even know, until the following morning, that she was a widow, her husband's ship having gone down in the Atlantic the previous winter.

'Poor Bill,' he was such an optimist,' she said, as she referred to the event. 'He always used to say, "Be seeing you, my girl. Me and my Mae West are more than a match for any Jerry torpedo." One of his mates who was picked up came all the way from Portsmouth to visit me after he got back. He said that when Bill was last seen he was helping another bloke to climb up into a lifeboat. Just like him. It's the sort of thing he would have done.' Momentarily, Betsy turned away. Then, looking Katy straight in the face, she continued, 'That's why I believe I ought to do what I'm thinking of doing . . . what I want to talk to you about. You see . . . well, you know a bit more about life. You're sort of . . . well, you're like the parents of the other children Paul has made friends with at school, poor little blighter.'

'What is it,' Katy asked, gently, 'that you're thinking of doing, Betsy?'

'Marrying again,' came the unexpected reply. 'You see, there's this elderly chap who's a regular at the Green Dragon. I've known him years, long before I met Bill. He lives in a posh place up on the hill. Last year his wife died and he's lonely. He's asked me to become his wife. He's prepared to adopt Paul. It's a sort of solution, isn't it? There'd be no need for you to help out any more. Arthur Mead — that's his name, by the way — is rich. And I've always wanted children. But, of course, I don't *love* Arthur, if you see what I mean. I'm just sorry for him, like I am for Barbara and Paul. Maybe, for everyone's sake, that's what I should do.'

Katy was silent. She thought what an extraordinarily nice person Barbara's sister was. It was certainly an answer to the situation, one which she had never remotely envisaged.

'Would you,' she asked, after a while, 'be happy, Betsy?'

'Well, I suppose so. Doing what I could for Arthur and the child would be very worthwhile. And, do you know, in a funny way, I think Bill would have wanted it. And it isn't as if I haven't been quite honest with Arthur. He understands how I feel. I haven't kidded him along or anything. You could have knocked me down with a feather the night he saw me home and popped the question. You didn't come into the bar last night or you'd probably have noticed him sitting in a corner by himself. Very correct-looking. Well turned out. Of course, he's several cuts above me, if you see what I mean. He was a jeweller in his time.'

Katy had not noticed Arthur Mead the previous evening, although she had become aware of another woman watching her covertly throughout the meagre statutory five-shilling meal.

'Perhaps you would care to come down before lunch today and I'll introduce you,' Betsy continued. 'Then you can judge for yourself.'

Katy found Arthur Mead all that Betsy had made him out to be and more. He appeared to have been waiting for them and stood up courteously as soon as they entered the bar. He then insisted on buying them each a glass of sherry, although Betsy was obliged to leave them almost immediately to attend to other customers who had started to come in.

'I should do my best, Mrs Mason,' he said. 'I've known the Woodley family a great number of years. Betsy's pure gold. As for the boy, he's a fine lad. Mind you, I haven't seen as much of Paul as I should have liked because, fortunately for him, he's spent most of his school holidays with friends. Evidently a popular chap. But he needs a stable background. I think I could give them both that. Life hasn't been easy for Betsy lately.'

'No. I realize that. I think it all seems an excellent idea although . . .' She hesitated, not quite sure how to word her next sentence. 'I wouldn't like you to think I'm saying this just because it lets me out,' she finally went on.

He smiled. 'I'm sure you're not, Mrs Mason. You've been very good, under the circumstances. Barbara's getting in touch with you after all these years must have been painful.'

'Not . . . altogether. It was such a long time ago. Although, I must admit that I occasionally have a great desire to see Paul, but it would obviously not be wise, especially *now*.'

'You must be the best judge of that, Mrs Mason. You would, of course, be at liberty to visit us at any time.'

Presently she left him and went into the dining room, where she noticed the same woman in the corner, now staring at her with undisguised interest. After the meal, she sauntered across to Katy's table.

'I hope you don't mind my approaching you, Mrs Mason, but I happened to see your name and address in the visitors' book soon after you arrived. Wilhampton is not a part of England I know personally, although I know someone who lives there very well indeed.'

'Really?' There was something about the woman which both repelled and yet fascinated Katy. Though dissimilar in looks, she had about her the same air of arch knowingness which she felt sure Barbara Woodley must have had when she was young and fitter.

'Yes. Lord Fairfax, as a matter of fact. It's a small world, isn't it. I seem to recall having read in *The Times* quite a while ago that his nephew was engaged to your daughter. How is Edmund, by the way?'

'Very well, as far as I know.' Katy was annoyed to feel the colour coming to her cheeks.

'Good. Do give him my love when next you meet. I expect with your respective families linking up, as it were, you see quite a lot of each other. I suppose the young couple are married by now.'

'No,' replied Katy, shortly. 'I'm afraid my daughter's fiancé is a prisoner of war.'

'Oh? What a *shame*. I *am* sorry. How *horrid* for you all.'

Katy stood up. 'If you'll excuse me. I have a train to catch,' she said, and walked deliberately to the door.

As she was saying goodbye to Betsy, she asked, 'Who is the rather expensive-looking blonde who's staying here?'

'You mean Chloe? Or I suppose I should say Miss Ford.' Betsy gave an exclamation halfway between a sigh and a snort. 'She's well . . . one of those. God knows how she manages to avoid doing any war work these days. She's been staying here on and off since London was bombed in the Battle of Britain. She has . . . well . . . gentlemen friends.'

Just before Katy got into the taxi, Betsy said, 'I hope you won't get too much of a shock when you see Bar. I don't think she can last much longer.'

'Thank you for warning me. But I've seen quite a lot of illness where I work lately, even if the patients' troubles are rather more mental than physical.'

And I have, Katy thought grimly as the taxi bore her away, seen someone dying of cancer before. My eldest sister. It was a long time ago but I shall never forget. It was summer then, just as it is now. I swear the inside of the Mill House was almost as hot as the coal range which we had to keep going for cooking purposes. Poor Flo. I can see her lying in bed in the front room and the way her sunken eyes lit up whenever I went in, and how valiantly she tried to pretend she was getting better all the time.

Barbara Woodley made no such attempt as an elderly nurse showed Katy into the ward and placed some screens round her bed. She barely opened her eyes. It seemed doubtful that she knew who her visitor was, so Katy simply sat down on a chair and held one of her hands in silence. Only when she got up to go did Barbara appear to rally a little. 'Paul?' she enquired.

'Paul will be well taken care of, Barbara. There's nothing for you to worry about. I promise you.'

Suddenly she became conscious that the woman in the bed was staring at her, that her lips were trying to form a whispered. 'Thank you'. Then the eyes closed and Katy knew that Barbara had lost contact with the world again.

Miserably, she made her way out of the ward and down the dim depressing corridor, hating herself for having given the totally misleading impression that it was she and not Betsy who was taking on Paul.

'It's not too bad here,' Helen Swayne's letter ran. 'I'm in charge of thirty cooks and orderlies on Hayling Island. Mostly I sleep there, but I come back to Portsmouth on the ferry for a night at our officers' mess once a week, when I pick up the girls' wages for the following pay day.'

Emily sat in the nurses' common room at Ashmore, glad to have heard from Helen and not John. For a long time now, she had been finding her correspondence with the latter an increasing burden. In fact, so much of her present life seemed a burden these days. Sometimes she felt that letters from Helen and Frank François were the only thing she looked forward to. 'I've got an absolute shocker in my platoon,' Helen's recent one went on,

> She went absent without leave the other day. The military police hauled her back and she then informed us that she had just got married. It turned out that she'd gone through some kind of ceremony with a *bigamist*. I ask you. Every evening I'm meant to have her into my office and give her a pep talk. My CO seems to think I exert a good influence and that I shall get her to mend her ways, but half the time I think she's simply laughing up her sleeve at me.
>
> Incidentally, I called to see the parents of those evacuees you had at the Hermitage at the beginning of the war and also the sister of Mrs Sherston, who's still at Bulbarrow. They all seemed awfully grateful to everyone at home and I think the mother of that youngest kid you took care of regretted having had her back to Portsmouth again. Apparently, poor little Pearl got terribly scared when the bombs eventually did come. She's rather a cowed child now. I didn't look up Porty's family because I felt they wouldn't want to see me. He's so happy working at Bulbarrow and living with your Aunt Edith that I felt it would be a pity to stir anything up . . .

Emily put down the letter and stared at the inadequate coke stove which was the only form of heating in the large draughty room. It was autumn now. She had come back to Ashmore at the beginning of September, physically a little fitter but older-looking and most of the time fighting with whatever courage she could summon up, an overwhelming depression.

Just before her return, Maurice Fitzherbert had talked to her in his consulting room for almost an hour. He had tried to give her something to hold on to, to point out that probably the end of the war was, if not immediately, at least in sight, that she might feel very different when it was over, glad that she had remained constant, true to her natural sense of right and wrong. But he knew that his words lacked conviction and that the girl herself sensed this.

Yet Emily was not perhaps so much conscious of any failure in Maurice's attitude, as her own. After Vernon's departure she had hoped, for a long time, that he would write. But the weeks had gone by and no letter arrived. She realized that, probably purposely, he had not given her his address, although she knew that she could send a letter via the camp on Barbury and more than once she had composed such a missive. But, subsequently, she had torn it up. What, after all, could she say in the face of his very definite and reasoned pronouncement that their affair must end. Though extremely limited in her knowledge of the opposite sex, she knew that for her to adopt any pleading woebegone role would have the effect of lessening rather than strengthening his feelings towards her. He had asked to marry her once and she had demurred. Missed opportunities rarely, if ever, returned. She could not write now and say, 'I don't want to wait to see John William. I know I'll never love him as I love you. Please? Can we be married? Next week . . . ?' Besides, during her illness, she had allowed time to slip by. She had an uneasy feeling that Vernon would scarcely have been living like a monk the past few months. In wartime London he would have found plenty to occupy himself off duty, far more than in Wilhampton and Westonbury. Perhaps she had just been an interlude, incidental to his life, a rather naïve country girl with whom he had enjoyed a light-hearted dalliance . . . Possibly he had only mentioned marriage because – and when she thought like this Emily found herself becoming hot all over – he simply wanted to get her into bed.

'Aren't you coming, Emily?' The Honourable Monica appeared suddenly in the common room *en route* for the ward on which they were both working. 'It's almost four-thirty. You know what Sister Matthews is like if anyone's a second late.'

Quickly pushing Helen's letter into her apron pocket, Emily got up and followed Monica outside, where they both hurried along the covered way in the early evening twilight. They were on quite friendly terms now, especially since Monica's cousin, the Honourable Jane, had married the Guards officer on whom her mother had been 'awfully keen' and had just borne him a son and heir. Because Emily herself was now engaged to a member of the aristocracy, Monica often tended to seek her out, even if their relationship, owing to basically very different characters, never went particularly deep.

'D'you know what I think?' said Monica, as they hung up their cloaks on their respective pegs at the end of the passage. 'I believe this place needs waking up. A bloody good air raid on Westonbury would put everyone on their toes.'

'*Monica!*' Emily stared at her, unable to credit that anyone could make such a remark, even in fun.

'Don't look so shocked, Em. But don't you ever feel that, well, here we are . . . over three bloody years emptying spittoons and bedpans and plumping up pillows and saying "Yes, Sister. No, Sister" and nothing to show for it. One day perhaps one of our kids will ask what we did in the war and I'd like to be able to say I'd hauled somebody out of a bomb crater, or made some mad dash in an ambulance applying a tourniquet which saved a poor chap's life. I don't mind telling you, I wish to God I'd got out of nursing before Ernie Bevin clamped down so that people couldn't switch their jobs. Or at least done what Liz Brewer did and gone to London to get a proper nurse's training in one of the big teaching hospitals . . .'

The rest of Monica's diatribe was lost as they entered

the ward and a voice said, 'Hurry up, Nurses. The laundry has come. There will be clean draw-sheets for Sergeant Boon and Corporal Fellows and, Nurse Mason, can you explain how it was that at lunchtime Private Weston was given an egg from the very limited number we have, when you know perfectly well he is on M & B?'

Emily looked at Sister Matthews blankly. She seemed to remember Bunty Carrington coming into the kitchen and saying something about poor Private Weston wasting away and needing better nourishment than 'that foul Woolton pie' – a concoction named after the Food Minister, consisting of carrots, turnips and potatoes covered in a mess of white sauce and soggy pastry – which Emily herself had always balked at. Possibly because of this and her general apathy, she had paid little attention. It was no good blaming Bunty. Besides, she would never dream of doing so. It was she who had been put in charge of dinners that day, wasn't it, because Sister Matthews had had to deal with an emergency admission and the Staff Nurse was away sick. Emily was well aware that patients on M & B were never allowed eggs. What would happen? Would Private Weston die? Mercifully, she could see him now, halfway down the ward, giving the thumbs-up sign to a patient in the opposite bed.

'I'm sorry, Sister,' she replied. 'It was a complete error on my part.'

'Well, don't let it happen again.'

Don't let it happen again. It was by no means the first time such words had been directed at her lately. It seemed that so many older people kept treating her in a vaguely disapproving way. Even Aunt Chip had been obviously very upset with her over the Vernon episode. She could remember overhearing a remark she had made to Katy which had remained constantly in her mind: 'There's no excuse, when you think of that poor dear young man eating his heart out in Germany.' As for John's mother, she had made it very plain how hurt she had been when Emily had not gone to stay at Bishopsdown that summer. Alicia's subsequent letters had all been couched in a kind of veiled criticism. She was always slipping in phrases such as 'I think John would – or would not – like it if you were to do this, that or the other'. 'I'm sure John is anxious that you don't overdo things again'. 'You must stop if you feel your work is becoming too much for you. After all, when John comes back – which we all hope and pray will be sooner than anyone thinks now – he won't want to find a worn-out fiancée. You and he will be able to have such *fun*, my dear . . .'

Fun? Would she? With Vernon, yes. But not with John. There was a song from a popular revue which was constantly being played on the wireless these days: 'I'm Gonna Get Lit Up When the Lights Go Up in London' . . . If only she could go to London, *now*. There would be no need to *wait*. She would be so happy to get lit up with Vernon, to show him that there was another side to her character, one he might not have even suspected.

She was so *tired* of waiting. After all, the Second Front hadn't come this year, although all the signs pointed to it being inevitable in 1944. It was impossible, living in the south of England, not to feel that things were moving, building up to something. It seemed as if heavy transport of army personnel and equipment was forever trundling through Westonbury *en route* to the coast. And the news from abroad was definitely encouraging. Montgomery was in Italy. Naples had fallen. The Russians had taken Kiev. Emily knew that she should have felt excited. If it had not been for Vernon, perhaps she would have. Now, however, she only felt empty – empty and extraordinarily alone.

It was not until the beginning of the New Year that she saw the news. She happened to pick up Monica's discarded copy of *The Times*, open at the only page in which its owner really took any interest – the Court Circular. Idly, Emily glanced down the Engagement column. When she at first saw the names she looked away quickly, as someone unwilling, even unable, to witness something repugnant. Then, slowly, she turned back to stare at some words which seemed to bounce back at her, stark and hideously irrefutable:

The engagement is announced between Elizabeth Brewer,

youngest daughter of Mr and Mrs Donald Brewer of Broad-
stones, Nr Westonbury, and Captain Vernon Keeler of the
United States Army.

18

'There will be no direct communication, you understand,
Mrs Mason, for three weeks.' The woman's voice was
unattractive, guttural.

'*Three weeks?*'

'Yes. Having assessed your daughter's case very care-
fully, Dr Schmidt has decided that is the length of time
she should remain in deep sleep.'

'But Matron . . . I understood from the doctor yesterday
that she might have to be under heavy sedation, but I did
not know that meant she would actually be *asleep*.'

'Every case is different, Mrs Mason. Dr Schmidt goes to
infinite trouble over each one, as I am sure you are aware.
That is why he achieves such spectacular results. He had
a long talk with your daughter after you left Charlton
House and realized what severe strain she has been under
for several years.'

'Yes . . . but . . . Could I speak to Dr Schmidt, please?'

'I am afraid the doctor is with a patient at present, Mrs
Mason.'

'Then later, perhaps. When would be the best time to
catch him?'

There was a pause. Katy knew quite a bit about Matrons
now. They were a difficult type to deal with, but she had
certainly never come across one to whom she had taken
such a dislike. The woman on the other end of the line
was one of those humourless enigmatic foreigners, like the
doctor. Katy suspected she was in love with him and her
next words seemed to lend support to such a supposition.
She was undoubtedly the zealous protective type.

'I'm sorry, Mrs Mason, Perhaps I should explain. Once
a patient has been committed to Dr Schmidt's care it makes
his work so much easier and more effective if relatives do
not interfere.' Then, on a slightly more conciliatory note,

she continued, 'You are quite at liberty to telephone for a report from time to time should you so wish but, of course, you will appreciate that while the initial treatment is taking place there is never a lot to say. Let me just assure you that we shall do all in our power to see that your daughter returns home a very much fitter and happier person than she has been for a long time. Once her brain has been given a total rest, she will be able to adopt a completely different attitude to her problems. But this three-week suspension of all mental thought processes is of vital importance.'

Miserably, Katy came away from the telephone and sat down by the fire. Opposite her, May remained silent, her knitting lying idle in her lap. It was snowing outside and they had managed to leave the Hall early, partly because of the deteriorating road conditions, but chiefly because Katy had been anxious to put through a call to Charlton House.

She had felt uneasy all day – uneasy, in fact, ever since she had taken Emily there by train the previous afternoon and left her, looking like some defeated waif, in Dr Schmidt's dark and oddly furnished consulting room. She had never been sure that she was doing the right thing and knew that May felt the same. Neither did she feel that Maurice Fitzherbert was by any means a hundred per cent certain that Charlton was the place for Emily. But the girl had been acting so strangely ever since she had been sent home from Ashmore for the second time, that it was obvious something more positive than ordinary sick leave was needed. She was so withdrawn and detached from everything around her, spending her days staring silently out of the window, her nights pacing her bedroom floor. Desperate with anxiety, Katy and May had been forced to take alternate days off from the Hall in order that she should not be left alone.

It was a surprise visit from one of their previous patients which finally resulted in Emily's being sent to Dr Schmidt's nursing home. One day, when Katy – who had been up with her daughter most of the previous night – was trying to prepare some notes at the Hall for one of the visiting psychiatrists, a man in civilian clothes appeared at her office door. For a moment, she did not recognize him. Then, to her astonishment, she realized that it was Corporal Watts, their one-time shell-shocked patient of private means who had been discharged with, as it was thought, incurable psychoneurosis. The figure now before her exuded health and self-confidence and was, apparently, engaged on some highly technical, top-secret and demanding war work. His cure, he informed her, was entirely due to a wonderful German refugee Jewish doctor.

Katy's mind raced. It seemed little short of a miracle. Here was a man who had been so shattered by his experiences at Dunkirk that he would come running indoors with his hands over his ears at the faintest sound of an aircraft overhead – and now he was utterly transformed. If someone could do this for Corporal Watts, what might he not do for Emily?

Katy was on good terms with the expected psychiatrist who, on arrival, was obviously just as impressed as she was over the restoration to normality of what had appeared a hopeless case. After lunch, she had taken Colonel Tetbury aside and asked him whether he could possibly find out more about Dr Schmidt from the point of view of helping her own daughter. Within a few days he sent her a report. It appeared that Dr Schmidt had only set up his own nursing home the year before, sponsored by the rich and grateful wife of a major who had been in a similar state of shock to Corporal Watts. Prior to this he had been practising in the north of England but, owing to red tape and medical etiquette, his methods had often been ignored or frowned upon. He was, however, a bona fide doctor – at one time attached to a famous Berlin hospital – and he was now having an unquestionable success treating overstrained service personnel as well as civilians.

All the same, neither Dr Schmidt nor his nursing home had been quite what Katy had been expecting. Already possessed of an innate distrust of all foreigners, she found his manner too esoteric, his accent difficult to follow, the muted atmosphere at Charlton disconcerting and weird. And she had not at all liked the way a nurse had turned and locked the front door after ushering them in. The place wasn't a lunatic asylum, for goodness' sake. She thought now of all the presumably inert and helpless bodies lying there in his charge — Emily's amongst them — and shivered.

Noticing this, May said suddenly, 'We must just hope and pray. I don't suppose a good long sleep will hurt her.'

'But . . . it's all so *artificial*. And the problem will still be there when she wakes up.'

'Yes, but, as they said, she might be better able to face it. Besides, she wasn't doing any good here, was she?'

'No.'

They lapsed into silence again, each immersed in private thoughts. May had tried to sound encouraging for Katy's sake, but in her heart she felt far from confident. She knew her niece had suffered a severe blow, but surely she should have been able to get over it without resorting to quite such drastic measures. After all, she wasn't the first young woman whose love life was seemingly in ruins. May recalled how both she and Flo had had their share of troubles with the opposite sex during the First World War. But, of course, she had to admit to herself that neither of them had been placed in quite such an unusual and difficult position as Emily. They had not had a fiancé in the background incarcerated in a German prisoner-of-war camp. Poor Emily. Everyone had expected far too much of her. They were all to blame. What must the girl have gone through by herself. That was the trouble with being an only child. She had always been too serious, had taken things far too much to heart.

Katy's thoughts ran on very similar lines to her sister's, except that there was an additional problem bothering her, one which she knew would have to be faced — and soon. She must let Alicia Moreton know the present position. She had already told her that Emily was home on sick leave again but, as yet, she had said nothing about Charlton. Should she, perhaps, write? Explain carefully why such a course had been chosen? Or should she try to *see* Alicia, give her some hint of the basic trouble? Or would that be disloyal to Emily? But surely John's mother must have suspected something by now? Of course, it was more than probable that Alicia had been in touch with Rachel or Edmund, in which case it was all the more imperative that she acted quickly. Although Rachel, bless her, was always so discreet. Katy had a feeling that she had always known a great deal more than she would ever divulge. Then what about John himself? She knew that there were often periods when letters got held up for an inordinate length of time, but if Emily was going to be *drugged* — she could think of no other word for it — for three weeks, there would now be a very long gap, particularly as she suspected that her daughter had not written to Germany for some little while.

The ringing of the telephone made her start, although it was May who got up to answer it. Quickly, she handed it over to her sister.

'You mean she's bad enough for a *nursing home*?' Alicia Moreton's voice sounded querulous when Katy was forced to tell her the news.

'I'm afraid so . . .'

Peremptorily, Alicia cut her short. 'Then I must go to her. At once. The poor girl. Where is she?'

'Near Woking, but I'm afraid it won't be possible to see her. You see . . .'

Again, Alicia interrupted her, almost rudely.

'What do you mean? Not possible. Why on earth not?'

'She's being put to sleep.'

'*Put to sleep?* Oh, my God.'

The voice had taken on an altogether different tone now. It was plainly accusatory.

'Emily's suffering from a bad breakdown. It is thought a complete rest is the only answer.'

'Rest? I can understand that. I always did think she went back to that ghastly place Ashmore sooner than she should have last year. But she can rest at home, can't she? Or at Bishopsdown? You don't mean to tell me you've sent her somewhere where she's going to be *put out*?'

Katy felt suddenly faint. She sat down and paused before saying, quietly, 'It's a new form of treatment but I understand it has an amazing success rate.'

There was quite a long silence before Alicia said, 'Give me the address. I must see her. John would be appalled. Thank God he doesn't know. I shall go tomorrow.'

With all the strength she could muster, Katy replied, 'Alicia, please. Can we meet? In London, perhaps. It would be so much easier to explain.'

Again there was an uncomfortable pause. Presently, and obviously grudgingly, Alicia said, 'All right. When?'

'Saturday perhaps? I could get away from the Hall then. I've taken rather a lot of time off lately.'

'Saturday's a bad day for me, but . . . well . . . if that's the best for you. What about the ladies' annexe of the Army and Navy in Pall Mall? Lunch, one o'clock?'

'Yes, I'll be there.'

And I could stop off at Woking to see Emily, Katy thought, as she put down the receiver – except that she'll be *drugged* or, rather, *put out*, as Alicia says. Dear God, after that conversation, I feel I could do with a bit of Schmidt's treatment myself.

19

Rather to her surprise, Katy found Clare Fitzherbert waiting on Westonbury station at nine-thirty the following Saturday morning. She was wearing a fur coat, high-heeled shoes and a jaunty red pill-box hat. In her left hand she carried a small suitcase. For once, her manner was positively affable.

'Taking a well-earned breather, Katy?' she quipped, as some puffs of steam away to the west heralded the arrival of the London train.

'I suppose you could call it that,' Katy replied, anxious not to strike up too long a conversation lest she might find herself obliged to sit in the same carriage as Clare. The latter, however, appeared to have no such fears in that connection. She simply raised a free arm in salute as the train drew in and disappeared in the direction of one of the front first-class carriages. Thankfully, Katy darted into another.

Idly, she wondered what Maurice's wife was up to. A night in town, obviously, judging by the suitcase. It was, of course, no business of hers and she had far too many serious and urgent problems on her mind to let it occupy her thoughts for more than a minute or two. She merely felt sorry for Maurice that Clare was the subject of so much speculation these days. She knew that there had always been gossip about the Fitzherbert marriage, but surely his wife's previous, ungracious, touch-me-not manner was preferable to the strange unbalanced woman she seemed to have become. Captain Bradley Butler had long since left the area and, so far as Katy knew, there had been no more billetees at East Lodge; but Clare was apparently often to be seen at some function or other organized by the officer in charge of entertainments at Barbury, who had personally escorted her to their last Thanksgiving party. Poor Maurice. He deserved so much better. Katy recalled how concerned he had been when he had called at the Hermitage the night before she had taken Emily to Charlton House. He had, for once, seemed confused, out of his depth, obviously wanting to give her every encouragement and support now that the decision had been taken, yet prevented by a basic honesty from pretending to a confidence that he did not altogether have. For the first time in her whole life she had looked on him as a man rather than a doctor: vulnerable, weary and so very definitely middle-aged. What must he be now? Getting on for fifty, yet he looked a great deal older.

'This train will call at Andover, Basingstoke, Woking and Waterloo . . .' They were off. Katy sat back and stared out of the window, registering the cold bare landscape, the patches of snow lying in sheltered places. No doubt there would be more to come. What was it Sarah used to say? 'When it hangs about there's always another fall on the way.' Well, she was prepared. Like Clare, she was clad in a fur coat bought long before the war, but she had been careful to put on an old pair of warm boots. Hardly glamorous wear for London, but that no longer mattered these days. Besides, she felt fairly certain Alicia would be similarly attired. And there was always the possibility,

Katy thought, that she might decide to stop off at Woking on the way home where taxis might not be easy to come by. After all, they couldn't shut the door in her face at Charlton, could they? Or would such an attempt put their backs up, make them less careful over Emily? But surely, as a mother, she had a *right* to see her, even if she was asleep. Dear God, it was *they* who had no right to act as gaolers.

She began practising what she should say to Alicia: 'Emily has had a love affair . . .' 'Emily temporarily became fond of someone else . . .' 'I blame myself . . .' 'Of course, John has been gone a very long time now . . .' 'I mean, it's understandable that . . .' But would Alicia understand? Oddly enough, Katy felt that her mother, the old dowager, would have been far more likely to be sympathetic. Behind that autocratic façade, Maud Fairfax had far more compassion than most people gave her credit for. And she had a much better grasp of human nature, too. She had never been blind to the faults of her own kith and kin. Alicia was somehow too blinkered. She was obsessed by her son. The sun rose and set over John William's head. She would certainly not make an easy mother-in-law, although, perhaps, after all that had happened there would be no question of that, so far as Emily was concerned.

Katy found Alicia tense and agitated when she arrived at the Army and Navy a little before one o'clock. As soon as she saw Katy at the door of the lounge, she jumped up and promptly dropped her handbag, scattering its contents all over the floor, so that both women – perhaps somewhat conveniently – became engaged in retrieving them.

'Sherry?' Alicia said, standing up but without smiling, when order had at last been restored.

'That would be lovely, Alicia.'

All at once, Katy realized that it was she and not John's mother who was the more at ease. She felt suddenly extremely sorry for the woman before her, so obviously troubled and unhappy and, it would seem, on the defensive. Once they were seated with their drinks, she noticed that one of Alicia's eyes appeared to have developed a nervous tic, the lid closing up every so often while, at the same time, her shoulder jerked involuntarily, as if she was impatiently trying to shake off such an embarrassing handicap. As Katy had surmised, Alicia was dressed as she was, sensibly and suitably in boots, a tweed suit beneath a fur coat and a small velvet beret on her now almost white hair. There was little to distinguish the baronet's wife from the daughter of the one-time manager of the Wilhampton Felt Mills who had, many long years ago, looked after the former's baby son. The passage of time, Katy's rather surprising marriage and subsequent widowhood, the gradual levelling of the classes due to the war, had somehow made them equals, both today sisters in distress, mothers of two betrothed and possibly ill-starred young people.

'I know a little,' Alicia volunteered abruptly. 'I talked to Edmund after we last spoke. He didn't tell me much and Rachel, of course, closed up like a clam, but I gather . . . well . . . there's another young man in Emily's life.'

'Was.' Katy felt infinitely relieved. At least she did not have to explain the situation from scratch.

'How do you mean: was?'

'He's engaged to be married to someone else.'

'Oh. Oh, I see. And she's completely broken down over it?'

'Yes.'

Alicia's eye closed and opened again. Her shoulder jerked.

'This man . . . Schmidt. What on earth can *he* do about it?'

'I don't know. But at least . . . she's getting a rest. She couldn't have gone on . . . as she was.'

'I see,' Alicia said again. Then, after a pause, 'Perhaps we should go in to lunch. They don't like it if you're late. The food was never all that good here before the war, but I believe the five-shilling meal is just about the same as anywhere else now.'

Throughout the meal Katy told her, little by little, what had happened, that Vernon Keeler had been billeted at the Hermitage, that he was a well-mannered, pleasant enough young man, that Emily and he had enjoyed each other's company. Yet, as she talked, she noticed Alicia's nervousness becoming more pronounced, sensed the way her mind was working. It seemed somehow necessary quickly to allay her fears.

'There was no question of . . .' Katy hesitated, her mind hunting about for the right word or expression, 'things going too far,' she said, at last, with embarrassment.

'Thank God for that.' Alicia was visibly relieved. 'These Americans . . . I mean, in Suffolk, on the estate, the illegitimacy rate is quite alarming.'

Katy flushed. She felt angry. The remark was in such bad taste. It was wounding to feel that Emily was being lumped together with the daughters of the Bishopsdown ploughmen and tractor-drivers. Yet, if she were honest with herself, she was well aware that the American troops seemed to have had a devastating effect on the women of Britain – both maidens and matrons – and quite irrespective of social distinctions. What about Clare Fitzherbert, for instance? And she had heard a most disturbing rumour which she did not propose to mention to anyone, not even May, that Vernon's marriage to Elizabeth Brewer was to take place within the next week. If it were true, she could not help wondering exactly why. Was Elizabeth pregnant? Was it possible that Emily, but for the grace of God, might have been in her shoes? On the other hand, supposing she had? Would it not have been better than having her lying, to all intents and purposes, dead to the world in some nursing home run by a Jewish refugee whom she neither liked, understood, nor, for that matter, trusted?

'I'm sorry,' she heard Alicia saying. 'I didn't mean to imply . . . It's just that poor dear John, when he does come back, it would be too awful if . . . that is, of course, if Emily feels it is he whom she really loves after all. Perhaps when she's had this rest, she may come to realize just what he means to her.'

'Yes,' Katy said quietly, but without conviction. What you're really saying, Alicia, she thought grimly, is: I don't want my son marrying soiled goods. You're back in that closed unrealistic world of yours where no one, not even

529

the Virgin Mary, is good enough for John William and where it is impossible for you to believe that any girl could ever, for one moment, prefer any other boy to him.

After they parted, Katy went to a call-box and telephoned Charlton House. It took some little while and several more coins before she was eventually put through to the Matron. The answer was as she had feared: 'I'm sorry, Mrs Mason, but it would really be pointless for you to stop off at Woking this evening. You would be unable to see your daughter but, I assure you, her treatment is going according to plan.'

20

'She'll be coming round the mountain when she comes,' sang Bradley Butler into Clare Fitzherbert's ear as they danced, cheek to cheek, thigh to thigh, on the Savoy Hotel dance floor. 'She'll be coming round the mountain when she comes . . .' He seemed to have devised his own little steps to the tune, which necessitated him and his partner coming to a halt every so often and standing locked together in a swaying movement, during which he would slip an arm lower so that a finger and thumb could give a playful pinch to a certain part of her anatomy. The lights were low, the floor crowded. No one noticed. In any case, they were by no means the only couple given to the same kind of brash indelicate gestures. Clare giggled a little. She had had quite a lot to drink. Through her short straight Utility dress, for which she had given eleven coupons, she could feel Bradley's body harden against her own. Perhaps it was time they went to bed. She laid a head on his shoulder.

'Tired, honey?'

'A little.'

'One more tune, then.' He gave her bottom another tweak. She knew that he was looking forward to the rest of the night, but that he also loved to dance. 'There'll be blue birds over the white cliffs of Dover . . .' he crooned as, without a pause, Carroll Gibbons swung into another tune. This time Bradley held Clare so tightly that, with both arms twined behind his neck, she let her body go limp and found herself being virtually lifted round the dance floor.

They were not staying at the Savoy. Like many another West End hotel, it was fully booked and Brad had not been sure, until the last moment, if he could get away at all. He was stationed in Essex, his unit engaged on extremely hush-hush activities. Even he was not quite sure what they were all about. He only knew that it was necessary to guard serried flotillas of dummy landing craft which kept appearing in the creeks around the Thames estuary, and that dummy gliders made of plywood were being assembled on nearby redundant airfields. It was coming this year, of course, the Second Front. Everyone was aware of it, although God knew when and where it would take place. Naturally, Bradley had said nothing to his companion about his present duties. He was sworn to secrecy. In any case, Clare would hardly be interested and, at the present moment, he simply wanted to enjoy himself, forget all his responsibilities, including his wife, Luella, back in Nashville, Tennessee. 'We'll *meet again*,' he murmured, somewhat inappropriately, as 'The White Cliffs of Dover' melted into Vera Lynn's signature tune.

They did not leave the Savoy until well past midnight. There had been an air-raid alert just beforehand but no one had taken much notice. Since the blitz of 1940, although Londoners still often heard the voice of the sirens, they had come to look on it almost as that of an old friend. There had been nothing to compare with the appalling destruction in the second winter of the war although, oddly enough, just recently there had been some short sharp attacks when bombs of a much more powerful kind had rained down on the capital. Even so, Bradley and Clare were far too taken up with each other to give much thought to the searchlights now sweeping the sky behind them as, unable to get a taxi, they began walking round the Aldwych towards Holborn, where they were booked in at a small hotel in Russell Square.

Suddenly, from the direction of Battersea, there came

the sound of an unexpectedly loud barrage. The new rocket guns went into action, their crash and swoosh drowning all else. The din was unprecedented.

'Christ!' Bradley Butler, his arm round Clare, stopped and turned. He had not been in England during the first appalling onslaught by the Luftwaffe. Now, he could only look back in horror and amazement at what was happening in the night sky on the other side of the river.

'Guess we'd better make base quickly, honey,' he said, hurrying Clare along. She did not demur, although her high heels were making walking difficult. But she was far too inebriated to mind. If the worst came to the worst she expected that Bradley would pick her up and carry her.

Towards the top of Kingsway, he did just that. All London seemed to be lit now by a bright menacing glare. Realizing that they could not possibly get to Russell Square, he attempted to seek shelter in Holborn Underground, where the few other people still about were being hustled by tin-hatted wardens.

He was a second too late. They were level with Twyford Place when a bomb fell on the opposite side of the road at the corner of Gate Street. The building they happened to be passing collapsed instantaneously. Clare Fitzherbert and Bradley Butler went down together, buried under several tons of falling masonry.

The news did not reach Maurice until the following Sunday night. The inhabitants of Wilhampton heard nothing until Monday, except that London had fairly 'copped it' again. Katy, working late at the Hall that evening, was surprised when Maurice failed to call in for a promised half-hour before his evening surgery, but she supposed some emergency must have prevented it. When the telephone rang in her office, she imagined she would hear that this would be the explanation.

'Katy?' Ethel Sharman's voice seemed rather more high-pitched than usual, her lisp more pronounced. 'I'm afraid . . . Maurice won't be coming. He's had to go to London.'

'*London?*' There was a pause.

'Yes. Clare was killed on Saturday night. A bomb. I gather it was one of those big raids again.'

There was another pause. Eventually Katy replied quietly, 'I see. Thank you for telephoning, Ethel.'

She put down the receiver. *One of those big raids again.* She must have just missed it herself. There had been more bombs, too, on Bristol and Hull, according to the news, although the BBC always played down the extent of the damage. But she had noticed a journalist in one of the Sunday papers refer to the 'Little Blitz'. Would the Germans, with their extraordinary unpredictability, pick on Woking? Could she get Emily away, home, out of whatever there might be in store? She checked herself. Woking was a small town. Besides, Charlton was well outside it. Almost in the country. She started to wonder about Maurice. When would he return? She so wanted to extend her sympathy. Or would that be hypocrisy? She hated herself for the thought, but was not Clare's death, horrible as it seemed, more a cause for relief than grief? Poor wretched woman. She hoped that her last hours had been happy. She had certainly never appeared to have had much of it before.

Katy did not see Maurice Fitzherbert until the end of the week. She had been typing out a rather complicated report one afternoon and had not noticed him standing at the open door of her office. When she did so, she stood up quickly without quite knowing why.

'I'm so *sorry*, Maurice,' she said, feeling in a way that it was quite true. She was sorry for so many things: for him, for Clare, for their whole miserable marriage and the part which, however inadvertently, she had played in it. She became suddenly shy. 'I ... haven't written, or anything,' she continued. 'I was just hoping to see you.'

'Thank you, Katy,' he answered quietly, and smiled.

She wanted to go across to him, put out a hand, make some tangible gesture of sympathy or comfort. But it was difficult. Embarrassed, she turned away.

'Emily?' he enquired, gently.

'They say the treatment is going according to plan.'

'Good. Try not to worry. I've heard another excellent report about Charlton.'

'Really?' She brightened. Then he was gone.

Afterwards, she wondered how long he had been watching her before she had looked up. She had been trying so hard to concentrate on the report, which she had been having to do a second time. She knew her typing was far from perfect and these days, especially, it was difficult to avoid making mistakes. Yet she supposed, in many ways, her work at the Hall had helped her to become a more disciplined efficient person, better able to take responsibility, even if it was mostly for people she knew little about rather than her own kith and kin. Several times lately she realized that she had managed to tackle problems from which, years ago, she would simply have shied away. The business of Paul, for instance; and even, recently, going to lunch with Alicia.

If only she could feel that she had done the right thing over Emily. Perhaps she had. What was it Maurice had said? Another excellent report. Maybe she had misjudged Dr Schmidt. He was obviously very clever; and he must have seen such a lot of life, must know so much more than she herself who was, after all, just a middle-aged provincial woman whom fate had elevated into a rather different stratum of society from that into which she had been born. She must have faith. She would hang on to Maurice's words. She would try to believe that Emily would start to face up to life again in . . . what was it now? . . . another ten days' time.

21

'You can see, can't you?'
    'Yes.'
    'And your arms and legs?'
    'What about my arms and legs?'
    'They work all right?'
    'Yes.'
    'A lucky young woman.'
Emily stared at Dr Schmidt. What was the man getting at? Did he expect her to have gone blind or paralysed under his diabolical treatment? She sat in his consulting

room on the other side of what could hardly be called a desk – simply a large glass table with nothing on it save a little Chinese mandarin swaying about as he balanced an arc of gold on his shoulders.

'So many people in this world,' Dr Schmidt continued, 'cannot see or move.'

There was complete silence in the room then, except for the hissing of the gas fire behind her. Outside the window the sky appeared unnaturally white and bright. She wondered whether it was because she had been kept in the dark for so long. She seemed to be encapsulated in the moment, alone with this strange man in his strange room. She was aware that it was the beginning of March, but time was at a standstill. It was as if there was a wall blocking off both yesterday and tomorrow. Yet it was not an altogether unpleasant sensation. In spite of Dr Schmidt's unaccountable conversation, she felt safe here.

'How do you visualize your future life, Emily?' His eyes, beneath their large shaggy eyebrows, stared at her intently.

'I . . . haven't thought.'

'Should you not do so?'

'I . . . suppose so.'

'Vat vere you doing before the var, before you became a nurse?'

'I was at art school . . . and I've always been interested in writing . . . in plays . . .'

'Ah. Zat is good. Do you have a local theatre in Vestonbury?'

'Yes. That is . . . I believe it's run mostly for the forces these days. I'm not sure.'

'Ve must find out. Such an occupation might suit you vell.'

'But . . . I mean . . . I'm a nurse. Won't I be returning to the hospital?'

Dr Schmidt sat back in his chair. 'Some people,' he said, 'are excellent at tending the sick. Indeed, in a var many vomen turn themselves into Florence Nightingales with the most creditable results. Others show an amazing ability to adapt to unprecedented situations: hardship, danger, partings from loved ones. They accept, in other vords, vat *is*. Make the best of it. They live, if not on faith, then certainly hope. Although, of course, hope deferred does tend to make the heart sick. You must know your biblical proverbs, I'm sure.'

She waited. What *was* the man getting at?

'There are,' he went on, 'usually three ingredients necessary to make up a balanced existence. Here again, I'm not saying that they are *always* necessary. Only that they are desirable from most people's points of view. They are vork, sleep and recreation. I suggest that for some time you made do vith the first two. The diet was unbalanced. Being somevat starved, ven the third ingredient presented itself, you . . . vent overboard. Yes?'

She looked away miserably. Out of the corner of her eye she saw the mandarin bow ceremoniously towards her.

'Now.' Dr Schmidt started talking again. 'Ve vill forget about Emily Mason, the nurse, Emily Mason, the devoted fiancée of the young officer in a prisoner-of-var camp, Emily Mason, the girl who vanted to go to bed vith an attractive American captain, Emily Mason, the dutiful daughter of the vidowed Mrs Mason. Ve vill try to think about Emily Mason, the individual, and vat she is now going to give, *villingly*, to the vorld – who, by doing vat she is best suited to do, vill be no more trouble to her family or doctors. You haf a lot to give, Emily, if you did but know it. For people like you, serious-minded, fond of the arts, var is alvays more difficult. But this var, I think, thank God, is in its final stages. At this point perhaps ve can afford to relax a little over the . . . how do you say in England? . . . square pegs in round holes? Yes?' He smiled. 'Ven your mother next comes to see you, ve vill ask her about the Vestonbury theatre.'

Emily stayed at Charlton House until early April. As the weeks went by, she became quite fond of Dr Schmidt. He found an opportunity to talk to her every day, sometimes for only five minutes, sometimes for an hour. Gradually, she came to understand a little of what he was trying to say. It was not always easy. In many ways his philosophy was a harsh one, yet she had the wisdom to realize that it was based on sound practical common sense. He had, moreover, an uncanny knack of knowing exactly what was going on in her mind.

On the day Katy came to fetch her away for good, he put a hand on her shoulder and said, 'I hope you vill come and see me sometimes, Emily. I don't like to lose touch vith any of my patients. You haf been one of the youngest, certainly the youngest female. Let's see, you vill be twenty-three at the end of the year. You are still very young. Remember, time is very much on your side.'

She had, at last, got back her sense of time, except for the blank in her life between the day she read about Vernon's engagement until a short while ago. But she had come to accept it, just as she had come to accept the news of his marriage which Katy, on the advice of Dr Schmidt, told her about on one of her visits. Her mother had mentioned it quietly, almost in passing, along with other items of information, such as Clare Fitzherbert's death and a visit which Phoebe Moreton, looking every inch the glamorous FANY, had paid them one evening when she had been driving some general to the army headquarters at Netherford Grange.

'A lot seems to have been happening at home,' Emily said to Dr Schmidt the following day, and he had replied, 'Λ lot is alvays happening, Emily, if you look around enough. Has no one ever suggested that to you, pointed out that life is like a river. It never stops. Ve are all afloat on it together. Unfortunately, your own boat all but capsized a little vile ago and you had to be taken in tow, but you should be able to cast off again on your own soon. I suggest that you paddle along slowly at first, letting the future take care of itself. You don't know how you may feel in, say, a year's time, ven you've got round a few more bends.'

Suddenly, his words brought back the memory of some others which John William had used when they were still children. They had been standing on top of the Barbury turnpike looking down on the Willon as it wound its way through the valley below. And he had said, 'It's a bit like being in an aeroplane up here, isn't it? It reminds me of something one of our English masters said the other day.

When you look down on a river from a great height, it's as if you can see the past and the present and the future all at once.'

Of course, when one was actually on the river, one could only ever recall the past and see the present. The future was always an unknown quantity, but she would try to do what Dr Schmidt said and let it take care of itself. Somehow, these days, she did not feel quite so afraid of what might be round the next bend.

She started to work for the theatre company in Weston-bury at the end of April. Since the emergence of three large cinemas in the town, the old picture house had been used for a variety of purposes: amateur operatics, concerts, conferences. Lately, however, it had been given over entirely to a semi-professional group of mostly middle-aged actors and actresses under the management of a retired theatrical agent called Milroy Stevens. For a while, Emily felt embarrassed and out of place. She was afraid people would wonder why she was not still nursing. But Milroy, having been told about her illness, soon put her at her ease; and the realization of the pleasure which each of his productions gave to packed audiences – of civilians and servicemen and women alike – soon made her feel her work was more than worthwhile. For the moment, she simply acted as general dogsbody – prompting, changing scenery, seeing to make-up or rushing out to beg some prop or other from the local inhabitants; but Milroy had promised her a small part in a play he was putting on shortly, written by a young unknown soldier called Peter Ustinov, for whom he prophesied a great future.

One day, when Emily was walking along Westonbury High Street, she saw a figure coming towards her whom she at first failed to recognize. Then, as the obviously pregnant woman drew closer, she realized who it was.

'Liz!'

'Emily!' Vernon's wife flushed.

There was a pause. She could feel the colour sweeping into her own face, her heart racing. She would have given anything to have been able to sit down. Then, from some-where in her inner consciousness she seemed to hear six little words: *your arms and legs, they work?* She stood her ground.

'How . . . are you, Liz?'

'I'm . . . all right. A bit tired, sometimes.'

'And . . . Vernon?' There, she had said it. Her legs were not going to give way. Possibly Liz was the one who needed to sit.

'I haven't seen him for some time. He's at an unknown destination. I mean . . . well, these days . . . no one quite knows, do they?' Liz's voice trailed away, uncertainly. Suddenly she put out a hand. 'I know you've been awfully ill, Em. And why. I'm terribly sorry.'

She smiled. 'I'm fine now, Liz. Please remember me to Vernon when you can.'

'Of course.' Liz seemed to be considering something before she continued, slowly, 'I'm living with my parents now, just waiting for the baby. It tends to get a bit wearisome. If you ever felt like coming to Broadstones, you'd be very welcome.'

'Thank you, Liz. Sometime, maybe.'

They parted. What was the other thing Dr Schmidt had said: we are all afloat . . . your boat all but capsized, but you'll soon be able to cast off again on your own . . . *paddle slowly at first . . .*

No, she wouldn't go to Broadstones just yet. But she was glad to feel that she had navigated one little bend all right today. Poor Liz. What must it be like? Emily knew what she'd been hinting at. Vernon was going over to France. That was obvious. He was probably this very minute incarcerated behind barbed wire, not far away but unable to get leave to see her. She feared that Frank François was somewhere there, too. And Helen, down at Portsmouth – not perhaps going across the Channel, but definitely in the war zone. Her last leave had been cancelled at twenty-four hours' notice. Virtually the whole of southern England was one vast military camp. No one said very much, of course. But everyone *knew*. There was a kind of expectancy, a hush, more meaningful, even, than the clatter of heavy tanks lumbering down the roads to the coast.

22

In the small hours of Tuesday, June 6th, 1944, the waiting was over. The skies above Westonbury and Wilhampton were filled with the sound of throbbing engines and a mass of twinkling red, green and white lights, as wave after wave of aircraft passed overhead with unceasing regularity. These were not the forlorn and gallant few of earlier days, but hundred after hundred of mighty planes, like a heavenly host on the march, making the earth shake beneath them as they roared southwards to the Channel and their rendezvous with destiny.

The Second Front had begun.

After the nine o'clock news that evening, the BBC broadcast the first of its eyewitness accounts from the French beaches. The following day it became known that a hundred and fifty-six thousand troops had reached France. The ordinary people of Britain, going about their daily tasks, snatched up newspapers or listened to the wireless during whatever opportunity they had, still only able to make wild guesses as to what was really happening on the Normandy coast. No one then – save a few VIPs – knew of the appalling responsibility shouldered by the Supreme Commander, how General Eisenhower, having postponed the invasion for twenty-four hours owing to adverse weather reports, had finally said, 'OK. Let's go', and had prepared two communiqués: one for success, one for failure.

For anyone who had loved ones 'going over' or about to 'go over', it was a time of tense anxiety, yet pride. Here was Dunkirk in reverse. When convoys of fresh troops on their way south stopped at appointed places, women and girls rushed up with jugs, even pails, of tea and thrust packets of cigarettes into soldiers' hands, cheering as they drew away. Towards the end of the month, Henry wrote to say they had heard from Frank François. Tim Swayne, unknown to Emily, had apparently also been one of the first to step ashore on the Cherbourg peninsula. His letter home, which arrived in mid-July, was typical of the whole family's courageous attitude to life. Dick and Dorothy hardly knew whether to laugh or cry when they read, 'Ye gods, I'm glad you couldn't see the things our tanks did to standing corn.'

One Sunday, a few weeks later, Emily decided to visit Liz. She found her pale and troubled, but infinitely glad to see her. As yet, there had been no news of Vernon. Mrs Brewer, after ushering her in and making a little desultory conversation, soon left them alone. Emily sensed a certain disapproving unsympathetic attitude in the older woman, as if she felt that her daughter had no business to be in her present state of suffering and that she resented the fact that Emily had escaped any such predicament. It was obvious, after Liz's opening remarks, that Mrs Brewer had no time for her son-in-law.

'You see, she hates Vernon, Em. Oh, I know, it was partly my fault. I should never have let him ... well, I should never have gone to bed with him. I think he looked on me as a more sophisticated person than I actually am. Anyway, there I was, doing my best to become a bit more than an ordinary VAD and Vernon called at the nurses' home one night to ask to take me out. He seemed awfully cut up about breaking off with you. I felt so sorry for him. He really did love you, you know.'

Emily sat there, quite quietly, wondering what to say. Yet Liz appeared not to notice. She was in full spate now, obviously relieved to be able to unburden herself. 'You see, I don't *want* this baby, Em. I know it sounds awful, but I didn't think. And Vernon said, or I thought he said, that he'd take precautions. And then, when I realized I was pregnant ... well, we just married. He was anxious to do the right thing. I mean ... he's a nice guy. But I'm sure he didn't want to get so involved.' She hesitated for a moment before continuing, 'I know I've no right to ask this. Under the circumstances, you might think it an infernal cheek. But, when the baby comes, will you be its godmother, whatever happens?'

'Yes. Yes, of course.' She thought: Dr Schmidt was right.

One never knew what was coming round the next bend, but one just had to float along and accept it. Well, she was learning. She had agreed to become godmother to the child of the man with whom she had been desperately in love. Suddenly, she realized that she had put the affair in the past tense and that, surely, could be no bad thing. The most important one at the moment was for Liz to hear from Vernon. She knew he would have written, if he had been able . . . But allowances had to be made. She tried to sound reassuring, to talk about the appalling problems of communication in an operation of such magnitude, to try to divert Liz's mind from what was happening in France to what was happening in England, now that the German pilotless planes had begun their attack on London and the south-east. But such a strategy seemed to have little effect on her companion, except to make her remark, 'I wish to God I was back at Thomas's, in the thick of it. If Vernon's killed, what am I going to do, here, with a baby who'll never see its father and a mother whose own mother would like to be shot of us both.'

'Liz, hush.' She had not expected quite such a frank and bitter outburst. 'You mustn't think like this. Remember, you've got other friends, not just me. There's Bunty still at Ashmore. I'm sure we'll all of us rally round.'

'Oh, I know.' Liz had begun to cry now. 'Bunty called the other day. But I could tell. She thinks I've been such a fool. I mean, you'd never catch her becoming pregnant. God knows how many men she's slept with. She used to tell me about them. We stopped saying anything much to you because . . . well . . . you always seemed so *good*. I hope you won't mind my saying this now, but you were easily shockable. Of course, we all realized you'd fallen heavily for Vernon and thought it was probably doing you good. We didn't dream that you never actually went to bed with him.'

She thought a lot about what Liz had said on her way home in the bus. She knew that most of it was very true. She was hopelessly young and naïve for her age. And she supposed that she had been easily shockable, at least up to the time when she had almost done what Liz had evidently done. It was so easy to be good, to be censorious, even, of others, when one had never been tempted.

She was surprised to see two bicycles propped against the gate of the Hermitage as she went in: a man's and a woman's. Then she heard the sound of voices and laughter coming from the garden at the back of the house. She began to hurry. Could it possibly be . . . ? It must be. She would know that cheerful giggle anywhere.

As she rounded the corner, Helen Swayne got up and ran to greet her. In the background, a short, fair, pleasant-faced young man rose also and came forward more slowly. She realized at once that it must be Colin Mackay. What she was quite unprepared for was his opening remark, 'Hello, Emily. I've been looking forward to meeting my wife's best friend.'

She looked in astonishment from one to the other of them: happy, smiling and so manifestly in love.

'When . . . ?' she managed to ask.

'Yesterday,' answered Helen, promptly. 'We found we could get forty-eight hours' leave together. Now that the Second Front is well under way, the authorities have relaxed a little. A very nice padre in Portsmouth performed the ceremony. We always reckoned on going to London for our honeymoon and staying at the Ritz, but the doodle-bugs rather put paid to that idea, so we spent last night in *Basingstoke* of all places . . .' She went off into peals of laughter. 'And we're staying at Bulbarrow until tomorrow afternoon. Colin's got to catch a train to Chester but, believe it or not, Em, I'm being posted to Larkhill, so you'll be seeing quite a bit of Junior Commander Mackay.'

'*Junior Commander!*'

'Yes. Isn't it a scream? Married and promoted all at the same time. Three pips and a batwoman to clean every button.'

There was the sound of a car drawing up in the lane outside, a door slamming and then footsteps along the flagstones. Maurice Fitzherbert was with them.

'I happened to see your parents, Helen,' he said, 'as I was passing Bulbarrow just now. They told me you were here. I've come to offer my congratulations.'

Emily noticed her mother suddenly disappear into the house and return a few minutes later, carrying a tray on which were some glasses and a bottle of champagne. She handed the latter to Maurice.

'Will you,' she asked, almost shyly, 'open it?'

He smiled. 'I'll do my best. Although it's a long time since I performed this small operation.'

For a moment, Emily had that curious feeling of *déjà vu* which she had experienced quite often of late. The scene in which she was taking part seemed like that of a stage set, predetermined, inevitable, enacted in slow motion in a tiny moment of time, preserved for eternity in the golden light of the summer evening. Even the Willon seemed to be hardly moving, waiting for the players to float along again on their normal course.

It was only a fleeting impression, yet it remained with her long after she had gone to bed that night, as did the recollection of the way Maurice Fitzherbert, while raising his glass to the newly-weds, seemed to be raising it to her mother at the same time.

23

One late September afternoon May Lodge, having finished checking all her supplies and working out the menus at the Hall for the following week, left a little earlier than usual and walked up to see her sister on downside. She did not take the car for, ever conscientious, such petrol as she and Katy were allowed was used strictly for getting themselves to and from their work.

For some time, May had been feeling that they did not see quite enough of Edith. Certainly, they had done their best from the material point of view. Katy had been generous to a fault over her monthly cheques, insisting on them being accepted despite Edith's constant protests. They were as anxious as Herbie had been that their sister should never be forced to undertake any menial task, yet realizing that it was not good for her simply to remain at home caring for Porty and Georgie – and that in any case she would be obliged to take on some kind of part-time war work — they had agreed that Edith's decision to do her bit, as she put it, by offering her services to the local NAAFI was probably a good thing. It got her out and about and prevented her from brooding too much on what was happening to the rest of her scattered family.

'Donald's somewhere in Italy, moving north all the time, I suppose,' she informed May, as she set about making some tea. 'But I haven't heard from Ernest for quite a while. I think he's probably still in Egypt. He's never been much of a correspondent, though. Debbie's the one for letters. She always was the best of the bunch. I'm not surprised they've made her a sergeant. I wish our Della took after her. And Mavis, too, for that matter.'

'How often does Mavis get home?' May asked. She was aware that her youngest niece, earning good money at the munitions factory, was not as dutiful a daughter as she might have been, and Edith's reply somewhat confirmed this.

'About one weekend in three,' she said, guardedly, before quickly adding, 'How's Emily?'

'Better than we ever expected. She seems to have settled down to working at the theatre.'

'Well, she always was keen on that sort of thing, wasn't she? Runs in the family, I dare say, when you think how Katy had that fling on the stage when she was first married. Is Emily over that other affair?' Edith picked up the kettle and poured out a little hot water to heat the teapot.

May paused before answering. She did not suppose that Emily would ever quite get over something which had affected her so deeply. Nevertheless, the girl was definitely putting a calm and brave face on things. 'In a way,' she said, slowly. 'The young man was badly wounded in France, you know. He's in hospital in East Anglia now.'

'Oh, I'm sorry. What about his wife?'

'She's had a little boy.'

This time it was Edith who remained silent, a troubled look in her eyes as she stared out of the window where the outline of the downs showed black and somehow forbidding in the fading daylight. 'Sometimes you can't help wondering,' she muttered, half to herself.

'Wondering what, Edie?'

'Oh, I don't know. What life's all about. Especially nowadays. I often think of poor dear Mother and what she would say if she could see us all now. I'm afraid I haven't made a very good job of bringing up my brood. Sarah was so strict that I suppose I went the other way. D'you remember how dead against my marriage Father was?'

'Yes. We had to hide your wedding dress in a cupboard while we were making it.'

'And you could hardly hear his responses in St Mark's when he gave me away. D'you know, it would have been Herbie's and my thirtieth wedding anniversary last July.'

'Oh, Edie. And to think. Katy and I forgot.'

'Why should you remember? I took some flowers to the cemetery and sent up a little prayer, although . . . well, with so much killing going on I think I've become a bit cynical about life after death. And even life after birth, for that matter,' she added, to May's consternation.

It was unlike Edith to talk like this. She was usually so acquiescent, ready to accept her lot. May blamed herself again for not seeing more of her.

'Why don't you bring Porty and Georgie down to the Hermitage next Sunday?' she said. 'Come to lunch. It's not a bad walk this time of the year.'

Edith shook her head. 'Thanks, but it's the day Porty's set his heart on them both taking the barrow and going wooding. The dear boy's determined to get me in as much as possible before the end of the month. I'm told the shortage of coal is going to be worse than ever this winter. I must say, the Fairfaxes giving us the right to gather kindling in Breconbury Woods is one of the blessings about living on downside.'

May did not pursue the point. The need for fuel was, she knew, a good enough reason for such a refusal. Yet she sensed that it was one which Edith had fastened on to with relief. Since Emily had become officially engaged to Edmund Fairfax's nephew and she and Katy so involved at the Hall, she realized that Edith never really wanted to visit them. It made May feel sad. It was something no one mentioned, but she knew that their respective ways of life were now so totally different that they had grown apart. Still, if Edith would not come to Netherford, she would at least make every effort to visit downside at least once a week.

Suddenly, she remembered the time and stood up. 'I must be going, Edie. The car's at the Hall and Katy will be waiting to drive home.'

At the mention of their youngest sister, Edith said unexpectedly, 'You know there's been talk, don't you?'

May reddened. They were the selfsame words she recalled Edith having used once before, about ten years or so ago, when Katy had become rather too friendly with an elderly bohemian neighbour of theirs. 'Yes,' she replied, levelly, 'I expect there has. But not bad talk this time, surely?'

'Oh, no. Just people wondering if Katy's going to become the doctor's wife at East Lodge after all.'

'I don't know,' May answered, putting on her coat. 'I honestly don't know, Edie. I wish I did.'

'It would be nice, really, wouldn't it.' Edith's voice had taken on a wistful gentler tone now. She seemed more like her old self. 'I mean, he's waited long enough,' she added as she came to see her off.

'Yes, he's waited a long time.'

A very long time, May thought, after they said goodbye. Twenty-four years, in fact, since that poignant never-to-be-forgotten summer of 1920 when Katy had come home from London to help nurse poor Flo. She could see Maurice as if it were yesterday, standing at the Mill House door: tall, handsome and so obviously smitten from the very beginning. And she could see yet another scene a few months later: Maurice arriving to take Katy to her first dance and the look of wonder, almost reverence, in his eyes when he caught sight of her in the blue taffeta dress which May had made specially for the occasion.

It was almost dark now, as May hurried down the steep winding road, trying to avoid the potholes which occasionally showed up beneath the dimmed unsatisfactory lighting. Were they in for another winter of war? Long, blacked-out evenings, rationing, shortages of almost everything she could think of? It looked like it. The British and American forces under General Montgomery and General Bradley were gaining ground, but they had not swept across Europe as, in the temporary euphoria of the successful cross-Channel operation, people had hoped. The recent disastrous British airborne landing behind the enemy lines at Arnhem had definitely cast a gloom over proceedings. But the Allies were closing in, all right. Paris was liberated. French and American troops had come ashore on the Riviera, completely unopposed. General Alexander's forces had reached the Lombardy plain. The Russians were nearing Warsaw and advancing into the Balkans.

Please God it would soon end, May thought, as she at last reached East Street. It was five years now since those pathetic evacuee children had arrived at the Hermitage, only to be whisked back to Portsmouth again by their parents before the Battle of Britain ever began. It was four since John William had been taken prisoner. And since then, so much had happened: Bob Swayne killed at Alamein, Clare Fitzherbert a victim of the 'Little Blitz', Emily with a bad nervous breakdown, Vernon Keeler a physical wreck. Thank God Helen Swayne's husband was still in England, as well as May's own brother. But there was no knowing what would be the fate of Henry's son, Frank François, or Tim Swayne, or Edith's two boys, or the Farleys' son from Sweetacres, who she believed was somewhere in Burma. It didn't bear thinking about. Yet one had to have hope. The end was coming, even if it was on the slow side.

There was a message for May when she arrived at the Hall to say that Dr Fitzherbert had been called out to Netherford and had given Mrs Mason a lift home. She was both surprised and pleased. There was so little time in which the two of them could ever be alone. It was not as if they were able to conduct some ordinary courtship. Maurice was such a public figure, one who neither could nor would ever put a foot wrong. He was so highly respected, so hard-working. She did not believe that he had taken any time off since the war began. Certainly, he had never had a holiday. She sensed that there was something going on between him and Katy these days, even if it was only a kind of mutual shyness of each other, a fear of betraying their private feelings. Katy, especially, seemed the more nervous, as though she had some extra problem which she could not quite resolve.

May could see no car parked outside the Hermitage as she drove down the lane; but that was only to be expected. For one thing, Maurice evidently had a patient to see and would, in any case, have to get back for evening surgery. Yet, irrespective of this, May was very conscious of the fact that theirs was a home he would not dream of visiting unless it was for a strictly professional purpose. The evening he had suddenly turned up when Helen and her husband had been with them was the only time she could remember that he had called for a purely social reason. She suspected that he must have welcomed such an opportunity.

When she got indoors, she found Katy smoking a cigarette by the sitting-room fire, which she had evidently just lit. There was no other light in the room.

'May?' she said, as her sister came across and sat down opposite her.

'Yes?' She waited, aware that something important was coming.

'Maurice asked me to marry him tonight.'

May wanted to get up and embrace her, but something in Katy's manner made her desist. In the flickering firelight she thought her face wore an anxious, almost embarrassed expression. 'I'm so glad, my dear,' she said, quietly, and then could not refrain from adding, 'and you accepted, I hope.'

'Well . . . yes, although there's so many things to be taken into consideration. You . . . Emily . . .'

'But you know Emily would be delighted, my dear, as I would, too.'

'Yes, I thought you'd say that, bless you. I'm sure you're

right about Emily, but I can't help thinking . . . well, poor child, she'll be bound to feel everyone around her is getting married, won't she? I mean, there's her best friend, the man she was so in love with and now her own mother. If only her life could straighten out. It's such a shame it's so uncertain.'

'We must just hope. She's still very young, Katy. No one can foretell what might happen when John William gets back.'

'No, but I can't help worrying about her. And you, too. Would you be quite happy living here alone? I'd make the Hermitage over to you, of course. But you must have become so used to having me and Emily around. You know, May, I'm ashamed now to think I never realized all you gave up by coming to live with us after Philip's death. You were always so keen on your independence. Have you ever regretted leaving Cob Lane?'

May paused a moment before replying. 'Well, just at first, maybe. But perhaps I'll go back to Wilhampton, too, one of these days, if some little place turns up. The Hermitage does seem a bit on the big side for me.'

'Maurice suggested you came to East Lodge. You'd be so very welcome.'

'No, my dear. I appreciate being asked, but I think you and he ought to have some time to yourselves after all these years.'

Katy gave a short laugh. 'We're a bit old to worry about that sort of thing, aren't we? Besides, I have a daughter, remember. Although I have a feeling that Emily might well decide she'd like to divide her time between East Lodge and here.'

'Perhaps.' They were silent for a while. Katy stubbed out her cigarette and threw another log on the fire. 'There's something else,' she said, at length. 'Paul.'

May frowned. 'Paul?'

'Yes. There wasn't time to tell Maurice tonight. But if we're to marry, I want him to know. I don't want any skeletons in the cupboard. I often long to see the boy.'

'But surely, that wouldn't be wise. Particularly now that he's . . . well, settled.'

'No. I suppose not.' Katy sighed.

For a moment May found herself becoming almost angry. The past was the past. Couldn't Katy let it alone now? She had the chance to make a new life, to make a man happy who deserved it more than anyone she had ever known.

'How soon,' she asked, briskly changing the subject, 'does Maurice want to get married?'

It came as no surprise when she received the reply, 'As soon as possible. He'd like to put the banns up in St Mark's next Sunday. But I said I thought that was rushing things a bit.'

'But we could surely ask him to lunch that day, couldn't we?' May stood up. 'Seeing that you'll be an engaged couple, it's high time we did away with so much protocol, isn't it? There'll be no more need for him to be quite so chary about crossing the threshold.'

How fortunate, she thought, as she bustled away, already planning the best meal which rationing would allow, that Porty had decided to go wooding that day after all.

24

'I always knew there was a child.'

'You *knew*?'

Katy stared at Maurice Fitzherbert. They were sitting, one on either side of the fireplace, rather as she and May had done a few days earlier. Maurice had accepted, with alacrity, their joint invitation to lunch and, the meal now over, May had discreetly absented herself while Emily had gone to Broadstones to see Liz and her baby. Katy had brought up the subject of Paul as soon as she and Maurice were alone, but was totally taken aback by his revelation.

'Barbara Woodley got in touch with me some time after the inquest,' he continued, quietly. 'I don't suppose it was difficult for her to find out the local doctor's name and address. She wanted to know the circumstances of Philip's death and how you were. She had apparently heard the news through telephoning the Moat at some stage where, presumably, she talked to May. I don't think she was all that bad a character, Katy. I got the impression that she found herself actually wanting to have the child. She must have had some compassion. Whatever she may or may not have intended to do at that time, once she heard from me how ill you were and that on no account was she to attempt to get in touch with you, she promised me that she would never do so unless she found herself in dire straits.'

'She certainly kept her word there. She did get in touch with me, Maurice, but not until three years ago. She'd been injured when the Café de Paris was bombed. She lost her home, too, the same night. She was living with her sister in Colwyn Bay when she came all the way to see me. It was just after she'd read the announcement of Emily's engagement in *The Times*.'

It was his turn now to express ignorance of such a meeting although, when Katy went on to explain about her own visit to Wales the summer before last, he said, 'I thought something like that might have been the case when you sent Emily away with May.' He smiled. 'Sixth sense, perhaps, although this is a very small place, Katy. Knowing that your sister had taken some unexpected leave, I was surprised when they told me at the Hall that you had gone away for the weekend also. A lot of the patients expressed their disappointment that your usual tea parties had been cancelled at short notice. I just hoped that whatever you were doing wasn't going to cause you distress. Of course, I realized that I could have been wrong. You might have been off for a . . . well, romantic assignment. One or two officer patients at the Hall . . .' he added, and broke off, a little embarrassed.

She laughed. 'Oh dear. You must have been checking up on me. I'd no idea my movements were that important.'

'Whatever you do, Katy, will always be important to me.'

She was overwhelmed by the emotion in his voice and found herself blushing like some young girl. She was forty-two, Maurice was fifty. But the way he was looking at her and the manner in which he spoke left her in no doubt that their marriage would not be simply a Darby and Joan affair. After all these years she would be sharing a bed with a man again. She had a feeling that now she had at last agreed to become his wife, he could hardly wait. She became all at once apprehensive, praying that he would not be disappointed.

They were married on the first Saturday in November. Rain and storms had set in early that winter, yet the sun broke through with a sudden, almost spring-like, touch as Katy and Maurice Fitzherbert came out of St Mark's church and Porty, cheered by an enormous crowd of well-wishers, rushed forward and placed one of Blossom's old horseshoes, tied with white ribbon, round their linked arms.

They had hoped to have a quiet wedding and, as far as the actual ceremony was concerned, had managed to confine this to family and close friends. Much to Katy's delight, Henry had come down from Catterick to give her away and, to add to her pleasure, at the last moment Marianne had decided to accompany him. Debbie and Mavis had also made a point of being there with their mother and Georgie, as well as two of Maurice's sisters and their husbands. Apart from Emily and May, the rest of the small congregation had consisted of Dick and Dorothy Swayne and Helen, Robert and Frances Farley, Rachel Fairfax – without, not surprisingly, Edmund – and Ethel Sharman; but as soon as news of the marriage had got around, it became quite evident that East Lodge, large as it was, would be quite inadequate for the reception and the town hall was therefore commandeered instead. And if, owing to wartime restrictions, the catering was on the austere side, the warmth and goodwill of the gathering more than made up for it.

It was dark by the time Katy and Maurice were able to get away, driven in one of the Parkers' taxis to Westonbury station, whence they set out to spend their honeymoon at the same guest-house to which May had once taken Emily. 'Not,' as the former remarked to the latter, as they waved the newly-weds goodbye, 'where he would have taken her if there hadn't been a war on, but at least it's as good as they'd get nowadays and I sent a cheque to that nice manageress earlier this week asking her to put a few flowers in their bedroom.'

Emily nodded, blinking back tears. She thought she had rarely seen her mother looking so radiant as she had that afternoon, dressed in a lavender-blue suit made by May – who had forgone most of her own clothing coupons to ensure Katy had as good a trousseau as times permitted – and wearing on her still luxuriant hair a most becoming velvet toque to match. But as she watched Maurice and his new wife smiling at each other, noticed the protective way he was constantly placing a hand beneath her elbow as he shepherded her carefully through the crowd, she was made very aware that her mother had entered into that other mysterious relationship, one about which, even now, she remained so ignorant. Katy's loyalties would be divided again, as they had been when Emily was a little girl. She would try not to mind. Indeed, she had no right to do so. She was grown up, wasn't she? Besides, she knew that Maurice Fitzherbert, as a stepfather, would be unfailingly kind, a tower of strength. She kept reminding herself that this was what she had always hoped would come to pass.

And Maurice, sitting opposite Katy in the train heading for Oxford, also kept telling himself, with a kind of awed wonder, the same thing – that the woman for whom he had held a torch for nearly a quarter of a century was his at last. Quietly, exultantly, he looked across at her in the dimly-lit carriage, her lovely face enhanced by that shy half-smile which had so captivated him on a summer evening back in 1920, when he had found her sitting all alone by the Willon. Suddenly, unable to contain his joy any longer, he abandoned a lifetime's propriety. Completely disregarding the other passengers, he leant forward, took her hand and said just two words, 'My wife'.

Much joy also overflowed back at the Hermitage that night, where a little party continued to celebrate the wedding: Henry and Marianne (who were staying with May), Edith and her two daughters, Porty and Georgie, the three Swaynes, the two Farleys and Ethel. Henry, particularly, went out of his way to talk to Emily, mostly about Frank François and to make conjectures as to where exactly his son might be at the moment. With his bright intelligent eyes and tall commanding presence, she did not find it difficult to think of him as Frank's father.

But it was hard, just at first, to reconcile herself to the fact that Marianne was his mother. She was such a reserved little person, all the volubility with which Emily usually associated her race seemingly quite lacking. She realized, however, that Marianne had made a big gesture in coming to the wedding at all and that she was probably still very much on the defensive. As the evening progressed, she thawed visibly. She told Emily how much Frank François had enjoyed meeting her and how often he referred to this in his letters home. 'He takes after his father and, I think, my eldest brother,' she said, still in a strong French accent, 'the one I haven't seen in years. I feel sure Edouard would have joined the Resistance. He was always so full of life, so anxious to . . . how does your Mr Pickles put it, "Have a go"? It would be nice to get news,' she continued, rather wistfully. 'I haven't heard from any of my family for such a very long time. Frank François was going to do his best to find out but, of course, the poor boy can't do much. He's probably right up front with Montgomery's forces. There's some as say if only we could get to the Ruhr, the war could be over by Christmas.'

By Christmas! That would mean John William being released from prison camp. She had a curious mental vision of her cousin opening the gate so John could run out and start for home. He would suddenly arrive at the Hermitage or, perhaps, East Lodge — wherever she happened to be. How should she greet him? What should she say? She had been writing such very stilted mundane letters to him of late, trying to cram them with purely factual news, making the most of her mother's forthcoming marriage, her work at the theatre, which she explained had been taken up on doctor's orders but that she was really quite well again now. In the few replies still getting through she had sensed that he had not been altogether satisfied with this kind of information. He wished to know more about her 'illness'; why, if she was better, had she not returned to Ashmore? Could she not pay a visit to Bishopsdown again? He was sure it would please his parents.

Many was the time she regretted never having sent him one of those 'rejection slips' to which he had once alluded, expressing at the same time a kind of blind naïve faith in her fidelity which, however unintentional, had nevertheless acted like a form of moral blackmail. Surely it would have been so much better to have told him the truth, wouldn't it? Now, it was too late. They were too near meeting again. If only she could delay it. She wasn't ready. But that was tantamount to wanting the end of the war postponed. She began hating herself for harbouring such wicked selfish thoughts when the whole world was waiting and praying for peace.

Agitatedly, she slipped away from the others and went upstairs to her bedroom, where she pulled back the black-out curtains – now no longer quite so necessary since the war on the home front was running down – and sat looking out across the meadows. Intermittently, she could see the Willon quite clearly as the moon shone down from behind high scudding clouds. Not for the first time did she think how strange it was that the river always seemed to be there in times of crisis. She remembered the September day when war had been declared and she and John had sat beside it, how he had slipped his grandmother's eternity ring on her finger and asked to marry her when he was twenty-one. Then there was the summer day when it had flowed past the garden of the Black Horse and Vernon had told her he was going away. So much had happened during the past five years. She felt a lot older, although she doubted she was really any wiser. She might have experienced quite a slice of life, but she was not at all happy about the part she had played in it, especially the breakdown bit. So many others had faced up to far greater troubles and danger with so much more courage. She felt ashamed to have become ill enough to be sent to some-where like Charlton House, although she was grateful to Dr Schmidt for helping her when, as he had put it, her boat almost capsized. She must try to remember his advice: Paddle slowly at first. Let the future take care of itself . . .

There were signs that the party below was breaking up. Hastily, she pulled the curtains together and went down to say goodnight.

The next morning she walked up to the Barbury turnpike with Henry. He was interested to see the American camp but, except for a rather bored-looking sentry at the gate, it seemed practically deserted. 'I suppose they're all over there, poor devils,' he remarked.

Knowing that he, too, had been 'over there' during the last war, she asked him, diffidently, if it had been very different.

He did not answer at once. Then he said, 'Wars are always different, Emily, but the same. It's human nature that doesn't change. Last time we were stuck in the trenches. This time the fighting's been much more mobile. Last time there was comparatively little aerial activity. This time supremacy in the air was paramount and civilians as well as combat troops have been in the front line. Last time there was no Dunkirk and no D-Day, but we had all those terrible losses at Ypres, Passchendaele and on the Somme. Last time we certainly made a hash of the peace . . .'

He stopped and turned round to look at the Willon valley, his home ground. Almost to himself, he added, 'It would be nice to think that this time the powers that be will have learnt a lesson from the Treaty of Versailles.'

25

Maurice passed her *The Times* one morning a few weeks before Christmas.

'I see Arthur Mead has died, Katy,' he said, quietly.

'Arthur Mead? Oh, *no*.' In dismay, she read the obituary notice and handed the paper back to her husband. 'I must write to Betsy at once.'

She received a reply by return, sad, simple and curiously appealing — not for help in any material way. It would appear that Arthur had more than lived up to the promises he had made when he married Betsy; but she was so obviously distressed and lost in the position in which she now found herself. 'I knew it was bound to happen sooner or later,' the letter went on,

> I mean, he was seventy-six. But I'd hoped that he might have been spared until Paul was a few years older. The boy goes to his public school next year and I'm so ignorant about all that sort of thing . . . seeing masters, speech days. Arthur was so good. He always knew just what to do. Fortunately, Paul has a great friend who wants him to spend Christmas at his home in Gloucestershire. I don't feel I should be very good company for a whole five weeks . . .

But who, thought Katy, as she showed Maurice the letter, will be keeping you company? She did not think Betsy had much in the way of family left now. There she would be in a large house, twice widowed, lonely and anxious. Yet it was typical of her not to be thinking of herself. It was also typical, Katy realized afterwards, of her own husband immediately to offer some practical help.

'How about asking Betsy here for Christmas?'

'Oh, Maurice!' She was taken aback. 'Could we? It would be such a kindness. Only . . .'

'Only what, my dear?'

'Well, it would mean . . . explanations. Emily . . .' she said, and stopped.

'Emily will have to know sometime, Katy. Now might be as good as any. Remember how you didn't want to keep what you called "skeletons in the cupboard" when you married me?'

'Yes. But . . . Emily isn't getting married yet. Or at least we don't know.'

'Of course we don't. No one does. But she's twenty-three. And she's doing awfully well at the theatre, isn't she? I was most impressed by the way she stepped into the part at such short notice at the recent ENSA show. I believe she's found her feet at last.'

'Yes, I know. I expect you're right.'

Maurice was, she found, right about so many things, not in any superior or infuriating way, simply that his judgement seemed better than anyone's she had hitherto known. Having for so long only had May to turn to for companionship and advice, Katy was beginning to wonder how she had ever managed without his constant support and encouragement and, above all, love. She knew that she had done nothing to deserve it — almost the reverse, in fact. Yet it was there, all around her, lifting her up, often astonishing her and making her realize that whatever joys she had experienced in her marriage to Philip, they had always been too precarious, all too often followed by pain and disappointment. Now, there was a feeling of security, tenderness, a well-being which she had never known.

She hoped that Emily had not felt excluded from her new-found happiness. Somehow she did not think so. She was constantly coming across her daughter and Maurice deep in conversation, usually about Emily's work at the theatre in which he took particular interest. Katy was immensely pleased and grateful about this, for she knew that when the child had been small she had felt left out, had resented her and Philip's absorption — albeit intermittently — in each other, and had unfortunately become aware of that private union between them which, however incomprehensible, both shocked and frightened her. It would certainly not be easy to talk to her about Paul but, whether Betsy accepted their invitation for Christmas or not, she was determined to take Maurice's advice at the first opportunity which presented itself.

It came, quite naturally, one Sunday evening when Maurice had been called out to an unmarried woman living on downside who was having a baby. It was Emily herself who suddenly brought up the subject of illegitimacy.

'The child . . . will it be given its mother's surname?'

'Yes, darling. I expect so.'

'But won't it ask questions later on?'

'Possibly. Although one never knows what might happen. The mother could marry the father after all, or perhaps some other man, like your own cousin, Della. Or she could just call herself Mrs So-and-So. Wear a wedding ring. That sort of thing. It depends so much on the circumstances, how her family take it.'

'What would you have done,' Emily said, taking Katy completely by surprise, 'supposing what happened to Liz had happened to me, and Vernon had turned out to be a married man?'

Katy was silent for a while, as she laid aside her sewing. Having given up her duties at the Hall, she was now often to be found in the tiny workroom she had made for herself on the first floor and it was here where Emily had come across her, surrounded by odd bits and pieces from an old rag-bag at the Hermitage. With the limited amount of material available these days, Katy knew that there was not a lot she could do to relieve the sombre interior of East Lodge, but at least brighter cushion covers in the drawing room would be a help. When at last she spoke, she chose her words with care, thinking what a very different answer her own mother might have given: *never darken my doors again* ...

'It's a difficult question, darling, but I hope Aunt Chip and I would have done our best. It would have been very sad, but ... well ... these things do occur. And now we're talking about them there's something I want to tell you. I probably should have done so a long time ago.'

She saw her daughter give a wary look.

'You mean about my father?'

'Yes.'

'Was there a child? I often wondered.'

'Yes. A boy. Paul.'

Katy felt somehow infinitely relieved and touched by Emily's spontaneous reply. 'It must have been absolutely ghastly for you, Mummy.'

'At the time ... when I suspected ... yes.'

'What happened? Where is he? And his mother?'

'His mother is dead. He's being brought up by her sister, Betsy, who has just lost her second husband. Maurice wants us to ask her for Christmas.'

'Oh. What about Paul?'

'He's apparently going to friends.'

'Have you ever seen him?'

'No.'

'Do you want to?'

Again Katy paused before answering. 'I think, now, a lot depends on how you and Maurice feel about that.'

She watched her daughter pick up an empty cotton reel and absent-mindedly wind some thread round it. It was quite a while before Emily replied, 'He wouldn't mind. He wouldn't have suggested having Betsy to stay if he did. He obviously adores children. It's so sad he . . . well, that you and he couldn't have married before and had some.' She looked up and, staring her mother straight in the face, continued, 'I suppose Paul and I could be the next best thing.'

Although they did not actually see the boy those holidays, Betsy's visit proved a great success, the person with whom she seemed to have most in common being May. Many was the evening the latter would call at East Lodge after leaving the Hall and drive Betsy back to the Hermitage in the second-hand Baby Austin she had recently acquired. Gradually, she came to learn more and more about Paul and his mother, her heart going out to the child who had had such an unfortunate start in life.

'Barbara was a funny mixture,' Betsy said, on one of these occasions, as she sat knitting while May was turning some sheets from sides to middle. 'There had always been a lot of men in her life, but I really think she fell for Philip in a big way. I gather he was . . . well, very attractive to women. I don't think she actually meant to trap him by having a child, but once she found she was pregnant I suppose she hoped . . . well, who's to say. She certainly seemed to want the baby in the end. She loved Paul after her fashion. She was terribly ambitious for him. She'd be so proud of the way he's growing up. It's my belief he'll go far, if he's looked after all right. That's what bothers me so. I mean, now there's no man to guide him any more.'

'There's my brother-in-law, Betsy.'

'Yes. Yes, I realize . . . He's so nice, isn't he? I'd be very grateful if, perhaps, later on . . . But I don't want to upset anyone. I'm so happy for your sister. She must have had such a terrible time.'

'Well . . .' May broke off some cotton and took off her glasses. 'It wasn't easy.'

It certainly wasn't that, she thought, later on in bed that night. In her mind's eye she could see quite clearly the winter morning back in 1931 when Maurice had called at the Moat to break the news that Philip had been found drowned in the Willon, how Katy had suddenly seemed to come out of a trance and rush towards him, flailing her fists, imploring, even demanding, that he should take her to see her husband's body, how he carried her down the front steps into his waiting car. And then – the long, long haul until she eventually came to terms with her bereavement.

But that, thank God, was all in the past. It was the future of Emily and, now, Paul which required attention, as well as all those other young men and women whom she knew whose lives had been so changed and confused by nearly five and a half years of war.

26

Liz Keeler, with her baby, Jonathan, tucked under one arm, opened the door of Broadstones in response to Emily's knock. She looked startled and then embarrassed.

'Oh, Em. I didn't expect you on a weekday, knowing how hard you're working at the theatre.'

'Well, I've scarcely seen my godson since Christmas and when Milroy Stevens suddenly decided we were all getting a bit stale and needed an afternoon off, I thought rather than go home I'd pop along and pay you both a visit.'

Liz nodded and closed the door. Then she whispered, 'Vernon's here.'

Emily knew they would have to meet sooner or later but she would have preferred to have been a little more prepared. Liz had given her to understand that he would not be able to leave hospital for quite a while.

'They sent him home in an ambulance for a few days before he goes on to some rehabilitation centre near

Oxford,' she continued, still in a whisper. 'We hardly had any notice he was coming.'

'Oh, I see.'

'Em, I must warn you. He's different. Very difficult. Try not to notice. Look, I've got to feed Johnny. I'll just show you in and leave you.'

He was sitting staring into the fire when Liz took her through to the drawing room. It was impossible to fathom the expression on his face as he turned towards her. She could only see that this was not the Vernon she remembered.

He made an attempt to rise and stumbled. Realizing his difficulty, she said, quickly, 'Don't, please . . .'

Angrily, he answered, 'Not get up? It's polite, isn't it? Besides, the powers that be keep telling me it's a good thing to do. Exercise. Makes my tin leg work.' He gave a short bitter laugh. 'After all, your chap, Bader, apparently manages beautifully with two of the damn things. I ought to be able to do better with one.'

She did not know what to say. If she was unprepared for actually meeting him, she was certainly unprepared for the change in his personality, as well as his whole appearance. His immobility had resulted in his putting on a considerable amount of weight. His face was white and puffy. The dark eyes which had once so attracted her had a hostile resentful look in them.

'I hear,' he said, 'that you're Johnny's godmother.'

'Yes.'

'Nice of you, Em. Considering.'

'He's a dear little baby, Vernon.'

'I suppose so, poor little blighter. Though God knows what sort of a life he's going to have with a father who can't walk across a room without help.'

'But you will. It'll get better.'

'That's what they all say.'

There was silence between them. He managed to bend down and put another log on the fire. Presently, he said, 'A singer with a tin leg isn't going to get very far in the States. And I can't imagine being able to do any of my old jobs.'

She found herself saying, 'What exactly were your ol
jobs, Vernon?' She realized she could ask him this now
whereas when she had been so in love with him she ha
refrained, sensing that it was a subject he wished to avoid

'I've always been a bit of a rolling stone, Em. A kind o
loner,' he answered. 'When I could get work singing,
took it. Went anywhere. Hoped one day I'd get a rea
break. In between times, I just bummed around. Di
anything: truck-driving, travelling salesman, waiter at th
Waldorf, even. Then I joined the army. I had a shrew
idea America would come into the war sooner or later
After Pearl Harbor I couldn't wait to get over here. Bu
now . . . well, I've made a pretty good mess of thing
haven't I? You were well out of it. How the hell am
going to support a wife and kid with no home, no futur
to go back to? No wonder Mrs Brewer hates my guts.'

To Emily's deep consternation, Vernon sudden
covered his face with his hands and wept. She waited unt
the sobbing ceased and he took out a handkerchief.

'Vernon. When I was nursing a lot of men worried lik
you. And there was one at the Hall who had been s
affected by Dunkirk that no one thought he'd ever recover
But he's fine now . . .'

'But I bet he had both his legs, Em.'

All at once, as if from nowhere, Dr Schmidt's word
came back to her. *Your arms and legs, they work all right
A lucky young voman . . .* She heard Vernon repeat, 'I said
I bet he had both his legs, Em.'

'Well, yes,' she replied, 'but . . .'

He interrupted her, rudely, 'Don't say *but*, Emily. Don'
come that on me. I've had all the standard gush. So man
worse off than oneself, kind of thing. It doesn't really mak
it any easier. I thought you'd know better. Anyway, let
change the subject. Liz tells me that you were very il
yourself. I'm sorry. But I gather you're much better an
have taken to the stage these days?'

'Yes. That is, most of the time I simply help behind th
scenes.'

'And your intended? Still waiting for the Allies to releas
him?'

She paused for a moment. 'Yes.'

'We should have gotten around to it by now. Trouble ... well, the generals can't always agree. Your chap, Monty. A difficult customer to get on with. It's a pity he can't occasionally have a drink or light a cigarette ... or even use a four-letter word.'

She laughed then, feeling they were getting on to an easier footing. Presently, Liz came back by herself, having put Johnny down in his cot. Emily left soon afterwards, surprised and pleased that when Liz accompanied her to the door she said, 'I'm so glad you came, Em. I don't mind admitting I was worried at the beginning, but you've done Vernon a world of good. I noticed him becoming positively human.'

She went back to the theatre, cheered. A difficult situation had been faced, unexpectedly, and dealt with satisfactorily. She prayed that Liz, Vernon and Johnny would somehow surmount the appalling difficulties and challenges facing them, that she herself would be able, whenever she could, to give them genuine support.

There would be no need to worry about meeting Vernon any longer. Whatever there had been between them was definitely over. She wondered how much she had actually ever loved him. She had certainly felt desperately *in love*. Had it been merely an intense but transient sexual attraction? If they had married would it have developed into love? What would she have come to feel for this sad embittered man? What did Liz feel? She feared now that her own overwhelming emotion would simply have been one of pity. But then, pity was akin to love, wasn't it? She realized that Liz would need so much of the latter to get the little family through the next few years. Vernon was certainly right when he had said the future looked bleak.

She kept thinking about the different forms of love all the way back to Westonbury in the bus, wondering what she herself might feel for John William on his return. She had known him since a child, yet they would be strangers. And she had never once experienced with him a tenth of the emotion which had set her in such a turmoil whenever she had seen Vernon. She had thought she had been in love with John that day at the beginning of the war when he had slipped his grandmother's eternity ring on her finger, but she knew now it had been an illusion. Yet perhaps all love was that. One day she would like to try and write a play about it.

Milroy Stevens met her at the stage door when she arrived at the theatre. He had obviously been watching out for her.

'Emily, June Forbes has gone down with 'flu. Hers wasn't a big part. Can you possibly go on? You've two hours to swot it up. I'll put you in my office with a "Do Not Disturb" notice on the outside.'

It wasn't, as Milroy had said, a big part but she knew it was important. At the end of the evening, she was astonished when the audience seemed to accord her as much applause as those taking the leads, Milroy pushing her back on to the stage to take several curtain calls. Later he asked her to have a drink with him at the nearby Pheasant Inn.

'After the war, Emily,' he said, when, rather to her surprise, she found herself asking for and being given a shandy, 'what do you propose to do? You ought to go to London, you know. You've got a future in the theatre. I hope you realize it.'

She laughed. 'I don't know what I'm going to do at the moment. But sometimes I think I'd rather write a play than act in one.'

'Well, you're not exactly wasting your time here, if that's in your mind. At least we're showing you the ropes.'

She almost missed the last bus back to Wilhampton, where she found Katy and Maurice waiting up for her. When she explained what had happened and how Milroy Stevens had asked her to have a drink with him, she thought she saw a flicker of fear in her mother's eyes.

Later that week Katy said casually, 'Maurice and I thought we might invite Milroy to have lunch here one Sunday. Is there a wife we should ask? I really know so little about him.'

'Er . . . no. That is, I think she has a home somewhere

in Bucks.' Emily did not add that she believed the Stevenses were separated.

'So I just address the letter to him? Does he live in Westonbury?'

'Yes. He has some rooms off the High Parade. I can give you the address.'

'You've never been there?'

'No, Mummy.' She was suddenly angry. What did her mother take her for? Milroy Stevens was Maurice's age – or older. 'I can take care of myself, you know, now,' she continued. 'Don't forget I'm twenty-three. I've had my lesson. I've learnt a lot.'

'Though not enough, darling. None of us ever has time to do that. But anyway, it would be nice to meet this man who thinks so highly of your prospects in the theatre world.'

Or was he, Katy thought – and not for the first time since the evening Emily had returned so flushed and excited – thinking of something else? Her daughter had looked very beautiful as she had told them about her triumph. But there was no need for Milroy to have taken her to the Pheasant afterwards, was there, and almost cause her to miss the last bus home? Should she tell Emily now about the terrible evening way back in 1927 when she herself, fired by theatrical aspirations, had gone back to a certain Mr Marcus Kreiger's flat thinking she was to meet an impresario who would help to further her career? How there had been no impresario, only Marcus with his ageing execrable lust? It was the sort of thing one didn't talk about, at least, other than to one's husband. She had managed to get away, but only after a struggle. Even though she had been married six years and was the mother of a five-year-old child, she had still been hopelessly naïve. Yet though the war had possibly opened Emily's eyes rather more than her own, she was still a virgin, thank God. It might be as well, when the opportunity arose, to have a word or two with her about men, tell her that age seemed to make little difference to their desires. After all, she reflected – not without pleasure – Maurice was living proof of this.

27

Junior Commander Helen Mackay, still huddled in a khaki greatcoat, sat in her office going through the morning's post. Behind her, Private Mary Tilotson was trying to coax the sluggish anthracite stove into greater action. A biting March wind seemed to penetrate every corner of the Nissen hut and, outside its windows, Salisbury Plain stretched away for miles and miles — a rolling sea of grey: forbidding, mysterious and, in some curious way, eternal.

Presently, Helen came to what she was looking for: details of a new posting to her company. Since the sudden disappearance of Sergeant Whatley on compassionate grounds owing to a dying mother, Helen had been concerned about an insidious lack of discipline becoming noticeable amongst the girls under her command. She had had to put more than one on a charge for disorderly behaviour. This was especially apt to occur after the dances arranged for the troops throughout the neighbourhood, when many a junior officer or NCO had a difficult time of it as they tried to round up all the wayward members of their platoons and get them safely back to the barracks. Sometimes it actually became necessary to take physical steps to cut short the various goodnight embraces and make sure that there were the same number of girls in the lorry going home as there were when it had started out. Helen had discovered that poor Second Lieutenant Ansell was absolutely no good at this task at all. The bewildered young thing, just down from OCTU, was obviously becoming worn out and she had had to send her to the MO, with the result that Jill Ansell had been excused such duties for a while and the burden of seeing everyone in at night fell more and more heavily on to other people's shoulders.

How wonderful it would be, Helen thought, when the war was over. Somehow she did not feel it could possibly be much longer now. The Allies were well into Germany.

At long last there was no need to feel embarrassed about the song 'We're gonna hang out the washing on the Siegfried Line' which, after the tragedy of Dunkirk, everyone had tried to pretend had never been written.

Suddenly, Helen gave a start. Turning over the document in her hand she found the name *Deborah Lench* staring her in the face. So — Emily's cousin was to be her new sergeant. What an amazing coincidence and how splendid for both herself and poor Mrs Lench. Debbie would be able to get back to downside on her days off, just as she could visit Bulbarrow. All the same, Helen realized that she would have to be careful. It would be as well not to let anyone in her company know of the friendly pre-war relationship between them. It would be bound to give rise to criticism and jealousy. With a whole lot of women living at such close quarters there seemed to be no end to the petty bickering that went on; and there was always sure to be one troublemaker in each hut, someone who usually, sooner or later, had to be hauled up and put on a charge. She must try to have a quiet word with Debbie as soon as she arrived.

But when, a few days later, Sergeant Lench knocked on her office door and, with a deadpan expression, gave her a smart salute, Helen realized that there would be little need for any warning. Debbie obviously knew what she was about. She hadn't been made a sergeant for nothing. Besides, she was several years Helen's senior and had been in the ATS right from the beginning of the war.

Quickly, Helen sent Private Tilotson out on an errand which she judged would take her at least half an hour. Only then did the two of them burst out laughing.

'It's lovely to have you here, Debbie.'

'It's lovely to come.'

'I can't say Salisbury Plain is exactly the most congenial of places, especially at this time of the year, and the bus takes an even more roundabout route than usual to get to Wilhampton. But at least you can reckon on being home in under an hour and a half.'

'Yes. Something I couldn't possibly do from Derby!'

'Debbie, I can see I don't have to say anything to you

about not mentioning that we both come from the same place.'

'No. I understand completely. I'll be extra careful. I shall "Ma'am" and salute you at all times.'

'Though not too often, I hope. Somehow, it doesn't seem right. I mean, here I am, younger than you . . .'

Debbie smiled. 'I shouldn't let a little thing like that worry you. It certainly won't me.'

What a nice person she was, Helen thought, as, after discussing the immediate duties required of her, Debbie stood up and, just as Private Tilotson came back into the office, gave her Junior Commander another smart salute and went on her way. She was definitely the best of the Lench family. Apart from Edith herself, Helen had never had a lot of time for the others.

The following Sunday, when Helen was at Bulbarrow and Emily had come over to lunch, she started talking about Debbie as they set off together that afternoon to walk up to Breconbury Woods. The weather had miraculously changed by now. There was warmth in the soft spring sunshine and clusters of early primrose buds were beginning to show in the banks on either side of the lane.

'Have you any idea what Debbie's going to do after the war, Em?' Somehow the expression 'after the war' seemed to creep into most people's conversation nowadays.

'I think there's been talk of her hoping to run a village shop and having Aunt Edith to live with her. You can somehow see them, can't you, making a good job of it together. Maurice and my mother want to help them. Unless Debbie happens to marry, I suppose.'

Helen gave her friend a quick glance. She wondered whether to say anything about John William but decided against it.

'If that does happen, I wonder what Porty will do, because I can't see him ever going back to Portsmouth. He loves the country so much. He seems such a part of Bulbarrow now. The war has at least done him a good turn. I believe he could get a job as a farm worker anywhere. I suppose if your aunt moved and he decided to stay with Daddy he could always get lodgings in Wilhampton.'

'Yes.'

'Did you know that Colin wants to farm,' Helen went on. 'His godfather has just left him a bit of money. He hardly knows wheat from barley but if we took some place near here, Daddy's promised to hold his hand for a year or so. He teases me that we shall be landowners while he's quite content to remain a tenant for the rest of his life. But I know he'd like to have us around. Of course, I suppose Tim might come in with us for a bit, though I expect one day he'll take on the tenancy of Bulbarrow, just as my father did after my grandfather died.'

'That would be wonderful, Helen. You'd make such a perfect farmer's wife. Colin could hardly have married into a more suitable family, if that's what he wants to do. How is Tim, by the way? Have you heard from him lately?'

'No. But it's not surprising, is it? I mean, with all that's going on. We seem to be advancing pretty swiftly by all accounts.'

'Yes. It's quite a while since any of us heard from Frank François.'

Once again, Helen wondered whether to ask about John, but refrained. They had reached the edge of the woods now and, as if by mutual consent, they turned round and stood looking at the Willon valley below. It was a slightly different view from the one on the Barbury turnpike, yet both of them knew it equally well. It was their home ground, the place where all their formative years had been spent, the place they loved and the one for which Helen's brother, Bob, had given his life.

'It's funny,' she remarked, after a while. 'Do you remember the evening when we sat in that perishing bedroom of yours at the Fawcetts' and how I said I wanted to get away and see a bit more of the world . . . England, that is.'

'Yes. I remember very well.'

'You know, I don't feel like that any more. I want to come back here, settle down, start a family. Of course, I realize if I hadn't joined the ATS I'd never have met Colin.

From that point of view it was a wonderful move and somehow I don't think he'll be sent abroad now. I've been so lucky, Em.'

'No more than you deserve.'

'It's nice of you to say that. But you deserve some luck, too.'

As they walked on, Emily said, quietly, 'I told you I saw Vernon a little while back, didn't I?'

'Well, you mentioned it on the telephone, but only briefly.'

'He's still in a very bad way. Mentally more than physically, I'm afraid. It's going to be uphill work for poor Liz.'

'But I should think she's equal to it. I don't know her as well as you, but with all that nurse's training behind her, I believe she'll manage.' This time, Helen decided she would broach the question of John and was relieved when Emily started talking about him quite naturally.

'I haven't heard from him for some time either,' she said. 'His last letter was dated December 20th. He was terribly disappointed not to be home for Christmas. The thermometer was registering nineteen degrees below and they were still being locked in each night at 5 p.m. Apparently, they were saving up tins for a big meal on Christmas Day but I shouldn't think it could have been all that big, because he mentioned that the Red Cross parcels had been held up. He said he felt rather as if he was in some play stuck at the point where it says, "Same scene five years later", only he didn't really know what had happened meanwhile.'

'Poor John. It makes me feel so guilty. I shall try never to complain about anything else again, especially the cold on Salisbury Plain. Whatever do the prisoners do with themselves in the evening?'

'Play bridge, mostly. And I believe John goes in for a certain amount of amateur theatricals.'

'You and he will have something in common, then.'

This time there was a definite pause. 'Yes. Yes, I suppose so,' Emily replied and changed the subject.

Just how much *would* they have in common, she kept

thinking, later that night. She found it difficult to envisage John acting, how he could possibly have played the leading lady in *The Last of Mrs Cheyney*. He was altogether too aristocratic, too inhibited for such an undertaking. Yet, on the other hand, she recalled his ease of manner with people such as the matron at Ashmore, of whom she herself had stood in such awe. Would she feel as nervous of Miss Butler now, she hazarded? Probably not. Acting had certainly helped a lot in that connection.

She regretted that she had been so annoyed and upset about her mother asking Milroy to lunch. She realized it had been silly of her. She could see the logic of it and, in the event, his visit had gone surprisingly well. He had made no further attempt to ask her out since then and, for all she knew – and probably for all Katy and Maurice knew – he had simply meant well. It was good to have someone who seemed so genuinely encouraging and she was delighted that he had now given her the chance to play Elizabeth in *The Barretts of Wimpole Street*.

28

It somehow seemed perfectly natural, even inevitable, for Betsy to be bringing Paul to spend Easter at the White Hermitage. Having carefully consulted with Katy and Maurice, May had written to invite them both shortly after Betsy had gone back to Wales after Christmas. Almost immediately, she had received a most grateful acceptance.

Now, on the afternoon of Maundy Thursday, May stood on Westonbury station awaiting their arrival – a trim, white-haired little woman with gentle eyes, immaculately turned out, as usual, in a cream tussore blouse and grey flannel suit, both looking as good as when she had made them six years previously.

Being on the early side, she went into the waiting room for a few moments, remembering, almost in disbelief, some nights in 1940 when she and Katy had actually lain down there on the narrow wooden benches, until it was time to return to their posts ready to start handing out mugs of tea for the next train-load of survivors from Dunkirk. Today, thank God, it was the German army which was in retreat. The war in Europe was coming to an end. Berlin, as the popular press put it, was 'in sight'. Had May but known it, only a few hours earlier that day the last of Hitler's V1 and V2 rockets had fallen in Kent. After five and half years, the sirens had lost their occupation.

The bell rang heralding the arrival of Betsy's train and May went out on to the platform, sending up a little prayer as she did so that she had been right in initiating the visit of, to say the least, two rather unusual guests. Yet as soon as she caught sight of them her fears were allayed.

He was a quiet, well-spoken boy who shook her hand, better looking than Philip, yet unmistakably his son. There were the same dark brown eyes and thickset body, an inflexion in the voice, a certain positiveness which stopped short of his father's more aggressive manner.

On Good Friday, Katy and Emily drove over to Netherford and any further qualms on May's part were quickly dispelled by the ease with which the meeting took place. All five walked up to the Barbury turnpike, the boy and Emily a little ahead of the others. The fact that he had been brought to stay with some friends of his aunt's obviously seemed perfectly natural to him, as well as highly enjoyable.

Betsy had always been surprised that so far Paul had asked very little about his father; and even his mother's death, though taken seriously at the time, had not for long affected his basic cheerful and pleasant disposition. She supposed that the fact that he had had such a sketchy unsatisfactory home life, having to rely on and adapt to that of his friends, must have had a lot to do with it. But she knew that one day she must be prepared for questions. Surely he would begin to wonder why his mother – 'Mrs' Woodley, as Barbara had called herself – had the same surname as his aunt's maiden one?

Betsy had discussed this problem with Katy and Maurice and May the previous Christmas and it had been mutually agreed that, so far as possible, Paul should be told the truth, while omitting – at least until he was a great deal older – the question of Philip's suicide. After all, Emily herself had never known the full story for sure until quite recently.

The girl brought up the subject of her father later that day when she and Katy were alone. 'I suppose,' she said, 'that you went against Granny's wishes and married Daddy because you felt for him rather as I did for Vernon?'

'Something like that, I expect, darling.'

'Do you mind my asking? Were you really happy?'

'Extremely happy. At times.'

'But you're much happier now, aren't you. *All* the time.'

'Yes. But in a different way, I think. You must remember, I'm older.'

'You mean, and wiser?'

Katy laughed. 'If you put it like that.' She realized that her daughter had John William's return very much on her mind.

'It's a funny situation, isn't it?' Emily continued, changing the subject. 'I'm awfully glad to have met my half-brother. He's nice, isn't he?'

'Very nice.'

'Do you know what I think ought to happen?'

'No. What?'

'Well, Aunt Chip often says the Hermitage is a bit big for her by herself, but she can't seem to find anything more suitable in Wilhampton. And you heard what Betsy said this morning about finding her house in Wales far too large. They've become such friends, even though I know Aunt Chip was dead against your having anything to do with the situation in the beginning. But now you're happily married to Maurice and she likes Betsy so much and approves of Paul, I think the two of them ought to come down here and live with her.'

As it turned out, Emily's suggestion proved not nearly such a flight of fancy as even she herself originally supposed. Before Easter was over, the selfsame idea had actually been mooted by the parties concerned, something to be carefully considered during the coming months and, if undertaken, done so on a strictly shared financial basis. 'And if there's talk,' said May to Katy, one evening after she had obtained her sister's and brother-in-law's blessing, 'well, as far as I'm concerned, the boy and his aunt will simply be friends from the past.'

But that April most of the talk in and around Wilhampton was of a wider and more significant kind than the usual local gossip. It seemed but a question of days before hostilities ceased in Germany. Although when President Roosevelt died on the twelfth the shock was great and mourning sincere, at the same time there was another kind of unacceptable shock to be faced when the Allies overran the Nazi concentration camps and discovered the horrors within Buchenwald and Belsen. So quickly now did events overtake one another that it was sometimes difficult to appreciate all that was happening: the meeting of the Russian and American armies on the Elbe, the death of Mussolini and his mistress, their bodies strung up head downwards from meat hooks by the Italian partisans, the surrender of the German armies in that country and then Hitler's suicide in the Berlin bunker with Eva Braun on the last day of the month. When, at midday on May 7th, the news was picked up from the German radio that there had been unconditional surrender by the German Supreme Command at Eisenhower's Headquarters at Rheims, the bells of St Mark's, Wilhampton, rang out that same afternoon.

May, whose duties at the Hall were gradually slackening off, happened to call in on Ethel Sharman just when it was announced and the two of them sat talking together over a cup of tea. During the thirties it had always been Ethel who had feared that there would be another war before the decade was out, while May, almost up to the end, had put her faith in the League of Nations. Magnanimously, the latter now reminded her friend of the fact.

'You were so right, Ethel. I shall always remember how you said you wanted to know what Hitler was rearming *for*. Back in 1935, I think it was.'

'Yes.' Ethel smiled. 'I believe I said he had a shifty face.'

'Worse than shifty.'

'Much worse.'

'Please God they'll make a better job of the peace this time.'

'Amen to that.'

The bells rang out again, loudly, jubilantly, even if not with the perfection to which Wilhampton was once accustomed. But that was only to be expected. The ringers were, after all, somewhat short of practice. During another lull, Ethel said, 'Forgive my asking, May, but what about Emily now? John William will soon be home and coming to see her, I suppose?'

There was a short pause. 'Yes. Yes, I expect so.'

'Will they marry, do you think?'

Again May hesitated. 'I really don't know, Ethel. No one knows, It's been so long, you see.'

'Yes, it's been a long time.'

As May left to call in on both Katy and Edith, there was an announcement on the wireless that, as expected, the following day would be a national holiday. Already one or two flags were beginning to appear at windows. While waiting to turn out of Cob Lane, she could see people running about in the market square. One or two were shouting. A few had begun to dance. From an open doorway someone at a piano could be heard playing 'There'll always be an England'. When she pulled up at East Lodge it seemed as if the whole of Wilhampton had started to sing, lustily, only this time it was 'Roll out the Barrel'.

29

The dress cost forty-nine and elevenpence plus eight clothing coupons in Elaine's on the corner of Westonbury's High Parade. It was blue with a white piqué collar and a white bow in the centre. Although it was made of ordinary utility material, it seemed to be of a rather better design than the majority of ready-mades to be bought in the town nowadays.

Normally, Emily would have asked May to make her a new dress, but there simply hadn't been time. John William had telephoned from Dover to say that he would be arriving the following morning. His parents were meeting him in London and they would all be spending the night at Brown's Hotel, where he would be able to change into what he called 'a little more respectable attire' which they would be bringing for him.

'I hope Alicia won't be upset,' Katy said to May, when she rang up to tell her the news, Emily having taken the bus into Westonbury to do some shopping once she had obtained Milroy's ready agreement to a week's holiday. 'I mean, I expect she imagined her son would be going to Bishopsdown first.'

Emily, too, had wondered the same thing, but she had not made any mention of this to the disembodied voice on the other end of the line: faint, rather nervous and hurried, giving her little time to say anything very much at all. She was not quite sure why she wanted a new dress to wear when she met John. After all, she already had one or two quite suitable ones, even if they were several years old. It was just that it seemed appropriate and might give her the confidence which appeared to be disappearing with every minute his arrival drew nearer.

She could never remember feeling quite so apprehensive and confused as she stood on Westonbury station the next day, not even when she had been a raw young nurse at the beginning of the war. At least then there had been others equally unsure and scared of doing or saying the wrong thing. But now she was quite alone, the problem intensely personal. She knew no one else in a similar position, had no girl-friend who had become engaged to a prisoner of war with whom, for four and a half years, the only contact had been by letter – and heavily censored ones at that. What would John look like? He would be bound to have changed. No one could be shut up in such conditions for so long and emerge quite the same person.

She had not long to wait now. The warning bell had rung. The London train was coming out of the tunnel. She could see the first few puffs of steam as it rounded the bend. A shaft of summer sunlight filtered down to where she was standing: a slim, pretty young woman with large sensitive eyes and dark shining hair which lifted a little in the breeze. Nervously, her right hand went up to her throat where she fingered the bow, rather in the same way as her Grandmother Lodge had been apt to finger her cameo brooch in moments of acute anxiety.

Slowly, the train drew to a halt, doors opened. She looked up and down the platform. At last she saw him coming towards her: tall, painfully emaciated, with an enormous black bruise on his forehead and a shiny dome where once there had been fair wavy hair. She found herself thinking, quite irrelevantly: I suppose he must have worn a wig when he played Mrs Cheyney.

'Emily!'

'John!'

He put down the small suitcase he was carrying and, again to her surprise, she became aware that they were shaking hands in an almost formal fashion.

Without saying more they went out through the ticket barrier together and she pointed to her mother's car. 'I was allowed to bring it,' she said, shyly. 'On an occasion like this I don't think anyone is going to query the use of petrol.'

'Oh. I was forgetting. Is there none for private motoring?'

'No. Not since 1942.'

He put his case in the back and got into the passenger seat beside her. As she drove off, he remarked, 'I'm afraid I look rather a sight. I got this bump in Antwerp the night before last. A Belgian family did us rather too well and I fell over a tank trap afterwards. We all got rather drunk. Not used to alcohol, you see. We've been warned to watch the amount we eat and drink for a while. I suppose it stands to reason. When you've been so hungry sometimes that you've swapped orange peel for a raw mouse, your stomach shrinks.'

Appalled, she crashed the gears badly at the bottom of the station approach. 'Did you *really* do that, John?'

'Yes. And much worse on occasions. I mean, when one is desperate for food, there's hardly anything one wouldn't do to get it. Do you mind if I smoke?'

'No. No, of course not.'

He lit up and inhaled deeply. 'Sorry, I should have asked. Do you, now?'

'No.'

'Just as well. I'm glad. I smoke whenever I have the chance. Of course, there were periods when we didn't have any at all in the camp. That was hell. The Red Cross parcels were very erratic, especially towards the end.'

'Who finally liberated you?'

'The Yanks. Part of the Ninth Army. But do you know we'd become so conditioned to the Germans taking roll call three times a day that we simply went on taking it amongst ourselves. Couldn't get used to the idea of freedom, somehow.'

She drove him home over the Barbury turnpike and at the top she pulled up at the point where they had so often stopped before; but apart from saying 'Good Lord' when he saw the American camp, he hardly seemed to register the rest of the scene, the Willon valley below them looking at its best in the bright May sunshine. There was something distant about him, as if his mind was back in Germany, still reliving the experiences of the past, unable to accept and appreciate the present. He did not attempt to kiss her and for this she was grateful, for she did not know how she would have reacted. He simply lit another cigarette and said, 'I must tell you about Stanton.'

'Stanton?'

'Yes. Stanton Pearson. I thought when we go back to Bishopsdown I'd get him to come and stay. I'd like you to meet him.'

She frowned, a little hurt at the automatic assumption that she would return with him without being actually *asked*.

'He's been my bridge partner for the last year and a half, after he was sent on from an Italian prisoner-of-war camp. We became almost unbeatable. Talk about Culbertson. We're thinking of teaming up together sometime. Going in for championships. That sort of thing. I suppose having so little else to do, other than taking part in amateur theatricals, it was a question of practice making perfect.'

'Didn't you ever study? I thought you once wrote that you were going to do some course on philosophy?'

'I meant to. But ... I don't know ... when you're herded together in a room with three hundred beds, end to end in two rows, and a gramophone constantly going and people hammering makeshift stoves out of old tin cans and others talking and trying to swat flies or catch fleas ... well, it isn't easy.'

'No. I suppose not.' She felt infinitely compassionate. The idea of John having to contend with *fleas* was somehow wholly shocking. She started the engine. 'I think perhaps we should be getting on. Mummy and Maurice will be expecting us for lunch at East Lodge.'

He made no objection. He did not even remark on the fact that they would be going to Wilhampton and not Netherford because her mother had remarried. As they descended the hill, he was busy explaining how he had thought of escaping.

'There was a time,' he said, 'when we were being moved in convoy. We had to get up in these trucks and I reckoned if I sat in one at the back which was open, perhaps I could jump off just after we'd gone round a bend and hide in the hedge before the next one followed. I almost did it, but in the end my heart was beating so fast, I didn't dare. Just as well, I expect. I wouldn't be here if I'd been caught. The Gestapo would have shot on sight. I'll never know how some of us managed to get away, although I must say it was absolutely amazing the ingenuity people showed. And we did have very clever back-up services. You know, chaps we called "tailors" who were always transforming uniforms into civilian clothes, as well as a forgery department which turned out the most authentic-looking identity documents. Stanton and I had the idea of posing as two foreign workers if the tunnel we were helping to dig was never discovered. But of course it *was*. And there would always have been trouble with the language problem once we'd got out. I knew a bit of German, so that I might just have been able to get away with pretending to be an alien travelling home to visit a sick mother, but Stanton didn't know any.'

'Where is he now?'

'At home. In Sussex.'

'Was he a prisoner long?'

'Not quite as long as me. He was captured in the desert at Sidi Barrani and, believe it or not, he was transported across the Med from Benghazi to Taranto in an Italian submarine which was actually depth-charged by the British.'

'What is he going to do when he's demobbed?'

'I don't think he knows. Rather like me. His parents run some pub.'

She was surprised. Somehow she did not associate John with making such a firm friendship with the son of a publican.

Katy and Maurice came out into the hall of East Lodge as soon as they stepped inside the front door. After some initial greetings, John began talking rather as he had done ever since Emily met him at the station. Beginning with an explanation about the bruise on his forehead, she found herself listening to a repeat performance. Both her mother and stepfather were naturally extremely interested and sympathetic, yet when the meal was over and she and John went out into the garden alone to sit in the summerhouse, she wished that the conversation had not been quite so one-sided. When, after a while, he said that he would like to go and see his uncle and aunt at the Hall, she felt a certain amount of relief.

'Come along then.' He stood up.

'You mean you want me to come, too?'

'But of course. They'll be expecting me to bring my fiancée.' For the first time he looked down at her left hand. 'Why aren't you wearing the ring Mummy sent?'

'I . . . John . . . There's something I've got to tell you. Two years ago . . .' She stopped and then went on, with a rush, 'I had a love affair with someone else.'

'*A love affair with someone else?*'

She had all his attention now. He stared at her, incredulously. 'Who?' he asked.

'An American officer.'

'An *American officer*,' he repeated. Then he said, quickly, 'Emily, you didn't sleep with him, did you?'

'No.'

His relief was undisguised, yet there was still an accusing look in his eyes. 'What happened?'

'He went away . . . when he realized . . . well, there was you. He married someone else. He was wounded during the D-Day landings.'

'Why didn't you tell me?'

She flushed. 'I sometimes wondered whether to . . . but it was so difficult, John. There you were, shut up in Germany . . . and then . . . I got ill . . .'

'So *that* was what was the matter. I never could understand what was wrong, why you didn't carry on nursing.' He paused and then, all at once, his whole manner seemed to brighten. 'Anyway,' he said, 'it's all over now. And you didn't go to bed with him, thank God. I couldn't have stood that. There's really nothing to stop us getting married quite soon, is there? I suppose you'll want a bit of time to get your trousseau together but, knowing your aunt, I dare say she'll soon see to that. How about the middle of June? It would be a lovely time for a wedding.'

30

'Maurice, I wondered if I could have a word with you, if you're not too busy.'

'Of course, my dear. Come into my consulting room.'

One of the nicest things about her stepfather, Emily thought, as he courteously opened the door for her, was that he always seemed to have time for her mother and herself. He was the sort of man she could invariably rely on, whose judgement was sound and with whom she could discuss anything – or practically anything. The subject she was about to bring up was certainly not an easy one; but with John having gone to the Headquarters of Southern Command to find out when Netherford Grange might possibly be de-requisitioned, she was anxious to take the opportunity.

He motioned her to the chair usually occupied by his patients and she sat down, registering the reassuring faint but familiar smell of furniture polish and antiseptic.

'It's about John,' she said, coming straight to the point.

He smiled. 'I thought it probably was.'

She hesitated a little. 'He's not . . . himself, Maurice.'

This time his expression changed. 'We all realize that, Emily,' he answered. And then, when she appeared to be finding it difficult to go on, he continued, 'No one can go through what he has gone through for four and a half years and be the same.'

'No. But . . . it's something much more. It's hard to explain. He used to be so sensitive. And now . . . well . . . he behaves quite abnormally, does things he would never have dreamt of doing. Sometimes, when we're walking along the street he keeps looking in the gutter. He says one never knows what might come in useful, that scavenging has become a habit. And the other evening, when we went to supper with Aunt Chip and she happened to leave a tiny piece of bread on her side plate, he picked it up and ate it himself, giving her a terrible lecture on wasting food.'

'These things will pass, Emily. They're understandable. For many years he's been concerned with sheer survival. But that's not what you're really worried about, is it?'

'No.' She looked at him, mutely. His heart went out to her. He would have done anything for this young girl whom he had watched grow up and loved as the daughter he had never had.

Suddenly, she burst out, 'It's not that I don't feel desperately sorry for him, but it's this other man, his friend, Stanton. John keeps talking about us getting married, but it's almost as if he feels it was . . .' she broke off while she hunted for the right word. '*Ordained*,' she went on, 'as if it's *got* to happen, something he and his family have been expecting. Yet last night he suggested that once we *are* married, Stanton might come and live with us. It's not . . . natural, Maurice.'

He was silent. She was still twenty-three, but she had been through a lot, seen a good deal of human nature one way or another, nursed men who were seriously sick and often extremely difficult; yet not, he suspected, in the way John William was. He wondered if she had any inkling. After all, she was well-read and she had understudied in two of Oscar Wilde's plays recently. Emily was no fool. And he had noticed the speculative look she had given John the previous evening, when they had all gone to the theatre to see *There's Always Juliet* and the boy began telling her in the interval how he himself would have played the part of Leonora.

Maurice Fitzherbert had never been a bitter man, but he felt now a great rage welling up inside him because of the way the war had torn apart the life of the young woman before him. She should never, of course, have become officially engaged. She had been 'used', particularly by Alicia Moreton. There was a time when it had been obvious that John's mother had not considered Emily Mason good enough for her precious only son. Yet she had been all for announcing their betrothal when she realized how much it would help John during his incarceration. When that American had come along, Emily should have broken the thing off, written to John William, however cruel a blow it might have been at the time. She should have followed her instincts, married Vernon Keeler. Except, *no*. Of course not. He was forgetting. The poor chap was in a pretty bad way now, by all accounts. A wife and child, only one leg and no job to go back to. Either way Emily was at the losing end. She'd had a raw deal.

'What,' he asked, gently, 'have you said to John about marriage?'

'I've said that I think we've both changed, that we aren't sure and that we ought to wait a while. I've suggested that he goes back to Suffolk to spend some time with his parents.'

'And what did he say to that?'

'Not a lot. Sometimes, he seems so wrapped in himself that he doesn't really appear to be listening. I thought . . .

later on . . . I would simply write him a letter. You know, the one I never sent when he was in Germany.'

'Have you,' he asked, 'told your mother about this?'

'Not exactly everything. But I'm sure Mummy knows. She's pretty perceptive.'

'Yes.' He sighed. Katy and he had doubted for many months that Emily and John would ever marry, but they had been practically certain of it as soon as he had stepped over the threshold of East Lodge. Yet neither of them had envisaged the extra underlying complication which made the whole idea impossible, even repugnant.

When his stepdaughter left him, he sat for a long time lost in thought. The girl had a future in the theatre. He felt fairly certain of that. She ought to get away, go to London as Milroy Stevens had advocated, even if she was more interested in writing plays than acting in them. She needed a break. She might have had plenty of unusual experiences for someone of her age, but she had scarcely left her home ground. Helen Swayne, or Helen Mackay, as she was now, had seen much more of the world than Emily. He would talk to Katy about it. They could surely find somewhere for her to live. He believed his sister had some friends in Kensington. The trouble was that conditions wouldn't be easy in post war Britain. The 'old country', as the Americans called it, would be bursting its seams with all the GIs waiting to go back to the States or even to the Far East. He prayed that Emily's cousin, Frank Lodge, and Helen's brother, Tim, wouldn't be sent on out there. He had not forgotten that the Allies still had the Japs to contend with.

It was, perhaps, May who took Emily's tragic situation most hard. She had quickly forgiven John for his sudden tirade at supper. She had told Katy that the poor boy was overwrought, like many of their patients had been at the Hall. He needed a long rest and Emily's love. She was quite prepared to admit that possibly a June wedding was rushing things. A month or so later would give her more time to produce the kind of trousseau she had always dreamed of. Thirty years ago it had been one for herself. Five years after that, when she had more or less given up the thought of marriage, it had been for her youngest sister, Katy. There had always been a vision of a cream satin wedding dress and a veil of Brussels lace somewhere in the back of her mind. And if only Emily had been going to marry this August or September, a going-away outfit in pale gold shantung would have been just about perfect.

But now, sadly, apparently it wasn't to be. No final link-up would take place between the Fairfax family and the Lodges of the one-time Mill House, Wilhampton. It was as if fate had severed, with a knife, that strange, undeclared, indefinable relationship which had lasted getting on for half a century. She could see the April afternoon, as if it were yesterday, when she and Flo had first been summoned to the Hall to make clothes for John's grandmother; she could remember the shining summer morning on Westminster Bridge when she had taken Katy to London to start working as nursery-maid for Alicia Moreton, who was expecting her first baby; she could recall the time that same child, nearing his tenth birthday, had first met Emily at the mill. Her niece must have been about seven and a half then. And she thought of that July day ten years later when John had taken Emily to the Eton v. Harrow match at Lord's, and the look in his eyes on catching sight of her in the white dress May had made specially for the occasion. It was the same look which she had noticed him give her when he was home on leave from the RAF the following summer. And now everything had gone wrong.

Typically, May began taking much of the blame on her own shoulders. She should never have let Katy agree to having an American billetee. Surely that was at the bottom of it. If Vernon Keeler hadn't come into their lives, with his bold impulsive ways, Emily would never have been swept off her feet, never have had that illness, would have now been staying at Bishopsdown with John and his parents, planning the wedding and, in the fullness of time, her favourite niece would have become Lady Moreton. How pleased Sarah would have been.

At the thought of her mother, May's eyes strayed to the photograph in the silver frame standing on the small antique escritoire at her side. It had been taken by Philip during that glorious summer of 1929, before the winter floods arrived and Sarah had died in May's arms on that terrible December night, when Bulbarrow sluice had collapsed and all the water came pounding down through the mill and hit the house. He had caught his mother-in-law at her best, however much she might have denied it simply because, in her eyes, Philip was rarely able to do anything right. All the rest of the family had realized it was a wonderfully lifelike snapshot, revealing all the proud elegance of an elderly woman: the determined, almost aristocratic profile, the immaculate coiffure, the erect figure wearing her best black moiré dress with the little tucker of snow-white lace at the throat. Sarah could well have been an actress, except that she had always looked upon theatre folk with the utmost contempt, carefully concealing the fact that her own grandmother had run away from home to go on the stage. What would she say now if she knew that her own grand-daughter was so interested in the profession? But surely it was in the blood somewhere?

It was the kind of thing which got handed down, May reflected, as she made her way slowly to bed. It might occasionally skip a generation, but somehow or other it would always be there, like the mill-race.

31

Colonel Frank Lodge, MC, came down the steps of a Dakota which had just landed at Old Sarum aerodrome. It was August 5th, 1945. He was returning from Germany on ten days' leave and had eagerly taken the unexpected chance of being able to fly rather than travel by train and boat. He had quickly sent a telegram to his relatives in Wilhampton, asking if he could spend the night either at East Lodge or the Hermitage before going on to his parents' home in Catterick. Although May would dearly love to have had her favourite nephew to stay with her, she had immediately realized how nice it would be for Emily if the young man went to Katy's house and, with her usual unselfishness in such matters, had told her sister to wire back to that effect.

Now, as Frank François went into a call-box to say he would be arriving around 8 p.m., he found himself greatly looking forward to the visit, particularly to seeing his cousin again. When he discovered that she was at the theatre in Westonbury taking part in a special Sunday evening charity concert, he had asked his aunt if, provided it would not upset any arrangements she might have made, he could pick Emily up there and take her out for something to eat afterwards.

Having obtained Katy's whole-hearted approval, he glanced at his watch. With any luck, he might just be in time to see the end. There was a car waiting for the Wing Commander who had flown him from Leipzig and this same benefactor had kindly offered to give him a further lift into the centre of the town.

As Frank walked along the High Parade, he tried to remember when it was he had last seen Emily. With a shock, he realized it must be getting on for three years. They had, of course, corresponded, although there had been times when circumstances had prevented it. He was aware that she had been very ill at some stage. He was not quite sure why. Letters from the family had never been very forthcoming on the subject. He wondered what had gone wrong when her fiancé had come back from the prisoner-of-war camp. She had simply written to say that they were not marrying, that she was busy working at the local theatre and in the autumn she would be going to London to attend the Royal Academy of Dramatic Art. Poor Emily. She had always aroused his compassion. There was something vulnerable about her. She was different from any of the other young women he had known. He hoped she hadn't been hurt too much.

It was quite difficult getting into the theatre because the box office had shut up shop. In the end, he simply barged his way through a side entrance, explained what had happened and was allowed to sit down in the only empty seat available. So well made-up was Emily that he hardly recognized her when she came on; but he was sufficiently knowledgeable about the theatre to appreciate her talent. When he went round backstage as soon as the show was over, he was able to congratulate her with the utmost sincerity.

She looked very different across the small table at the White Lion in the special room where late snacks were served. She was obviously older and much more mature than when he had last seen her, but she was still very beautiful. There was no doubt about that. It was her eyes which most affected him: haunting, luminous, the kind which seemed to speak volumes without her having to utter a word.

'Fill me in with all the gaps,' he said, when some sausages and mash had been put before them.

She smiled. 'I'd sooner you did that. After all, look what *you've* done. I rather let the side down, getting ill and then having to give up nursing. I often feel guilty about it.'

'You needn't. I bet you're doing far more good than if you were tying a bandage round some chap's arm. A lot of women can do that. Not many can do what you were doing tonight.'

'Nice of you, Frank. But you always did make me feel better about things. I've missed seeing you. But please tell me about yourself. Are you going to be demobbed soon?'

'I hope so. The powers that be have been a bit sticky about it. I suppose . . . well, I got this promotion rather quickly and pressure's been put on me to become a regular. But I've got my own plans, once we've finally licked the Japs. You may not remember, but when I was a kid I wanted to go into the printing trade. That's changed slightly. There's someone in the regiment who was in publishing before the war. With any luck, he's going to give me an opening.'

'How splendid. Then you'll be in London?'

'All being well. If you're up there, too, we should be able to get around a bit together.'

They dropped into the easy uncomplicated relationship they had once known. It was as if they had simply picked up where they had left off, any intervening experiences coming into their conversation quite naturally. Even her love affair with Vernon and the time she had spent in Dr Schmidt's nursing home was no embarrassment. Only when she touched on John's return, and the reasons for calling everything off, did she hesitate. He did not press her. He had the Lodges' sensitivity coupled with a good deal of intuition, some of the latter possibly also derived from his French mother. He reckoned Emily would tell him all about it in her own good time.

It was late when they got back to Wilhampton, having walked the whole three miles. But it had not seemed long. There was a brilliant moon and the summer-scented air was soft and warm. When they neared East Lodge they could hear the mill-race in the distance, immutable, insistent, as always.

By mutual consent they turned into River Lane and paused where the Willon flowed past the mill gates. A willow tree had been felled close by and they sat on its stump, silently watching the water, its surface brimming and bright in the moonlight.

Suddenly, Frank François said, 'I wish to God you weren't my cousin.'

She turned towards him, a puzzled, almost fearful look in her large eyes.

'I've never met anyone I'd sooner marry, Emily,' he continued, by way of explanation.

She did not speak for a while. When at last she did, she said slowly. 'I appreciate the compliment, Frank, more than I can say. But . . . I don't think I shall ever marry anyone, now.'

'I wouldn't be too sure of that,' he replied. 'One day you might change your mind.'

Again they lapsed into silence. An owl hooted and then flew low overhead. Back at East Lodge, Katy Fitzherbert stirred a little in her husband's arms. At the Hermitage, May Lodge lay peacefully dreaming, having that very day received a long letter from Betsy Mead confirming that she was looking forward to coming to live with her in the autumn. Up on downside, Edith Lench slept soundly, too, happy in the knowledge that her two eldest sons, as well as her son-in-law, were safe and that Debbie would soon be home for good. In her small back bedroom Georgie and Porty snored.

At Bulbarrow, Helen and Colin Mackay were still awake, whispering excitedly about the prospective farm that Dick Swayne was taking them to see in two days' time and where, though he was still in Germany, they hoped Tim might soon be joining them. At the Hall, someone else was also awake. Rachel Fairfax was thinking about wedding plans for her eldest daughter, Belinda, who had just got engaged. Edmund was in London, ostensibly staying at White's, but she did not mind. She suspected he had yet another inamorata. She believed that nowadays they were considerably younger than Chloe Ford, who she felt must be getting rather long in the tooth. Life was really much easier when her husband was out of the way. Somehow she no longer felt unequal to the many tasks which confronted her, such as Belinda's marriage and, in due course, moving back into the Hall. During the war years she seemed to have come into her own. She felt that Wilhampton had accepted her, even if she was not the same *force majeure* as her late mother-in-law, the old dowager.

Thinking about the Fairfax family, Rachel wondered what was happening to John William these days. Alicia had been curiously reticent about him, even rather short-tempered when she had enquired. She was glad that he and Emily had not married after all; although she hoped the girl would find some suitable husband soon. It was a pity about that love affair with the American. She had not known what had happened in the end. Neither was she aware that at this very moment the Keelers were on the high seas, returning to the United States in the SS *Argentina* which, being still converted as a troop ship, meant that Vernon was segregated each night from his GI bride and baby son. He spent much of the time on deck, his expression inscrutable as he gazed silently at the white-capped waves. Soon, they would be seeing the Statue of Liberty.

Even further away from Wilhampton, on the other side of the world, in a land where the sun had already risen heralding a new day, a little Japanese boy called Taro Suzaki looked up from where he was playing by a stream. Suddenly, in the distance, he saw a strange dark mountain rising into the sky, its top spreading out like a mushroom and becoming larger and larger. Panic-stricken, he ran indoors screaming, 'Okaa-san, Okaa-san,' and his mother came at once and held him close, while she, too, stared at the terrifying sight – then quickly turned the other way.

What had been the city of Hiroshima at 8.15 a.m. on Monday, August 6th, 1945, had now gone up in a cloud of dust-filled smoke. The Second World War was over.

Back in England, Emily looked at her watch. It was twenty past midnight, time to go home to bed. Yet still she and Frank lingered, unwilling to disturb the peace of the moment as the Willon flowed serenely on under a starlit sky.

Unto the Fourth Generation

Part One

1

'And it's definite I'm pregnant?'

'Yes, Mrs Vandenburgh.'

'When do you think the baby will arrive?'

'From what you have told me, I should say the beginning of September. Round about the third.'

'Thank you, Dr Peterson.'

She wished him goodbye and drove home slowly along the back road, trying to accustom herself to the situation which had now been confirmed. At the turning which led into Lower Hensford, she drew into the side and stopped the car. A little below her, lying in a small hollow, she could just see Hensford House, a grey stone early Georgian building, still half hidden by trees even though, except for a few evergreens, their branches were bare. In the summer, when the leaves were out, when her child was born, it would not be possible to see it at all from the surrounding Cheshire countryside. She had always thought of it as a secretive place. People said it was beautiful and, objectively, she knew that was true; yet to Emily it was too cold, too impersonal, almost as if it resented its inhabitants. And it seemed so very much Richard's home, not hers.

Of course, a child, or children, would make all the difference. Perhaps that was what it needed, what it was waiting for. As far as she could make out, there had not been a young family at Hensford for a long while. It had changed hands many times since the turn of the century, most of its owners, for one reason or another, leaving because of adverse circumstances. The last occupant had apparently sold up because his wife was suffering from melancholia.

At the time of Emily's wedding in 1947, she had given little thought to the history of the place of which she was about to become mistress. Like other possible drawbacks, such as the gap in her and her fiancé's ages – Richard was thirteen years older than she was – his extraordinary mother and the necessity for abruptly ending her own drama training, she had ignored everything except the fact that she was in love. When, two years previously, she had told Frank François – the cousin who was in love with *her* – that she did not think she would ever marry, he had replied that one day she might change her mind. She realized now how right he had been. She had changed it overnight at a party in London, because the man to whom she was introduced looked exactly like Vernon Keeler, the American officer for whom she had fallen so heavily during the war.

But that, sadly, seemed to be as far as the similarity went, as she was gradually coming to find out. Richard Vandenburgh might have been dark, good-looking, attractive and amusing – in public. But there was another side to him, one she was still at a loss to understand, however hard she tried. Whereas poor Vernon, hardly surprisingly, had shown a certain bitterness after he had lost a leg during the Normandy invasion, her husband would become moody and depressed for no apparent reason at all.

On such occasions she had tried a little gentle probing, only to be angrily brushed aside. Puzzled and hurt, she had learnt to keep her own counsel. She knew that Richard had not had a bad war in that, possibly because of his age, he had mostly been given staff jobs. He had not been wounded in action like Vernon, nor had he been shut up in a prisoner-of-war camp like John Moreton, the young man to whom she was once engaged. She sensed that the difficulties afflicting her husband were of a totally different, more complex kind and hoped that perhaps one day, in his own good time, he would come to talk to her about them. At least his curious bouts of malaise did not appear to affect him for very long at a time. A trip to London or one or two friends in to dinner and he would be back on form. She was expert now at thinking up distractions.

Their life together might not have been quite as she envisaged when, starry-eyed, she had come down the aisle of St Mark's, Wilhampton, wearing the cream satin wedding dress that Aunt Chip had long been hoping to make for such an occasion. But she was by no means unhappy, Emily reflected, as she sat now, looking at the house which was, and yet was not, her home. It was, of course, always a little more tricky when Sybilla, her mother-in-law – or Ma, as she called her – came back from her travels and took up residence on the top floor. And Emily could have wished that Richard was not so keen on social life, that he would be content to spend more evenings alone with her, that he would take greater pleasure in reading or listening to music. Even, perhaps, that he wanted sex more often. She was still, physically, very much in love with him. There were times when she would see him walking towards her across the garden and she could have sworn it was Vernon. It was all she could do, then, not to run and throw her arms around him. But she knew that would never do. Richard disapproved of too overt demonstrations of affection.

She wondered what he would say when she told him about the baby. She felt he would be pleased, although disappointed if it turned out to be a girl. She did not think he really cared for children, although he might be different with one of his own. Possibly, because of his rootless upbringing, he showed a great desire to lead a fairly conventional existence, to give the impression of a typical English country gentleman and this, surely, would be greatly enhanced by the existence of an heir.

As for herself, she hardly knew what to think about the forthcoming event. Since her marriage, she had always imagined that she would one day become a mother, but she had never longed for children as she believed many women did. She knew that her baby had been conceived by accident, because she had deliberately made advances to Richard one night when they had gone over a fortnight without any sex. They had taken a chance and that chance was going to alter the rest of their lives.

There were many times when Emily wished she was more like Helen Mackay, her lifelong friend with whom she had grown up back in the west country, who now had two children and seemed set on having four more. Although how she and her husband were going to combine rearing such a large family with running the dairy farm which they had taken on at the end of the war, Emily could not imagine. Their circumstances were so very different from her own that she had often felt guilty when visiting them. Helen had no help in the farmhouse, yet at Hensford she herself had a married couple living in the staff flat and two excellent dailies, to say nothing of a gardener and a boy.

Sometimes she wondered where exactly her time went. She supposed that in spite of continuing rationing and shortages of one sort or another, it was spent on entertaining or being entertained. If she hadn't been so anxious to turn herself into the kind of wife she believed Richard wanted, she felt she would like to have got started on the play she had always intended to write. But somehow such an undertaking invariably faded into an ever-receding future. Perhaps now, with the baby on the way, she would be able to sit back with a clear conscience and get down to it. After all, marriage might have forced her to give up any thought of acting, but it should not necessarily preclude her earlier ambition of creating characters out of her own head.

She was surprised to pass a taxi coming away from Hensford House as she drove up to the front door, and not a little disconcerted when she discovered her mother-in-law standing in the hall surrounded by suitcases, with Mrs Draper, the housekeeper, hovering in the background. Sybilla Vandenburgh had not been expected for another week, although Emily had begun to accept her comings and goings as but one manifestation of her totally unpredictable character.

'My *dearr*!' Ma now came towards her, arms outstretched, and kissed her on both cheeks. She was a small pale woman, Scandinavian by birth, her once fair hair now dyed ash-blonde, her big blue eyes curiously opaque, her outward appearance of frailty belying the steeliness within, as hard as the diamonds on the numerous rings which always covered her fingers.

'You don't mind my arriving early, *dearr*, do you?' she continued. 'But suddenly Paris was no more *fun*. All my bridge friends were leaving. So I say to myself I need my son and daughter-in-law and some sunshine. I go back to England and whisk them up and then we all take the Olsen Line to Madeira and maybe I go on to the Cape. Yes?'

'Well . . .' Emily hesitated. She had no desire to go abroad with Ma, especially now she was pregnant. She had already begun to feel sick although, contrary to what might have been expected, only in the evenings. But, in any case, the government restrictions on foreign travel were still such that she and Richard would be obliged to let Ma finance the trip with money which came from her late husband, a South African who had made a fortune gold-mining in that country. Being continually indebted to Ma might not bother Richard, but it certainly bothered her.

'Don't look so worried, Emily darlink. I tell my friends how my beautiful daughter-in-law is always so full of *Angst*. You must live for the moment, like me. Anyway, I talk to Richard about it. Where is he? Out with the shooters?' Ma had never lived long enough in England to be able to use the correct phraseology, especially when it came to country pursuits. She had once highly embarrassed both Richard and herself at a local meet by referring, loudly, to the 'dogs'.

'Yes, I don't suppose he'll be back till about six. He generally stays on for tea and a drink with his host and hostess.'

'Ah. Then I think I go to my quarters.'

After Mrs Draper had brought up some tea and Emily had switched on several heaters and settled her mother-in-law in, she went to her own bedroom and lay down. It was already getting on for the time when she expected to feel queasy. She wished Ma had not appeared on this particular day. She had been looking forward to telling Richard her news when they were quite alone. Now, he would almost certainly be distracted by his mother's arrival, fussing that she had all she needed, possibly pleased and preoccupied with her suggestion of going to Madeira. The shooting season would soon be over and

Emily recalled how last year this time he had been more than usually bored and moody, chafing at the inactivity in the countryside during January, February and March. With a manager running the place there was no reason why he should not go away.

Idly, she wondered how much of a problem Ma might become as she got older. She had already passed sixty, yet was apparently still fit enough at the moment for endless globe-trotting. But there could come a day when she might be forced to take up permanent residence with them at Hensford. Presumably, she would feel quite entitled to do that. After all, it was she who held the purse strings, although Emily had never been able to understand all the complicated provisos connected with the will Ma's husband had made on his deathbed. Richard had then been but a child, one in whom he had never shown any interest and would appear to have almost actively disliked. If ever there was a case of dead hands stretching out from the grave it seemed those of Frederick Vandenburgh. Knowing the kind of lifestyle his wife would expect to lead after he had gone but also that she could become prey to fortune hunters, he had set up several trusts. On the condition that she did not marry again, Ma enjoyed a large income, but was only able to draw on capital at the discretion of her trustees. The buying of Hensford for Richard after the war, together with a thousand acres of Cheshire, had been one such contingency which she was adept at never letting her son forget. One day, when Ma died and the trusts terminated, all the monies would come to him outright. It was sometimes difficult for Emily to appreciate that Richard was a potentially very rich man unless, of course, Ma *did* marry again when, apparently, everything was to go to charity.

She heard his car coming down the drive now, saw the lights sweep across the bedroom window, for she had not yet bothered to draw the curtains. There was the scrunch of gravel, the slamming of doors, a shout to Brandy, his golden labrador, the sound of footsteps along the passage leading to the gunroom and then Richard's voice calling, 'Emily?'

She knew that he liked her to be around whenever he came home. Hastily, she threw herself off the bed – then retched, violently. It was all she could do to get to the bathroom in time.

2

'It will be lovely to see you, Emily. How will you be travelling?'

'I'll drive, Maurice.'

There was a slight pause on the other end of the telephone and then her stepfather said, 'The roads could be tricky at this time of the year. But there's another reason, my dear. You've got quite a bit of foot and mouth up in your part of the world, haven't you?'

'Yes.'

'I was thinking of people like the Swaynes and Helen and Colin with their dairy herds. You know, cars coming from an infected area.'

'Oh, my goodness. How awful of me. I hadn't thought. We're so lucky at Hensford, being mostly arable.'

'Of course, they're taking every precaution round here. Disinfectant at all the farm entrances. Discouraging any unnecessary callers. That sort of thing.'

'Nevertheless, I couldn't bear to think I might be helping to spread the wretched disease. I'll certainly come by train.'

'How long can you stay?'

This time it was she who hesitated. 'Well, could you put up with me for, say, a week?'

'As if we couldn't. Make it longer if you can. Your mother will be delighted when I tell her. She's sure to give you a ring as soon as she gets back from Westonbury. Then you can arrange the date and what time we should meet you at the station.'

Did he think it odd, she wondered, as she put down the receiver, that Richard was going away without her? Probably. But then she hadn't told him her real news yet. That must wait until she was at Wilhampton. She had merely said, briefly, that Richard was having a little break with his mother and she felt she would like to take the opportunity of paying them a visit. She had not said anything about the fact that he was going abroad and possibly would be gone for two or three weeks. Maurice would definitely have thought that very odd indeed. She doubted that he could bear to be parted from his own wife for even a day now that, at long last, he had been able to marry her.

There were marriages and marriages, she thought, after saying goodbye to Sybilla and Richard. And so many different kinds of love. She recalled how that was to have been the idea behind the play she was hoping to write. Perhaps it wasn't exactly original, but there were surely infinitely new ways of putting it across. Of course, it was possible she wasn't old enough to tackle the subject yet although, one way and another, she felt she'd had a certain amount of experience.

There was the business of her failed engagement, for instance; the long years of waiting for a young man incarcerated in a German prisoner-of-war camp who, when he finally came home, appeared to have a predilection for the same sex. She had known him since she was a small child, for he had been the grandson of the late Lord and Lady Fairfax at the Hall, Wilhampton. She had thought herself in love with him when he had first asked to marry her on the day war broke out, but it was scarcely to be wondered at that they had both changed during their long separation. She realized that she hadn't really known what it was to be in love until Vernon Keeler had come to England at the beginning of 1942 with the first contingent of US troops. As time went by, if only she – and more especially Vernon – hadn't been quite so conscious of Pilot Officer John William Moreton eating his heart out – or so they imagined – all those miles away in Oflag VA, she might well be in Chicago now, married to a man with one leg who, according to his wife's last letter, was mercifully holding down a job in a real estate firm.

Then there was her cousin, Frank François. Dear Frank. What was it he had said on that starlit August night back in 1945 when they sat beside the Willon at just about the same time – had they but known it – that the bomb which ended the war was being dropped on Hiroshima? 'I wish to God you weren't my cousin, Emily. I've never met anyone else I'd sooner marry.' Frank was in London now doing well in a publishing house. He had made several subsequent references as to the possibility of their marrying, that many people considered it an old wives' tale that cousins produced abnormal children. He had even suggested that if she was not all that keen on motherhood, he would be quite happy to forgo the idea of children, altogether. And she had simply repeated, 'I appreciate the compliment, Frank, more than I can say, but I don't think I shall marry anyone now.' To which, one day with uncanny foresight, he had made the astute rejoinder, 'Unless the man in question happens to resemble Vernon Keeler.'

When Richard Vandenburgh had come along, Frank was one of the first people in whom she confided. She felt she owed it to him. She had even persuaded Frank to come and have dinner with them both one evening. It had been disappointing that the two men did not seem to get on better. There was a superficial cordiality and an exchange of war experiences, but Frank seemed to drop out of her life more and more after that. At the time of her wedding he told her that he himself would shortly be marrying – a girl whom Emily had only met once. She prayed the union would not turn out to be as disastrous as the one into which Maurice Fitzherbert had entered, obviously on the rebound, when her mother had first turned him down way back at the end of 1920.

But it wasn't just the man–woman relationship which still occupied her thoughts during the evening she started packing for Wilhampton. There was the love a mother gave to her children, even – as in her case – a stepfather to a stepdaughter. She hoped she would have enough of that sort of love to give to the young life within her. She remembered hearing someone once saying that the love for a child was the only purely unselfish kind. One didn't expect anything back – although Emily felt it must be very rewarding if one happened to get it. She wondered if maybe she was too selfish to have a baby, too wrapped up in being a wife. It was extraordinary how Richard Vandenburgh seemed to absorb her whole being, to put a check, however unintentionally, to any former desires and ambitions, although perhaps it was as well not to have too many of those once one was married.

It suddenly came into her mind what a marvellous wife and mother Aunt Chip would have made, especially the latter. It was ironical to think how often the people who should have married and had children seemed to remain spinsters. May Lodge, her mother's eldest living sister, was so totally selfless. It would be good to see her again soon. Even though Emily was missing Richard terribly, she could not help looking forward to her prospective visit. She had been very disappointed that there had been no family reunion at Christmas. Although she knew that there were perfectly valid reasons – their own overwhelming social commitments at Hensford, such as the Boxing Day shoot, and her stepfather's inability to leave his practice in Wilhampton where, since time immemorial, the doctor had been on call – she suspected that such obstacles were a relief to Richard. She had noticed more than once that, however hard he tried to conceal it, he was ill at ease in the presence of her family, even her friends. Helen and Colin Mackay were but a case in point.

The following day, after she had changed trains at Bristol and was nearing Westonbury, she began to feel almost childishly excited as she stared out eagerly on the well-known wintry landscape. There seemed something curiously protective about the majestic shoulders of the downs as they lay in echelon on either side of the windows, bare save for the small clumps of trees on the skyline which, at this time of the year, were no more than dark brown smudges, but later on would turn into what she had always likened to green velvet pincushions. Every so often she caught a glimpse of a small village or hamlet, a thatched cottage, grey smoke spiralling upwards, a flash of light on the River Willon or a chalky white-bright road. It was all so different from the flat Cheshire plain and made her think of yet another kind of love: that for the place where she was born and bred. Although she might now have got a home of her own, this seemed to be her real one, her *home ground*, where she belonged. With every mile that the train bore her closer to Westonbury, she felt as if some unseen umbilical cord was being pulled tighter and tighter.

As she expected, her mother was standing on the platform to meet her. Katy Fitzherbert was nearing fifty yet, since her second marriage during the last winter of the war, she seemed to have shed several years. There was a serenity, almost a radiance about her, which Emily could never remember seeing while she was growing up. Today, as usual, Katy was faultlessly dressed, her small still-youthful figure clad in a well-fitting camel-hair coat, a brown corduroy beret set at just the right angle on a head of hair still far from grey, which she now wore in a softer style than the rather severe bun which she had adopted while working for the Red Cross. A pair of thick suede gloves and boots completed her outfit. At the sight of Emily her enormous eyes lit up and she hurried towards her.

'Darling!'

'Mummy!'

But for the affectionate way they greeted and embraced each other, a stranger might not have thought them mother and daughter. Emily was a good three inches taller. Her eyes might have been almost as large but they were brown, not greeny-grey. Her hair, which she still wore in a long page-boy bob, was also very much darker than her mother's. Yet, although the younger woman had the more robust physique, there was a similarity about them, which any discerning person could not fail to appreciate. They had a certain something in common – an elegance, a quickness of expression, a sensitivity – which had been handed down through the generations, from handsome indomitable Grandmother Lodge to Katy and to Katy's daughter.

'I can't tell you how pleased we all are about your visit,' Katy said, as they went out into the station yard to the car. 'Aunt Chip can hardly wait to see you.'

'Did she say "Oh, chippatoo" when you told her I was coming?'

'Several times over.'

Emily smiled. No one knew from whence her aunt had coined the phrase, only that since May had been a small child she had always used it when she was particularly happy and hence had acquired her nickname. How many more times would her aunt use it, Emily wondered, when she heard about the baby? When should she tell them all? She was longing to say something this very minute, but felt it would be better to wait until at least Katy and Maurice were together. How should she put it? 'I've got news'? 'I'm going to have a baby'? No, 'Richard and I are going to have a baby.' Yet, strangely enough, she could not think of it like that, especially here, on her home ground. Richard seemed to have so little to do with it. Richard was far away on the high seas with Sybilla. How was she going to explain that? 'I didn't go along too because I decided it wasn't a very good idea. You see, I've started being sick every evening'? Would they understand?

She told them, quite quietly, just before tea, before the time when the nausea came on.

'You're going to be a grandmother and grandfather,' she said. There seemed no reason to use the prefix 'step'. Maurice seemed much more of a father to her than the one who had committed suicide when she was ten years old. She saw a look of incredulous joy come into their faces and she smiled back at them. 'In September,' she continued, 'about the first week in September.'

3

Sunlight sparkled on the frost-covered hedgerows as Emily walked down the lane to Netherford the following morning. Her mother had wanted to drive her to visit May at the White Hermitage, but she had insisted that the exercise would do her good. It was therefore arranged that Katy would call for her after lunch and take her on to Edenbridge to see Helen and Colin, and that the latter would bring her home.

She went slowly, delighting in each familiar landmark:

he bus-stop at the corner where she had so often stood waiting either on the way to school or, later, as a VAD in he war, when she was returning for duty at the emergency ospital near Westonbury; then there was the stile at the eginning of the right of way through Sweetacres Farm; he huge chestnut trees at the entrance to Netherford Grange, the one-time home of the Dowager Lady Fairfax, which, just conceivably, had she married the Dowager's grandson, might have become her own; the little hump-acked bridge over a tributary of the River Willon, and inally the Willon itself as it ran parallel with the lane. They were all there, indelibly printed in her heart and mind, for this was where she had spent most of her forma-ive years. It was to the White Hermitage that May Lodge ad shepherded a grieving sister and young niece after the ragedy which had threatened to overwhelm them.

That event was but hazy in Emily's memory now. At he time, she had simply been told that her father had been aken ill and fallen into the mill-race. Not until she was nuch older did she come to learn that he had committed uicide because of his involvement with a woman in London who, several months after his death, had borne his son. It was a strange story and even stranger when Emily thought how, a few years ago, her half-brother, Paul Woodley, had also found refuge at the aptly named Hermitage. She was sorry that she would not be seeing the boy today, because he would be away at boarding school. But she was looking forward to seeing Betsy Mead, the widowed sister of Paul's late mother, whom Katy and Maurice and May had befriended.

Emily had been pleased when, after her mother remar-ried, May had suggested that Betsy and Paul might like to live with her. She had been even more pleased when she heard how well the unusual ménage was working out. If, at the beginning, there had been speculation as to the identity of the pleasant-looking woman from Wales and her sturdy bright-eyed nephew, it had luckily soon died down. It seemed that May and Betsy, both alone in the world and each having known hardship and suffering, were more than a match for the gossip-mongers. Besides,

May was liked and respected by all and sundry. Sadl
Emily realized, it was only her own father, Philip Maso
who was still talked about disparagingly, when someor
or other started raking up the past.

She would occasionally try to console herself by thinkir
that there could have been few people who had real
known what had happened. As always, in times
adversity, the Lodge family had kept its own counsel ar
closed ranks. Even Edith, her widowed aunt who live
on downside, had only confided in her eldest unmarrie
daughter although, as time went by, Emily suspected th;
the rest of her children probably guessed the truth. Silenc
on the subject had also been helped by the fact that it w;
not until years later during the war, when more importai
matters were uppermost in people's minds, that Paul's sic
mother had appealed to Katy for help and the child
existence was gradually acknowledged. Somehow, t
Emily, there had always seemed a curious inevitabilit
about the way Paul Woodley had come into their lives an
eventually been brought up, just as she had been, at th
White Hermitage on the banks of the Willon.

Today, as she unlatched the garden gate, the front doc
opened immediately and May, who had obviously bee
watching out for her, stood on the step: a welcomin;
white-haired, gentle-eyed little woman who still, at th
age of fifty-nine, gave the impression of almost childlik
innocence, often confounding strangers by the wisdom an
acute perception that went with it. Although, on hearin
Emily's news, her reaction was one of enormous excit
ment and pleasure — as the constant use of her pe
expression made only too clear — May confessed durin
lunch that she had felt almost certain that was what he
niece had come to tell her.

'You must be psychic, Aunt Chip,' Emily said.

'No. I just thought it was about time, my dear,' Ma
replied. 'And September is a splendid month to have
baby. They can't do other than lie down for the first si;
months, so yours can be kept nice and snug throughou
the winter and then, as soon as it's able to sit up and tak
notice, the spring will be here.'

'I hadn't thought of it like that.' Emily marvelled at May's practical way of looking at things. Moreover, there had been no silly questions about whether Emily wanted a boy or a girl. Aunt Chip was so full of common sense. And she had appeared to accept, with perfect equanimity, the fact that Richard had gone on holiday with his mother. She had merely remarked, 'Well, naturally you wouldn't want to be on a boat at a time like this.' There was nothing in her manner to suggest that she might be thinking that, under the circumstances, Richard could or should have stayed at home.

After lunch was over, they got on to the subject of Paul. Betsy told Emily that he was doing well at school and hoped to go on to Oxford to read English. 'And then?' she enquired, tentatively.

For the first time there was a slight constraint in Betsy's voice. 'I'm . . . not sure,' she replied, slowly. 'He's mentioned the possibility of something in the book line. Of course, his mother . . .' She broke off, with obvious embarrassment.

Emily nodded. It was no good, now, pretending Barbara Woodley had never existed. She had been a literary agent who had worked her way up in the world. Philip had consulted her about the novel he had been trying to write, after he had come into some money and settled down in Wilhampton. From all accounts, Barbara Woodley had been somewhat of a manipulator. No two sisters could have been less alike.

'My cousin, Frank, might be able to help Paul there,' she said, as the garden gate clicked, announcing that Katy had come to collect her and drop her off at Ladywell Farm.

It was a very different scene which greeted her when she arrived. After the immaculate interior of the White Hermitage, Helen's kitchen seemed to overflow with dogs and cats, pots and pans, a pram and a pushchair, an assortment of gumboots and mackintoshes and Helen herself, older-looking, but unconcerned and smiling as she presided over the grand miscellany. It was hard for Emily to credit that this was the wartime Junior Commander who, with buttons and Sam Browne polished, would smartly return a private's salute or dress someone down for slipshod appearance or behaviour. Today, she was so very much the farmer's wife, the proud and indulgent mother.

'Here's your god-daughter,' she said, happily handing Emily a small, fair-haired, chubby-cheeked child of two and a half, who immediately clutched at the headscarf Emily was wearing, only to receive the mild rebuke from Helen, 'Oh, Joanna'.

'I'm sorry, Em,' she went on. 'But at this age they're into everything. They call it "the terrible twos". And I hate to keep saying "no". Robert's at a much easier stage, of course. Come and have a look at him.' She led Emily over to a pram in the corner where all that could be seen of the small form within was the top of his head. 'He'll wake soon, I expect,' she continued. 'Then you can see him properly. He's the spitting image of Bob.'

A flash of memory suddenly jerked Emily back over six years to that terrible November evening when her mother had come to meet her on Westonbury station, after she had been staying with her fiancé's parents. She had known at once from Katy's face that something was seriously wrong. She could hear again those fatal words, 'Bob Swayne was killed at Alamein. Helen will be coming home on forty-eight hours' compassionate leave tomorrow. I thought you should know. I expect you may want to see each other.'

'Your parents must be so pleased, Helen. About another Bob in the family.' Emily stood looking down at the pram which apparently held the spitting image of Helen's eldest brother.

'Oh yes. Tickled pink. Mummy comes over here as much as she possibly can. She's a tower of strength. I must say I didn't know bringing up kids meant quite so much work.'

'Are you still set on having six?'

'Well . . .' Helen laughed. 'We might make it four. But we still want a proper family.'

Faced by so much compliant chaotic domesticity, Emily felt somehow embarrassed about telling Helen that she herself was pregnant. She knew that she would have a nanny when the time came. Richard had made that quite plain. Children, according to him, were barbarians until they were at least six or seven years old. He would be delighted to have a son and possibly a daughter, but he really did not want to see too much of them until, as he put it, 'they were safe at both ends'.

When at last Emily did get around to imparting her news, she felt somehow disconcerted, even saddened by Helen's response. It was not that it wasn't initially just as full of genuine delight as the others she had received within the past twenty-four hours. It was simply that Helen had qualified hers by adding, 'I've been so hoping to hear that you and Richard were planning to start a family.'

Didn't she realize, Emily wondered? Had Helen not even considered it possible that there were no plans, that the child she was carrying was accidental, conceived because she had desperately wanted sex one night with a husband who happened to look just like Vernon Keeler?

There was the sound of heavy male footsteps outside the back door and presently Colin and Tim — Helen's younger brother who had joined them as a working partner after the war — came into the kitchen. Both men, like Helen herself, looked considerably older than when she had seen them a year ago. There were signs of weariness in their faces, yet they greeted Emily cheerfully enough, obviously delighted at seeing her. Only during tea, when the subject of foot and mouth disease inevitably cropped up, did all three custodians of Ladywell become unusually grave.

'Maurice warned me not to drive south,' Emily said. 'There's quite a bit of it where we are.'

'Just like him to think of that. Thank you, Em,' Colin replied. 'But it's a funny plague. I've heard of a farm with the disease next door, yet somehow it escapes. Then you suddenly find the wretched thing has hopped several hundred miles to some isolated place, for no apparent reason. It's the thought of seeing all our cattle compulsorily destroyed if it comes to Ladywell that gets me. We've taken such care building up the herd. However, it's getting colder every day now, thank God. Much healthier. Foot and mouth seems to prefer wet weather. Let's change the subject. How's Richard getting on at Hensford?'

She did her best. It was a question she had been hoping to avoid. How could she explain that Richard had gone to Madeira to escape the rigours and boredom of an English winter? She had a sudden mental picture of him and Sybilla in some cocktail bar. Her husband lived in another world. She felt like a person with a foot in two camps, a quisling. She was aware that Helen was watching her, carefully. Then, mercifully, just at that moment the telephone rang and baby Robert woke crying. The Ladywell ménage had more important matters to attend to.

With her parents otherwise engaged, Joanna came round the table and placed a sticky hand on Emily's knee. She picked the child up, wondering what it would be like when she had one of her own.

4

She was large by the beginning of June, larger than she expected. At a routine examination she thought Dr Peterson took a little longer than usual. When she had dressed again and was facing him across the desk, he said, 'Is there a history of twins in the family?'

She looked at him, incredulously. '*Twins?*' she replied. 'Oh, no!'

Then she remembered. Of course, Aunt Edith, who had lived on downside but who now, with the help of one of her twin daughters, ran a village shop twenty miles from Wilhampton. She had paid them a brief visit when she was last down there. She supposed that because Della – Debbie's other half who had brought disgrace on the family by almost, but mercifully not quite, becoming an unmarried mother – was so rarely mentioned, she had practically forgotten her existence.

'I'm sorry,' she said, making a quick apology. 'Yes, I made a mistake. One of my mother's sisters had twins.'

'Ah.' He smiled at her, encouragingly. 'And that seems to be what you are going to have, Mrs Vandenburgh.'

She remained silent for a few moments, her mind racing. She thought: what on earth will Richard say? I'll need two of everything. I'll have to get in touch with that nanny we've engaged. Will she be prepared to take them on? And what about the monthly maternity nurse, too? She felt a kicking inside her. Which one? A boy? A girl? Dear God, I don't think I feel equal to *twins*.

'Don't worry.' The man in front of her had sensed her agitation. 'Twins can be an enormous blessing. They entertain each other. You wait. But under the circumstances, I should like you to see Dr Hedley in Stoke Wallington. Just as confirmation, really. I see no complications. I'll make an appointment, shall I, and let you know?'

'Yes. Yes, thank you,' she managed to say, at last.

She drove back to Hensford, shaken and apprehensive. She must ring her mother. Ask if there had been any other twins, further back . . . a long time ago. After all, what did she really know about her ancestors? She had a dim recollection of Grandmother Lodge at the Mill House, some time when she was about seven years old, ticking her off for trying to dance the Charleston – but little else. It was only now, now that another generation was on the way, that she had begun to think more and more about the past, about heredity, whether the baby would take after Richard or her. Of course, there would be little she could find out about her father's side of the family, although her mother must know something. She believed Katy had a box with keepsakes in it, but it would hardly contain Philip Mason's family tree.

'*Twins*?' Richard said, when they were in the drawing room that evening, with the sun slanting through the mullioned windows. 'You don't mean to tell me you're expecting *twins*?' His incredulity matched her own when she had first heard Dr Peterson's pronouncement.

She watched her husband get up and go across to the cocktail cabinet, where he poured himself a large whisky and soda. When he came back and sat down again, there was an expression on his face which she could not quite fathom. 'So I'm to be the father of *twins*,' he went on. She wished he wouldn't keep repeating the word, that he would say something encouraging like Dr Peterson, or simply give her a kiss. Suddenly, she got up and left him. She no longer felt sick at this time of day, but she felt she wanted to be alone.

She went upstairs to the nursery she had created and sat in the window seat. She looked at the trimmed cot which would have to be duplicated, to the chest of drawers which would need another set of nappies, a second layette. I've made a mistake, she thought. I'm not cut out for motherhood. Or marriage. I should have abided by what I told Frank François at the end of the war. How I wish he were here now to hold my hand. I'll ask him to be a godfather. Good heavens, there'll even have to be two sets of godparents, I suppose.

There were footsteps on the stairs and then Richard stood in the doorway. 'I'm sorry, darling,' he said. 'I feel I've upset you. I realize it must have been one hell of a shock.'

She was mollified. He so rarely apologized. She smiled at him. 'It's all right. I'll get used to the idea.' She noticed he had refilled his glass.

'It's a pity,' he continued, 'that you can't drink. I should think you could do with one right now. But you haven't got much longer to go. And I've been thinking . . . it could be all for the best. So long as one of them's a boy we'll have got the production business over and done with. You won't have to go through it all again. It'll be like killing two birds with one stone.'

She shivered suddenly, in spite of the warmth of the evening. She wished he had not used that particular expression. It was such an unfortunate way of referring to a birth. And he had made it abundantly plain that he was really only interested in a son and heir. What if she had twin daughters?

'I thought I might put through a call to Ma in Cannes,' he said. 'I'd like her to know. I'll just about catch her before she leaves for the States.'

'Yes, do. And you might ask her if she knows of any twins on your side of the family.' Forlornly, almost childishly, she did not want to accept the whole responsibility, even though she had twin cousins.

He frowned. 'I don't think Sybilla would have a clue. She's never been concerned about that sort of thing. She lives for the present. Besides, I should have thought we've only got to look to your own forbears.'

She nodded, knowing his words made sense. 'Will Ma be here for the christening, do you think?' she asked.

'Oh yes. That will probably appeal to her. When do you think we might have it?'

'I should say sometime in October, if possible. November's such a horrid month and Hensford church will be freezing then.'

He left her and presently she heard him downstairs, telephoning – something she would do a little later on. But for the moment she simply sat there, watching the shadows lengthen beneath the huge cedar tree outside on the lawn, absently registering the vivid colours in the herbaceous border, now at its best, the honeysuckle and wisteria clambering over the old red brick wall behind it, the willows trailing their delicate green foliage in the pond at the far end of the garden, the blue haze beyond, where sky and horizon merged in the flat Cheshire plain. There was plenty of space, yet she felt trapped, trapped by her own body, by Richard, by Hensford. She was caught up in a situation over which she had no control. She knew it was wrong to feel like this. Guilt overwhelmed her. She had always been prey to a tender conscience. That was what her breakdown had been all about during the war: the worry over falling in love with Vernon Keeler and out of love with her fiancé, miles away in a German prisoner-of-war camp. Of course, this time it was a very different story. At least she was not involved with two men. Or was she? There was Richard Vandenburgh, her husband, and the ghost of Vernon always in the background. The thought came to her, horrifying, shocking. She was in love with the ghost, the man whom she used to meet clandestinely in the woods behind the emergency hospital back in the spring and summer of 1943 – not the man whom she had just heard putting down the telephone receiver.

Later on, when she had spoken to her own mother who, as she expected, had been kind, sympathetic and reassuring, Richard asked her to go out into the garden with him. She noticed that he was still being unusually considerate. 'If they're the same sex,' he said, 'we'll have to think up some more names.' They had already chosen Charlotte for a girl and Mark for a boy.

She began to feel infinitely weary; the fact that every problem seemed to have doubled within the last few hours was something she wanted to forget. She had received two shocks today: she was going to be the mother of twins and their father was no longer a man with whom she was in love. Some words of the Jewish refugee doctor who had treated her during her breakdown came suddenly into her mind: 'Your boat almost capsized . . . I suggest you paddle along slowly at first . . .' Well, she had to go slowly now, at least physically. She couldn't do much else. She had felt so ungainly walking across the lawn. This uncomfortable swelling up. The things nature did to one. Had Helen minded pregnancy? Or just accepted it? Rejoiced, even? She wished her best friend lived closer, that they could have one of their heart-to-hearts, as they used to do in the war. But even if Helen were not so far away, things between them could never be quite the same now. They each had a husband, husbands poles apart in every respect, yet to whom, as wives, they owed their first allegiance – although it was an allegiance which, in Helen's case, was obviously a pleasure.

There was a seat down by the pond and now, by mutual consent, she and Richard sat down on it, looking back towards the house, its austere grey stone mellowed by the evening sun. Here and there, a pane of glass flashed like some enquiring eye. She had a ridiculous feeling that the place was watching them. She saw Mrs Draper, in her white coat, cross the small courtyard at one end and disappear into the old dairy, now used as a store room but where her housekeeper also made butter, for rationing had still not ended, even though the war had been over for four years. Presently, she noticed Hardiman, the gardener, walking purposefully along the wide grass path to do some nightly watering in the greenhouses. In the distance, a car could be heard coming down the front drive and then turning off in the direction of Hensford Hollows. That would be Bert Chandler, their manager, going home. They had so many people, she thought, working for them, serving them. They were so lucky, when she compared their lot to that of Helen and Colin. And yet . . . There seemed no doubt who were the happier, who were living the more worthwhile life. Thank God the Mackays' and Swaynes' herds had escaped foot and mouth last winter.

'By the way . . .' Richard broke the silence almost, she felt, with diffidence. 'I hadn't realized, until I spoke to Ma tonight, that she's spending a little while in England before sailing for New York. She's not catching one of the Queens at Cherbourg, as I imagined. She said she wouldn't have time to come up here, but she's suggested that you and I might go down to London next week and stay at the Dorchester with her. She'd like to take us to see Ivor Novello's *King's Rhapsody*.'

'Oh.' She realized why he had waited until now before telling her. It was to let her calm down a little before broaching the subject. He must have known, surely, that she wouldn't want to go to town just now. All that travelling. And it was so *hot*, the hottest summer for years. Besides, Richard drove so fast in his new Jaguar, reputed to be able to do 120 m.p.h. although, with the roads still in the same state as they had been in at the end of the war, he often grumbled that there was nowhere that he was able to 'let her out'.

'Can you leave Hensford just now?' she asked, cautiously.

'Well, I'm not exactly needed, Em. I mean, Chandler's an excellent man. And even though it's going to be an early harvest, it'll hardly start in *June*.'

'No, I suppose not.' She made an effort at brightness. 'You go, darling. I'll be quite happy here. After all, I've got more than enough to see about at the moment.'

5

'Dearly beloved, forasmuch as all men are conceived and born in sin: and that our Saviour Christ saith, None can enter into the Kingdom of God, except he be regenerate and born anew of Water and of the Holy Ghost . . .' The Reverend Mr Egerton, pale, pious, elderly and suffering, so uncharitable people said, from anaemia of the brain, stood by the font in Hensford church, conducting the christening service of Charlotte Sybil Vandenburgh and her twin brother, Mark.

The former's godparents – Helen Mackay, May Lodge and Harry Bartholomew, a shooting companion of Richard's – stood on one side of the rector. Mark's godparents – another neighbour called Sheila Renton, together with Frank Lodge and Colin Mackay – stood on the other. That Emily's nearest and dearest constituted three-quarters of the little group was accounted for by the fact that, sadly, Richard Vandenburgh appeared to have no really close friends or family and had been quite relieved when Emily seemed to have so many from whom to choose.

All the same, he hadn't been prepared for the business of putting them all up for the occasion, including Emily's mother and stepfather. There was a *limit*. Hensford only had three spare bedrooms now that there was a night nursery, a day nursery and a nanny's room, although he had supposed that May Lodge could be accommodated up in the top of the house with his mother. But Sybilla had firmly vetoed the idea. Her quarters were apparently sacrosanct. Emily's cousin, Frank, and his wife, Elaine, had therefore been booked in at a nearby guest-house. Richard had told the proprietor to send the bill to him, although Emily was emphatic that Frank would never allow that. He realized she was probably right. Her cousin was such a damned independent fellow. He watched him now standing by the font, tall, good-looking, successful in the publishing business, by all accounts. Apparently, he'd won an MC during the war. Emily said he'd wanted to marry her afterwards, but she'd turned him down. Quite right, too. But anyway, all that was in the past. Frank appeared to have a perfectly presentable wife and he had no objection to his being Mark's godfather.

But Richard wasn't too happy about May Lodge and the Mackays, now that he had seen them again. May was altogether too old and as for Helen and Colin, well, it was obvious there wasn't much money there. Not that that mattered. The twins would be all right financially, more than all right, so long as Ma didn't marry again. But Sybilla had just been telling him what a good time she'd had in the States, how she had met some investment banker and had a 'ball', as she put it – although his mother always seemed to have a man in tow wherever she went. She seldom actually produced them, at least not in front of Emily and himself. Sometimes Richard wondered how much of her so-called conquests were pure fantasy. The way she spoke, one might have thought she was a *femme fatale*, when really she was rather a faded little coquette. He did not imagine she ever slept with anyone these days, although she might have been quite bedworthy some years ago, before she became stringy, before the wrinkles arrived. Yet, when he came to think about it, he'd been surprised how sprightly she was looking when he'd fetched her from the station earlier that week. She must have had something done to herself in New York. It was probably the reason why she went. If only, now, she hadn't chosen to wear such a ridiculous pink felt hat with white feathers. It simply didn't go with her age or her dyed hair or her mink coat.

He wished the rector would hurry up with the service so that they could all get back to Hensford for the champagne. Donald Egerton's intonations seemed to be taking an inordinate length of time, his quavering voice rising and falling monotonously, unintelligibly, as if his mind was elsewhere, certainly not on the job in hand.

All at once, it was more than evident that this was the case. With Helen ready to present him with Charlotte – already taking advantage of her prerogative: ladies first – the rector, for once firmly articulate, pronounced, 'Grant that all carnal affections may live and grow in her, and that all things belonging to the Spirit may die in her.'

There was a second's horrified silence, and then Sybilla Vandenburgh's voice could be heard in a loud stage whisper, saying, 'Richard, he's got it the wrong way round. Stop the service.'

Embarrassed, her son muttered, 'It's the meaning that counts, Ma. He *meant* the right thing.'

Oblivious of the commotion behind him, Donald Egerton was already carrying on, asking Helen if, in the name of the child, she would renounce the devil and all his works. It was too late. Sybilla Vandenburgh sat back, unconvinced, affronted, the feathers in her hat shaking like those of an angry White Wyandotte.

Back at the house, when the christening party was well under way and the Reverend Mr Egerton had bidden them a bemused farewell, she did her best to make a joke about what had happened. She agreed that it was possible the rector might have been even more put out of his stride had he been stopped mid-stream.

'He'd have probably got the sexes mixed up,' said Harry Bartholomew, with a slightly drunken guffaw. 'Called Mark a "her", or some damn fool thing like that.'

Emily was surprised to see her husband wince. Richard did not usually object to Harry's rather tasteless jokes. She herself could have wished that he was not one of the godparents. On the other hand, it hadn't seemed right for her to select them all. And Harry wasn't a bad sort, really. Neither was Sheila Renton. They were both kind and generous, even if they were rather apt to talk too much and shared a tendency for wearing rather loud checks.

Looking round, Emily could not help feeling how well her own family and friends compared with the other people in the room, even if they were, in almost every respect, worlds apart. Clothes rationing having been abolished earlier that year, she suspected that all the ladies amongst them had new outfits. Her mother was wearing a beige cashmere two-piece with one of her little velvet toques, which always suited her so well. May was all in navy, except for a white silk blouse with a high-necked collar. Helen, though never having had the same kind of dress sense as the Lodges, was nevertheless looking her best in a soft green woollen ensemble, with a suede beret in the same shade. It was the first time she and Colin had been away from Ladywell since they had taken it on and, with the children left in the care of her parents, it was obvious how much they were enjoying themselves. Frank's wife, too, looked extremely smart in dark brown velvet. Of the four of them she was by far the most sophisticated, but she seemed pleasant enough to talk to. Emily hoped that she and Frank were happy. She could see him now over in a corner talking with Sybilla. Trust her mother-in-law to have got hold of one of the most attractive men in the room, although Emily felt sure that Frank would be more than equal to her blandishments.

'Wouldn't you like to sit down, my dear? You've been on your feet all day.' Maurice was suddenly beside her and she turned to him, gratefully.

'It would be rather nice.' He pulled up two chairs and she felt how lucky she was to have him for a stepfather.

'You must be glad to have the christening over,' he said.

'Yes, although it was a lovely excuse to get you all up here. I wish Wilhampton wasn't so far away. Then perhaps you could look after the twins!'

He smiled. 'But you know the unwritten rules. Doctors don't usually treat their own families.'

'No. But Charlotte and Mark are once removed, so to speak. And poor little Charlotte needs such a lot of attention. Leaving aside that awful gaffe old Egerton made in the church, I'm worried about her. She's so frail compared to Mark. She's not putting on weight as she should.'

'Are you still feeding her at all?'

She coloured. 'No. I didn't want to stop, but I . . . gave out. I wouldn't have made a very good cow, I'm afraid,' she replied, apologetically. She did not add that Richard had been delighted.

'I shouldn't worry too much. Your nanny seems quite competent. I'm sure she'll watch Charlotte carefully. Give her a bit more time over the bottle.'

'Oh yes. We're already doing that. I try to be there to

take on one or the other of them.' Again, she did not say that Richard had complained, had even suggested getting a nursery maid. 'I didn't marry you,' he had said, 'to become one yourself. You're my wife.'

Nervously, she put up a hand to her forehead and became aware that Maurice was watching her, carefully. He had probably been doing so for some time. That must have been why he had asked her if she would like to sit down. She realized, now, how exhausted she was. There had been so much to organize, although Mrs Draper and her husband had given her infinite support. But it was only six weeks since the birth, not an easy one, either. Richard had suggested putting the christening off till the spring, but she had said that she would like to go ahead with it. It was possibly something to do with Charlotte's health. She remembered the difference in the way they had arrived in the world. Mark had greeted it lustily but his sister had given little more than a mew. At her husband's insistence, Dr Hedley had delivered them in a private room in Stoke Wallington hospital. Emily felt she would have been happier with Dr Peterson, whom she found more sympathetic, even if he did not have the older man's experience. But it was no good looking back. It was all over now, thank goodness. She had produced a pigeon pair.

Momentarily she closed her eyes and some words came back to her. 'As long as one of them's a boy,' Richard had said, 'you won't have to go through it again. It'll be like killing two birds with one stone.' She found herself shivering, just as she had done when he uttered them.

She got up, suddenly. Nanny Corbett must be struggling with feeding time.

'Will you excuse me, Maurice,' she said. 'I think I'll just see how everything's going in the nursery.'

'Of course, my dear.'

She did not look back, but she felt his kind concerned eyes were following her as she left the room.

6

The letter and parcel arrived just before the twins' first birthday. The latter contained two large identical teddy bears and a beautifully bound book of nursery rhymes, labelled, 'For use in riper years'.

The letter, written on business notepaper and dated Tuesday, August 29th, 1950, ran:

Dearest Emily,

Many happy returns to Charlotte and Mark. Not being particularly expert in the buying of children's presents, I hope the enclosed will give reasonable pleasure at some time or other.

I also hope that all goes well with everyone at Hensford. I can hardly believe it is almost a year since we last saw you, when we came up for that splendid christening. When you and Richard are next in town with any time to spare, do give us a ring and come to dinner. We've had quite a lot done to the house lately. Publishing seems to be looking up . . . There's more paper about now, for one thing. God knows how our firm managed in the war.

Which brings me to another point. We've decided to go in for attacking the younger generation. There is a very go-ahead new girl on the staff called Clare Carpenter, who is looking out for original stories. (The enclosed book is one of her first productions.) It suddenly came to me the other night that you might be interested in writing something for us. I mean, you've not only got the talent and originality, but you've recently acquired *first-hand material* to draw on. Of course, I realize it's rather a far cry from your intention of writing plays, but do think about it. I believe there's quite a future in this direction . . .

She put down Frank's letter and let it lie idle in her lap. She was sitting in the morning-room, which faced the front drive. The sounds of Hensford, the background to her present existence, went on around her: commonplace, cloying, restrictive. Mrs Rafferty, one of the dailies, was brushing down the stairs. Mrs Draper's husband went by the open door carrying a tray of silver to be cleaned. (They were giving another dinner party that night.) Outside, the boy who helped Hardiman was attacking some weeds at the edge of the gravel with a brand new hoe. From somewhere above, there was a thump and then a child's cry. Should she go and investigate? It was the kind of thing which sent shivers down her spine. But, for Richard's sake, she had tried to curb over-reacting. All was now silent. Presumably everything was well.

Presently, she got up and went into a small writing room. It was the one place in the house which she now considered essentially hers. Sitting at a little antique escritoire, she began a reply to her cousin's letter:

Mr dear Frank,

How lovely to hear from you and what gorgeous presents you have sent the children. Thank you so very much. I agree it's too long since we saw anything of you and Elaine. We haven't any immediate plans for coming to London, as Richard and I are driving down through France in September, leaving Nanny and the twins with Mummy and Maurice on our way. We shall stay the night at East Lodge and then go straight on to Southampton for the crossing to Cherbourg – like you did, in 1944!! But when we get back, perhaps you and Elaine would come and spend a weekend here? Anyway, I'll be in touch, and thank you again for being such a good godfather and uncle.

About your writing idea. I'm flattered. But, oh dear, motherhood seems to have knocked all that out of me. I can't imagine ever having another original thought in my head. I've been rather run down lately. That's why we're going away. Although, what with worrying about Charlotte and Mark – especially Charlotte, she's *so* delicate – when we've gone, I can't see that the holiday's going to do much good. But, of course, they couldn't be left in better hands. I keep telling myself that.

As I said, we'll be in touch. Meanwhile, my love and gratitude.

Emily.

She did not show Richard either letter. She did not think he would be particularly interested. Her one-time desire to write and natural aptitude for the world of drama had always left him singularly indifferent. As far as he was concerned, Emily was his wife: beautiful, well-dressed, a competent if rather over-indulgent manager of staff and a quiet but intelligent hostess, who could possibly do better if she were more light-hearted. As a mother, he had not expected such dedication, and this manifestly irritated him. He had been doing his best to get her away from the twins all the year. As he had pointed out to her soon after they were born, he had not reckoned on his wife becoming a nursery maid.

They left for the continent in the middle of the month, Nanny Corbett creating a host of last-minute difficulties. She was an experienced, middle-aged, rather taciturn woman — at least, so Richard felt, whenever he had occasion to converse with her — who was now making it quite clear that she resented taking her charges where they would be supervised by grandparents, as it cast doubts on her own capabilities. However, such was the welcome they all received at East Lodge that she became slightly mollified, even to admitting later on that night that it was perhaps as well, with Charlotte's tendency to pick up every passing germ, that the twins were under a doctor's roof.

Emily was relieved, on setting off next morning, that, for once, Richard did not drive too fast. In any case, when they reached France, the roads seemed even worse than those in England and he was far too careful of his car to risk any shaking about on the cobbled surfaces. The second night they came to a small village in Saône-et-Loire where they stopped at an inn, recommended by Harry Bartholomew and his wife, who had stayed there the previous summer.

To Emily, it was everything she most longed for on a holiday: quiet, beauty and an overall sense of peace. After an excellent dinner, having put through a call to England and discovered that all was well with the twins, she suggested that they might spend two nights there.

'What? Hang around here for another whole day?' Richard frowned. 'Why ever do you want to do that? What would we do?'

'Nothing much. Go for walks. It's such lovely country. I

might do a bit of sketching. And the *patron* said something about a château nearby which is well worth a visit.'

'Don't you want to get to the Riviera? I thought you said you wanted to learn to water-ski?'

'Did I?' she laughed. 'Well, there's plenty of time. We've got three weeks.'

'Don't forget, some of it's already gone. I specially haven't hurried, knowing you wanted to take things easily. But honestly, Em, I don't see any point in stopping here. It's just another village like Hensford, only in a foreign country. I brought you away for a complete change, remember. And Ma would be awfully disappointed if we didn't turn up at the Mirabeau in Monte Carlo the day after tomorrow. After all, she's booked us in.'

Emily did not demur. She could see his point, although she couldn't help feeling that they would hardly be having a *complete* change, not with Sybilla deciding what they would do each day.

Her assumption proved to be just as she had feared. Sybilla greeted her effusively, wearing a black and green tubular sun dress, enormous dark glasses and a wide-brimmed black straw hat with a fringed edge. She reminded Emily of an animated miniature palm tree.

'*Darlink!* I am so glad you haf come. We must do something about you. Build you up. Get you brown. You are so *white*. As if you haf crept out from – how do you say? – *au dessous d'une pierre!* And Richard, he does not look much better. He has been working too hard. Now, you must both forget all your troubles. Tonight we go to the casino.'

It was the last thing Emily wanted to do. She wondered if she might ask to be excused. They had had a long tiring drive over the Alps and she had a bad headache, probably exacerbated by the height and the terrifying tortuous hairpin bends. But after a bath and a short rest on her bed, she decided to say nothing. She couldn't, mustn't, send Richard off alone with his mother as soon as they arrived.

Emily had never been inside a gambling establishment before and the whole atmosphere depressed her, in spite of the fact that Sybilla had insisted on giving her some francs and she immediately succeeded in winning a thousand. But the croupiers' repetitive calls of 'Rien ne va plus', the tense concentration of the players surrounding the various tables — the ladies all with heavily painted faces and loaded with jewellery — the combined smell of scent and cigar smoke, the occasional cheers or, more often, groans of disappointment as the wheel came to a standstill, made her long to escape. When, at last, about two in the morning, they were back in their bedroom at the Mirabeau and Richard asked her why she hadn't seemed to enjoy herself more, she burst out, uncharacteristically, 'But *surely*, what is there to enjoy? I mean, it's all so . . . so . . .' She hunted for the word and finally ended, 'artificial'.

She was surprised, even puzzled, by his answer. He was standing at the window looking out on the harbour lights, on to a place where, according to its own standards, the night was still young. 'Is there,' he said, 'so very much wrong with artificiality? It's a stimulus. People need it sometimes. It's a form of art. We can't always be natural and down to earth. That would be very dull. After all, you used make-up this evening and wore that very attractive, rather oriental-looking outfit.'

He made love to her a little later with an intensity that she had scarcely known. She found herself responding in like manner. They lay, afterwards, for a long while, naked and entwined. She thought, why can't it always be like this? What had happened? She was glad that he had persuaded her to come on holiday.

Their lovemaking never reached quite the same heights during the rest of their time in France, but she was well content. She began entering into the spirit of things far more than she ever imagined she could do, occasionally managing to equal Sybilla with some frivolous nonsensical repartee. Only when they reached Le Touquet, on their return journey, did she suddenly become serious again. The war still seemed so very much in evidence. They were five years on now, yet the desolation remained, the effect of the bombing on this particular part of the coastline by no means erased.

The memory of the conflict came back to her now with startling clarity: the evacuation from Dunkirk, her duties at Westonbury Emergency Hospital, her fiancé, John Moreton, missing and then taken prisoner by the Germans, Helen going off to join the ATS and her brother, Bob, being killed at El Alamein, the arrival of American forces in England and her love affair with Vernon Keeler, their parting and her subsequent breakdown after learning of his engagement to Liz Brewer, the increasingly tense but carefully camouflaged build-up to D-Day, the knowledge that Frank Lodge, Vernon Keeler and Helen's younger brother, Tim, were 'over there' somewhere, fighting. Fighting, possibly on ground where she was now standing, so that she and people like her could enjoy a holiday on the continent . . .

As they drove aboard the ferry at Calais, the words 'Rien ne va plus' seemed to echo, unceasingly, in her mind.

7

Although Mark Vandenburgh was sturdier than his twin sister, nevertheless Charlotte was by far the more advanced mentally, as well as in learning to walk. Apart from both being auburn-haired – something which surprised Emily, considering her and Richard's dark colouring – they did not seem like twins. Sometimes, she thought that Charlotte, with her big blue eyes and small frame, took after Sybilla or, possibly, one of her own twin cousins, the one who was 'no better than she should be' and whose links with the family had suffered in consequence. Such thoughts distressed Emily. She had no wish to see her daughter growing up to resemble either Ma or Della.

When she mentioned the twins' appearance or progress to Richard, as often as not he merely smiled and said that, as far as he was concerned, all babies were the same. It really wasn't worth discussing until they were several years older. His one concession to fatherhood had been to give up his sugar ration so that the children could have an adequate amount of demerara in their bottles. But, as time went by, Emily noticed that he occasionally gave Mark a vague pat on the head in passing, something he never did to Charlotte.

'I want to plant some more trees,' he said to Emily, one day in the early part of the following summer. 'I don't suppose I'll live to see them properly established, but Mark will. He'll inherit a first-class shoot at Hensford.'

Out of the window she caught sight of her son staggering across the lawn beside Nanny Corbett, with Charlotte toddling on a few steps ahead. She was seized by irrational panic. The twins were not yet two. The time when Mark could be entrusted with a gun seemed a century away. Besides, who was to say he would be keen on the sport? She recalled how her one-time fiancé had hated it. It was impossible to legislate for something so far ahead, even though she realized it had been necessary to put Mark's name down for a school at birth. To her regret, but not altogether her surprise, Richard had insisted that it must be Eton. He had always had a chip on his shoulder about his unconventional nomadic upbringing, apart from the few years he had spent at a boarding school just outside Durban.

Cautiously, she enquired, 'Where are you thinking of planting the trees?' She did not want to upset him. They had been getting on better since their holiday the previous autumn. There had not been so many of Richard's black moods.

'Just above the Hollows. Merton, the new keeper, is all for it. So's Chandler, I'm glad to say.'

She knew that quite often those particular employees did not see eye to eye, the needs of the farm clashing with those of the shoot. That was why their previous keeper had left. For a while, she remained silent as she picked up her sewing. During the past winter she had started to do *petit point*. It was something which could be done at odd moments and she found it relaxing. When, a few minutes later, Richard came out with a rather more startling suggestion, she kept her eyes on the rose she was working.

'I've also been thinking of buying a flat in London,' he

said. 'It would be nice to have one. Ma could stay there when she comes to England.'

This time she replied, quietly, 'Surely she would always prefer a hotel? Where she's waited on.'

'Possibly. But, anyway, you and I could use it. I'd like to spend more time in town. Make a base where we could be contacted. I reckon we could get hold of somewhere quite cheap now and do it up. Harry and his wife have just found a *pied-à-terre* near Grosvenor Place. We could have small parties. I might be able to get a little poker school together. I mean, apart from the shooting season and a certain amount going on midsummer, there isn't an awful lot to do here, is there? We could have the best of both worlds.'

She stopped stitching now and looked up at him. 'I suppose it depends what you want out of life.'

He was sitting with one leg slung over the side of an armchair. She noticed his foot begin to move up and down, a sure sign that he was irritated.

'Well, I certainly don't want just to stagnate in the country, Em. I'd like a bit of fun. So would you, if you'd only admit it. You perked up no end on that holiday in France.'

She supposed he was right. She often felt she would like to get away, although not perhaps in the same manner or for the same reasons as he did. The people and parties Richard hankered after bored her beyond measure. But going to a good play, meeting up with some of her former contemporaries, dining with Frank and his wife, that would be a different matter. Yet, she knew it was impossible. She had no particular love for Hensford, but she was too involved with the twins to spend much time in London. Besides, where was all the money coming from? Was he intending to ask Sybilla for it, or was he hoping that she herself would come forward as she had already done once or twice before? Because she so deplored their dependence on his mother she had dipped into the inheritance she had received at the age of twenty-one, firstly to help him over a bad harvest and then to put up some money for a new drying plant. She had been pleased to feel that the farm seemed to have picked up since then, although she suspected that much of it had to do with the acquisition of a first-class manager, Bert Chandler. But, however it was doing, their fortunes would surely not extend to the kind of extravagant lifestyle which Richard had just proposed.

Aware that he was waiting for her reactions, she did her best. 'An occasional holiday's one thing,' she replied. 'But until the twins are older, I can't see myself often going to town.'

Again, he took her by surprise. He appeared to have got everything worked out.

'I'm coming to that, Em. I've had a splendid idea. Charlotte's much easier to look after now, isn't she, and Merton's got a daughter who's just leaving school. I believe her name is Janine. He volunteered the other day that she's devoted to kids. I'd like to take her on. She could live in. I think her parents would be delighted. Their cottage isn't all that big and they've obviously bred like rabbits. I always did want an extra pair of hands in the nursery, so that you'd be much more free.'

She bent over her tapestry again, trying to digest his suggestion, consider the implications. Did he realize just what he was letting himself in for? Dear God. A nursery maid *as well* as a nanny? A keeper *and* a flat in town?

'Is she the young woman with red hair who comes flying down the drive on a bicycle?' she asked, trying to play for time.

'Yes.'

'I can't think Nanny Corbett would approve.'

'To hell with Nanny Corbett. Really, Em. You and she are as bad as each other. Set on making difficulties. Most wives would be over the moon at all I'm suggesting. One's only alive once.'

He got up and stormed out of the room. She heard the front door slam. She wanted to run after him, say, 'I'm sorry,' but then she was conscious of the twins and Nanny coming through a side entrance and simply stayed where she was. It was so difficult, even in a house as large as Hensford, not to feel there were eyes and ears everywhere.

Nanny Corbett might not *say* very much, but Emily had a feeling she missed nothing and that she kept her employers under constant surveillance, mostly of a disapproving kind. Occasionally, Emily had contemplated replacing her with someone younger and more congenial, but she was good with the twins who, for all her censorious attitude towards their parents, appeared to be fond of her. She might be old-fashioned and strict, yet she seemed to give them something — a security perhaps — that Emily herself did not or could not give them, however hard she tried. Often, she despaired. How *did* one combine successfully the role of wife and mother? Other women did it. Helen, for instance. She was pregnant for the third time and absolutely delighted. She did not appear to have any problems in this connection. But then, Helen had always longed for a family and did not have a starchy uniformed nanny about her home, nor a restless husband forever bent on getting away from it.

What *was* the matter with Richard? Was it all her fault? Perhaps, as with the twins, he wanted something from her that she was unable to give. She was probably far too serious-minded for him. He needed a wife like Ma, although the thought of her husband married to a youthful Sybilla made her shudder. She tried to think of other possibilities. Sheila Renton or Harry's wife, Mabs? Yet, no. They weren't attractive enough. They might be fun-loving, but they weren't smart or sophisticated. Richard tended to go after the latter. Although 'go after' was not exactly the right expression. He might notice that type of woman but, oddly enough, he never seemed to chat them up. It was almost as if he was nervous of them. He had never given Emily any reason to think he had been unfaithful. She still felt that, in spite of her failure in many aspects of their marriage, he needed her, as she needed him.

And she did need him. That was the strange part about it. She still wanted him sexually and wished he wanted her more that way. The fact that they were poles apart and often at loggerheads, as they had been a little while ago, made no difference. It made it, in fact, even more important that they should now make up quickly in the bedroom before Richard went into one of his black moods. She must see what could be done about it.

Suddenly, for no apparent reason, the memory of their last holiday came to her mind and what he had said about stimulus and artificiality. Although she had not been feeling well, she had taken a lot of trouble over her appearance that first evening. On leaving for the casino, she had wondered whether she had overdone it, worn too much make-up, too exotic a dress and sandals – whether, in fact, she had really looked rather tarty. But it had obviously appealed to him.

After she had gone into the nursery and seen the twins safely into bed that night, she went to her own room and, from a cupboard, extracted the very same clothes she had worn at Monte Carlo. Strictly speaking, they were not suitable for Hensford, nor was the weather yet warm enough. She might just get away with the gold open-toed sandals at a midsummer cocktail party, but the dress – made of Egyptian cotton printed with a pyramid design and gathered at the waist by a gold chain belt – was altogether too revealing and outré. Nevertheless, with unaccustomed recklessness, she decided she would drape a shawl over her shoulders, at least during dinner. Richard couldn't fail to see that she was trying to make amends.

She was in the bath when she heard his footsteps on the stairs and then the bedroom door opening and closing. Usually, he went straight through to his dressing room, but tonight he appeared to have halted by the bed.

Still wrapped in a towel, she came in to find him sitting on it. He had gathered the dress and sandals in his arms and appeared to be burying his face in them. She remained motionless, bewildered, a feeling of nausea beginning to well up inside her. For a while, he seemed too preoccupied to notice her presence. Then he turned and jumped up, letting all her articles of apparel slip to the floor.

'I'm sorry, Em,' he said, sheepishly, as he disappeared into his bedroom.

8

In his house overlooking Hampstead Heath, Dr Carl Schmidt sat re-reading the letter which had just arrived in the morning's post. He was sixty-nine, but his memory was excellent. He could remember the sender well. Emily. Emily Mason, or Emily Vandenburgh, as she now signed herself. It was over seven years since he had treated her for a severe breakdown in the early part of 1944. She had been the youngest of his female patients, one whom he considered just as much a casualty of the war as any of the servicemen he was trying to help, even if her shattered nerves had been due to the anguish of a love affair during the abnormal times rather than armed conflict.

Now, apparently, she wanted his advice again, although he was relieved to find that she did not appear to be exactly ill. She explained that she had gone to some trouble in order to track him down, having been informed that his nursing home near Woking, where she had been a patient, had since had several private owners. She went on to say that she would quite understand if he was not able to see her now he was retired, but she would be very grateful if he could. It was a delicate matter and she knew of no one else whom she could approach.

Carl Schmidt picked up his pen. He was actually only semi-retired, as he still occasionally saw a few patients and employed a secretary two mornings a week. But this not being one of them, he decided he would write to Emily in his own hand. He had always been a spontaneous and unconventional man. As a Jewish refugee who had escaped from Germany before the war, he had finally overcome the opposition of the strictly orthodox medical profession in Britain and been allowed to practise his advanced, but surprisingly successful, methods of treating nervous illness.

Emily's case was quite clear in his mind. He knew that she was not the sort of person to have got in touch with him like this without very good reason. He would be more than interested to see her again, to find out what seven years – during which, according to her letter, she had married and produced twins – had done to her. His recollection was of a tallish beautiful young woman with large, strangely appealing eyes. She had been sensitive, imaginative and intelligent – the worst possible combination from the point of view of leading a happy life.

When, the following week, he rose to greet her, he was glad to discover that his mental imagery had not failed him, although time had inevitably cast a layer of maturity over his former patient. She looked older, wiser but, in many ways, still vulnerable.

'Emily!'

'Dr Schmidt!'

She was wearing a black and white silk suit with a large fetching black straw hat. He remembered how both she and her mother had always dressed well, in spite of the exigencies of wartime. It came back to him that during one of their talks, Emily had told him that her maternal forbears were in the clothing business.

'Vat,' he said, after they had exchanged initial pleasantries, 'can I do for you, my dear?' His foreign accent was still pronounced. He had fled Germany too late in life for it to change.

He noticed the colour sweep into her cheeks, the way she seemed to be bracing herself for an unpleasant task.

'It isn't easy,' she began, slowly. 'and I'm not sure that there *is* very much anyone can do. It's just . . . that I wanted to talk to someone about a problem which has just cropped up. It's nothing I could tell my family. It's . . . well, unusual. You know,' she managed a small smile and his heart went out to her, 'the sort of thing you read of in books.'

He nodded, watching her stare, just as she used to do, at the little bowing Chinese mandarin he always kept on his desk.

'It's about my husband,' she began again. 'Something that happened to him in the war. Something he can't get over. I never knew about it until the other day.'

'I see.' He waited, noticing how her colour had heightened. Agitatedly, she put up a hand to her face. He remembered the gesture well. 'How did you find out?' he asked, at length.

'He told me. A certain incident occurred and he felt he owed me an explanation. I'd always thought he had some kind of secret. He gets these black moods. He needs a lot of diversion.'

'To get away from himself, perhaps?'

She became thoughtful. 'Yes, that could well be. I've often puzzled about it. Wished he would tell me what was wrong instead of . . .' She broke off, and he felt he had to help her.

'Instead of vat, Emily?'

'Well, . . . shutting himself away . . . sometimes drinking more than is good for him.'

'Did you know about these moods before you ver married?'

'Oh, no. The wedding took place less than three months after we first met.'

'You ver in love, Emily?'

'Yes. Yes, very much,' she repeated, and then added, almost defensively, 'Richard . . . my husband . . . is extremely good-looking. He's thirteen years older than I am. He's very like Vernon Keeler.'

'Your American?'

'Yes.'

Carl Schmidt thought of the war, the time when she had been placed under his care. Poor Emily. He could see it all. She had a propensity for misfortune. Even if to the world, as well as herself, she had appeared to recover from that doomed love affair, there had obviously been some part of her which had never quite got over it. And so, when Vernon's look-alike had come along, she had made a mistake. He felt sure of that, although as yet she had not told him much about it. Gently, once again, he tried to help her out.

'You referred to an incident, my dear, which prompted your husband to confide in you?' Purposely, he framed his question more as a statement, in order to draw her out.

She hesitated and then, as if she had at last decided to

get her story over with, she replied in a rush, 'We'd had a row . . . well, difference of opinion, really, about Richard's constant desire for amusement. He proposed buying a flat in London. Holding poker parties. I felt I'd been altogether too discouraging. I wanted to make it up. I put out some special clothes to wear that evening which I knew he admired. I mean, I thought . . .'

'You hoped you vould make it up in bed, yes?'

'Yes,' she answered, keeping her eyes on the little mandarin. And then, unconsciously, she made the kind of throw-away remark which always told Carl Schmidt a great deal more than his patients intended. 'I mean . . . we don't have sex all that often.'

'I see,' he said. 'And your little ruse? It did not vork?'

'No. I came in to find him sitting on the bed . . . his face sort of buried in the dress. He was very embarrassed. Later he told me that it reminded him of one worn by someone he knew in the war. In Cairo. When he was a staff officer there. She was a . . . a . . .'

'A voman of the vorld?'

'Yes.' Emily's voice had dropped to not much more than a whisper now. 'It was about the time of Tobruk. He'd known her for several months. On this particular day he shouldn't, by rights, have left his HQ. The Eighth Army was still retreating, well inside the Egyptian frontier. But she'd telephoned him. I think Faza – that was her name – had some kind of hold over him. Anyway, he got a junior officer to man his desk for the afternoon. She lived right across the city in one of the poorest areas. Because of the ghastly news the whole place was in an uproar, so it took him some time to get to her. I gather her apartment was pretty sordid. When he arrived he found she wasn't well. He felt very annoyed that she'd dragged him such a distance and wasn't prepared to . . . Well, in the end, he *made* her. He said it had somehow seemed terribly exciting having sex with the Germans almost knocking on the door. But afterwards, she collapsed. She kept putting a hand to her chest and begging him not to leave her. He knew that he had to get back, that he might be court-martialled if he was found absent from duty, and he panicked. She didn't seem to know of a doctor, so . . . he left her, saying he would come again the next day. Because of the emergency, he couldn't go back for two whole weeks. When he did, he discovered she'd died.'

They were both silent now. Carl Schmidt had heard many a strange story during his long career, had done his best to help many an anguished mind, but his speciality had lain mostly in the treatment of sudden severe nervous collapses, when he put his patients to sleep for weeks at a time in order to give their minds a complete rest before talking to them. Richard Vandenburgh's trouble was something entirely different. The man had not 'gone under'. He was evidently too tough a character, mentally, for that. He had managed to suppress his guilt for nine years, getting over his black moods with the help of drink, diversion and taking things out on his wife, or so Carl suspected. He did not hold out much hope for the marriage, nor did he feel that he himself would be of much assistance although, for Emily's sake, he was willing to try.

'Are you,' he asked her, when she had recovered a little composure, 'still in love vith your husband, my dear?'

He was not surprised when she replied, 'No. Not like I was, but . . . well . . . we're married . . . there are the twins . . . And even a few nights ago we still . . . I would like to help him. I feel sorrier for him now.'

'Do you vant me to see him?'

Again, he was not altogether surprised when she replied, promptly, 'Oh, no. I mean, that would be out of the question. Richard would never dream of consulting a doctor or telling anyone else. As a matter of fact, I feel disloyal in coming to see you myself. He begged me to keep it a secret between us. He said there was no reason for me to feel that our marriage or sex life was in any way in jeopardy. Now that I knew he thought it would make everything easier.'

'But you haf not found that is so? Othervise, you vould not haf come to see me?'

She inclined her head. Then she said, 'Although, oddly enough, we've made love more often since. But I get the feeling, when we do, that Richard is . . . how shall I put it? . . . re-enacting that time in Cairo. Before Faza died. I think maybe it helps him to feel she's still alive. He keeps wanting me to wear the same clothes. Sometimes he even wants to have sex where we might be discovered. That really does make him very excited. It's all so . . . bizarre. I don't quite know what I ought to do about it.'

He looked at the young woman facing him across the desk. She was still evidently emotionally attached to her husband, seemed to be more or less asking him whether she should indulge his whims. If it had been anyone else seeking his advice he might have considered the possibility of a small amount of give and take. But with Emily, no. It would never work. She was too natural, too straightforward, probably even too passionate for being party to any kind of contrived sex. Yet, for the very same reasons, she was unlikely to come to terms with her husband taking a mistress. Carl Schmidt was an old man now, but he had seldom come across any individual whom he wanted to help more, while aware that he was powerless to do so. The only thing he could think of which might be of positive assistance was for Emily to become interested in something outside her marriage. It would stand her in good stead if things took a turn for the worse.

'Your acting, my dear?' he enquired. 'Have you given up all thought of that?'

'But, of course. How could I now?' The retort was quick and to the point. 'A hundred and fifty miles from London,' she went on. 'And I don't think I mentioned . . . Charlotte, my little girl, is very delicate. I want to be around. She needs a lot of attention.'

'Vat about the play you once told me you vanted to write? Vould you haf no time for that?'

She shook her head. 'Oh no, not now.'

He could see she was trapped, trapped by circumstances, an over-developed conscience, the way she had been brought up. He did not think she would break down again as she had in the war unless, of course, some further unforeseen catastrophe overtook her. It was a thought which haunted him long after she had gone.

Carl Schmidt had never felt more inadequate than when he had watched her walking down the drive, hearing again her final words in response to his exhortation to come and see him again whenever she wished. 'Oh yes,' she had said. 'I'd be so grateful to feel I could do that. You don't know what a relief it's been just talking to you about everything.'

But it was only a palliative, he thought, sadly. It was no solution to her plight. She was as fettered as, presumably, her husband was with his understandable guilt though possibly not quite so understandable fantasies about the past. But he was aware that the workings of the human mind were so often incomprehensible. He remembered an English judge once telling him that. There were always some situations in life to which there was no remedy. Only the day-to-day business of simply keeping on keeping on.

Part Two

9

'*Come on, Mark!*' Richard Vandenburgh leant forward on his seat, clearly willing his son to win Form III's hundred yards race at the annual sports day held by Chantry's Preparatory School. Emily had seldom seen her husband show so much emotion, especially in public. When the boy seemed to be losing ground and came in third, Richard sat back not only disappointed but obviously extremely put out.

'He should have won,' he muttered to Emily, under his breath. 'I can't think what was the matter with him.'

'Never mind. I didn't think he was looking too well at lunch time. He hardly ate anything.'

'That was probably just excitement.'

Richard sat frowning. He had no further interest in the remaining events. His son was not taking any part in them. As far as he was concerned, Mark had the makings of a first-class athlete who had, unaccountably, let the side down, let his parents down. At tea, Emily did her best to stop her husband cross-questioning the child. It was plain to her that Mark was sickening for something, possibly the summer 'flu which was going around. She was not unduly perturbed. The boy was tough. It was Charlotte's health about which she was always concerned.

Only that very morning, she had had misgivings about leaving the little girl in Janine's care for the weekend. Yet she had known that it would have been hopeless to try to take Charlotte with them. Her daughter was invariably sick in the car after travelling more than a few miles. All the same, it had been distressing to see the small forlorn figure standing at the front door of Hensford, waving frantically as they disappeared up the drive. Emily hoped she would not be too miserable while they were gone. It was not that Janine wouldn't do her best. She was kind and reasonably intelligent, but she did not have Nanny Corbett's years of experience behind her, that special art of knowing exactly how to cope with tears, tantrums, sudden accidents or illness and, it had to be confessed, sometimes nowadays faked illness.

Emily knew that she should never have let Nanny Corbett go. Richard had been dead against it and he had been right. But when Mark had gone away to boarding school at the age of seven, it had seemed ridiculous to keep on both a nanny *and* a nursery maid, even though Richard had suggested that Janine might come under the jurisdiction of Mrs Draper during term-time. Emily had argued that Janine's parents might consider domestic work a come-down and that she, personally, wanted a chance to inaugurate an altogether different régime in the nursery, because of the bronchial–asthmatic attacks to which her daughter seemed to have become increasingly subject. It was impossible to do this while Nanny Corbett ruled the roost. Richard, anxious to keep on good terms with his keeper, gave in. Nanny Corbett, sensing what was in Emily's mind, gave notice. Emily – mistakenly, as she now realized – set about taking charge herself, adopting a variety of measures to combat Charlotte's affliction, according to the dictates of a Harley Street specialist whom she had consulted.

None had made the slightest difference. Her efforts at rigid dieting, creating entirely dust-proof nursery quarters by installing a hospital bed, rubber mattress and pillows and insisting that Janine wash all the curtains and blankets once a week, seemed, if anything, to accentuate the problem. No sooner was the child over one bout of illness – usually triggered off by a common cold – than she was into another, for now that she attended a small private school in Hensford, it was inevitable that she was constantly coming up against a virus. At the height of her attacks, Emily would often sit up with her daughter all night, fearing each gasp for breath in the skinny body might be the last. When morning arrived and, unwillingly, she left Charlotte in the care of Janine for an hour or two, she would creep back to her own bedroom utterly exhausted.

Yet Richard's entreaties that she should either get Nanny Corbett to return or try to find some other equally responsible woman, fell on deaf ears. Emily's only concession to any alteration in the ménage was to suggest that she might employ a daily governess during the coming winter. She felt that by not going to school Charlotte would be saved from catching quite so many colds. Still angry, Richard had retorted that the child would lack companionship, that a daily governess was not going to prevent every cold coming into the house, nor Emily spending nights on end in her daughter's room. In many ways, she knew that his attitude was justified, that she was becoming obsessed by her duties as a mother at the expense of those of a wife. Yet she seemed powerless to alter course.

Richard Vandenburgh was not the only one who deplored the unfortunate situation. Emily's mother and stepfather had become as concerned over her as they were over Charlotte. 'She can't go on like it,' Maurice said to Katy, one day after they had received a letter describing the little girl's latest attack. 'Emily will crack up. She needs a break. Why don't we have Charlotte and Janine down here for at least a month?' To which Katy had replied, 'I'll ask, Maurice, but she'd never allow it. I'm sure of that, much as she trusts us. She seems to have got it into her head that it's a mother's duty to be always there when needed.' Her observation proved only too correct.

They had, however, been pleased to hear that at least Emily was going off with her husband to Mark's sports day and spending the Saturday night at a nearby hotel in order to take him out next day. Richard, until his son's failure to win the hundred yards, had been pleased about this also. He did not much care for the tedious business of entertaining Mark throughout the Sabbath, especially if the weather was wet and they were forced to hang around indoors playing idiotic games; but he had been looking forward to dining the previous evening with some of the other parents. He felt that possibly he and Emily might even engage in a little sex afterwards when they got to bed. Oddly enough, since she had become so wrapped up in Charlotte, it was he who often wished that their marital relations were more frequent.

Not that he allowed it to bother him too much. Since that fatal night getting on for nine years ago, he had tried to forget that he had ever spoken to his wife about his guilty secret. He had managed to push it further and further from his mind, to pretend he was as normal as Emily had imagined him to be when they married. In many ways, he felt he had succeeded. He had directed his energies on to more worthwhile things. He had concentrated on Hensford and the farm and less on purely frivolous pursuits. It was true that he had got his way about employing a nursery maid, as well as acquiring a small flat in London; but he had eschewed any idea of holding poker parties there and, apart from a few brief holidays with Sybilla, he had spent an increasing amount of time at home, building up his shoot and taking an interest in the day-to-day running of the whole estate. In short, having unburdened himself to his wife, he had done his best, apart from occasional lapses, to settle down and turn over a new leaf.

The trouble was, to his great disappointment, Emily appeared not to have noticed. She had become completely blinkered — as he saw it — by her own misguided reasoning. He sometimes wondered whether, had he never disclosed his own failings, she would have given quite so much attention to Charlotte. He realized that she had been upset by his revelations, even though she had tried not to show it. By a kind of unspoken mutual agreement, they had never mentioned the subject again. But there was no doubt that her obsessive care of the child had become more marked since then. It was as if, in determinedly burying their separate anguish, they had gone their separate ways.

Richard studied his wife now as she sat at the end of the dining table which they were sharing with two other sets of parents at the Garston Grange Hotel. She was looking as beautiful and well turned-out as ever, but obviously strained. He regretted that he had shown such ill humour when Mark failed to win his race. He supposed that he set as much store on his son's athletic achievements as Emily did on bringing about an improvement in Charlotte's health. He must make amends for his churlish behaviour. They need not stay too long chatting after the meal. He would take her to bed early.

He was surprised when he saw the waiter coming across the dining room and then leaning forward by Emily's shoulder. He saw her turn, visibly blanch and jump up. He rose also, aware that something untoward had happened. With a hasty 'Forgive me' to the rest of the party, he hurried after her and waited while she went into a small telephone booth. He did not think it could be anything to do with Charlotte, because less than an hour ago Emily had telephoned Janine and found all was well at Hensford. Possibly it was connected with a member of her own family. He was totally unprepared for her words when at last she emerged.

'Mark,' she said flatly. 'It's Mark. The school have had to call an ambulance. He complained of a severe headache after we left. We're to go to Garston hospital at once.'

'Hospital?' He stared at her, uncomprehendingly. 'But what do they think it is?'

The answer seemed no more than a movement of her lips, yet it was loud and clear in his brain as they drove rapidly away down the narrow country lane: *polio*.

He found himself thinking: My God, I believe I'd sooner he died than see him confined to a wheelchair all his life.

10

She did not cry at the funeral. Neither did Richard. At their special request, only the two of them were present, standing, numb and expressionless, while the new young rector of Hensford conducted the short simple service. But afterwards, outside in the graveyard, when the tears began pouring down her face as the small white coffin was lowered into the ground and she turned to her husband for comfort, she found him staring at the cross above the steeple with a look of something akin to hatred in his face.

Despite her own grief, she thought: I must help him – but how?

For Richard Vandenburgh had refused to allow his son to be inoculated against polio when the child was seven years old. Both he and Emily had been spared making any categorical decision at that time because, owing to the fact that the vaccine was in its infancy and there was therefore a strictly limited supply, only children with birthdays in August and November became eligible to receive it. The following year, however, in 1957, when there was more to go round, Richard had still maintained that he wasn't prepared to risk it.

In an anguish of doubts – albeit encouraged by the advice of her stepfather – Emily had decided that Charlotte should be immunized. She could remember the bright June morning when a medical team in a mobile county council van drew up on the village green at Hensford and, clutching Charlotte by the hand, she had led her towards it, feeling as if she was sending her child to the guillotine. She could see again the pale-faced, high-shouldered little figure walking bravely up the steps at the back of the van, where a lady doctor in a white coat plunged a needle into the skinny arm. She recalled the agony of watching out for days afterwards for any adverse repercussions, an inevitable summer cold which she feared heralded the worst and then the relief when enough time had elapsed to realize that all was well.

Emily had then felt justified in tackling Richard again about Mark being inoculated likewise, but her entreaties fell on deaf ears. The boy, he said, was not one who succumbed easily to infectious diseases. He was a strong healthy type. With Charlotte it was different. Even though he had not approved of having his daughter inoculated, he could see that Emily had grounds for feeling the child might need extra protection. He had still considered his wife was taking an unnecessary chance, but he certainly had not shared any of her attendant anguish over it. Having got his way with regard to his son, he had simply refrained from making any further comments.

Although the tragic consequences of Richard's stubbornness could not now be anything than uppermost in both his and his wife's mind, they did not mention the subject again. On the evening after the funeral, Richard disappeared out of the house and Emily eventually found him sitting beneath the trees at the end of the garden, staring, unseeingly, into the pool. She had sat down beside him and put out a hand, but he had angrily brushed it aside. As the days turned into weeks, his silent unapproachable attitude did not change. As with the moods she recalled in the earlier part of their marriage, the whisky bottle was never far from his hand. In despair, she began to sense that not only did he resent her presence, but that he acutely resented Charlotte's. Whenever the child came into a room where he happened to be, he got up and left. Once, as they both caught sight of her running across the lawn with one of the dogs, Emily thought she heard him swear under his breath.

Many was the time when she longed to talk to her former mentor, Dr Schmidt, but sadly, not long after she had consulted him when the twins were small, he had died of a heart attack. There were, however, others with whom she felt she might at least safely discuss a little of the present situation.

When August came that year she said to Richard, 'Janine will be going away for her holiday later this month. I should like to take Charlotte down to Wilhampton for a fortnight then, if that's all right by you.' She felt that, if for no other reason, it was important to get the child away from Hensford. Not only was she grieving for her twin brother, but she was becoming puzzled by, even scared of, her father.

'Good idea,' he replied. 'As a matter of fact, Harry and his wife are going up to Scotland for the Twelfth. I thought I might join them for a week and then go on down to Biarritz. Sybilla will be staying there.'

'Oh.' The fact that he had given her no indication of what was in his mind, had obviously been planning such moves behind her back, distressed her beyond measure. We ought to be closer now, she kept saying to herself. We have both lost a son, *our* son. But it's as if Mark's death has driven us even further apart.

They left for their respective holidays more or less at the same time. Because Charlotte was such a bad traveller by car, Emily took her by train, arriving at Westonbury station one hot sultry evening, tired and somewhat dishevelled. Her daughter had still been unable to manage the last part of the journey without being sick.

If Katy was alarmed at her own daughter's appearance she did her best not to show it. She had wanted to come to Cheshire after Mark's death, but sensed that it would not have been wise. It was obvious from Emily's letters – not so much by what she put in them as what she left out – that things were difficult between her and Richard. When Emily suddenly asked if she might bring Charlotte to stay at Wilhampton, Katy had been pleased and relieved, although the brief reference to Richard going away elsewhere had perturbed both her and Maurice.

Now, as she drove her daughter and grand-daughter the short distance to Wilhampton, she hoped she would gradually learn more, although she knew she would never be the recipient of the full story. Loyalty to one's husband or wife was something which had been handed down in the Lodge and Fitzherbert families throughout countless generations. She and Maurice were not likely to hear any complaints from Emily, even though they had long suspected there was something fundamentally wrong with the marriage. All they could do was to play as supportive a role as possible, and this they did their utmost to fulfil during the forthcoming weeks.

'Richard should not,' Maurice said to Katy one night after they were in bed, 'have left her just now. I realize how hard it must be for him, but he's not going to find the solution in running away. Besides, Emily needs him.'

'I know.' Katy put out a hand which was instantly taken unlike, had she known it, the one which her daughter had tried to extend to her husband not so very long ago. There were, she reflected, marriages and marriages, husbands who could always be relied upon when most needed – rocks of Gibraltar, as her mother would have said.

Maurice was one of them. Philip Mason, her first husband, was not; neither was her son-in-law.

As the days passed, she began to despair. Once again, it was not so much what Emily said as what she did not say which caused Katy the gravest anxiety – that, and the pathetic way her daughter seemed constantly trying to make excuses for her husband.

One evening, when Charlotte was in bed and the three of them were sitting out in the garden after dinner, she became even more alarmed when Emily opened up a little more. 'You know,' she said, 'having an heir to Hensford meant everything to Richard. I suppose it's understandable that . . . well, he's come to look on Charlotte as a kind of . . . reproach.'

'Perhaps,' said Maurice, gently, 'Charlotte's husband might one day fill that role.'

'Yes. I know. I've thought about that. But I haven't liked to mention it. It's too soon. Besides, I'm so scared now, about the future. Things happen so quickly. I can't look that far ahead.'

He nodded. He realized that there was little chance of his stepdaughter having another child. What was Emily now? Coming up thirty-eight. Too late. Too great a risk, especially after what she had just said. And if it turned out to be another girl . . .

Something of the same gentleness and concern was shown by the inhabitants of the Hermitage and Ladywell Farm whenever Emily called there. Inevitably, not having seen any of them for some time, she noted signs of ageing, even though Helen, now surrounded by four children, remained basically the same calm, easy-going person she had always known. Rather to Emily's dismay, on her very first visit, her godchild, Joanna, immediately whisked Charlotte off out of sight. 'Will they be all right?' she asked, anxiously, to which Helen replied, 'Oh, I'm sure they will, Em. Jo knows exactly what she's allowed to do and where she's allowed to go. Colin and I have laid down pretty firm rules. She's a sensible kid. They won't come to any harm.'

Emily wished she had the same kind of confidence, that

inner tranquillity, a knack of looking after children which no amount of teaching could ever bring about. Helen wa a born wife and mother and manager. There was a happi ness at Ladywell which, long before Mark's death, had been so sadly lacking at Hensford. Helen's youngest child a little girl called Tess, was upstairs asleep. The two boys Robert and Derek, were playing some kind of make-believe game on the overgrown lawn. Sitting with Helen on an old garden seat beside it reminded Emily of the time when they themselves were round about the same age as the two children they were watching, of the friendship forged then which had grown into a lasting bond which nothing could sever.

Helen did not avoid the subject of Mark, but neither did she dwell on it. She simply said, 'I'm not good at writing, Em. I hardly knew what to say in my letter. I still don't, for that matter, except that Col and I think of you every day.'

It was enough – all Emily wanted. 'Thank you,' she replied, quietly. And then they remained silent for quite a while. Presently, she continued, 'How are your parents? I should have asked before.'

She noticed there was a slight hesitation before Helen answered, 'Mummy's all right, but . . . I'm not so sure about Daddy. It's difficult to tell, because he never complains. But he seems to have aged a lot in the past few months. He takes longer to do things. He used to be such an expert at everything. I've never seen anyone handle an animal or a piece of machinery better. But, well, the other day he actually backed his car into the petrol pump in our yard. It's awfully unlike him.'

'I'm terribly sorry. Have you spoken to your mother about it?'

'Just a little. Mummy's no fool, of course. She's already discussed his health with your stepfather. Maurice makes it his business to call at Bulbarrow whenever he can, without allowing his visits to appear too obvious. I don't know what we'd do without him, Em. I was just so happy when he married your mother after all those years.'

'Yes, it's nice, isn't it. I never really realized all she must have gone through while I was growing up.'

Emily noticed Helen give her a quick look before changing the subject. 'I expect Col and Tim will be back soon,' she said. 'They reckoned to finish combining our winter barley this afternoon. The wheat isn't ready yet. Knowing you were coming, they said they'd make a point of getting back for tea. I'll just go inside and put the kettle on and wake up Tess.'

Towards the end of Emily's holiday at Wilhampton, the telephone rang late one night when Maurice was out on a call. On answering it, Katy was delighted to hear her nephew, Frank Lodge, on the other end of the line. It transpired that he was driving down to Dorset at the weekend on some business connected with one of his authors and wondered if he might call in at East Lodge. It was arranged that he would come to lunch that Friday, a lunch to which May and Betsy were naturally invited, particularly as Paul Woodley was now doing so well in Frank's kind of world.

Although Emily had received the kindest of letters from her cousin after Mark's death, she had not actually seen Frank for almost two years, a gap in time during which, she now noted, he had obviously prospered and put on weight. Yet, like Helen, he was still just the same Frank she had always known. Despite his success, there remained his habitual unassuming manner, the insight and concern for others, a concern which today, she felt, was very much for herself. He was so manifestly pleased that his visit had coincided with hers and did his best to manage a few quiet words with her before he left.

They wandered down the garden together and he pushed open the small door that led into River Lane. For a few moments they sat down on the very same tree stump by the Willon, where they had sat on that starry August night in 1945. She sensed, without being told, that he, too, was thinking of that night. She wondered how happy he was in his own marriage. There had never been any children, yet he had spoken of Elaine frequently and quite naturally during lunch, even to explaining that she had not accompanied him because she found this particular author 'too tedious'. Emily was aware that she and Frank would probably never know much about each other's private lives. It went without saying that they would always maintain a 'front', that they would present to the outside world as good an image as possible of their respective 'better halves'.

Only when they rose to go and he took one last lingering look at the Willon, flowing along in its usual unhurried impervious way, did his remark make her feel that, beneath his bonhomie, there was a certain sadness.

'It's been a long time, hasn't it, Emily,' he said. 'So much water under the bridge.'

11

'I think you should seriously consider sending Charlotte away, Emily.'

'*Away?* Where to?'

'Boarding school. You could start her in the summer term, when she's coming up for eleven.'

'But *James* . . .'

Emily had long been on Christian name terms with her local doctor. Over the years she had had to call James Peterson out to Hensford far too often for them to be anything than otherwise. He had been unfailingly kind and understanding, but she looked at him now askance as they sat, one on either side of the fire, in the little room where she spent much of her time – that is, when she was not upstairs battling with Charlotte's bronchial troubles. When, momentarily, she failed to continue speaking, he broke in with much more assertiveness than usual.

'Look, Emily. It's hard to say this, but I'm not sure you aren't your daughter's worst enemy at the moment. Your anxiety shows. It's possible you're helping to make her ill, as well as yourself. For some time I've been just as concerned about you as I have about her. If the child could be got away into . . . well . . . more happy-go-lucky surroundings, I honestly believe these attacks might lessen, both in frequency and intensity.'

'I can't see any school matron coping with them, James.' Agitation had made her voice peremptory.

'You'd be surprised. And the very fact of having someone kind, trained, but completely unemotional, nursing her could work wonders. Anyway, please think about it. There are several good schools I know of. I could give you a list if you like. Then you might care to go and see some of them. Charlotte needs to be amongst kids of her own age now. Hensford isn't . . .' This time, it was he who stopped speaking, abruptly.

Almost involuntarily, she completed the sentence for him. 'Yes, I know, James. It's not the happiest of places for the child to be at the moment. I realize that.'

He looked at her keenly. He knew there was something very wrong somewhere. Emily had never before gone so far as to admit it. He noticed that she had flushed and was probably regretting what she had just said. He wished he could get to know her husband better, but he hardly ever saw the man. Richard Vandenburgh always seemed to be away, unless it was the shooting season when he was out four or five days a week – which came to practically the same thing – leaving Emily and Charlotte to mark time in his large and somehow unfriendly house. James knew that neither parent would ever be able to get over Mark's death and the particularly distressing circumstances connected with it; and it had not altogether surprised him when he became aware that Richard was now rejecting his daughter. The man's frantic and hedonistic activities were probably the only way he knew of living through a well-nigh intolerable situation. Yet, when James came to think about it further, he recalled how Richard's behaviour had been somewhat the same in the early part of the marriage. Emily had been so hauntingly beautiful at the time, but he had often speculated on just what it was that always made her look so sad.

As he said goodbye to her now, James Peterson wondered what she would do if, by any chance, she did send Charlotte to boarding school. It would leave a gap

in her life, but he knew she had literary leanings. It wou[ld]
be nice to see her getting interested in something el[se]
although, for a start, she ought to go away for a goo[d]
long holiday with, or even without, her husband. An[d]
here, James found his thoughts straying into an area wher[e,]
as a doctor, they probably had no right to stray. All th[e]
same, he couldn't help feeling that this particular patie[nt]
needed some other man. He could not see her actuall[y]
taking a lover. Would a divorce, perhaps, be the answe[r]
in the end?

Left alone, Emily did not at once go back upstairs t[o]
her daughter's bedroom. She knew that Janine was aroun[d]
and Charlotte was recovering from her latest bout [of]
illness, albeit slowly. For a while, she simply sat o[n]
considering James's advice. It was impossible to believ[e]
that she would take it. And yet . . . she had come to hav[e]
great faith in him as a family doctor. She had a shrew[d]
suspicion that much of what he had just said made sens[e]
and that her stepfather would, in all probability, back hi[m]
up. Besides, Richard's attitude since Mark's death ha[d]
exacerbated the whole situation. That alone was enoug[h]
reason for getting Charlotte away from Hensford. Sh[e]
wished she could discuss James's proposition with hi[m]
even though she could already guess at his reaction. H[e]
would be all for such an arrangement. But Richard was i[n]
the Cape with Sybilla and not due back till the beginnin[g]
of March. Meanwhile, she supposed that there would b[e]
no harm in simply going to *look* at a few girls' schools.

In the end, she took herself off one late February da[y]
to visit two of them: Waverley, eighty miles away an[d]
Eaton Grange, only twenty. The first had been one o[f]
James's list; the second name had been given to her by [a]
friend of the Bartholomews. The fact that it was nearer t[o]
Hensford had already made her more favourably incline[d]
towards it, even though James himself knew nothing abou[t]
it and remarked, quietly, that it was not necessarily a goo[d]
thing for a child to board too close to home.

She found a great difference in the two establishments[.]
Waverley was a large Victorian building with a mass o[f]
outhouses converted into extra classrooms. Her firs[t]

mpression was of little girls running in and out all over he place, none of them wearing coats. Before she had got s far as the headmistress's study, she had decided that Charlotte would never survive under such conditions, even hough the atmosphere seemed happy and relaxed and the hildren obviously full of health and high spirits – very lifferent from the subdued waif to whom she had said oodbye that morning at Hensford.

For politeness's sake, she allowed herself to be taken on detailed and unhurried inspection, partly by the deputy ead and partly by the pupils themselves, who showed her vith pride their various pets which they had been able to oring with them including, to her amazement, a few ponies. With the memory of her own serious riding accident when he was a child, Emily had been secretly relieved that Charlotte had never shown much interest in horses and he child's increasing asthmatic tendencies had rendered keeping one out of the question.

At Eaton Grange, however, there were neither horses nor any other kind of pet. It, too, was a Victorian building, out there the similarity with Waverley ended. The interior vas warm and comfortable. There appeared to be no converted outhouses. The grounds were spacious and beautifully kept. The headmistress herself took Emily on he whole tour of inspection, throwing open doors on clean bright classrooms, in which pupils automatically umped up from their desks and stood to attention until hey withdrew. The dormitories were equally immaculate, ll fitted out in delicate shades of pinks, blues and greens. Yellow was reserved for what Mrs Mather had referred to as the 'sick bay', although, on opening and closing the door quickly, she said, 'We get remarkably little sickness here. We have no one in bed at the moment.'

'And you feel you could cope with a child who gets bronchial asthma after almost every cold?'

'But, *of course*.' Mrs Mather swept Emily on down the corridor. 'We have had more than one asthmatic here. They have invariably benefited from being at Eaton Grange.'

And it was only twenty miles away, Emily thought, as

she drove home. *And* they appeared to have a vacancy fo:
the coming summer term. She felt suddenly inclined to giv
in. It would be such a relief to pass over the responsibilit
for Charlotte for just a little while, however much it was
and always would be, ultimately hers in the end. Bu
perhaps, after all, James was right. It would be wonderfu
to see the child fitter and coming out of herself a little. Sh
was such a buttoned-up little thing at the moment.

Emily began, albeit with misgivings, to make th
necessary arrangements. By the time Richard returned sh
was able to present him with a *fait accompli*. As antici
pated, he approved heartily, saying he was sure she wa
being extremely sensible and practical. On the fateful day
when Charlotte was due at Eaton Grange, he actuall
drove them both there, stopping at regular intervals, wit
admirable thoughtfulness, to avoid any car sickness. O:
the way home, having said goodbye to a quiet, but no
exactly tearful, daughter, she found herself silentl
praying: Please God it will work out.

She was surprised but immensely relieved when Char
lotte appeared to survive the first three weeks with n
mishap, so much so that when the telephone rang one lat
May evening, she did not automatically fear it was bad
news. Nor was it. As the voice on the other end of the lin
said, 'Hi, Emily,' her spirits lifted further. Nearly twent
years seemed to have been suddenly wiped away. She fel
all at once exhilarated, even carefree.

'Hi, Vernon,' she answered. She might have been in he
early twenties, nursing at Ashmore, eager for whateve
jaunt he was about to propose. 'Where are you speaking
from?' she added, quickly.

'London. I'm back in the old country, Emily. By myself.
For just the inside of a week. The firm's sent me over. I'm
Carson Incorporated's blue-eyed boy right now. They've
chosen me to try to pull off some deal over here. The
reckon, with my wartime experiences, I know the English.

She laughed. 'And do you?'

'Some of them. You, in particular. Is there any chance
you could come to town?'

'Well . . .' She hesitated, but only momentarily. 'I could . . . unless you might be able to get up here?'

She was instantly relieved when he replied, 'Not a chance, I'm afraid. My employers have worked out a pretty tight schedule. I'll have to fly back at the weekend. But I wondered . . . Friday night, Emily? Would you be free?'

His voice sounded just as it had always done when he was fixing a date. Behind the charming, simulated diffidence, there had always been a kind of assurance. Would she be free, indeed. She had always been free. Had made it her business to be so. Unconsciously, she did the same thing now. She heard herself saying, 'We have a small flat in town, Vernon. In Kensington. I daresay I could come up. Just for that night.'

This time it was he who laughed, and she regretted her choice of words. Embarrassed, she asked, hastily, 'How is Liz?'

'Fine. She sends her love.'

'And my godchild and the rest of the family?'

'They're fine, too. Johnny's sixteen now, would you believe it. Taller than me. I've got photos to show you. And of the two girls. It'll be good to see you again, Emily. Sorry to have sprung it on you, but I only knew I was coming forty-eight hours ago. I'm staying at the Cumberland. I'm afraid Carson's didn't think me quite important enough for the Dorchester or the Ritz.'

After she rang off, having agreed to let Vernon at least give her dinner at the Dorchester, she wondered what she would say to Richard. It was unusual for her to go to London quite alone, apart from matters connected with Charlotte's health or her visits to Dr Schmidt, which she had managed to pass off under the pretext of some other appointment, usually a dental one. It was such a pity that Richard was at home just now. He could so well have been away. Somehow, since Charlotte had been packed off to boarding school he had seemed a little more settled. He had said nothing about going away again, other than referring to the possibility of them both visiting Norway in the autumn. For once, there had been no mention of Sybilla.

The telephone ringing a second time interrupted any further meditation. As she went to answer it she found herself thinking, guiltily: If it's Mrs Mather about Charlotte, maybe I shan't be able to go to London after all . . .

Totally unexpectedly, she found herself speaking to Sybilla. The latter's voice sounded harsh and over-excited. 'Darlink? I'm coming up to Cheshire tomorrow as ever is. So unfortunate. I had this little operation in Harley Street. The wretched man . . . how you say? *Bungled* it. I shall sue 'im. Meanwhile, I need to *hide*, darlink. My poor face. I don't want to see *anyone*, you understand?'

12

She felt nervous in the taxi on the way to the Dorchester – nervous and slightly guilty. By the time it reached Hyde Park Corner she began to wish that she had not come.

Not that there had been any difficulty about leaving Hensford. She had decided to tell Richard about Vernon's telephone call and he had taken both that and the news of Sybilla's imminent arrival with complete equanimity. He had said that he felt it would do her good to get away for a little break on her own. There was no need, he added, for her to be home just because her mother-in-law was arriving, especially as Sybilla had stressed her desire for complete privacy. He himself would be around in case anyone was needed. The fact that his wife would be going off to meet an old flame did not seem to concern him one way or the other. Emily had long realized how much she was taken for granted.

She knew that he had absolute faith in her, for she had never given him the slightest cause for anything otherwise and, despite their curious marriage, she sensed he still needed and relied on her in some indefinable way. She had been content to let that be so, to remain Mrs Richard Vandenburgh, irreproachable wife, conscientious mother and competent – if somewhat retiring – chatelaine of Hensford. Very occasionally, when she was more than usually over-strained, she wondered what it would be like to get right away and kick over the traces. Often, she speculated to what extent Richard might have already done so, particularly since Mark's death when he had started his wanderings again – ostensibly with Sybilla – just as he had in the early part of their marriage. But having failed to get closer to him in their mutual grief, she had now given up trying. During the last year they had seldom made love and, after each occasion, she had thought how misleading was the description of an act which, she felt, had given little pleasure to either of them – even though deriving pleasure from anything since the tragedy seemed not only impossible but somehow out of place.

Nevertheless, as she walked up the steps to the revolving doors at the Dorchester's main entrance and was conscious of one or two admiring male glances, she felt suddenly and unexpectedly light-hearted. It might be nearly sixteen years since she had last seen Vernon, her face might have acquired a few more lines, but her figure had certainly not acquired any extra pounds. She was still as slim and supple as when they had first met and this evening she had taken great care over her appearance, putting on one of the most becoming outfits in her wardrobe.

'Emily!'

'Vernon!'

He must have been waiting just inside the foyer because all at once he was by her side, the expression on his face one she recalled so well: a mixture of eagerness, amusement and, she had to admit, undisguised admiration. There was no hint now of the bitterness which had overcome him after he had lost a leg in the Normandy landings. Oddly enough, he seemed in better form than she ever remembered. He was lean, alert and deeply tanned. All the extra weight which he had put on at the time of his injury had disappeared. As he leant forward to kiss her cheek, he exuded vitality and an air of knowing exactly what he was about.

She was vaguely aware of his arm under her elbow, of being shepherded further inside to a small table which he had reserved and where, having ascertained what she would like, he ordered their drinks. Then he turned and gazed at her for a full minute without speaking. At last he said, 'Em, I'm not just laying this on. Don't get me wrong. But I honestly didn't think I'd have the pleasure of taking out the most beautiful woman in London while I was over here. Maturity suits you.'

She flushed. 'Nice of you, Vernon. But I've been thinking . . . well, you haven't done badly yourself. I'm longing to hear about everything, Liz, my godchild, the whole family. I hope you've brought those photographs.'

'Sure. But first of all there's something else I want to say. I know Liz wrote after . . . what happened to your little boy. I feel badly that I didn't, although God knows what I could have said. I thought maybe you'd sooner not mention it now, but I just had to say something.'

'I understand, Vernon. Thank you. I don't mind talking about Mark. In fact, it's a relief. It's Richard who . . . can't bring himself to, yet.'

He nodded. 'I guess I might be just the same, if it were Jonathan. It sure was one hell of a thing to have happened. How's Charlotte nowadays?'

She paused, glad of the slight interruption while the waiter brought a Martini for her, a whisky for Vernon. She did not want to go into details. She certainly wasn't going to give the slightest hint of Richard's attitude towards his daughter. In the end, she simply said, 'I was advised to send her away to boarding school. The doctor felt it would be best. Goodness knows if it was the right decision, but time will tell and so far she's survived better than expected. With all her bronchial troubles, I think he felt I was overdoing the mothering. Of course, I realize in the States you don't go in for boarding school at that age, whatever the circumstances.'

'No. Maybe not. But then, I guess a lot of things are different where I live, Em. I wish sometime you'd come and see, pay us a visit. Do you think you ever could? We'd love to have you – and Richard and Charlotte,' he added, quickly, as an afterthought.

'Well, sometime maybe, who knows.' But even as she said the words, Emily knew that it was extremely unlikely that she would ever take him up on the suggestion. What was more, she knew that he knew it also. As the evening progressed, she simply sat there, grateful for his company, happy to listen to his description of life in Chicago as lived by the Keeler family, picturing the fairly large apartment which they rented in one of the more fashionable parts of the town, hearing how they were hoping soon to move out to a house in Lake Forest. She chided herself for feeling a slight stab of jealousy when he touched on how well Liz had adapted to living in America and did not appear to miss the 'old country', as he still called it.

'Of course,' he remarked, drily, at one stage, 'her mother never forgave us. You know, Jonathan being born only seven months after the marriage.' For the first time he looked slightly abashed, before adding, 'Well, with no love lost in that direction, I suppose it made things easier for Liz not to feel homesick.'

Emily gathered that financially they had been very much up against it in the beginning but latterly things had greatly improved. Vernon did not actually produce his photographs until they were almost at the end of their meal. To her consternation, in nearly all of them, she found herself looking at a woman she scarcely recognized. There was such a great deal more of Liz than the young girl with whom she remembered making beds at Ashmore Emergency Hospital. Her former contemporary must have put on another stone at least, even since the photograph sent as a Christmas card a few years ago. Yet she looked cheerful enough, especially in one sitting outside a log cabin surrounded by her three children.

'We've been going up to the mountains these last few summers,' Vernon explained. 'The heat in Chicago gets pretty unbearable at this time of the year. We'll be going again soon after I get back.'

She nodded, carefully going through the photographs a second time. This, presumably, would have been *her* life, had she married him. Or perhaps not. Probably she wouldn't have adapted to America nearly so well as Liz had obviously done. She might even have been a drag on Vernon, longing for England and Wilhampton and all the familiar people and things which had given her such deep irreplaceable roots. Or would her passion for Vernon have surmounted all difficulties until such time as, with luck, they settled down into calmer waters? So difficult to tell. Besides, what business had she to be making such conjectures at this point? They were both married to others – Vernon, she imagined, much more happily than she. Just because on a certain June night in 1960 when they were both middle-aged and spending a pleasant few hours in each other's company, there was no reason to get starry-eyed about the past.

She gathered the photographs neatly together, preparatory to handing them back. As she did so, she found him staring at her and, when their hands touched as she passed them over, he said, 'Em, I'm sorry. I've done all the talking. Let's hear about you, for a change. You minded a lot, didn't you, about . . . us? So did I. Only, I mean . . . we couldn't have gone on as we were. You being engaged to that chap who was a prisoner of war. What happened to him? Why didn't you marry in the end?'

She looked away. What, indeed, had happened to John William Moreton, only son of Sir Charles and Lady Moreton, her one-time fiancé, the young man for whom she had waited throughout the war and who, when he returned at the end of it, she found had become emotionally involved with a member of his own sex and was now, so far as she knew, living an unconventional life in Tangier.

'He . . .' She began hesitantly and then, knowing that whatever she said would be instantly understood, continued, 'turned out to be homosexual, Vernon.'

'Oh, *Em*.' His distress was so obvious and sincere. 'And you'd waited . . . all that time. I . . . we sacrificed ourselves for *that*?'

'Yes.'

'My God.'

He became suddenly angry. 'Why did you marry Richard Vandenburgh?' he asked, shortly.

'Because he looked awfully like you, Vernon.'

'And is he?'

'No. Not at all.'

'Have you been happy? I mean, before what happened to Mark?'

'No.' She felt it was important to be honest.

'But you managed?'

'Yes, I managed.'

There had been a band playing throughout dinner to which a few couples had been dancing, but she and Vernon had been too engrossed in conversation to pay much attention to it. Now, as they fell silent, it suddenly launched forth into a well-known hit from the early forties. He put out both hands and drew her to her feet.

'I'm not too good at this sort of thing, nowadays,' he remarked. 'Having one tin leg and all that. But if you feel you could cope . . .'

Effortlessly, almost unconsciously, they were suddenly back in time. They could have been on the small dance floor at the White Lion in Westonbury, as he held her very close and they started off – slowly at first and then with increasing confidence – to the strains of 'We'll Meet Again'. Only once did he pause while she heard Vernon ask the pianist if he would play 'a few more from the same era'. Smilingly, the man acquiesced. Tune followed tune: sad, nostalgic, humorous – 'As Time Goes By, Yours' and 'Chattanooga Choo-Choo, Won't You Choo-Choo Me Home?' Vernon did not immediately release her as 'Sentimental Journey' brought the medley to an end. He simply stood holding her, until they eventually became aware they were alone on the dance floor and that it was necessary to return to their table.

Once seated, she glanced at her watch, amazed to find that it was past midnight. 'It's been lovely, Vernon,' she said, 'but I think I must be going. I didn't realize it was getting so late.'

She was just a little disappointed when he merely nodded and called for the bill. In the foyer, she began thanking him once more, but he cut her short. 'Wait here. I'll ask for a cab.'

She had been expecting that he would probably suggest seeing her back to Kensington, even though he himself was staying but a few steps away from the Dorchester. What she was not expecting was that as soon as they were inside the taxi and he had given instructions to the driver, he swiftly closed the sliding glass partition, turned and took her firmly in his arms. She made one half-hearted attempt to resist, which he instantly suppressed by kissing her harder.

She said nothing as they walked towards the door of the building where she lived. She knew that it was useless trying to prevent him coming up to the flat. Once there, she switched on the hall light and, partly out of nervousness, partly convention, she said, 'Would you like a drink, Vernon?'

He shook his head. 'There's only one thing I'd like, Em. I think you'd like it too. We've waited long enough and there might not be another chance – ever. Don't tell me it's wrong. Can't we just think of it as one little taste of what might have been? A sort of memory that we'll each be able to carry with us for the rest of our lives?'

13

'Darlink. Be honest, now. Do you zink my scars are better than when you returned from London?'

'Much better, Ma.'

'You *really* mean it?'

'Of course I do.'

Sybilla Vandenburgh, dressed in a negligé, sat by the window in her bedroom wielding a hand-mirror while twisting her head this way and that.

'But it's a *fortnight*, darlink. And I hoped to go to Lord's later on in July.'

'Lord's?' Emily was not aware that such an event had ever been on Sybilla's social calendar before although, doubtless, if little Mark had lived to go to Eton it might have been different.

'Yes. With this *divine* man, Stephen Cartwright. I met him at a party just before I went into the clinic. I said I was coming straight to you. After all, I didn't want him visiting me, did I? It is such a problem making up excuses for operations which are *visible*. One can't always say one is having a cyst removed in one's neck or one's sinuses straightened. And an eye job is *always* far more tricky. I know one woman whose scars took ages to fade. She used to tell new acquaintances that she'd got her neck stuck between the banisters when she was a child. Of course, I suppose if I kept my dark glasses on all the time, the ones with the very wide sides . . .' The mirror was suddenly switched to the other hand. Sybilla's head went on turning like a small inquisitive bird's.

Emily watched her, fascinated, thinking of two July days in 1939, just before the outbreak of the Second World War, when she, too, for the only time in her life, had gone to Lord's in the company of her prospective fiancé, John William Moreton, and his parents. It had been the big event of her youth. But, surely, Sybilla, so faded, so manifestly the wrong side of sixty, couldn't be getting excited about such a prospect now?

All at once, her mother-in-law stopped looking in the mirror and stared Emily straight in the face. 'How I envy you, darlink. You are so *young*. You look even younger than when I was last here. I said to Richard when you came back from London that he really shouldn't have allowed you to go off on your own like that.'

Emily found her colour mounting. It was not the first time Sybilla had made a similar remark since her return. With a hasty, 'I can see the postman cycling down the drive, Ma. There might be a letter from Charlotte,' she left the room.

There was only one letter for her, but it was not from her daughter. It was an airmail one, in Liz Keeler's handwriting. She felt suddenly uneasy as she went into her study to open it. She had not been expecting to hear from either Vernon or his wife. For one thing, she knew that as soon as he had reported to his firm they would be off to the mountains on holiday. What could Liz possibly be writing about? Could she have suspected something? Found out, even? Abruptly, Emily took herself in hand. That was an impossibility. What had happened on a single June night all those thousands of miles away from Chicago was something quite apart, isolated, unique. It had never happened before and it would never happen again. It was, as Vernon had said, a memory which they would have for the rest of their lives, a secret they would share to the grave.

She read the words and then read them again, experiencing the same kind of disbelief as the writer:

> . . . And so Vernon is dead, Emily. I can't really take it in yet. When he telephoned from New York he sounded so happy. He said the trip had been a great success and he had decided to stop by and get me a present on the strength of it, something he'd always wanted me to have. I guess it was a mink. He'd managed to change his flight to another one on a smaller airline and reckoned he would be home around 10 p.m. So the children and I just waited. I even kept little Lindy up. When it was getting on for eleven, I got a bit worried. There had been a few electric storms rumbling around, but we didn't really know anything was wrong until Jonathan switched on the radio. There had been this crash twenty miles short of Lake Michigan. I'll write again, Em, when I can . . .

You stopped by, Vernon, Emily kept saying to herself, not because you wanted to buy Liz a present due to any business success. But because you wanted to make it up to her in some way. Because you felt happy – but guilty for being so. If you hadn't spent that night with me in London, you'd probably have gone straight home. You wouldn't have changed flights. You'd be still alive, off to the mountains with the family. Oh, Vernon, now it is only I who have the memory. Oh, my God, what have I done?

She was still sitting with the letter in her lap when she heard footsteps in the hall and Richard stood at the door.

'I've just bumped into Harry. He and Mabs want us to go over for drinks tonight and bring Sybilla. It would be nice to see her getting about again. Anyway, I said you and I would be there around six-thirty. I'll have to check with Ma, of course.'

He was gone, without waiting for her reply. She felt a wave of anger at his assumption that *she* would automatically acquiesce, yet he displayed none of the same kind of assurance with regard to his mother. She wanted to run, anywhere, to leave this house in which, more than ever, she felt eternally trapped.

She was unable to cry. For the rest of the morning she went about numb and silent. Knowing that Richard would be out to lunch because he had to attend a meeting in Stoke Wallington, she told Mrs Draper to take her mother-in-law her usual salad and fruit on a tray, but that she would require nothing as she was not feeling well. Then she went up to her room, drew the curtains, lay down on the bed and closed her eyes.

Almost immediately, with painful clarity, she saw again the photographs Vernon had shown her at the Dorchester: Liz and the children, laughing and happy. She thought of the log cabin where now, by rights, they all would have been. She had a vivid image of Vernon on a plane, some gift-wrapped box amongst his hand luggage. The fatal crash she would not, could not, visualize. But, against her will, there then came a feeling, almost tangible, of his arms around her, his lips on hers, his voice saying, 'Don't tell me it's wrong.'

With an effort, she brought her mind back to the present. What would Liz do – a widow with three children all at crucial stages in their upbringing? Would she remain in Chicago? Somehow, having severed so completely her family ties, Emily doubted that she would return to England. But would Vernon's firm help out sufficiently? Whatever compensation his widow received, it could scarcely be enough. At least there was something which she, Emily, could do. After all, she was Jonathan's godmother, wasn't she? She had not let Richard have all her inheritance. She could certainly see Jonathan through college. Perhaps help with the two girls if Liz would let her. The thought of being able to give some practical material assistance gave her a modicum of comfort. She would get up and write to Liz at once.

On the stairs she met Richard. A look of irritation came over his face. 'Aren't you ready? You don't seem to be.'

She frowned. 'Ready for what?'

'The Bartholomews. I'm just going up to collect Ma. She's decided to come.'

'I'm sorry. I forgot.'

'Well, buck up and get dressed. It's getting on for six.'

'Getting on for *six*?'

He looked puzzled now. 'Yes. Whatever have you been doing all afternoon?'

'I'm sorry. I was lying down. I had no idea it was so late. I ... had a bad headache. Would you make my excuses?'

'But you didn't come last time, remember. Mabs won't like it. She'll think you're avoiding her.'

'I'm sorry, Richard. But I really don't feel I can.'

He shrugged and went on up to his mother's apartment.

Emily was scarcely conscious of their departure as she sat in her study and picked up a pen. It was one of the most difficult letters she had ever had to write and draft after draft went straight into the waste-paper basket. She was still not satisfied with her last effort when she heard the car returning and felt obliged to go into the dining room and make some attempt at sociability during their evening meal.

It was a pretence which she did her best to keep up in the days that followed. When Sybilla made some reference to her not looking as well as she had done, Emily merely brushed it aside by saying it was possible she might have picked up a slight virus. It was a relief when Richard suddenly announced that he would be driving his mother back to London and staying for a while in the flat. At least she would now be alone and there would be no need to conceal her distress.

She sat by the pool late one evening, her thoughts, as always, on a situation which she knew she would never be able to disclose or discuss with anyone. For once, it took precedence over her concern for Charlotte. Her mind seemed to go round in kaleidoscope fashion: Vernon, their brief moments of ecstasy, his death and the feeling of the part she had played in it. Light kept turning to shadow, love to remorse.

Yet would she have acted differently? *Could* she have?

She felt there had been something curiously fatalistic, preordained about the way things had turned out. Had not Vernon himself implied that what they had done could not have been wrong? Remembering their love-making she could almost believe he was right, could give herself, if only for a few moments, absolution. But then the thought of his widow obtruded. Poor, poor Liz. Emily had not heard from her again yet, but that was understandable. She would have so much to do. It had been good of her to write so quickly in the first place. After all, it was still less than a month since the tragedy . . .

The thought of time passing made her, momentarily, reflect on something else. It was only a thought which flitted in and out of consciousness. It did not really amount to anything until a few days later, when she was looking in her diary. Even then, she was still able to dismiss it. She had already gone to James Peterson earlier that year about her irregular periods and he had told her she could well be starting an early change of life. She had ceased to bother too much about contraceptive precautions. She had lost interest in sex. In any case, it was something which hardly came into the picture nowadays.

Except, of course, three weeks ago when, in one single night, it had been more wonderful, more fulfilling than anything she had ever known.

14

The woman in a white coat, seated behind a desk, was small and nondescript-looking, with straight sandy-coloured hair and rimless spectacles.

'Your doctor said you wanted a complete gynaecological check-up, Mrs Vandenburgh.'

'Yes.'

'What seems to be the problem?' Dr Veronica Cole raised her pale blue eyes from the letter in front of her and gazed at Emily in a curiously dispassionate and, she felt, almost disapproving way.

'I . . . well . . . I consulted Dr Peterson some time ago

about irregular periods. He thought I might be starting an early change of life.'

'How old are you?'

'I shall be thirty-nine at the end of the year.'

'Hmm. It's always possible, though unusual. Do you and your husband have regular sexual intercourse?'

'I . . .' She found herself blushing, furiously. The eyes behind the spectacles continued to watch her in the same disconcerting fashion. 'We don't have sex all that often,' she replied.

'Why?'

Dear God. What an insensitive cold-blooded type she was. Besides, Emily thought, I haven't come here to be catechized about my sex life. I've come to know whether I'm pregnant.

Not having wanted to go to James Peterson direct, it had been a relief to find that it was not quite so difficult to bypass him as she had imagined. She had simply rung him up and said that, in view of what they had already discussed, she thought she would like to see a lady gynaecologist and he had been quite agreeable, saying he would arrange an appointment with a Dr Cole in Wimpole Street as soon as possible. Only at the end of their conversation had she felt slightly mean when he had said, 'I'm sure there's nothing wrong, Emily, but it'll put your mind at rest.'

Her mind was feeling far from rested at the moment. She was certainly not prepared to tell her interrogator just why her marital relations were so infrequent. In any case, the real reasons were so strange, so intensely personal, far too complicated to explain in one brief interview.

'My husband and I have . . . grown apart, I suppose,' was all she volunteered.

She watched Dr Cole write something down and wondered what it was. Neurotic? Frigid? There seemed something altogether distasteful about discussing the subject with this singularly sexless little woman. With a shock, Emily noticed that Dr Cole was wearing a wedding ring. Had she ever, or did she *still*, somehow, somewhere, have sex with Mr Cole, or whoever he was? It was unimaginable, unthinkable.

'Had you thought that perhaps it was not very wise to let such a situation deteriorate?' The voice kept to the same flat inquisitorial tone.

'Well . . . I mean, I don't quite see what I could have done.'

'You could have talked to someone professionally. I don't necessarily mean a gynaecologist. A psychiatrist or some marriage counsellor, maybe. After all, sex is mostly in the mind, isn't it?'

Emily thought suddenly of Dr Schmidt. She *had* asked for advice, once upon a time. A long, *long* time ago. Perhaps she should have gone on seeking it after he had died. But then, what would have been the good, if Richard hadn't been willing to co-operate.

'I'm sorry,' she replied, at length, 'but I think I would sooner just talk about why I've come today. It's possible I'm pregnant.'

'From one of your rare copulations?'

She looked down at her hands, inwardly wincing, as she gave a slight nod. How outspoken Dr Cole was. Could she possibly have guessed her secret?

'Well, we must find out, mustn't we,' the voice went on. 'Have you brought a sample with you?'

'Yes.'

'Did you not take any precautions on this isolated occasion?'

'No.'

'Was that not rather irresponsible?'

'I haven't for some time. I mean . . . I thought . . . my age, and after what Dr Peterson said.'

'All the more reason, Mrs Vandenburgh.' Dr Cole stood up and motioned Emily to a corner where there was a bed behind a screen. 'Some women get caught out at this time of life,' she continued, as she left her to undress. 'Just let me know when you are ready.'

But if Dr Cole's manner seemed sharp and unsympathetic, she certainly conducted her physical examination with the utmost gentleness and care. When Emily had dressed and was once more facing her across the desk, she said, 'You will appreciate that I cannot make a positive diagnosis until the result of the usual test comes through, although I think it more than likely that you are, in fact, expecting. There are all the signs. How would you feel about another baby at your time of life?'

Emily looked down at her hands again, now so tightly clenched that the knuckles showed white. When she did not speak, Dr Cole said, a little more kindly, 'There is always a risk, of course, giving birth as late as this. In certain cases, if we envisage problems, it is sometimes advisable to terminate the pregnancy.'

'Terminate?' Emily's head jerked up. Kill Vernon's child? It was she who now stared the doctor straight in the face. 'Oh no. I couldn't . . . I would never have an abortion.'

'No?' Dr Cole's manner became even more conciliatory. 'Well, I just wanted to find out how you felt. You seem a very fit woman. I don't think you need worry. Ring me about this time tomorrow and I will let you know the final verdict.'

She went back to the flat. It was the first time she had been there since the night she had spent with Vernon. Although there were signs of Richard's recent visit, she knew from now on she would always connect the place with one man only. She lay on the bed and gave herself up to thinking about him. She was carrying his child. There was no doubt in her mind about it now, even though she had been told to wait until the next day for confirmation. She put her hands on her stomach, on the secret she must carry to the grave. But how? She and Richard had not had any sex since her last period. He would know, that is, unless they . . . The thought seemed hideous, totally immoral, against all her principles.

She arrived back at Hensford the following evening, the report of her pregnancy coming as no surprise, merely something about which, out of courtesy, she had felt obliged to enquire. She found her husband in a more expansive mood than usual. The harvest prospects looked good. The Rentons, discovering that he was on his own, had apparently asked him to dinner the previous night. He remarked that he was glad, now that Charlotte was away at school, Emily was at last finding the London flat useful. He hoped she had had a successful visit to — as she had let him believe — the dentist.

She went upstairs to bath and change and then, because it was still so hot, she put on a strapless sundress and some new high-heeled sandals which she had not yet worn that summer. Already the dress seemed to strain a little over her bust and hips. When she came down to the drawing room, she noticed Richard's eyes on her more than once. To her surprise, he complimented her on her appearance, something which had not happened for a very long time.

Suddenly, she knew that it would be possible to put into practice that night the idea about which she had felt so ashamed. She tried to tell herself that it was quite accidental that she had decided to wear this particular outfit, not unlike that which she had worn with such devastating effect in the early part of their marriage. When he suggested walking down to the pool together after dinner, she made no objection. When, in the shelter of the weeping willows, he began to stroke her bare arm she did not at first recoil; although when a light snapped on back in the house and there were the sounds of Hardiman making his nightly visit to the greenhouse, she tried to make him desist. But it was too late. He was already pulling her down on the grass, obviously excited by the thought of having intercourse in the open with the risk of discovery, even though he kept saying, 'Don't be silly, darling. No one can see.'

She began to fight him then. However much she might have contemplated letting him make love to her for expediency's sake, the thought was now replaced by a feeling of utter revulsion, both at him and herself. To have him touch her, after Vernon, seemed wholly shocking. She flailed out with her fists, twisting her body this way and that. But he was too strong for her. Soon, he had her pinioned beneath him, one hand tearing at her underwear. She heard the ripping of silk as still she struggled, unaware that she was simply intensifying his desire, giving him the hitherto unexpected pleasure of raping his wife.

In the early hours of the following morning, she staggered, bleeding, to the bathroom. Her pregnancy was at an end.

15

'I'm sorry, Emily. Very sorry.'

Richard stood with his back to her, looking out of the window, as she lay in bed the following day. Although she was feeling far from well, she knew the trouble was much more mental than physical. There had been no need to send for James Peterson. Presumably, he would soon have received – or might already have received – Dr Cole's report. In due course, it would be a comparatively simple matter to let him know that she had miscarried; and Richard need never know that she had ever been pregnant – only that she was now suffering from shock after the way he had treated her.

What was more difficult was to know how to handle her life from now on. When she did not reply to his apology he turned and stared at her, an expression on his face which she had never seen before: contrition mingled with fear.

'It won't happen again. I promise you.'

She looked away. It came to her, far more intensely than ever before, that Faza must have been willing to satisfy his sadistic impulses all those years ago. It was the hold she had obviously had on him. It was something Emily had long suspected, but the thought had been so distasteful that she had never allowed her mind to dwell on it. She knew little of sexual aberrations; that her own husband was inclined towards any unnatural practices was totally repugnant. It was preferable to pretend otherwise.

But now, after what had just happened, she realized only too well how its memory would always come between them. Their marriage was doomed yet, on the other hand, divorce seemed equally impossible. She would have to admit to adultery, the secret she had promised Vernon she would always keep. For she wasn't the type to lie, even though Vernon was dead and no one could gainsay her. But then poor Liz would get to hear of it, as well as her own relations, even her daughter. She had no proof that Richard had ever strayed, certainly not with anyone she knew, only the suspicion that there must have been other women in his life like Faza, the kind to whom, for obvious reasons, he was much more attracted. She supposed that was why he had never appeared particularly interested in the ones they knew socially, which at one time had lulled her into a false sense of security from the point of view of their marriage.

All these things kept running through her mind, just as they had done throughout the previous night. Always they came back to the same urgent overriding problem: Charlotte. She would be breaking up for the holidays next week. Hensford might not have been an exactly happy home when the child had left it, but it was the only one she knew. If there was a divorce Emily realized that, whatever happened, she would be the one who would have to leave, go off into the unknown because, to all intents and purposes, she was living in a tied house. It belonged to the estate. And would a judge grant her custody of her child when he heard she was a scarlet woman? Would necessarily believe her story that her husband had raped her? Hardly. Besides, how could she go into a witness box and actually *say* that. The idea was abhorrent. It was out of the question. It was the sort of case which would get into the papers. Charlotte was quite old enough to read them now. She wondered if Richard was thinking along the same lines.

'I said it won't happen again, Emily.' He made a move towards her, as if to sit on the bed and then, seeing her recoil, went back and sat on the window seat.

'Yes,' she replied at last. 'I heard you the first time.'

'I don't know what came over me. You were looking very seductive, as if . . . well, you wouldn't mind. You've never resisted like that before.'

'Which made you all the keener?' She surprised herself by her unaccustomed acerbity.

'I suppose so.'

'Presumably Faza . . .'

He cut her short. 'Don't,' he said. 'Please don't, Emily.' He seemed to be pleading with her. There was almost a whine in his voice. Would he, she wondered, have reacted like this if he had been in possession of all the facts; known her guilty secret? But had she been so *very* guilty? She felt suddenly angry that it had never seemed to occur to him that another man might desire his wife or that she would desire anyone other than him. She remembered, suddenly, how some barrister whom she had met at a party a short time ago had said, apropos of a much-publicized matrimonial dispute, 'There's bound to be a change in the divorce laws soon. Another ten years and adultery won't be the chief grounds for a divorce. Marital breakdown, incompatibility, living apart, all that kind of thing will be much more important.' 'Oh,' she had replied, 'do you really think so?' And he had answered, 'I don't think. I know. May I get you another drink?'

But, nevertheless, divorce hadn't got that far yet. It was still, primarily, at the 'sleeping with someone else' stage. And she had *slept*, hadn't she? Although, once again, like the term 'making love', it seemed such a euphemism. You did not *sleep* when you made love. It was exactly the reverse. And you certainly did not always 'make love' when, according to law, you 'slept' with a man. Last night was but a case in point.

Wearily, after Richard's last outburst, she said, 'All right. Let's change the subject. Charlotte comes home next Wednesday. I think I'll take her down to Wilhampton earlier than I intended. We might spend a little time there and then go on to the seaside, that's if I can get in anywhere at such short notice. I believe there's a very good hotel at Studland Bay which caters especially for children. I might suggest taking Joanna Swayne, my god-daughter, with us. She'll be company for Charlotte. The two of them get on very well, in spite of the difference in ages.'

He looked obviously relieved at the temporary respite.

She imagined that he thought she was going to announce she was leaving him at once. She was well aware that, for none other than financial reasons, he would not want a divorce. Besides, she had a feeling it might not be all that easy for him to find another wife, one who would enable him to go his way yet present to the world the kind of front on which he set such store. So far, she had fulfilled her role admirably.

'That seems like an excellent idea,' he replied quickly, as he got up and left the room.

They barely spoke again before she and Charlotte went south. On the day the child had to be fetched from Eaton Grange, Emily arranged to go there driven by the young garden boy who had turned out to be an unusually competent driver. The actual journey to Wilhampton was, once again, undertaken by train, partly because of Charlotte's propensity to car-sickness, partly because Emily herself still did not feel up to driving. If, later on in the holiday, she felt she needed a car, it seemed much more sensible to hire one.

The warmth of the welcome which the two of them received on their arrival did much to alleviate the suffering of the past weeks. She lay in bed the first night, listening gratefully to the familiar sounds, safe, comforting. Even the mill-race, which had for her both joyful and tragic associations, seemed, by its very timelessness, to give her a sense of peace. It was eternal. It had been there before she was born and it would be there long after she was dead. One day, she was not sure when or how, she believed she would return to end her days somewhere near to it. Maybe this would not be for quite a while yet, but the feeling that it would eventually come to pass was strong within her.

The following morning she did her best to explain away her pallor and lack of vitality to Katy by telling her that she was probably having an early change of life. She felt her mother was by no means convinced although, with her customary tact, she did not press her on the subject. But both she and Maurice said that they thought her idea of a seaside holiday was excellent and Helen was overwhelmed and overjoyed at the thought of Joanna accompanying them.

'It's awfully good of you, Em,' she said. 'But Col and I will insist on paying Jo's hotel bill.'

'No way. I've only got two godchildren. It's a poor lookout if I can't sometimes do something for your Jo or Liz's Jonathan. Besides, think of the pleasure it's going to give Charlotte. The holiday wouldn't be the same without having Jo for a companion.'

And this, Emily realized as the days passed, was more than true. Her daughter was certainly different after a term at boarding school. She was curiously withdrawn when alone with her. There was a knowingness, a kind of unnatural early maturity about her, a guarded secretive look in the elfin-like little face. Could Charlotte possibly have guessed anything in the short time she had been at Hensford? Hardly, other than being aware of a certain lack of communication between herself and Richard, which was by no means unusual.

Yet, one evening, when Charlotte and Joanna were in bed and she had returned after dinner to fetch a shawl with the thought of taking a short stroll along the cliffs, she overheard them talking. In the suite which she had managed to take after a sudden miraculous cancellation at the Three Rocks Hotel, there were two bedrooms and a bathroom leading off a small hall. She had entered the latter quietly, hoping the children would be asleep, but was brought up short by overhearing her daughter say, 'You see, Eaton Grange is really a special school for misfits. Mostly for children whose parents don't get on.'

'How do you mean?' Jo, her voice low with a marked west-country accent, was obviously anxious to learn more.

'Well, nearly all the mothers and fathers are divorced. Mrs Mather, the headmistress, sort of trades on that. You know, sucks up to them. They say she plays one off against the other. She's a terrible tyrant, really. We're not allowed to stick up the envelopes with our letters home because she has to read each one before it gets posted. I wrote something about having carrot stew for dinner when I first went there and she hauled me up and made me re-write the whole thing. "You must think of your mother," she said. "She wouldn't want to hear such a silly piece of news as that. Besides, all the stews at Eaton Grange have many more things in them than carrots. They are always full of vitamins because they're worked out by a . . . " ' Here, Charlotte stumbled slightly, before coming out with '*nutritionist*'. 'How *terrible*,' Joanna, clearly appalled, said. 'Why don't you get your parents to take you away?'

There was a pause. Emily held her breath. Charlotte's next words made her feel suddenly sick.

'I don't know which is best, Jo. I mean, a holiday like this with you is heaven, but if I had to spend it at home at Hensford, well, I can't explain. There's such a funny . . .'

Charlotte broke off and Joanna, the elder by three years, provided the word she wanted. 'Atmosphere, you mean?'

'Yes. That's right. There's a funny atmosphere. Besides, I haven't had quite so much bronchitis at Eaton Grange although, of course, so far I've only been there in the summer.'

Emily withdrew and closed the door as quietly as she had opened it. The shawl and her evening walk could wait. Back in the lounge, she found her hand shaking as she picked up her coffee cup. A jolly, middle-aged father whom she had seen once or twice on the beach tried to engage her in a little conversation. She did her best to be polite but her daughter's remark kept interfering with her responses: *such a funny atmosphere*.

The four words, accusing, challenging, kept repeating themselves over and over again in her mind throughout the rest of the holiday.

16

The house seemed singularly dark and cheerless. Mrs Draper had locked up and drawn the curtains soon after five, but a bulb had gone out in one of the chandeliers in the hall so that much of the area was now in shadow. As Emily came downstairs, she made a mental note to ask Fred Draper to replace it, but not until the morning. He seemed far from well these days and she often wondered whether something more than advancing age was afflicting him.

A gale was getting up outside and she went into her small study, closed the door and sat down by the fire. She realized it was one of those occasions when she had time to do several jobs which she had put off during the summer. She could even, she supposed, at last start thinking about a little writing. After all, she was quite alone. Charlotte was back at school and Richard was in London because Sybilla had telephoned, agitatedly, saying she wanted to see him in connection with some urgent business before she flew to the Cape. He had left immediately, although he informed Emily that he would probably only be away for a couple of nights. The shooting season was upon them, which always meant he was loath to leave Hensford.

She wished very much that this was not the case. Just at the moment, she would have welcomed his prolonged absence. Since that fatal night in the summer they had maintained a kind of silent truce. Neither had referred to the subject again. She felt as if she were in some kind of limbo, waiting for events to take their course, to point the way and tell her what to do. She knew that this was a hopeless, cowardly attitude. It was no solution. She was merely drifting, letting her mind continue to revolve around the memory of Vernon, their short ecstatic but ill-fated reunion, his death, her secret, Richard's assault and the possibility of divorce. Lastly, and now overruling all other considerations, was the question of Charlotte.

Restlessly, she got up and went across to her desk on which the child's last letter was lying. She picked it up and reread it. There were no kisses at the end and this perturbed her. Having overheard last summer that all letters home were censored by Mrs Mather and having subsequently elicited the same information from her daughter direct, she had said, as casually as she could, before Charlotte returned to Eaton Grange for the winter term, 'I should like to feel you could let me know if you weren't happy at any time.' And when, quite reasonably,

Charlotte had asked how, she had said, 'Well, if you're *really* miserable just leave out the kisses. Then I would know and perhaps be able to do something about it.' Afterwards, she was aware that it was a highly reprehensible thing for any parent to have entered into such a devious conspiracy with a daughter, but it was too late. The damage was done. Now, it was as if Charlotte was saying, 'Over to you'.

Yesterday, as soon as she had received the stilted formal little missive minus any kisses at the end, she had telephoned Eaton Grange and asked to speak to Mrs Mather, excusing such a call by saying that because of the sudden appalling change in the weather she could not help wondering how Charlotte was faring. She had gone on to explain that often, at this time of the year, the child's chest was at its worst.

There had been a distinctly unfriendly pause on the other end of the line and then Mrs Mather's voice, cold, clipped and accusatory, 'Charlotte is quite well, Mrs Vandenburgh. She was a little indisposed at the end of last week. Some slight tummy pains, but at her age that is only to be expected, isn't it? After all, she is eleven now. Many children begin to menstruate well before they reach their teens.'

'I see. Yes, I'm sorry to have troubled you.' To her mortification, Emily found herself apologizing, awkwardly. She thought it unlikely that her daughter was anywhere near starting her periods. If she herself was anything to go by there would have to be another five years before such an event took place. On the other hand, she was aware that girls matured much earlier these days and Charlotte had certainly grown up a lot since she had been away from home.

Mrs Mather's voice had then taken on a more conciliatory tone. 'I quite understand, Mrs Vandenburgh. But please remember that if there is ever anything really wrong, I shall naturally telephone you at once. Goodbye.'

All the same, Emily thought, as she put down the receiver, *something* was wrong. If the same thing happened in the next letter, she would find an excuse for making a personal call at Eaton Grange. It was only twenty miles away. She could, ostensibly, just be passing or maybe she could think of a parcel which she wanted to deliver to her daughter. For goodness' sake, one surely did not spend all that money to send a little thing away to school and then find that one was barred access to her, for all the world as if she were in some prison.

At eight o'clock, Mrs Draper brought along Emily's dinner on a trolley. She had long let it be known that whenever she was by herself she preferred not to use the dining room. She had found it a nerve-racking business to be seated there alone, waited on by one or the other of the Drapers, looked down upon by a whole galaxy of bogus ancestral portraits which Richard had acquired. However well she might have adapted to the role of chatelaine of Hensford, it was not one which came naturally to her, although she was at a loss to know what kind would suit her best.

As she lifted the lid off the dishes and started her meal, an extra loud splattering of hail beat against the windows, forcing the long red velvet curtains to sway slightly inwards. Fancifully, she had often felt that Hensford seemed to attract such storms, to take a certain malevolent pleasure in showing how well it could withstand the elements. She had never before been frightened in such circumstances, even though she had often been, as now, alone; for the Drapers' flat was right at the other end of the house and completely cut off by a small courtyard. Yet tonight she felt on edge. The letter from Charlotte had probably triggered off her uneasiness. She wished Richard had not always been so adamant about refusing to allow any dogs indoors. His new black labrador, Prince, would have been company tonight.

At ten-fifteen she went up to bed. She was in the bath when the telephone rang. She was not expecting to hear from Richard, but it was on the late side to receive a call from anyone else. Quickly enveloping herself in a towel, she hurried to the bedroom to answer it.

'Hullo?'

'Hullo.' She recognized the voice at once. She had

already spoken to it less than forty-eight hours ago. She sat down, still dripping, on the bed. The towel slipped from her shoulders. A mantle of fear replaced it, cold, clammy. She found herself clutching the telephone with both hands as she heard Mrs Mather saying, 'I wonder, Mrs Vandenburgh . . . Is your husband there?'

'My husband?' Her voice had risen. It was unnatural, abrupt. Politeness was nowhere in it. 'No, he's not,' she answered.

'Ah.' Maddeningly, the woman seemed to procrastinate. 'I . . . er . . . don't want to alarm you unduly, Mrs Vandenburgh, but I'm afraid . . .'

'Afraid of what?' Emily found she was almost shouting now, trying to force the woman to come to the point.

'I'm afraid Charlotte has been playing tricks with us.'

'*Tricks?*' She seemed to be screaming inside: oh for God's sake, Mrs Mather, stop playing tricks yourself. She was wildly angry at being spoken to in riddles, almost as if she were a child.

'Yes, well, you see . . .' The voice went on, hesitant, placatory, embarrassed, 'We haven't been able to find her for a while.'

'*Find* her? You mean she's *missing*?'

'Oh, I wouldn't go as far as to say that, Mrs Vandenburgh. She's probably hiding somewhere.'

'Hiding? How could she be? How long has she been missing?' Emily had suddenly taken complete charge of the conversation, her nurse's training in the war standing her in good stead. There had always then been the strange unprecedented emergency. The woman on the other end of the line was at a distinct disadvantage as her interrogator wasted no time, asking questions, eliciting facts. The situation was completely reversed since they had spoken to each other the previous day. It was Mrs Mather who was now the apologetic one.

'We didn't suspect anything was amiss, Mrs Vandenburgh, until Charlotte did not appear at cocoa time.'

'But that's six-thirty, isn't it?'

'Yes, but . . .'

'You mean she's been missing over *four hours*?'

'Well, yes, but we thought . . , we *still* think . . . she must be hiding. Naturally, we are continuing to search . . .'

'The police. Have you informed the police?'

'Er . . . no. Not yet. We felt you and your husband should be consulted first.'

'What is the number of your nearest main police station?'

Mrs Mather had evidently had it to hand because this time she replied at once, 'Stavorley 382.'

'I will ring you back.'

Emily put down the receiver and picked it up immediately. The duty officer to whom she spoke was helpful, took all the particulars and promised that an immediate search would be set in motion. 'Your daughter could well by trying to get home to you, ma'am. We will alert all the relevant bus and railway stations.' He then took her telephone number and that of the school, as well as a full description of Charlotte, and promised to keep her informed. For good measure, Emily then telephoned both Stoke Wallington and their own local police station herself.

It was obvious to her that Charlotte had run away from Eaton Grange, the omission of the kisses proving that she was unhappy, so unhappy, in fact, that she could not wait for her mother to do something about it, as Emily had so rashly promised. What a fool she had been, she thought, firstly to have ever proposed such a strategy and then, when it was put into practice, not to have foreseen that a child of Charlotte's age would expect instantaneous action on a grown-up's part. Children who were desperately unhappy did not know the meaning of waiting, holding on. And she knew that her daughter showed all the signs of turning into an impulsive headstrong character. She was by no means pretty – yet. She was far too thin, her features too pointed, her manner gauche; but there was something about her, she was unusual, fey, there was obstinacy, even wildness, under that veneer of obedience. She had already suffered more than any eleven-year-old had any right to do. She had been the victim of so much illness, had lost her twin brother, followed by an unfortunate relationship with her father and, Emily felt, a not altogether satisfactory one with her mother. Moreover, had she not told her friend, Joanna Swayne, that there was a 'funny atmosphere' at home.

Where was she now? Walking along some isolated country road? Molested by some sex-fiend? Lying dead in some ditch? Knocked down while running to catch some bus or train? And there was no knowing that she would actually be trying to get to Hensford, especially as she did not find it a happy place. But where else would she try to go? Wilhampton? She so obviously loved it there. But she wouldn't have the money. Mrs Mather kept the ten shillings with which each girl started the term. Charlotte would probably have little or no money on her. The thought came to Emily with all its hideous implications.

Countless appalling hazards kept racing through her mind as she picked up the telephone once more. Her husband might not be on hand to turn to for help but there was another man who was. Their farm manager, Bert Chandler. It was another quarter of an hour before the last bus would come rumbling along past the Hensford stop. She would get Bert to meet it, *just in case*. It was a forlorn hope, but not to be ignored. Every avenue must be explored. She wished she could go herself, take some positive action, but she knew that it was imperative for her to remain manning the telephone. She could, she supposed, wake up the Drapers, but however loyal and helpful they were, she realized that if there was news of any sort, it was she who would be needed to cope with it.

Bert Chandler understood at once, both the situation and the urgency of her request. Within what seemed no more than seconds, she heard his Land-Rover roar away up the drive. While she was waiting, she dialled the number of their London flat, but was hardly surprised when there was no reply. She then tried her mother-in-law's hotel, only to be informed that Mrs Sybilla Vandenburgh had left for Heathrow two hours previously. Richard could, she supposed, have driven his mother there, but she thought it unlikely. It was much more likely that he had other fish to fry. That was of no concern to her. She merely experienced a feeling of anger that he was, as so often, unavailable when she most needed help.

Quickly re-dressing, she went down into the darkened hall and drew back one of the curtains, instantly letting it fall in place again. The night seemed so wild, so black and although she did her best to pull herself together, trying to believe that it was simply due to her overwrought imagination, a vision of Charlotte's face, white, pathetic, pleading, had come before her eyes from out of the storm. Presently, she heard the Land-Rover returning, slowly now. She knew the answer even before she managed, this time, to open the front door and peer out.

'She wasn't on the bus, Mrs Vandenburgh,' Bert Chandler said, 'but I've a mind to go back along the road. If Charlotte did, by any chance, get to Wallington somehow and couldn't make the connection to Hensford she might have tried to walk.'

'Walk? From *Stoke Wallington*?' She stood on the steps, oblivious of the rain streaming down upon her, conscious only of what it might be doing to Charlotte. Silently, she watched Bert get back into the cab.

He was gone a long while, during which she spoke again to the school, the police and tried, unsuccessfully, to contact Richard. At one-thirty, she went along to the kitchen and made some tea, careful to keep all the connecting doors open in case the telephone rang. She was standing in the hall drinking it when in the distance her ears, now alert to the slightest sound, heard the Land-Rover returning. She put down her cup and ran to open the front door. The gale seemed to have abated somewhat and a fitful moon lit up the forecourt. She saw the head-lights turn into the driveway. Then she lost them as Bert rounded a few bends. He was going fast, faster than she had ever known him do. No one drove down the Hensford drive, with its sign 'Speed Limit 10 m.p.h.', at this rate unless it was urgent, very urgent . . . She was standing at the bottom of the steps by the time he swung into the forecourt, this time sounding his horn as he drew up with, as she remembered afterwards, a very definite flourish.

Then he was out and round to the passenger door,

passing a bedraggled, exhausted and tearful Charlotte into her arms.

Emily was crying now, the tears pouring down her face just as the rain had done a few hours earlier.

'Thank you,' she said. 'Thank you, Bert.'

He stood there, smiling. 'I didn't see anything on my way to Stoke, but I dunno. Something made me take the back road home. I reckoned the little mite had probably figured out it was that much shorter. I damn near missed her, even then. She was that done in. All of a heap, like. I drove past and then I stopped and went back . . .'

'Thank you, Bert. I'll never be able to thank you enough.'

He smiled again. 'You don't need to do that. I've got two of my own, remember?'

Part Three

17

'You will appreciate that this is a question I am obliged to ask, Mrs Vandenburgh. Have you yourself ever committed adultery?'

'No.' She was surprised at how clearly and firmly she brought out her answer.

'Thank you. You would, of course, have been entitled to ask for discretion of court.'

She merely nodded. Was this little man across the desk trying to give her a second chance? Did he believe her? She noticed he had reached for his pen, presumably with the intention of writing down her denial in black and white. It would soon be on file, her lie. She felt curiously detached from it, as if it had been uttered by someone else. She had imagined that she might have been consumed by guilt. Instead, she only experienced a sensation of infinite weariness, almost a physical ache to have the whole thing over and done with and be divorced from Richard with the least possible fuss.

'And you have no one?' Mr Bellamy went on. 'I mean, you aren't thinking of marrying again yourself?'

'Oh, no. Nothing like that.'

'What about your husband? Is he going to marry the co-respondent?'

She hesitated, slightly. 'I know very little about the co-respondent, Mr Bellamy, other than her name. But I don't imagine my husband is thinking of marrying her because . . .'

'Because what, Mrs Vandenburgh?' He was quick to take her up during pauses. His questions seemed like little poisoned darts coming from all directions, goading her into saying more than she intended.

'Because . . . my husband doesn't want me to leave him. If I were prepared to accept . . . his mistress, then he would be most relieved. He would like me to remain at Hensford.' She did not add: I'm sure Maisie Fripp isn't the type Richard would ever *marry*.

'But you would not find that situation acceptable?'

She stared at him, incredulously. 'Of course not,' she replied. 'How could I?'

He raised his shoulders slightly. 'Some women react differently. Status, security, mean more to them. But if your husband doesn't want to marry Miss Fripp, perhaps he might be persuaded to give her up?'

'It's always possible, I suppose.' She spoke more slowly now. 'Although even if he did,' she continued, 'I would still want a divorce, Mr Bellamy.' Again, she did not add: because sooner or later there would be someone else, or Richard would return to the Fripp woman. There would be more deceit. Until recently, it's seemed more convenient to ignore it. But now, I've had enough.

There was a short silence between them and then Mr Bellamy said, 'You do realize, Mrs Vandenburgh, that if you were prepared to wait a year or so, when the new laws come into effect at the beginning of 1971, a two-year separation would be grounds for a divorce – that is, of course, if both parties agree. If one or the other of them still objects then divorce would simply become automatic after they had lived apart for five years. It occurred to me that if neither you nor your husband are anxious to re-marry, perhaps . . .'

Two years? *Five*, if Richard went on being bloody-minded. Both periods seemed a lifetime. Couldn't Mr Bellamy understand that she wanted *out*? *Now*. Did he not wish to take her case on? What was the matter with him? Surely he wasn't going to obtain much custom for his firm if he behaved in such a putting-off fashion with every prospective client.

Almost as if reading her thoughts, he suddenly said on a kinder note, 'Forgive me, Mrs Vandenburgh, but I did not think you looked at all well when you came in. Divorce is never easy, at the best of times, especially for a woman with no other emotional attachment, as it were. I just felt you should be aware of all the alternatives before we proceed with your petition.'

'Thank you,' she replied. 'But I have made up my mind.'

'You have friends and family, I take it, other than the daughter you mentioned?'

Should she go into details? Explain how cancer had carried her mother away in '63; that Maurice, in retirement, had thereafter appeared to lack the will to live and had followed her to the grave six months later; that Aunt Chip, now cared for by Betsy, was frail and nearing eighty; that her favourite cousin, Frank François, was thousands of miles away in charge of his firm's publishing house in New York. There only seemed Helen, dear Helen, to whom she could turn.

'Sadly,' she answered, at length, 'my family has rather dwindled during the last few years. The person I'm closest to is a lifelong girlfriend.'

'I'm glad,' he said, picking up his pen again. 'It is always helpful for a woman to have one good friend at a time like this.'

Would she, she wondered, as she watched him writing, have answered any differently if he had explained all about the new laws before she had perjured herself? Might she have been prepared to wait, even five years, with Richard maybe putting pressure on her meanwhile? It had seemed so straightforward when she had first walked into Mr Bellamy's office. She had felt that she had known just what she was about. There would be no need to tell him all that much, go into details, delve back into the past. The passing of time had put a different complexion on things. Charlotte was out in the world leading her own life – a highly unsatisfactory one, she had to admit; but the problem of custody no longer entered into things, even if Emily still believed, as she had done nine years previously, that she would be unable to lie about her one isolated act of adultery. But her qualms on that subject were, she hoped, over. If, today, she had technically done wrong, surely it would have been a greater wrong to have told the truth. She had kept her promise to Vernon. She would not be bringing distress and disillusionment to Liz after all these years nor, so far as she could help it, to Aunt Chip — although the latter would be bound to dislike the idea of divorce even if, privately, she had never cared very much for Richard.

Emily was well aware that she had become harder nowadays, that her once easily aroused conscience had grown a thicker shell, especially when she paused to compare what seemed to her to be one pardonable sin with the enormity and frequency of her husband's. Besides, she had reasoned, she would really be letting him off quite lightly. She had no intention of suing him for anything other than common or garden adultery. She was simply petitioning for a divorce on account of his liaison with a woman whom he had, apparently, for some time been keeping in Maida Vale.

Once again, as if reading her thoughts, she suddenly heard Mr Bellamy say, 'The co-respondent, Mrs Vandenburgh, how did you find out about her?' He had finished writing for the time being and was evidently anxious to proceed with his interrogation.

'Because of a cheque book.'

'A cheque book?'

'Yes. I found it in our London flat. I happened to come across it at the back of a drawer.'

'And what about it?'

'The stubs were all blank, except for some funny little hieroglyphics in one corner. I thought it strange. I took it back with me to the country.'

'And then?'

'I asked my husband about it.'

'And what did he say?'

'Well, at first he tried to bluff his way out of it. He said he thought he'd lost it, that it was an extra one he kept for emergencies in town. When I asked why he hadn't filled in the payees' names, he broke down and admitted the payments were to his mistress.'

'Had you any idea of her existence before?'

She did not answer at once. When she did, she said, 'My husband is often away. I've always thought . . . but I have never had proof.'

'You mean the marriage has been unsatisfactory for a long time?'

She merely inclined her head.

'Did you not think about obtaining a divorce earlier on?'

Again, she hesitated. 'Yes . . . often. But my daughter was young . . . It seemed difficult.' She could not add: those were the days when I worried about the question of my own guilt, whether I might lose Charlotte, whether some judge might take Richard's side, would never believe me if I had said my husband had no time for his daughter.

'But now you have changed your mind?'

'Yes.'

She waited a moment or two while he wrote something down. Then he looked up. He seemed a prematurely aged man, balding, with piercing blue eyes which, when raised above his half-moon spectacles, seemed to bore into her. All at once she felt unmasked, as if he knew there was more to her story than she had divulged. Yet, with his next remark, he was off on another tack.

'Why did you not leave at once, Mrs Vandenburgh, when your husband admitted his adultery and you decided to petition for a divorce? Why did you remain at Hensford for . . . let me see . . . you mentioned a week?'

'Because a godchild of mine, the daughter of the friend I mentioned, was coming to stay with her husband. I couldn't very well put them off at short notice.'

'Was it not difficult . . . going ahead with their visit under the circumstances, having just had what must have been quite a show-down with your husband?'

'Yes. Very difficult.'

'But you managed to keep everything to yourself?'

'Well, naturally. Joanna might have thought me rather quiet, I suppose. But my husband went off to our London flat in order, so he said, to give me time to think again.'

'So you were not actually under the same roof after his confession?'

'No.'

'But now *you* are occupying the flat, that is, the smaller part of the marital home?'

She stared at him. 'I don't quite follow . . .'

'Look. Mrs Vandenburgh.' He spoke slowly and quietly now. There was a weary expression on his face as if he had gone through all this before, as though he was having to explain something for the umpteenth time to a backward pupil. 'In divorce cases, one has to establish certain facts, one of the most important being who leaves who. And it could be argued that by remaining with your husband for a week you were actually condoning his adultery. It is also an irrefutable fact that although you may have left him, you are still living, as I said, in part of the marital home. All these things affect a divorce, especially from the financial point of view.'

'Financial?' She stared at him again.

'Well, that's what divorce is all about, isn't it?'

'Is it?'

This time he whipped off his bifocals, placed both elbows on the desk and rested his chin on his cupped hands. She did not think she liked him at all. He was not an easy man, not a comfortable solicitor like the old-fashioned one in Westonbury with whom she knew that her mother and aunt had occasionally had dealings. But then, she supposed that if one consulted such a well-known London firm of divorce specialists – whose name she had once happened to overhear being recommended at a smart cocktail party – one should not, perhaps, expect tea and sympathy thrown in. Nevertheless, she felt that she and Mr Bellamy had somehow got off to a bad start. Possibly getting a divorce from Richard was not going to be as easy or clear-cut as she had imagined. Mr Bellamy's next question made her all the more uncertain.

'About alimony . . . your settlement . . . How much do you think you would need to live on?'

She frowned. 'I hadn't really thought.'

'No?' He was obviously surprised.

'No. I mean, well, I imagine my husband will provide something, but I have money of my own.'

'Ah!' He looked at her more keenly. 'How much?'

'I came into around thirty thousand pounds after the death of both my mother and stepfather.'

'I see.'

'And I also inherited ten thousand pounds when I was twenty-one. Back in 1942. It was from my late father's stepmother.'

'Quite a considerable sum in those days.'

'Yes, but . . .'

'But what, Mrs Vandenburgh?'

'Well, in the early part of our marriage, I lent . . . gave . . . round about half my capital to my husband to help with the farm.'

'*Lent* or *gave*, Mrs Vandenburgh? Which? This is important.'

'I don't really know.' She had begun to feel utterly miserable, as well as very tired. 'There was no legal agreement, if that's what you mean. It didn't seem necessary.'

For answer, Mr Bellamy momentarily covered his face with his hands in a gesture of despair.

'How wealthy is your husband, Mrs Vandenburgh? You must have some idea. You have this place in the country. A thousand acres, I think you said. A London flat. He must be fairly rich. When the new laws come into effect you would be entitled to something like half, bearing in mind your own assets.'

'Would I? But his capital is so tied up. In Cheshire. In Kensington . . .' She did not add: in Maida Vale, although she thought Mr Bellamy was possibly thinking that. 'And, of course, he no longer has the expectations he once had,' she added.

'How do you mean? What? Where from?'

'From his mother. Before she died, back in 1961, she had remarried. Suddenly and rather disastrously, as it turned out. By doing so, under the terms of my late father-in-law's will, neither she nor my husband had any further claim on his estate.'

'I see.'

She looked away but she felt that his eyes were on her, studying her, probably thinking she was a complete fool. Outside the window, the dome of St Paul's rose stark and black against a wintry skyline. It was uncomfortably hot in Mr Bellamy's office with its double-glazing, thick carpet and air of luxurious, artful concealment.

'Have you,' she heard him saying, as if from a long way off, 'brought your marriage certificate with you?'

'No,' she answered. She felt completely exhausted, as though she was being taken on some difficult journey with a not particularly sympathetic guide. Did Mr Bellamy really think that when she was packing her things at Hensford, trying to decide what to take and what would have to be collected at some later date, whether to drive or go by train – she had never, at the best of times, felt happy negotiating London traffic – how to cope with Mrs Draper's tears when she told her of her departure, that she would have had enough foresight to get her marriage certificate out of the safe?

'Never mind,' he said, and his voice sounded gentler now, even if it still seemed strangely distant and disembodied, 'we can get a copy from Somerset House. But I must warn you, after all you have just told me, there could be complications. Whatever you do, please remain in the London flat.'

18

'How nice to see you, my dear.'

'Nice to see you, Aunt Chip. But whatever have you been up to? Falling over like that. You'll have to get Betsy to see you take more water with it.'

Be bright, Emily kept saying to herself. Talk about anything, however banal. Lie through your teeth. You're becoming good at it these days. She looks worse than you thought, doesn't she? She's obviously had a bad shaking up. Don't breathe a word about divorce. Not today.

The face from the bed smiled. It was very pale but still beautiful, the skin soft and delicate, the wrinkles carefully powdered, the white hair which framed it immaculately coiffured. Emily could never remember a time when Aunt Chip – or her mother, for that matter – had not been perfectly groomed. There had always been an unmistakable elegance, a dress sense, a flair for possessing the right clothes for any and every occasion. What was it Maurice had once said? 'I do believe, Emily, that if your mother and aunt were suddenly asked to breakfast with the Queen, they would have the ideal outfits waiting in their wardrobes.' And she had smiled, knowing only too well that, as she was growing up, there was never any last-minute scurrying round to buy something. She felt sure that the pink satin lace-trimmed nightdress and crocheted bed jacket to match, which May was now wearing, must have been hiding in some bottom drawer, having been specially made at an earlier date for use in an emergency such as today's.

'You shouldn't have come all this way just to see me,' May was now saying. 'I've only sprained an ankle and acquired a few bruises. It isn't as if I've broken anything. And as for bringing such gorgeous flowers and fruit, I don't deserve such spoiling.'

'Of course you do, Aunt Chip. And anyway, I was already in London when I got Betsy's message. What could be easier than coming on down to Wilhampton, especially as I happened to have the car.' There you are, she said to herself again. You made it sound as if you were simply up in town on a fleeting visit, not an enforced sojourn in 'the smaller part of the marital home', as Mr Bellamy calls it. When Betsy rang Hensford, thank God Mrs Draper was discreet enough not to tell her anything other than my whereabouts. It would be as well not to let either May or Betsy know the present situation at the moment. After all, Betsy must be over seventy and she's obviously had a bit of a shock herself.

'And how is Charlotte, my dear?' May asked, firmly switching the conversation away from her own health.

Again, Emily remained guarded, realizing, sadly, that there was need for even further dissembling. She could not say: living in some commune in Wales. Doing a kind of back-to-the-land act with a whole lot of hippies.

'She's well, Aunt Chip,' she answered. At least, I hope she is, an inner voice said. I haven't heard for several weeks now. 'She's decided to give up cooking those directors' lunches,' Emily went on, 'but I don't think she's quite decided what to do next.'

'Marry, perhaps? She was so pretty the last time I saw her. Whatever happens, that domestic science training she took after leaving school should always stand her in good stead.'

'Yes. Yes, I'm sure it will.'

Dear Aunt Chip. In many ways so naïve and romantic and yet, underneath, often remarkably wise. Emily knew that May wasn't going to press for further news of her great-niece. She also knew that although her aunt had referred to a domestic science training, she probably had a shrewd idea that Amberley House was more of a finishing school than anything else. May had always kept up with the times, even if, privately, she considered that all the domestic arts were – or should be – something which a child learnt naturally at home. In her young days they were absorbed, never *taught*. Emily had a sudden vivid recollection of leaning against her aunt's chair at about the age of seven or eight watching, fascinated, as May worked a buttonhole on the Dowager Lady Fairfax's dress; of standing at the kitchen table while May broke an egg into a bowl of flour and then being allowed to stir the mixture, as her aunt gradually added milk in order to make a Yorkshire pudding for Sunday lunch – or dinner, as Grandmother Lodge always called it. Then there were those precious never-to-be-forgotten occasions: Eastertide, when she and Helen Swayne were sent primrosing in Breconbury Woods, returning with overflowing baskets to help decorate the font in St Mark's church; or, when autumn came, they would beg a sheaf of corn from Helen's father for harvest festival and transport it, together with marrows and Michaelmas daisies, all along East Street in a hand-cart. Later still, in December, they would go off to the Barbury Turnpike, collecting hips and haws and old man's beard to make the church look colourful for Christmas. Nowadays, children were never sent alone to the woods or the downs. It was a pleasure her own child had missed. There was too much danger, too many muggings, rapes even. Dear God, how life had changed. It had all been so much simpler, once upon a time. She could recall, as if it were yesterday, the faint, musty but not unpleasant smell of St Mark's, the jam jars of water carefully camouflaged by moss, the dust sheets spread out on the stone floor to collect debris as they worked, the way May never said, 'You must do this,' or 'You don't do that'. The knowledge handed down through the generations had been much more subtly imparted.

Presently, Betsy came into the room with a vase in which to arrange the flowers Emily had brought and the conversation, understandably, turned to Paul and how successful he was in the publishing world, thanks to Frank's initial introduction and advice. Although he was not a member of Frank's firm, he was now a senior editor in another equally well-established one.

'And he's married such a nice girl,' Betsy volunteered, proudly. 'They seem made for each other. They've just bought a lovely house near Guildford where it's easy for him to get up to London each day.'

'I'm so glad,' Emily said. Yet she had an uncomfortable sensation that her mind was operating on two levels, the nicer one saying: 'Yes, of course I'm glad. I only wish Charlotte could follow suit. That's what ought to happen to all young people.' But a smaller darker voice kept interrupting: 'It's just that I can't see my daughter ever marrying, not now, not with the life she's leading and the way she's let herself go so much. Besides, she's got a mother who's petitioning for divorce. Charlotte's cynical enough as it is. She'll think me a failure. I suppose I am, except I don't feel so much a failure right now as horribly overwhelmingly *tired*.'

The latter fact was remarked upon as Emily took her leave after lunch.

'You haven't been overdoing things, have you, my dear?' May asked. 'You look as if a holiday would do you good. You couldn't stay down here for a while, could you?'

She flushed. 'No, I've got to get back, I'm afraid, Aunt Chip. But I'll hope to come down and see you both again very soon.'

'That would be nice. But only if you've got to be in London, mind.'

Only if I've got to be in London. If May did but know I've got to be in London all the time now. I've another appointment with Mr Bellamy tomorrow. He's going to have some draft petition ready for me to approve before it goes off to what he calls 'the other side'. It's almost as if he might be a medium or, at any rate, some general waging battle. I suppose he is, in a way. He will keep telephoning me about maintenance. How can I possibly tell what I need? He says Richard must be made to pay for all the outgoings of the flat *pro tem*, as well as provide some 'spending money' for me. I suppose he's right. I'll have to trust him. But it's so difficult to know what to say. I wonder how long it's all going to take and whether Aunt Chip will be well enough to be told next time I come.

'Betsy,' she said, as she finally took her leave at the front door, 'please keep in touch. If there's anything, *anything* that either you or May need, you must let me know. Try the London number first. For various reasons, I might have to be there quite a bit during the next few months.'

As she drove off to see Helen at Ladywell Farm, Betsy's answer kept echoing in her mind: 'Of course, my dear. But we're really very lucky. There's nothing we need, except for May to get well again and, perhaps, to see you whenever you can spare the time. Your visit has done us both such a lot of good.'

What a pity, Emily thought, as the car gathered speed, that she hadn't done more good in her life. After all, it was such a small thing which Betsy had just asked of her. She wished she had spent more time at Wilhampton in recent years instead of being so wrapped up in her own problems. True, she had come down to help nurse her mother during those last agonizing weeks. But it hadn't been enough. The trouble was that she had never realized it until it was too late. And she could have been more of a comfort to Maurice afterwards, when he refused to come to Hensford. She should have travelled south and spent more time with this gentle elderly man who had done so much for her over the years. She had no excuse, other than her own unhappiness, her concern over Charlotte – no longer just from a medical point of view, for her bronchial troubles had improved, but because of the child's increasing waywardness – and then the constant strain of maintaining a 'front' to a crumbling marriage. How aware of the situation, she wondered, had Katy and Maurice been? Was that why they had always been so reluctant to visit her home and why Maurice, after his wife's death, had been so adamant about remaining at the small cottage in which they had both hoped to have spent a long and happy retirement? How distressed would they have been about the divorce? Possibly not as much as she imagined. Maybe they would have welcomed it as, to her great relief, Helen appeared to do when she told her the news soon after arriving at Ladywell.

'It was never really right, was it, Em? I often thought that you never really got over Vernon.'

'Was it so obvious?'

'Towards the end. Even though I never saw much of you. Jo said that she'd never seen anyone look so wretched as you did on their last visit. I almost wrote to you, but I thought you might have resented interference. What do you think you'll do now? Come back here to live? I do hope so.'

'Eventually, I expect. But for the moment my solicitor says I've got to stay put. Till everything's settled. I didn't realize that getting divorced is so full of pitfalls and complications. I'm beginning to think it's like a maze, impossible to find the way out.'

'Poor Em. Look, whatever happens you'll come for Christmas, won't you? And Charlotte. And May and Betsy. I was going to ask them, anyway.'

'It's terribly kind of you, Helen. Yes, I'd love to. Mr Bellamy can't expect me to stay in the metropolis *then*. And I'll find out about Charlotte and let you know.'

'Good. We'll be quite a party. Jo and her husband will be here and our three other kids, of course. And Tim and his family and Mummy will all be coming over to lunch.'

'How is your mother? I should have asked before.'

'She's wonderful really, considering. Madly independent

as you might imagine. After Daddy died and Tim took on the tenancy of Bulbarrow, he and his wife begged her to stay on and live with them, but she refused. She's settled down in the carter's old cottage and made it so attractive. I think she probably took the right decision. One or another of us sees her every day. And she dotes on her grandchildren, of course, especially the new arrival at Bulbarrow. She's always adored babies.'

'Like you, Helen.'

'Did I? I suppose so. I must say I'm longing to have a grandchild of my own.'

'It doesn't seem possible.'

'You wait. It'll be your turn next.'

Emily looked away. Would it? It was so difficult to imagine Charlotte married, Charlotte with a baby. A picture of her daughter as she had last seen her came unhappily to mind: pouting, lank-haired, unkempt. Could it be just a phase which she would grow out of? It would be nice to think so, yet Emily feared otherwise. It seemed as if she'd failed as a mother as well as a wife. She had gone horribly wrong somewhere. So far she had said little to Helen about Charlotte's latest exploits. Perhaps she should now do so. After all, Helen was the child's godmother, just as she was Joanna's. What a lot of water had flowed under the bridge since the day of the twins' christening back in 1949. Twenty years, in fact. Was it altogether too fanciful to think that the ageing absent-minded rector's unfortunate mistake was now having repercussions?

Emily could see them all standing round the font: Richard and Sybilla in her ghastly hat, Katy and Maurice and May, Helen and Colin, Frank François and Elaine, the Rentons and the Bartholomews. She had never forgotten how, with Helen all ready to hand Charlotte over to the Reverend Donald Egerton, he had intoned: 'Grant that all carnal affections may live and grow in her, and that all things belonging to the Spirit may die in her.'

The depression deepened with the arrival of Charlotte's letter, made somehow worse by its incomprehensible Welsh *poste restante* address. 'I'm glad you and Daddy have got around to getting divorced,' it ran:

> I've thought for ages that's what ought to happen. Of course, I expect you realize that I'm against matrimony on principle. I suppose it works for some people but it seems to me a ridiculous state of affairs, dreamt up by ancient ecclesiastics.
>
> Which brings me to the other point in your letter. Christmas. Please thank Helen for her invitation (Charlotte had dispensed with 'aunt' years ago), but I simply don't believe in it, any more than I do marriage. It's a pagan festival, again kept going by those who simply have to have something to cling on to, no matter what. In any case, none of us here could get away then. We all have our duties. We've a cow, three goats, as well as quite a few hens and we've pledged ourselves to renovating a derelict shed which none of the locals appear to claim or want.
>
> I wonder if you could send those thick furry boots of mine if you're going to Hensford to collect the rest of your belongings? Or perhaps Mrs Draper could post them on. They say we're in for a hard winter . . .

She sat looking out over the London rooftops. There was a small square patio outside the sliding French windows in the sitting room. At least, she supposed it could be called a patio, but at present it was just a kind of dirty prison-like yard. It was a very dark day and she thought, as she had so often done, that if one had to live here permanently, the area could be turned into a garden, brightened up by tubs and flowers and a lick of white paint. But she wasn't going to be here all that long – she hoped. This was just a temporary abode while Mr Bellamy went to work on her case. It was not worth doing anything to it because she was a bird of passage, caught for a while in a small claustrophobic flat, marking time until she got her divorce. The only thing saving her from utter despair over her incarceration was the fact that the place held the bitter-sweet memory of Vernon – that, and her frequent evening telephone conversations with Helen.

It came to her that she ought to do something positive while she was waiting, but she couldn't think what. The idea of writing, forever at the back of her mind, somehow appeared to be more impossible, even though she had time and enough to spare. Because whereas at Hensford there had always seemed perfectly valid reasons for keeping busy in other ways, now a feeling of total inertia held her back. Besides, she had not brought her little typewriter – nor, for that matter, a hundred and one other things which, in her desire to get away, she had left behind. She supposed she would have to write to Mrs Draper and send her some money to post on Charlotte's boots as well as some personal items of her own. Somehow, she did not see herself going back to Hensford to fetch anything this side of Christmas.

She began wondering about Charlotte's other companions in Wales. She remembered her daughter having once spoken of some boy called Benedict. It seemed a singularly unsuitable name for any male living in such surroundings. It made her think of monks and she was sure that there was neither celibacy nor virginity amongst the weird little group. Charlotte must be sleeping with someone, probably Benedict. Apparently, although there were two caravans, some people were still under canvas. Now that the nights had drawn in, what did they do, other than fornicate? Or – and here her mind tried to shy away from the idea, but failed – smoke pot.

She recalled the years she had spent bringing up Charlotte and nursing her through the countless anxious nights, how she had often not expected the child to survive until morning. Yet now, here she was, sleeping rough like a gipsy and asking, in a matter-of-fact way, to be sent her furry boots, with no more interest in or concern over her parents' divorce than if one or the other of them had decided to undergo some minor operation which ought to have taken place years ago.

She supposed she should go out and buy Charlotte a

present for Christmas but she was unsure what to get. A blanket, perhaps? Or would that be frowned upon, contravening the insistence on self-sufficiency. On the other hand, the girl had not repudiated her expensive furry boots. Whatever happened if she got ill in such a godforsaken spot? Would someone fetch a doctor? Would a doctor *come* to that kind of camp? She felt certain none of its inhabitants would have bothered to register with one. They were outlaws, outcasts, misfits in society. Where had it all started in Charlotte's case? The night she ran away from Eaton Grange? She had at least run *home* then. But would she do so now – or, rather, come to the flat – if things went wrong? It would be nice to think so. But whatever happened, Emily knew that she had lost her daughter, even if not with the same finality as she had lost her son. She wanted to weep, but no tears came.

Idly, her mind turned to Richard and what he would be doing at Christmas. Spending it with Maisie Fripp? Now that he could no longer use the flat when he came to London, did he stay with her in Maida Vale? Somehow Emily sensed that the co-respondent's abode was not particularly luxurious. Richard could hardly take her to Hensford. Maybe they would go to a hotel – or possibly abroad somewhere. But if he left the country for any length of time, it would surely hold up the divorce. Already, Mr Bellamy seemed annoyed at what he called the 'tardiness of the other side'. She was having her third interview with him later that day and not looking forward to it. She was unused to being questioned in such a pertinent manner. There seemed something extremely distasteful about revealing details of her private life to a stranger.

She found him looking more serious than ever when she entered his office promptly at 3 p.m. After rising to shake hands and motioning her to a chair, he picked up a sheaf of papers and, with no further preamble, went straight into the inquisition.

'Has your husband always been a very difficult man, Mrs Vandenburgh? Particularly over money?'

She hesitated. 'I suppose I could say yes to both those questions. Although, he's always been more than happy to spend money on . . . things which appealed to him. It was just that our tastes were very different.'

'So it would seem.'

'How do you mean?'

'Well, although he cannot do other than admit to adultery – having already admitted it to you – he is contesting the proposals we put forward for a settlement. He is alleging that you yourself were primarily responsible for the break-up of the marriage.'

She felt the colour flooding into her cheeks. Her hand went up to her throat. Vernon? Had Richard brought up Vernon? She wondered if Mr Bellamy noticed her acute discomfiture.

'What . . . ?' She managed to ask.

'It would appear to do with your . . . er . . . mental stability.'

'My *mental stability*?'

'Yes. Did you have a breakdown at some time?'

'Yes. But long before I met my husband. In the war.'

Mr Bellamy nodded. 'He has referred to this. I am sorry, Mrs Vandenburgh, but I must explain that your husband has described you as . . .' he glanced at his papers and then went on, 'extremely nervous, uncooperative and obsessed by your daughter's health. He also maintains that you do not like entertaining, that he would have liked to lead a far more social life but you have always vetoed it.'

She frowned. 'But that's ridiculous, Mr Bellamy. Especially as he appeared not to want me to leave him. I've always done what I could. Given shooting lunches and returned hospitality. It's true that, when my daughter was younger, this sometimes had to be limited because she was ill a great deal and I had to nurse her.'

'This would seem something which your husband greatly disapproved of. He says . . .' here, Mr Bellamy flipped over a page and went on, 'he was only too willing to provide you with adequate help, but you refused this in the same way as you apparently refused to go away with him, so that he was forced to go alone. Is that true, Mrs Vandenburgh?'

This time she looked away, miserably. 'Up to a point, I

suppose. But my daughter needed . . . at least, I thought she needed, my personal attention, much more than my husband realized.'

For the first time since she had known him, Emily thought Mr Bellamy looked slightly doubtful. 'We shall have,' he said, 'to come back on these allegations. You'll have to swear an affidavit. You see, your husband is also maintaining that as you rarely came to London with him and seemed to dislike the flat in Kensington, he requires it for his own use. He is prepared to buy you a small place somewhere in the country and pay you fifteen hundred a year alimony. That is not good enough, Mrs Vandenburgh. The flat must be worth something in the region of seventy thousand, from what you have told me about it. Your husband is hoping to get away with half that. You do see, now, how important it is for you to remain there, possession being nine tenths of the law.'

She stared at him, mutely. 'But I don't want to live in London, Mr Bellamy. A small place in the country would suit me fine.'

'On fifteen hundred a year, less tax?'

'And what I get in dividends.'

'Not all that — although naturally we shall insist on the return of the capital you lent your husband. Meanwhile, I'm afraid you must stick it out in town and he must be made to pay all your outgoings, rates, service charges, rent, telephone etc., until such time as a satisfactory settlement is reached.'

'But sometimes . . . I don't think I *can*. Unless . . .'

'Unless what?'

'Unless I get out, get a job, maybe.'

'What sort of a job?'

'Anything. I don't know. There's a flower shop at the corner of my street. Perhaps I could help with the Christmas rush.'

'*Mrs Vandenburgh.* Please be reasonable. By all means do some voluntary work if you wish. But for heaven's sake, don't do anything that's *paid*. That would upset the entire applecart. Affect the settlement. You've been, if I may say so, the chatelaine of a large country house. You

715

tell me you are forty-eight and you have never earned your own living, except in the war when you were a nurse. It would be most inadvisable to work for remuneration now, as well, I should have thought, as rather demeaning. Don't you agree?'

'No,' she found herself saying, with unaccustomed assertiveness. 'No, I don't agree. I should welcome a little independence.'

'Independence is one thing,' replied Mr Bellamy. 'Fool-hardiness is another. Shall we make a start on your affidavit?'

20

She knew what was the matter. She'd gone out too soon after the attack of 'flu which had laid her low a week or so previously. She hadn't felt at all well ever since and suspected it must have been the Asian kind which was sweeping the country. This morning, when she awoke, her head hurt so badly and her throat was so sore again that it was all she could do to stagger along to the bathroom.

It was two days before Christmas.

'Oh, *Em!*' Helen's voice on the other end of the tele-phone was not only full of disappointment but genuine alarm. 'You can't be ill all alone over the holiday. Who's your doctor?'

'I haven't got one,' she croaked. 'I never thought I'd be here long enough to bother.' So much for presuming Charlotte's irresponsibility in this connection, she thought. She herself had been just as lacking in foresight.

'Em, you must get hold of a good GP. *Now.* Surely one of the other residents in the building would tell you of one.'

'There's not much a doctor can do, Helen. I mean, I shall simply have to stay here and dose myself with Disprin until I'm better.'

'But you've just done that. And look where it's got you. And it's *Christmas*, Em. Please be reasonable. Promise me you'll at least get hold of the *name* of a doctor. And what about sustenance? I bet you haven't anything in the fridge, thinking you were going away.'

'I don't *want* any sustenance. And anyway, there's a very nice shop near here which actually delivers. I've never troubled to open an account, but I'm sure they'll oblige.'

'I'll ring back tonight to see what you've arranged. Em, I can't bear to think of you being holed up there by yourself just now. Especially with the divorce going on. Who do you know in town?'

'Hardly anyone, really. It was Richard who led the social life up here. But I'll be all right. Besides, I don't want anyone coming near me. I certainly wouldn't want to give whatever I've got to my worst enemy.'

They rang off. Momentarily, Emily lay back on the pillows, too exhausted to embark on another telephone call. In any case, she had a feeling that most of the other tenants in the block had already departed. For several days she had been vaguely aware of cars outside in the street being piled with luggage, of children shouting, of the exotic-looking model on the fourth floor, smelling of *Je Reviens* and surrounded by expensive luggage, standing on the landing as she waited for the lift. Emily had been glad to think that she, too, would soon be going away, not left high and dry in a top floor flat with only the saturnine Portuguese caretaker and his wife in the basement. But now, presumably, that was exactly what was going to happen. There was just a chance, she supposed, that Mrs Braithwaite, the elderly sad-eyed widow on the ground floor, had not yet left. Emily seemed to remember that one evening, when they had come through the main front door together, she had mentioned something about going to her sister's on Christmas Eve. Mrs Braithwaite would be sure to know of a doctor. She invariably looked as if she was at her last gasp.

The poor woman certainly sounded both breathless and agitated, when Emily eventually summoned up strength to ring her.

'Oh, my *dear*, I *am* so sorry. A *second* bout of 'flu, you think? Asian, I feel sure. Half London is down with it.' Mrs Braithwaite's voice had gone faint, as if she had pushed the telephone away from her mouth for fear of the disease spreading down the line. 'Yes, yes I do have an excellent GP. Dr Pratt. He's private, of course. They all are in the West End. I think he may be away himself but he has partners. Young ones. I always try to see Dr Pratt if I can. I'll give you his number. I'm afraid I'm just leaving. Otherwise . . . I'm sorry I can't be of more help. Do mention my name . . . You poor thing . . . I can't even wish you a happy Christmas under the circumstances, can I . . .'

Later in the day, Emily discovered that Mrs Braithwaite had been slightly distorting the truth about 'just leaving'. In the middle of the afternoon the driver who had evidently been booked to take her to the station pressed the wrong bell on the intercom, forcing Emily to heave herself out of bed to answer it. But by now she was feeling too ill to register anything other than vague resentment that she had bothered to see who it was. It was perfectly understandable for her ground floor neighbour not to want to become more involved. Women living completely by themselves needed to take special care, as she was just beginning to find out.

Since coming to live by herself at the flat, it had begun to dawn on her that there was a lot more to being alone or lonely than she had bargained for. It was true that, mentally, she had experienced much of the latter during her marriage. But, physically, she had never been totally devoid of company, even if that company had simply been the intermittent presence of Charlotte or Richard, the proximity of the Drapers, Bert Chandler, the dogs, or a neighbour or two. Now it was different. She was cut off. She had had to get used to a loss of identity, of returning from any sojourn to a place where no one knew where she had gone, when she would be coming back – and cared less. But for Helen's solicitude and possibly the caretaker's curiosity, she had a nasty feeling that she could be dead for quite a time without her body being discovered.

It was not until the middle of Christmas night that she began to have real difficulty in breathing and the pain in her chest became acute. Earlier that evening she had managed to have a word on the telephone with everyone

t Ladywell, had even joked with May in order to allay
er fears and informed them all that she had contacted a
octor in case it was necessary to ask him to call. She had
hen refilled her hot-water bottle, poured out a stiff brandy
nd soda and forced herself to drink it while attempting
o watch television in the sitting-room. Afterwards, she
vas violently sick. Once more back in bed, she began to
hiver uncontrollably. Several times she stretched out a
and to ring one of Dr Pratt's partners and stopped herself.
She hated to feel she was making a fuss, possibly dragging
ome young family man out on this particular night.
Besides, by this time the front door of the building would
be bolted and she would also have to wake the caretaker
o let him in. Surely she could hang on till morning.
Presently, she seemed to float, in and out of consciousness,
unable to move, the pain coming and going as the hours
wore on.

It was 11 a.m. when she heard voices, female ones,
outside the door of the flat. Daylight was showing through
the curtains. Was she dreaming? Delirious? Why was
someone trying to get in? Using keys? She turned over and
cried out in agony. Suddenly, she was looking up into
the troubled faces of Helen and the caretaker's wife, Mrs
Santos.

She was not very clear as to what happened after that,
except that a doctor was sounding her chest and then
giving her an injection. She heard him saying,
'Hospital . . .', and then Helen's quiet reassuring words,
'But I shall be staying . . .' She thought she heard her
own voice whispering, 'You can't . . .' and then Helen's
rejoinder, 'Of course I can. I've left Joanna in charge at
Ladywell.'

Four days later, when she was sitting up in bed, with
Helen perched on the end of it, Emily said, 'Whatever
made you *come*?'

'Well, I rang on Boxing morning and got no reply. I
think you must have knocked the receiver off the hook.
You mentioned that you kept hesitating about ringing the
doctor. Like an idiot, I found I hadn't got your caretaker's
name or number. I just felt things were bad. So I got in

the car and did the journey in splendid time. Nothing on the roads. Not much traffic in London, either. Easy a wink.'

'I'll never be able to thank you enough, Helen. But look you must go now. They'll be needing you at home and you could still catch this wretched bug from me.'

'Rubbish. Jo's arranged to stay on longer. And you know I've got a built-in resistance. I'm going to talk to that nice young doctor when he comes today and ask him when he thinks you might be well enough to come back with me.'

'But, Helen . . .'

'Don't argue. The worst is over. I'm quite enjoying things now. Do you realize I haven't had a holiday by myself in years. The sales are on. I'm going to Oxford Street tomorrow and God knows what I'll come back with. A fur coat, I shouldn't wonder.'

Emily laughed – then winced. The pain had not quite gone and she was still horribly weak, but Helen's cheerful presence seemed to make everything better.

London was getting back to normal again by the time they set off for the west country early in the New Year. Sensing that her friend wanted to concentrate on the traffic, Emily said nothing until Helen herself broke the silence after they reached the motorway.

'When you were so ill, Em,' she said, 'I wondered whether to get hold of Charlotte somehow. How do you actually contact her?'

'Letters. *Poste restante*, I suppose a telegram . . . But I'm glad you didn't. I mean, I don't think she . . . well, she's very different from Joanna.'

There was a slight pause and then Helen replied, 'Everyone's different, Em. Poor old Charlotte hasn't had it all that easy. Those ghastly bronchial attacks as a child . . . Losing her twin brother. . . . and you did mention once that Richard took against her for a while afterwards.'

'Yes. But all the same. She and I are so out of touch. She seems to resent both her parents now. I'd hoped she might have rung Christmas Day. From a call-box. I believe it's why I drank all that brandy. I was trying to pretend.

You know, that I wasn't ill or alone and she wasn't shacked up in the Welsh mountains. It seems only yesterday that I took her and Jo for that seaside holiday, remember?'

'I remember. They were kids together. Like you and I were once.'

'But I'm afraid their friendship hasn't lasted. It couldn't now, in the very nature of things, with Charlotte having turned into a hippie. I wish to God she'd seen more of your Jo. She was such a good influence on her. It was a thousand pities that after Charlotte ran away from Eaton Grange she failed the entrance exam to Wickfield House so that they were never at the same school.'

'It's nice of you to say that, Em. But you can never tell. And, remember, there's a much greater age gap between them than there was between you and me. They would probably each have made other friends. We always had so much in common.'

They lapsed once again into silence, immersed in private thoughts, in memories of a lifetime. How very true, Emily reflected, was Helen's last remark. Here they were, both getting on for fifty, bound by lasting ties which only death could sever. What had originally forged them? The same home ground? Those early lessons with Ethel Sharman? A mutual passion for ponies? Emily's love for Bulbarrow and all that it had to offer? Their friendship had certainly deepened after her father's suicide and Dick and Dorothy Swayne had taken her with open arms into their happy-go-lucky rambling farmhouse and – although she had never realized it at the time – carefully shielded her from the full impact of the tragedy, of witnessing her mother's collapse and the overwhelming burden which May was having to bear alone. Then there had been their schooldays, travelling to Wickfield House together on the bus. Hardly a day went by without their seeing each other. Even at weekends they were always in and out of their respective homes. Later, of course, they were separated when Helen joined the ATS and she became a VAD. But they had written, constantly. Emily still had bundles of letters: immature but strangely revealing about those times. Oddly enough, they had become almost closer in the war years, each working for a common goal, sharing a unique experience which neither of their daughters had had at the same age.

Later still, marriage had naturally brought a different element into their relationship. But it had not weakened the bond. Nothing could do that. Today, as the west country opened up before them, the rolling downs familiar and welcoming in the clear January sunlight, Emily thought of all that Helen had just done for her. Often, she felt their friendship was too one-sided, that Helen invariably gave while she, weakly, took. She tried to say as much now, but was instantly rebuffed.

'I wouldn't have come to town if I hadn't wanted to, Em. Naturally, I was worried about you and it seemed the sensible thing to do. It was a bit of a challenge, too. I don't mind admitting, now we're safely out of it, that I've never driven in London before. But there's always a first time. Like when I had to take over an army truck to bring a whole lot of girls back from a dance at Tidworth because the driver had had one too many. Sometimes I feel that you and I were lucky. We were always having those kind of things thrown at us. The young nowadays seem to miss out on such challenges. Could be that's why Charlotte's making herself battle with nature in the back of beyond. You and I were continually up against it in our youth. Jo's always asking me what it was like. I think she's quite envious ... you know ... that our generation had the war.'

21

Our generation had the war. Helen's words came back to her as she sat in Mr Bellamy's office one day at the beginning of March. He himself would have missed it, she felt, by a few years. That is, she judged him to have been a schoolboy at the time, possibly even an evacuee like the ones she had known in Wilhampton. True, he would have recollections, but they would surely be of others shouldering the responsibility, possibly leading him to air-raid shelters, protecting him to the best of their ability. He wouldn't have been brought back from the hell of Dunkirk in a Thameside tug, incarcerated in a German prisoner-of-war camp, lying in some hospital ministered to by an inexperienced VAD such as herself. For all his air of smooth expertise – even paternalism – she surmised that he would not have embarked on his career until sometime in the late 'forties, rising, twenty years later, to the post he now held: a senior partner in a firm of eminent London solicitors, specializing in complicated divorce cases like Vandenburgh v. Vandenburgh, parties who had made a mess of things, who should never have married in the first place and were having difficulty untying the knot.

'Your husband,' Mr Bellamy was now saying, 'appears to be in South Africa. Most unsatisfactory. I suppose, as he has no plans to remarry, he doesn't mind prolonging the issue. Especially as you mentioned that he did not really want a divorce. The other side has simply informed us that he will be replying to your affidavit in due course.'

'You mean it is impossible to get on with things?'

'Naturally. Until we have secured a proper settlement we cannot fix a hearing for the *decree nisi*. I know of some ill-advised people who have been in too much of a hurry, whose solicitors have allowed them to become, as it were, half-divorced. The *nisi* has gone through but the absolute has then had to be held up indefinitely owing to further financial complications. I know of one case like that which went on for years.'

'*Years?*'

'Yes, Mrs Vandenburgh. In fact, I always bear in mind the classic example of one poor lady who was so certain that her husband would do the gentlemanly thing, that she became completely divorced, only to end up completely unprovided for. You will, I fear, have to be patient. Your husband is being extremely difficult and elusive, but as long as you remain in the flat you have the whip hand. I have, at least, got the other side's confirmation that Mr Vandenburgh will pay your rates and service charges *pro tem*. Keep sending me the bills as they come in. Incidentally, you mentioned in one of your letters that you had 'flu very badly at Christmas. I hope you have quite recovered.'

She did not answer at once. She had been feeling more and more depressed since then and today's conversation had certainly done nothing to help. 'I think I should feel better,' she replied, 'if the divorce were over and done with and I could leave London. Make plans for the future.'

'Such as . . . ?'

'I want to go back to the west country. Where I was born. Where I have friends. Buy some small cottage. Settle down.'

She was conscious of him staring at her, speculatively.

'Might you not find that rather too quiet? After all, Mrs Vandenburgh, you have been the wife of a very rich man for getting on for . . . let me see . . . twenty-three years. Might you not miss the kind of life to which you must have become accustomed? Servants . . . A certain standard of luxury. I should hope that the settlement which we eventually reach would enable you to live on a somewhat grander scale than that which you seem to envisage. When the new laws come into effect you would be entitled to half your husband's wealth — that is, after taking into account your own much smaller assets, as I believe I mentioned during our initial talk.'

So he was still thinking about that, was he? He didn't approve of her modest ideas. She was an unsatisfactory client, from his point of view, one who needed pushing, tempting, being made to ask for more.

'I don't think you quite understand, Mr Bellamy,' she answered, surprising herself by a sudden burst of assertiveness. 'I wasn't *happy* in those kind of surroundings. And I certainly don't like the ones I'm in at present.' She did not add that she was also becoming daily more and more conscious of a still small voice which kept saying: I'm suing Richard for something of which I, too, was guilty, once, a long long time ago. I shall be getting money dishonestly, illegally. If only I could get over to Mr Bellamy that it's not money I'm after. I just want my freedom.

'I realize that you are not . . . how shall I put it . . . a London person, Mrs Vandenburgh,' she heard him saying.

His voice sounded tetchy now, as he went on, 'But the delay is no fault of mine. It is entirely to do with the other side. Have you thought any more about the possibility of doing some voluntary work while you are waiting?'

She wished that he wouldn't keep referring to the 'other side'. She was beginning to find both that and the word 'settlement' getting on her nerves.

'Yes. I'm going for an interview at St George's Hospital tomorrow,' she replied. Although how, she thought, I shall be able to cheer up others when everything seems so black, I haven't any idea.

She found Miss Gordon, the almoner, brisk and business-like when she arrived to see her next morning. She informed Emily that they would be glad of her help for as many hours a week as she felt able to give. Her duties would include attending to the flowers in the wards, chatting to patients — especially those who lacked visitors — performing small tasks for them such as shopping, writing letters and occasionally accompanying them on journeys home. If Emily could ever spare any extra time at a weekend, so much the better. Miss Gordon said she was sure she would find the work rewarding and that they would expect her, wearing the blue overall the hospital provided, at two o'clock the following afternoon.

As she walked back to the flat, she realized that she had forgotten to mention that she had once actually been a VAD. But then she reflected that it probably would not have greatly interested her interviewer. She suspected that Miss Gordon, like Mr Bellamy, had missed the war by a few years. The fact that today she had been confronted by some unknown woman who, more than likely, she had mentally classed as 'idle rich', would mean nothing to her, other than the necessity for sending a memo to the Sister in charge of Ward D North, to the effect that a Mrs Vandenburgh would be lending her services there on Wednesday, March 11th, at 2 p.m.

The old familiar smell of antiseptic and polish greeted her as soon as she arrived at the entrance of the ward at the appointed hour. But after that she became aware of many differences. For one thing, this was no long low

725

makeshift hut in the heart of the Wessex countryside. D North was huge and high-ceilinged, with the roar of London traffic drifting up from the street below. Curtains round one or two beds bore evidence that all of them could be partitioned off if necessary. Moreover, the patients were not soldiers but women, women who were in for major surgery, one or two who glanced at Emily apathetically out of sad lack-lustre eyes.

'Sister's office is in there,' a nurse said, jerking her head towards a door halfway down the ward, as she went by with a bedpan. She was a buxom young woman with straight mousy-coloured hair falling either side of her face in a fashion which Emily knew would never have been countenanced at Ashmore Emergency Hospital. Indeed, remembering how strict the matron had been about every stray wisp having to be tucked well out of sight, Emily had found herself that morning taking extra care to look neat and tidy. She knew it was ridiculous but, as she approached the Sister's office, something of the same feeling of intimidation came over her. It was therefore quite a shock when she was confronted at the desk by a most attractive female with golden curls beneath a very fetching cap, who smiled pleasantly and said, 'Ah, Mrs Vandenburgh. Do sit down. Would you like a cup of coffee?'

A sudden recollection of a certain Sister Matthews dressing her down in the summer of 1940 for having perched on a patient's bed, made it hard for Emily to credit the present relaxed atmosphere. But surely this was better, she thought, as she began her duties, removing vases of flowers from lockers and taking them into the sluice-room, throwing out the dead ones and salvaging others. She worked quietly and efficiently, saying little at first, but gradually, as the afternoon wore on, she struck up a conversation with several patients, aware that a rather more ill-looking one, a Mrs Core, seemed to be taking a special interest in her. As she left the ward, she went across and asked her if there was anything she wanted.

'Maybe. I don't know yet.' The voice was cockney, weak but on the defensive. 'When are you comin' again?'

'Tomorrow. Every afternoon.'

'OK. I'll think about it.'

The woman's face haunted her all the way home. She had that fatal look about her, the one she had come to recognize in the war, the one she had seen on both her mother's and stepfather's faces towards the end. Mrs Core was going to die. Of that, she had little doubt.

It was not until a week had gone by that Mrs Core beckoned Emily over to her bed as soon as she saw her arrive.

'I bin watchin' you. You've got a kind face. Will you do something for me?'

'Of course. If I can.'

'I want you to see Mabs.'

'Mabs?'

'Yes. Me daughter. She don't know I'm 'ere. We bin out of touch for years. She left home to lead 'er own life. No questions asked. I dare say you know what I'm drivin' at. I never put 'er down as next-of-kin because . . . well . . . I don't think of 'er like that. At least, not till now. But she's all I got. 'Course, if the 'orspital authorities knew I 'ad a daughter, they'd be on to 'er like a shot. They'd ask 'er to take me away. They don't like you to die in these places. You see, I'm for the chopper. When the doc came round this mornin', 'e didn't say much, but I could tell. I shall be goin' out of 'ere feet first. I'm down to seven stone and the pain's come back something terrible. So I thought I'd like to see Mabs, for old times' sake, now I'm near the end. She needn't come if she don't want to. She knows I don't approve of 'er, but well, I'm prepared to let bygones by bygones now. She was a nice little thing, once.'

Emily sat on the bed and put out a hand, trying to hide her emotion. She mustn't break down. Not now. Not here. She'd witnessed plenty of others facing death, even her own mother. But somehow this unknown unfortunate woman's story affected her profoundly. It made her think of her own relationship with Charlotte. The girl had only sent one hastily scribbled note since Christmas.

'Of course I'll go and see Mabs, Mrs Core. You must give me her address.'

'And you won't let on to the Sister, will you? I mean, it's not as if Mabs could possibly help in any way.'

She hesitated. 'No. If that's how you want it. I'll just let your daughter know the circumstances and say you'd appreciate a visit.'

Mrs Core pointed to the drawer of her locker which, according to instructions, Emily opened and extracted a small plastic writing case. She then handed it to the dying woman, who pulled out a ragged piece of paper and passed it back to her.

'Not far from here, is she, dear? I wouldn't want to put you out in any way.'

To her astonishment, Emily read the address: Flat 2, 18 Shepherd Market, W1. She knew enough now about London to realize what the area stood for and why Mrs Core and her daughter were estranged.

22

'Hello?'

'Hello. Is that Miss Core?'

'Who?'

'Core. Miss Mabs Core. I have a message for her.'

Emily stood in the narrow street, hardly more than an alleyway, pressing her ear against the intercom.

There was a silence and then the woman's voice shouted, 'Sorry, can't hear you.'

'Core,' Emily shouted back, desperately, 'Are you Miss Core?'

'Hang on.' There was a longer silence, after which there came the sound of a door banging overhead, footsteps descending the stairs and along a passage, the sliding of bolts and, suddenly, Emily was confronted by an apparition in a shiny blue dressing gown who might have been anything from twenty to forty-five years of age. She had dyed blonde hair, a sallow unmade-up complexion and a lighted cigarette in one hand. Although it was eleven in the morning, she seemed oblivious of her appearance and of the vaguely curious glances from the people round about, who were browsing amongst the bric-à-brac displayed outside the adjoining shop.

'I'm looking for Miss Mabs Core,' Emily repeated.

'There's no one here by that name. I'm Lilian. Lilian Forman.'

'Oh. Perhaps someone else in the house would know . . . ?'

'I don't think so. There's only me and Sylvie up aloft and she's away. Besides, she came later than me.'

'You've been here some time?'

The woman's eyes narrowed. She took a pull on her cigarette. 'You aren't from the fuzz, are you?'

'Fuzz?'

'P'lice. They're always snooping around.'

'No. Of course not. I'm a helper at a hospital. I'm trying to trace Mrs Core's daughter for her. Mrs Core is . . . . dying.'

'I'm sorry, dearie. I'd help if I could. Why don't you ask Mr Samuelson, the bugger at the shop who rents us our rooms. If you'll excuse me, it's perishing standing here like this.' Lilian closed the door and, utterly frustrated, Emily could only act on her suggestion.

She was met with the same discouraging response. Mr Samuelson informed her that he could not recall ever having had a Miss Mabs Core as a tenant. Prior to Miss Forman there had been . . . He had then paused, rubbed the side of his nose and continued, 'Well, I don't think it was a Miss Core. You must understand that it's a question of here today and gone tomorrow in these parts. Let me see now . . . There was a Maisie someone or other, I believe, before Lilian. That is, I *think* it was Maisie. She was married, at least, she wore a wedding ring. But I've completely forgotten her surname. My memory isn't as good as it used to be.'

She put out a hand and steadied herself against a table on which there were countless small silver-plated and brass ornaments and a china figurine of the Virgin Mary with child. Despite her anguish, Emily was conscious that the shopkeeper was watching her carefully not, she felt, out of any solicitude, but because he was probably concerned lest she might pocket one of his nick-nacks. She did her best to pull herself together. She knew it was ridiculous to associate the Maisie whom he had mentioned with the unknown unseen Maisie whom she was citing in her divorce case. It was also unlikely that Mr Samuelson's Maisie was Mrs Core's daughter. Mabs was short for Mabel, wasn't it? How stupid she had been not to ask Mrs Core for Mabs's full Christian names.

'And you've no idea,' she asked, 'where she went? This Maisie?'

'No. I'd tell you if I did. I only recall her rent was paid up. By some gent, I think. She went off, sudden like.'

She forced herself to ask the next question. 'I don't suppose her surname could have been Fripp, by any chance?' After all, Mr Samuelson had seemed quite definite that the woman in question had been married.

He frowned at her and once more rubbed his nose. 'Sorry, love. I really couldn't say. It's not as if I keep records. It's cash every Friday night. Like as I said, there's always been such a turnover round here.'

'Thank you.' She left the shop. Having no desire to eat anything before going to St George's, she wandered round and arrived at the ward well before time, staring in stupefaction at the strange face regarding her from Mrs Core's bed.

'Haemorrhaged,' said the buxom nurse whom she had first encountered. 'Soon after you left last night. Best thing, really, poor old soul. She asked for you just before she passed away. But there was no time to telephone. I mean, she snuffed out pretty quick in the end.'

I should have done more, Emily kept saying to herself, as, mechanically, she went about her duties. Mrs Core had obviously had something on her mind from our first encounter. I should have gained her confidence sooner. Then I might have had time to do some proper sleuth work. Discover more about this curious Maisie, even tried to make anonymous contact with the Maida Vale address I've got, broken my vow never to go and even look at the outside of the place. But it's too late now. Mrs Core's dead and Mabs, wherever she is and whatever she's called, will never know.

In bed that night, she was unable to sleep. As the clock struck 1, 2, and then 3 a.m., she began to feel the cramping pain in the middle of her stomach which had bothered her more than once lately. It was far more acute now. Possibly she ought to make an appointment with Dr Pratt's nice young partner. But she was fairly sure what it was. She was simply over-reacting these days. Jumping to conclusions. Letting her imagination run riot. It had been ridiculous to get all steamed up and confused yesterday over nothing at all. Although Mrs Core's death was hardly 'nothing at all'. She kept wishing she had done better in Shepherd Market.

Several weeks later, as she was drinking an early morning cup of tea, the caretaker pushed a letter through her box addressed in well-known handwriting. She took it back to bed with her and slit open the envelope. 'Dear Madam', it ran,

> I do hope you are keeping well and have quite recovered from that nasty 'flu. Also that you are eating enough. You are always in my thoughts.
>
> I hope you don't mind my enquiring, but there have been stories going round that Mr Vandenburgh is selling Hensford. He seems to have lost interest lately and is hardly ever here, so perhaps it is for the best. If this is the case, I should like to go and live with my married sister and her husband who have asked me. I'm not getting any younger and it is very lonely here all by myself, now Fred has died. Of course, I may have been misinformed and I would never dream of leaving if you ever thought of returning. But if you could let me know the position, it would put my mind at rest.
>
> May I say how much I and everyone at Hensford miss you.
>
> I am, Yours respectfully,
> Clara Draper.

I must ring Mr Bellamy at once, Emily thought. Find out if he has any inkling that Richard intends to sell up. Poor Mrs Draper. It must be ghastly for her all alone there. I'll write and tell her I'll find out all I can as soon as possible.

I've been so wrapped up in my own problems, I haven't taken enough account of others with equally pressing ones.

Unfortunately, Mr Bellamy proved as elusive as usual. His secretary said that he would be in court all that week and probably the best part of next on an extremely complicated case. Perhaps Emily would care to make an appointment for the one after. At the moment he was still awaiting a reply to his last letter to the other side. Despairingly, she made an appointment for three weeks' time and put down the receiver. Solicitors' letters, she was beginning to feel, were like communications exchanged at increasingly lengthy intervals by participants whose chief aim in life was to avoid any actual curtailment of their correspondence. They seemed to be engaged in some leisurely and enjoyable bat-and-ball game while their clients remained pawns in the background.

It proved, however, to be not Mr Bellamy but Emily herself who was responsible for delaying matters on the day of the appointment. She was almost out of the door of the flat when the telephone rang. Other than her frequent conversations with Helen, she received comparatively few calls. Sometimes, when she was particularly depressed, she had been dismayed to find that a wrong number, especially at weekends, helped to allay the feeling that she was cut off from the rest of humanity. She had noted, not without a certain cynicism, that friends and acquaintances in Cheshire seemed to be a little uncertain as to whom they owed their allegiance. She sensed that the women were sympathetic towards her, but were held back from making overtures by their husbands because, as Sheila Renton had put it one day when they bumped into each other in Piccadilly, 'Geoff has enjoyed so much shooting from Richard. I don't think he'd like it if I came to see you. It's so difficult, darling. I'm sure you'll understand.'

Today, as Emily went back to answer the telephone, she wondered who it could possibly be. As soon as she heard Betsy's voice, the 'fear' pain, as she had come to think of it, gripped her.

'I'm sorry, my dear. It's . . . bad news, I'm afraid. May . . . A stroke . . . early this morning.'

'Is it . . . was it fatal?'

'Yes. She didn't suffer at all.'

'Thank you, Betsy. I'll drive straight down.'

But, for just a few moments after she replaced the receiver, she sat quite still, trying to take in the news. May was dead. May, who had looked after her since she was a child, for whom, guiltily, she had often felt more love than for her own mother. May, who had never had an enemy in the world. May, the last of that generation of Lodges to go. Thank God she had managed to keep her recent troubles from her.

She reached for the telephone again and put off her appointment with Mr Bellamy. Then she started to pack. May's sudden death so soon after Mrs Core's, even Mrs Draper's prospective retirement, made her suddenly and sadly conscious of age, of time passing, of the fact that she was entering on another phase of life.

As she left for the west country, she realized that she herself could now definitely be said to belong to the older generation.

23

'I cannot advise you too strongly, Mrs Vandenburgh, against the course you wish to adopt.'

It was June. London was stifling. The journey to the City on the Underground had been almost unbearable and, surprisingly, Mr Bellamy's office did not appear to have air conditioning. There was a fan making a distracting noise in the corner.

Although Emily was still deeply saddened by the loss of May, she had come to a decision which, ultimately, she felt would bring some solace. She had known that Mr Bellamy would not approve but, nevertheless, she had told him quietly and firmly that she wanted to waive any claim to a settlement from her husband, asking for nothing except the return of the money she had passed to him and certain belongings of hers which were still at Hensford. Her circumstances, she had explained, had altered. She had been left the White Hermitage, together with its contents, by her late aunt on the understanding that Mrs Betsy Mead, her aunt's friend and companion, could remain in it for her lifetime. As it had turned out, however, Mrs Mead's nephew, Mr Paul Woodley, was anxious that she should go and live in separate accommodation available in his country house, where he and his wife could keep an eye on her. This, Mrs Mead had elected to do. There had always been a particularly strong bond between her and the young man whom she had cared for so devotedly.

Emily was aware that Mr Bellamy had looked more and more distressed as he heard her out and, after she had finished and he had said his little piece about 'strongly advising' her against any such action, there had been quite a long silence, save for the whirring of the fan in the background and one of the telephones buzzing on his desk, which he had instantly switched off.

'Although we now know that your husband is, indeed, selling up and that Hensford has been heavily and unaccountably mortgaged of late,' he said, at length, 'there is bound to be something left after the sale. And, of course, the London flat in which it has been and, in my view, still is imperative for you to remain.'

'But I wish to live at the Hermitage, Mr Bellamy. It's like a family home. I was brought up there.'

He drummed his fingers on the desk. 'Yes. Yes, I dare say. But there would be nothing to stop you keeping the flat as well. Having two homes, if we obtained a proper settlement.'

'I have no desire for a flat in London, Mr Bellamy.'

She could almost read his thoughts. He had hoped she would be a compliant lucrative client and she had turned out to be awkward and financially disappointing.

'You do realize, don't you, Mrs Vandenburgh, that even with your altered circumstances, your actual income will not be great. With inflation . . . You will have to live quite simply. There will be the rates and upkeep of the White Hermitage, the necessity for refurbishing from time to time.'

'Yes, but I would prefer it that way.' And I shall feel better now, said a still small voice, about that lie I told you in the beginning.

'I still feel it is important for your future security that you should receive some form of capital from your husband. The transfer of the flat is the obvious answer. It would be yours to do what you liked with, to sell, if you wished. It would be an asset whatever happened, even if you remarried. Any alimony, you appreciate, would cease on remarriage.'

'I do not intend ever to remarry, Mr Bellamy.' Suddenly, there came into her mind an echo from a long way back, at the end of the last war in fact, during the early hours of the day that the atom bomb was dropped on Hiroshima. She had said almost the exact words to her cousin, Frank François, while they had been sitting by the Willon and he had intimated that he would like to marry her. To her consternation, she now heard Mr Bellamy making the self-same reply.

'I wouldn't be too sure of that. One day you might change your mind.'

For answer, she simply shook her head.

'Then what do you want me to do? Write to the other side? Let them know of your decision? Fix a date for the hearing? It will be merely a formality now.'

'Yes.'

'Costs?' he said, abruptly. 'We shall insist your husband pays your costs.'

'Yes,' she replied, again. She was tired of arguing now.

As she rose to go, he remarked, 'One can never tell. I have steered countless ladies through divorce cases, but I would say that you have been my most unusual client, Mrs Vandenburgh. I hope you won't regret your decision and that life will treat you more kindly in future.' He held out his hand. Was there, she wondered, on parting, almost a flicker of admiration in his eyes?

Now that she had something definite to look forward to, her desire to get away from London did not seem quite so imperative. She wrote to Betsy, whom she had by now taken into her confidence about the divorce, reaffirming that there was absolutely no need for her to hurry over moving and she could take all the time in the world. She also wrote to Charlotte, saying that when she was eventually settled she hoped she might come for a holiday, that she would always be welcome at the Hermitage and Emily would like to think that her daughter would regard it as a family home, now that Hensford was being sold and it was thought that Richard might possibly emigrate. She decided to keep on with her hospital work, while letting the authorities know that she would be obliged to give it up in the not-too-distant future, as she would be leaving London.

There was, however, one pressing and painful task which she knew had to be faced and that was the necessity of going to Hensford to arrange for the removal of the rest of her belongings. Although Mrs Draper had sent Emily many of these over the past few months, there were certain pieces of furniture inherited from her mother and stepfather which she naturally wanted to keep for sentimental reasons, together with some smaller items which would be impossible for anyone, other than herself, to sort out. She knew that Mrs Draper would be leaving shortly and that she should not delay much longer, particularly as Mr Bellamy had said it would be advisable for her to list and label such effects when Mr Vandenburgh was absent but in the presence of her housekeeper.

He therefore arranged that she should go back to Hensford for twenty-four hours during the first week in August. As she neared the house, she could see a combine harvester at work at the top of the home field, a scene painfully familiar but from which she now felt strangely detached. She had opted out. She was no longer part of the place, even though she had often felt little more than a figurehead. But she realized that whatever difficulties the one-time occupants of Hensford might have got themselves into, the harvest would still have to be gathered in. Bert Chandler would see to that. She wondered if he would be staying on with a new employer, dedicated to the land which he had tended so faithfully, even though his efforts of late would appear to have been sadly dissipated. She trusted things would turn out well for him, whichever decision he took, and that Hensford itself might become a happier place. She recalled how she had once hoped that children would bring it alive, but it had certainly been a forlorn one as far as the Vandenburgh family was concerned.

Mrs Draper greeted her with a distressing show of emotion. She had aged considerably since Emily had last seen her. Abandoning all her usual reserve, she informed her that the last year had been the unhappiest of her life, even more unhappy than when her husband had died. 'It's never been the same since you left, Mrs Vandenburgh. Sometimes I don't know how I've stood it. If you ask me there's a jinx on the house. You know, back in the 'twenties, when some people called Harcourt were here, they asked the rector to come and conduct a service . . . an excise, or whatever it's called, because they felt there was such a nasty atmosphere. I never mentioned it to you, naturally, when you were here. I mean . . . you were alone such a lot of the time. But when the bad things happened . . . you know, little Mark and then Charlotte running away from school and you leaving . . . well, I couldn't help thinking about it.'

She was appalled. 'That was very kind of you, Mrs Draper. I'm terribly sorry you've been so unhappy. I wish you'd said something about it in your earlier letters.'

'Well, I kept thinking perhaps you might be coming back. Divorce is never . . . easy, is it? You might have changed your mind. And I also felt that if Charlotte wanted to come at any time, I should be here. I hope she's well?'

'Yes . . . Yes, thank you.' Was her daughter well? She felt obliged to lie. She did not really know. She had, as yet, had no answer to her last letter.

She began on the downstairs rooms first, with Mrs Draper never far away. When she was in doubt about some article, she carefully refrained from claiming it but, as she passed by the tallboy in the hall, she remembered the photograph albums which had always lain in the bottom drawer. When a marriage broke up, to whom, for good-ness' sake, did they belong? She didn't suppose that

Richard would want them. She could never recall him giving them a second glance. On the other hand . . . She pulled open the drawer. They were still there, exactly as she had left them. She turned to a fresh page in her notebook, put a question mark at the top and scrawled 'Photograph Albums' underneath.

It was a long arduous day. She had not realized that there would be quite so much to attend to, that her cupboards still contained clothes she had forgotten ever possessing. After Mrs Draper's carefully prepared dinner – to which she was unable to do justice – she slipped out and called on the occupants of various nearby cottages and then went on and spent a longer time with the Chandlers, who were delighted to see her. As she had surmised, Bert wanted to stay on. Tactfully, neither she nor they made any reference to Richard.

The moon had risen as she made her way back to the house. At the gate of the churchyard, she turned in and stood for a long while looking down at Mark's grave, grateful to find that her requests for its maintenance, which she had made on leaving Hensford, had been so faithfully carried out.

She did not sleep that night. The only thing which, under any other circumstances, she might have found welcome after London was the silence. But, as the hours passed, even that seemed to have its drawbacks. It allowed too many memories to keep flooding in, of little Mark, of previous nights spent all alone in this strange unfriendly house when Richard was away, of others battling with Charlotte's illnesses in the night nursery, making up the fire, spooning out the antibiotics at the appropriate times, praying while she listened to the child fighting for breath, opening and closing windows, wondering whether she dare telephone James Peterson and drag him out ten miles during the early hours so soon after the last attack.

Other than to visit Mark's grave, Emily did not think she could bear to come to Hensford again, not now. A whole enormous slice of life was over. Finished. She was longing to get away in the morning, even more to getting to the Hermitage. Dear May, thank God for her legacy.

Had she, with that uncanny perception of hers, known that Emily might have need of a refuge at some time or another? It was more than likely.

But it was not quite so easy to break with the past when it came to wishing Mrs Draper goodbye. She found herself saying, 'Later on, when I'm settled in the west country, perhaps you would like to spend a holiday with me?' She was pleased to note the obvious pleasure which her invitation had given. As she drove away, she reflected, not for the first time, that so often there were far stronger bonds between friends and associates than between relatives.

One afternoon in September, a week after she had moved into the White Hermitage, she was staking and tying up some late flowering chrysanthemums in the herbaceous border when she heard footsteps in the lane and the click of the latch as the garden gate opened. She straightened up, wondering who her caller might be. She had always felt that one of the nicest things about living in the country was that people frequently dropped in to see each other without any formal invitations. Nothing like that ever seemed to happen in London.

She went round the house to greet her visitor. Standing at the front porch, wearing an old duffel coat with a knapsack on her back, stood Charlotte. Even before she turned to face her, Emily could see that her daughter was heavily pregnant.

Part Four

24

'Where is my Mummy, Elly?'

She knew that the question had to come sometime, but she had hoped it might not be just yet. The child was only three and a half.

'Your Mummy went . . . to India, Tom.'

'Where's India?'

'India is . . . a long way away.'

'Why did she go there, Elly?'

'She went to see . . . a wise man. To listen to what he had to say.'

'Oh.'

The little boy on the sitting-room floor resumed playing with the model tractor and cardboard trailer she had made for him. The conversation, Emily thought, was over. But she was wrong.

'What did the wise man say, Elly?' Tom asked, after a few minutes.

What indeed did the wise man say, Emily wanted to shout. Who knows? I don't. I've had less than half a dozen cards from Charlotte since she left. These days the young just seem to up sticks and go off to sit at the feet of some guru, leaving all their responsibilities, including offspring, to a generation who never had the time or opportunity for meditation and were obliged to get on with the actual process of living or, in the war, dying.

'I think we'll have to wait a while, Tom, to hear that,' she answered. 'Perhaps Mummy will tell us when she next writes.'

'Tomorrow?'

'Maybe not as soon as that. Would you like me to make you another trailer?'

'Yes please. A red one.'

'Oh dear. I don't know if I've got any red cardboard. I

shall have to paint it. I'll see what I can do when you've gone to bed. It's really time for your bath now.'

'Not yet.'

'Another five minutes then.'

Thank God, Emily thought, after the child was asleep and she was doing her best to keep her promise about the trailer, that I managed to change the subject. At least he hasn't started to ask about his father. I suppose it's bound to come, though. And what do I say then: I'm not sure where your father is, Tom. I'm not even sure *who* he is. He might be called Benedict. On the other hand, he might not. He might be in India with your mother but, once again, he might not. In fact, both of them might be anywhere now. The last card was three months ago. No address. Only an indecipherable postmark which might or might not have been 'Lahore'. And what is Charlotte doing for money? She must have got through the small legacy Aunt Chip left all her nephews and nieces by now, which she apparently drew out of the bank soon after that ghastly winter's night when I came back from visiting Helen and found the note pinned to the baby's cot: 'Forgive me. But you're so much better at looking after Tom than I shall ever be'. But *surely*, doesn't Charlotte want to know how he is? What he looks like? He's such a lovely child. I expect I'm prejudiced, but I reckon he takes after the maternal side of his family. He's rather like little Mark was at the same age. And . . . I don't know . . . there's something about him which reminds me of those old photographs I've got of my father as a boy. I must hunt them out when I've got a spare moment.

But there were not many spare moments in Emily's life nowadays, not that she minded. She kept to a strict routine. Every weekday morning she drove Tom to a small nursery school in Wilhampton and fetched him again at twelve-fifteen. After lunch a young girl called Gilly Parker, the great-great-grand-daughter of the town's first garage proprietor, arrived at the Hermitage on a bicycle where, during the first part of the afternoon while Tom slept, she spent the time washing up and doing a little housework, after which she took him for a walk. Apart from weekends and holidays, these arrangements enabled Emily to shut herself away for several hours each day in May's old workroom – and write.

It had taken courage to start – even more to continue – but after the third effort she had sold, through an agent, a short story to a women's magazine. The remuneration seemed surprisingly good and, to her delight, she had subsequently had two more accepted. While waiting for further inspiration, she had decided to embark on something rather different: the book for children which her cousin, Frank François, had once, long ago, suggested and which she intended to illustrate herself. She was aware that, at best, all her efforts were unlikely to supply the wherewithal necessary for bringing up her grandchild in the way for which she might once have hoped. Tom's schooling, for instance. She wanted him to have a first-class education but, with inflation rocketing, this would scarcely be possible. It would be foolish in the extreme to imagine achieving anything but the most modest of incomes from writing. As a last resort she could, she supposed, sell the Hermitage, but the thought distressed her and she felt that in some way it would be disloyal to May and not at all what her aunt would have wished.

She realized that she might have obtained help from other sources. She could have appealed to Richard when Tom was born, although she doubted that she would have received much response, except under pressure. Sickened by all the financial wrangling, she had let the divorce go through without ever mentioning that a pregnant unmarried daughter had descended on her. Since then, she had lost track of her former husband's whereabouts, although rumour had it that he had settled abroad. It would appear that Richard had opted out of his responsibilities in much the same way as his daughter. Was their behaviour simply because they possessed many of the same genes? Emily had often pondered on the importance of heredity compared to that of upbringing, of nature versus nurture and those unmistakable character traits which seemed to come down through the generations no matter how a child was actually reared.

Then there was another form of assistance which Emily felt she might well have accepted in the beginning, even though she would have remained supportive financially. Many was the sleepless night she had spent wondering whether she had been right in refusing the generous offer made by her god-daughter soon after Charlotte's departure. Joanna, now with a small daughter of her own named Sarah, had suddenly called to see Emily at the Hermitage. She would always remember how the girl, as she still thought of her, had stood over Tom's cot, concerned, eager, warm-hearted – just like her mother – saying, 'I've talked it over with Matt, Aunt Em, and we'd love to have him and bring him up as one of our own.' Emily had hesitated, realizing only too well the advantages her grand-child would have: a loving happy home, companionship, and probably far better up-to-date care than that which an ageing grandmother, living by herself, could give him. Had it been selfishness which had made her reply in the end, 'It's wonderful of you, Jo. I appreciate it more than I can say but . . . you see, one day Charlotte might come back.'

Had she really thought that? It seemed such a forlorn hope, especially as time went by. When Tom was about eighteen months, Helen had mentioned that she was sure the offer which Joanna – now the mother of two – had originally made, still held good. But by then Emily knew it was too late. She couldn't let the little boy go. She sensed that he felt secure at the Hermitage, that he relied on her. She hoped she was not being fanciful in thinking that they seemed to belong to each other. The difference in their ages did not appear to matter. She was at a loss to explain it but she was aware of a curious growing affinity between them. She looked on the child, despite his tender years, as a character after her own heart. Nevertheless, she was glad to feel that, even though she had not parted with him, she had asked Joanna if she would become his official guardian in case anything happened to her.

Sometimes, in the small hours, she awoke in terror of such an eventuality coming to pass, even though she had legislated for it. She wanted so desperately to see Tom grow up. She loved the child. She suspected that she had never really known the meaning of love before. Was it, she wondered, possible that one had more to give as one got older, that she was now being granted a second chance in an area where she had failed so lamentably earlier on? But although she had elected to keep Tom, she was constantly reminding herself of the pitfalls connected with such a decision, that it was especially important not to become over-protective. For this reason, she had promised Joanna that she would let him spend a week or so with her during the coming summer holidays at her home near Oxford, where her husband was a schoolmaster. When she deposited Tom there and watched him happily trotting off to play with Sarah, without so much as a backward glance in her direction, she felt that, however much it might have cost her, she had so far been proceeding along the right lines. For all his unusual upbringing, Tom Vandenburgh was by no means a clinging child.

It seemed strange to be quite alone back at the Hermitage, something which had never happened before, other than for the very short period before the arrival of Charlotte. She proposed to put the time to good use, tidying up the manuscript and drawings on which she had been working, while trying to steel herself against what she felt sure would be a firm letter of rejection. Her only consolation at present was the knowledge that at least Tom had enjoyed *The Scarecrow of Sweetacres*, even if some of it was a little above his head. 'Talk it, Elly,' he kept repeating, when she had read one or two passages and shown him a few rough sketches; and, obligingly, Emily had 'talked it' again and again until she was more certain than ever that no publisher would accept such nonsense. Perhaps, she mused, I ought to have stuck to my lifelong ambition and tried to write a play, but I've been so out of touch with the theatre world since my marriage that a book for children seemed so infinitely less of an undertaking. And, as Frank once intimated, I do happen to have some personal experience of the young, especially just at the moment. At least my opening words: 'One day a bird of paradise flew down into the field where the Scarecrow of Sweetacres lived' seem to have fired Tom's imagination, although I still haven't quite been able to get over to him what paradise is. I expect he thinks it's just a question of blue and green and gold feathers.

It was in this somewhat uncertain frame of mind that, one evening after supper, Emily wandered down to the Willon and sat on the bank, thinking how much the river had witnessed her hopes and fears, joys and sorrows. There seemed a strange inevitability about returning to live by it, as if her life had come full circle, that this was where she was destined to spend whatever was left of it. When I'm nearing sixty, she said to herself – and then corrected it to *If I get to sixty*, because she was feeling so lacking in confidence – Tom will be eleven; if I reach sixty-five, he'll be sixteen. Would that be too much to hope for? Would I by then have steered him far enough along the right road?

Suddenly, there was the sound of parting rushes. She looked up, expecting to see a fisherman. Instead, a young man stood before her, long-haired, bearded, wearing a torn faded shirt and jeans. She stiffened, experiencing a momentary fear. But despite his dishevelled appearance, there was something sensitive and vaguely aristocratic-looking about him.

'Mrs Vandenburgh?'

'Yes?'

His eyes held hers and she knew, at once, that she had been wrong in supposing that Tom only took after the maternal side of his family.

'I'm sorry to surprise you like this,' he continued, 'but your door was open. As there was no reply, I guessed you could not be far away.'

When she did not answer, he sat down, diffidently, a little way away from her. Together, they stared across the water to the opposite meadow, where a mist was rising in thin wispy patches. She remembered how, when she had been a little girl, with May's dressmaking in mind, she had called it 'nun's veiling'.

'Why have you come, Benedict?' she said, at last. It seemed perfectly natural to use the name and he himself showed no surprise.

'I'm afraid I have . . . bad news.'

'Charlotte?'

'Yes.'

She waited. Presently, he said simply, 'She died, Mrs Vandenburgh. A month ago. In Bangkok.'

She had felt that this was what he had come to say, almost as soon as she saw him. Now that he had actually said it she found, incredibly, that her first overwhelming reaction was one of relief. Tom was safe. Her daughter was not coming back to claim him. This young man beside her had no legal right, however obvious it was that he was the child's father. Besides, would he want such a responsibility? Still a drifter. Penniless. She had nothing to fear. All the same, she was glad Tom was away.

'How . . . did it happen?' she asked, even though, once again, she could have foretold his answer.

'I thought she was only taking marijuana,' he replied, bitterly. 'I'd been trying to get her off it. I believed I was succeeding and that we'd come back to England. Make a fresh start. I realized we'd behaved abominably. We'd no right to ask your forgiveness, but . . . it seemed worth a try. On the night before . . . she died, she agreed, said she wanted to see Tom. Then, I suppose, I don't really know. I think she became scared, felt she couldn't face you. Deep down she was consumed by guilt.'

'She took an overdose?'

'Yes.'

'What of?'

'Heroin,' he replied, quietly.

The mist had thickened now. She shivered and stood up.

'The little boy,' he asked, also rising. 'Is he . . . ?'

'He is well, Benedict.'

'But not here?'

'Not at the moment.'

They began walking back to the house. 'I suppose,' he said, 'you would not wish me to see him?'

'No,' she answered. 'At least, not just now. I shall have to think. What would be best. For him. After all, that is the only thing which matters.'

'Yes. I thought you might say that. I quite understand. But . . . should you ever change your mind . . . perhaps could leave my address?'

'Have you one?'

For answer, he stopped and pulled out a small notebook from the pocket of his jeans, scrawled something on on of the pages, tore it out and handed it to her. 'It's m' father's home,' he said. 'I'm hoping for a reconciliation.'

She did not ask him to come into the Hermitage and h made no attempt to do so. Only after she had watched him disappearing into the lane, did she look at the piece of paper in her hand. It came as no surprise to read 'Kilochry Castle, Perthshire'. She realized she still had n idea of his surname.

25

'Is that Wilhampton 8549?'

'Yes.'

'One moment, please. I have a call for you from New York.'

Her spirits lifted. When Frank François came on the line she felt as if he was with her in person.

'Emily, dear. I've only just got your letter. I've been in San Francisco the last two weeks or I'd have been in touch sooner. I'm so desperately sorry about . . . your news. Are you all right?'

'Yes. I'm all right, Frank.'

'And Tom?'

'He's fine. He doesn't know, of course. One day . . . I'll have to think how best to tell him.'

'Yes. Look, Emily. I'm coming over. Quite soon. I've been uncertain whether to attend the Frankfurt Book Fair but your letter's clinched it. In any case, I would have had to come before Christmas for a rather important meeting in London. I'll see if I can get it put forward. Could I spend the weekend of October 11th at the Hermitage?'

'Oh, Frank! How marvellous. Of course. Will Elaine be with you?'

'No.' His voice suddenly seemed to go flat. 'I'll ring you as soon as I'm in England. Take care of yourself, my dear.'

'And you.'

She sat quite still after they had said goodbye, looking out on the leaf-strewn garden, thinking she must tidy it up, get the Hermitage all shipshape, as May used to say, before Frank's visit. It would be so *good* to see him again, especially in such surroundings. There would be so much to talk about. She had missed him since he went to New York, even though they had never seen a lot of each other before that. Somehow their respective marriages had precluded many meetings, other than the odd lunch if she happened to be in town. They had maintained contact mostly through correspondence, rather as they had done during the war years. Emily had always been acutely aware of the antipathy between Richard and Frank; but while she could not say that there was any such feeling between herself and Elaine, she sensed that the latter, who had remained childless, had little time for family life and that her husband's relations probably bored her. Emily also suspected that the fact Elaine had never had any children was deliberate on her part, for Frank so obviously adored them. He had once seemed on the point of saying something to Emily about it but had suddenly changed his mind at the last moment. She had respected this, loyalty to one's spouse being one of the countless things they had in common.

As the next few weeks went by, she found herself looking forward with increasing pleasure to her cousin's visit and, on the evening of October 11th, she felt an unaccustomed wave of excitement as she waited on Westonbury station in the fading daylight for the arrival of the London train. Ever since the war, meetings on this well-known platform had always greatly affected her emotions, even though it wasn't quite the same these days when there was no steam shooting upwards as the train came out of the tunnel and rounded the last bend. Nevertheless, she found her heart quickening quite ridiculously as the warning bell rang and she stood, eyes searching the slowing carriages as they slid by, wondering if Frank

would have altered much, whether he would find he
altered, too. Nervously, she put up a hand to the came
brooch at her throat which had once belonged to Grand
mother Sarah, then Katy and now handed down to her
She did not think she would have worn it a few years ago
Today, it somehow seemed perfectly appropriate. After al
I am a grandmother now, she kept reminding hersel:
though I'm still as thin as when I was twenty and I haven'
gone grey. At least, only a little. But I do sometimes fee
my age. I'm glad I had my hair done this morning. I expec
I ought to do that more often, not let myself get too boun(
up with my grandson and my work.

Happily, however, any fears as to her appearance wer
instantly allayed by Frank's first words.

'Emily! More beautiful than ever.' He put down th(
small grip he was carrying, caught her hands in his an(
kissed her firmly on both cheeks – a habit no doubt derive(
from his French mother. She felt as if the moment wa
suddenly out of context, that she was once again living fo
a little while in that world of no problems, similar to thos(
all too brief evenings which she and Frank had spent i
wartime, making a kind of private oasis for themselves
where they purposely did not mention the fighting bu
talked instead of all the things that mutually intereste(
them: books and plays, the countryside and what eacl
would ultimately like to do with their lives. She had alway
felt better for Frank's company, uncomplicated and easy
going. Because of a shared heredity and certain principle:
inculcated in their respective upbringings, there neve
seemed any need to explain anything. They automaticall)
took it for granted how the other would feel and react.

Now, as they waited to go through the ticket barrier.
Frank saved her from making any return comment on his
own somewhat changed appearance by saying, 'I'm afrai(
there's even more of me, Emily, than when we last met.
Publishers' lunches and launches are the very devil for
one's waistline.'

She laughed. 'But you . . . like America?'

'It was all right. At first. I'm glad to have had the experi-
ence. But I'm looking forward to coming back.'

'When will that be?'

'Hopefully, not long. A lot depends on the meeting in town next Monday.'

She noticed that he did not mention Elaine in this connection and she did not ask. She could still recall the curious flatness in his voice on the telephone, when he had said that she would not be coming with him on his present trip.

Tom was by no means in bed, let alone asleep, when they arrived back at the Hermitage. Dressed in pyjamas and dressing gown, he was on the landing peering through the banisters, shouting 'Great-uncle' as soon as they came through the door. The word had evidently appealed to him when Emily had first explained about their forth-coming visitor and he had been repeating it ever since. Now, he fairly bellowed it out as he hurled himself down the stairs and into Frank's outstretched arms.

'Hullo, Tom.' He lifted him high into the air and then, putting him down again, asked if he would like to unzip his case as there were two presents inside. 'The one wrapped in gold paper is for your grandmother, Tom. The one in red is for you.'

With an impressive show of good manners, Tom did as he was bidden, handing Emily her own present before asking if he might open his.

'How on earth did you know *just* what to get us both?' Emily asked, after thanks had been duly given for a mammoth bottle of Chanel Number 5 and a model of a combine harvester, together with a tractor and trailer which really tipped.

'Well, I seem to remember that was the scent which was always your favourite and was so difficult to get in the war. And I guessed that as Tom was now living in such close proximity to several farms, he was bound to have become interested in what sort of operations went on there.'

The child looked up from the hearth rug where he was now playing. 'Oh yes. That's right. When I grow up I'm going to be a big big farmer.'

'You mean you're going to have a big big farm,' said Emily.

'Or both, perhaps,' Frank broke in. 'Farmers are usually big fine fellows,' he continued, and they all laughed.

When Tom was at last in bed and she and Frank were sitting having a drink, he remarked, 'He's a marvellous kid. What are your plans for him, my dear?'

'I'm not sure. There's a very good preparatory school in Westonbury where I'd like him to go a bit later on. After that, well . . . I'll have to see. Rather optimistically, I've put him down for two public schools, Marlborough and Winchester, but . . . that may not work out.'

'You mean, financially?'

'Yes.'

'Emily, you do realize, don't you, that I'd be only too happy to help in that direction. Please let me.'

'Oh, Frank. Just like you to offer. I do appreciate it. Truly. But . . . I'd like to be as independent as possible. You see . . .'

She hadn't meant to say anything about her writing, at least not the first evening, but now it all came spilling out. 'I know it's a long shot, that authors never make much unless they hit the jackpot. You'll be sure to think me mad to imagine I could send Tom to boarding school on the little amount I'm likely to earn. But if I can't, well, he could still be a day-boy in Westonbury. Half of me says that's what I would really prefer, but I'm trying so hard not to be a doting grandmother, not to let him become tied to my apron strings. I want him to learn to stand on his own feet early in life. It's something which will be more important for him than for other boys.'

It was difficult to see the expression on Frank's face in the light of the fire and the one lamp now illuminating the room, but there was no mistaking the feeling in his voice when he said, 'Tell me more about *The Scarecrow of Sweetacres*. Where have you got to with it?'

'It's finished. I've sent it, with illustrations, to the agent I mentioned,' she replied, quietly.

'You've *what*?'

'I've sent everything to my agent,' she repeated.

'Oh, Emily. When you could have come direct to us. I explained that I once asked you to do a children's book. Clare Carpenter's no longer in charge of our juvenile department but, thanks to her, that side of the business got off to a good start and it's now doing splendidly under Clare's successor, a Mrs Miller. I suppose that independent streak of yours got the better of you.'

She smiled. 'Something like that. Although I daresay I could have just submitted it to your firm without saying anything. I write under the name of Emily Mason, incidentally. But this agent has been so good about placing the short stories. I value her opinion and I thought I'd like to see what she had to say about *The Scarecrow*. I'm very keen for my work to stand or fall on its own merits. Doing it any other way seems to me to smack of . . . well, nepotism.'

'In spite of your wanting so much to earn money for Tom?'

'In spite of my wanting to earn money for Tom,' she repeated. She wondered whether to go ahead and tell him the rest of the saga and decided that she would have to. 'The irony of it is,' she continued, 'that my agent wrote a little while ago to say that your Mrs Miller was the first person she was going to approach.'

'So the manuscript and drawings are actually with us now?'

'Yes, but . . .'

'All right. I know what you're going to say. I won't. Although sometimes, my dear, you do make it awfully difficult for your nearest and dearest.'

She thought about those words after Frank had gone back to London on the Sunday night. She supposed they were only too true. So many people of late had offered help of one sort or another, yet some obstinate streak in her had made her refuse every time. There was Mr Bellamy, for instance, not that she could exactly class him amongst her nearest and dearest. Then there was Joanna. And she had been well aware that both Frank and Paul Woodley would have been delighted to have given her every assistance in connection with writing. I don't know why, she said to herself as she lay in bed that night, I have to go it alone. It's just something which seems to have come to the fore since leaving Hensford. There's a part of me that I'm only just beginning to find out about.

The letter came on Monday morning, just as she was about to take Tom to nursery school. 'Dear Ms Mason,' it ran, 'I am pleased to tell you I have now heard from Mrs Miller and enclose a copy of her letter . . .'

She turned quickly to the photostat:

> I found *The Scarecrow of Sweetacres* a most unusual and appealing book. The illustrations are enchanting. I have no hesitation in saying we should like to publish it. It seems to me it is crying out for a sequel. As to terms . . .

Her eyes blurred. There would be just time to let Frank know before he returned to the States.

26

When Tom Vandenburgh was six and a half, Emily Mason – her maiden name by which she was becoming increasingly well-known – had three illustrated children's books to her credit: *The Scarecrow of Sweetacres*, *The Scarecrow's Secret* and *School for Scarecrows*. Their success surprised not only Emily herself but her agent and publishers as well. The stories were soon to be adapted for television. There were models of scarecrows in the toy shops and negotiations with a clothing manufacturer were taking place as to the possibility of using scarecrows as decoration on juvenile tee-shirts.

Every penny Emily had earned from her efforts had gone into what she called the 'Tom' fund and, one sunny April afternoon while she was sitting by the Willon reflecting on the extraordinary twist her life had taken, she wondered whether she could now afford to branch out in another direction. Although immensely cheered and grateful for her unexpected good fortune, she had to admit to herself that she was becoming just a little tired of scarecrows.

She was well aware that her agent would not approve

her idea any more than Mrs Miller. She knew that they
~~lly~~ expected her to go on in the same genre. During
~~cent~~ meetings they had even made tentative suggestions
~~to~~ future scarecrow titles. Emily was their goose who
~~l~~id the golden eggs. The one person she knew who would
~~u~~nderstand how she felt was Frank but, although he was
~~w~~ back in England, she hesitated about bothering him. It
~~as~~ not because he was now chairman of his firm, for she
~~new~~ only too well that, however busy, he would always
~~t~~ake time to see her. It was because she happened to
~~now~~ he had personal problems of a very distressing kind.

His usual reserve on such matters had broken some
~~m~~onths previously when he had been giving her lunch in
~~L~~ondon. Ever since he had returned from America he had
~~b~~een singularly reticent on the subject of his wife,
~~c~~onfirming what Emily had long suspected: that there was
~~s~~omething seriously wrong with their marriage. She knew
~~th~~at they had bought a house in Hampstead but she had
~~n~~ever been invited there, for which he had apologized more
~~th~~an once. 'Elaine,' he had said on one occasion, 'has not
~~b~~een too good lately,' and on yet another, 'I'm afraid
~~E~~laine's finding life back here a bit trying after the States.'
~~It~~ had never occurred to Emily that these were anything
~~o~~ther than perfunctory excuses and that Elaine was, in
~~f~~act, actually ill.

Things had come to a head at the end of the meal at
~~th~~e Connaught that day when she had asked, somewhat
~~d~~iffidently, whether he and Elaine or he by himself might
~~c~~are to spend a weekend at the Hermitage. She could recall
~~th~~e despairing look which had crossed his face as he had
~~r~~eplied, 'I'm sorry, my dear. I'm afraid it's impossible. I'd
~~l~~ove to come alone if I could but . . . well, I can't leave
~~E~~laine at weekends. She's sick.'

Even then, Emily had not been prepared for his appalling
~~r~~evelations. Once started, it seemed as if Frank could not
~~s~~top. He explained that Elaine was a confirmed alcoholic,
~~th~~e trouble having started not long after they had arrived
~~i~~n New York. 'I blame myself,' he had said, typically. 'I
~~w~~as so busy in the beginning, working late at the office.
~~S~~he was bored and lonely. There was this guy – one of

our authors, actually – who was a pretty good rotter . .
Emily remembered how Frank had seemed almost to bra
himself before continuing with a rush, 'He took h
around. They had an affair, naturally. Then he pushed o
back to Florida. But she'd got a taste for the bright spo
by then. And, unfortunately, highballs. God, they mal
them strong out there . . .' He had gone on to descrit
how Elaine had kept vowing she would stop, how he ha
trusted her and had then come home unexpectedly ear
one day to find she had passed out on the bedroom floc
of their apartment, a bottle of Scotch and a broken gla:
beside her. He was unable to persuade her to jo
Alcoholics Anonymous. In the end she was constantly i
and out of clinics from which she invariably discharge
herself. During the interim periods he was forced to engag
private nurses who usually left after a few weeks.

'And now?' Emily had asked. 'Now,' Frank had replie
grimly, 'she's pretty far gone most of the time. I look afte
her at weekends and I've managed to get hold of a retire
Sister, a saint, who stays with her during the week.'

Ever since that conversation, the thought of Frank an
his wife had never been far from Emily's mind. Elaine ha
always been so smart, so soignée. She could remember he
at the twins' christening. Whatever did she look like now
What kind of torment did she and Frank go through eacl
weekend? How was he able to hold down such a
important job? What made someone like Elaine, once s
very much in command of herself, turn to drink? The
said alcoholism was a disease, that people couldn't hel
it. Or could they?

Sitting now by this sunlit river, waiting for Tom to b
brought back from school in Westonbury by Helen, who
had suggested undertaking the task as she would be shop
ping in the town that afternoon and afterwards virtuall
passing the Hermitage door, Emily felt how lucky she was
There had been times when it would have been so easy t
start fortifying herself with alcohol: when she had firs
found out about Richard, for instance; when Charlotte':
health had given her so many sleepless nights; when littl
Mark had died; when she had been quite alone in Londor

fter leaving Hensford; when Charlotte had descended on
er, unmarried and pregnant; later still, when Charlotte
ad disappeared. What exactly had saved her? All at once,
came to Emily that it had always been the thought of
he younger generation, their needs, those of her children
nd then her grandchild, however badly she might have
ailed them. Elaine had never had any children. For all
mily knew, she had possibly misjudged her cousin's wife
n thinking that she had never wanted any. That was
omething she might never know. Poor Elaine. Poor Frank.
he wished there was something positive she could do to
elp them both.

In the distance, she could hear the sound of a car coming
lown the lane. She rose and walked back to the house in
ime to hear Tom's piping voice saying, as he came through
he front gate, 'You must stop for tea, Aunt Helen. Elly
aid she would buy indigestibles.'

'And I did,' Emily assured him, while greeting them both
nd smiling at the well-known description of the kind of
:akes which Wilhampton bakers seemed to have produced
rom time immemorial.

'And me topping ten stone,' remarked Helen, cheerfully,
ifter agreeing to stay.

It was into this settled straightforward way of life that
he letter from Scotland arrived the following day, sending
ill thoughts of Elaine, Frank and her own writing out of
Emily's head. She had often wondered whether she would
:ver hear from Benedict again. Having met him, she had
lecided that he would not constitute a threat. She had
actually felt sorry for him after saying goodbye and wished
that she had behaved in a more kind-hearted fashion. She
had more or less told him to keep away. But she had never
got in touch with him and, as time passed, she imagined
that their lives would never cross again, that the fact he
had fathered an illegitimate son at a very young age would
become, for him, simply a memory pushed further and
further to the back of consciousness. All the same, he had
taken the trouble to give her his address. He was possibly
not quite the callous irresponsible youth she had once
supposed him to be and when she had realized that she

did not know his surname she had made it her business
if only for interest's sake, to find out who was the owner
of Kilochry Castle, Perthshire.

She was surprised to find that the letter which had now
arrived was not from Benedict after all, but from his father
Sir Duncan Rawlinson. It appeared that the latter would
be in the Westonbury area at the beginning of May and
wondered if he might call on her. It was a courteous, old-
fashioned, rather formal missive, written, she suspected
after a great deal of deliberation, not because the writer
was not in command of perfect English but because of the
delicacy of the request. She noted in particular such
phrases as, 'You may well consider I am intruding on your
privacy' and 'I fully appreciate that you might find my
suggestion unacceptable, even distasteful'; and then the
final words, 'I do not know, of course, whether you still
reside at Netherford but trust, if not, that this will be
forwarded and I might be favoured with a reply . . .'

There was no positive reference to Benedict or Tom, but
Emily could not help thinking that it was not entirely
accidental that Sir Duncan had asked to come on a
Saturday. He must surely have reckoned that he might
then have a better chance of seeing his illegitimate
grandson than during the week when Tom would more
than likely be at school. Although why he should wish to
do so at this particular juncture, she had no idea.

For forty-eight hours she turned the question over and
over in her mind. Once or twice she considered talking to
Helen about it. Certainly, if she did decide to see Benedict's
father, she would let both her and Joanna know. Apart
from all else, Jo was Tom's official guardian. But some-
thing made her hold back until she had made up her own
mind. She was well aware that one of the reasons for
wanting to meet the boy's grandfather was that, quite
frankly, she was *curious*. And, however strange their
relationship, Sir Duncan was of her own generation and
they had a vital link in common. It was obvious from his
letter that he was, to put it bluntly, a gentleman. He could
not harm Tom by seeing him. He had no claim on the
boy. But there was something else, she realized, which,

although irrational – even deplorable – kept urging her towards a meeting. It was a fierce motherly – or, rather, grandmotherly – pride. She wanted to show him the child she had brought up single-handed and was eventually proposing to send to public school with the help of her ever-increasing 'Tom' fund.

Next day, as she picked up her pen to write to Kilochry Castle, she prayed she would not be punished for indulging in one of the seven deadly sins.

27

He was one of the old school all right – impeccably dressed, manners faultless. Yet, for all that, soon after they met she suspected his son might possibly have the greater insight, the more sensitivity. She watched him: a tall lean figure sitting upright on the garden seat – he had declined a deck chair – his features distinctly patrician beneath a head of fine white hair.

'It is good of you to have allowed me to come,' he began, slowly, once she had sent Tom off for a short walk with Gilly Parker, who still came to help on occasions. 'You must have wondered what prompted me to write.'

She nodded, a little uncertain what line to take, her natural courtesy making her enquire 'Benedict?' In an effort to help him.

'Benedict married a year ago,' he answered.

'I hope he is happy . . . settled?'

'Yes and no.' Her visitor's voice became more clipped now. 'He is running the estate extremely well. Has been for some time. Turned over a new leaf. All that youthful rebellion . . . a thing of the past. And my daughter-in-law Melanie, a charming girl. Charming. It was a great releif to me suddenly to find all the domestic cares of Kilochry taken off my hands again in such a capable fashion, just as they were in my dear late wife's time.'

She felt he might not have extolled his daughter-in-law's virtues quite so much, considering the circumstances. She waited for him to continue.

'But . . . we have had a tragedy. A great tragedy. Last winter Melanie was breaking in a young thoroughbred. She comes from a riding family. Superb horsewoman. Unfortunately . . . she was thrown. She's paralysed from the waist down. A wheelchair for the rest of her life.'

Even as Emily murmured her condolences, she could foretell his next words more or less exactly.

'There will be no question of children.'

'Yes. I see.'

I see only too well, she thought. She felt a surge of pure anger. Her colour mounted. So – they wanted Tom after all, did they? She remembered how keenly Sir Duncan Rawlinson had looked at the boy on arrival, sizing him up, as it were. She wanted to shout: How dare you? No communication all this time but now, when it suits you, you want to see what kind of a child your only son fathered out of wedlock. You're dynastic, blinkered, obsessed with heredity, just like my former husband and the parents of my one-time fiancé. Do you really think you could uproot a child of six and a half and spirit him away to some remote castle in Scotland to satisfy your desire for an heir?

'I know what you're thinking,' he went on, and she became calmer, feeling that perhaps she had misjudged him, that her love for Tom had frightened her into jumping to irrational conclusions. 'Please let me explain,' she heard him continue. 'My visit here today is entirely due to my daughter-in-law. It was she who suggested it. As I said, she is a charming girl, a very remarkable one in every way. Benedict told her about the child before they were married.'

'She . . . they . . . could adopt a baby, couldn't they,' she replied, defensively, without any of her usual compassion.

'Yes. I realize that, except none of us feels . . . well, flesh and blood, you understand . . . and Tom having no mother. For all we knew, you yourself might have been . . .'

'Dead?' she hazarded, amazed at the hardness which had crept into her voice.

'Well, yes. Or, at any rate, unable to cope. As one gets older . . . I mean, the child might have had to be sent to a less favourable environment. But I can see how well you have managed. I hope . . .' and here he paused, embarrassed, 'that it has not been too difficult in any way.'

She could only suppose what he really meant was 'financially', but was unable to bring the word out.

'No,' she answered, coldly. 'There have been no difficulties.' She did not mention how her writing had helped.

'He is a delightful little boy. Delightful. He does you great credit. I can see how fond you are of him and he of you. You must believe me. Having seen you both in this charming home I have no wish to disturb the . . . er . . . status quo.'

'Thank you,' she said and they fell silent. In the opposite meadow the Sweetacres herd was returning from its afternoon milking. She saw him watching it in an abstracted way, as if there was something else he wished to say but did not quite know how to broach the matter. Presently he turned and looked at her out of very direct blue eyes. It was only momentary, but she had an impression that she could see both Benedict and Tom in them – and even more. There was admiration, not simply for the way she had brought up her grandchild, but because she was still an attractive woman.

'I suppose,' he said, at length, 'that you will consider this an extraordinary suggestion, but I was wondering whether you would care to bring Tom to Kilochry for a holiday.'

She stared back at him, astonished.

'I know it is a most unusual situation, but the longer I live,' he went on, 'I find that no family seems to escape . . . irregularities. Should you come to Scotland it would give me the greatest pleasure. I promise you that there would be no strings attached.'

She became flustered, out of her depth. 'Tom,' she said, at last, recalling how she had once made the same kind of remark to Benedict, 'I hardly think it would be wise.'

'Does he know anything about his parentage?'

'I have explained to him that his mother has died. As he could not remember her, I'm glad to say he took it quite philosophically. Of course, death, for a child of his age, does not have the same meaning – the grief, the finality.'

'I am very sorry,' he said, quietly, 'about your daughter. It must have been terrible for you.'

She did not answer for a while. Then she replied, 'It was not altogether the shock it might have been. I think I knew ... all along ... that it was inevitable. Charlotte was not a happy person. She was looking for something which I feel she may never have found. It was probably my fault. Something to do with her upbringing. I like to think I have done better with Tom.'

'You must not be too hard on yourself. Have you never thought about inherited tendencies?'

'Oh yes. Often. One never quite knows. I just feel grateful to have been given a second chance at looking after, at *loving* the younger generation.'

'What have you said to Tom about his father?'

'He has only asked about him once. I explained that as he travelled quite a lot and had no wife to help him, he had left Tom with me to look after. This seemed to satisfy the child. At least, he has never mentioned the subject again.'

'Until he does, there would be no point in saying anything else at this stage. If you accepted my invitation, I envisage no difficulties. He could simply call my son by his Christian name. I notice many young children address their elders in that way nowadays.'

'It is kind of you,' she answered. 'But I shall have to think.'

'Of course.'

She left him alone while she went indoors to put the kettle on and she did not go back to the garden until she began wheeling out the tea trolley, by which time Tom had returned from his walk and was sitting on the grass in earnest conversation with his grandfather. As she approached the two of them she could hear the child saying, 'When I grow up I am going to be a big big farmer,' to which Duncan Rawlinson replied, gravely, 'That seems to me like a splendid idea.'

She was aware that the car which had come to collect

their visitor was waiting in the lane a long while before he actually stood up to go. It was as if he was loath to leave them. She sensed he was a lonely man, that the loss of his wife followed by his daughter-in-law's tragic accident and the realization that Kilochry might fall into strangers' hands had affected him profoundly.

'This afternoon has been one of the most pleasant I can remember for a very long time,' he said, as he finally took her hand. 'It would be nice to feel we might meet again before long, whether you decide to come to Scotland or not.'

28

You're being too possessive, she kept saying to herself over the next few weeks. You've known it for some time. In a few years you'll be sixty. Supposing something happened to you.

But then there would be Joanna, another voice answered. Tom would be well taken care of. Don't be so fearful. Why not take him to Kilochry? Think how thrilled he would be to stay in a *castle*. And you yourself haven't had a holiday in years, even if you've allowed him to go and stay with Jo and her family. Duncan Rawlinson said there would be no strings attached and I'm sure he's a man of his word, although I can't help remembering the way he looked at me once or twice. But that's not the problem. I'm through with the man–woman thing now. It's funny how impervious I've become to the opposite sex. At least, perhaps that isn't quite the right word. I still like men, but only in the same way as I like women. I certainly don't want to marry again. I simply want to bring up Tom. There wouldn't be the time for a man as well. It's as if I've reached another plateau, a much more tranquil one. I can't help looking back in amazement at what seems like another existence, in which sex at various times played such an important part. No, it's not Duncan Rawlinson who's the stumbling block but once his young people clap eyes on Tom, they couldn't help being captivated.

Everyone is. I'm not being silly about this. I've heard it from all sides. Supposing they put on the pressure.

In an agony of doubts, Emily felt unable to do any writing, even if it had been clear in her mind what she was going to write. She spent the summer days gardening furiously, carefully avoiding going anywhere near her small workroom. The only time she was able to relax a little was when Tom was back from school, or during the weekends when she would take him for expeditions into the surrounding countryside.

It was on one such occasion that they called in at Ladywell on the way home. Although Emily, by herself, had made the decision to see Duncan Rawlinson in the first place, it was inevitable that she had discussed his visit afterwards with her oldest friend and had told Helen of his invitation. Now, while Tom played at the far end of the lawn with one of Tim's grandchildren, who had been parked at Ladywell for the afternoon, the question naturally arose again.

'You know, Em,' Helen said, after a while, 'I think you *should* go. It's not as if they're people who are ever likely to snatch Tom and do a bunk with him. And if the child got used to seeing a bit of his father at this age, wouldn't it be a good thing? Not come as such a shock later on? God knows, it won't be easy to explain when the time comes, but if Benedict and Tom have already formed a good relationship, he won't feel he had ever been abandoned, as it were. Besides, in a way, he wasn't. I mean, Benedict obviously wanted to keep in touch when he first came back from India.'

'Oh, I know. I never gave him a chance.'

'And even if Melanie and he do adopt a baby, there's no reason why Tom shouldn't see a bit of them as he grows up.'

'No, I suppose not.'

They set out for Scotland in the first week of September, Tom wild with excitement at the thought of sleeping on an overnight train. The sheer pleasure which the journey alone gave him suddenly seemed to make the whole enterprise not only inevitable, but extremely worth while.

Even though it was only 6 a.m., Duncan Rawlinson himself met them with a chauffeur at Perth and, having ascertained that they had had some light refreshment before arriving, he suggested, as long as Tom could wait, that they breakfasted at Kilochry. Emily had never been quite so far north and the scenery in the early morning sunlight, particularly at this time of the year when the trees were beginning to turn red and gold, had the effect of making her fall silent while Tom produced a constant stream of questions addressed to his host. 'Sir Duncan, what are those cattle called?' 'Will I see a deer?' 'What happens on the other side of that mountain?' 'Is that snow?' 'Does your castle have turrets?' – to all of which he received grave and courteous answers, occasionally enhanced by additional gratuitous information such as, 'In this part of the world we have a bird called a grouse. Over there is a grouse moor. We will take you over one while you are here.'

As they neared their destination, Duncan Rawlinson said, 'Look Tom. You were asking about turrets. Can you see one just above those trees? That's Kilochry Castle.' And the boy himself now fell silent, his eyes full of wonderment.

Melanie was waiting to welcome them in the hall, a beautiful dark-haired girl, her own eyes now lighting up as they came towards her. Emily had warned Tom that their hostess was unable to walk and could only move about in a wheelchair and he shook hands quite naturally, without a trace of awkwardness or embarrassment.

'Breakfast is all ready,' she said. 'Perhaps you would both just like to see your rooms and then come along down. Benedict has had to go to Aberfeldy today, but he will be back by tea time. He is so looking forward to seeing you.'

Emily imagined that it had been pre-arranged they should meet him alone. In spite of Tom's protests, she made him lie down after lunch and he quickly fell asleep for the rest of the afternoon. When they descended the wide oak staircase they saw Benedict sitting in the hall by the huge fireplace, where a fire had already been lit. He got up as soon as he heard them and came across to stand at the bottom. Through the high windows a shaft of evening sunlight fell on his upturned face. It was no longer the face of the boy whom Emily remembered. It was older, careworn, but infinitely kind. The resemblance to Tom was unmistakable.

'I hope,' he said, as the child jumped the last few stairs and he caught him in his arms, 'that you are both going to enjoy staying here. There isn't a lot to do but, if Tom likes farms, there's quite a few of those to see. In fact, tomorrow there's three on my list. I don't know if that would interest you, Mrs Vandenburgh. The roads are not all that good. You might prefer to stay at home.'

'I'm in your hands,' Emily replied. 'I'm sure I'll be happy doing either.'

And she was. Some days, Tom went off early with Benedict for the whole day. Sometimes she accompanied them but, on others, she remained at Kilochry, getting to know Melanie, pushing her out on short walks, taking others by herself or in the company of Duncan Rawlinson.

She found his daughter-in-law, as he had said, a charming and remarkable girl, especially for one so young who had suffered such an affliction. The entire lack of bitterness or self-pity amazed Emily. And Melanie's interest and delight in Tom was so obviously genuine. 'I've always adored children,' she said, simply, at one point. 'The more the merrier, of whatever creed, nationality or circumstances. Before my marriage I worked for a kids' home in the East End of London. Of course, occasionally I couldn't help feeling a bit of a hypocrite, helping the under-privileged all week and then going home to spend the weekends riding and hunting in Cheshire.'

'Cheshire?' Emily asked. 'I used to live there.'

'Really? Did you know the Bartholomews, by any chance?'

'Of course. Harry was a godparent of Tom's mother. But we've been out of touch for some time now.'

'Harry died, I believe,' replied Melanie. 'It all seems such a long time ago. Life before my accident,' she added, by way of explanation.

It was the first time she had referred to that in such a

direct fashion and Emily took the opportunity of saying, quickly, 'I am so *sorry*, my dear. I admire the way you have taken it more than I can say. Especially as it has deprived you of the one thing you wanted so desperately.'

'You mustn't feel sad. I have Benedict, his father and now a splendid new friendship which I hope I have established with you and Tom.' Emily felt that at the age of twenty-two this paralysed girl in a wheelchair had attained a wisdom, a maturity, which she herself might never achieve. 'The future is always so unpredictable for everyone,' Melanie went on. 'I try to count my blessings each day. Your coming to Kilochry has most certainly been a very special one.'

Towards the end of their stay, Duncan Rawlinson said the same kind of thing on one of the walks they took together. 'I can't tell you how much your visit has meant . . . to us all.'

'And to us,' she answered. 'Tom has been in his element. I'm afraid he's going to find the Hermitage rather dull when we get back.'

'Perhaps you would care to make it a more frequent event. You would always be so welcome. I had no idea that you were such a countrywoman, that your former husband had an estate in Cheshire. It has been the greatest pleasure getting to know you, hearing about your writing and talking about other matters which are so . . . dear to my heart. I was wondering . . .' He paused. They were standing looking westwards towards the mountains. In the distance a Land-Rover came into view along one of the narrow roads. Tom and Benedict returning. She had an intense feeling of *déjà vu*, that she and her grandson had both been here before. Duncan Rawlinson's next words came as no surprise.

'I shall be coming to London in a month or so's time for several meetings. I'll be staying at my club, the Athenaeum. Would you, by any chance, be able to dine with me in the Ladies' Annexe one evening? I imagine you'll have to come to town sometime to visit those publishers and the agent you told me about.'

'I . . . well, yes. I shall have to see them before too long.

Thank you very much for the invitation. Could I perhaps think about it and let you know?'

'Of course. I was envisaging the middle of October, but I could always alter anything to suit you.'

They began walking back to the castle. The Land-Rover had disappeared into the valley and the light was beginning to fade. As they neared the forecourt, Duncan suddenly stopped and laid a hand on her arm.

'I meant to wait until I next saw you,' he said, diffidently, 'but I'm afraid I can't. I promised you that by coming here there would be no strings attached and I want to stick to that promise. I don't want you to say anything now. It's just that while you are thinking about what I've suggested, might you be able to think about something else. Would you do me the great honour of becoming my wife?'

29

'Have some more chocolate mousse, Em. With your figure, you don't have to worry.'

Frank was giving her lunch in the smart new dining room which his firm had just installed at the top of the building. A girl had come in to cook and wait on them, but she had now disappeared into the small kitchen to make some coffee. She was doing the kind of job, Emily realized, that her own daughter had started off doing – before the rebellious stage, as Duncan Rawlinson called it, when she had gone off to live with Benedict in a commune in Wales. 'In a way, you and I were luckier,' she recollected Duncan having said. 'We had Hitler to fight rather than our parents and the Establishment. By the time the war was over, we'd cut our eye teeth and grown up enough not to need to prove to them and ourselves how well we could cope.'

She took another spoonful of pudding and switched her mind back to Frank and the subject which they had been discussing throughout most of the meal. 'Mrs Miller is worried, Em,' he was saying. 'She wants more scarecrows, as I told you. She said your agent knew you had other ideas in mind but she wasn't sure what.'

'Yes. She's right. As a matter of fact, I nearly got in touch with you about it some time ago, only I didn't want to bother you.'

'Wicked of you, Em. You know you'd never be a bother to me.'

She smiled. 'Yes, well . . . I dare say I would have got around to coming to see you before, only . . . other things intervened.'

'You mean your and Tom's holiday in Scotland?'

'Yes.' She had told Frank on the telephone that they were going and he had been cautiously non-committal.

'Did you enjoy it?' he now enquired.

'Yes.' This time it was she who became guarded. 'And, of course, Tom adored every minute of it.'

'Will you be going again, do you think?'

'Some time, yes.' She looked away. The girl came back with the coffee and put it on a low table at the far end of the room.

Frank stood up. 'I suppose,' he said, as they went across and sat down in two easy chairs, 'that Tom's more keen than ever on becoming a big big farmer now.'

'Yes.' Again, she remained uncharacteristically reserved.

'What is it, Em?' he asked quietly.

There seemed no point in procrastinating any longer. 'I had dinner with Benedict's father last night, Frank. He wants to marry me.'

She saw him put down his coffee cup with great care. A look of something like pain came over his face. 'And are you going to?' he asked.

'No, Frank. I'm not going to marry anybody any more.'

His relief was obvious, despite his next remark, 'You said that thirty-two years ago, my love. August 6th, 1945. Twenty past midnight. By the banks of the Willon. Remember?'

'I remember, Frank.' The term of endearment did not escape her.

'I realize,' he continued, 'it would have been . . . well, neat. You'd have still had Tom. Tom would have had

Kilochry. Both your futures assured. Many women would have jumped at the chance. But, of course, you've never been "many women". Don't answer this if you don't want to. Perhaps I shouldn't ask, but why didn't you accept the proposal?'

'It would have been like selling my soul.'

'Even if it were for Tom's sake?'

'Yes. Even if it were for Tom's sake. I have no feelings for Duncan Rawlinson other than ordinary liking. I don't love the man.'

'Dear Em. Always the romantic. At our age love doesn't necessarily come into it. People marry for all sorts of other reasons. Companionship, usually.'

'I expect so. But I've learnt to live alone now, that is, except for Tom.'

'Have you thought what it will be like when he goes to boarding school?'

'There will be my writing.'

'Will that be enough?'

'I think so, Frank. To get back to what you were saying during lunch. I want to write a play. I've always wanted to write a play.'

He poured out some more coffee for them both. 'It's quite a tall order, Em. Difficult, unless one is very lucky. I'm not saying for a moment that you mightn't pull it off. You're damn good at writing dialogue. But there are so many hazards and disappointments lurking along the way, even if a management company does buy it. You know, actors' and producers' quarrels, strikes, even the weather, once a play's actually put on. A hot summer and people stay in the parks. But I suppose I oughtn't to deter you. It's just that . . . you've been doing so well. You realize, don't you, that you've become one of the foremost writers for children in the country.'

'Others have been known to write for grown-ups as well.'

'Yes, I know. Dodie Smith, for example.'

Her mind went back to her childhood. When had it been? 1933? '34? Her mother and May had taken her to see *Autumn Crocus* while they had all been on holiday in

Bournemouth. Was it that which had prompted the idea, one that had lain dormant all these years?

She heard Frank continue, 'You know, my dear, I believe your mind's made up, really. You've probably got to do it. Get it out of your system. Can I ask what it's to be about?'

She coloured. 'Love. Sounds pretty trite, I suppose. But I'm thinking about all the different kinds of love, particularly between the generations. It's something which has always interested me.'

'And no one can say you haven't had quite a bit of experience over that, one way and another. I wish you all the luck in the world, Em. I'll look forward to an invitation to the first night. But don't forget all of us here completely, will you? It would be nice to have the name of Emily Mason still featuring in our lists from time to time. Who knows, you might even write a novel for us one day.'

Just before leaving, she said, tentatively, 'Elaine? Is there any change?'

He sighed. 'No. Things are pretty much the same, I'm afraid. I wish I could ask you to Hampstead. But it's difficult. I don't want to upset her. She seems to think any visitor would only come to spy on her.'

'I'm so desperately sorry. Please don't apologize. I understand. I just wish there was something I could do to help.'

'There's nothing much anyone can do, Em.'

'But it doesn't seem right that you should have to shoulder all the burden.'

'There's Sister Hayward, don't forget.'

'But doesn't she ever go on holiday? What happens then?'

'So far, the miracle is that she's the kind of person who doesn't seem to like them. I suppose if she did have to go away for any reason, it would mean a clinic again for Elaine. I've heard there's a very good one near Woking.'

'Woking? It's not called Charlton House is it, by any chance?'

'Yes.'

'That's where I was sent in the war when I had that breakdown. It was run by a man called Schmidt who took care of nervous wrecks. I suppose it now caters for . . . people like Elaine,' she ended, not liking to use the word 'alcoholics'.

He nodded. 'Of course, I do have another alternative in sight. I'm pushing sixty, Em. I've been thinking about retirement.'

'Oh *Frank*. But you couldn't . . . just stay at home all the time looking after Elaine.'

'No. P'raps not. I'm no saint. I must admit it's a hell of a relief to get out of the house during the week.'

She left him, more distressed than she could remember having been for a long time. Her dinner with Duncan Rawlinson had, in comparison, been far less painful, however much she had initially dreaded it. But afterwards there had been none of the depression which now engulfed her on her journey home. Duncan had taken her refusal well. Though obviously saddened, he had said that her answer did not surprise him. Having got to know her for only a short time, he realized that she was not a woman who would ever marry for expediency's sake and that beneath her air of vulnerability there was a strong streak of independence. In fact, it had been this combination which he had found so irresistible right from the beginning. 'Along,' he had added, rather charmingly, 'with a great many other things. You are very beautiful, Emily,' he had continued as they sat in the almost empty annexe after dinner. 'You must have broken many hearts. In the war, when you were nursing, I can't imagine how you managed to remain single. Was there no one, other than the fiancé who was a prisoner all those years?' And she had replied, 'Yes, there was someone. An American.' She had looked away then and he had not asked anything else of her other than, while wishing her goodnight at the door of the ex-nurses' club in Kensington of which she had become a member, he had said, 'You will still bring Tom to Kilochry, won't you, Emily? And perhaps dine with me from time to time in London. Having come into my life so swiftly and naturally, I really don't think I could bear it if you went out of it again in the same way.' To which she had answered, 'Thank you, Duncan. Of course.' And he had taken her hand, raised it to his lips and kissed it.

Could that possibly have been less than twenty-four hours ago, she wondered, as the train went into the long tunnel before reaching Westonbury. Only when she saw the small figure of Tom standing on the platform with Gilly, who had fetched him from school and given him tea in the town, did her spirits lift. She opened her arms as he ran towards her and then, bending down to kiss him, she said, 'I managed to get to Hamley's toy shop, Tom. I found what I think you wanted. Anyway, it's an animal that looks as near to an Aberdeen Angus bull as you're ever likely to get.'

30

By the end of the following year, Melanie and Benedict had adopted a three-year-old girl called Shirley. Six months later they decided she needed a sister and Alison, aged two and a half, joined the Rawlinson household. Both children had been abandoned by their parents and came from the same home in the East End where Melanie had worked before her marriage.

Duncan could have wished it otherwise. It was not that he altogether objected to the adoptions, particularly as they were girls and would not interfere with the plans he proposed making – with an ever-increasing certainty as to their rightness – for the future of Kilochry. It was simply that he would have liked the children to have been babies, preferably orphans, whose parentage was known and who had not already picked up a cockney accent and questionable manners. But witnessing the astonishing improvement which took place in the children within a relatively short time under Melanie's loving care and guidance, and the obvious joy that it gave her to be an adoptive mother, he became, firstly, reconciled and then glad on her account.

The young couple had not adopted babies for several reasons, not the least being the fact that Melanie's disability would have precluded her from doing much in connection with the handling of a small baby and a trained nanny would have had to be installed. Feeling about children as she did, Melanie had always reckoned on looking after a baby herself. She did not think she could bear to see any infant of hers in the hands of some stranger, whose methods and ideas might not be compatible with her own. By adopting Shirley and Alison, she felt she would not only be helping two deprived children, but she would be able to manage with the services of two young sisters from the village who would be willing to care for them in the way she wanted.

Tom had by now got to know the little girls well, for he had spent several holidays at Kilochry although, at the advanced age of nine and with his passion for farming, he much preferred being taken about by Benedict to wasting any of his precious time within the confines of the castle. It seemed to Emily that he could hardly wait to get up to Scotland whenever there was a chance and when, a year later, the spring holidays came round again and she explained that, as the play she had written was to be put on in London that April, she would prefer to remain at home, his disappointment was so great that she had felt forced to compromise. Because he was still too young to be taken to see it and because they had already travelled north together once or twice by air, she agreed to letting him fly alone in the company of a stewardess. 'Although some time during the summer,' she said, 'you really will have to spend a few days with Aunt Jo and her family. You mustn't neglect old friends.'

As Emily saw him off at Heathrow, she had a strong feeling that it was but the first of many such partings, that from now on Tom would gradually be moving away from her and, although they would always remain close, the time spent in each other's company would become less and less, their lives following predetermined and totally different directions. She tried not to feel sad. After all, she knew she had much to look forward to.

The play which she had outlined to Frank some time previously had inadvertently not turned out quite as she had intended. Her agent had sold it all right, but not to a theatre company but for television. Initially, Emily had been disappointed. Visions of a London first night receded before the far less exciting business of switching on her TV at the appropriate time in the sole company of Helen and Colin. But, after reading the subsequent notices, her spirits rose. She realized she had been extremely well paid. *The Love Line*, as she had called it, had been shown at peak viewing time and watched by millions. Believing in playing her luck, she had immediately sat down and written a shorter play, *The Stalking-Horse*, which was also favourably received. The name *Emily Mason* was becoming known, not merely as the author of children's books.

But the ambition to write a stage play lingered on and the idea for it came to her one night while travelling south on a sleeper from Scotland. Emily had often marvelled at the way such ideas seemed to drop into her head, quite unexpectedly, out of nowhere, as if she was simply some cipher who put them on to paper for presentation in one form or another for the benefit of a wider audience. She recalled how someone at a literary party had once told her that he reckoned most creative work was all ready and waiting for the right person either to reach out and claim it or itself insisting on entering into the mind of whomsoever it happened to choose. This did not mean that writers or artists or musicians did not work extremely hard at transmogrification. It was simply that originally it had nothing to do with them at all. Emily was by no means a believer in the supernatural, yet she could not help feeling there was something uncanny taking place when a certain character or situation took hold of her to such an extent that she felt completely possessed and that whatever she was writing came from 'somewhere other'. As the overnight express roared through the Midlands, she remembered how she had envisaged an entire three acts in between Crewe and Rugby and, before arriving at Euston, three small words kept dancing in front of her eyes. *Angels in Waiting* had been conceived.

Now, after all the long-drawn-out labour pains, it was actually about to be born. Duncan and Frank, whom she had introduced to each other some time earlier and who had obviously got on well, seemed to have joined forces and arranged the whole evening from the social point of view. There was to be an early dinner party at the Savoy – not that Emily thought she would be able to eat anything – consisting of the three of them and her agent, together with Helen and Colin, who were driving up from Wiltshire, and Joanna and her husband who were coming from Oxfordshire. After the play, a private room had been booked at the same hotel for a reception where the cast, producer, director and various others would be joining them.

Emily was sorry to find Frank looking unusually strained during dinner and could only suppose that Elaine had been making things difficult for him at home. She had always sensed that she had been jealous of Frank's attachment to her. Duncan, on the other hand, was at his most expansive, saying that he had one or two things he wanted to tell her the next day. For a fleeting moment, she wondered if he were going to announce he was getting married again, but soon nervousness pushed all thoughts except the play out of her head. She could not imagine what he would think of it. It was modern and several scenes might be considered rather too explicit. She hoped he would not be shocked.

When, during the first interval, he said to her, 'If the next two acts are anything like the first, I think you've got a winner, my dear,' she was immensely relieved, especially as this seemed to be the unanimous opinion of their entire party. Even so, she was determined to remain braced for disappointment, despite the unquestionably enthusiastic response from the audience at the end. She was well aware there were still the words of the critics to come, still time which had to pass before it could be said that anything approaching 'a good run' had been achieved. All she could do was to think how extraordinary it was that an idea which had come to her on an overnight express had now developed into something quite tangible, for which the public were prepared to pay good money to see and which had given work not just to producers and actors but to countless others behind the scenes. Yet it had been such an ephemeral thing in the beginning. It was like something built out of a dream, one that did not die, as the hymn put it, at the opening day. Later that night, she wondered whether there was not a good title for another play somewhere in that thought.

Surprisingly, she slept. It was Duncan who woke her by telephone at 7 a.m. to tell her that, according to the papers, he had prophesied aright. She had rather hoped it might have been Frank imparting such information, for he had always been so interested in and such a staunch supporter of her literary work. Then she recalled how strained he had looked the previous evening and, when he still had not rung by 10 a.m., she telephoned his secretary. 'Mr Lodge,' the girl said, 'will not be coming in today. His wife has been taken very ill. He is with her now at the hospital.'

The news took away much of the pleasure she had received after reading the notices Duncan had mentioned. She was due to lunch with him before being driven home by Helen and Colin that afternoon but, when Frank eventually got through to her just before she left for the Athenaeum telling her that Elaine was in a coma, she decided to remain in London for another night, sensing that he might need some support. She had little doubt in her own mind that Elaine's condition had been self-inflicted and not unconnected with her husband's absence at *Angels in Waiting*.

'You don't,' said Duncan, 'look like a successful playwright,' when they met and she was obliged to tell him why. It was not until the end of the meal that she remembered he had mentioned there were one or two things he wanted to say to her and she now asked him what they were.

'I wanted to tell you,' he replied, slowly, 'that Tom knows Benedict is his father.'

'He *knows*?'

'Yes. It all came about quite naturally. Tom's grown up a lot lately, hasn't he? I've noticed that he's become very aware of the happy family atmosphere at Kilochry now that the two little girls are there. The day before yesterday he remarked that he wished he had a father who would come and see him sometimes and that he would be like Benedict. So Benedict just said, "*I* am your father, Tom." '

'And whatever did the child say?'

Duncan smiled. 'He just said "Yippee". Children are marvellous, aren't they, at the way they react so simply and matter-of-factly. Kilochry will be his one day, my dear. There's no doubt about that. I've made provision for the girls but the boy was made to take care of the estate. I feel the time is soon coming when, provided you agree, this is something else he should be told. I've been watching him. He's beginning to know more about the day-to-day running of the place than I do. You've made a marvellous job of bringing him up, Emily.'

As she took a taxi back to the nurses' club she realized that Duncan's last words meant more to her than any amount of praise for *Angels in Waiting*.

31

He looked small and somehow extraordinarily defenceless, standing on the platform in the company of a young master and five other boys. The expression on his face was eager yet apprehensive, his uniform so obviously new and immaculate.

She had deemed it better for Tom to travel to boarding school by train at the beginning of his first term, rather than to drive him there herself. For, even if *he* stood up to the ordeal of parting well – and she had no doubt that he would, particularly as he was by now accustomed to going off on his own – she was not at all sure how *she* would react. This way, she would be able to say goodbye quickly, the tears held in check until she was back in the station car park.

It had been a long time, she thought, as she sat there trying to regain her composure. A whole lifetime. Tom's lifetime. It was exactly thirteen years, to the month, since that September day when she had been tidying up the herbaceous border at the Hermitage and Charlotte had suddenly appeared, heavily pregnant. And today, the bringing-up process had just about come to an end. True, there would still be the holidays, some of which they would always spend in each other's company, either at Kilochry or Netherford, but Emily was acutely conscious that she was starting off on her own again. Although she knew well enough what it was like to be alone, nevertheless the house seemed singularly cheerless when she eventually arrived back there.

She recalled how Frank had asked her what she would do when Tom went away to school and how she had replied that there would always be her writing; and he had asked 'Will it be enough?' Now that the situation had actually come about, she did not feel quite so sure. She was nearly sixty-two, aware that she was not getting through quite so much in a day, that she did not spend quite so long at her typewriter, that she was suffering from more than a few twinges of rheumatism. Often, she was in bed by nine.

A year ago, a sudden stroke had carried off Duncan Rawlinson at the age of sixty-eight, a man who had appeared so fit. Although people tended to live longer these days, Emily felt that it could well be that she might only have a few more years. After all, her Grandmother Lodge had died at sixty-one, her mother at exactly the same age. She was overcome by a feeling of great sadness.

Unable to settle, she wandered aimlessly about the house. Tom's room was in chaos and she wondered whether to start tidying it, but faced with a heap of dirty shirts, piles of books, a discarded cricket bat, some old trophies and an assortment of model farm machinery together with some torn-out pages from a farming journal, she did not have the heart to start. She went out, firmly shutting the door behind her. Her new daily help could sort it out in the morning. Having decided that her own workroom was equally uninviting, she went downstairs and poured herself a drink. As the autumn evening closed in on her, the ringing of the telephone came as a welcome interruption.

'Elly?' Nowadays, Frank often adopted Tom's pet name for her.

'Oh, *Frank*. How lovely to hear from you.'

'Well, I thought you might be feeling a bit low. wondered if I could invite myself down for the weekend?

'But *of course*. I can't think of anything nicer.'

'Friday, then. Round about seven. I'll be driving.'

'Splendid. AFD.' That was a small private joke between them, meaning she would arrange to have all their favour ite dishes. She put down the receiver, feeling annoyed with herself for having temporarily given way to despon dency. Surely she was old enough to know that, sooner or later, life invariably came up with compensations.

Frank arrived, as usual, bearing presents: a copy of a new biography, two bottles of a very special hock and a photostat of a letter in some literary journal which she had missed, the writer asking why there was such a dearth of good television plays for older children and whether someone such as the authoress Ms Emily Mason might be persuaded to fill this need.

'Your public isn't going to let you rest, my love,' he said the following morning when they were leaning on a bridge over the Willon. 'I think you should seriously consider taking up this lady's suggestion in between your grander efforts. I have infinite faith in your pulling off whatever you set your mind to.'

She laughed. 'But I don't want, or need, to work quite so hard these days, Frank. I'm slowing up.'

'And I am, too. I'm definitely retiring at Christmas.'

'Have you any plans in mind for after that?'

He was silent for so long that she wished she had not asked.

Presently he said, 'I'm not like you, Elly. I haven't learnt to live alone. Although my life has certainly been easier since Elaine's death, the Hampstead house seems to have died also. I've still gone on working to get out of it, just as I did when she was alive. But I know I'm not the man I was. I've slipped up badly over one or two things lately. The time's come to pack it in. Incidentally we've decided on some completely new blood for our next chairman. Paul Woodley, believe it or not.'

'Really? I'm glad. I haven't seen quite so much of him

and his wife since Betsy died. But he's always struck me as being an extraordinarily capable sort of person. And nice, with it.'

'Yes.'

There was silence once again between them. The Willon sparkled in the autumn sunlight. A large trout rose to the surface and then disappeared beneath the undulating weeds. The special rivery smell she had loved since childhood was strong in the air. Away to the right, the Sweetacres herd was still grazing the meadows, not yet quite ready for the move to higher winter pastures. But that would not be long now. The seasons seemed to come round so quickly. She remembered how, a few days ago, she had been thinking of thirteen years as a lifetime. Yet she seemed to have experienced so many separate lifetimes: her childhood, school, the war, her long unhappy marriage to Richard, the shorter but intense period of the divorce – and then Tom. Dear Tom. She wondered how he was getting on. She would probably get a letter soon, but she did not doubt that the news in it would be good. He seemed to be one of those fortunate children who were popular with their contemporaries and grown-ups alike. She wished her mother and grandmother and Aunt Chip could have seen him. They would have been so proud whatever, individually, they thought of his mother.

'Elly.' Frank's voice broke into her reveries. 'There's something I want to ask you. You needn't answer now. I don't want to take advantage . . . because I realize this is rather a vulnerable moment for you. It's . . . well, even if you don't believe in marriage and you still just want to write, do you think you could go on doing that with me around? I loathe the expression "this day and age", as I'm sure you do, but it's awfully apt on certain occasions. Surely in 1983 we could join forces, live here together without too many eyebrows being raised?'

A heron flew low and vanished somewhere downstream. She watched the Willon flowing beneath them. The past came flooding back now: little bright hurting jewelled memories. She could see a glorious summer day in 1929 quite clearly in her mind's eye: her mother convalescing in the mill house garden after two serious operations, Aunt Chip sewing in her honeysuckle-covered workroom, her grandmother standing over a vat in what they called Main Building, doing her washing. She could hear again her voice – surprisingly soft and melodious for so forceful and independent a character – as she sang her favourite hymn. Some of the modern generation would call it hackneyed, Emily supposed, so much old cant. Yet it was still sung by people of all ages each November at the service at the Cenotaph, wasn't it? One couldn't get away from its beauty or its truth. Time *was* like an evening gone and it *was* like an ever-rolling stream bearing all its sons – and daughters – away. She didn't know, and neither did Frank, what was round the next bend, but what was it Dr Schmidt had once said: 'We are all afloat together . . . I suggest you paddle along slowly at first, letting the future take care of itself.' It was worth taking a chance, wasn't it? Frank was such a steady, endearing sort of person, infinitely kind, just as her stepfather had been. He had always seemed to be *there*, in the background of her life. She had come to the conclusion that was one of the most important things about relationships, simply being *there*, even if it was only on the end of a telephone, around to help in times of trouble. When Frank had been thousands of miles away in America, he had never failed her. True, she had learnt to stand on her own feet now but suddenly, with great clarity, rather as when an idea for writing dropped into her head, she knew that something, somewhere, was telling her what to do.

She moved her hand towards him along the rail of the bridge and he closed his own over it.

'Thank you, Frank,' she said. 'I can't pretend that I'll make you nearly as good a wife as you deserve, but . . . perhaps it would be as well to marry, while we're about it. I mean . . . even if we *are* cousins and even if it is *this day and age*, I think the local inhabitants of Netherford and Wilhampton would still prefer it.'

'And Grandmother Lodge too, I guess,' he replied. 'God rest her soul.'